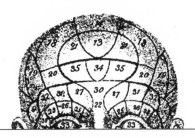

A Measure of Perfection

A Measure of

Perfection

PHRENOLOGY AND THE FINE ARTS IN AMERICA

Charles Colbert

The University of North Carolina Press   Chapel Hill and London

© 1997
The University of North Carolina Press
All rights reserved
Manufactured in the United States of America
Designed by Richard Hendel
Set in New Baskerville
by Tseng Information Systems, Inc.
The paper in this book meets the guidelines for
permanence and durability of the Committee on
Production Guidelines for Book Longevity of the
Council on Library Resources.
Library of Congress
Cataloging-in-Publication Data
Colbert, Charles, 1946–
A measure of perfection : phrenology and the
fine arts in America / by Charles Colbert.
p.   cm. — (Cultural studies of the United
States)
Includes bibliographical references and index.
ISBN 0-8078-2370-8 (alk. paper). —
ISBN 0-8078-4673-2 (pbk. : alk. paper)
1. Phrenology—United States—History—19th
century.   2. Arts, American—History—19th
century.   3. United States—Intellectual life—
19th century.   I. Title.   II. Series.
BF868.c65   1998
139'.0973—dc21   97-8449
CIP

01 00 99 98 97   5 4 3 2 1

To Agatha P. Colbert

Contents

Acknowledgments

I would like to take this opportunity to thank a number of individuals who provided advice and assistance in the preparation of this text. At the outset, Madeleine B. Stern offered insights that came from a long familiarity with phrenology, and William Gerdts generously allowed me to peruse the material he had collected on the topic. In examining documents at the Archives of American Art, I had the help of Robert Brown, while Richard Wolfe provided similar guidance at the Countway Library of Medicine. Discussions with Frederick Voss about the patronage of the Boston Athenaeum were extremely useful in determining its implications, and when information about Rembrandt Peale was wanting, the suggestions of Carol Eaton Soltis proved fruitful. Good neighbor George Litterst saw me through many computer crises. Colleagues Jeffrey Howe and Kenneth Craig listened patiently to what must have seemed interminable discussions about ideas that appear in this text. During the summer of 1993, while attending an NEH seminar titled "Hudson River Valley Images and Texts," Wayne Franklin, John Seelye, and H. Daniel Peck read portions of one chapter included here and gave the encouragement necessary to complete a project that seemed faltering. The completed manuscript profited immensely from the thoughtful criticism of Alan Trachtenberg and the close scrutiny of Ron Maner and Stephanie Wenzel of the University of North Carolina Press.

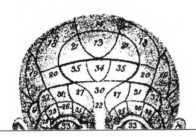

Introduction

Phrenology, the discipline dedicated to ascertaining the mind's orientation from the shape of the skull, was an invention of the late eighteenth century. From the Enlightenment it inherited a desire for transparency, insisting that external bodily attributes disclose unambiguous meaning. From Romanticism, however, it absorbed a commitment to diversity, particularly as this quality pertained to race and gender. The resulting combination was not without its contradictions, for, while followers claimed that their conclusions were universally applicable, there was no single mind, no uninflected intelligence, that could validate the assertion. Evidence had to filter through individual minds, no two of which were identically constituted. Despite such contradictions, or perhaps because of the latitude for interpretation they allowed, the theory managed to attract a large number of supporters who remained undaunted in the face of stiff opposition. We should not be blinded by the disingenuousness of its defenders to the real virtues also present in the teachings of phrenology. I thought it best to address these issues at the outset, not with the intent of resolving them, but to alert the reader to the need for open-mindedness in evaluating the doctrine's legacy.

The prominent attraction of phrenology was its promise to delineate the natural causes behind mental phenomena, a development that is incorporated in this text under the rubric of "physical metaphysics." The conviction that science could account for the life of the mind was a mixed blessing.[1] If it placed accountability for insanity or disease on the sufferer, for example, it also proposed humane remedies that were often preferable to the alternatives. If it divided humankind by racial categories that were qualitative as well as quantitative, it obliged followers to respect the merits they discovered in those who differed from themselves. If it tended to equate femininity with maternity, it also encouraged women to assume responsibilities beyond those prescribed by conventional wisdom. All these subjects receive extended treatment in the chapters that follow; here I would like to review briefly what I consider the defining paradox of the doctrine's reception in the United States.

As a program of personal improvement, phrenology was warmly embraced by Jacksonian America. The theory lent itself to a land of "self-made" individuals because it valued initiative and perseverance above the preferment that advanced the careers of the privileged. At the same time, it maintained that the parameters of mental and physical ability were largely drawn by heredity, and one could only make the best of endowments received at birth. This conundrum was easily resolved, for no one is ever truly self-made; phrenology set out to alert prospective parents to the measures that would enable them to bequeath their children even greater prospects for success than they themselves enjoyed. Self-made men and women could take an active part in the formation of their offspring, and as each generation surpassed the preceding in its potential for betterment, a future of perfect human beings emerged as a real possibility.

In this utopian scheme the *Greek Slave*, by Hiram Powers, played a pivotal part. Her unclothed form could furnish the model of uncorrupted beauty that would guide Americans to the physical and moral perfection necessary to usher in the millennium. She was the mother of self-made men. As such she stands at the center of the argument offered here, and her appearance in the penultimate chapter represents the culmination of the possibilities inferred in preceding ones. She is the goal toward which landscape, portraiture, genre, and history all strive, while the architectural ventures of the phrenological Fowlers discussed in the final chapter were likewise attuned to her interests. This deference of all creation to the ideal resulted from a commingling of Platonic and scientific notions. If (wo)man was the measure of all things, then precise knowledge of her proportions, of her healthy constitution, could come only from modern physiological

wisdom as expounded by phrenologists. The quest for the perfect figure had little use for vague notions of inspiration, the voluptuous imaginings of antiquity, or the conceptions of anatomy fostered by fashion plates.

Several conclusions follow from this insight. First, if we wish to locate the paradigmatic expression of Manifest Destiny, we would do well to look elsewhere than to the imprecise prospects offered by landscape painting. Americans of the antebellum era still thought the human figure the most subtle and expressive of God's creations, and for them, phrenology translated its lessons into tenets applicable to the circumstances of modern life. While the *Greek Slave* is usually shunted aside in histories of these decades as an anomaly or as a naive attempt to raise the national standard of taste to levels set by Europeans, it actually spoke directly to aspirations and anxieties that were especially endemic on this side of the Atlantic. The heroic maiden was seen as the source of the hardy pioneers who were going to civilize the continent and as an image of the bounty that awaited when the process was complete. She embodied collective assumptions to a degree rarely approached by the contemporary landscape and, as such, deserves a place at the center of Jacksonian visual culture. Sculpture, in any case, was more apt to speak to public issues than was painting, which tended to offer itself for private delectation, and Powers's work belongs to a series of ideal figures, including those executed by Erastus Dow Palmer, Thomas Crawford, William Wetmore Story, Joel Hart, Joseph Mozier, and Harriet Hosmer, that were similarly didactic in intent. Further, in searching for evidence of the pressures that increasingly troubled society in the 1850s, it is again sculpture that serves as the most sensitive barometer. I know of no landscape painter who agonized over the prospect of civil war to the degree Powers did in distant Florence. Below I argue that his *Daniel Webster* and *America* plead the case for union in terms drawn from phrenology and physiology.

A second conclusion that follows from the proposals presented above is that Powers's contemporaries were more sophisticated in their analysis of style than is generally recognized. Much modern criticism of the *Greek Slave* has focused on the supposed dilemma experienced by viewers as they gazed on the naked figure and tried to remember why she should inspire only chaste thoughts. It is my belief that this litany has resulted from consultation of a limited number of documents relating to the reception accorded the slave. Examination of a wider range reveals a frank acceptance of her sexuality in conformity with the intentions of the sculptor.

Scholars have been impeded in their recognition of this discourse by an unfamiliarity with the terminology and issues promoted by phrenology. Despite my review of these in the leading journal of art history, the six or seven extended discussions of the slave that have appeared in the intervening decade have failed to cite this article, let alone acknowledge its content. This rather blinkered approach has been taken by proponents of traditional methodologies as well as followers of more fashionable ideologies, but the major obstacle to understanding how form reinforces content in this and similar statues has been disregard of the values they were designed to embody. Contrary to modern perceptions, phrenology was not an arcane science shared by a few eccentrics; its wide popularity meant that an audience for the *Greek Slave* already existed by the time she arrived on these shores.

Among her admirers was Walt Whitman. The frequent parallels between his poetry and Powers's statuary make them mutually illuminating, and I have thus relied on the former to clarify issues related to the latter. There is hardly a figure of the American Renaissance who did not have an opinion about phrenology, and a number appear in the pages that follow. Some sense of the theory's pervasiveness can be gained by considering that both Uncle Tom and Moby-Dick came under its scrutiny. The doctrine served as a cohesive cultural factor, uniting phenomena that might otherwise seem disparate; it was not, however, without opponents. There is surely some significance in the fact that genteel authors with academic inclinations tended to question its claims. The emphasis phrenology placed on innate talent undermined the grounds for their authority and made them wary of the entire venture. This attitude is evident, for example, in the contention of Oliver Wendell Holmes that one cannot ascertain the contents of a safe by feeling its knobs, but even this skeptic could find much of value in the discipline. I have selected Ralph Waldo Emerson's objections for particular attention because they offer a useful foil to the opinions held by Whitman; this antithesis sheds much light on contemporary approaches to the theory.

As mentioned, the progress of phrenology in the early nineteenth century was not unopposed. From a philosophical standpoint, Hegel criticized the doctrine as unsystematic; the act of murder was a direct expression of the will to do so, but what was to be done with the cranium that exhibited a propensity to kill although its owner never committed the deed? It was rather like the washerwoman who claims that every time she hangs out the laundry, it rains. The phrenologists, Hegel continues, confused the relation of cause and effect and, in so doing, ossified the powers of reason, making self-consciousness subject to the physical condition of the skull.[2] Theologians argued along similar lines; phrenology deprived the individual of free will and accountability for his or her deeds. It was dismissed by them as the invention of French infidels intent on duping the gullible.[3] Although the theory was generally well received in medical circles, there were those who disputed its claims. Thomas Sewall, for example, could not locate during dissection the divisions of the brain identified by phrenologists. He also contested their assertion that size was a measure of power and doubted that the skull possessed the uniform thickness necessary to ensure an accurate reading of the brain. Further, he reported, the frontal sinuses interfere with many of the faculties, making it impossible for the latter to modify the shape of the head.[4]

Echoes of these debates can be heard in contemporary literature; Melville's remark that "the brain [of the whale] is at least twenty feet from his apparent forehead," and thus a puzzle to phrenologists,[5] for instance, seems to reflect the sort of reasoning advanced by Sewall. It is difficult, however, to find an equal degree of skepticism among artists. Of course, they were less given to articulating their beliefs in writing and may have simply kept their reservations to themselves. But they often profess their belief, quibbling, at most, with specific tenets, and several reasons can be postulated for their allegiance to the theory. Artists, generally, were less educated than authors and may not have given the matter the critical scrutiny it deserved, but even relatively literate figures such as Thomas Cole remained unimpressed by the arguments against phrenology. What made the science so seductive to him and his colleagues was its dependence on visual indexes to assay character. This fact made artists valued recruits in the crusade to reform humankind while bestowing the blessings of science on their calling in the process. Few could resist (although Horatio Greenough, for one, did), and in the absence of documentation relating to their indifference to its appeal, the history of its decline in popularity is not especially relevant to this narrative. It seems to have died of neglect, a process that does not readily lend itself to detection.

All sources agree on the fact that the phrenological seed fell on particularly fertile soil when it arrived on these shores.[6] Even after scientists began to apply electrical stimulation to the brain in the 1860s and thus dispel the localization of functions proposed by Gall and his followers, phrenology enjoyed an interest here that it did not sustain elsewhere.[7] Its penetration into popular culture, where it survived into the early decades of this century, is only briefly mentioned in this account. Much remains to be done in this area. Its influence on folk art, popular art, caricature, and photography warrants further examination; but such material would have made this text far too cumbersome, so analysis was limited to the "fine arts." Whatever one's feelings may be regarding the validity of this category, I have adopted it as a means of restricting the range of my investigations. Indeed, even within its confines, I have been compelled by considerations of length to limit or remove the review of certain individuals, such as Bingham and Eakins, because the material on them was perhaps not as compelling as that for others.

Much of phrenology's appeal was due to the conviction that the blessings of material progress would prove nugatory if a corresponding moral progress was not also sustained. It taught the individual how to adapt and prosper in times of rapid change. In siding with the party of progress, it sought to root out customs that were contrary to what it defined as natural law. This outlook motivated it to unite with a wide range of reform movements that emerged in the antebellum period with the intent of hastening the millennium. As suggested at the outset, the blessings of these campaigns were not unalloyed, and the cause of truth is hardly served by regarding them as either entirely beneficial or unrelievedly sinister. Certainly much of what they promoted was intended to produce conformity to middle-class, patriarchal values, but the liberating and even anarchistic currents that flow through American culture were also fed at this source. And in suggesting that such attitudes are still viable for present social problems, Steven Mintz contends that "it would be a mistake of the highest magnitude to cynically conclude that antebellum reform was in its essence an instrument of class hegemony or control."[8] I would likewise argue that even the pristine marble nudes produced under phrenology's aegis require attentive scrutiny that eschews facile judgment or the inclination to see them solely through the spectacles of ideology. Just as we can only appreciate the integrity of others by granting their right to confound our expectations, so a work of art confesses most candidly only to those who are willing to listen.

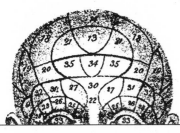

A Measure of Perfection

1

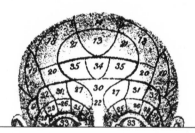

A Plausible Rascality

"A young man, named Ralph Waldo Emerson, and a classmate of my lamented son George, after failing in the everyday avocations of a Unitarian preacher and schoolmaster, starts a new doctrine of transcendentalism, declares all the old revelations superannuated and worn out, and announces the approach of new revelations and prophecies. Garrison and the non-resistant abolitionists, Brownson and the Marat democrats, phrenology and animal magnetism, all come in, furnishing each some plausible rascality as an ingredient for the bubbling cauldron of religion and politics."[1] So wrote a beleaguered John Quincy Adams in 1840 as he surveyed a world that seemed bent on uprooting the moral order he held so dear. The culprits he names, Emerson, Garrison, and Brownson, scarcely require introduction to the reader even moderately acquainted with the history of antebellum America; that same reader, however, may well be hard pressed to recall the relevant issues associated with phrenology and animal magnetism, the final entries on the list compiled by the elderly statesman. This circumstance suggests that our perspective on the age diverges in an important respect from that held by Adams's contemporaries, for they flocked to these "plausible rascalities" in far greater numbers than to the other causes he mentions. The particular reticence of art historians to address the subject of phrenology is especially curious, since its primary concern was to identify the moral code inscribed in the human form. Obviously, artists had much at stake in the outcome of this venture, but their enthusiasm for the doctrine is rarely accorded the serious attention it deserves. This book was written in hopes of rectifying some of the consequences of this neglect by recognizing phrenology as a crucial ingredient in the "bubbling cauldron" of Jacksonian culture.

For those intent on probing the mysteries of the psyche, few subjects have proved more enigmatic and enticing than the human countenance. Where else, it was asked, would the soul be more likely to divulge its secrets with equal candor? The tongue might deceive, the eyes dissimulate, but the face was presumed guileless. The question of identifying the pertinent indicators, however, long remained a topic of debate.[2] Were the fixed features more reliable than the mobile? In either case, how did one translate the visual evidence into a systematic discipline? The inquiries into these matters conducted in the waning years of the eighteenth century by Franz Joseph Gall (1758–1828), the man whose theories evolved into the doctrine eventually called phrenology, took place against a backdrop delineated by the encyclopedic publications of Johann Caspar Lavater, whose name had become virtually synonymous with the study of physiognomy at the time.

Lavater assumed that bodily features testified to moral condition based on the belief that a fixed set of correspondences existed between the intangible spirit and the corporeal form.[3] In pursuing his studies, he examined the figure from top to toe, but the head was the object of prolonged attention. The height of the forehead, the profile of the proboscis, and the arch of an eyebrow all furnished clues in his search for the soul.[4] And despite the intuitive nature of his conclusions, he claimed they were scientific,[5] while chiding his predecessors for their want of objectivity.[6] Because his theories offered access to regions of the personality that had hitherto escaped objectification, artists and authors were among his most avid readers.[7]

Far more than Lavater, Gall qualifies as a standard-bearer of science. He still holds an honored place in the annals of medicine as an innovating anatomist.[8] In this capacity he developed a novel technique for dissecting the brain to examine its structure. Instead of slicing indiscriminately, Gall endeavored to tease out the individual fibers and follow them through the entire structure. His pronouncements about the form and functioning of the brain came to be considered authoritative even by those who may not have agreed with his conclusions.[9] In championing the brain as the sole organ of thought, he made short work of those who clung to the belief that ideas and emotions originated in the bodily viscera. He also took Lavater to task for his ignorance of anatomy. Without an intimate knowledge of the vital organs, how could one hope to comprehend the forces that mold the figure? Those few instances where the Swiss physiognomist had proved accurate were, Gall contended, the consequence of chance insight rather than reasoned investigation.[10]

The labyrinthine structure of the brain encouraged Gall to draw a number of deductions about its operation. It was hardly possible, he argued, that a single idea could occupy the entire organ. Thought must take place in certain nodes along the convolutions; each of these, in turn, was the locus of a particular mode of thinking that could not be duplicated elsewhere. Confirmation for this hypothesis came not from dissection but from his experiences as the attending physician to an asylum for the insane, a position he assumed shortly after earning his medical degree in Vienna in 1785. This appointment afforded him ample opportunity to observe the behavior of monomaniacs, persons who exhibited a species of mental alienation that had important implications for his enterprise. Victims of monomania were enthralled by the urge to commit a specific form of aberrant behavior, be it theft, amatory excess, or whatever. When not so engaged, these same inmates conducted their affairs in a seemingly normal manner. If the brain were uniform in nature, no function would escape the irrational promptings of the diseased mind, but here was clear evidence to the contrary. It followed that these diverse functions must operate in relative isolation as a consequence of their physical separation from one another within the matrix of the brain. While Gall endeavored to promote his system on the basis of his superior insight as an anatomist, it was actually this sort of inference that furnished the substance of his argument.

Like physiognomy, faculty psychology was not a new discipline when Gall took it up. As ancient as the Greeks and as current as Scottish commonsense philosophy of the eighteenth century, the notion that thought could be compartmentalized served as a convenient device for theoretical discourse. By combining this concept with the principles of physiognomy, however, Gall gave the enterprise a new twist. Why not locate the "faculties" at specific points along the convolutions of the brain? In adopting this approach, he sought to divorce the doctrine from the purely speculative use made of it in the past. If successful, he would deliver the psyche from its captivity among theologians and philosophers by consigning it to physicians.[11]

As his study of lunatics suggests, Gall's beliefs were rooted in the tangibility of the evidence he could procure. He had no patience for the abstract categories of thought created by philosophers or for their tendency to wander off into the mazy realms of conjecture.[12] Therefore he aimed to establish his faculties in conduct observable in the real world. This ambition led him from the asylum to the prison, where he hoped to identify the physical consequences of a predisposition to violence. But such goals could only be realized if one further condition were met. Gall invoked the example of the muscles to explain the organic constitution of the mental faculties. Like muscles, the faculties expanded in size with use, overcoming the resistance of the skull by modifying its shape. A penchant for violence, then, would betray its presence if a substantial proportion of the prison population exhibited a uniform peculiarity in the cranial structure. Much to Gall's delight, a positive correlation did appear, and he designated the protuberance associated with this finding the organ of *Murder*.

Not satisfied merely with studying antisocial tendencies, Gall turned his attention to the benefactors of humanity. Equipped with novel investigative methods, he scrutinized those who had distinguished themselves in some profession or calling. The singular form encountered regularly among composers and musicians, for example, permitted him to designate a faculty of music. By long and "tedious experiment," Gall managed to locate some twenty-seven aptitudes that signaled their presence by sending up protuberances. Born of this marriage of physiognomy to faculty psychology was the cerebral diagram often taken as the embodiment of the theory (fig. 1.1). In viewing such images, it is important to remember that they were not conjured up by divination but were determined by procedures then thought rigorously empirical.[13]

A number of tests were devised to assist in affirming the identity of the particular faculties. If, for example, the victim of a severe head injury began to sing uncontrollably, then the point of impact might reasonably be assumed to be the seat of the faculty governing musical talent. The phenomena associated with dreaming furnished additional evidence of the multiplicity of faculties; were the mind pervaded by a uniform consciousness, it would remain entirely dormant during sleep, but dreams indicated that some portion of the brain had not succumbed to slumber. Further, Gall noticed in collecting accounts of such reveries that their content was neither random nor unpredictable. Certain kinds of dreams occurred to certain kinds of people. The regularity of this pattern was due to the

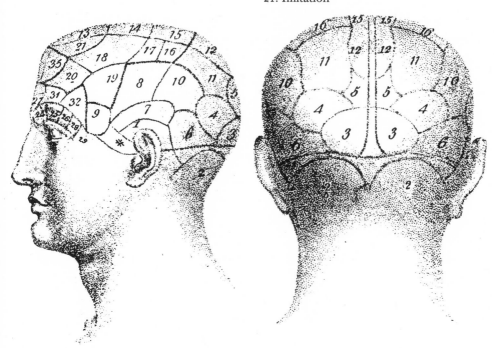

POWERS AND ORGANS OF THE MIND

Affective	Intellectual
I. Propensities	*I. Perceptive*
† Desire to live	22. Individuality
* Alimentiveness	23. Configuration
1. Destructiveness	24. Size
2. Amativeness	25. Weight and Resistance
3. Philoprogenitiveness	26. Coloring
4. Adhesiveness	27. Locality
5. Inhabitiveness	28. Order
6. Combativeness	29. Calculation
7. Secretiveness	30. Eventuality
8. Acquisitiveness	31. Time
9. Constructiveness	32. Tune
	33. Language
II. Sentiments	
10. Cautiousness	*II. Reflective*
11. Approbativeness	34. Comparison
12. Self-esteem	35. Causality
13. Benevolence	
14. Reverence	
15. Firmness	
16. Conscientiousness	
17. Hope	
18. Marvellousness	
19. Ideality	
20. Mirthfulness	
21. Imitation	

FIGURE 1.1. *Spurzheim's Phrenological Head*, frontispiece from J. G. Spurzheim, *Phrenology or the Doctrine of the Mental Phenomena* (Philadelphia: Lippincott, 1908)

predominance of particular faculties as a consequence of their habitual exercise. Dreams afforded the researcher direct access to the workings of the faculties unencumbered by the contingencies and distractions of the waking state. They were especially useful in determining the number and range of the diverse mental functions.

Another source of insight was comparative anatomy. Animals were not driven by blind instinct, Gall maintained, and in their brains resided many of the same faculties that operated in humans. The broad head of the bull-dog, for instance, resembled the heads of the criminals examined during his prison tours, a similarity he attributed to the ample organ of *Murder* in both man and beast. The differences observable in skulls of the two sexes also proved informative. Men and women did not think alike; how could their crania be alike? Gall suspected that the faculty of *Love of Offspring* operated in the posterior portion of the head, but he would not publish this notion until extensive data confirmed that the region was consistently larger in women. In like manner, all those factors that contribute to the di-versity of humanity, including race, nation, class, and religion, were seen as promoting variations in physical structure and moral constitution.

To prove his ideas, Gall gathered skulls, casts, and pictures, but as contemporary critics remarked, he never managed to make a direct con-nection between his anatomical efforts and his theories about the brain.[14] As noted, his precepts were drawn from inference and, as such, shared many of the prejudices of the age.[15] Their failure to meet present stan-dards of science, however, does not negate their importance as a cultural phenomenon, and the peremptory dismissal of the entire venture so often encountered in modern histories is unwarranted.[16]

Although Gall considered size an indicator of the relative power of a faculty, he soon realized how imperfect this measure was. Intelligence, probity, and like virtues could not be ascertained merely by surveying the faculties from which these qualities derived; much depended on the total organization of the brain. Two heads, for instance, could be the same size, but if one favored the organs given to the gratification of animal appe-tites while the other favored those devoted to spiritual concerns, the two personalities might be diametrically opposed. Nor did this qualification relieve the examiner from further considerations. Most important among these was the physical condition and constitution of the subject. Since the effort of thinking drew on the reservoirs of bodily energy, the activity of the brain could not be isolated from the entire vital economy.

Phrenologists borrowed the theory of the temperaments devised in an-tiquity that divided mankind into four types: lymphatic, bilious, sanguine, and nervous. But in adopting this system, they did not intend to endorse the idea that personality was subservient to bodily organization. It was instead proposed that organic constitution harmonized with mental orientation. The color of the hair, eyes, and skin; the ratio of fat to muscle; and height to weight all had to be factored into one's calculations. It might be anticipated, for example, that artists would appear among the fair-complexioned, frail beings who belonged to the nervous temperament, for these attributes were all indicative of an exquisite sensibility.

Phrenology, of course, was more than the sum of its analytic techniques. By asserting that the mind was subject to the same conditions that prevailed throughout the organic constitution, Gall opened himself to charges of materialism. This perception caused authorities to forbid him from lecturing on several occasions,[17] but he countered adversaries by asserting that there "is a God; because there exists an [mental] organ for knowing and adoring Him!"[18] The visible presence of a faculty devoted to worship stood as a divine signet on the forehead of man. Embedded in the very matrix of sublunary existence, then, were ciphers of a higher order; traditional religion ignored these, but science promised to give them their due. This predisposition was neatly summed up in the term "physical metaphysics," a concept we shall return to repeatedly.[19]

Citizens of Jacksonian America were, according to de Tocqueville, apt to "conclude that everything in the world may be explained, and that nothing in it transcends the limits of the understanding." He goes on to note that such persons possessed "an almost insurmountable distaste for whatever is supernatural,"[20] and we may well surmise that individuals of this inclination swelled the ranks of phrenology's followers. An easy comprehensibility earned it praise as "a science for the people,"[21] and Lydia Maria Child expanded on this commendation when she declared phrenology to be "the democracy of metaphysics."[22]

Contemporaries were particularly enthralled by Gall's suggestion that the mind be investigated according to the standards employed in the study of nature. The belief that the same laws applied to both suited the needs of rising urban professionals, the new "thinking class" as Cooter calls them, who shared an aversion for mystery, which they viewed as an obfuscatory tactic designed to perpetuate the privileges of the landed gentry. Phrenology constituted a potent weapon in this skirmish because it enlisted science on the side of the insurgents by projecting their hierarchy of intellectual values and notions of specialization onto the "natural" order of the mind.[23] As the scion of an old Boston family and a custodian of tradition, John Quincy Adams turned a rather jaundiced eye on the rascalities advanced by Gall and his followers, but like Canute, his gestures did little to turn the tide. Phrenologists had this in common with Emerson; both were resolved to place reasoned principle above unexamined tradition even if doing so provoked the ire of the old guard.

To this point, the term "phrenology" has been used somewhat negligently. Gall could not abide the word and instead favored "craniology" to designate his science. "Phrenology" was first coined in 1815.[24] Soon it entered general circulation, but the matter was complicated by the inclination among many to employ "physiognomy" when referring to Gall's doctrine, a usage that testifies to the proximity of the two theories in the minds of contemporaries despite the efforts to distinguish them.[25] The circumstances that caused "phrenology" to prevail over all other appellations are closely tied to the career of Johan Gaspar Spurzheim (1776–1832).

Well before Gall began publishing his discoveries in 1798, word of his ideas spread through much of Europe. Among those who thronged to his lectures in Vienna was Spurzheim. In 1800 he arrived as an aspiring medical student, but his ardor and intelligence soon earned him an invitation to collaborate on research.[26] The two embarked in 1805 on a tour that took them through much of Germany and did not end until they settled in Paris two years later. Eventually, professional rivalry eroded their relationship, prompting Spurzheim to return to Vienna in 1813 to take his degree. The next year found him in Great Britain, and he subsequently crossed the channel frequently to lecture before English audiences.

Spurzheim's auditors were not treated to the same philosophy heard by those who sat to Gall. The latter prided himself in his painstaking research and berated his erstwhile colleague for drawing conclusions from data he considered provisional. But one man's prudence may be another's timidity. Why, Spurzheim asked, should findings of such potential consequence for humanity be withheld merely because every foreseeable objection had yet to be answered? In part, then, Spurzheim appropriated the term "phrenology" (derived from two Greek words meaning "mind discourse") to signal the ideological rift with his former mentor.

In seeking to place the mind on a continuum with nature, Spurzheim adopted the nomenclature of botany and arranged the faculties according to order and genera, a step designed as well to emphasize his scientific intent.[27] He also took exception to Gall's habit of naming each faculty after a single mode of conduct it induced. The organ of *Murder* was a case in point. This label failed to encompass the types of behavior motivated by the faculty and compounded the error by naming it after an abuse of the functions it governed. Spurzheim sought neutral titles that granted greater latitude for the kinds of activities promoted; *Murder* became *Destructiveness* and had among its purposes the procuring of nutriment. The organs of *Cunning, Religion, Poetry,* and so on were transformed and given suffixes such as "ive" or "ness" or "iveness" to suggest their range. By Spurzheim's count, the number of faculties reached thirty-five, and all were designed for some useful purpose that might, however, be corrupted by ignorance or willful neglect.[28]

Gall entertained no such optimism and expressed little hope that the follies of mankind might ever be eradicated.[29] Some sense of his dour outlook can be gained from the account of his examination of Giuseppe Ceracchi.[30] This noted sculptor and self-proclaimed champion of freedom had twice traveled to the United States in the early 1790s with the intention of erecting a colossal monument honoring liberty. Although the commission never materialized, he did manage to create a number of busts of the founding fathers, including George Washington. His meeting with Gall in 1800 stands as the first documented encounter between a figure associated with the history of American art and a practitioner of the new science.

The sitting began with Gall running his hands over the organ of *Pride* and then that of *Mechanism*. Both were large, and though the latter might have destined Ceracchi for a simple life as a laborer, the former goaded him on to higher things. A career in the fine arts would satisfy the needs of these faculties, but *Color* scarcely merited notice; this head, he concluded, must belong to a sculptor. As the craniologist's fingers glided over the region of *Murder*, his expression darkened momentarily, for here was a protuberance that loomed above all others. Carnage and mayhem were subjects that one so organized represented with alacrity; indeed, he must admire even "the name of a great general."

Since the two were strangers, Ceracchi was impressed by the accuracy of his examiner's deductions, which were made in ignorance of the favor the artist had found with both Washington and Napoleon. Having scored a "hit," Gall could not suppress the more ominous implications of his reading. Noting a tendency to disguise sanguinary propensities beneath a veneer of democratic sloganeering, Ceracchi was admonished to shun imprudent ventures. The perilous urges so readily apparent to the craniologist could not be forestalled indefinitely, and within a year the sculptor was implicated in a plot to assassinate Napoleon. The guillotine made its contribution to Gall's collection, and there the sculptor's skull was exhibited as evidence of the contempt for legitimate authority engendered by an overweening *Pride*. This and a penchant for violence had sealed Ceracchi's fate.

Specimens gathered at the acquiescence of the executioner were not particularly informative about the prevalent qualities of human nature, according to Spurzheim. He chided his mentor for excessive interest in

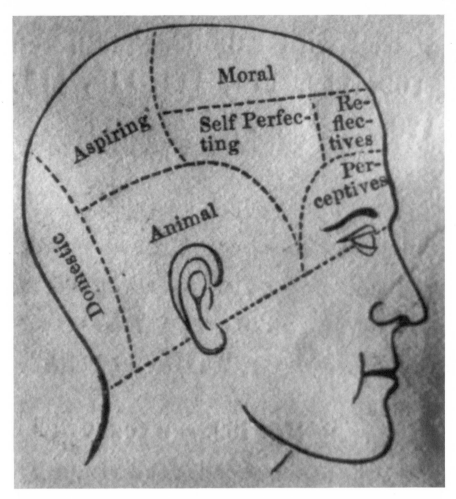

FIGURE 1.2. *Grouping of Organs*, from O. S. Fowler, *The Practical Phrenologist* (Boston: O. S. Fowler, 1869), p. 9

the outlandish and exceptional, a tendency that led to concentration on one or two protuberances and to derision of the discipline as a "bumpology." Instead of turning to the ends of the spectrum, why not fix one's gaze on the middle, where many distinguished heads formed by the expansion of a number of related faculties might be found (fig. 1.2)? These types could be evaluated by the gradual anterior or posterior lean of the cranium rather than the isolated eruptions of individual organs. Where the craniologist saw depravity and adversarial relationships among the faculties, the phrenologist found goodness and neighborly cooperation.[31] The latter's emphasis on harmony and the possibilities for improvement garnered him a wide readership in Jacksonian America.

Precisely when and how these ideas reached America remains a matter of conjecture, but the efforts of Nicholas Biddle warrant attention. The year 1806 saw him busily engaged in crating and shipping some fifty plaster casts of classical statuary donated by Napoleon to the Pennsylvania Academy of Fine Arts.[32] Biddle had just attended a series of lectures delivered by Gall in Carlsruhe, Germany, and there was presented a skull marked with the location of the faculties by Spurzheim.[33] This treasured artifact also crossed the Atlantic. Biddle's cargo, then, was divided between the testimony of antiquity and that of modern science about the nature and ideals of humanity. The dialogue engendered by these sometimes complementary, sometimes contradictory visions was one that would engage American artists through much of the century.

The prestige of the Biddle name and Nicholas's own rise to eminence as a banker lent an air of authority to his endorsement of phrenology,[34] and these factors certainly figured among the reasons for its early popularity in Philadelphia. The first society devoted to the theory in this country was established there in 1822.[35] In the same year, Dr. Richard Harlan delivered a series of lectures on the subject at the Peale museum.[36] These events, in turn, must have influenced the directors of the Pennsylvania Academy in the following year to appoint Dr. John Bell professor of anatomy.[37] He held this position until 1839 and was described in this capacity as "a zealous phrenologist who impresses his students with its value."[38] The generation that matriculated during his tenure was, according to Bell's own testimony, duly impressed. "In my lectures on the Anatomy of Expression, before the Artists of this city last spring," he wrote, "I had occasion to point out, as I believe to their satisfaction, the necessity of a knowledge of the outlines of Phrenology to the painter and sculptor."[39]

By 1824 the journal of the Edinburgh phrenological society could report that the theory of Gall and Spurzheim had been well received in medical, legal, and scientific circles of the United States.[40] Many of these same professionals were instrumental in giving the republic's fledgling artistic community an opportunity to flourish. The large collection assembled by Nicholas Biddle is suggestive in this respect. Nearly two dozen of the images gathered were portraits of himself, and while a certain epicene comeliness doubtlessly nourished the venture, vanity could not serve as the acknowledged justification.[41] Phrenology urged its followers to monitor their features repeatedly in search of indexes that might reveal changes in character,[42] and its involvement in this instance seems all the more plausible when we consider, for example, that Luigi Persico's bust of 1837 was praised for exhibiting the "fine forehead" of the prototype.[43]

To the north, the budding cultural life of New York City benefited from much the same civic pride that prompted Philadelphia's professionals to support the arts. The efforts of Dr. John Francis were exemplary in this matter. His name often finds its way into biographies of the city's artists, and like Biddle, he was an early devotee of phrenology, having attended the lectures of Gall and befriended Spurzheim while in Paris in 1815. On his return in 1816, he loaned a book by the latter to John Wesley Jarvis,[44] a leading portraitist about town. After perusing its pages, the painter declared art and science to be united in a single cause. "If I have any merit as a portrait-painter," he added, "so be it; I may have depicted Lavater: but Spurzheim renders the artist the phrenological delineator."[45]

Both parties benefited from the association; to Jarvis it meant an enhancement of the status of his profession, while Francis relied on the portraitist's talents to furnish the evidence needed to demonstrate the theory's validity. Considerations of this sort certainly spurred the doctor's interest in art, and it can hardly have been coincidental that, shortly after his return from Europe, he conferred with John Trumbull about the possibility of adding a lectureship on anatomy to the American Academy. While the idea was well received, no steps were taken toward its realization.[46] Undaunted, Francis remained active in the art world, perhaps most noticeably in the assistance he provided William Dunlap. As we shall see, the latter's history of American art bears traces of the former's interest in phrenology, an enthusiasm that peaked precisely when the chronicler was engaged in his monumental undertaking. During the early 1830s Francis labored to found a phrenological society, an effort that was rewarded by his election to the presidency of the body by members who wished to acknowledge his preeminence in the field.[47]

Proposals to establish a phrenological society had already been advanced almost a decade earlier by Dr. Frederick Gore King. In 1824 he had sounded out his colleagues on the prospect, and after several months of deliberation a consensus arose that an athenaeum with a chair devoted to phrenology would best serve the interests of all parties concerned.[48] From this decision arose the New York Athenaeum, an institution of considerable importance in the cultural life of the city because it provided the forum for the lectures delivered by William Cullen Bryant and Samuel Morse on poetry and the fine arts. These were read in 1825 and 1826, and in them we find several allusions to the principles of faculty psychology that suggest an attempt to insert the new theory into a critical discourse.[49] Both addresses served to put the community on notice about the crucial part played by the creative imagination in the collective identity of the nation, and as such they appear regularly in histories of American literature and art; but the introduction to phrenology furnished by King to the same audience has not received due notice. He made his presentation in 1826, the same year he joined Bryant and Morse in a position of leadership at the National Academy of Design. His appointment was to the professorship of anatomy,[50] and here, with the set of phrenological casts he had recently imported from Europe, he fulfilled the ambitions John Francis had previously entertained for the older academy.[51]

The weight of evidence suggests that most artists in New York possessed some degree of familiarity with phrenology by the end of the third decade of the century. A dispatch sent in 1831 by Samuel Morse to the academy, for example, includes a discussion of Spurzheim that assumes a knowledge of his identity and accomplishments.[52] When Spurzheim arrived in person on these shores in the summer of 1832, Asher Durand received a letter from an acquaintance detailing his thoughts about the phrenologist's teachings.[53] No doubt such exchanges were common at the time. This was the frightful choleraic summer when a hitherto unknown strain of the disease swept through the city, leaving thousands dead in its wake. The sobering statistics of its ravages were duly recorded by Philip Hone, former mayor and diligent diarist, but he interrupts his doleful entries on 7 August to report that Spurzheim, "the celebrated phrenologist, a disciple of Dr. Gall," had arrived from France.[54] Clearly, here was an event of some consequence.

Actually, Spurzheim's ship had docked on the fourth; but the perils associated with the epidemic prevented public assembly, and after a week's stay, he departed for Boston in anticipation of finding more favorable conditions for lecturing. His progress between the cities was not uneventful, and a number of encounters serve to remind us of the close affiliation that developed between phrenologists and artists. After being warmly welcomed in New Haven by the faculty of Yale, he managed to find time for an interview with Hezekiah Augur, the self-taught sculptor. As Spurzheim examined his head, Augur lamented the unavailability of models and want of encouragement that were his lot. Despite the disadvantages, a number of faculties, including *Constructiveness, Form, Size, Imitation,* and the "reflective faculties," arose in impressive array from the artist's skull.[55] To what avail was this auspicious constellation of talents? Did Augur redouble his efforts to fulfill the destiny so plainly written on his physical organization? Since he soon abandoned the chisel, apparently not. Others, as we shall see, were inspired by their phrenological prognosis to overcome the sort of limitations Augur bemoaned.

Spurzheim soon boarded the stagecoach for Hartford and then journeyed to Worcester, where he enjoyed the hospitality of Alvan Fisher. Known today primarily as a pioneering painter of landscapes and genre scenes, Fisher had spent much of 1825 in Paris attending Spurzheim's lectures and copying the old masters at the Louvre.[56] Despite the reminiscences the two must have shared, the phrenologist could not tarry long, for Boston beckoned from just over the horizon, and there his arrival was eagerly anticipated.

As in other cities, the citizens of Boston had been expertly tutored in the intricacies of phrenology during the 1820s by a number of eminent physicians. Dr. John Collins Warren, who seems to have learned of craniology as early as 1801, discoursed on the topic at Harvard Medical School,[57] while Charles Caldwell, a prominent physician from Philadelphia, delivered a series of lectures in 1828.[58] His success, along with that of Warren and doubtless many others, can be measured by the pace of Spurzheim's schedule after his arrival on 20 August. In addition to teaching at Harvard, Spurzheim also presented a popular course at the Boston Athenaeum until this setting proved too small for the numbers seeking admittance, and it was moved to the more capacious Masonic Temple.[59]

The distances traversed by some artists to attend measure the degree of their enthusiasm. From Philadelphia came John James Audubon with an offer intended to entice the phrenologist away from Boston. The ornithologist soon realized that the many obligations assumed by the visitor precluded an immediate departure,[60] and any hopes he continued to entertain were shattered within a month when he witnessed "the melancholy death of the lamented Spurzheim."[61] This sad turn of events also altered Rembrandt Peale's plans, for he managed to arrive in town only to hear one lecture before illness brought the series to an unanticipated end.[62]

After several weeks of confinement, Spurzheim breathed his last on 10 November. Immediately thereafter a group of distinguished citizens, including such luminaries as Josiah Quincy, Nathaniel Bowditch, Joseph Story, Thomas Wren Ward, and Charles Follen, gathered to dispose of Spurzheim's effects and arrange his funeral. Thousands witnessed the cortege as it wound through Boston to the tolling of church bells on its way to the bowered environs of Mount Auburn Cemetery, where the phrenologist was just the second to be interred.[63] These were not the last rites accorded a charlatan or quack. The presence of the entire medical faculty of Harvard and the membership of the Boston Medical Association indicates the respect in which the deceased was held. Years later a writer for *The Crayon* described the tomb, modeled on that of Scipio, as reflecting "glory upon the New World for paying homage to a man of science of the Old."[64]

Consistent with Spurzheim's own wishes, his skull, brain, and diverse bodily organs were preserved at the Athenaeum. These were subsequently acquired by the Boston Phrenological Society, an organization founded shortly after Spurzheim's death with the intent of testing the veracity of his claims.[65] In answering this charge, over five hundred objects, includ-

FIGURE 1.3. *Thompson, Executed for Rape* (date unknown, plaster cast, Warren
Anatomical Museum, Harvard University)

ing Spurzheim's material, were procured and still survive at Harvard. Most
are life masks (fig. 1.3); in quality they do not diverge significantly from
the busts of John Browere, but in quantity they comprised one of the most
extensive collections of portraits then in America.

This resource was bound to benefit Boston's artistic community, which lacked the academic facilities available in Philadelphia and New York. That the casts came to constitute something of a standard is suggested by one journalist's comparison of Washington Allston's rendering of Coleridge to "the well-known cast of [him] by Spurzheim." [66] Here the young Henry T. Tuckerman (1813–71) served as curator in 1835,[67] honing the critical acumen that later made him a leading commentator on American art. For a period the collection apparently did provide aspiring artists of the city with material for study in a formal context. This occurred when an invitation was extended to William Rimmer, the town's famed artist and educator, to conduct his classes in the collections,[68] and as the following account suggests, he would have had much to impart in these surroundings. "This lecture consists of drawing by the Doctor, which represents the human anatomy in its different forms of repose and action; the different expressions of the face; the phrenological formations of heads; and the general outlines of the human body, with full and succinct remarks upon each subject." [69]

The desire to honor Spurzheim was acutely felt by Bostonians, and nowhere was this sentiment stronger than among the fellows of the phrenological society. Being both a member and an acquaintance of the phrenologist, Alvan Fisher was uniquely qualified to record his likeness in an appropriate manner and did so by painting a pair of portraits. Although the images were once criticized as "naive," Tuckerman thought well of them, and recent opinion has followed his lead.[70] Fisher exhibited one in his studio and the other at the Athenaeum,[71] where the public confirmed, the artist reported to his friend Asher Durand, "that I have painted a very fine head of *Spurzheim*." [72]

Fisher was obliged to work from memory, but he must also have consulted a bust made available commercially by the phrenological society.[73] Both images present Spurzheim lecturing, a pose Bostonians were likely to associate with him. The frontal (fig. 1.4) and profile (fig. 1.5) views enable the observer to assess the anterior and posterior faculties, to phrenologize the phrenologist and judge for oneself the validity of the doctrine he preached. In essence, Fisher's portraits were the artistic counterpart to the task the phrenological society set itself.

Given the reception accorded Spurzheim by the members of the Boston Athenaeum, one might anticipate that the library's patronage would furnish evidence of the initial impact of his teachings. Shortly after the phrenologist's death, a number of busts were ordered from John Frazee, and the two events might seem unconnected were it not for an anomaly in the commission. Three of the seven personages selected were already represented on the institution's walls by handsome paintings. Images of

FIGURE 1.4.
Alvan Fisher, *Portrait of Johann Gaspar Spurzheim* (1832–33, oil painting, Harvard University Portrait Collection, gift to Warren Museum by Dr. John C. Warren, 1927)

FIGURE 1.5.
Alvan Fisher, *Johann Gaspar Spurzheim* (1833, oil painting, Harvard University Portrait Collection, gift of Boston Phrenological Society, 1840)

John Marshall, Daniel Webster, and Thomas Handasyd Perkins had been acquired previously at considerable expense,[74] yet these same individuals now had to be immortalized in marble as well. Why? A glance at the circumstances surrounding the initial negotiations may furnish some clues.

In 1833 Thomas Wren Ward, treasurer of the Athenaeum as well as caretaker of Spurzheim's collection and preserved mortal remains,[75] happened into Frazee's studio while visiting New York and was enthralled by what he saw there. On returning to Boston, he persuaded his colleagues to order busts of Nathaniel Bowditch and Daniel Webster. Both Ward and Bowditch figured prominently in the preparations for Spurzheim's funeral, and Webster soon earned a niche in the phrenological pantheon of distinguished Americans. Among the subsequent commissions, that for

Joseph Story also involved a name conspicuous in accounts of the Spurz-heim ceremonies. Although no definitive program survives, circumstances suggest an underlying motivation. Fisher had been obliged to render two likenesses in order to capture the sitter's entire mental life; sculpted busts, such as those executed by Frazee, would obviate this solution by includ-ing all the faculties in a single piece. The advantage would not be lost on members of the Athenaeum, many of whom, no doubt, were well aware of Spurzheim's directive to "take a complete cast from the head of every man of great talents or remarkable character, and to hand down mental as well as personal likenesses, and also to preserve and multiply the proofs of phrenology." [76]

The prospect that portraiture could provide an objective record of the sitter's character now became a distinct possibility, and the more complete the account of the cranium, the more it would be cherished by future his-torians. Stylistic flourishes that obstructed the reading were not welcome regardless of the conventional notions of beauty they were designed to gratify. Just as phrenology took much of the mystery out of religion, it re-moved the vagaries from aesthetic appreciation. John Marshall appeared in the Athenaeum on canvas and in marble (fig. 1.6), but only the sec-ond medium provided access to the complete scope of the jurist's power-ful mind. Indeed, Frazee's "remarkably accurate bust of Judge Marshall" caught the attention of one phrenologist who proceeded to measure and analyze it precisely as he would the living individual. [77]

While the 1820s were a time of tentative acceptance and institutional-ization of phrenology, the 1830s witnessed the dissemination of its ideas to all levels of American society. Reformers such as Horace Mann and Samuel Gridley Howe toiled in the fields of education and care for the disabled to effectuate the promises held out by Spurzheim, while prisons and asylums were increasingly administered by sympathizers. [78] Its incur-sions were most warmly resisted from the pulpit, whence thundered warn-ings about the perils of materialism. The letters of Horace Mann illustrate how this debate played out between supporters and their orthodox oppo-nents and afford a glimpse of countless such exchanges that took place in parlors and debating societies across the country. In attempting to as-suage the doubts of an acquaintance about the possibility of reconciling phrenology with religion, Mann suggests that the moment of spiritual re-generation so essential to faith be considered a step in the progress of the moral faculties in their struggle for ascendancy over the lower, ani-

(Opposite)
FIGURE 1.6. John Frazee, *John Marshall* (1834–35, marble bust, Boston Athenaeum)

mal propensities.[79] This tack represents a common stratagem adopted by phrenologists; they translated the language of traditional metaphysics, particularly that of Calvinism, into the psychological mechanisms of their science while glossing over the significant differences that remained.

If the clergy vociferated against phrenology, they were not joined by the medical community. One observer estimated that about half of the physicians in Boston were favorably disposed toward the doctrine,[80] and this statistic may be considered as approaching a consensus in an era when numerous philosophies of healing contended with one another. Members of the profession were heavily represented in the Boston Phrenological Society, which during the 1830s earned an international reputation as one of the leading scientific bodies in the United States. Its decline in the following decade was not precipitated by a sudden recognition of phrenology's failings; on the contrary, having passed the tests stipulated in the founding charter, the theory no longer inspired the missionary zeal that stimulated the society when initially organized.[81]

With the death of Spurzheim, the mantle of leadership came to rest on the shoulders of George Combe (1788–1858) of Edinburgh. Unlike his predecessor, Combe was educated as a lawyer and drew on this training to write his *The Constitution of Man.* This text offered readers a rather distant, legalistic divinity, not unlike the one who ruled over Calvin's world. Prayer exerted no influence on the eternal order of nature, and the time devoted to such petitioning was better spent in self-evaluation and personal improvement. The message obviously struck a chord with Americans, for in the three decades before the Civil War they bought some two hundred thousand copies of the volume, which was said to be surpassed in circulation only by the Bible and John Bunyan's *Pilgrim's Progress.*[82] Henry Tuckerman had these developments in mind when he praised Combe for "clearly explaining to the masses the natural laws of human well-being."[83] Under the Scotsman's guidance, phrenology became a doctrine of self-help that appealed immensely to the citizens of the young republic.

Even more than Spurzheim's tour, Combe's travels through the United States might be characterized as a triumphal progress.[84] He arrived on 25 September 1838 and stayed for more than two years. While his predecessor had managed to visit a few cities, Combe traveled up and down the eastern seaboard, attracting large crowds wherever he went.[85] Again, artists sought out Combe just as they had his forerunner. A number of these encounters will be discussed later; here his meeting with Rembrandt Peale will illustrate further some of the concerns that brought members of the two professions together.

Having painted Gall's portrait in Paris in 1810, Peale now sought to enshrine Combe in his gallery of notables in like manner.[86] As Combe toured the studio, his gaze fell on Peale's *Washington before Yorktown* (1824–25, Corcoran Gallery of Art, Washington, D.C.). The auspicious organization of the general's cranium was bound to catch the phrenologist's attention, but he regretted that developments above *Benevolence* were obscured by the wig, a fashion frequently condemned for raising artifice above nature.[87] Peale's fondness for quoting Combe's pronouncements on art suggests that the latter's words fell on attentive ears.[88] Nor was the artist adverse to exercising his own faculties in this manner, finding, for example, *Veneration* large in his portrait of Doctor Priestley and *Form* only moderately developed in Combe.[89] Such statements, like those discussed earlier with regard to Frazee's portrait of Marshall, place art and nature (Combe himself) on a single continuum, with phrenology serving as the unifying ideology.

While on tour, Combe was approached by a fellow traveler curious to know if he was Frederick Coombs, the noted phrenologist. The latter, it turned out, was an itinerant practitioner who attracted crowds by parading a dwarf and a giant before the hall where he was about to lecture.[90] These types were known as "practical phrenologists" because they were more apt to offer concrete answers to the quandaries faced by their clients than did their more theoretically inclined counterparts. A paltry two bits entitled the sitter to sage counsel about vocational aptitude or marital prospects, and in a nation where social and geographic mobility were increasingly the norm, such advice was in great demand. As a result, the practical phrenologists soon outnumbered those who eschewed pecuniary considerations.[91]

It was not the ambition of practical phrenologists to introduce the kinds of institutional reforms undertaken, for example, by Horace Mann. They regarded private consultation as the primary means for bettering society, and if they made some money in the process, it was only just recompense for their efforts. A few books and a fancy for the open road liberated the enterprising youth from the grinding toil of the farm. He was not obliged or even likely to make phrenology his sole field of expertise; by cultivating other areas, including geology, poetry, and the like, he acquired the requisite flexibility to meet any contingency. When the rigors of itinerancy lost their luster, he might turn to a more settled calling such as teaching. One authority has calculated that about twenty thousand practical phrenologists plied the trade in the nineteenth century.[92] Whatever the number, there were certainly enough to visit every hamlet in the union. Add to this the claim by one that he examined over two hundred thousand heads in his career,[93] and the mathematics suggests that such persons were a pervasive feature in American life.

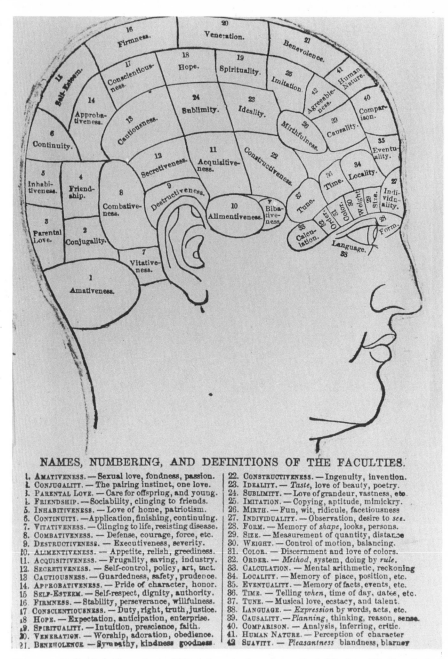

NAMES, NUMBERING, AND DEFINITIONS OF THE FACULTIES.

1. AMATIVENESS. — Sexual love, fondness, passion.
2. CONJUGALITY. — The pairing instinct, one love.
3. PARENTAL LOVE. — Care for offspring, and young.
4. FRIENDSHIP. — Sociability, clinging to friends.
5. INHABITIVENESS. — Love of home, patriotism.
6. CONTINUITY. — Application, finishing, continuing.
7. VITATIVENESS. — Clinging to life, resisting disease.
8. COMBATIVENESS. — Defense, courage, force, etc.
9. DESTRUCTIVENESS. — Executiveness, severity.
10. ALIMENTIVENESS. — Appetite, relish, greediness.
11. ACQUISITIVENESS. — Frugality, saving, industry.
12. SECRETIVENESS. — Self-control, policy, art, tact.
13. CAUTIOUSNESS. — Guardedness, safety, prudence.
14. APPROBATIVENESS. — Pride of character, honor.
15. SELF-ESTEEM. — Self-respect, dignity, authority.
16. FIRMNESS. — Stability, perseverance, willfulness.
17. CONSCIENTIOUSNESS. — Duty, right, truth, justice.
18. HOPE. — Expectation, anticipation, enterprise.
19. SPIRITUALITY. — Intuition, prescience, faith.
20. VENERATION. — Worship, adoration, obedience.
21. BENEVOLENCE — Sympathy, kindness goodness.

22. CONSTRUCTIVENESS. — Ingenuity, invention.
23. IDEALITY. — *Taste*, love of beauty, poetry.
24. SUBLIMITY. — Love of grandeur, vastness, etc.
25. IMITATION. — Copying, aptitude, mimickry.
26. MIRTH. — Fun, wit, ridicule, facetiousness.
27. INDIVIDUALITY. — Observation, desire to *see*.
28. FORM. — Memory of *shape*, looks, persons.
29. SIZE. — Measurement of quantity, distance
30. WEIGHT. — Control of motion, balancing.
31. COLOR. — Discernment and love of colors.
32. ORDER. — *Method*, system, doing by *rule*.
33. CALCULATION. — Mental arithmetic, reckoning
34. LOCALITY. — Memory of place, position, etc.
35. EVENTUALITY. — Memory of facts, events, etc.
36. TIME. — Telling *when*, time of day, dates, etc.
37. TUNE. — Musical love, ecstacy, and talent.
38. LANGUAGE. — *Expression* by words, acts, etc.
39. CAUSALITY. — *Planning*, thinking, reason, sense.
40. COMPARISON. — Analysis, inferring, critic.
41. HUMAN NATURE. — Perception of character
42. SUAVITY. — *Pleasantness* blandness, blarney

FIGURE 1.7. *Fowler's Phrenological Head*, frontispiece from O. S. Fowler, *The Practical Phrenologist* (Boston: O. S. Fowler, 1869)

Combe held them in low esteem because he thought soft flattery the inevitable reward for hard cash. His own monetary anxieties had been relieved by marriage to an heiress, a circumstance that permitted him to indulge his true interest exclusively. The expertise so acquired did not enhance his estimation of itinerant lecturers or their representations of the science to the public. It is easy to imagine how frictions arose between the theoretically oriented, usually physicians and lawyers, who appended the subject to their professional studies, and those of less exalted social standing, who embraced it as a means of getting by. Less obvious, however, are the substantive issues, other than commercialism, that separated the two factions. Practical proponents could point to Spurzheim's efforts to open the discipline to a wider range of types as the origin of their own endeavors. In any case, this attention to financial viability sustained the doctrine well into the twentieth century, long after its theoretical advocates had vanished.[94]

By the middle of the nineteenth century, phrenology held a place in the American mind not unlike that occupied by psychiatry in the 1930s. Its terminology and tenets entered the language of daily conversation. In literature it proved a convenient means of summarizing behavior and character,[95] but its complete demise often makes such allusions inaccessible to the modern reader. The following lines by Walt Whitman, for example, are best read with a phrenological chart nearby (fig. 1.7): "Extreme caution or prudence, the soundest organic health, large hope and comparison and fondness for women and children, large alimentiveness and destructiveness and causality, with a perfect sense of the oneness of nature and the propriety of the same spirit applied to human affairs . . . these are called up of the float of the brain of the world to be parts of the greatest poet from his birth out of his mother's womb and from her birth out of her mother's."[96]

Not all authors, however, were similarly disposed; while John Quincy Adams tossed Emerson into the "bubbling cauldron" with phrenology, the latter would have been less than thrilled by the gesture. The reasons for his distaste will be discussed later, but it should be noted here that this stance distanced him from Whitman. The poet embraced physical metaphysics, while the philosopher could not abide the formulaic salvation it promised. In reviewing the quest each man pursued to penetrate the core of personal identity, one critic has aptly remarked that "Emerson seeks this in what purges him of physicality. Whitman finds it in what immerses him most deeply in the physical."[97] This polarity merits prolonged consideration because it pares down preferences to their basic constituents, thus clarifying a number of issues. Hence, we will consult these two exemplars through much of what follows.

Just as Whitman relied on phrenology to situate his ego within the float of moral and material developments of the day,[98] so artists employed the theory to express like sentiments succinctly. Again, the implications may not be readily apparent to the modern reader. While strolling with his young daughter, sculptor Thomas Ball noted that an incongruous action struck her "funny bump" (*Mirthfulness*). While the event is trivial, the report of it reveals, almost inadvertently, a partiality to the doctrine. Alerted to this preference, a reader can draw further inferences from remarks in Ball's autobiography that might otherwise seem casual. His description of William Morris Hunt, for example, includes praise for his "well developed, intellectual forehead" and "nervous and imaginative temperament."[99] By recognizing that these features were integral to the phrenological evaluation of artistic talent, we learn not merely about Hunt's appearance but, more importantly, about Ball's conception of genius and how this would figure in his own self-image. Henry Tuckerman shared these thoughts, remarking that it was "impossible to associate with Hunt, however casually, without recognizing in him the artistic organization and perception."[100] As we shall see, a major strain of Victorian criticism embraced this approach by seeking to trace the correspondences between the physical constitution of the creator and the aesthetic tenor of the artifact.

Mention of Whitman in this context leads us to the Fowler brothers, the phrenologists with whom he frequently associated at the outset of his career. Orson Squires (1809–87) and Lorenzo Niles (1811–96) parlayed their interest in the theory into a substantial business venture that survived for several generations.[101] Combe's program of physical and mental hygiene they translated into a doctrine of perfectionism, molding the entire scheme into a project that harmonized with the millennial notions then prevalent in America. They wrote extensively about daily regimen, diet and digestion, work and play, education and marriage, and conceiving and raising children. From their offices in New York and elsewhere issued a stream of publications designed to appeal to a wide public, and that audience responded, purchasing some half a million books and pamphlets by mid-century. They also produced the *American Phrenological Journal*, a magazine with a readership of fifty thousand, while their *Phrenological Almanac* reached three times that number.[102] In addition to these undertakings, the Fowlers encouraged, edited, and distributed books and journals devoted to allied reforms. Temperance, hydropathy, and vegetarianism were among the movements that benefited from their support.[103]

The inventory drawn up at the death of Joseph Whiting Stock (1815–55), an artist active in Connecticut, illustrates how infectious this enthusiasm could be. Besides several issues of the *American Phrenological Journal*, he owned a book by Combe and several devoted to hydropathy and the water cure. Still others dealt with vegetarianism, temperance, the dangers of tobacco, and the "Natural laws of man."[104] Nor did Stock confine himself merely to reading about such matters. He provided speakers with likenesses of Napoleon, Jackson, Sir Walter Scott, and similar notables.

One such patron was Dr. Swan, a lecturer whose discourses ran the gamut from temperance and dyspepsia to phrenology.[105] And in the list kept by Stock of the subjects he had rendered, there appear the following entries:

The Millenium [*sic*]
7 Illustrations of the Stomach for Dr. Swan.[106]

Given the artist's reading habits and Swan's interests, it is likely these were related commissions. Only half facetiously it might be said of phrenologists that their voyage of life progressed down the alimentary canal. Salvation and mastication were two sides of the same coin. Abrupt juxtapositions of the sublime and mundane similar to the one above appear frequently in their texts, and Stock would not have thought the following maxim by Orson Fowler incongruous: "When the devout Christian or profound thinker has eaten to excess, or induced severe colds or fevers, or in any other way clogged or disordered his PHYSICAL functions the former can no more be 'clothed with the spirit,' or 'soar on the wings of devotion,' or the latter bring his intellectual energies into full and efficient action, than arrest the sun."[107]

Whatever merit this system may have in the eyes of modern readers, it is important to realize that it proved inspirational to Stock's contemporaries. There is no reason to suppose, then, that for all its involvement in the minutiae of bodily functions, this faith precluded flights of the imagination among its believers. It moved Whitman to write,

The head well grown and proportioned and plumb, and the bowels
    and joints proportioned and plumb.
The soul is always beautiful,
The universe is duly in order . . . every thing is in its place,
The twisted skull waits . . . the watery or rotten blood waits,
The child of the glutton or venerealee waits long, and the child of the
    drunkard waits long, and the drunkard himself waits long.[108]

While Stock's accomplishments were far more modest than those of Whitman, they were both motivated by similar notions. I suspect that had Stock's painting of the millennium survived, his place in the history of American art would be far more prominent than it presently is. This loss, no doubt, has diminished our appreciation of much of the depth and contemporaneity of his oeuvre, and he might well have taken a place beside Edward Hicks and Erastus Salisbury Field.

The Fowler firm owed Stock the substantial sum of $166.63 at the time of his death.[109] No indication is given of the services performed, but he may have provided the sort of illustrations and diagrams the company

FIGURE 1.8. Winslow Homer, *Circassian Girl and Prize Old Man* (ca. 1897, drawing, Bowdoin College Museum of Art, gift of the Homer family)

made available commercially.[110] Artists were also engaged to make portraits and take plaster casts of persons with exemplary heads. Taking advantage of lessons learned from his father, Albertus Browere (1814–87), son of John Browere, made the masks exhibited at the Fowler museum and designed their phrenological chart.[111]

When the Fowlers settled in New York City in the late 1830s, they began to assemble a collection that was housed during the 1840s and early 1850s in Clinton Hall, the building vacated by the National Academy of Design in 1840. The museum, which moved to various locations in subsequent decades, became one of the city's premier tourist attractions, drawing hundreds of thousands through its doors before their final closing.[112] By viewing the assembled treasures, the visitor could test his or her ability to judge character. This challenge would have appealed especially to artists, and evidence that Winslow Homer made the visit survives in a rather caustic caricature of his father (fig. 1.8). Situated side by side are two busts; one, labeled "Prize Old Man," represents the paterfamilias, and the other depicts a "Circassian Girl." Circassia, a region located on the shores of the Black Sea, was fabled for the beauty of its women, who according to the testimony of travelers, were highly valued as slaves by the Turks.

This circumstance afforded artists the opportunity of rendering scantily clad damsels brought to the auctioneer's block or some equally enticing vignette.[113] Few scenes could have been more alien to Homer's creative temperament, and, of course, that is not what he depicts. The subject becomes comprehensible when we learn that the Fowlers proudly displayed the Circassian skull they chanced to acquire. A bit of doggerel written by a visitor to the museum provides further illumination:

> The smooth skull of the fair Circassian girl
> Stands where the wild gorillas—savage pair,
> Threatened to crush the gentle maiden there.[114]

Where else would the artist have seen two such heads so displayed? Recognition that his father stands in for the gorilla makes Homer's updating of the old tradition of the "ill-matched couple" particularly acerbic. We shall have occasion to return to Circassia.

As their collections expanded, the Fowlers were able to increase the number of faculties. They identified several, including *Conjugality, Vitativeness,* and *Bibativeness,* that had escaped the scrutiny of Gall and Spurzheim, but it became apparent that this line of research could not continue indefinitely. There were limitations to the nuances discernible by the finger, and those anxious to sustain the pace of progress searched for a means of overcoming this apparent impasse. To such seekers, the advent of mesmerism seemed heaven-sent.

Franz Anton Mesmer (1734–1815) claimed the distinction of discovering a universal ether that possessed traits akin to those of electricity and magnetism.[115] This vital energy, which bounded across the emptiness of interplanetary space, also sustained the internal functions of the body. When unbalanced, it was a source of disease, and the magnetizer's task was to restore harmony by the ministration of iron rods, specially treated water, and similar devices, all of which were designed to transmit the fluid in prescribed doses. The patients who slipped into a trance during treatment intrigued Mesmer's disciples, for marvelous phenomena often ensued. Some wondered if the clairvoyance and ecstatic visions experienced by those *en rapport* were powers granted a soul disencumbered of its earthly trammels. Did it traverse the globe at will? Speculation abounded.

Some time elapsed before mesmerism, or animal magnetism, as it came to be known, attained a level of popularity in America comparable to that it enjoyed in Europe. The lectures delivered by Charles Poyen in the late 1830s did much to narrow the gap,[116] and by 1840, as we have seen, John Quincy Adams could condemn it along with phrenology as one of the plausible rascalities that had bewitched the populace. Inquiries into the nature and abode of Mesmer's mysterious fluid caused many to connect the two disciplines.

If the magnetizer's touch could activate the forces residing within the cranium, then the brain could be mapped without recourse to the skull's shape. A faculty could be awakened merely by placing a finger in its vicinity. Upon performance of this act, the sensitive sitter would respond to the dictates transmitted by the energized organ. *Self-Esteem* induced haughtiness; *Veneration,* piety; and so on. This confluence of disciplines became known as phreno-magnetism or phreno-mesmerism. Because practitioners were not obliged to discern a protuberance, they could make finer distinctions than their more orthodox colleagues. Theoretically, every sentiment and instinct might have its seat, and this realization led to a precipitous rise in the number of faculties. Why stop in the vicinity of three dozen when, by forging on, 80 or 100 or 150 organs divulged their locale? Beside established faculties such as *Benevolence* and *Ideality,* exotic upstarts named *Money-Making, Love of Keep-Sakes,* and *Tattling* vied for attention.[117]

As the 1840s progressed, it became increasingly difficult for those of Combe's ilk to dictate the priorities for phrenology. The commercialism that now dominated the discipline set each practitioner against potential competitors. Prospective customers had to be persuaded of the advantages that accrued to a particular system.[118] The dilemma was exacerbated by the phreno-mesmerists because none could replicate the results published by others. No consensus emerged among them; hence they did not challenge the practical phrenologists seriously. In any case, the boundaries between the two were ill defined and often traversed. The Fowlers, for example, claimed for themselves the initial insight into the potential of phreno-mesmerism,[119] but they had to contend with Robert Collyer, La Roy Sunderland, and Joseph Rodes Buchanan for the honor. The last named came closest to institutionalizing the system by training students in the techniques of manipulating the "nervauric fluid." [120]

Among those bitten by the mesmeric bug was Rubens Peale, who made his museum in New York a center for research on the subject.[121] Here, in 1838, La Roy Sunderland instructed him in the techniques of phreno-mesmerism. On inducing a magnetic sleep, Peale would rub the sitter's forehead to stimulate the intellect. He then touched the various faculties and observed the outcome. Stimulation of *Tune* in one instance engendered vocal feats "utterly impossible" in the waking state.[122] After witnessing one such performance in 1842, Henry Inman took the stage and succeeded in transmitting the image of a phantom to an entranced girl. The artist later wrote a friend about the incident, declaring that it "absolutely demonstrated the thing [mesmerism] to my own mind." [123]

Inman and his colleagues would have had good reason to pay close attention to these demonstrations, for they offered them the prospect of witnessing behavior unconstrained by convention, and this possibility promised to enhance the level of artistic expression.[124] Orthodox phrenologists had sought to identify similar instances of unfeigned behavior without the aid of the hypnotic trance. They were obliged to scrutinize habitual stances, gestures, and demeanor for evidence of the control exercised by one faculty or another. The body thus became a living hieroglyph written by the cerebral scribe; whenever a faculty was in ascendance, it dictated bodily deportment. This "natural language" of the faculties, phrenology's adaptation of pathognomy, provided investigators with another means of access to the secret workings of the mind, and while an individual might strive to conceal his true feelings, the alert observer could always detect telltale signs.

The vocabulary of the natural language was limited by the number of faculties in the brain, each of which governed a circumscribed range of activities.[125] Those initiated into the discipline could read a portrait even if the sitter's cranium did not offer itself advantageously. Woodcuts based on Gilbert Stuart Newton's likeness of Washington Irving (fig. 1.9) were often published with the following commentary: "Ideality throws the head slightly forward and to one side, as in Irving a man as gifted in taste and imagination as any other writer; and, in his portraits, his finger rests on this faculty."[126] Irving's familiarity with phrenology predates the portrait and makes at least possible its influence on the choice of pose. Had you

FIGURE 1.9.
Washington Irving, from
O. S. Fowler, *The Practical
Phrenologist* (Boston: O. S.
Fowler, 1869), p. 60

inquired further into the matter, however, a phrenologist would have explained that the impulse to comply with the dictates of the natural language was universal, rendering largely irrelevant the question of Irving's or Newton's knowledge of the doctrine.

We might wonder whether our phrenologist friend had discovered something like the modern subconscious. What was this animating principle that motivated meaningful behavior at a level other than pure volition? Gall's teachings initially drew fire for being merely the latest form of atheism—charges that were not entirely without substance—but by the 1840s, phrenology had become entirely reconciled with religion.[127] By then, few in the movement were actively committed to materialism, and most, on confronting the issue, would have repeated the standard response regarding the faculties that attested to a divine plan.[128] Phreno-mesmerism did nothing to discourage the growing affinity between the theory and the occult. Its preoccupation with vital fluids, often thought to be either a form of refined electricity that bridged the gap between body and soul, or the soul itself, enhanced the expectation that the spirit would one day be as accessible to scientific scrutiny as the anatomy presently was. It seemed that Mesmer had stumbled onto the spiritual essence adrift in the remote vastness of the universe, and phrenology would now delineate precisely how this soul stuff generated mental activity as well as flesh and bone in conformity with the dictates of supreme wisdom.

For those dedicated to this belief, the writings of Emanuel Swedenborg (1688–1772) appeared prophetic of the discoveries of their own era.[129] On a spring evening in 1745, an angel visited this great mystic and commenced his initiation into the secrets of the spirit world and the hidden meaning of the Bible. Based on the insights gained during these sessions, Swedenborg came to realize that his mission was nothing less than the regeneration of Christianity, which, he believed, had declined precipitously in his time.

Deeply embedded within Swedenborg's moral teachings was the kernel of a physiognomic system. He maintained that mankind had once been blessed with facial features so highly expressive and mobile that they had served as the principal means of communication. Only as selfishness supplanted innocence did the expedient of dissimulation arise. Indurated by the influence of evil, the visage became a mask, losing much of its ability to convey the ideas that once played so swiftly across its surface. These developments necessitated the invention of language, but language was a slow and imperfect substitute for the mode of imparting information once allotted primitive humanity.[130] Some vestige of the relationship between the internal and the external person survived, though the connections were no longer so readily apparent. Needless to say, Lavater recognized the importance of these ideas to his project, as the phrenologists did to theirs,[131] but to understand the use made of them, the theory of "correspondences" must also be considered. According to this doctrine, heaven and earth are so intimately connected that any entity or event that appears in one has its correspondence in the other. Man, being the most refined inhabitant of the terrestrial sphere, is most closely tied to the spiritual; he is sustained by the continuous outpouring of divine love and wisdom, any interruption of which would mean immediate annihilation of him and the entire material realm.[132] The emanations that compose this outpouring are called "influx,"[133] and due to its operation, all phenomena are symbolic of the moral order present in the universe.

The last two decades of the eighteenth century saw the establishment of Swedenborgian communities up and down the eastern seaboard.[134] Although never a major denomination in terms of membership, the New Jerusalem Church managed to attract creative thinkers in numbers out of all proportion to its size. Hiram Powers and William Page both belonged,[135] but as we shall see, those who have endeavored to trace the influence of Swedenborg on their work have neglected the contributions made by commentators in the nineteenth century. The seer had encouraged followers to expand the theory of correspondences by turning to the ongoing revelations of science, and this adaptability enabled the religion to respond to the radical changes of outlook that shook the faith of so many Victorians.

The preceding helps explain the popularity of Mesmer in New Church circles well before his wider acceptance in America. The Frenchman's discovery of a universal ether permeating mind and body recalled the seer's discussion of influx, and the similarity of the latter's visions to the clairvoyance associated with the trance state of mesmerism strengthened the bond. The advent of spiritualism as an organized religion after the "Rochester rappings" of 1848 cast yet another ingredient into the bubbling cauldron of antebellum society and vastly expanded the audience receptive to these notions.[136] Followers soon noted the parallels between the communications with the deceased made by the Fox sisters and those conducted by Swedenborg, while the latter's descriptions of heaven as a place resembling earth also found favor with the former. Likewise, the odylic fluid of the spiritualists, again a sort of rarefied electricity that constituted the soul's substance, resembled both animal magnetism and the theory of influx. While reviewing these matters, one partisan contended that "Emanuel Swedenborg is therefore deservedly ranked as the first Spiritualist."[137]

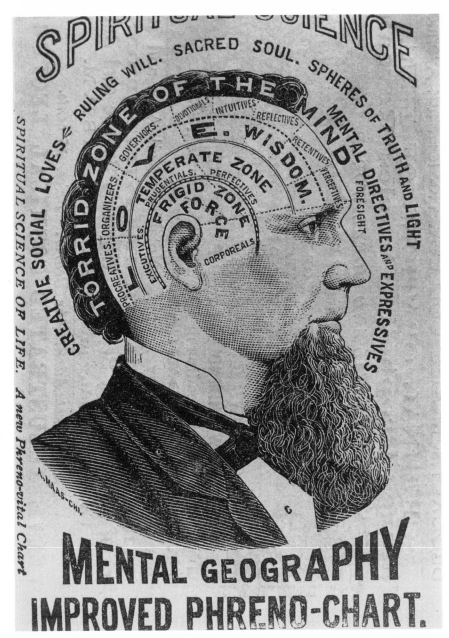

FIGURE 1.10. *Franklin's Phrenological Head,* from Prof. Zeus Franklin, *Private Marriage Guide* (Boston: Mutual Benefit Co., [ca. 1883])

Phrenologists also regarded Swedenborg as having anticipated many of Gall's discoveries. These included the contention that the brain was the organ of the mind, that its health depended on the condition of the body, and that character determined the shape of the skull.[138] Also, by extending the theory of correspondences to include the entire human frame, they derived further justification for the mapping of mental functions onto the body that had already commenced with the phreno-mesmerists. Such considerations cemented the ties between the theory and metaphysics[139] and encouraged a mutual admiration of the sort expressed by James John Garth Wilkinson, a prominent author of Swedenborgian tracts, when he praised phrenology as a "science of sciences," explaining that it went beyond mere descriptive anatomical analysis to include qualitative and moral considerations within its purview.[140] The label often applied to this confluence of spiritualism, Swedenborgianism, and phrenology was "spiritual science."

Familiarity with the tenets of this philosophy enables us, for example, to decipher the notes written by William Sidney Mount after attending a lecture delivered by Andrew Jackson Davis, the famed spiritualist.[141] In his address the latter contrasted the dominion held by Moses over the back of the head to that of Christ over the top; the explanation for this cryptic statement comes from the spiritualist's writings. There we read that the Jewish prophet's philosophy of "an eye for an eye" emanated from the selfish sentiments and propensities, while the admonition of Jesus to love one's neighbor as one's self represented a higher stage of spiritual development embodied by *Benevolence* and contiguous faculties. Democracy, Davis explained, was the final flowering of this precept because it implied that all were entitled to equal respect and consideration; soon American civilization would realize man's innate but long-suppressed desire for justice and liberty.[142] It was to phrenology that Davis could point when he sought tangible evidence for his account of human evolution, and this appeal was not lost on Mount, who likewise shared the seer's vision of the future.

The charts devised by the spiritual scientists reflect the eclecticism of their discipline. That published by Zeus Franklin (aptly named for one so devoted to studying the electromagnetic forces of the soul) exhibits a series of generalized phrenological faculties combined with Swedenborg's spiritual essences, love and wisdom (fig. 1.10). In conformity with the seer's teachings about the correspondence between man and his environment, various geographic zones are thrown in for good measure. The universality so achieved was designed to restore a measure of holism to an age of growing specialization. Science and philosophy were increasingly undermining the foundations of phrenology in the later decades of the century,[143] and the best defense seemed to be a strategic retreat from the field, thus cutting losses to a minimum. Subjects that had been dismissed by Gall and Spurzheim, such as traditional physiognomy and chiromancy, were now recruited into the cause in order to put on as good a front as possible. This explains the particular appeal of Swedenborg's correspondences, for they transformed the study of anatomy from the plane of scientific investigation to that of metaphysical speculation while blurring the distinctions between the two.

A passage drawn from a later phrenological treatise epitomizes this approach. "Prominence of the nose undoubtedly indicates strength, energy, power-full manly development. Prominent noses are of several different forms, depending upon the relative development of different portions of the ridge. In all of them we find indications of a disposition to fight, contend, dispute, argue, or in some form, or under some circumstances, to manifest Combativeness."[144] Commingled here are elements of the older form of physiognomy as it pertains to the nose, with phrenological tenets relating to the organ of *Combativeness*. The former is made to comply with the latter, and this logic granted phreno-mesmerists and spiritual scientists the license not merely to chart the body but also to tap a faculty, much as one might a telegraph key, to send messages of healing electricity to the corresponding portion of the body that was in distress.[145] Few perceived the potential of this method more clearly than Warren Felt Evans, an advocate of mind-cure who anticipated much that Mary Baker Eddy later introduced as articles of faith in the Christian Science Church.[146] In the late 1860s Evans could still claim that phrenology was "a branch of human knowledge yet in its infancy and formative stage. There are many discoveries not made by Dr. Gall, in relation to the sympathetic connection of the various organs of the body, with particular parts of the brain, whence they receive vital stimulus, which are of great importance in the system of Mental Hygiene."[147]

Uniting all these beliefs was a faith in progress. For the spiritualists this implied that revelation itself was progressive. The intermittent communications made by the divinity of the Old Testament became increasingly frequent in the New, but they did not terminate with its concluding book. Moderns might expect the process to continue until access to the spiritual world would be available to all.[148] To the phrenologist, progress meant that the spirit of history would ascend from its ancient residence in *Amativeness* and *Combativeness* to a more exalted post in *Benevolence* and *Veneration*.[149] To persons such as Andrew Jackson Davis, whose philosophy was a compilation of these doctrines, both were headed in the same direction; thus he could urge listeners, including William Sidney Mount, to "incline to that which your mind admired most—and perfect yourself."[150]

These notions of self-perfection and the immanent millennium may help resolve a seeming paradox in Mount's intellectual and artistic development. His paintings often depict persons of moderate circumstances who share a sense of well-being as they go about their tasks in an orderly environment; the tenor of this imagery has caused many to equate it with the egalitarianism of Jacksonian politics. But the artist remained loyal to the conservative wing of the New York State Democratic Party that opposed the "fiscal radicalism" of the Jacksonian faction. His proslavery views eventually put him at odds with the Republicans, whom he called "Lincolnpoops,"[151] yet he could also write that spiritualism "teaches us progression here and here after, upward and onward forever and that God is ever present and full of love." "All human souls are," he added, "unfolded from the exhaustless fountain—Deity. They are inherently pure, and destined to progress forever."[152] Leashed together in his mind, then, were social and metaphysical views that would seem to pull in opposite directions, with the need for fiscal responsibility tugging against a utopian vision of future liberation and harmony among all peoples. The dichotomy, however, would have been less apparent to Mount. Government, from his perspective, was not so much a vehicle for the betterment of mankind as a means of maintaining a sufficient degree of stability so that advances could take place elsewhere. That elsewhere was the individual psyche whence all progress flowed. The spirit of the Reverend Samuel Dean stressed this lesson in a seance attended by the artist. "Each person must be true to himself," the ghost uttered, "and all the world will be right. A departure from the right by one person mars the harmony of the world."[153]

Some idea of Mount's sentiments toward reform can be surmised from T. S. Mackintosh's *The "Electrical Theory" of the Universe*, a copy of which found its way into the artist's library. Like the phrenologists, the author of this work seeks to devise a system of morality from natural laws. He takes as his paradigm the precept that every action has an equal and opposite reaction. Extreme positions in politics are bound to invite equally harsh countermeasures; hence Mackintosh proposes the best recourse is to press forward, avoiding violent action, so that the violent reaction that might otherwise follow can be circumvented.[154] No doubt Mount wanted to press forward as well, but not at the pace demanded by radical Jacksonians or Republicans. The world depicted in his paintings is also one of moderation, and there the individual may pursue his own perfection unimpeded by outside forces.

The tippler in *Loss and Gain* (fig. 1.11) does not resort to banditry, does not beat his wife and children, does not commit suicide while in delirium tremens; although Mount praised the virtues of teetotalism, he did not resort to the extreme rhetoric of prohibitionist pamphlets and broadsheets. What defeats the drinker's designs? Gravity, the most fundamental of all nature's laws. Carelessly, he has placed the jug on a pebble, and now its contents pour forth. The phrenologists endlessly reminded their readers

FIGURE 1.11. William Sidney Mount, *Loss and Gain* (1847, oil painting, Museums at Stony Brook, bequest of Mr. Ward Melville, 1977)

that the laws of physiology, including those that prohibited the imbibing of spirituous liquors, operated with the same universality as other laws of nature, including gravity.[155] No exceptions were granted, and prayerful remorse could not save those intent on destroying themselves. The edition of Spurzheim owned by Mount begins by claiming, "Nature is constant and ever within the reach of those who would examine for themselves, and by self-examination, obtain self-conviction of truth."[156] Beyond the grasp of the inebriate in Mount's painting is the jug; within his reach are the natural laws that can transform his loss into gain if he will only examine himself honestly.

In an attempt to dissuade an acquaintance from an inclination to drink, Mount sent words of encouragement, reminding him, "You have firmness—say no."[157] The choice of words here is interesting; it may be coincidental that the term "firmness" appears, but it may also be an instance of Mount's habit, one we shall encounter again, of employing the vocabulary of phrenology to elucidate his convictions. The fact that the letter goes on to describe the misshapen heads of drunkards is suggestive, just as the bald pate of the figure in his painting provides us an advantageous view of his phrenological developments. We are even afforded a glimpse of *Firmness*, which is located in the upper posterior region of the skull; presumably it is not well developed in this case, but its cultivation will constitute the first step in recovery.

In *Loss and Gain* we encounter "one person [who] mars the harmony of the world." The point of this analysis has been to suggest that Mount's perception of that harmony was deeply influenced by his familiarity with phrenology and spiritualism, and these, in turn, guided him to such allied reforms as temperance.[158] Perfection was the goal of such movements, and if this possibility has eluded the protagonist of Mount's little drama, he could at least improve his moral and physical being. Those who had not so injured their person might even aspire to reach or surpass the ideal offered by the Greeks and Romans. Just as science had propelled modern civilization beyond the level achieved by antiquity, it could also raise the stature of contemporaries to heights hitherto unattained. The representatives of progress, however, would have to be attuned to the laws of nature. Such individuals could inaugurate the millennium not by withdrawing from the world but by embracing it even as it pertained to the most intimate functions of their own bodies.[159]

The agenda promoted by phrenology made no great demands on believers; exercise, the proper diet, comfortable clothing, and circumspection about the physical and mental attributes of a prospective spouse were seemingly enough to usher in the golden age. Its standards were basically those of the middle class, and its emphasis on self-improvement was alluring to individuals intent on leading a life of respectability. Cooter's contention that the theory was even more deeply entrenched in the popular consciousness of England in the second half of the nineteenth century than the first is probably also true of the United States.[160] This very ubiquity, however, dissipated much of its ability to inspire the crusading fervor of the antebellum years.

Its system of criminal anthropology entered obliquely into the writings of Cesare Lombroso and Havelock Ellis,[161] and its protoeugenic teachings anticipated the movement inaugurated by Francis Galton.[162] While these developments are significant, they are beyond the scope of this book. The place of phrenology in late Victorian society was aptly summarized by one authority who notes that "its principal credo—that the scientific, experimental approach should be made to operations of the human mind—had suffered scientific euthanasia, incorporated without acknowledgment into contemporary thought, and phrenology was left with the dry husks of its eccentricities—'bumps on the head.'"[163]

Many readers may have first encountered phrenology as I did, by reading *The Adventures of Huckleberry Finn*. There, the dissolute "Duke of Bridgewater" boards Huck's raft and lists his occupations: "Jour printer by trade; do a little in patent medicines; theater actor—tragedy, you know; take a turn to mesmerism and phrenology when there's a chance."[164] The plausible rascality about which John Quincy Adams complained so bitterly has finally come full circle in this implausible rascal. It should be remembered, however, that when Twain created the character, the halcyon days of phrenology had long passed, and the author enjoyed the advantage of hindsight in ridiculing the foibles of an earlier generation. Only by moving beyond such caricatures do we come to a just appreciation of the science advocated by Gall and Spurzheim. It then takes its place among the sanguine beliefs of a sanguine era. Artists in particular were charged with the task of documenting the doctrine's truths and, in doing so, with advancing the cause of humanity. This heady challenge meant that the visual culture of Jacksonian America was involved in a venture of far greater consequence than that of merely furnishing a veneer of taste over a rough-and-tumble society. Rather, with the aid of phrenology, art fully immersed itself in the bubbling cauldron of those turbulent times.

2

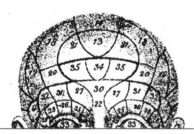

Know Thyself

If, by the wave of a wand, we could be whisked back to Jacksonian America and there accompany one of its citizens on rounds that included visits to a phrenologist and then a portraitist, we would doubtlessly be struck by the similarity of routine followed at each place of business. At the first, our companion would take a chair to have his head scrutinized, measured, and otherwise examined for the testimony it divulged about character. If our gaze happened to wander during these proceedings, it would alight on the numerous busts and paintings requisite for the trade (fig. 2.1). We would encounter much the same paraphernalia on entering the artist's domicile, and again our escort would sit while his features were inspected, perhaps measured, and rendered with the intent of capturing personality. Artists themselves were not unaware of these affinities, and the consequences of this recognition, which caused them to rethink

FIGURE 2.1. *Prof. Burton's Consulting and Class Room*, from C. Burton, *Phrenology: Evil and the Devil* (Birmingham: C. Burton, 1903)

their professional identity and studio practices, are the thread that ties what follows.

Some sense of the symbiotic relationship that evolved between the two callings arises from consideration of Josiah M. Graves, a practical phrenologist who took up the brush to furnish himself with the images needed to illustrate his lectures. According to accounts, he produced several hundred of these, and one can easily imagine their impact on the inhabitants of the isolated hamlets he visited. Those enticed by an exhibition provided gratis would then proceed to the consultation room, where fees were charged. Another phrenologist, recognizing the potential of this tactic, purchased Graves's entire collection of more than a hundred oil paintings. The latter set about replenishing his stock posthaste, while the former gloated that the additional income generated by the "gallery" enabled him to recoup his initial outlay within three months.[1]

Here, then, was a phrenologist who, while operating within the purview of his own profession, adopted the practices of an artist. In turn, Joseph Whiting Stock carried not only a number of portraits, but also a phrenological bust when he went on tour.[2] The bust no doubt presided over sittings, offering its example whenever patron or painter sought to resolve some point relevant to the likeness. The relationship between the Fowler firm and Stock may have developed for reasons other than those postulated in the previous chapter; he may, for example, have been attracted by the prospects that drew John Quidor to the cause. The latter endeavored to found a phrenological society in Columbus, Illinois, during the summer of 1848 as a means of selling subscriptions to the *American Phrenological Journal.* The remuneration offered by the Fowlers for this service may have helped stave off the wolves that perpetually lurked around the door of this impecunious artist.[3]

Poverty was less likely to have figured among the motives that led Hiram Powers to mold a bust and distribute phrenological pamphlets from his studio in Florence. The resolve to take these steps grew out of personal conviction, and some idea of its depth can be gained from an essay he wrote on the detrimental consequences of prejudice. All great scientific innovators, he observes, have encountered setbacks engendered by this vice. The travails faced by Franklin and Fulton stemmed from the ignorance and prejudice of their opponents; likewise, the followers of Gall and Spurzheim had to surmount similar barriers before their theories could benefit mankind.[4] Here was a cause that warmed Powers's enthusiasm, but when the Italians remained indifferent to his efforts, he concluded that they did not "care half so much for their heads as they do for their bellies."[5]

Besides contributing their labors to the cause, artists also sought to bring the practices associated with their metier into conformity with the principles of phrenology. Sculptors were particularly responsive because, as noted in the case of Frazee, they modeled the entire head and hence had access to faculties that were not generally available in a painting. Busts created around mid-century are frequently disparaged for their prosaic execution in modern histories, but this analysis often glosses over the conflicting motives that alternately came into play. Artists knew they were enjoined to accuracy but were equally convinced that imitation alone was inadequate. The images that emerged from this tension are often more complex than critics of our time will allow. We broach this theme by considering first those factors that pulled the artist in the direction of scrupulous fidelity to the model.

Gall realized that one prerequisite for the acceptance of his theories was a means of calculating the absolute size of the faculties. An astute observer might wonder, after all, about the assessment of a large organ if it were surrounded by even larger neighbors; how could one do justice to the former? Again, Gall's knowledge of anatomy served him well. During his dissections he discovered that the convolutions of the brain gathered directly behind the orifice of the ear. From this point they radiated out to the extremities of the skull, and since the power of any faculty was a function of the length of the convolution that contained it, both could be ascertained by measuring the distance of the protuberance from the ear.[6] Calipers were useful in making these determinations, but the ultimate in accuracy was the craniometer (fig. 2.2). By resting this device in the ears and rotating it over the skull, the operator could establish the actual dimensions of each organ.

During his formative years Powers had been advised against reliance on calipers; their continued use, he was warned, would diminish the capacity for invention. Hadn't Michelangelo claimed the eye to be the most discriminating instrument available to the sculptor? These admonishments went unheeded by Powers, who continued to employ the device because it enabled him to record the small "differences upon which all the infinite variety in the human countenance depends."[7] In any case, Michelangelo's example left Powers less than impressed. He had seen a cast of the famed *Moses* (fig. 2.3) but came away asking, "Where is the place for his statesmanlike brains?"[8] It was apparent that "phrenology would deny him common sense,"[9] and one was forced to conclude that this shortcoming was due to the Italian's failure to take measurements.[10]

The gist of Powers's thinking is at cross-purposes with Michelangelo's, and we encounter in these remarks the divergence of two ages and two approaches to sculpture. For the Italian, inspiration could only be imparted to the recalcitrant marble by a chisel held in the hand of the master; the American, however, was content to leave much of the labor to assistants, a luxury he could afford because the system of measurements and pointing had been so thoroughly developed in his day. It is also apparent that Powers made a connection between this method and the precise calculations that were crucial to a dependable phrenological reading.

The opinions expressed by Powers were hardly his alone. George Combe also thought the prophet's forehead undistinguished, and could not reconcile the stupendous mental energy stamped on the face with the obvious deficiency in the region of *Firmness*.[11] A review of Combe's book on art printed in *The Crayon* repeated these observations, adding, "The head has low qualities, fired out with the wrath of a low mind, instead of that of a high minded and inspired prophet; but there is a sign of tremendous mental energy given to the uncovered arms, which even seems to pierce the drapery of the body."[12] Rembrandt Peale attributed these deficiencies to the impatience and accompanying fatigue suffered by an artist who was overwhelmed by commissions. Had Michelangelo availed himself of the techniques presently in favor—again, an apparent allusion to rela-

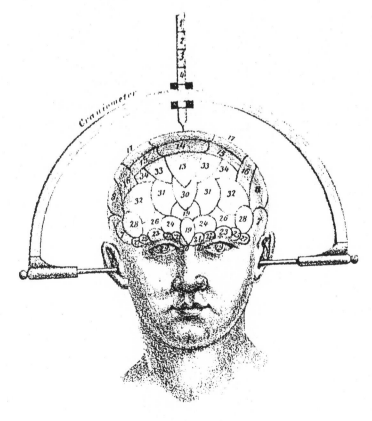

FIGURE 2.2.
The Craniometer, from Thomas Sewall, *An Examination of Phrenology* (Washington, D.C.: Homans, 1837)

FIGURE 2.3. Michelangelo Buonarroti, *Moses* (1513–14, S. Pietro in Vincoli, Rome, Italy, Alinari/Art Resource, N.Y.)

tively recent improvements in the pointing machine that enabled modern sculptors to make a precise transference of the clay or plaster model to marble—his efforts would have had a happier outcome.[13] This reasoning is given its most comprehensive expression in the writings of William Wetmore Story.

Story's debt to phrenology can be measured by his response to the monks he observed in Italy. Applying the criteria of physical metaphysics to them, he finds confirmation of the customary Protestant antipathy toward the vocation:

> If you are a convert to Romanism, you will perhaps find in their bald heads, shaven crowns and bearded faces a noble expression of reverence and humility; but, suffering as I do under the misfortune of being a heretic, I could but remark on their heads an enormous development of the two organs of reverence and firmness, and a singular deficiency in the upper forehead, where there was an almost universal enlargement of the lower jaw and of the base of the brain. Being, unfortunately, a friend of Phrenology, as well as a heretic, I drew no very auspicious augury from these developments; and looking into their faces, the physiognomical traits were narrow-mindedness, bigotry or cunning.[14]

When this same eye was brought to bear on Michelangelo's *Moses*, similar defects were detected. What should be a figure of great sanctity is found to be "of a lower grade."[15] Not only has the back of the head (*Firmness*, as mentioned by Combe) been chiseled down to "impossible" dimensions[16] (hence disadvantaging him in any test of wills with Pharaoh), but the entire body betrays the impetuosity of a hand simply loosed on marble.[17] The cumulative weight of this criticism implies that, while inspiration has its place, it must not be overly indulged. Science gives direction to the ramblings of the imagination,[18] and it is this philosophy that makes the technical procedures shared by phrenologists and sculptors so telling.

Indeed, there is reason to believe Powers actually applied a pointing machine directly to the heads of his sitters,[19] a step that represents the logical culmination of these ideas. The practice was adopted by his son, Preston,[20] and was taken up as well by their colleague in Florence, Joel Hart.[21] The latter's device resembled a mask perforated by long, blunt needles. These he advanced until they touched the subject, and, by reversing the operation when modeling the head, he achieved complete fidelity. Given the interest of all three men in phrenology (Hart's preferences will be discussed in a later chapter), the example of the craniometer is again pertinent.

Powers's devotion to accuracy led him to dispose of a bust of Professor Farrar when an assistant removed an eighth of an inch in excess from the nose.[22] The convictions that prompted such extreme measures were reinforced during the sculptor's several visits to the Fowlers. There he learned that the organs necessary for his profession, including *Ideality, Constructiveness,* and *Order,* were all well developed, but it was his *Form* that attracted particular attention. Its ample size, he was told, assured "correct ideas of shape and configuration."[23] The pains expended on his work, then, can be seen, in part, as the quest to satisfy an innate disposition as explained to him by phrenology. And when he confronted a portrait of himself by another artist, he was not above employing the ruler to aid in analysis. Measurements indicated a disparity of half an inch between the eyes when compared to the original,[24] and since this was the seat of *Form*, the very engine of scrupulosity, the irony could not have gone unnoticed. Because the organ was so powerful, it could not contemplate with equanimity the consequences of such heedless execution.

These issues—the nature of style and its relation to an individual's phrenological organization—assumed critical importance in the case of Shobal Vail Clevenger, a Cincinnati sculptor who followed in Powers's footsteps. Like the latter, Clevenger attracted the attention of Nicholas Longworth, but the assistance proffered by this wealthy patron to the aspiring youth came with decided reservations. He thought the artist quite proficient in rendering portraits but discouraged his ambitions when they aimed at the ideal. What set this otherwise generous Maecenas against a project even before it had materialized?[25] The answer comes in a letter to Powers praising the progress Clevenger was making in portraiture. "I do not believe he has any bump thereby developed," Longworth explains, "but the bump of imitation. (That stands permanent [? almost illegible].) He took my Bust when here last, and devoted much time and attention to it. He labored under some disadvantage, as I was not well, I had lost 10 lbs. of flesh. But he succeeded so well that Drake said to him 'Clevenger, you are inferior to Powers, but you have taken a more accurate likeness of Longworth than the one taken by Powers.' Clevenger was delighted with the compliment for none is more disposed than he to admit your superiority."[26]

Longworth goes on to express his reluctance to finance a trip to Italy. Clevenger might well profit from a visit to the eastern cities, he wrote elsewhere, for it would furnish him an opportunity to cultivate his aptitude for portraiture,[27] but with only *Imitation* well developed, the young sculptor was not adapted to the higher branches of art and hence would gain little from the experience of European monuments. Imagine Clevenger's dilemma! Somehow he had to cajole his skull into complying with Longworth's standards.

The contribution made by *Imitation* to the creative enterprise was not inconsiderable. It was an invaluable asset to those intent on copying or describing the world around them (fig. 2.4).[28] As a rule this faculty attained an early ascendancy, prompting the child to delight in mimicking its elders.[29] The exception was likely to attract attention, as William Dunlap observed in the case of Henry Sargent, who since youth had "evinced a taste for poetry and music, not withstanding which, the talent or faculty for imitating forms remained dormant, and the craniological bump undeveloped, almost to the age of maturity, although several fine portraits by Smibert, and finer by Copley, adorned the walls of his father's house."[30]

True genius, however, was not the offspring of *Imitation* alone; above accuracy stood beauty, and the organ most devoted to its attainment was *Ideality*. Its refining influence extended to portraiture, causing George Combe to assert that a "cast of the human head is a plain transcript of nature, a bust is nature elevated and adorned by the Ideality of a Chantry, a Joseph, or a Macdonald."[31] Apparently, Clevenger's hopes foundered on this rock, for Longworth wrote Powers that the young sculptor was "in his line [portraiture] right with you, but for the want of one bump. He can equal you in delineating the features, but falls far short of you in strength of expression. He is sensible of this."[32]

Of course not everyone was susceptible to the enticements of *Ideality*, and among such individuals the unaided efforts of *Imitation* sufficed. The complacency of Americans in this matter earned them a few choice words from the pen of Henry Tuckerman. "In this country especially," he wrote, "where there are so few standards of judgment or prescribed ordeals in Art, a faculty of imitation rare enough to excite wonder is hailed as prophetic of future triumph—and in many cases results in disappointment." The popular press nourished this taste with its excessive praise for "the exercise of a faculty regarded by the ignorant as next to miraculous." Artists were well advised, the critic continued, to ignore the "puffs" so liberally bestowed on them by journalists.[33]

FIGURE 2.4.
Imitation, from Mrs. L. N. Fowler, *Phrenology, Designed for the Use of Schools and Families* (New York: Fowlers and Wells, 1847)

If Americans were content with the handiwork of *Imitation*, what need had Clevenger for Europe? This, in any event, seems to have been Longworth's sentiment, and only after the artist came into his father's inheritance was he able to make the long-anticipated journey.[34] He soon discovered, however, that a transatlantic voyage provided no refuge from the onus of *Imitation*. Previous to Clevenger's arrival in Florence, Hiram Powers knew of the shortcoming and was unlikely to ignore it, given his standards for sizing up strangers. While still in Washington, for instance, Powers had set down the reasons for his aversion to Luigi Persico, an Italian whose knack for winning important public commissions did not endear him to native artists. "I have seen enough of his [Persico's] treacherous character to deter me from ever counting on his society, which, by the way, I have never done, for his face and head[,] if there be truth in physiognomy and phrenology[,] are sufficient warnings for me not to trust him."[35] By contrast, when Henry Kirk Brown landed in Italy, Powers confided to Longworth that he was "an ambitious and energetic man and judging from appearances (I have not yet seen any sculptures of his) he will succeed in his profession."[36]

Clevenger was less favorably endowed; Powers had the word from his benefactor in Cincinnati and was not inclined to ignore it. So while he was impressed by the busts Clevenger arrayed before him,[37] he could not bring himself to encourage the young sculptor's ambitions to model an Indian warrior and his daughter. On several occasions Powers sought to dissuade Clevenger, at first telling him that the subject would find no patrons and, when this stratagem failed, proposing instead something less fanciful, perhaps a narrative that could take full advantage of the models available in Florence.[38] This advice surely reflects the misgivings expressed by Longworth, who in turn concurred with the suggestion, adding, "To succeed he [Clevenger] should have material subjects to copy."[39]

That he persisted in spite of these obstacles says much for Clevenger's resilience, but the project was ill starred from the beginning and remained unfinished at the sculptor's early death.[40] Perhaps Henry Tuckerman was answering Clevenger's critics when he wrote the following about the artist: "To develop the instinctive powers of his character seemed to him the true end of life. He desired nothing more fondly than to give shape to his particular endowment. This was the art of statuary. It was obviously his vocation. A physiognomist would have detected at a glance no little aptitude to deal with form in the marked size of that organ. An uncommon space between the eyes indicated that in this sphere his faculty lay."[41]

To the virtues of *Imitation* could be added those of *Form*, but even this observer stops short of *Ideality*. For others it was not merely a matter of a few faculties; the size of the entire head might also foretell one's prospects for success. As noted in the previous chapter, Gall did not make size his sole criterion, but all things being equal, it correlated positively with ability.[42] Hence, when Chester Harding informed one aspirant that he could never hope to achieve fame as a painter "because his head was not big enough" (while promptly adding that his own was really quite enormous),[43] he was merely giving the unfortunate the benefit of his wisdom as "a full believer and convert to the doctrine" of Gall and Spurzheim.[44] During the 1840s Harding was instrumental in founding and guiding the Boston Artists' Association, a society established to provide the city's youth with some of the opportunities for academic training long enjoyed by their counterparts in New York and Philadelphia,[45] and his directorship provides yet further evidence of the close affiliation that arose between phrenology and the institutions intended to raise the national standards of artistic accomplishment.

Did Harding examine every prospective student similarly? Certainly the practice was not uncommon at the time. John Wesley Jarvis had only to glance at Henry Inman to declare the boy in possession of "the very head for a painter." With these words still ringing in his ears, Inman entered an apprenticeship, only to discover, as he later disclosed with mild amusement, that his efforts did not immediately fulfill the expectations aroused by his auspicious phrenological organization.[46] Nevertheless, it was phrenology that provided the initial impetus in his choice of career. Ephraim Brown was already established as a sign painter in 1837 when, finding little demand for his services in Indianapolis, he resolved to spend some of his dwindling cash reserves on a visit to a phrenologist. The account of what followed is wonderfully evocative of the forgotten customs of a distant time:

> "Well, sir, I think you must be a portrait painter—fine head for this business! Is it so?"
>
> I answered, "No: I never painted a portrait in my life."
>
> "Never painted a portrait!"
>
> He put his hands over the front of my head again, and looked me in the eye.
>
> "Never painted a portrait!—But you are a painter?"
>
> "Yes," I answered, "I paint signs."

Overcoming an initial skepticism, Brown executed a portrait of Washington. When the success of this effort was followed by others, he reported, "Now here I am, having as much as I can do, painting portraits at fifteen dollars a piece."[47]

The Fowlers were besieged by persons asking how they stood "as a painter or artist? Would I make a mechanic: if so what branch best?"[48] What is striking about these questions is the apparent absence of any clue as to the vocation that might best suit the inquirer. Creator of sublime images or factory operative—did it matter so long as science sanctioned the decision? When Lorenzo Fowler told (Obadiah?) Dickinson that he was "an artist by nature," the latter abandoned carpentry and took up painting. Ten years later, in 1846, he had cause to celebrate his resolve.

> I have made the dream a reality. I have painted five of the Governors of our State [Connecticut] for public places, and many of the finest people in the State have been my patrons and friends. I have improved myself not a little in general culture, have a lovely wife and children, a pleasant house and a large library, a welcome place in excellent society, and a good deal more property than my brother, though I thought him well-off when I left him, and he has been earning and saving ever since; in short, I have been successful, and I owe it to Phrenology, and I always acknowledge it with pride and pleasure, and never fail to patronize and otherwise aid every worthy worker in that field.[49]

Perhaps the most dramatic of these conversions occurred when Clark Mills chanced upon an itinerant phrenologist.[50] The account merits quoting at length because it is so revelatory of the circumstances that might induce a youth of Jacksonian America to adopt the fine arts as a career:

> He [Mills] told us he was a good house plasterer in Charleston, and did not know that he possessed any faculty whatever for sculpture or taking likenesses. One morning as he was going to his work he passed by a door where a Phrenologist had hung up his sign, with a notice that skeptics were not charged for the examination of their heads. This induced him to go in and have his head examined. The Phrenologist said to him, "you have the organ of sculpture in a very eminent degree, and if you were to cultivate your talent you would be a very distinguished artist." Mills replied to him, "you have confirmed me in my skepticism. I never had any confidence in your pretended science, but if I had, your account of my own head would utterly destroy it. I am, Sir, a house plasterer, and know nothing about sculpture whatever." The Phrenologist replied, "I don't care for that; you have the organ in a most wonderful degree, and should cultivate your talent." Mr. Mills said the idea that he possessed a rare and valuable talent, which he was not conscious of, haunted him night and day. But still he never thought of trying his talent, for he did not know how to begin. One day he saw an Ital-

ian going through the streets of Charleston with a bust of Napoleon in plaster, and he asked him how it was moulded. The Italian promised to show him, and did so, he caught the idea instantly, and was enraptured with it. First he commenced a likeness in plaster of his father-in-law, who had very prominent features. It was the wonder of all who saw it. He then commenced taking busts, as he was doing when we formed his acquaintance. Next he chiseled in marble a beautiful bust of that distinguished statesman, Mr. Calhoun. His friends now declared their willingness to send him to Rome, where he might study sculpture and cultivate his genius. For this purpose they provided him with funds, and as he was passing through Washington he was there engaged to make the Equestrian Statue of Jackson. In his poverty and obscurity in Charleston while working at his trade of house plasterer, he kept a bear and a dog, which he would make fight for fourpence. Between this exhibition of his dog and bear, and with the assistance of his trowel, he made his living in a sort of way, and would in all probability, have died in these humble pursuits, but for the Phrenologist. Who can laugh at Phrenology, after this, as a humbug, and not a science.[51]

This report reaches us through an intermediary who has doubtlessly taken certain liberties. It is unlikely, for example, that an "organ of sculpture" was identified unless an especially singular interpretation of the theory was professed. One suspects it was invented by the writer to advance the narrative; perhaps the faculty identified was *Form*, the one that announced Clevenger's abilities to Tuckerman. Aside from this lapse, the story complies with what is known about Mills.

In attempting to determine how Mills positioned himself in relation to those who had received an academic training, it is helpful to consider Whitman's venture into literature. The poet took comfort in the belief that talent was the offspring of phrenological organization, a contention that put him on equal footing with the likes of Henry Wadsworth Longfellow and James Russell Lowell despite his want of formal education.[52] Similar sentiments would have sustained Mills through the trials he undoubtedly faced as he acquired the technical skills necessary for his calling, and they would have pushed his career in directions others preferred to leave untried. A more sophisticated artist would hardly have essayed an equestrian with all the brassy novelty that enlivens his *Andrew Jackson* (fig. 2.5). The rearing stallion makes a spirited claim for primacy among the herd of bronze geldings whose staid poses betray a tamer aesthetic. The sculptor's ability to remain undaunted by the prospect of balancing his steed on its back legs was described by Lorado Taft as the "intrepidity of ignorance," but there may be something more significant at work here. Mills drew the sanction for his innovations from within, from the reservoirs of talent that only the phrenologist knew how to tap. He was, then, a self-made man, the epitome of Jacksonian ideology, and where better to declare these virtues, disencumbered as they were from the tired conventions of Europe, than in an exuberant image of "Old Hickory" himself?

Not every encounter with a phrenologist came as the thunderclap that awoke Clark Mills. In the case of John James Audubon, the prevalence in society of notions inspired by the theory proved conducive to his ambitions. After years of toil in relative obscurity, the naturalist traveled in the fall of 1826 to Edinburgh, a town then so completely in the throes of a phrenological mania that, it was reported, doctors and lawyers were frequently seen carrying "craniometers about in their pockets to measure heads with."[53] George Combe's leadership of the local phrenological society accounted for its preeminence among all such institutions. Another member was William Home Lizars, the man who, on 2 November, agreed to engrave Audubon's work, thus inaugurating the artist's ascent to international fame.[54] The next day, seemingly among the assembled guests at Lizars's house, the ornithologist met Combe, and the company resolved on the spot that a portrait of Audubon should be painted by John Syme and engraved by Lizars.[55] Does this sequence of events have a unifying thread? Was there a reason behind Lizars's interest in Audubon's personal appearance as well as his illustrations of birds?

The answer may reside in events that were to unfold one night some three weeks later. On that evening Lizars escorted Audubon to a meeting of the phrenological society, where he was introduced to the famed flutist Charles Weiss. The two were seated, and William Scott, president of the organization, entered. While professing to know neither man, Scott readily complied when asked to distinguish the painter from the musician. As his fingers ran over the naturalist's skull he declared "there cannot exist a moment of doubt that this gentleman is a painter, colorist, and compositor." While *Form, Size, Weight,* and *Locality* were all duly noted (fig. 2.6), it was *Color* that earned Audubon a place beside Titian and Rubens (fig. 2.7) in the annals of phrenology.[56]

Such judgments convey some idea of the sensation caused by Audubon's head, but it is clear from accounts that these events were merely the culmination of an interest that had been initially aroused at the time of

(Opposite)
FIGURE 2.5. Clark Mills, *Andrew Jackson* (1848–53, Lafayette Park, Washington, D.C., courtesy of the National Park Service)

FIGURE 2.6.
William Howland, *John James
Audubon,* from Rev. Edward Guibert,
"Auduboniana," *Phrenological Journal
and Life Illustrated* 53 (1871): 7

FIGURE 2.7.
Rubens, from O. S. Fowler, *The
Practical Phrenologist* (Boston: O. S.
Fowler, 1869), p. 140

his arrival. Earlier, Combe "begged" to be granted the privilege of taking
a cast of his head because it "exhibited and verified" the truth of phrenology.[57] Assent was eventually obtained,[58] and the resulting bust was treasured by the society on the grounds that a "better-marked development"
could scarcely be found.[59] It is difficult to believe that all this commotion
did not register with Lizars and contribute in some manner to his decision
to publish Audubon's work. The engraver's perceptions had been trained
by those of his close friend Combe, and scrutiny of the American's features must have confirmed what the paintings led him to suspect. The
convergence of testimony from both sources promised success for their
joint venture, and in this respect Lizars resembles the cabman mentioned
by Emerson, who, on being paid his fee, was "a phrenologist so far—he
looks into your face to see if his shilling is sure."[60]

The relationship between Audubon and phrenology was not without its
ambiguities. On one hand he found in phrenologists close allies in defense
of some of his more controversial proposals; they supported him, for instance, when he claimed that the vulture detected carrion by sight rather
than smell. His reasoning, which included the contention that the olfac-
tory nerve of the bird was smaller than the optical and therefore less sensitive, accorded with their belief that the capacity attainable by an organic
function was in direct relation to its size.[61] They also scoured his essays for
information about the human species. In describing the renowned wood

engraver Thomas Bewick, Audubon remarked that "his eyes are further apart than those of any man I remember just now."[62] He doubtlessly intended this as a reference to *Form*, and the phrenologists took the hint, for they entered Bewick into their own discourse based on this evidence.[63]

On the other hand, Audubon's allegiance vacillated. While his ruminations about the death of Spurzheim suggest a continued interest in the theory, he could equivocate. At one point he is in accord with Combe, but another lecturer then persuades him to question these convictions.[64] In another passage he confesses to being "neither a craniologist nor a physiognomist,"[65] but these words seem contrived for dramatic effect and, in any case, are contradicted by his writings.

In describing the intellect of "the eccentric naturalist . . . M. de T.," Audubon claims his brow was accessible to "any tyro in phrenology."[66] Especially telling in this regard is Audubon's description of Lord Stanley. His forehead, we learn, "would have suited Dr. Harlan, his brow would have assured the same old friend of his great mental powers."[67] This old friend is Richard Harlan, whose lectures on phrenology in the spring of 1822 were mentioned in the previous chapter. The doctor was an adviser and defender of Audubon,[68] and the conclusion that the latter was acquainted with the theory before his departure for England in 1826 is inescapable. It may have been the desire to portray himself as Natty Bumppo before his European hosts that led him to express such surprise about the analysis given in Edinburgh.[69]

Harlan's discussions with Audubon about phrenology would certainly have touched on concerns that were central to the ornithologist's enterprise. Gall had relied on the study of animals to establish the identity and functioning of the faculties, and a notice of Harlan's lectures describes the speaker as harboring a "zealous interest in natural history and comparative anatomy."[70] If for some reason Harlan failed to broach the subject, then "the master in Phrenology," whom Audubon met at the house of the Reverend Mr. John Bachman of Charleston, might have taken it up.[71] Nor can we preclude the possibility that Spurzheim himself explained the subject, perhaps over dinner, since both men lodged in the same boardinghouse in Boston.[72]

While George Combe applied the calipers to Audubon's head during an examination, the latter mused that his "skull was measured as minutely and accurately as I measure the bill or legs of a new bird, and all was duly noted by the scribe."[73] Despite the comparison, he limited his explicit phrenological commentary to the featherless bipeds he encountered. We need not wonder at the reticence. He was well aware of his limitations in matters of anatomy and often had to rely on others to supply his commentary with the requisite degree of scientific precision.[74] In any case a text full of phrenological data would have proved unwieldy.

These circumstances do not necessarily imply that his publications were uninfluenced by phrenology. While he did not indulge in its penchant for statistics, the theory did encourage his inclination "to anthropomorphize his subjects, portraying them as having human feelings and attributes."[75] The novelty of this approach can be measured by the resistance it engendered among naturalists of the old school. "Monday Captain Hall called to speak to me about my paper on Pigeons," wrote Audubon. "He complained that I expressed the belief that Pigeons were possessed of affection and tenderest love, and that this raised the brute species to a level with man. O Man! misled, self-conceited being, when wilt thou keep within the sphere of humility that, with all thy vices and wickedness about thee, should be thine."[76] The attribution of human feelings to brute creation is a habit of greatest antiquity, and Audubon was not insensible to the enchantment of La Fontaine's narratives;[77] but he was writing neither fable nor poetry. His text was offered as a scientific treatise, and here phrenology came to the rescue. By maintaining that humans and animals shared many of the same sentiments and instincts, Gall sanctioned those passages in the ornithologist's works that are given over to the emotional life of birds.

Gall stated that the procreative and nurturing impulses, Spurzheim's *Amativeness* and *Philoprogenitiveness*, were universally distributed throughout the animal kingdom, proposing "that all young naturalists might commence their research by these two organs. Both are easily recognized and it is very rare to find, as an exception to this rule, a male animal assume, as far as these two organs are concerned, the character of a female."[78] Audubon's description of the alternating emotions awakened in the female ruby-throated hummingbird when her nest is menaced by the scientific investigator and then left undisturbed on his departure suggests an acquaintance with such ideas. To understand her plight, he asks the reader to imagine "how pleasing it is to a mother of another kind, to hear the physician who has attended her sick child assure her that the crisis is over, and that her babe is saved."[79]

Passages of this kind raise questions about the role of experience in Audubon's work. He claimed to be no scholar, relying instead on personal familiarity with his subjects,[80] but much in his work gainsays the assertion. Harlan's discourse allowed him to read into animal behavior more than he could possibly have known from impartial observation. The doctrine of natural language as it ran through the entire spectrum of living creation stands as a distinct presence behind his many passages on the activities and emotions entertained by birds. His remarks were sufficiently explicit in this respect to permit phrenologists to employ them for their own ends. They cited, for instance, his account of the constancy of the eagle and the shape of its head in their efforts to establish the existence and location of *Union for Life*.[81]

The pages of Audubon's books come to life because instead of the dry descriptions of plumage and anatomy that characterized previous ornithological treatises, he supplies the reader with vivid anecdotes about the habits and sentiments prevalent among the feathered tribe.[82] This same practice appears in the works of contemporaries who were often more forthright than he in acknowledging the contribution of phrenology. Denton Offutt, Abraham Lincoln's political adviser, relied on the theory as the basis for his treatise on horses.[83] While reviewing the paintings of William Dana, Henry Tuckerman marveled at the artist's ability to capture the natural language of various animals,[84] and then there is Herman Melville's whale. Noting that Gall and Spurzheim had thrown out "some hints touching the phrenological characteristics of other beings than man," he goes on to deliver a gently ironic discourse on the topic. Humor alternates with perceptive insight into the theory's deficiencies. These are beyond the scope of this discussion; in passing, however, it merits notice that his resolution to designate the hump on the sperm whale's back an outpost of the organ of *Firmness* is not entirely a concoction of his fantasy but, instead, a delightful parody on the sort of reasoning employed by the phreno-mesmerists.[85]

Among the names of those whose contribution Audubon wished to acknowledge is that of George Combe. This was no empty gesture, for the ornithologist was "astounded" by the Scotsman's brilliance as a speaker and wrote of one evening's discourse that it would "remain in my mind all my life."[86] But what remained? From this and other sources he acquired the habit of judging individuals by the shape of their heads, a practice he could undertake with impunity because he would not be held to accounts. This amateur standing, however, would not suffice when it came to his scientific publications, and there he refrained from explicit reference to phrenology. Nevertheless, the theory continued to exercise its influence in oblique fashion, permitting the mind to listen to the dictates of the heart, and in this context he could compare the nesting instincts of humans to those that prevailed in the wilds. Finally, we should not ignore the benefits Audubon reaped from the favorable analysis of his own head. The repeated invocation of the old masters could only spur his ambitions, and when his cranium was once compared to that of Raphael, he felt compelled to admit "the merit of the science."[87]

FIGURE 2.8. William Sidney Mount, *The Painter's Triumph* (1838, oil painting, courtesy of the Pennsylvania Academy of the Fine Arts, bequest of Henry C. Carey, Carey Collection)

Perceptions of self also enter prominently into William Sidney Mount's *The Painter's Triumph* (fig. 2.8), where a studio setting serves to articulate ideas about the profession. The nature of those ideas, however, remains open to interpretation; does the profile of Apollo, the deity who personifies artistic inspiration, look away from the commotion to signal his distaste?[88] That would depend on the quality of the painting that is the source of so much excitement. If it is good, then the response of the two protagonists is merited; if poor, then they are a pair of hayseeds deserving ridicule. Since the painting is turned from us, we have no means of resolving the issue. An alternate approach is offered by the figures themselves. What clues do they reveal about their moral and mental condition? The genius loci of Mount's own studio was the phrenological bust that enabled him to judge the merits of those who entered his domain,[89] and this circumstance invites us to follow his lead.

Some years ago William Oedel and Todd Gernes did just that, and their conclusions reflect favorably on the triumphant painter but less so on his companion. By their calculations the former is well endowed with *Form* and *Color*, while his protruding forehead reveals ample perceptive and reflective faculties.[90] There is every reason to believe Mount would have encouraged a reading of this kind. He praises the old masters, including Michelangelo, Raphael, and Rubens, for demonstrating "a mastery and knowledge of the skull" in their work.[91] Artists of their stature, he speculates, must have possessed "perceptive and reflective faculties . . . of the first order" and especially large "ideality and constructiven[ess]."[92] The similar conclusions reached by Oedel and Gernes suggest that the central figure of Mount's painting embodies many of the virtues the artist thought present in himself.

To search only among the aesthetic faculties for evidence of artistic disposition, however, ignores Spurzheim's dictum that any organ might be put to positive ends if subordinated to a propitious mental constitution. This precept guides Mount's ruminations about the endurance required of Michelangelo and Raphael in their unrelenting quest for excellence. They must have enjoyed, he surmises, a powerful temperament bolstered by "large firmness."[93] This same thought reached him during a seance via the spirit of Rembrandt, who attributed his success to a dependence "on my own individual resources of mind, and a *good eye for local color*, [by means of which] I launched forth on my sea of adventure, with a *firm determination* to avoid the style of any artist whatsoever."[94] Given the confluence of phrenology and spiritualism in spiritual science and the enthusiasm shown by Mount for its pronouncements, we might expect the advice transmitted through these diverse channels to concur on the benefits of *Firmness*.

The above remarks did not exhaust Rembrandt's ideas about color. He went on to inform the enthralled circle that the "brown and somber tints and broad masses of transparent shadow" popular in ages past were inappropriate to the present era.[95] Here again Mount found confirmation of a precept he had inscribed some years earlier in his notebook: "A painter should have *large combativeness*—to make him contrast his colors continually."[96] Like *Firmness*, *Combativeness* might seem to have little to contribute to the creative act, but spiritual science told Mount otherwise. By means of this faculty he could resist the temptation to employ murky tones and instead devise a style appropriate to his own time.[97]

Both Mount and his acquaintances relied on phrenology to set down their perceptions of traits that otherwise seemed elusive. One example appears in a letter sent to the artist, but discerning its intent requires considerable familiarity with the theory. "Friend Mount, if during your life instead of painting pictures, playing music, and cracking jokes, you had been spending money to make other people happy, you would have got rid of more of the filthy lucre than did Mr. Gosse who gave away two fortunes. And if instead of generously doing deeds of benevolence, and serving out to others the milk of human kindness, you had been investing money as seven percent, you would now have a greater income than William B. Astor."[98] This passage effectively delineates one side of Mount's personality by means of phrenology, for Mr. Gosse appears regularly as an example of the consequences of an excessively developed *Benevolence* (fig. 2.9). Accompanying illustrations of his head are words recollective of those above. "Gosse was noted for his kindness, generosity, and unselfishness. He could not say no. He gave away two fortunes, and having inherited a third, he wisely appointed a treasurer or agent to take care of it for him."[99]

While not as rich as Gosse or Astor, Mount enjoyed a life of music and art and was as liberal as they in dispensing favors among friends. No doubt he appreciated the comparison and in turn was fond of alluding to the "lump of benevolence" in others, including patrons.[100] So it would seem fair to include this faculty among the others identified previously as contributing to the prominent forehead exhibited by the artist in *The Painter's Triumph*. More importantly, these reports suggest that the relationship between Mount and his clients was not unlike that depicted in the painting. He did not feel alienated by class antagonism, and neither should we imagine the visitor to be some monied boob, insensitive to the beauties set before him. When we remember that Mount came to regard *Benevolence* as the epitome of progressive Christianity, the tenor of much of his imagery comes into focus. He was not one to mar "the harmony of the world" by anything he did or created, and an innate affability, such as that rendered in this composition, would, if generally dispersed among the populace, be sufficient to usher in the millennium.

No. 166. — MR. GOSSE — GAVE AWAY
TWO FORTUNES.

FIGURE 2.9.
Benevolence, from O. S. Fowler, *The Practical Phrenologist* (Boston: O. S. Fowler, 1869), p. 122

FIGURE 2.10. Thomas Cole, *The Architect's Dream* (1840, oil painting, Toledo Museum of Art, purchased with funds from the Florence Scott Libbey Bequest in memory of her father, Maurice A. Scott)

In painting *The Architect's Dream* (fig. 2.10), Thomas Cole investigated many of the same issues that appear in *The Painter's Triumph*. Both works set out to examine the implications of creativity, but Cole labored at a disadvantage. The artist's studio was a popular subject in the nineteenth century, and Mount exploits its potential for picturesque incident and props. Cole's subject was less ensconced in this tradition, and since the architect consigns his plans to others to execute, the activities associated with the profession would seem to offer fewer possibilities for pictorial representation. The ingenious solution devised by Cole was to project the architect's schemes onto a backdrop that occupies most of the canvas. By making the viewer privileged to the cogitations of the protagonist, Cole concocted one of the most extravagant compositions bequeathed us by Romanticism in America.

I want to emphasize the cerebral nature of Cole's piece because, while others have studied the architectural setting,[101] the dreamer and the implications of dreaming as they were understood at the time have received relatively little attention.[102] The painting presents the visions of an architect who slumbers atop a stack of enormous volumes set upon a gigantic column. His musings range from the sun-drenched world of antiquity to the dark forests of Gothic Europe. The idea was to celebrate the talents of New Haven architect Ithiel Town, but he anticipated a rolling landscape with buildings set at various intervals in the manner of Claude Lorrain and thought Cole's solution excessively fanciful. Curiously, the artist did not attempt to justify his imagery, and the rift between the two men never entirely closed.[103]

Cole was far less reticent to express his opinions about phrenology, and when Samuel Taylor Coleridge disparaged the theory, he answered with obvious fervor. "He [Coleridge] says that Spurzheim was the most ignorant German he ever saw; he must have seen only a few of them. Any person who will read Spurzheim's work will be astonished at his being called ignorant. The fact is that Coleridge & his Editor in their remarks on Spurzheim's system have shown themselves utterly ignorant of the subject. Neither of them can possibly have read Spurzheim."[104] This rebuke could only come from one who *had* read Spurzheim, and Cole's writings bear this out.

In debating the relative merits of decorating churches with trompe l'oeil paintings, Cole argued against the practice, calling it deceptive and therefore unworthy of a house of worship; for his adversary to think otherwise, he continued, his "organ of marvelousness must be exceedingly large & give him great pleasure."[105] Spurzheim's *Marvelousness*, the *Spirituality* of the Fowlers, was a fickle faculty that might be indulged only with circumspection. Behind its delight in deception for its own sake lurked the perils of excessive credulity.[106] Thus, when Cole learned that certain parties were heralding the advent of photography as sounding the death knell of painting, he again attributed the commotion to an "enormous bump of Marvellousness."[107]

In preparing a treatise on the comparative virtues of painting and sculpture, Cole again relied on phrenology to validate his ideas. While the text never advanced beyond a few preliminary jottings, he did manage to articulate one telling concept. "Taking painting in all its departments," he contended, "its influence is certainly more extensive than that of sculpture; and to excel in painting requires *a combination of a greater number of faculties* than to excel in sculpture. He who cannot distinguish one colour from another may be a sculptor."[108] This brief passage belongs to the venerable tradition of the *paragone*, a debate concerning the virtues of the different media begun in the Renaissance. Cole's thoughts diverge in one important respect from those set down by Leonardo and Michelangelo. Whereas the latter concentrate on the ease or difficulty involved in the mastery of materials, Cole turns his attention to the innate endowments of the artist. In adopting this approach, he couches his argument in terms familiar to the phrenologist. One, for example, observed that, while the sculptor was well endowed in *Form, Size, Individuality, Causality,* and *Ideality,* "a picture is a more complex object than a statue, because to figure and size it adds colouring. Either to execute it, therefore, or to judge it, the faculty of colour must co-operate with those already enumerated, as concerned in producing and criticising a statue."[109]

Each of these quotations shifts the evaluative criteria to the organic and mental constitution of the artist, which as Audubon might testify, was the touchstone of genius. The relevance of these precepts to the architect in Cole's painting will appear shortly, but as a preliminary inference, it is clear that the scene recapitulates the critical method employed by the phrenologists. We see the creator, we see his creation; our task is to identify the correspondences between the two.

These considerations entered Cole's assessment of Washington Allston. He thought the elder artist unduly influenced by the old masters, a tendency he attributed to the sway exercised by the "faculty of imitation." His seemingly casual remark that Allston's "forehead retired rapidly" proves especially revelatory in this light.[110] Even more disconcerting was the figure of William Turner, the English landscapist; Cole found him to be a man of "common form and common countenance," with "nothing in his appearance or conversations indicative of genius."[111] By contrast, a death mask of Torquato Tasso, the Renaissance poet, exhibited a width of brow that caught Cole's eye, just as it did the phrenologists', who illustrated it to demonstrate the "breadth at the region of Ideality."[112]

Cole himself came under similar scrutiny from his close friend and biographer Louis Legrand Noble. "His [Cole's] head was one of the very finest. So well constituted was his brain, as to quantity and balance, as to give him, according to the laws of phrenology, a combination of intellectual and moral qualities of the rarest kind. Thought had, prematurely, so thinned his soft brown hair as to require it to be brought up from the temples across the head, in order to cover a partial baldness. *His forehead, beautifully proportioned, was much his finest feature when his countenance was in repose*: when enlivened, his eyes."[113] These words bring us close to the image of the reposing architect, who obligingly offers his profile.

We come even closer in the phrenological portrait of Cole rendered by Lorenzo Fowler in 1837. According to standard procedure, the phrenologist began by evaluating the figure for its qualities of temperament. The "Nervous" was found to predominate; hence he was given to "extreme delicacy of feeling and excitability." In the skull, *Comparison, Benevolence, Imitation, Ideality, Veneration,* and *Constructiveness* all contrived to expand the bulge of the anterior region.[114] The size of the last of these was particularly well known among Cole's acquaintances, for they teased him about it. When his son was born, for example, his brother-in-law, Dr. George Ackerley, sent a tongue-in-cheek inquiry on whether the promptings of this organ would cause him to model the child's head into fanciful form.[115] As both men knew, the faculty was the engine that drove architectural talent, and when it was combined with the *Ideality* that also welled up in Cole's forehead, one could anticipate that the buildings so engendered would satisfy the most discriminating eye.[116] In the last years of the decade, Cole enjoyed some success in designing the plans for the Ohio state capitol,[117] and it is difficult to believe that these events did not contribute in some way to the imagery devised for Ithiel Town.

The intent of *The Architect's Dream* is to render a physical and mental portrait of the ideal architect. Further specificity can be attached to the former by recalling the diagnosis of Cole's temperament. The Nervous or Mental type of the Fowlers designated an individual whose brain made heavy demands on the body. Such persons were likely to "have a small stature; light build, [and] small bones and muscles."[118] The Fowlers claimed the disposition was well suited to the profession of architect, and if one examines their illustration of the Refined and Spiritual type (fig. 2.11), the twin brother of Cole's slightly built dreamer appears. In both, an auspicious forehead and cranium, delicate features, weak chin, and wavy hair stamp the seal of genius upon the figure. The means of identifying *Constructiveness* as the prevailing muse comes from the background. Just as Cole could reason back from the folly of a writer's argument to the size of his *Marvelousness*, so he asked the viewer to draw like inference from the spectacular setting of his composition.

This connection becomes all the more compelling when the teaching of phrenology on dreams is factored into the equation. The phenomenon, as indicated in the first chapter, was crucial to the logic of faculty psychology. Dreaming was a form of incomplete sleep, with the stronger faculties remaining most resistant to the embrace of Somnus. It warrants repeating that Gall looked askance upon the speculative categories devised by philosophers and turned instead to individuals, including architects, whose involvement in practical affairs yielded the solid evidence required by scientific investigation. Such types exercised a few faculties habitually, and this enhanced the prospect that their dreams would be woven from the stuff of their trade or profession. One phrenologist explained that "a person's natural character, therefore, or his pursuits in life, by strengthening one faculty, make it less susceptible, than such as are weaker, of being overcome by complete sleep; or, if it be overcome, it awakes more rapidly from its dormant state, and exhibits its proper characteristics in dreams."[119]

The protagonist of *The Architect's Dream* has not merely devoted himself to the calling; he has even fallen asleep while reading the literature of his profession. This could only enhance the predictability of his dreams:

> Whatever has much interested us during the day, is apt to resolve itself into a dream; and this will generally be pleasurable, or the reverse, according to the nature of the exciting cause. If, for instance, our reading or conversation be of horrible subjects, such as specters, murders, or conflagrations, they will appear before us magnified and heightened in our dreams. Or if we have been previously sailing upon a rough sea, we are apt to suppose ourselves undergoing the perils of shipwreck. Pleasurable sensations during the day are also apt to assume a still more pleasurable aspect in dreams. In like manner, if we have a longing for any thing, we are apt to suppose that we have it. Even objects altogether unattainable are placed within our reach: we achieve impossibilities, and triumph with ease over the invincible laws of nature.[120]

These factors magnify the phantasmagoria conjured up before our eyes; fueling an already powerful faculty are the reveries engendered by the learned tomes beneath the dreamer. Pleasures abound, ambitions swell, and the contingencies of mundane existence are suspended. William Cullen Bryant, who described Cole's scene as one that "might present itself to the imagination of one who had fallen asleep after reading a work on the different styles of architecture,"[121] also wrote that in his search for

FIGURE 2.11.

Refined and Spiritual Type, from "Lessons in Practical Phrenology," *Phrenological Journal and Life Illustrated* 61 (1875): 14

complete repose he "avoided in the evening every kind of literary occupation which *tasks the faculties*, such as composition, even to the writing of letters, for the reason that it excites the nervous system and prevents sound sleep." [122]

Dreams were not an arid wasteland where irrationality brazenly unfurled its banners; rather, they were a fertile field that nourished the budding aspirations of the middle class. Gall suggests that dreaming might even enhance career skills:

> The whole vital strength is concentrated in a single organ or a small number of organs, whilst the others sleep; hence their action must of necessity be more energetic. The sentiments and ideas awakened in dreams are, sometimes, perfectly free from every thing irrelevant. It should therefore no longer be a matter of astonishment if, like Augustus Lafontaine, we occasionally compose exquisite poetry in sleep, or like Alexander, sketch the plan of a battle, or like Condillac, solve difficult problems, or like Franklin, we find furnished in the morning, a plan designed the preceding eve; or, if we discover during sleep, the true relations of those things, which, amid the confusion of sentiments and ideas, had defied our penetration. It is a mistake, to believe that dreams are always a recurrence of sentiments and ideas, previously entertained. Man may invent in his sleeping, as he does in his waking hours; for, the internal sources, whence the sentiments and ideas flow, are the same in sleep as in wakefulness. [123]

Something like this takes place in *The Architect's Dream.* We are not, after all, transported to the ruins left by a departed civilization; rather, we are invited to survey the history of architecture "free from every thing irrelevant," so that the sequence from Egypt to the Gothic can readily be traced. Had Cole obliged his patron, this program would have been seriously compromised. As it is, the viewer is treated to "the true relations" of things, and from this understanding even greater wonders may one day spring.

Among the antecedents to Cole's painting is Henry Fuseli's *The Nightmare* (1781, Detroit Institute of Arts). The tormenting imp here belongs to folkloric beliefs still strong in Europe, while other details suggest a bodily indisposition brought on by food or drugs. [124] Cole pointedly avoids the supernatural beings of traditional dream imagery, and he does not imply that the architect's inspiration has come from intoxicants. His version merely projects the sleeper's reverie, which, upon reflection, winds up looking a lot like Piranesi's *capricci.* Unlike his Italian predecessor, however, Cole includes the visionary—the mind, if you will—responsible for the panorama spread out for our consideration. The stroke of genius behind *The Architect's Dream* derives from its forging of a new synthesis out of these two traditions.

Cole's painting is more than a diagrammatic illustration of dream theory. Personal aspirations cast a veil of enchantment over the scene that manages to soften much of its programmatic asperity. If the architectural yearnings engendered by his *Constructiveness* remained unrequited in real life, they could at least be consummated in the musings of his imagination. Perhaps it was the resolution born of personal conviction that prevented him from making the changes requested by Town. The contribution of phrenology to Cole's sense of identity may have had consequences that extend well beyond this one work. He was often obliged to choose between the "compositions" inspired by European art and the less structured "views" of his adopted homeland.[125] Generally his preferences leaned toward the former, and one feels he would have agreed with the critic who wrote that "nothing less than [the] epic could engage all his faculties."[126] By translating this into Cole's own understanding of mind, we realize that *Imitation* unaided would not suffice for painting any more than it did for sculpture; it could only produce those scenic representations that did not fire his enthusiasm. His more epic undertakings, such as *The Voyage of Life*, required the contribution and polish prompted by several faculties, including *Ideality*, *Veneration*, and *Benevolence*, all of which he knew to be well developed in his own brain. Only by engaging the entire range of his endowments could he honestly answer his calling.

The strain of eccentric Romanticism that runs through American art extends from Cole to Elihu Vedder, but while the writings of the former are replete with the earnestness of Victorian sermonizing, the latter adopts the pose of the raconteur, filling his pages with bons mots and other diversions that often bemuse the reader. These inclinations cannot be ignored by anyone seeking a common theme in his literary and artistic productions. What are we to make, for example, of the following account of a childhood spin on a rocking horse that ended in near tragedy when he was thrown from his steed and hit his head on the mahogany arm of a sofa? "That first ride, which easily might have been my last, has often made me wonder if my bump of memory was not the part affected. Having lost my phrenological chart, which I with others received when I had my bumps examined at Fowler and Wells's, as was the custom in those days, I am unable to locate the bump, and time has obliterated the wound. Yet I wonder . . . my memory has been very bad since the day of that fall."[127]

The bump of memory identified here was not a regular feature of phrenological charts. When it did appear, it arose in the forehead.[128] Vedder does not identify the precise point of impact, stating only that his head was shaved to dress the wound. Data of this kind was often gathered by phrenologists. A fall from a horse, for instance, deprived one individual of his memory of names after *Language* became befuddled.[129] The standard interpretation made memory the resident of every organ—*Locality* remembering places, and so on[130]—and Vedder's proverbial inability to recall dates suggests that *Time* was the injured party.[131]

It probably will not do to insist on the particulars. Rather than trying to pin Vedder down, we would do better to recall the refrain that runs through his autobiography: "What am I to do with a memory like mine?"[132] This lament arose from a childhood trauma, and Vedder sought to assuage his doubts by visiting the offices of Fowler and Wells. The Fowlers, in any case, were quite willing to expand the domain of memory to its widest latitude, locating it "all over the forehead."[133]

What possible significance can this childhood accident have had for Vedder the artist? A perusal of his autobiography reveals a number of youthful encounters with death that later found their way into paintings. *The Dead Alchemist* (1868, Brooklyn Museum) is one example; in this case the figure slumped against the wall evokes a scene he chanced upon years earlier. Sent one morning to awaken a boarder for breakfast, he discovered that the guest had expired during the night.[134] The painting that eventually resulted does not simply document the event; rather, it makes transformations to encompass his interests in the occult. The artist's facade of joviality hid a profound disquietude, a circumstance that prompted Joshua Taylor to remark that "for all his flamboyance and high spirits, there was always an unexpressed depth of seriousness in Vedder that early showed itself in his work."[135] Far from being the mere offspring of fantasy, his compositions are often imbued with a sense of mortality fostered by personal experience. One such piece is *Memory* (fig. 2.12).

The title picks up the lament of his autobiography and recalls the phrenological prognosis, but how do these circumstances correlate with the image? Above a vast expanse of ocean arises an ominous thundercloud from which emerges the features of a young woman or child. Certainly this painting is even less documentary than that of the alchemist. Any connection it may make with past events must come through his affiliation with spiritual science, an interest he shared with Kate Field. This aspiring author was a devotee of spiritualism and Swedenborg when she befriended the artist in Florence in the 1850s.[136] Her enthusiasm was con-

(Opposite)
FIGURE 2.12. Elihu Vedder, *Memory* (1870, oil painting, Los Angeles County Museum of Art, Mr. and Mrs. William Preston Harrison Collection)

tagious, and the parallel evolution of each is suggestive of shared beliefs. Thus, while Vedder was drawing the floating heads in 1867 that were to be the source for *Memory*,[137] Field was attending seances where a pencil in the medium's hand "started off, and made the most extraordinary looking heads I ever saw, and executed in the most peculiar manner."[138]

These were also years when Vedder undertook the study of Swedenborg. He reports of the mystic's works that he "read about three feet, or a good yard of them."[139] The expertise so acquired surely acquainted him with the Swede's teachings on memory, and these have some bearing on his own imagery.

> When a person's deeds are being laid bare to him after death, the angels who are given responsibility for examining him look carefully at his face. The examination then spreads through his whole body. . . .
>
> This is why the things that are written in a person's memory, that have come from intention and consequent thought, are not written on the brain alone, but on the whole person. . . .
>
> It is indeed the fact that everything—both deeds and thoughts—is written on the whole person, seeming to be read in a book when called from the memory, and to be seen in visual likeness when the spirit is examined in heaven's light.[140]

This examination could be seen as the celestial counterpart to the phrenologist's task, for he or she likewise scrutinized the entire body but devoted particular attention to the head. Such parallels contributed to the wide popularity of the disembodied head as a subject among European artists.[141] A collection of essays published in 1868 by Theophilus Parsons, a copious contributor to New Church literature, further elucidates the tenor of Vedder's thought. Phrenology, Parsons maintains, serves as the ally of theology; hence the theory of correspondences originates in the "organ of comparison," which must have been large in Swedenborg's forehead.[142] His delineation of the correspondences between the sea and memory provides instructive reading in the presence of Vedder's painting:

> Because thought, being indestructible, all lies stored up in the memory,—not the recollection, for by that we mean only what can be by our own effort recalled; but in the memory,—Swedenborg frequently speaks of the sea as denoting, by correspondence, the natural memory; and sometimes the natural man, because he lives almost wholly in the natural mind.
>
> The depths of the sea! Profound, dark, and inaccessible as they are, are they one whit more profound, more inscrutable, or more inaccessible, than the depths of the human intellect?[143]

It is possible, the author adds, that these waters will one day yield their secrets thanks to methods recently devised for fathoming their depths. The allusion here is to Swedenborgianism and phrenology, and whether or not Parsons's works were on that yard-long shelf of books read by Vedder, such ideas were in circulation. Like any Swedenborgian or phrenologist, we can examine the face to assay the memory. Its treasures far surpass those of recollection, which have been plundered by worldly affliction. The index of memory written on the forehead finds its correspondence in the ocean below, conflating science, religion, and personal trauma into an imagery that has much in common with Symbolism.[144] By this means Vedder exacts compensation from an environment that was no respecter of childhood innocence. The cloud-borne visage promises restitution of all that has been lost during life's stormy passage,[145] for all that befalls the natural man lingers in the chambers of "the sea of the mind."[146]

Both Thomas Cole and Elihu Vedder addressed their deepest concerns by resorting to fantastic imagery. But whereas the former's proves on analysis to be rational, didactic, and almost diagrammatic, the latter's divulges its content reticently and is involved more intrinsically in the occult. No doubt a number of factors contributed to this divergence, but it cannot be entirely coincidental that the epistemological basis of phrenology evolved in much the same direction. Unlike the optimistic individualism endemic among his predecessors of the antebellum era, Vedder extracts a poignancy from the doctrine that transcends personal anxiety and mirrors, at some level, the legacy of the Civil War and the enervating disillusionment of the Gilded Age.

Who better epitomizes the social mobility of nineteenth-century America than William Sidney Mount? When he embarked on his career, the status of the painter was still in the process of shedding its affiliation with the crafts and aligning itself with the professions. He never settled down and married, a fact that had its symbolic embodiment in his studio on wheels. In essence, he forsook the outward trappings of respectability as understood by his parents' generation in favor of a calling that was still regarded as marginal by most. As a consequence, he was subject to doubts that prompted much soul-searching. His notebooks contain exhortations to "Try, Try, we do not know ourselves until [w]e Try."[147] At one point he expands on the theme: "Why should men strive against their nature? Some have great talent for dancing—Hornpipes, Jigs, and Reels—but they think it beneath them—and those who play comedy to perfection think they are best calculated to play tragedy. So with painters—some will take portraits indifferently, when they make good landscapes, and others again who would excel in comic pieces will endeavor to paint contrary to their genius. Oh man, try to know (yourself [crossed over]) thyself."[148] The last phrase echoes the famed inscription engraved on the temple at Delphi; it was also the favored motto of phrenologists, who seem to have installed it in Mount's mind.[149]

In a culture where traditional wisdom governing the choice of calling and spouse seemed increasingly irrelevant, the obligations enjoined by this dictate were all the more compelling. As with the lawyers and physicians discussed in the previous chapter, the capital brought by artists to their enterprise was ensconced in the cranial vault, where only the right combination could withdraw it. The phrenologist's sensitized digits were often deployed in the task, for he or she could determine not only whether an individual was fit for brush or chisel but also whether success would follow from portraits, landscapes, or comic pieces. Beyond meeting this need, the theory directed the resources of patronage, spoke to matters of technique, and encouraged new types of imagery. Our comprehension of these matters can only be enhanced by inquiring just how persons such as Mount came to know themselves.

3

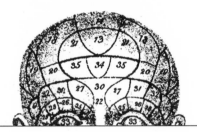

Tired of Looking at Small-Headed Venuses

Phrenology did more than identify the attributes required of those who sought to pursue a career in the arts. It also set out a theory of art that was tailored to the aspirations of Americans. How were the citizens of the young republic to fulfill their destiny if they possessed no standards by which to measure their progress? The science of Gall and Spurzheim offered just the gauge many sought by providing followers with models they might emulate. The art of antiquity and recent times was surveyed for images of diverse types that would provide the requisite instruction. Artists and critics were not likely to remain indifferent to this development, and the efforts made by several of their number to incorporate this method of analysis into their own endeavors constitute the theme that runs through the following pages.

The first of these, Dr. John Bell, wrote extensively about the history of art in a book devoted to household hygiene. His tendency to draw examples of health from statuary and paintings is comprehensible if we recall that he lectured on anatomy at the Pennsylvania Academy. Here he was requested to "deliver a course of lectures on the Statues in the antique gallery,"[1] and what he might have said on such occasions can be surmised from his medical manual. A basic premise of this text contends that the pervasive frailty of American womanhood imperiled the republic. This perception was widely held. Travelers routinely claimed that the buxom types regularly seen in Europe were rarely encountered on these shores, a circumstance often attributed to the ignorance of physiology imposed by Puritanism. This false modesty proved opportune for the pernicious example popularized by fashion plates. To comply with the latter, women submitted their figures to the corset and like devices, which compressed and dislodged bodily organs in a manner that was positively injurious. The antidote Bell prescribed was art; there nature's intentions could be studied without recourse to expedients that might coarsen the viewer's moral constitution.[2]

Bell appropriated this line of reasoning from the phrenologists, one of whom told skeptics to "ask the sculptor what he thinks of a fashionable waist, pinched till it rivals the lady's neck in tenuity; and he will tell you it is monstrous. Consult the physician, and you will learn that this is one of those follies, in which no female can long indulge with impunity; for health and even life are often sacrificed to it."[3] This same writer goes on to recommend a stratagem often advanced as the best means of toppling dame fashion from her throne: juxtapose an ideal figure with one whose form had been warped by constricting garments, and the risks assumed by the latter would become patently obvious to all (fig. 3.1). How could anyone remain unmoved, it was asked, by the contrast between the ample waist of the *Venus de' Medici* and "the same form squeezed into fashionable proportions by the steam-power of modern corsets"?[4] The most celebrated incident in this campaign occurred in 1839 when George Combe recommended to an audience in Philadelphia "the study of the human figure in statuary and painting, not only as an interesting object of taste, but as capable of conveying knowledge of great practical utility." The maternal eye so trained could keep a vigilant watch over her brood, thus enabling timely intervention should a daughterly chest fail to bloom or a head become excessively large.[5]

Bell's volume was intended to acquaint young ladies with "what may be termed beauty-training."[6] To accomplish this he relied on aesthetics, contending that the diverse teachings of physiology could be subsumed under a single principle, the "line of beauty." William Hogarth had coined this term a century earlier to describe a serpentine line thought to distill the essence of taste, but Bell employed it for ends that surpassed those of mere visual delectation. The "fullness of parts and swelling and undulating outline are pleasing to the eye," he claimed, "because they give proofs of fitness and health, necessary conditions for beauty."[7] No one need fear that the "nobler faculties" would be compromised by such study; throughout history the appreciation of beauty had accompanied "progressive perfection" and "mutual happiness." The healthy human form had enabled Greek artists and philosophers to embody their highest imaginings, and an aura of "ambrosial respect" had filled the temples wherein stood statues of "the goddess of Love and Beauty." Misgivings about the enervating influence of beauty were quelled by the example set by ancient Athens and Renaissance Florence, cities that cherished both "liberty and high art."[8]

Beauty, "the irradiation of mind through the corporeal frame," also encompassed natural language, that quality of deportment which eluded all but the most adept artists.[9] A stroll along our urban thoroughfares, however, offered only "fantastic figures, called fashionably dressed persons, moving in a constrained and artificial manner." The "fairer part of cre-

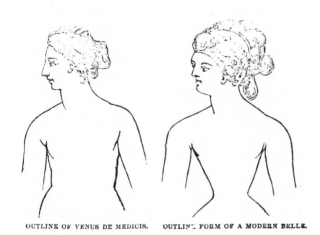

OUTLINE OF VENUS DE MEDICIS.   OUTLINE FORM OF A MODERN BELLE.

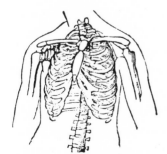
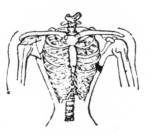

SKELETON AS NATURE FORMED IT.   SKELETON AS ART DEFORMED IT.

FIGURE 3.1.
Venus de Medicis and a Modern Belle, from A. P. Dutcher, "Anatomy and Physiology," *American Phrenological Journal* 16 (1852): 54

ation" was particularly hobbled by bizarre apparel, and emulation of the loose drapery and graceful gait seen in "the paintings on Etruscan and Grecian vases" would prove salutary.[10]

Hogarth's line set the standard. Even the head could be brought into conformity. Its outline should not be subject to the whims of the coiffeur, for a well-organized brain constituted woman's greatest ornament. Part the hair in the middle, Bell advised, and comb it in a manner that featured the upper, arched portion of the cranium. Tresses should be pulled away from the forehead and, without obscuring the ear, gathered behind in a bun. An occasional curl might wend its way over the temple, but a woman should aim for the intellectual air that came from exhibiting the "higher observing faculties." One need only glance at "the representations of the more elevated personages by the ancient sculptors, and in the heads of Guido and Rafael" to recognize the beauty of this arrangement.[11]

The sinuosities of the line of beauty, however, could only be fully realized in the torso, and in denouncing the deleterious consequences of modern attire, Bell holds forth with all the eloquence at his command. The corset damaged the organs of circulation, digestion, respiration, and reproduction, and the same compression that rendered them dysfunctional also sallowed the complexion and oppressed "the faculties of the mind" by obstructing the free flow of blood. Again he delves into the history of art to provide an alternative to artifice. In praising the full figure, with its ample bosom and natural waist, he argues that

> its superiority over any molding by fashion would be admitted by all of either sex, if the two figures divested of drapery, that on which corsets have been used, and that left to its natural growth and proportions, were copied on canvass [*sic*] or in marble. The proper contrast would be to place the figure made by fashion with its long, straight, flat, and disproportionately narrow waist and upforced breasts beside the Venus de' Medici, or the Juno of the Capitol, or Diana, or any admittedly beautiful female, painted by a Titian or a Vandyck, a Guido, or a Rubens. Every spectator, whilst admiring the one, would turn away with ill concealed dislike for the other.[12]

Not content merely with working its mischief on the torso and viscera, fashion also set out to blight the extremities. The feet, for example, it confines to tiny shoes, and Bell bemoans the mincing step of modern belles that compares so unfavorably with the barefooted liberties taken by the ancients. Among the latter a well-turned ankle or a rounded arch was enough to inspire the muse of many a poet and philosopher. Anyone desirous of experiencing the emotions engendered by a truly beautiful "locomotive system" need only consult the statue of the Grecian Diana.[13]

One might suppose from the tenor of Bell's remarks about classical art that his admiration was unqualified, but this was not the case. Before the academy's cast of the *Venus de' Medici*, for example, he undoubtedly praised the amplitude of waist and bust, but his commendation would not have extended to the head. This feature he judged disproportionately small, a verdict, again, reached in concurrence with the established views of phrenologists for reasons we shall examine shortly.[14]

Bell's text sets the artistic nude at the center of efforts to effect the physiological salvation of American society. Statuary and painting might rescue womankind from the "barbarism of tight lacing," enabling future generations to become worthy successors to the citizens of Athens and Florence. From this perspective the artist stood in the foremost phalanx of civilization, dispatching with brush or chisel all those who in the name of propriety would retard the march of progress.

Bell was not a particularly original thinker, but the forum in which he delivered his remarks should alert the historian of American art to their importance. The heady concoction of aesthetic and scientific theory appealed to artists, and one need not have attended his lectures to learn their content. Erastus Dow Palmer, for example, acquired much the same philosophy from sources available in his native Albany. A visit to Mrs. Thompson's phrenological museum would have acquainted him with these ideas,[15] and the collection assembled by the city's phrenological society no doubt provided a welcome opportunity to supplement the education he felt had been so woefully neglected in his youth.[16] He also conversed with prominent citizens to expand his horizons,[17] and although their names are not reported, one likely candidate is Amos Dean, a lawyer and professor of medical jurisprudence who sat for a cameo portrait in 1847. Their exchanges can hardly have overlooked phrenology, for Dean staked his reputation as a lawyer on its veracity,[18] while also publishing a book based on the lectures he delivered before the city's young men's association.[19]

Much of our understanding of Palmer's outlook comes from an essay he sent to *The Crayon*. There he diverges from Platonic ideals by situating them elsewhere than in the mind of the artist. Instead of adjusting the sitter's features to a preexisting idea, he proposes that every face "is but a type of its own ideal" that the sculptor modifies toward an "order of perfection to which the character belongs, so as to portray that spirit, whose absence we so much feel." In explaining himself Palmer employs a phrase that has already appeared a number of times in this text, "physical metaphysics." His reliance on the term was engendered by a determination to avoid the mannerisms that inevitably follow the abandonment of "nature." By bringing spiritual science to bear on the task, he could trace the imprints left by the soul as it modified the physical constitution. This process sanctioned those improvements in the likeness that did not compromise its individuality.

Much of this sounds mysterious, but Bell had already explained many of these notions. Palmer also realized, for example, that expressive modifications could be made in the coiffure without diminishing the likeness (fig. 3.2). The first image, he explains, "shows how the hair is arranged as usual when the wearer presents herself to the sculptor or painter for a portrait. This is what we are directed to 'copy as we find it.' It elongates the head, in effect, from the chin to the crown, gives the front part of the head a depressed appearance like some of the animals, while the hair is brought down at the sides like the ears of an elephant, thereby concealing the forehead, by which so much that is high and intellectual may be expressed, and also concealing that beautiful feature, the ear." These assertions become more coherent in light of the second design, which, we are told, represents the transformations appropriate "when the ideal is aimed at." [20]

Although Palmer does not elaborate, he does provide a few hints. The two profiles are exactly the same. Hence no changes in the shape of the head have been made to meet the demands of the ideal; rather, it is achieved by alterations in the hair. The preferred arrangement lowers the bun, endowing the occipital lobe with a gradual downward slope where *Firmness*, an unladylike attribute, might otherwise arise. By contrast, the first profile rises continuously from front to back, so depressing the apparent inclination of the forehead, according to the sculptor, that it appears to resemble those of animals. The "ideal" hairdo emphasizes the vertical thrust of the forehead and the general development of the "moral faculties." Further, the references to the ear are significant. The second diagram exhibits it just as the discerning phrenologist would desire, while no such index to the faculties is provided in the first, where the tresses fall in a manner that suggests "the ears of an elephant." These repeated allusions to animals are suggestive because Dean also discusses the "gradual slope backwards" characteristic of the foreheads exhibited by brute creation,[21] and Palmer may well have derived his ideas from this source.

Palmer's diagrams invite close examination for other reasons as well. The first profile, he claims, conceals "much that is high and intellectual," and the basis for this contention is apparent when we perceive just how far over the forehead the hair descends. In the second illustration it is withdrawn, permitting scrutiny of the region governed by the intellectual and moral faculties. This contrast recalls Bell's assurance that "the fair, ample forehead will be lauded by all."[22] Some exercise of our own bump of history is required to realize how extensively phrenology contributed to perceptions of beauty current in the antebellum era. When Miss Blackwell caught the eye of a classmate at Geneva Medical College in 1847, for example, he wrote that she was "a pretty little specimen of the feminine gender. . . . She comes to class with great composure, takes off her bonnet and puts it under the seat (exposing a fine phrenology), [and] takes notes constantly."[23]

Then, as now, preferences in hairstyle often entailed assertions about one's standing vis-à-vis the accepted norms of society. A newspaper report of 1855 reveals the depth of feeling aroused by these issues.

> The notion that high foreheads, in women as well as men, are indispensable to beauty, came into vogue with phrenology, and is going out with the decline of that pretentious and plausible "science." Not long ago more than one "fine lady" shaved her head to give it an "intellectual" appearance, and the custom of combing the hair back from the forehead probably originated in the same mistaken ambition. When it is considered that a great expanse of forehead gives a bold, masculine look—that from frons (forehead) comes the word "effrontery"—it will not be wondered at the ancient painters, sculptors and poets considered a low forehead a "charming thing in woman," and, indeed, indispensable to female beauty.

The author then goes on to cite various ancient authorities who sanction his views and concludes by ridiculing the presumption of those who would attempt to improve on "nature."

The editors of *The Crayon* were not about to let these assertions go un-

Example No. 1

Example No. 2

FIGURE 3.2.
Erastus Dow Palmer, *Two Heads*, from "Philosophy of the Ideal," *Crayon* 3 (1856): 19

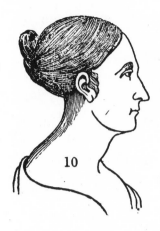

FIGURE 3.3.
Female Head, from O. S. Fowler, *Fowler's Practical Phrenology* (New York: Fowlers and Wells, 1847), p. 55

challenged, so after printing the above, they refuted it point by point.[24] Because the Greeks and Romans "were unconscious of the existence of any spiritual nature either in themselves or in their wives and daughters," their pronouncements about beauty were of limited relevance to the modern age. Their sensualism, the editors continue, thwarted efforts to comprehend "spiritual perfection," and since women were deemed little better than slaves, they were afforded scant opportunity to develop their minds. Three types of womanhood were embodied in the art of antiquity: Venus, the voluptuous; Diana, the active and physical; and Minerva, the intellectual. Of these the last exhibited a head "which any nineteenth century woman would acknowledge as fine and noble." The advent of Christianity brought with it recognition of the true "worth of woman," as any comparison of Raphael's Madonnas with the pagan Venus would testify. The essay concludes by asserting that a high forehead, incorporating active moral and intellectual acumen, as opposed to facile cleverness, is an adornment to its possessor.[25] Feminine allure, however, did not terminate with the forehead; its enticements were also announced by large domestic faculties, which could be enhanced by a bun (fig. 3.3).[26]

The hair of the *White Captive* (fig. 3.4) displays none of these niceties, nor should we expect them, she having been untimely ripped from her humble abode and rudely escorted into the wilderness by her captors. But the fact that the hair does not completely conform to the skull did not inhibit critics from offering their opinions about the mental organization of Palmer's most celebrated nude. Indeed, phrenology resolves one quandary that has puzzled viewers since the statue's initial exhibition.

(Opposite)
FIGURE 3.4. Erastus Dow Palmer, *The White Captive* (1857, marble, Metropolitan Museum of Art)

The figure of the captive is relatively mature, suggesting late adolescence, but the proportions are hardly womanly. The large head accounts for the disparity and seeming immaturity.[27] Contemporaries, however, thought it integral to the statue's meaning. One reviewer proposed,

> Palmer's aim has been to give the world the highest ideal of American Womanhood. To effect this he has not blindly followed the antique models. He has sufficient original force to reproduce nature as he finds it, and the courage to mold into marble the character of the inner life, as well as the mere external forms of physical beauty. The world is tired of looking at small-headed Venuses, which belong, like the De Medici, to a voluptuous rather than to an intellectual age. Palmer has accordingly given us the broad brow of a large-brained and cultivated woman. Her head and face bespeak not only intellectual superiority, but high moral culture.[28]

Palmer shared the reservations of phrenologists about the head of the *Venus de' Medici* and even called the statue "paltry."[29] His own work proclaimed the superior endowments of modern women, and critics concurred, offering the captive's large head as evidence of her "American" nativity when compared with the goddess.[30] One even opines that the progress of civilization might be inferred from this difference, remarking of the latter that "the form is all that could be desired, but the head and features are positively insipid, and a phrenologist would tell you by the development of the cranium that female education was not part of the Grecian policy."[31] Another reviewer supposes some familiarity with the particulars of phrenology, for when we read that the "fine arch of [the] head shows a presence of dignity," we are left to surmise that this refers to a combination of spiritual faculties and *Firmness* equal to the adversity she faces, while praise for the "breadth behind the temples" as an indication "of affectibility to music and beauty" translates into large *Tune* and *Ideality*.[32] Other critics were content to provide more summary assessments, finding in the maiden's ample brow testimony of her intellectual superiority to her captors.[33]

The gap that separates our culture from Palmer's appears in the contention of his modern biographer that "nothing is said in the articles about style or form or the manner of handling the subjects."[34] Quite the contrary, these passages are devoted to stylistic analysis, but not one divorced from content, and here emerges the darker side of antebellum culture. The proportions of the figure, eminently a concern of style, are also an expression of racial theories given currency by phrenology. The large head not only places the captive above her counterparts in antiquity as the consequence of Christianity; it also exhibits the benefits of race, raising her to an eminence not attainable by those with the mental organization presumably possessed by her Native American tormentors. We will return to this topic, but it seems in *The White Captive*, where circumstances of the narrative precluded reliance on those indexes he diagramed for *The Crayon*, Palmer set out to ensure that the viewer would not confuse the nakedness of the subject with intimations of promiscuity. By making the head unmistakably large, by pushing it, perhaps, to the limits of credibility, he created quite a different scenario, one where innate moral purity, warmed by indignation, confronts its polar opposite.

Among those gathered around the captive were certain "jaunty gentlemen" whose patronizing jests about her ample hips and bosom reached the ear of a visiting reporter.[35] These creatures of fashion, no doubt accustomed to the fantastic forms of their female companions, were scarcely prepared for the experience that awaited them within the gallery. There they encountered no wilting hothouse flower, but a hardy perennial of the wilderness, whose solid frame and sturdy limbs made her capable of enduring life's most demanding trials. Like Bell, Palmer equated beauty with health,[36] a conviction that caused him to remark, after surveying the constricted chest and sloping shoulders of one young lady, that whatever was attained " 'at the cost of health, vitality or usefulness' cannot be called beautiful."[37]

Contemporaries were impressed by Palmer's ability to combine precision of anatomical detail with power of expression. One interpreted the captive's response accordingly: " 'Touch me not!' she says with every tensely-braced muscle, with lineaments all eloquent with imperious disgust, 'Touch me not!' "[38] The pose is a variation on *contrapposto*, displaying, however, none of the repose associated with that stance. Instead the maiden remains rigid and withdrawn in the presence of those she surveys with undisguised contempt. Inspiration for this arrangement could have come from Amos Dean, who maintained that the natural language of *Firmness* and *Self-Esteem*, faculties sufficiently prominent in the captive to have drawn attention, prompted an upward and backward motion of the head and torso, accompanied by a stiff and unyielding appearance.[39]

Americans had much to learn from *The White Captive* when she was displayed in 1859. The soundness of her bodily constitution served as a reminder that physical stamina was a primary condition for the progress of civilization. Further, the pace of that progress could only be sustained by those whose mental faculties exhibited the superior organization possessed by Caucasians; hence the maid's disdain for her captors. One critic alluded to these themes when he reviewed the marble in tandem with

Frederic Church's *The Heart of the Andes*. His words have a familiar ring, comparing as they do the undeveloped "intellectual and moral faculties" seen in Greek statuary with the superior organization of Palmer's figure. The latter, he adds, "has given us what is seen, more or less, in all the cultivated and Christian women of the 19th century."[40] Church's landscapes also testify to the beneficial influence of Christianity, since the crosses and steeples that dot his settings indicate that the improvements brought by settlement are moral as well as material. Such panoramas present the Protestant vision of the New World as the fulfillment of God's covenant with his people; the wilderness becomes a theater where human destiny will be played out and salvation achieved.[41] Palmer's captive also speaks of renovation and salvation; she exhibits in an even more precise manner the beneficial effects of religion on untrammeled nature. The implications of such correspondences will be examined in greater depth subsequently.

Palmer's *Indian Girl* (1856, Metropolitan Museum of Art, New York, N.Y.) has taken a first step toward moral improvement, having chanced upon a cross during her rambles in the wilderness. Of her, Henry Tuckerman wrote that "the feet, and the bosom challenge scientific scrutiny,"[42] and to see the figure aright, this observation should be connected with the girl's gesture. Sound physical condition is the first step toward true piety, a philosophy summed up by Harriet Beecher Stowe when she asserted, "Good health is physical religion."[43] Viewers were asked to emulate the seminude figure in this respect, and while Palmer apparently belonged to no organized religion,[44] his claim to have lived a life free of illness, despite evidence to the contrary,[45] suggests he thought himself an exemplar of physical metaphysics in a manner analogous to his statues. "Scientific scrutiny" did not betoken allegiance to prosaic realism, but the pursuit of spiritual insight.

Many of these convictions were shared by William Rimmer, whose career as a physician gave them a particular urgency. We have seen that he relied on phrenology as a foundation for his anatomical instruction, but scholars have questioned its importance to his famed *Art Anatomy*.[46] In its pages the artist asserts that "there can be no such thing as fineness of proportions in any person in whom the head is too large especially in those in whom there is that disgusting protrusion of the frontal portion of the brain so much admired by phrenologists. Anything that increases the apparent size of the head belittles the general body." He adds, "It should be noticed in reference to its artistic uses that the size of the Head relates rather to the perfection and activity of the whole Physical Economy than to the Intellects. The size of the Brain has no special connection with the strength of the understanding, other than described above."[47]

Neither of these remarks, however, constitutes a refutation of phrenology. The first simply proposes that the anterior development favored by some was inappropriate for art; the second actually enunciates a precept often repeated by phrenologists themselves, who also held size alone an inadequate measure of mental power.

The relaxation of professional standards during the Jacksonian era meant that aspiring physicians were often obliged to set their own educational agenda.[48] Rimmer did so by reading Cruveilhier's *The Anatomy of the Human Body*, which served as his primary source of knowledge about the subject.[49] It reviews many of the claims made by phrenology, and while the author is not equally enthusiastic about all, he concludes that Gall "established a new era in the study" of the brain.[50] More telling is the evidence left by Rimmer's subscription to the *American Phrenological Journal*; Weidman could locate only one issue, but others were among the artist's effects that passed down in the family.[51]

Also significant is Rimmer's involvement with other reform movements. Among these were the water cure and vegetarianism. Patients of Rimmer who succumbed to typhoid or smallpox were treated with the gentle doses prescribed by homeopathy rather than the invasive measures of allopathy.[52] Further, one associate noted that "he [Rimmer] was sensitive to spiritual influences" and added that "Rimmer cured his patients with his hands and sympathy, rather than with medicine."[53] By including the artist's gift of clairvoyance, belief in spiritualism,[54] and Swedenborgianism[55] on this list, a single philosophy of healing emerges. This approach, recently labeled "transcendental medicine" by one authority, sought to revive the afflicted by restoring harmony to the vital forces flowing within him or her.[56]

The qualifications requisite for one intent on employing touch as a therapeutic mode were outlined by Walt Whitman in his poem on mediums:

> They shall report Nature, laws, physiology, and happiness,
> They shall illustrate Democracy and the kosmos,
> They shall be alimentive, amative, perceptive,
> They shall be complete women and men, their pose brawny and
>   supple, their drink water, their blood clean and clear.[57]

We must imagine William Rimmer as an individual who regarded himself similarly endowed, not only in terms of the phrenological faculties mentioned in the third line but also as a highly charged battery who could spark the depleted resources of his patients. This telegraphing of health through the faculties to the body was linked by famed mind-curist Warren

Felt Evans to theories that derived from spiritualism and Swedenborg.[58] "Magnetic" cures flourished in the 1840s, and Boston alone could boast of over two hundred such practitioners plying the trade when Rimmer commenced his career.[59]

Rimmer's activities as a physician, then, cannot be divorced from his beliefs as a spiritual scientist. We learn something about the integration of the two from his unpublished epic titled "Stephen and Philip." The reader's progress through this lengthy excursion into Rimmer's metaphysical beliefs is facilitated, as in the case of Whitman, by a familiarity with phrenology. "'Are there in the sphere of human consciousness only perceptions and reflections?' asked Stephen earnestly, 'Holding these at their full value what estimate shall we set upon our moral qualities, and the special faculties that constitute (the highest attributes of the soul? [crossed out]) What of all the endowments necessary to make us what we are? And if intelligence alone, as such is equal to the universe, what field shall we assign to our emotional or devotional life and instincts.'" He continues, "Hath being's Provider given us eyes for sight, ears for sound, tongue for taste, and the faculty of numbers and a sense of the infinite only there—but to cheat us and deceive us in the nobler qualities of our being? Whom shall we honor for all these excellencies? Shall it be the dumb and silent (? [crossed out]) soil that is beneath our feet? Oh blessed and holy dust if this be so."[60] We learn here why Rimmer was so set against the "disgusting bump" mentioned above; it arose in the realm of the "perceptions and reflections" and thus did not belong to "the special faculties that constitute the highest attributes of the soul." Among these "moral qualities" were *Veneration* and *Benevolence,* whose location at the top of the head proclaimed their superiority to the intelligence generated by "the faculty of numbers," which comprehended numerical but not spiritual infinity.[61] When Rimmer declared that the "faculty of reason is below the faculty of worship,"[62] he was speaking literally as well as figuratively, for *Veneration* was indeed above *Comparison.*

More is learned about *Comparison,* again a denizen of the disgusting bump, from a maxim Rimmer delivered to his students. "Some possess the faculty of comparison to so perfect a degree as to enable them to do in an hour what others could scarcely do in a day; yet, in kind, the faculty is the same in all, and is possessed by some in the highest excellence who are quite destitute of every other power of art. To make a literal copy requires, for the time being, the subjection of every faculty but comparison, and, if followed long for itself, destroys the higher love for art in worth of imagination and the ideal."[63] This declaration was vouchsafed by the liberties enjoyed by spiritual scientists; as Clevenger might have informed

Rimmer, *Imitation* was the faculty responsible for proficiency in copying. The latter, however, was unlikely to relinquish theories that allowed him to acknowledge the function of *Comparison* while regarding it unfriendly to the imagination. The tone of these remarks accords with the decided preference given the affections over the intellect in writings of the Swedenborgians and spiritual scientists.[64]

The reader who came to the *Art Anatomy* hoping for "how-to" advice was likely to be disappointed, for its diagrams were not primarily intended to provide tips that would ease the travails of the novice. It is both a work of art in its own right and a theoretical treatise, enlisting the ideas of Swedenborg, Lavater, and Spurzheim, among others, to delineate the ends of figurative art. Rimmer, however, rarely acknowledges his sources and is not as systematic as one might wish. The understanding he shared with the circles of genteel Bostonians who attended his lectures—circles where Transcendentalism and transcendental medicine met on familiar terms—is left for us to reconstruct.

Members of this select society would have recognized the reference to the "Museum of Natural History, Boston"[65] in the *Art Anatomy* as the Warren Museum,[66] the repository of the Boston Phrenological Society's collection and the institution that issued Rimmer an invitation to bring his class. The diagrams that come under this heading must reflect his study of this material; hence his "Skull of [an] Anglo-American" would derive from the study of the English skulls gathered there. Nearby appears the "Skull of [a] California Indian," and again the wide array of Native American crania in the collection afforded him ample opportunity to familiarize himself with the distinctive features of the race.[67] The comparisons set out here were not devoid of qualitative implications; without the insights provided by Gall's science into "the relative intellectual rank of the various races of mankind," wrote one contemporary authority, "ethnology is simply learned child's-play."[68] This assessment applies not only to Rimmer's work but to much of what follows in this and subsequent chapters.

Many of the same traits characteristic of the "lower races" were also present in degenerate Caucasians. One of the latter was Thompson (fig. 3.5), a rapist whose eventual rendezvous with the hangman was announced by the intimidating size of his *Amativeness*. The family resemblance to Rimmer's "Cunning, Rapacious, Treacherous, Hypocritical, Fanatical" type (fig. 3.6) may result from the artist's study of the cast, or it may simply derive from the general parameters of delinquency drawn by phrenology. Both heads exhibit ample "animal propensities" and a somewhat recessive forehead; unfortunately, as is often the case, Rimmer does not elaborate on the label. The similarity does suggest that the material he found in the

FIGURE 3.5.
Thompson, Executed for Rape (date unknown, plaster cast, Warren Anatomical Museum, Harvard University)

FIGURE 3.6.
Cunning, Rapacious, Treacherous, Hypocritical, Fanatical, from William Rimmer, *Art Anatomy* (Boston: Little, Brown, 1877), p. 30

Warren collection nourished his imagination in ways that the bland neo-classical works located in the Athenaeum could not.

Besides the Warren collection, another important key to the *Art Anatomy* is the one copy of the *American Phrenological Journal* that survived among Rimmer's effects. This issue, published in 1860, includes an account of George Combe's *Phrenology Applied to Painting and Sculpture.* Among the topics that book considers are the mental and physical qualities necessary for artistic talent, the natural language of the faculties, works that epitomized phrenological tenets, and the obligation of artists to respect the correspondences between mind and body as an essential component in expression.[69] The fact that two reviews appeared in *The Crayon* following its publication indicates the serious consideration given Combe's work by American artists.[70]

All the topics examined by Combe and his reviewer would have intrigued Rimmer, but he must have paid especially close attention to the last consideration. It directed artists to respect the unity between "particular mental endowments and particular corporeal forms."[71] As summarized in the article, this maxim could read as a prolegomenon to the *Art*

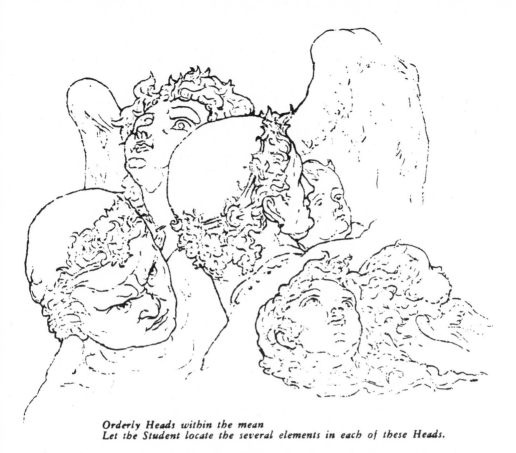

Orderly Heads within the mean
Let the Student locate the several elements in each of these Heads.

FIGURE 3.7. *Orderly Heads*, from William Rimmer, *Art Anatomy* (Boston: Little, Brown, 1877), p. 29

Anatomy: "Hence, a mistake made in bringing out this unitary character, by a failure rightly to adapt the expression of one part of head, face, or general form to the rest is surely exaggerated by the very circumstance of the intensity of the phases of life which it usually falls to the artist to depict."[72] Much of Rimmer's undertaking is devoted to this end, to demonstrating how differences in age, sex, and race find their correspondence in bodily proportion and mental acumen.[73]

The spiritualist bent of Rimmer's thought, including his communications with the deceased,[74] enabled him to project these precepts from this world to the next. Thus one diagram of "Orderly Heads" surveys the growth of identity from childhood to maturity and on to the angelic (fig. 3.7). This vision also extended downward, to the subhuman and animal species, and in each case Combe's tenets are interwoven with more arcane principles. The following is typical:

The lower races are in some instances more strongly marked in a Masculine and Animal way than some of the higher races. If it could be as-

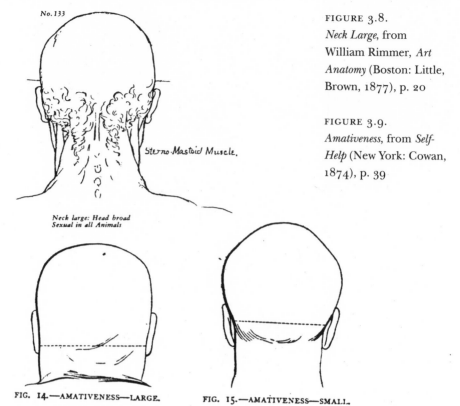

No. 133

Sterno-Mastoid Muscle.

Neck large: Head broad
Sexual in all Animals

FIG. 14.—AMATIVENESS—LARGE.   FIG. 15.—AMATIVENESS—SMALL.

FIGURE 3.8.
Neck Large, from
William Rimmer, *Art
Anatomy* (Boston: Little,
Brown, 1877), p. 20

FIGURE 3.9.
Amativeness, from *Self-
Help* (New York: Cowan,
1874), p. 39

sumed that the Cerebral Section represented the intellectual attributes
[moral and reflective faculties], the Maxillary Section, the nutrient and
combative or carnivorous appetites [*Combativeness, Alimentiveness,* etc.];
the Nasal Section, Forehead [perceptive faculties], and chin the sensibilities; the Eye, the purpose; the texture of the Hair and condition of
the Skin, the sensitiveness of the Constitution to the activities of the
Mind;—the Ideal Head representing the Ideal Character, and every
departure from it a departure toward one or other of the intellectual
or animal attributes—Physiognomy might be considered a Science ap-
proximating in some degree to that kind of exactness found in the
Science of Physiology.[75]

The irony of the last assertion hinges on its appearance in a book dedicated to delineating just such a science of physiognomy. The phrenological components of it are introduced in brackets, but these extend as well
to the texture of the skin and hair as a measure of sensibility.[76] Likewise,
the illustrations employed by Rimmer resemble those in phrenological
texts. The diagram of the neck as indicative of sexual appetite (fig. 3.8),
for example, resembles those of *Amativeness* (fig. 3.9).

To phrenology Rimmer also added the facial angle devised by Pieter

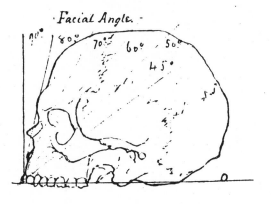

FIGURE 3.10.
Facial Angle, from
William Rimmer, *Art
Anatomy* (Boston: Little,
Brown, 1877), p. 3

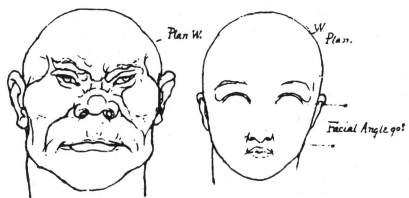

FIGURE 3.11. *Size Inverted,* from William Rimmer, *Art Anatomy* (Boston: Little, Brown,
1877). p. 5

Camper. The Dutch anatomist proposed that lines drawn along the bottom
of the skull and its profile gauged mental prowess (fig. 3.10)—the higher
the angle, the greater the intelligence. Allied to this was the concept of
prognathism, a term devised to describe the heavy jaw supposedly characteristic of inferior races; the Caucasian, with vertical profile, prominent
forehead, and relatively small jaw represented the standard from which
others departed. In one diagram (fig. 3.11) a head with Negroid features,
enormous jaw, and small cerebral section on the left bears an inscription
indicating that the facial angle is seventy-five degrees; to his right the measurement is fifteen degrees greater in an oval-headed Caucasian. Because
the views are frontal, information can be gathered that is not provided
by Camper. The former displays great breadth just above the ear, a trait
Combe equated with "cruelty and rapaciousness" since it was the seat of
Destructiveness and *Combativeness,* which corresponded in turn to Rimmer's
Maxillary Section. The second head expands above *Cautiousness,* a development signifying high moral standing.[77] Similar pairings appear in phrenological literature (fig. 3.12). The example included here is taken from the

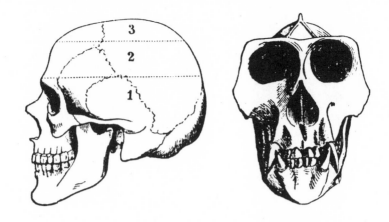

FIGURE 3.12. *Grades of Intelligence*, from Samuel R. Wells, *New Physiognomy* (New York: Samuel R. Wells, 1868), p. 600

writings of Samuel Wells, a Fowler associate whose approach reflects the increasing eclecticism of the later phrenologists. This greater latitude permitted him to advise readers "to observe the facial angle" as a convenient means of determining the relative strength of the anterior faculties.[78]

If phrenology guided Rimmer through the intricacies of racial ranking, it provided much the same service when it came to differences of gender. Here again his diagrams are not entirely self-explanatory. The implications of his *Man and Woman, Same Family* (fig. 3.13) become evident only in light of the theory's teachings on the subject. Because the professions required the cultivation of certain faculties at the expense of others, the skulls of males were more likely to exhibit irregularities than those of females, where diverse household duties provided a more uniform, if less vigorous, exercise of the faculties. In conformity with Bell's principles, the crania of women tended to be evenly rounded,[79] and the illustrations of this tenet in phrenological texts exhibit the same rugged male precipices and gentle female declivities seen in Rimmer's drawing (fig. 3.14). So, also, where "feminine characteristics" are in excess in the *Art Anatomy* (fig. 3.15), the curvature is extreme; where these qualities are deficient, the outline is correspondingly angular (fig. 3.16). On the male side, the deficient head is rounded (fig. 3.17), while the abundantly endowed is erratically formed (fig. 3.18).

Rimmer's discussion of the ear as indicative of brain size again reveals his reliance on phrenology,[80] while his preferences in coiffure recall Bell's reasoning. "Nothing," Rimmer writes, "can exceed the beauty of the natural outline of a well-formed Head. It should never be altogether obscured, nor its natural proportions defaced."[81] Granting a certain amount of artistic license, his vision of the "orderly" head (fig. 3.19) resembles the ideal

FIGURE 3.13.
Man and Woman, Same Family, from William Rimmer, *Art Anatomy* (Boston: Little, Brown, 1877), p. 19

FIGURE 3.14.
Profiles, from Samuel R. Wells, *New Physiognomy* (New York: Samuel R. Wells, 1868), p. 112

FIGURE 3.15.
Feminine Characteristics in Excess, from William Rimmer, *Art Anatomy* (Boston: Little, Brown, 1877), p. 29

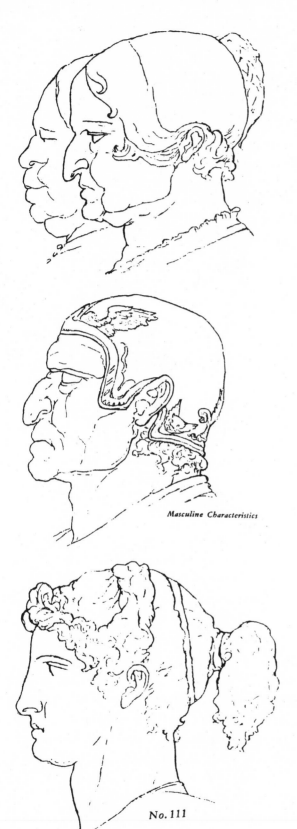

Masculine Characteristics

No. 111

(Above left)
FIGURE 3.16.
Feminine Characteristics Deficient,
from William Rimmer, *Art Anatomy*
(Boston: Little, Brown, 1877), p. 29

(Above right)
FIGURE 3.17.
Masculine Characteristics Deficient,
from William Rimmer, *Art Anatomy*
(Boston: Little, Brown, 1877), p. 29

FIGURE 3.18. *Masculine*
Characteristics in Excess, from
William Rimmer, *Art Anatomy*
(Boston: Little, Brown, 1877),
p. 29

FIGURE 3.19. *Hair, Female Form—*
Orderly, from William Rimmer, *Art*
Anatomy (Boston: Little, Brown,
1877), p. 16

of the phrenologists; the contour of the skull can be examined, the ear is visible, and the domestic virtues are reinforced by the hair in the back. The "artificial, disorderly" type (fig. 3.20) is less revelatory, and the conclusions drawn from her organization are likely to be less propitious. Rimmer also opposed the corset and offered readers a contrast between the ample proportions of the "natural waist" and the deformities inflicted by fashion (fig. 3.21), while lecturing audiences on the desirability of garments that conform to bodily contour.[82]

The figures in the *Art Anatomy* derive much of their identity from phrenology. The men generally exhibit the broad-necked angularity promoted by *Amativeness,* an organ that occupied one-fifth of the male brain but only one-eighth of the female.[83] Among its virtues was an ability to energize other faculties, prompting one phrenologist to remind businessmen that "a little animal power is more valuable than dollars can admeasure."[84] These notions prompted passages such as the following in the *Art Anatomy*: "In the Male body, through the great activity of the Physical Constitution, the Masculine Form passes over the Ideal, or the development of the principles of structure, toward the Animal to meet the requirements of actual use."[85] The wear and tear of the male world inhibited the ideal, while domestic life kept women well-rounded in both a literal and figurative sense. "The Mohammedans say that women have no souls," Rimmer remarked, "I say that they are all soul."[86]

Given the similarities, it is difficult to imagine that Rimmer's illustrations were uninfluenced by those in Samuel Wells's treatise on phrenology.[87] The latter's frontispiece (fig. 3.22) diagrams the doctrines that underlie the *Art Anatomy*. There are the familiar heads; the prognathous brute lurks at the bottom, while the bald-pated philosopher rules above. Caucasians dominate, relegating the representatives of other races to secondary status. In the center is woman. Her brain may not be as capacious as that of the bearded Nestor, but her moral sentiments hold the centrifugal impulses of mankind in check. On her descends the honor of transmitting the spiritual heritage of humanity from one generation to the next, and the dignity of her calling is evident in the noble head with its superior shape and fine-textured skin and hair.[88] The reader who brings these ideas to the *Art Anatomy* will progress through its obscurer passages more readily.

The stereotypes that appear in Wells's illustration were hardly unique to phrenology, but if they were shared by the culture at large, the theory gave them a specific visual dimension that exercised wide influence. Victorian standards of femininity, for example, imposed the sort of sedentary existence portrayed in *At the Window* (fig. 3.23), but we learn much more about the person confined to this dark interior by consulting the particu-

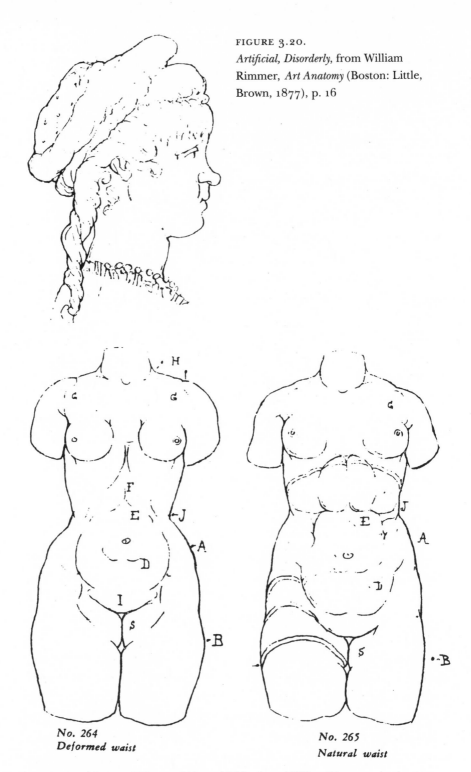

FIGURE 3.20.
Artificial, Disorderly, from William Rimmer, *Art Anatomy* (Boston: Little, Brown, 1877), p. 16

No. 264
Deformed waist

No. 265
Natural waist

FIGURE 3.21. *Deformed Waist and Natural Waist,* from William Rimmer, *Art Anatomy* (Boston: Little, Brown, 1877), p. 47

FIGURE 3.22. Frontispiece from Samuel R. Wells, *New Physiognomy* (New York: Samuel R. Wells, 1868)

FIGURE 3.23. William Rimmer, *At the Window* (1874–77, oil painting, National Museum of American Art)

lars of Gall's science. Her profile resembles that of the orderly type in the *Art Anatomy*, and judging from the high forehead and rounded skull, which expands in the region of the "domestic" faculties where the hair is gathered, her ruminations involve elevated subjects. The body complements the mind; a full bosom is apparent beneath the jerkin, while the dress flows around wide hips that declare their fitness for childbirth. Nothing is constricted or distorted, and had John Bell examined the figure, he would have praised the amplitude of its curves.

A similar response would have come from another opponent of tight lacing, Harriet Beecher Stowe. She decried the spareness of Americans when compared with the "opulence of physical proportions" rendered by artists such as Titian and Giorgione. "It would require one to be better educated than most of our girls are," she mused, "to be willing to look like the Sistine Madonna or the Venus of Milo."[89] This observation goes to the heart of the criticism inspired by phrenology. One should not simply look *at* an ideal figure; one should also aspire to look *like* it. Emulation went beyond the moral implied by the narrative to the physical organization of the protagonists. In this light Rimmer's image serves as an altarpiece in the religion of physical metaphysics, inculcating lessons of reason and health where the narrow considerations of dogma previously had reigned.

While Rimmer's women are often sequestered from the world, his men compete, sometimes literally, in the arena of life, and in doing so, sacrifice much of their spiritual nature. Such is the fate of the combatant in the *Lion in the Arena* (fig. 3.24). Weidman perceptively recognized the relevance to this scene of Combe's discussion of antique mosaics that depict similar subjects. According to the phrenologist, the deficiency of the moral faculties exhibited by these figures was symptomatic of the pervasive cruelty and sensualism of Roman society.[90] This opinion was shared by members of the artistic community, and William Wetmore Story left a graphic account of his reaction to these same images: "In the museum of San Giovanni in Laterano is a large mosaic pavement, taken from the Baths of Caracalla, on which are represented gladiators of the day. Their brutal and bestial physiognomies, their huge, over-developed muscles, and Atlantean shoulders, their low, flat foreheads and noses, are hideous to behold, and give one a more fearful and living notion of the horror of these bloody games to which they were trained than any description in words could convey. They make one believe that of all animals, none can be made so brutal as man."[91]

Their dedication to violence gave these Romans the stocky, awkward aspect also seen in Rimmer's gladiator, but the latter turns away from us. This fact, however, need not preclude the assessment of character, for an advantageous view of the neck is presented. The broad neck and head signal an active *Amativeness*, and when perverted, as is presumably the case, it occasioned "grossness and vulgarity in expression and action; licentiousness in all its forms; [and] a feverish state of mind."[92] As if to emphasize the point, all the other gladiators are also seen from behind.

FIGURE 3.24. William Rimmer, *Lion in the Arena* (1873–75, oil painting, Reynolda House Museum of American Art, Winston-Salem, N.C.)

Their helmets do not necessarily prevent analysis of the other faculties as well. Rimmer admired the headgear worn by Greek hoplites precisely because it revealed the skull's shape, and he lamented the absence of comparable fashions in modern times.[93] A glance at *Masculine Characteristics in Excess* from the *Art Anatomy* reveals an organization comparable to the gladiator's and protective gear that likewise conforms to the cranium. Weidman's suggestion, then, that the flat top of the gladiator's headpiece is indicative of the small cerebral section characteristic of "low" types,[94] and hence is consistent with other traits visible in the entire figure, accords entirely with the artist's pronouncements on the subject.

A different type appears in *The Falling Gladiator* (fig. 3.25), where personal sentiments underlie the ostensible subject. Its private meaning emerges in Rimmer's lines about his compassion for "the son of a great King who knowing not his heritance, was a Gladiator having no calling but to shed his blood at other's will."[95] The disinherited son mentioned here is an allusion to the artist's father, Thomas, who maintained he was the rightful heir to the French throne.[96] This belief became a consuming pas-

FIGURE 3.25. William Rimmer, *The Falling Gladiator* (1907 [modeled in 1861],
bronze, courtesy of Museum of Fine Arts, Boston, gift of Caroline Hunt Rimmer,
Adeline R. Durham, and various subscribers)

sion that filled his waking hours with apprehensions about possible assassination attempts, an anguish seemingly mirrored on the gladiator's face.

The Hellenistic marble then known as *The Dying Gladiator* stands behind Rimmer's piece, and George Combe's reflections on the former offer
intriguing possibilities for interpreting the latter. The phrenologist surmised that the stricken figure was not the type who joined the profession

with alacrity, "but a noble Gaul in captivity, compelled to assume this de-graded character." Everything about the body—its refined and intellectual qualities, vigorous thorax and limbs, and nervous sensibility—supported the conclusion. And although the head was perceived to be somewhat in-ferior to the other features, the Scotsman concluded that "the Gladiator is quite abstracted, and thinks of objects far away from the scene in which he is dying."[97] These words would have been especially meaningful if, as seems likely, Rimmer read the book as well as its review. Had not his father been "a noble Gaul" obliged to serve in the English army? Further, his death throes doubtlessly were haunted by visions of a distant homeland and a destiny now never to be fulfilled.[98] Combe's words, then, would have helped the artist expand personal experiences to a more comprehensive imagery.

The gladiator wears a close-fitting helmet that permits analysis of the cranial structure, and the shortcomings Combe found in the antique prototype were presumably edited out, since Thomas Rimmer was, in the eyes of his son, a man of superior endowments.[99] Further, this feature enabled the artist to avoid the shaggy locks of the ancient Gaul and, in-stead, to exhibit the shape of the head precisely, a matter of no small consequence given the likelihood that the statue presided at lectures.[100] The delicate modeling of the flesh and the ready visibility of the veins, tendons, and muscles all facilitated instruction while suggesting in turn a finely organized figure, not one of the rough-hewn types who entered the arena with enthusiasm, but instead a sensitive, "nervous" individual whose fate is undeserved.

Even higher up the ladder of humanity is *St. Stephen* (fig. 3.26), who, like the gladiator, faces imminent death. Both works reflect the high valua-tion the artist placed on antique statuary. In the case of *St. Stephen*, the source is the *Laocoön*, a relationship one critic stressed by calling the bust a "Christian Laocoon."[101] The deeper implications, however, emerge only when one takes into account the differences between the two. The most obvious are the retreating brow and abundant locks of the pagan priest when compared with the large forehead and want of hair in the martyr. No doubt phrenologists gasped at the size of Stephen's dome, but they also would have recognized the implications of its baldness. The frequency of this feature among those whose faculties of worship were in constant use caught Gall's attention,[102] a case, I suppose, of grass not growing on a well-

(Opposite)
FIGURE 3.26. William Rimmer, *St. Stephen* (1860, granite, Art Institute of Chicago, Roger McCormick Fund)

FIGURE 3.27. William Rimmer, *Flight and Pursuit* (1872, oil painting, courtesy of Museum of Fine Arts, Boston, bequest of Miss Edith Nichols)

traveled path. Charles Caldwell discussed the topic at some length, claiming that a fully developed *Veneration* "produces early baldness. Hence the heads of saints and pious men, are usually represented with that accompaniment."[103] By displaying the massive, well-constituted head of his saint in this manner, Rimmer affirmed his spiritual elevation. Impiety brought down the wrath of the gods upon the Trojan, while Stephen endures the persecution of mortals so that he might ascend to his God. Their fates are written on their faces.

The spiritual sciences offer the best prospect of solving the riddle posed by *Flight and Pursuit* (fig. 3.27): Who are the mysterious beings whose clamorous entry disturbs the tomblike silence of these fabulous halls? Why are their poses so insistently similar? Is the fugitive aware of the specter that shadows him? Conditioned as we are by the paintings of de Chirico and Magritte to yield to the enchantment of the inexplicable, there is an inclination to view Rimmer's work in the same manner. But did he also cultivate enigma for its own sake? An inscription written on a preparatory drawing of the fugitive suggests otherwise. It reads, "oh for the horns of the Altar,"[104] alluding to the custom in biblical times of granting asylum to the malefactor who entered the temple and grasped the horns of the altar within. Responding to this clue, Sarnoff proposed that the painting illustrates the tale of Adonijah, who, after failing to usurp the throne of Solomon, "caught hold on the horns of the altar." Others have drawn connections with specific events from recent history, including the assassination of Lincoln and the massacre of the Mamelukes by Mohammed Ali.[105]

A second school of thought proposes that *Flight and Pursuit* addresses issues of a more universal scope. Proponents of this interpretation maintain that the subject involves the soul's earthly tribulations, and mention of Emerson's "Brahma" is often made in this context, though the connection is tenuous at best. Weidman surely comes closest to the mark in suggesting that the mirrorlike figure in the background owes its identity to the doctrine of correspondences as it was employed by the Transcendentalists, with spirit and matter reflecting each other.[106]

Neither of these possibilities need preclude the other. Some particular incident may have launched Rimmer on an imaginative flight, but the case for a metaphysical reading is stronger. To make it, however, we must not rest content with the formulations of Transcendentalists but press on to their source, the writings of Swedenborg. The theory of correspondences enabled the seer to translate even the most harrowing events of the Bible into precepts of spiritual wisdom. In doing so, his insistence on the specificity of meaning, as seen in the following passage on the symbolism of the altar, was at variance with the more fluid approach taken by the New Englanders: "The altar was the representative of His divine Good, the horns were the representatives of His Divine Truth; that the truth was from good was represented by the horns being out of it or out of the altar." There follows a discourse on the wrongdoers who sacrificed on the altar to expiate their sins,[107] and the gist of this and other commentaries is that "the horns of the altar" correspond to articles of faith that shield the sinner. Reprobates, however, must approach these truths with humility; otherwise "the Divine does not flow into them, and all holy things with man are not holy but from Divine influx." "Accordingly, if the natural man is perverted, then the spiritual has no means of acting into him but in a perverse manner; and therefore the spiritual or internal man is then closed."[108]

In conformity with the timeless essence Swedenborg extracts from biblical history, there is little in *Flight and Pursuit* that leads us to a particular place or personage, least of all Adonijah. We might expect this offshoot of the venerable tree of Jesse to be robed in princely attire and cast in the mold of nobility, but no such attributes elevate the protagonist. His negative aura is reinforced by the demeanor of his ghostly pursuer; certainly this sinister presence cannot correspond to an elevated moral condition.

Malevolence haunts these corridors; the internal man is closed and can no more grasp the horns (which, incidentally, are not shown) than escape his true nature. The key to unriddling Rimmer's painting is less apparent in Emerson's poetry than in Swedenborg's declaration that "the things that happen in the material world do offer a kind of mirror-view of things in the spiritual world."[109]

Swedenborg wrote his *Heaven and Hell* not merely as a Baedecker to the afterlife but, more urgently, to remind readers that everyone, "dead or alive," partakes of the spiritual life during every living moment.[110] Each individual invites the community of spirits that corresponds to his or her moral condition; hence Rimmer's imagery reflects Swedenborg's claim that "there are spirits from hell and angels from heaven with every single person. The person is involved in his evil aspect by means of the spirits from hell, and in his good aspect from the Lord by means of the angels from heaven. In this way, he is in a spiritual balance—that is, in a freedom."[111]

The menacing aspect of both figures in *Flight and Pursuit* divulges the true nature of the fugitive. While he longs for the horns of the altar, he remains bedeviled by the influx from hell. Rimmer takes up the same theme in a poetic passage that comes especially close to the painting. "Alas! for adulterers and thieves, and murderers of who can fancy the shadows that follow them? things of another world on whom corruption hangs from their graves[.] Half on earth, ten fold in hell, whose only rest is in the passion that begets the blackest crimes! Demons that were once men, whose heavy load of wickedness from evil fortune, or evil heart, or both keeps them down to the dread level of their sad experience."[112] The Swedenborgian coloration here appears in the ascription of a positive existence to evil. Emerson and the spiritualists either denied that possibility entirely or were tentative on the subject, while the Swedish mystic and his followers dwelt on the topic at length.[113]

There is a phrenological coda to all this, which despite its relative brevity, forms an essential component of the imagery. The theological implications delineated above would have little consequence were the fugitive in *Flight and Pursuit* of angelic aspect. Were the latter the case, we might suppose him an innocent seeking refuge from unjust accusations, but this would undermine the entire Swedenborgian framework. As depicted, however, the figure corresponds to the ethical (and not merely the historical) implications of the horns of the altar. He exhibits those features that the *Art Anatomy* regularly associates with diminished mental and moral capacity. Weidman noted that the convex face, retreating forehead, Roman nose, and prominent chin all belong to the "aggressive or conquering races."[114] As we have also seen, Rimmer linked a low facial angle not only to impoverished intellectual and moral faculties but also to powerful *Combativeness* and *Destructiveness*. Add to this the dark skin and coarse beard (another sign of retarded moral development[115]), and the resulting type is one that is bound to draw up spirits from hell.[116]

Around each individual in Rimmer's universe swarmed armies of angels and demons who "come into our ears, our hearts, aye! into the very marrow of our sense from heaven and hell!"[117] Their incursions into the marrow of one's being meant that spirit served as the guiding principle behind physical development, thus making the disciplines of physiognomy and phrenology viable.[118] The implications of this philosophy went beyond Rimmer's artistic endeavors to include his activities as a physician, and in fulfilling his duties as healer and revealer, he had much in common with Whitman. A description of the latter, which identifies him as "the compassionate healer-persona who articulates the message throughout the poems, that bodily health is a key to spirituality,"[119] needs only minor adjustments in the wording to apply equally to the former.

The writings of Henry Tuckerman have been characterized as possessing "no strong convictions" on the contention that the critic was too deferential to the opinions of the artists with whom he socialized.[120] A different picture emerges, however, if we trace the thread of phrenological thinking that runs through his oeuvre. While yet a member of the Boston Phrenological Society, he published a review of Edward Bulwer-Lytton's *The Last Days of Pompeii* that sought to identify the passages in the novel that were indebted to phrenology. His interest in the visual arts is already apparent in this article, prompting him to speculate, for example, that an individual endowed with ordinary powers of observation would be likely to deduce from busts of Nero and Trajan many of the same conclusions reached by Gall and Spurzheim. The ideal heads carved by the Greeks to represent their gods, he continues, exhibit elevated qualities of character that reinforce their claim to embody divine attributes.[121] On one level, then, Tuckerman relies on phrenology to articulate a philosophy of expression; the artist who remains faithful to the model is most likely to capture the true nature of his sitter's personality. On another level, the assertion that the average person can intuit the principles of the theory and that artists in the past have unwittingly done so to project their understanding of the highest moral attributes promotes the contention that there exist objective standards in such matters that science will now clarify.

Another theme that appears in this essay concerns the value of the arts to an age mired in commercialism. It is by the "exercise of ideality," Tuckerman states, that "the ultra-utilitarian" mentality of modern times can be effectively tamed.[122] Subsequent writings reiterate this theme; *Ideality* testifies to an innate yearning for the beautiful, and like religion, art answers fundamental needs, which, if neglected, imperil society. Commingled sentiments of aestheticism and piety appear in the passages that urge this belief:

> Argue and moralize as bigots may, they cannot impugn the design of God in creating a distinct and most influential faculty in our nature, which has not merely a useful or temporary end—the sense of the beautiful. Ideality is as much a heaven-implanted element as conscientiousness. Nature's surpassing grandeur and loveliness hourly minister to it, and Art, in its broadest and highest sense, is its legitimate manifestation. When a human voice of marvelous depth and sweetness yields to thousands a pure and rich delight, or a human hand of ideal skill traces scenes of grace and sublimity, and bequeaths the features hallowed by love or glorified by fame,—then is the worthiest praise offered to God by the right and sacred exercise of those faculties which unite mortal to angelic existence.[123]

In essence, this line of reasoning follows that taken by phrenologists when they answered accusations of atheism. If faculties such as *Conscientiousness* and *Veneration* affirmed the existence of a higher being, then *Ideality* stood as a reminder to those whose waking hours were consumed with getting and spending that they were under an obligation to cultivate their better nature as well. This belief underlies all of Tuckerman's criticism.

Tuckerman's early article also mentions natural language, and again he touches on a topic that would become central to his philosophy. An entire chapter of his *Italian Sketch Book* is devoted to the subject. "Natural language," he states, expresses "innate sentiment" by means of "involuntary" movements and gestures. The stance of arrogance, for example, includes rigidity in the dorsal region and a protrusion of the chin that can scarcely be suppressed even when consciously acknowledged. Citizenship, too, carries with it a natural language consistent with national temper. While the Italian is likely to shrug off the casual slight of a waiter, the "combativeness" of an Englishman is not so easily placated or as likely to let the matter drop.[124]

Natural language rescued portraiture from the arid literalism that might otherwise have resulted from phrenology's demand for accuracy. It challenged the artist to convey a sense of the sitter's living presence. Tuckerman extols Thomas LeClear's likeness of Daniel S. Dickinson of Binghamton for capturing "the attitude, complexion, eye, mouth, costume, natural language, and expression, the very man himself," while

FIGURE 3.28. Emanuel Leutze, *Columbus before the Queen* (1843, oil painting, Brooklyn Museum, Dick S. Ramsay Fund and A. Augustus Healy Fund)

Charles Loring Elliott's full-length portraits of American officials were "very true, not only to the features, but the natural language of the subject. It gives us not only the form, but the very air of the man." These results were decidedly preferable to the traditional poses that ignored the individual and confined him or her to the straitjacket of convention.[125]

Success in depicting natural language depended on a felicitous accord between intuition and a capacity for objective analysis; only then could an artist hope to recognize which transient expression coincided with the relatively fixed structure of the skull. History painting permitted greater latitude in this respect than portraiture, and in no small measure the praise due Emanuel Leutze's *Columbus before the Queen* (fig. 3.28) resulted from the rendering of Isabella's "fine abandonment in her very attempt at self-control, and the manner in which the hand presses the temples is part of the natural language of subdued feeling."[126] The reference here is to those inadvertent gestures that bring the hand to the most active faculty. Tuckerman does not specify, but since she must decide the fate of one who has been imprisoned unjustly, it is probably *Causality*. The intelligent, vertical profile of the accused, which is isolated at the center of the composition, assures the viewer of his singular gifts and superiority to those who seek his downfall. This manner of setting off the protagonist becomes increasingly frequent at mid-century, and it is safe to conclude that phrenology contributed in no small measure to the popularity of the device.

Aside from these specific applications of the concept of natural language, Tuckerman also entertained more comprehensive ideas about its use. It provided a basic tool of analysis, obliging the critic to identify the pervasive natural language of a work. "There is no greater fallacy," he contends, "than that involved in the notion of an essential diversity between an author and his books: professed opinions do not reveal the truth of character, but unconscious phrases of style, habits of thought, and tones of expression, like what is called natural language, make us thoroughly acquainted with the man."[127] All art, then, is fundamentally autobiographical, "unconsciously" imparting "the tone of mind" of its creator while revealing his or her "constitutional idiosyncrasies."[128] These notions approach those of Combe, and the resemblance comes even closer in the following lines: "It is astonishing," Tuckerman asserts, "that with the new light modern science has thrown upon physiology, it is so seldom taken into view when mental phenomena are discussed. There is no fact better established than that the integrity of the nervous system is necessary to the felicitous exercise of mind. Yet biographers and critics seem blind to its influence. This delicate medium of intellectual acuity is refined and sensitive in all rarely endowed beings, for vivid impressions are the source of their power, and to these a susceptible organization is essential."[129]

Tuckerman thus disparages those who repudiate "the vital relation of genius to material laws." The adepts of this "shallow philosophy" seek to split mind and body asunder by ignoring "physiology in their analysis of character." Their devotion to "the abstract in mental phenomena" constitutes, in effect, a form of irreverence toward the muse who nourishes budding talent much as vernal zephyrs do the orchard. Just as fruit derives its flavor and color from earth and air, genius is "warmed, enriched and quickened by the agency of an animal organism—the channel of nature—by sensation, physical development, appetites, and sensations, as well as ideas."[130] It is evident, he adds, that the processes of reasoning and "descriptive limning" are the same for all; originality, however, is born of the "particular union of moral and physical qualities" present in the artist. Since such is not engendered by "pure abstract and spiritual emanation," it is incumbent upon the critic to approach his subjects "by the light of character; and from their human to deduce their literary peculiarities instead of the reverse, which is the method of superficial criticism."[131] The ascent from physical to mental character entailed by this methodology reflects the priorities of phrenology within the larger context of physical metaphysics.

Walt Whitman's call for a race of stalwart, brawny, poet-prophets, skilled in "the physiology [and] phrenology . . . of the land," to sing the virtues of America was premised on the same belief.[132] And when Tuckerman sets out to expose the shortcomings of Francis Jeffrey, editor of *The Edinburgh Review*, he begins by describing the "diminutive figure" of the Scotsman. We then learn of the "brisk movements" that bespeak arrogance and "clever argumentative ability." This bantam of body and mind had become "the Napoleon of the world of letters" by trampling the charms of poetry and scanning lines with "the bold curiosity of a successful attorney." Jeffrey's superior stature, then, appeared only in comparison with the tribe of pygmy scribblers whose species of "superficial criticism" he so consummately embodied. "With a practical gauge, regulated by the intellectual tone of an Edinburgh clique, and having for its highest standard only intelligence and the laws of outward morality," Tuckerman continues, "he discusses the lives of such men, without a capacity to enter into their motives, to appreciate the circumstances in which they were placed, or to estimate the trials and triumphs of their natures. He ascribes Franklin's self-education to the antagonism of an unfavorable situation rather than to his own perseverance and love of knowledge."[133]

Jeffrey concedes Benjamin Franklin only the negative virtue that comes from circumventing adversity. The innate qualities that enabled the sage to rise above circumstances were invisible to the critic; these qualities are, by contrast, the goal of Tuckerman's quest. The attentive reader will recognize this effort as a persistent feature of his biographies. At times the allusions are generalized, as we have seen in his reference to the "artistic organization" of William Morris Hunt; elsewhere the particulars of that organization are detailed, prompting him, in the case of Hiram Powers, to delineate the influence of "constructiveness" on his development.[134]

Tuckerman seeks to trace the connections between biographical, one might say biological, data and the singularities of an artist's oeuvre; to ignore this dimension of his analysis is to miss the deeper implications of his criticism. His tales are not mere homilies on the rewards of hard work;[135] success springs from a propitious constitution. In one essay, for example, the hopes of an aspiring writer are quickly dashed during an interview with a seasoned author, who, after the former's departure, informs the reader that the youth's forehead was "compactly rounded." Without some decided protuberance, or at least the angularity of the male brow, the neophyte's prospects were dim indeed, and on the narrator's advice he tills "paternal acres" and courts his muse only on "long winter evenings."[136]

Phrenology assisted Tuckerman in his defense of Clevenger and often served him in like manner. He writes that George Flagg was rescued from the consequences of an overweening "Love of Approbation" by the wise counsel of Washington Allston, while Charles Deas's career benefited from a well-developed "Color."[137] Those figures who had receded somewhat into the past afforded the critic an opportunity to judge their entire career on this basis without the reservations that inevitably arise in the consideration of a contemporary; hence he tends to be more definitive in his remarks about the artists of the preceding two or three generations. Another condition, of course, was the availability of biographical information. Many of the artists of the colonial era left little evidence about their lives and thus escaped this manner of scrutiny, but such was not the case with Benjamin West. Tuckerman commences his examination of West by tracing the painter's lineage back to the stalwart pioneers who settled the wilds of Pennsylvania. The wealth accumulated by their persistent toil was a mixed blessing to a boy with lofty ambitions. Some of the sharpness requisite for genius was blunted by the material comforts that softened his childhood. Tuckerman's reflections on these circumstances reveal the source of his lukewarm response to West's work. Regarding the artist's progress, it is proposed that "*spirituality* is the offspring of deep experience; he suffered no trying ordeal—he was not disciplined and elevated by the battle of life: his success was too easily achieved; order, calmness and regularity marked his experience not less than his character."[138]

Propriety, meticulousness, and decorum govern West's style, but Tuckerman thinks something more compelling is needed. *Spirituality* might have allayed this want were it not dormant. Nowhere is this more apparent than in the famed *Christ Healing the Sick* (1815, Pennsylvania Hospital, Philadelphia). While all the demands of taste have been met and the viewer is impressed by the dexterous depiction of the sufferings of the afflicted, the spectacle nevertheless leaves one unmoved. Beginning with the details, Tuckerman notes a violation of the principle of unity preached by Combe.[139] The hands of Christ do not exhibit the same qualities visible in the chest, and throughout there is lacking that uniformity of expression that is the "soul of art."[140] But beyond these particulars, West's ultimate shortcoming arose from an inability to comprehend himself. His skill in drapery and grouping, for instance, was not accompanied by "any commensurate reach of mind and sympathy of subject." The lesson, Tuckerman adds, is that the "artist's subject should spring from his natural powers and not from external dictation. He certainly cannot deal successfully with expression, unless at home with the idea or feeling to be expressed; and this depends more upon character than imitation."[141] The lacuna in West's mental profile occurred at *Spirituality*. How could he hope to sympathize with the sensations of those who had witnessed Christ's miracles?

If the recalcitrance of a single faculty stunted West's talent, the physical organization of Washington Allston promoted genius. Tuckerman describes the latter as offering an "appearance and manners [that] accorded perfectly with his character. His form was slight, and his movements quietly active. The lines of his countenance, the breadth of the brow, the large and speaking eye, and the long white hair, made him an immediate object of interest."[142] This portrait resembles the Mental or Nervous type drawn by the phrenologists, which also displayed "a high, pale forehead; delicate and finely chiseled features; bright and expressive eyes; slender neck; and only a moderate development of the chest. The whole figure is delicate and graceful, rather than striking or elegant. The hair is soft, fine, and not abundant or very dark; the skin soft and delicate in texture."[143] Allston's "fine fibrous texture" was also noticed by Tuckerman, who took it as an indication of his nervous temperament.[144] Lorenzo Fowler summed up much of this thinking when he wrote of the painter that "few heads and temperaments are more perfectly in harmony with their characters than [his]" and added that a "nervous" temperament inclined him to prefer mental over physical entertainment, making him vulnerable to dissipation by "nervous excitements." The prominence of *Sublimity* and *Ideality* furnished "him with an exquisiteness of emotion, fineness of feeling, scope and exaltedness of thought, beautiful conceptions, and powerful imagery, seldom equaled."[145]

Ideality appears repeatedly in Tuckerman's biography as well, finding its way into his account of the Italian sojourn, which, we learn, stimulated "the education and ideality of Allston."[146] In this context the author again takes the opportunity to express his deep reverence for this faculty. "In the moral economy of life," Tuckerman maintains, "sensibility to the beautiful must have a great purpose. If the Platonic doctrine of pre-existence be true, perhaps ideality is the surviving element of our primal life. Some individuals seem born to minister to this influence, which, under the name of beauty, sentiment, or poetry, is the source of what is most exalting in our inmost experience, and redeeming in our outward life."[147]

Such traits made Allston more receptive than his contemporaries to the influence of beauty. The perceptive abilities of Gilbert Stuart, for all their acuity, could not elevate his style to the level attained by the younger artist. While the latter "was inspired by ideality," the former merely followed the dictates of "sense."[148] Stuart exhibited "the hardihood rather than the susceptibility of genius," a circumstance attributable to the powerful physical organization and practical insight he inherited from his Scotch ancestors. These strengths, then, were unaccompanied by refinement, and in accordance with Tuckerman's convictions regarding the correspondence between physical and mental characteristics, it is asserted that Stuart's aptitude favored those sitters who possessed the same practical bent. He could hardly have done justice "to the ideal contour of Shelly," but was well suited to render "the dormant thunder of Mirabeau's countenance" or "the argumentative abstraction that knit the brows of Samuel Johnson."[149]

The career of John Wesley Jarvis was also hobbled by constitutional deficiencies. He was, according to Tuckerman, "almost destitute of what the phrenologists call the organ of order; social by instinct, convivial by temperament, capable of vigorous artistic effects, yet imprudent and reckless, with hosts of acquaintances." On entering his apartment one saw an array of "palettes in all conditions, decanters, dresses, a cradle, an easel, musical glosses, books, lay-figures," and similar paraphernalia scattered about with careless abandonment. Ruin inevitably awaited one so oriented, for "neglect, excitement, improvidence, never can produce the results of method." The irregularities of Jarvis's career represented for Tuckerman the bohemian excesses of an earlier generation that were gradually disappearing. Despite the appearance of the theories of Gall and Spurzheim during Jarvis's lifetime, "the deeper insight and more generalized experience of a scientific era had not quite dissipated the popular fallacy that genius is inevitably called to recklessness, and, in pursuit of art and literature, a valid excuse for despising the wholesome discipline of social conformity."[150]

A facile technique that eschewed the rigors of the profession prevented Jarvis from doing justice to his talent. The progress of Allston and Edward Malbone, in contrast, was decorous but not unharried by the perils of the calling.[151] An imperious muse often obliged these artists to neglect the organic laws of mind and body,[152] a danger magnified by their slightness of stature and vulnerability of temperament. Thus Tuckerman attributes Malbone's premature demise to a sedentary existence that sapped his "naturally elastic constitution"[153] and sees Allston as narrowly escaping an equally tragic denouement.

Allston's nervous temperament rendered him particularly susceptible to the maladies that attend serious application, but he spared no effort in completing *The Dead Man Restored to Life by Touching the Bones of the Prophet Elisha* (1811–14, Pennsylvania Academy of Fine Arts, Philadelphia). To the usual techniques he added the habit of throwing himself into the attitudes of the figures he was depicting, a practice Tuckerman describes as "a fine illustration of nervous sympathy—the engagement of the whole man, body and soul, in his work."[154] Such intense, unflagging devotion to the task boded ill, but the situation worsened when the artist decided to change his regimen. He adopted the English practice of eating early in the morning and again only when his labors for the day were done. While this permitted uninterrupted effort, it introduced an unaccustomed abstinence, which, combined with long hours of mental excitement, "produced a chronic derangement of the digestive organs" so severe that he was obliged to retire to Cliffton in hope of restoring his depleted resources. His woes were compounded shortly thereafter by the shock of learning of his wife's death, and for some time he could only intermittently summon the resources necessary to take up brush and palette.[155]

The close conformity of brain to body posited by phrenology made the discussion of diet seem perfectly natural to Tuckerman, but more than the hours chosen for dining, Allston's single-mindedness endangered his health. Overtaxing a faculty invited monomania, and George Combe never tired of warning the "ardent student" about the pitfalls of scholarship. Prolonged mental toil could only be sustained by diversity, by turning from drawing to reading at certain intervals, for example, and thus shifting the burden from one faculty to another.[156] In this manner, Tuckerman wrote, John Gadsby Chapman continued "at work, and seemed to overcome fatigue rather by changing his occupation than abstaining from labor."[157]

Allston set a standard by which Tuckerman measured others because he so completely exemplified the notion that an artist's habits, sympathies, and tastes—in short, his natural language—found their way into his work. He personified the virtues of *Ideality*, the faculty that figured so importantly in Tuckerman's calculations, and even his misfortunes were homiletic. The critic's didacticism deserves greater attention than it has hitherto received, for it often gives substance to passages that seem discursive to the modern reader. When Tuckerman writes that Allston's personal appearance coincided with "the testimony of his art,"[158] we need to resist the inclination to dismiss such inferences merely as instances of an inadequately conceived descriptive project; he knew what he was about. Only by following this reasoning do we arrive at the fundamental tenets of his outlook.

Basically he set out to decipher the moral order inscribed in the history of art. Just as his contemporaries in the Hudson River School scrutinized the environment for the evidence of design it might divulge, so Tuckerman surveyed the organic constitution of his subjects for similar testimony. Details were significant—the bosky foreground in the case of the former, the singularities of cranial form and bodily condition with the latter—and each proceeded from this point to a more comprehensive delineation. This sequence, both believed, would promote an agenda compatible with the priorities of physical metaphysics.

Phrenology obliged artists to think anew about several crucial issues. In choosing a model, they were asked to consider a range of criteria that pertained to moral as well as physical condition, and as seen in the statements of Bell, Palmer, and Rimmer, this venture gravitated toward the particularities of the female anatomy. With the writings of Tuckerman the focus shifted to the qualifications requisite for making art, and here again the discourse invoked the discipline of physiology as a means of anchoring the subject in objective standards. These considerations come together in Thomas Crawford's *Raphael* (fig. 3.29), a statue predicated on the principles outlined above.

Just where and when Crawford learned about phrenology is a matter of conjecture, but the course of his career constantly brought him within its sphere of influence. If he was not introduced during his apprenticeship with John Frazee, then associates such as Charles Sumner, himself a student of the doctrine,[159] may have initiated him. One thing is certain: when he married heiress Louisa Ward late in 1844, he married into phrenology. The two met during the winter of 1843–44 in Rome, where Louisa had journeyed to join her elder sister, Julia. The latter had recently married Samuel Gridley Howe, an enthusiast who, in the company of George Combe, was testing the theory against masterpieces from antiquity and the Renaissance.[160] Howe undoubtedly broached the subject when the young sculptor came calling on Louisa, but the most telling evidence appears in a letter sent by Crawford to *The Crayon* in 1855, the year he modeled his *Raphael*.

During a dinner party in Rome a cast of Raphael's skull was passed among the guests for their consideration. "The head is small, delicate, and full," Crawford reports, "and each organ is developed in the most beautiful proportions one to the other. Form, color, ideality, and amativeness, are equally balanced." A number of features are then described admiringly before attention turns to an accompanying cast of the right hand. The latter exhibits the long, tapering bones that made it "so faithful a *hand-maiden* to the fertile brain."[161] A preliminary glance at the statue indicates that these notions found their way into the composition. Although Raphael wears a hat, it sits high on his brow, permitting the viewer to survey, among other faculties, those of *Form* and *Color*. *Ideality*, the key

FIGURE 3.29. Thomas Crawford, *Raphael* (1855, marble, High Museum of Art, Atlanta, Ga., lent by the West Foundation)

to artistic immortality, causes the long hair to trail around its bulge. The right hand is also featured prominently and, according to the law of correspondences, exhibits the requisite delicacy.

Before proceeding further, however, we might ask how a cast of Raphael's skull came into Crawford's hands and why it enjoyed such renown in the early nineteenth century. Phrenology allowed those who grasped a moldering skull to ruminate on more than life's brevity. They now had access to secrets previously held inviolable by the grave. For several centuries a skull thought to be that of Raphael was revered by the members of the Academy of St. Luke in Rome. When a cast of this cranium was handed to Gall by Dr. Scheel, the former exclaimed "he 'had never seen the organ of Constructiveness so largely developed as in the head in question!' Scheel continued his interrogations. Dr. Gall then pointed out also a large development of the organs of Amativeness and Imitation. 'How do you find the organ of Colouring?' 'I had not previously adverted to it' said Gall, 'for it is only moderately developed.' Scheel replied, with much satisfaction, 'that it was a cast of the skull of Raphael.'"[162] This object frequently underwent such scrutiny, and it repeatedly confirmed Gall's findings.[163]

It is not difficult, then, to imagine the consternation that arose when papal authorities opened Raphael's tomb in 1833 and found a complete skeleton.[164] To those who would cite these circumstances as evidence of the latitude for subjective analysis permitted by the science, phrenologists replied that the academy skull, now proven false, belonged to the celebrated amateur Adintorlo, whose tastes and developments were likely to have paralleled those of the Renaissance master. Hardly losing stride, they now claimed that the whole incident actually reaffirmed their beliefs, for the head retrieved from the pantheon more closely embodied the talents of the great painter than had the pretender.[165]

Both answered expectations regarding *Ideality* and *Form*, but the large *Amativeness* raised questions about the contribution of this faculty to the fine arts. Some held the organ responsible for the voluptuousness of Raphael's imagery,[166] while others, including Combe, argued that it merely heightened the artist's appreciation of feminine beauty, which, judging from the Madonnas, was unsullied by animal passion. Speculation on the subject inevitably came around to the question of Raphael's mistress, a woman whose sobriquet, the Fornarina, identified her as the daughter of a baker. Combe surmised that the two were likely to have been united by a lively attachment; but their relationship never made the artist a slave of sexual passion, and the phrenologist could find no evidence that this admittedly "earthly woman" was ever employed as a model for the religious images.[167] In advancing this claim, Combe defied received opinion and the testimony of the paintings themselves, for the similarities between portraits of the Fornarina and such renowned works as *The Sistine Madonna* and *The Madonna della Sedia* are undeniable.

The interpretation given these circumstances by Tuckerman brings us closer to Crawford's imagery, and although these notions appeared in marble before they did in print, the currents of thought that ran through both men certainly suggest a common source. Tuckerman champions the Fornarina by informing those who think her "robust" charms antithetical to the refined taste of Raphael that their theories of love were founded on "imaginative" rather than "philosophic" principles. As children of "Nature," artists recognize intuitively those whose qualities complemented their own. Raphael was no exception in this respect, for the repose, latent emotion, impassioned eye, and "broad symmetrical bosom" possessed by the Fornarina indicate that she was "precisely the woman to harmonize by her simple presence, and to soothe or exalt by her spontaneous love, the mood of a man of nervous organization and ardent temper." She exhibits the "majestic simplicity, peculiar to the best type of Roman woman," and those of "over-tasked brain" were bound to find comfort in her company. A perfect match was this union of sensitive genius and tranquil baker's daughter, a pairing that merged "the irritable seeker in the serene and satisfied woman, the delicate in the strong, the gentle in the hearty, the ideal in the real, the poetic in the practical, [and] the spiritual in the human."[168]

The virtues listed here would seem to reverse contemporary sexual standards, but they are consistent with gender theories promulgated by phrenology. Refinement should seek out hardihood, and Raphael's skull and hand were judged feminine in their delicacy.[169] If consistently applied, the principle of opposites would do much to improve the institution of marriage, and phrenologists regularly touted its potential. Crawford's adoption of this philosophy made the statue something more than a journey into the past; it had a message for moderns, which if heeded could prove highly salutary. Women in particular could gaze at the *Raphael* as if they were his model, for the sketches on the scroll beside him tell us that he is about to commence the *Madonna della Sedia*.[170] In this manner they might measure themselves against the master's ideals as Harriet Beecher Stowe had hoped they would. Gussied up in finery that made them angular and ill tempered, one might search in vain among them for the Fornarina's equanimity and roundness of form. But how could great art be created without the latter? The symmetrical bosom so lauded by critics provided the apotropaic pendants needed to ward off the mono-mania that might otherwise have overtaken her lover; indeed, there but for the grace of a baker's daughter goes Washington Allston.

In examining Raphael's skull, Crawford had been struck by the size of *Amativeness*, but acknowledging the contribution of this organ was impeded by Renaissance conventions that favored shoulder-length hair. The resolution to this quandary comes in the choice of pose. We have seen that *Amativeness* guided Raphael to the beauties selected for his Madonnas, and that is the process taking place before our eyes. When William Rimmer wished to illustrate an individual under the sway of *Amativeness*, he did so by making the body rough and angular, but the sort of brutality characteristic of one for whom life was an unending struggle is not apparent in Crawford's work. Although Raphael seems to be in his adolescence, this is actually the mature artist, a man of thirty at work on one of his most celebrated masterpieces. Unlike Rimmer's types, he is healthy, but hardly Herculean. His gracile form is readily apparent beneath the close-fitting garb, an outfit that complies with the recommendations for male clothing published in *The Crayon*. The essay that advances this proposal mentions English and German fashions of the fifteenth century, but much that is claimed for these traditions also applies to the Italian. Comfort is the author's primary concern, and this is best served by clothing that fits "snugly enough to follow the shape of the limbs throughout." Artists, he adds, will declare that "there is no other so picturesque," and taste is most fully gratified "when the appareling of the outer being is in most complete harmony with the mental constitution." Then, in a passage that sounds like John Bell, he praises the curves indicative of grace and the straight lines and angles that denote strength.[171] All these conditions are met by the togs donned by the Italian artist. A combination of roundness and angularity suggests an organic constitution that is quite extraordinary, for it is able to subordinate the demands made by a powerful *Amativeness* to the inclinations arising from *Ideality*.

The ideas reviewed in this chapter constituted part of the matrix of theory and criticism from which American art of the nineteenth century emerged. Among the attractions of physical metaphysics was its effort to make art responsive to the needs of the people by shifting its justification from the aristocratic and elitist notions held by Europeans to ones that were decidedly more utilitarian. I suggested earlier that this philosophy brought William Rimmer into the orbit of Walt Whitman. Much the same might be said of the others reviewed in these pages. When, for example, the poet asks, "How dare a sick man, or an obedient man, write poems?" he offers a rather succinct synopsis of much that appears in the writings of

Henry Tuckerman. And before Crawford's statue, Whitman might have invoked the following sentiments copied from the writings of Orson Fowler: "Morality and talent are affected more by food, drink, physical habits, cheerfulness, exercise, regulated or irregulated amativeness than is supposed." Of Keats's poetry, he wrote it did not meet the "wants of the bodies and souls of this century," but he would hardly have lodged a similar complaint against John Bell's theory or Erastus Dow Palmer's figures.[172] Yet the latter's nudes continue to draw comparisons with the words of Emerson in modern criticism.[173] By looking to Whitman and the phrenology that stood behind his enterprise, we arrive at a more comprehensive understanding of the decisions that unified form and content in antebellum art.

4

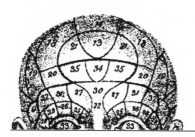

The Acorn and the Oak

The theoretical considerations set out in the previous chapter make it clear that phrenologists regarded human anatomy as the most sensitive gauge of the meaning present in mortal affairs. It was, however, not the only one. The body had to operate within an environment, and this relationship affected not only the soundness of the individual but also his or her ability to venerate the being who lent coherence to the vast diversity of creation. This chapter asks if the system of physiology outlined by phrenology and related reforms had an impact on the emergence of the Hudson River School. Was there an alternative to the Transcendentalist agenda so frequently advanced by modern historians? By concentrating on Asher Durand, the artist who did most to inaugurate the movement, and by reading what he read, we find that physical metaphysics stands as a seminal force behind the American school of landscape painting.

Of course a strong case can be made for awarding Thomas

Cole the title just given Durand, and there is no need to quibble about the matter; but I favor the latter because he was less committed than his colleague to the associationist aesthetic popularized by Archibald Alison.[1] As a consequence, the ruined monasteries and battlement-capped towers that call up Europe's fabled past in Cole's paintings appear far less frequently in Durand's, and in this respect he was more consistent in pioneering the American landscape. The whole subject was problematic for Cole, an emigrant from England whose praise for his adopted homeland could be ambivalent, and while this adds another dimension to his oeuvre, it set him apart from the other members of the Hudson River School. One reason for this divergence can be intimated from Tuckerman's remark that "veneration and ideality" were equally enthralled by the creations of genius and the marvels of nature.[2] Sentiments engendered by *Veneration* and *Ideality* were bound to undermine an aesthetic dependent on rumination, since the former occurred spontaneously while association involved the integration of memory with perception.

Phrenology can be said to have installed the landscape in the mind; hence when *Sublimity* was touched during a phreno-mesmeric session, the entranced subject exclaimed, "See there! see that rugged mountain; see the overarching cliffs, see the crags. Let us go on the mountain. Come, I see a good place to get up. There; that is a splendid view." And when *Ideality* was activated, the sitter envisioned "a verdant meadow, with a beautiful stream running through it."[3] The innate resources postulated by faculty psychology undermined the premises of Alison's doctrine. "Pleasure," Spurzheim declared, "does not derive from association only. Every faculty is in relation to certain impressions; these, being either in harmony with it, or the reverse, produce pleasure or pain. The power of configuration is pleased with certain forms and displeased with others. The faculty of coloring likes certain colors, and dislikes others."[4] Were we to press the phrenologist further on this point, asking him to identify the source of this pleasure or pain, he would revert to the precepts of physiology; when an individual resonated harmoniously with nature, he or she experienced positive stimulation. The superiority of this theory over traditional systems of aesthetics, he would continue, derived from its ability to trace sensations back to their corporeal source, a process that dispelled the connoisseur's murky *je ne sais quoi* with the clear light of science.

Durand's example permits us to specify these principles, for he often heeded the admonitions of transcendental medicine. One tenet in particular, the benefits of cultivating a beard, will receive extended treatment here. The advantage of this approach resides in its simplicity. By concentrating on a single precept, the outline of an entire philosophy can be more readily traced. Habits of hygiene and grooming have long served to signal loyalties or aversions to societal norms. A conspicuous example of this tendency is offered by the students of Jacques-Louis David who agreed to forsake the razor as a means of expressing their dissatisfaction with their mentor. By adopting the practices of the ancient Greeks, they sought to surpass David's own efforts to restore the spirit of antiquity, and the custom was revived in the 1830s under the aegis of Romanticism.[5]

Americans soon followed, but without the physical remnants of antiquity or the Middle Ages to capture the imagination, they sought inspiration elsewhere. Citizens of Jacksonian society in search of release from the dislocations brought on by rapid urbanization cast a longing gaze toward the wilderness that still covered large portions of the continent. A glance at Durand's chin likewise reveals untrammeled growth (fig. 4.1). The similarity was more than coincidental, and in accounting for the phenomenon, one critic explained that those who disliked the beard were expressing "their preference for the artificial, which shaving strongly gratifies. It was not by any means accidental that the beard movement should have originated with artists, who, however artificial their pursuit may be in itself, are brought more into contact with real nature, and are more observant of its beauties, than any other class of persons."[6]

More about this development can be learned by reviewing Durand's relationship with Sylvester Graham. Although the two were acquainted as early as 1821, their friendship has attracted scant attention despite the assurances of the artist's son, John, that his father profited considerably from his association with this famed advocate of dietary reform.[7] Graham's views resembled those fostered by transcendental medicine in that both endeavored to compose a program for health by reading the prescriptions of nature. His philosophy, then, tells us a great deal about Durand's beliefs concerning humanity, nature, and God before the advent of Transcendentalism or the arrival of John Ruskin's theories.

Graham concocted his own system during a stay of more than a year in Philadelphia that ended in 1831. There he studied with John Bell, who introduced him to the vitalistic doctrines of Xavier Bichat (1771–1802) and Francois Broussais (1772–1838).[8] These Frenchmen viewed existence as an unending struggle waged by organic life to sustain itself against the onslaughts of inorganic matter. Graham borrowed from the latter the notion that living tissue was characterized by contractility. Contact with

(Opposite)

FIGURE 4.1. Charles Loring Elliott, *Asher Brown Durand* (1864, oil painting, in the collection of the Corcoran Gallery of Art, museum purchase, Gallery Fund)

foreign substances caused the membranes to form "vital erections" that in turn induced an inflow of blood and other bodily fluids to mitigate the irritation. Ingestion of alcohol, coffee, tea, meats, and spices caused the stomach's lining to become highly excited without supplying nutritional benefit equal to the draw on the vital resources. The gradual dissipation that followed rendered the body susceptible to disease. Vegetable matter, by contrast, strengthened the system by providing it with a healthy stimulation. Graham's advocacy of vegetarianism was premised on the belief that a bland diet and moderate exercise expanded the reservoir of vital fluids and thus promoted resistance to the hostile forces present in the environment. Those who failed in this venture and went to a premature grave had, either willfully or inadvertently, disobeyed the laws written in the book of nature.[9]

Soon after Graham's return from Philadelphia, events of catastrophic proportions contrived to furnish a national audience for his ideas. During the summer of 1832 a strain of cholera hitherto unknown on these shores appeared in Canada and proceeded south to New York City, where its ravages inspired a dread that can be imagined from the following report:

> Our other plagues were home-bred, and part of ourselves, as it were; we had a habit of looking on them with a fatal indifference, indeed, inasmuch as it led us to believe that they could be effectually subdued. But the cholera was something outlandish, unknown, monstruous [sic]; its tremendous ravages, so long foreseen and feared, so little to be explained, its insidious march over whole continents its apparent defiance of all the known and conventional precautions against the spread of epidemic disease, invested it with a mystery and a terror which thoroughly took hold of the public mind, and seemed to recall the memory of the great epidemics of the middle ages.[10]

The impact this calamity had on Durand's generation can hardly be underestimated; like the plagues of old, it obliged survivors to examine anew their assumptions about the place of the Almighty in the affairs of men. Why had such sufferings been visited on the people of the New World? Had the burgeoning prosperity of recent decades blinded them to the corrosive effects of affluence on morality? Many thought so, and their numbers heeded the calls for fasting and prayer. Others were less inclined to attribute human misery to divine retribution, and while such individuals had the option of visiting the allopath, the ministrations offered by the latter were, as suggested by the above confession, of scant comfort given the unprecedented turn of events.[11]

But these alternatives did not exhaust the choices then available; much of Graham's popularity derived from his integration of the epidemic into a system of metaphysics dictated by a benevolent, if impersonal, divinity. It was man's ignorance, not God's wrath, that precipitated the events be- deviling society. Strict observance of the laws of nature fortified the body and enabled it to cast out afflictions, including cholera.[12] Some years later William Sidney Mount summarized this outlook when he claimed that a regulated diet would remove "all danger of cholera and contagious and epidemic diseases."[13]

The fact that urban dwellers proved most susceptible to the epidemic's lethal onslaught was not lost on Graham's followers, for they located the source of disease precisely in those enervating habits that lured the weak of will to the city. Where tables groaned under the weight of suc- culent viands, where the whims of fashion went unquestioned, and where the first rays of dawn espied revelers tottering down the avenues, there grim-visaged cholera lurked in the shadows. His knock, however, rarely sounded at the humble cottager's door, and many deduced that the towns were sapping the nation's constitutional fiber. Long-standing antipathies between urban and rural values evolved into a debate about physiology, and Graham's modern biographer contends that the epidemic was viewed as "the manifest expression of all those forces that had transformed the world and the people who inhabited it, from a source of vibrant resilience and inner serenity into an arena of irritation, disorder, and fevered, de- structive energy."[14]

According to John Durand, his father's consultations with Graham ex- tended from "intellectual" topics to regimen, and even his turn to gym- nastics as an atonement for the idleness enforced by his occupation was suggested by his friend.[15] The same idea stands behind Henry Tuckerman's report that the artist abandoned his lucrative career as an engraver be- cause it obliged him to labor in a "confined position," while as a painter he could enjoy "the free air which he breathed while exploring scenery, [and which] had become as requisite for health as a wider range for his mental development."[16] For like reasons Graham's followers decried the "noxious effects of impure air, sedentary habits, and unwholesome employments."[17]

By adhering to Graham's philosophy during the epidemic, Durand wagered his life, quite literally, on its efficacy, and a letter from John Casilear assuring him that no fatalities had been reported among the Grahamites must have bolstered his convictions. The same letter charac- terizes Durand as "a pretty good Grahamite,"[18] a conclusion the artist himself confirmed when he added his name to a list of endorsers included in a pamphlet published by Graham.[19] This gesture and the steps leading to it must be regarded as tantamount to a profession of faith on Durand's part. Gratitude for not having contracted cholera no doubt contributed to his decision to execute a print of Graham,[20] and the reformer wrote Durand about the "great system of truth established by creative Omnipotence in the nature and constitution of things, which I have been and am still endeavoring to bring to the knowledge of mankind."[21]

In explaining that "the nature and constitution of things" embodied in their form and functioning the intentions of "creative Omnipotence," Graham was arguing along lines adopted by many plausible rascalities of his time, but not by Emerson. Before "a rich landscape," the latter contended, "the problems to be solved are precisely those which the physiologist and the naturalist omit to state."[22] The tendency to associate the Hudson River School with the Transcendentalism of Emerson ignores the alternatives that enjoyed wide popularity. I will return to this theme shortly, but here it should be mentioned that there was already in place at the outset of Durand's career a doctrine that detailed the scientific and theological implications of nature. Indeed, the missives relating to his trip to Boston in 1832 make no mention of the brouhaha Emerson was then raising, but Spurzheim and the terminology peculiar to his science do find their way into the exchanges.[23] The topic was in the air, and Durand was anything but a disinterested party.

These circumstances form the background for what, judging by the frequency of its citation by modern scholars, is the most definitive evidence regarding Durand's religious orientation. During his voyage to Europe in 1840, the artist confided to his diary, "Today is Sunday. I have declined attendance in Church service the better to indulge reflection under the high canopy of heaven—amidst the expanse of waters—fit place to worship God and contemplate the wonders of his power."[24] Efforts to place this statement in context have prompted historians to peruse the liberal theologies of the day, causing some to conclude that it represents "a mild nature pantheism," while others discern the influence of Channing's Unitarianism.[25] Close attention to other events that occurred on board, however, yields different results.

It turns out that Durand and George Combe booked the same ship for the transatlantic journey. The phrenologist had just completed his triumphant American tour, and the artist's thoughts about this distinguished fellow traveler appear in a description of the informal gatherings of the passengers.

For instance, on the promenade deck one day my attention was directed to the various groups assembled around me, (and more or less of similar composition present themselves every fair day)—Immediately in front, flat on the deck on a small coiled-up rope squatted like a sailor sat Combe the Phrenologist Philosopher—near him, without even a coiled rope or any other seat than the bare deck floor were two or three fashionable ladies and, near them on a wooden bench sat an Italian Catholic Bishop surrounded by several of his confreres consisting of Priests and Laymen mostly with segars [*sic*] in the mouth (puffing forth more harmless fire & smoke than at some other times proceeded from the mouth of that description of personage).[26]

Durand's vignette evokes representations of Hercules at the crossroads, with a number of "fashionable ladies" now taking the part of the legendary hero. Will they be led down the primrose path of popery? The anti-Catholicism here is expressed in terms of physical metaphysics. What wisdom can possibly proceed from mouths that have been desecrated by tobacco? Those who partake of the indulgence pay for the initial stimulation with a subsequent exhaustion, and Graham anathematized the plant, calling it "one of the most loathsome poisons in the vegetable kingdom."[27] Its perniciousness, in Durand's eyes, was surpassed only by the dogma espoused by the Roman church, while the path of virtue was guarded by Combe, an unassuming figure whose sagacity earns him the appellation of Phrenologist Philosopher. With the artist in attendance, Combe discoursed about the prospects of democracy, noting that its ultimate success depended on the expansion of "Conscientiousness" made possible by "the gradual extension of our enlightened system of Education."[28] The same message had been delivered by the phrenologist to American audiences, and there he explained that without the cultivation of *Conscientiousness*, liberty might degenerate into anarchy. But, he concluded, "the process of improvement appears to me to be evidently begun," and the United States was leading the way.[29]

When the English coast finally loomed over the horizon, Durand was moved by the sight to extol the beauties of the world to Combe, who replied that he only regretted "man is not in harmony with it [that is, the world]." This response was not intended to cast a pall over his companion's enjoyment as has been suggested; rather, it encapsulates the message of *The Constitution of Man*.[30] We have seen that this text delineated the principles of hygiene most amenable to a rational system of metaphysics, and its full title, which promises to examine that constitution "in relation to external objects," recalls Graham's announcement to Durand that he was endeavoring to make known "the truth established by creative Omnipotence in the nature and constitution of things." Both men believed that the environmental factors that contributed to health, and not meditation abstracted from worldly concerns, held the key to spiritual progress.[31] If man were in greater harmony with the world, to reiterate Combe's shipboard musings, he would respond even more deeply to the beauties of nature, a thought that was not lost on his listener.

Durand's reasons for not attending church services are best understood in light of the insistent link between physiology and religion made by Graham and Combe. The artist prefers to remain on deck where he can observe the heavens, while the others, presumably, gather below. Shortly before, a similar sequence of events befell Combe during his travels in the United States. Again, the setting was aboard a ship, and again the passengers were invited to assemble in an unventilated cabin to offer prayers for their health. Realizing that lungs so employed would soon fill with devitalized air, Combe opted for the same alternative later taken by Durand, asking "whether rational beings should expect that God should work miracles in order to save them from the consequences of their own ignorance and neglect of his laws."[32]

Just when these ideas began to influence Durand's work is open to speculation. It seems reasonable, for example, to inquire if they had any impact on his engraving of John Vanderlyn's *Ariadne* (fig. 4.2). The project was undertaken in the early 1830s, when he was most pervasively under Graham's influence,[33] and this suggests that he may also have justified his essay in the nude for reasons similar to those encountered earlier. The reformer, who shared the antipathy of the phrenologists for the corset and like devices,[34] had recruited Durand to illustrate a poem titled "The Bustle." This piece was written "to satirize a form, which belied so villainously the chaste contour of a Venus or Diana,"[35] and while the effort was likely to have been slight, it does serve to indicate Durand's orientation toward the female anatomy at the time.

It was reported that Durand commenced the print without regard to remuneration, that it was entirely a "labor of love,"[36] but this statement only postpones a determination of his intent, for it does not tell us what he loved. Beyond the demonstration of technical mastery, what benefit did he hope his patrons might derive? The association with reformers certainly influenced his thinking about the implications of the human form at this time, and the accuracy of Vanderlyn's anatomical rendering, which lent itself admirably to their purposes, surpassed his own abilities. If nothing else, these notions would have helped him answer the charges of impropriety that originally had been leveled at the painting, for they warranted the enterprise as a didactic undertaking that was inspired by the love of humanity and not the baser instincts.[37]

The completion of the print coincided with Durand's decision to aban-

FIGURE 4.2. Asher B. Durand, *Ariadne* (1835, engraving, Metropolitan Museum of Art, Harris Brisbane Dick Fund, 1927)

don engraving in favor of painting, and perhaps the hours of confined labor over this image of supine salubrity contributed to his resolve. In any case he was heard to utter, "I leave the human trunk and take to the trunks of trees."[38] While no doubt spoken in jest, the remark provides another glimpse into Durand's habits of thought at this crucial moment in his career. These reflect the theory of correspondences as disseminated by physical metaphysics, and the analogy brings to mind John Bell's comparison of the detrimental consequences of the corset to those inflicted on a tree girdled with an iron band.[39] The habit of discerning qualities suggestive of the human form in the landscape was common at the time;[40] one contemporary, for instance, wrote of Mount Katahdin that the "grey of his scalp [was] undistinguishable from the green of his beard of forest."[41] But the processes that validated the doctrine of correspondences operated at a deeper level than the mere similarity of appearances. True affinity arose from influx or the imponderable fluids that united two entities.

The functions engendered by these vital forces could be seriously compromised by an unthinking submission to convention, and while fashion threatened the organic integrity of womankind, shaving was perilous to the male of the species. It diminished one's reservoirs of energy, according to Graham, who warned, "No physiologist can doubt that the habitual shaving of the beard serves in some measure to diminish the physiological powers of man and to abbreviate the period of his existence."[42] An explanation of this tenet was offered by Samuel Wells, who as Graham's assistant in the founding of his vegetarian society, may well have discussed the matter with him.[43] "Of the beard," Wells writes, "twenty-five years' shaving takes off *eight feet*. This cutting and shaving is attended with a great increase of the secretion of juices which nourish the hair, a part of which is lost by evaporation from the stumps of the hairs. Bichat, the celebrated French physiologist, attributes the superior strength of the ancients to the custom of wearing the beard."[44] Bichat was also a source of Graham's thinking, and mention of the irritation attendant upon use of the razor and the consequent loss of vital fluids recalls Broussais's vital erection. On this basis Wells claims that the beard "is believed to be also in some way conducive to health in other respects. We can not doubt but that this is so, because it is simply allowing Nature to have her own way, which is always the best way."[45] Where Nature has her way, man fulfills his destiny, and beards figure prominently in this formula.

Durand never set down his reasons for growing a beard,[46] but the decision should be seen as consistent with his vegetarianism, gymnastics, support for dress reform, and escape from the confinement imposed by the engraver's profession.[47] The resolve to let his chin revert to nature corresponded with the determination to rove the wilds in search of compositions; both aligned him with the influx of Nature. Of course Graham need not have been his sole informant on these matters. The reflections of Henry T. Tuckerman (fig. 4.3) after leaving Durand's studio alert us to the sort of conversation that transpired within.

Those fine old Roman heads!—who can forget them? For years have their possessors lived as models, drawing a more certain subsistence from the outside of their craniums than most authors do from their brains. The thick locks of "sable silver," the white flowing beards, the strongly marked sun-burnt faces and keen eyes—how venerable and

(Opposite)
FIGURE 4.3. Daniel Huntington, *Henry Theodore Tuckerman* (1866, oil painting, National Gallery of Art)

prophet-like! What an absurd profession is that of a barber? The man who first proposed clipping and shaving had no sense of the beautiful. Look at that handsome brigand—how his embrowned visage is set off by the full curving mustache! Razors are a vile invention. Not satisfied with arranging man in a way the best calculated to make him appear ridiculous, deprived of every thing like a becoming costume, to the deformities of a tail-coat and round hat, there must needs be added a gratuitous curtailment of "nature's fair proportions." We are infinitely obliged to artists for preserving such semblances of primitive, or, if you please, uncivilized humanity.[48]

The particular affinity with nature enjoyed by artists encouraged one contributor to *The Crayon* to remind its readers of the obligations of their calling. Writing under the nom de plume "Bumble-Bee," he explains that his compound eyes are indicative of "the huge power of language p[h]renologically referable to the size of those organs." Since *Language*, by virtue of its location, caused the eyes to swell, Bumble-Bee takes advantage of his obvious endowment to wax eloquent about those who would fly in the face of nature's dictates, and though his words may sound light-hearted, their underlying message is anything but frivolous.

I have heard men of thought and genius say, that they would instantly discard cravat, modish hat, razor, all complications of gear, and wear flowing beard and a more flowing dress, were it not that they would be accused of literary vanity, or a love of eccentricity. I have even heard grave clergymen assert that they would do the same, following the reasonable exterior of apostles, prophets, and the old reformers, were it not that they would be proscribed as dandyfied and heretical. I have heard noble women declare that they would apparel themselves according to beauty and comfort, were it not that they would be the laughing-stock of "society." A thousand similar things have I heard.

Now my suggestion—my conclusion of the whole matter—is this: men and women of mature years, of established position and character, of "high respectability," if not "fashion," of unassailable standing in general society, must take the initiative—must lead in all reforms of dress and fashion. There are enough of them who can see things in the light of reason, and can combine together on the side of reason. With them is the responsibility. On their heads will be all the blood of lacerated chins, choked arteries, deformed humanity, and disgraced nature. If any such persons will not use their impregnable position to promote the reform, they ought to be doomed to shave, to button, to lace, and to be squeezed up for ever, in a world of edges, angles, and stiffness, where nothing is soft, elastic, curved or flowing! They deserve to be boxed up and packed off to a square planet, where every leaf is a razor, every flower a button, every ocean starch, every cloud buckram, and where it rains pins, and snows hooks-and-eyes.[49]

The comprehensiveness of these lines lends them their particular relevance in this context. Many of the foibles that torment deformed humanity are listed here, and since Durand himself was a contributor to *The Crayon*, a publication coedited by his son, he likely read this essay. Judging from the portrait by Charles Loring Elliott, Durand need not have feared banishment to that square planet where lovers of disgraced nature sought the umbrageous cover of razors. His colleagues in the Hudson River School shared a predilection for beards that is in marked contrast to the generation of Washington Allston,[50] and perhaps they gazed on the stubbled chins of their elders with emotions akin to those engendered by the sight of a felled forest bristling with stumps.[51]

The pervasiveness of these ideas is suggested by the fact that even if Graham, Combe, Tuckerman, or *The Crayon* failed to inform Durand, he must have learned of them from Charles Loring Elliott.[52] So firm were his convictions that he agreed to do a portrait of William Sidney Mount only on the condition that the latter grew a beard (fig. 4.4). Our informant is Mount himself, who after obliging Elliott, wrote that "a man with a beard is nature in her glory."[53] We learn more about the implications of taking this step from the following:

I believe that if Sir Joshua Reynolds is permitted to know what is going on in this world, he quite regrets not having supported a flowing beard while President of the Royal Academy, knowing as he did that the early painters and sculptors wore beards—but the fashion of his time cheated him of that luxury. Place two portraits of two different Gentlemen side by side, one bare faced and the other with a full beard, and nature speaks with a trumpet tongue in favor of the latter as being the most natural. A man with a beard no matter what color is nature in her glory.[54]

The seemingly incongruous reference to Joshua Reynolds in the present tense is explained by Mount's spiritualism, a belief he integrated with transcendental medicine. Thus he committed to his notes the notion that the "desire causing principle is the electro-nervous flued [*sic*]. When equalized through the system, it is cause of health."[55] He added, "The Infinite Mind, or spirit, is above all, and absolutely disposes of and controls all. Hence mind and its agent electricity, are both imponderable, are both invisible, and coeternal."[56] Graham or some like reformer stands behind the artist's resolve to "abstain from greasy living and use more dry food [so] our health would be better and our [intellect] brighter: cause of my getting sick, painted too closely thru Nov and part Dec not enough exercise and too much greasy living—which brings on dyspepsia and colds."[57]

Further insight into Mount's decision to cultivate a beard comes from the writings of spiritualists. One contended that the "electro-physiological vital power" stored in the brain was also absorbed by the hair; shaving weakened the former by depleting its resources. If strong brains and smooth faces went together, the author reasoned in what he apparently considered irrefutable logic, women would enjoy a superiority over men.[58] Hence the whiskers that adorn Zeus Franklin's chart permit the faculties located above to attain their full potential. Mount's speculations about the former president of the Royal Academy, then, stem from the latter's likely regrets about the loss of his precious "electro-nervous flued." His disembodied identity was now sustained by the same essence, and when augmented in mortals, it enabled them to overcome the inertia induced by convention.

The social and aesthetic consequences of these beliefs are best studied by returning to Durand. I have proposed that his decision to take up landscape painting was in some measure a response to the perceived mental and physical deterioration caused by rapid urbanization in Jacksonian America.[59] The inroads made by cholera into the cities brought this message home, and Harriet Beecher Stowe spoke for many when she asserted that "one of Heaven's great hygienic teachers is now abroad in the world, giving lessons on health to the children of men." "What else," she continued, "would have purified the dark places of New York? What a wiping-up and reforming and cleansing is going before him through the country!"[60] As Durand peered into these same dark places, he also hearkened to the hygienic teacher lingering there. The lessons on health so inculcated weighed equally, if not preponderately, with other interests, including geology, botany, and meteorology, in the thoughts of members of the Hudson River School. Indeed, their priorities were likely to reflect Bruce Haley's claim that "no topic more occupied the Victorian mind than Health—Not religion, or politics, or Improvement, or Darwinism."[61]

Durand's famed "Letters on Landscape Painting" suggests that his discipleship with Graham remained an integral part of his outlook. Both

(Opposite)
FIGURE 4.4. Charles Loring Elliott, *William Sidney Mount* (1848, oil painting, courtesy of Museums at Stony Brook)

identify the weary businessman as the primary benefactor of their efforts. The artist proposes that, after a long day's drudgery, such individuals retire to their armchairs and gaze at a landscape. There the viewer encounters "no unhealthy excitement," that feature of urban life disparaged by Graham for depleting the vital reservoirs, because a painting is "soothing and strengthening to his best [phrenological] faculties," just as vegetarianism slows the metabolism and promotes longevity.[62] In like manner Durand declares that art must be spared from being "adulterated by the poisons of conventionalism." His wording here, with its reliance on a metaphor of ingestion, recalls Graham's campaign to prevent commercial bakers from adulterating their bread with poisonous additives intended to increase weight and price.[63] The most poisonous artistic habit is the muddying of summer's green with brown. Green is the first witness of organic life; it is the universal sign of unimpeded, healthy growth and, above all, is "the chosen color of creative Love for the earth's chief decoration." As such it is "grateful to the sight, and soothing to the mind"; it delights not only the poet but also "the dusty eyes of the tired citizen."[64]

Many artists, Durand continues, exhibit a fondness for warm colors, which they indulge "to a morbid degree," even though the prevailing hue of summer is cool. Again the sequence of ideas ascends from an experiential base to a metaphysical superstructure, for "there is wisdom in the provision—the sensation of coolness conveyed through the eye seems to allay the fervor of the feeling, and render the heat more endurable, so that it would appear a sacrilege to pollute its freshness by an undue proportion of warm color."[65] By proposing that a departure from actual appearances excites the emotions unduly, and thus disavows the healthful provisions of creative (divine) "wisdom," Durand parallels the theories of Graham and Combe. The latter contends,

> some philosophers and divines having failed to discover a consistent order or plan in the moral world, have rashly concluded that none such exists, or that it is inscrutable. It appears never to have occurred to them that it is impossible to comprehend a whole system without becoming acquainted with its parts; these persons have been ignorant of the physiology of man, of the philosophy of man, of the philosophy of external nature, and their relations, and nevertheless have not perceived that this extensive ignorance of details, rendered it impossible for them to comprehend the plan of the whole.[66]

Durand's insistence on detail as the starting point of composition finds its basis in doctrines that predate those of Ruskin. Like Combe, the artist brooks "no dissent from the maxim, that a knowledge of integral

FIGURE 4.5. Asher B. Durand, *Study of a Wood Interior* (ca. 1850, oil painting, Addison Gallery of American Art, Phillips Academy, gift of Mrs. Frederic F. Durand)

parts is essential for the construction of a whole—that the alphabet must be understood before learning to spell, and the meaning of words before being able to read." Time wasted in broad sketches, he continues, is better spent in close study of the rocks and tree trunks in the immediate vicinity.[67] These words trace the flow of Durand's own inspiration, for he advises the beginner to attain proficiency in such matters before turning to the more encompassing effects created by "the influence of atmosphere."[68] The echo of Combe's admonishments, perhaps reverberating through Graham, can be heard here. In life as in art the whole can be comprehended only after painstaking examination of the particulars. The premature conclusion, not the myriad of details themselves, ultimately promotes despondency before the vastitude of nature.

Durand's reliance on transcendental medicine accounts for much of the conviction that informs his plein-air studies (fig. 4.5). To appreciate their impact fully, we must see them not merely as preparation for more elaborate compositions but also as testimony of the painter's release from the city. They exhibit none of the facile execution common to sketches but are composed with a conscientiousness that derives from sincere devotion to duty. If the viewer can put in the back of his or her mind some sense of the perils of urban life in the early nineteenth century, then even such unassuming scenes begin to resonate with implications that might otherwise escape notice. The tonic benefits of nature and of representations of nature meant that talk about excessive fidelity to the motif was nonsensical, and Durand contended that "where the [phrenological] faculties exist to make a right use of all study of Nature, there can be no possible danger, no restriction to the freest exercise; on the other hand, where they do not exist, the fetter, if any be found, will be well applied, and fortunate for Art, if applied to arrest the multiplication of inane compositions and unmeaning details."[69] The details in Durand's own work are insistent but hardly devoid of meaning; they oblige us to contemplate the shrubs and sundry boulders located in the foreground so we may exercise our mental faculties just as profitably as did the artist when he initially drew them.

Of course, much the same can be said for Durand's composed settings. The emerald grass and foliage that invite us into *Early Morning at Cold Spring* (fig. 4.6), for example, contribute as much to the painting's content as the village whence rises the steeple. A lone figure stands amidst the towering birches and beeches while a procession wends its way toward the distant church. This contrast serves to emphasize the virtues associated with the avoidance of organized religion, an implication not lost on historians who have discussed the image in light of the artist's shipboard decision to remain on deck when Sunday services were announced.[70] More can be inferred by recalling that George Combe had acted similarly for specific reasons. A poorly ventilated church thwarted spiritual inspiration by inhibiting respiration. Harriet Beecher Stowe and her sister, Catherine, were equally adamant on this point, telling readers that

> no other gift of God, so precious, so inspiring, is treated with such utter irreverence and contempt in the calculations of us mortals as this same air of heaven. A sermon on oxygen, if we had a preacher who understood the subject, might do more to repress sin than the most orthodox discourse to show when and how and why sin came. A minister gets up in a crowded lecture-room, where the mephitic air almost makes the candles burn blue, and bewails the deadness of the church — the church the while, drugged by the poisoned air, growing sleepier and sleepier, though they feel dreadfully wicked for being so.[71]

Horace Mann attended a sermon "all based on phrenology and full of the most delightful religious spirit" given by a preacher who was "sensible enough to have but one service a day."[72] The point was to get outdoors as often as possible, and the further reflections of the Beecher sisters on

FIGURE 4.6. Asher B. Durand, *Early Morning at Cold Spring* (1850, oil painting, Montclair Art Museum, museum purchase, Florence O. R. Lang acquisition)

the subject are instructive: "While the bodies of men and animals are filling the air with the poisonous carbonic acid, and using up the life-giving oxygen, the trees and plants are performing an exactly contrary process; for they are absorbing carbonic acid and giving out oxygen. Thus, by a wonderful arrangement of the beneficent Creator, a constant equilibrium is preserved."[73] The symbiosis between man and the vegetable kingdom meant that the fresh air necessary for spiritual inspiration could never be exhausted.[74] Graham urged his followers to "exhilarate" themselves with "copious draughts of the pure air of heaven,"[75] while reminding them that "true religion consists then, in perfectly obeying all the constitutional laws of human nature."[76]

This message was especially pertinent to those professionals whose duties precluded exercise in the open air on all days but the Sabbath. Under such constraints, the Grahamites believed, the individual was well advised to roam outdoors.[77] The contemplative figure in *Early Morning at Cold Spring* is no rustic swain; the cut of his clothes suggests a prosperity acquired at the cost of long hours in the office or countinghouse. He has been given this day to forgive the trespasses against his constitution committed during the past week. We may suppose that his meditations are of the sort that occupied William Cullen Bryant when he rambled through the woods, for the parallels between the poet's imagery and Durand's idyllic bent have long drawn attention.[78] When the former sought to delineate the benefits derived from prolonged familiarity with nature, he wrote that it was bound "to exercise and strengthen the faculties of the mind, and to fill it with reverence and gratitude to the great First Cause of all things."[79] No doubt similar ideas engage Durand's figure as he strengthens his mental faculties and physical stamina in the nurturing countryside.

The science of Gall and Spurzheim contributed significantly to Bryant's evaluation of the virtues peculiar to the American landscape, and before the assembled membership of the National Academy of Design, he explained why their country surpassed Europe in its conduciveness to genius. It could hardly be doubted, he observed, "that, in the temperament formed by our diversified climate, the perceptive faculties are peculiarly awake and active, drinking in the sights and sounds of Nature, with a deeper delight than in climates of a more uniform character, and that the power of invention is quickened by the same causes to the same activity and energy." He goes on to enumerate the factors that energize the perceptive faculties, emphasizing the vicissitudes of a climate that passes from "polar cold to tropical heat." As a consequence, "the temperament of our people and the influence of our climate are, I think, highly favorable to the cultivation of the fine arts. Some quality in the air of our part of the world, which I do not pretend otherwise to define, promotes, unless I am greatly mistaken, the activity of those faculties which conspire to make the great painter and sculptor. The phrenological philosopher Combe used to call ours a stimulating climate, and he was right in so far as it tends to generate that poetic exhilaration to which the creations owe their birth."[80] The correlation drawn here between an invigorating climate and creative vigor was certainly encouraged by Bryant's devotion to the theory of correspondences,[81] but it should again be noted that his interpretation of the doctrine diverged considerably from Emerson's idealism. The former, like Durand, calls Combe the "phrenological philosopher," a designation meant to infer that the Scotsman would have approved of a theory of culture that commenced with the physical sensations instigated by atmospheric conditions and continued from these to the mental faculties so inspired.

In paintings such as *Landscape with Birches* (fig. 4.7), we encounter far less ostensible content than in *Early Morning at Cold Spring*. The first contains no narrative, no iconographic clues, and no emblematic devices to assist the viewer's search for meaning. The observer must instead cultivate a willingness to empathize with the artist's own comprehension of nature.[82] This response can be enriched by inquiring into the reasons why Combe's lament about man's being out of harmony with nature sounded so oracular to Durand. The answer lies in *The Constitution of Man*, a volume devoted to the philosophical ramifications of phrenology. It proposes that death be regarded as an institution devised for man's benefit, not only with reference to the afterlife but also in terms of terrestrial existence. Evidence supporting this conclusion came from coprolites. The presence of fish bones and similar remains in these petrified droppings of extinct reptiles testified to their predatory instincts before the appearance of humanity on the face of the planet. Further, since the faculties that constituted the brain remained constant, *Destructiveness* and *Combativeness* could not have been introduced subsequent to the transgressions of Adam and Eve but were, rather, installed at the beginning to adapt all living creation, including man, to an environment where strife and death were integral parts of the natural order.[83]

What made this natural order benign, what took the sting out of death, was progress. It constituted, according to Combe, the underlying condition of existence. Initially the physical mass of the globe cooled in order to make possible plant life, which as it accumulated and enriched the soil, gave rise to animals and the eventual arrival of humanity. The physical and moral advancement of mankind depended on a propitious alignment of the human constitution with the forces operative in the environment. Inhibiting this process were the theologians who claimed that Adam's fall had condemned humanity to perpetual turpitude, when, in truth, the blemishes of moral life were the consequence of disobedience to the dictates inscribed in nature. Combe was voicing this fundamental tenet of his philosophy when he expressed his regrets to Durand about the disharmony between mankind and the world. Pain and an untimely death were the wages of this sin, but they were not the ineradicable realities of the metaphysicians. They could inculcate lessons of great consequence

FIGURE 4.7. Asher B. Durand, *Landscape with Birches* (ca. 1855, oil painting, courtesy of Museum of Fine Arts, Boston, bequest of Mary Fuller Wilson)

to those prepared to learn from such misfortunes. The harmonious relationship with the environment that arose from this knowledge could add years of tranquil happiness, unmarred by bodily distress, to one's worldly sojourn, and this was testimony enough, in Combe's opinion, to the benevolent designs of the deity. "Like the acorn in reference to the oak," he wrote, this program of universal improvement was quietly exercising its influence on all creation.[84]

Looking again at the cycle of organic life that unfolds in *Landscape with Birches*, we are reminded by Combe's words that the organic dissolution in the foreground need not promote melancholy. Like the recumbent Ariadne, an aged tree stretches out in the foreground, assuming for itself the considerations of health and longevity that had previously resided in the figure. It has attained its destined span of years and now returns to the earth to enrich the soil. A similar idea underlies Bryant's "A Forest Hymn," where the cycle of woodland life provides evidence of divine presence,[85] but Combe delineates the implications of this process with a specificity not amenable to poetic diction. Nevertheless, the more evocative passages of the phrenologist's text bear reading before Durand's landscape.

> Now in the vegetable world, the effect of this law [of successive generations] is to surround us with young in place of everlasting stately full grown trees, standing forth in awful majesty, without variation in leaf or bough:—with the vernal bloom spring, changing gracefully into the vigor of summer, and the maturity of autumn;—with the rose, first simply delicately budding, then luxuriant and lovely in its perfect evolution. In short, when we advert to the law of death, as instituted in the vegetable kingdom, and as related to our faculties of Ideality and Wonder, which desire and delight in the very changes which death introduces, we, without hesitation, exclaim that all is wisely and wonderfully made. Turning, again to the animal kingdom, the same fundamental principle prevails. Death removes the old and decayed, and the organic law introduces in their place the young, the gay, and the vigorous, to tread the stage with renewed agility and delight.[86]

The laws of death and hereditary descent, as they extended from the vegetable and animal kingdoms to man, often moved Combe to such eloquence. It seemed that the mysteries of life were finally yielding before the advance of science as physiology engaged in amicable discourse with theology. The manner of adducing evidence to support this contention was especially consequential for the subsequent emergence of the Hudson River School; close observation of the minutiae of nature led to revelations about human fate. This process is most strikingly embodied in Combe's recognition that scatology recapitulates eschatology, that the destiny of mankind could be read in the particles embedded in fossilized feces. Death had been part of the divine plan from the beginning; its purpose was to make progress possible. Had but one generation of trees or persons prevailed throughout time, all would be mired in its short-comings. The present arrangement permits offspring to inherit the best traits of their parents and, if obedient to the laws of organic growth, to advance beyond them.[87]

The impact of these ideas on an intelligent reader can be gauged from a letter sent by Horace Mann to Combe. Significantly, the writer seeks to account for the present condition of the United States in terms of the Scots-man's theories. Just as the early geologic ages were a time when the earth's surface was formed by the eruption of magma, so the formative stages of society were characterized by a "wild commotion of all human propensities," each in conflict with the other. Mann believed that the republic would become less volcanic when its granite substratum was covered with the alluvial deposits of reform necessary for cultivating human welfare. He concludes with the hope that his life "may be as a single leaf cast off from this deciduous generation, whose decomposition may add a single particle to the mass of deep and rich marl on which the growth of some future age shall luxuriate, and gather nutriment for a glorious moral harvest."[88]

Many have remarked on the individuality and anthropomorphic qualities of Durand's trees,[89] an affinity likely to enhance the observer's identification with nature,[90] but the degree to which this recognition was premised on ideas about physiology has been largely ignored.[91] The cycle of organic life reminded viewers that each was called to fulfill a duty that, incidentally, was not inconsistent with goals of Manifest Destiny. By obeying the dictates of physiology, one could improve the race, a lesson Durand did not abandon with *Ariadne*, for the trunks of trees might teach it as well.

I have singled out the beard as a means of encapsulating these beliefs, but this custom should not be divorced from others, such as dress reform, vegetarianism, and efforts to procure good ventilation. The beard is a convenient symbol in this respect because it declared one's allegiance to all and hence provoked controversy. Emerson entered the fray with the alacrity of one who remained clean shaven all his life.

> Temperament puts all divinity to rout. I know the mental proclivity of physicians. I hear the chuckle of the phrenologists. Theoretic kidnappers and slave-drivers, they esteem each man the victim of another, who winds him round his finger by knowing the law of his being; and,

by such cheap signboards as the color of his beard or the slope of his occiput, reads the inventory of his fortunes and character. The grossest ignorance does not disgust like this impudent knowingness. The physicians say they are not materialists; but they are:—Spirit is matter reduced to an extreme thinness: O so thin!—But the definition of spiritual should be, that which is its own evidence. What notions do they attach to love! what to religion! One would not willingly pronounce these words in their hearing, and give them the occasion to profane them. I saw a gracious gentleman who adapts his conversation to the form of the head of the man he talks with! I had fancied that the value of life lay in its inscrutable possibilities; in the fact that I never know, in addressing myself to a new individual, what may befall me.[92]

A division of society into camps based on one's disposition toward the beard would have found Durand and Emerson glaring at each other across the breach. The larger implications of this disagreement extended to assumptions about the psychological mechanisms that attended spiritual enlightenment. Followers of transcendental medicine were wary of sudden outbursts of religiosity because they tended to unbalance the faculties. Insight into life's ultimate mysteries came through a slow, incremental expansion of consciousness. Momentary excesses could only compromise physical and mental health while true contentment was "made up of multitudes of successive enjoyments, no one of which is very exciting or ecstatic, but the united sum producing a calm, steady, satisfying happiness."[93]

Emerson, by contrast, could be made "glad to the brink of fear" by reflections in snow puddles at twilight. The free reign given the nervous sensibility in this response was antithetical to the model of mental health advocated by transcendental medicine; likewise, his elevation as a "transparent eyeball," made ecstatic by the currents of Universal Being,[94] suggests a disembodiment of mind incompatible with the physiological creed that promoted beards. The former is an image of vulnerability and emotional indulgence contrary to the latter's efforts to fortify the constitution and restrain temperamental excess.[95]

By granting this division its due, scholars would be relieved of the obligation they apparently feel to connect Emerson with the origins of the Hudson River School. While one, for example, admits that "it is doubtful how much direct effect Emerson's writing had on landscape painters outside of his Concord-Boston circle," he goes on, nevertheless, to discuss Durand's work in terms of the transparent eyeball.[96] The tenor of Durand's landscapes complies with the eschewal of Transcendental egoism advocated by phrenologists and, incidentally, by the editors of *The*

Crayon as well.[97] His prospects rarely display the spectacular effects associated with the sublime; rather, they invite us to savor some wooded or meadowy setting. When figures appear, they have about them an air of quiet contemplation, and one contemporary aptly characterized Durand's endeavors in the following manner:

> His position is assured. A quiet pastoral poet—a Thompson on canvas—always soothing—never inspiring—sure to please, equally sure not to surprise—a careful and loving student and imitator of the placid aspect of nature, and a genius that breathes pastoral peace over all his works—such was, in general, our feeling of Mr. Durand as an artist. It has been confirmed from year to year. There has been little marked advance, within our recollection, although certainly no retrogression. As with Bryant in poetry, it does not seem that the artist's experience deepens and widens with time. What they paint or sing today, they might have painted or sung twenty years ago.[98]

Much of this praise, with its commendation of the uninspiring, may strike the modern reader as left-handed, but it coincides precisely with Durand's theoretical program. Ensconced in an easy chair after a long day at the office, the harried urbanite could gaze on an inviting landscape to assuage the day's wear and tear. Such images soothed "the dusty eyes of the tired citizen" much as Graham's diet calmed the digestive tract and temperament.

Emerson's impatience with the phrenologists for their indifference to the "inscrutable possibilities" of experience extended to the Swedenborgians, who, he claimed, were equally rigid in their application of the doctrine of correspondences. He, no doubt, would have found the following lines wanting in the nuanced synthesis that imagination alone can bestow on metaphor. "Gall (the father of phrenology) came out of the cerebral well," writes one Swedenborgian minister, "and looking upon the surface found that it was a landscape, inhabited by human natures in a thousand tents, all dwelling according to passions, faculties and powers."[99] The gist of this statement rests on the resemblance between phrenological protuberances and tents pitched by diverse tribes; in each resides a different facet of human nature. Just as the surface of the skull corresponds to the personality within, so it corresponds to the world around man. The physical basis of this comparison (the phrenological bump) ignored, according to Emerson's outlook, the fact that in nature "each individual symbol plays innumerable parts, as each particle of matter circulates in turn through every system."[100] From the standpoint of his criticism, an image should not be equated with a fixed sign, for that failing belongs to traditional "mysticism," accounting for its tendency to petrify metaphysics into a set of unchanging and ultimately meaningless rituals. The obligation put on both poet and reader by the sage of Concord is that they remain open to multivalent symbolism and savor its protean nature.[101]

The viability of this stance derives considerably from the medium favored by the Transcendentalists. Their preference for the written word facilitated the expression of personal sentiments and correspondences that would resist articulation in other media. Henry Thoreau, whose faith in the superiority of the word rarely wavered,[102] could, for example, write that "a single gentle rain makes the grass many shades greener. So our prospects brighten on the influx of better thoughts."[103] There was no way, however, to evoke a similar response when composing a painting. The author could trace a sequence running from experience to the ruminations engendered by it; the possibilities available to Durand were not entirely analogous. In rendering grass or a tree, he had to depend on the observer's shared understanding of the implications of such details, and here resided the particular virtue of transcendental medicine and Swedenborgianism. By designating a specific response to nature, one that was based on verifiable data and not subjective musings, they allowed the landscape artist to address his audience in terms of mutual expectation. Returning again to grass, it serves a different end from that described by Thoreau. The purification of the noxious chemicals exhaled by animal species was accomplished by vegetation, and only air so vitalized and electrified could, when inhaled, energize the nervous system and so induce elevated thought. This was science, not the vagaries of poetry.

As such, it would readily appeal to the businessmen whom Durand identified as the persons most likely to benefit from his efforts. Such individuals were unlikely candidates for apotheosis as a transparent eyeball but were open to the sort of moderation advocated by Graham and Combe.[104] And while the tranquility that reigns in much of Durand's art would have answered their needs, it is obvious that this mode of expression was not universal among members of the Hudson River School. The volcanic scenes of Frederic Church constitute one alternative, and perhaps there is a chain that connects the tenor of this scenery with his more orthodox religiosity and beardless chin.

The precepts of transcendental medicine would seem to be most completely embodied in the forest interiors so frequently rendered by Durand and such bewhiskered colleagues as John Kensett.[105] To my mind, at least, the heavily wooded scene with its decomposing vegetation in the foreground represents the most original innovation of the Hudson River School prior to the advent of luminism. Abandoning the conventionalities of the sublime, these compositions capture nature with a directness that anticipates the intimacy later achieved by artists under the sway of Barbizon. Surely the sentiments that drove them in this direction were not merely aesthetic; rather, they arose from a visceral identification with the environment and from a recognition that the affinities shared by all organic life were destined to promote unending progress in this world as well as the next.

5

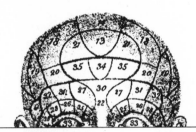

Faces

Sauntering the pavement or riding the country by-road,
  lo, such faces!
Faces of friendship, precision, caution, suavity, ideality,
The spiritual-prescient face, the always welcome common
  benevolent face,
The face of the singing of music, the grand faces of natural
  lawyers and judges broad at the back-top,
The faces of hunters and fishers bulged at the brows,
  the shaved blanch'd faces of orthodox citizens.

In these lines and throughout "Faces," the poem from which
they were excerpted, Whitman manages to capture the sense
of the anticipation felt by the urbanite as he ventured into
the street. We also discern in them the importance of phrenology to those who sought coherence beneath the diversity
offered by this kaleidoscopic environment. "Friendship," "cau-

tion," and "ideality" are all included regularly in the Fowler charts, while "suavity" appears intermittently. Similar translations can be made for the other faces; had Asher Durand entered Whitman's view, for instance, he would not have registered among "the shaved blanch'd faces of orthodox citizens." Those trained in the science of Gall and Spurzheim could banish the anonymity that was increasingly a part of city life in the nineteenth century and rekindle the older sense of community, even though familiarity was based on the most fleeting impressions. If such perceptions were a regular part of the daily routine,[1] their place in the analysis of portraiture was equally pervasive. No other genre was more susceptible to the probing of phrenologists, and their pronouncements were especially welcome in an age when the egalitarian impulse divested sitters of the aristocratic trappings that had previously proclaimed worth.

What *did* viewers presume to find in those plain paintings where no emblems or attributes bedecked the head and shoulders? The musings of the protagonist in a story by William Cullen Bryant conjure up a whole realm of discourse that must have taken place frequently in Victorian parlors. While regarding a likeness of Gil Polo, a much-venerated curate, doctor, and schoolmaster, the narrator opines, " 'It is a round, honest, jolly face,' said I, 'and not devoid of expression. There is a becoming clerical stoop in the shoulders, and his eyes are so prominent that my friend Spurzheim would set him down for a great proficient in the languages.' "[2] The posture (natural language) and cranial formation (*Language*) of the sitter testify to his abilities as a scholar; such qualities, deriving as they do from innate character, evoke his talents more convincingly than could an attribute such as a book.

Flattery, long the prerogative of princely patrons, acquired new implications with the discovery of phrenology. One had only to make minor adjustments in the brow or occiput to transform the dullest addlepate into a paragon of wit and wisdom. Hiram Powers received a letter urging adoption of this measure,[3] but his devotion to calipers precluded the possibility. Not all sculptors, however, were as unwavering in their search for the truth as he. Young Augustus Saint-Gaudens succumbed to the repeated demands of Edward S. Pierrepont that his portrait be improved (fig. 5.1). Pierrepont, a prominent lawyer and jurist, would admit no dissent to the opinion he reached after studying busts of Socrates, Seneca, Marcus Au-

(Opposite)
FIGURE 5.1. Augustus Saint-Gaudens, *Judge Edward S. Pierrepont* (1872–74, marble, National Museum of American Art, Smithsonian Institution, gift of Mary Pierrepont Beckwith)

FIGURE 5.2. Chester Harding, *Rev. Charles Lowell* (1833, oil painting, Massachusetts Historical Society, Boston)

relius, and Plato. All, he surmised, exhibited "very broad foreheads," and his entry into their distinguished company could be effected simply by enhancing his brow to like proportions. The artist complied, but with such want of enthusiasm that the patron demanded further additions until the head, in the sculptor's words, "seemed to be affected with some dreadful swelling disease." Nor did the importuning cease there; in a move that makes one wonder about his evidentiary standards, Pierrepont sought to give undue prominence to the perceptive faculties by having the artist excavate around the eyes. Again, Saint-Gaudens toiled until he "almost pierced through the back," achieving results that amply justified his wish "to get hold of that bust and smash it to atoms."[4]

At times the influence of phrenology seems to have operated almost subliminally. Chester Harding's avowal of the science in 1831 coincides with a marked departure from the normative proportions that previously governed his work. The head of the Reverend Charles Lowell (fig. 5.2), for example, is so large as to make the figure seem doll-like. Despite the declarations of phrenologists that size was no absolute guarantor of quality, Harding latched onto the second half of this tenet, which maintained that mental prowess might be gauged by cranial capacity if all other factors were judged equal. He employed it, as we have seen, to reject the entreaties of prospective students, and the general enthusiasm for phrenology in the early 1830s must have induced him to adopt a mannerism that subsided in subsequent years as familiarity with the doctrine encouraged a more measured approach.

On occasion, critics were willing to condone enlargement for the sake of improved moral stature. An article in *The Crayon* praises Richard Greenough's statue of Benjamin Franklin for Boston as "a true and earnest piece of idealism." Contributing to this conclusion was the perception that, compared with Houdon's bust, Greenough "had widened his [Franklin's] head, giving it a more comprehensive character—a broader tone of thought." The viability of providing "the mental being an idealized form" is then justified on the grounds that Franklin was "greater now than when he lived, because he is the guardian of a nation seven times as large as that he saw, and his fame and importance grow with its growth."[5] Well, maybe, but Hiram Powers spoke for the majority of those who were phrenologically inclined when he wrote of Horatio Greenough's *Washington* that it failed to satisfy anyone because "people want likenesses and not ideals of our great men."[6]

PORTRAITURE AND HISTORY

The philosophical underpinnings of this declaration were set down by Benjamin Paul Akers, a sculptor whose apprenticeship with Powers in 1853 must have been made especially congenial by the harmony of their beliefs. Like the latter, Akers read Swedenborg avidly,[7] and when evaluating an antique bust, he could discern in it "large benevolence and reverence, large perceptive faculties, and very large destructiveness."[8] From his devotion to phrenology grew the conviction that fidelity to "physical facts" would secure "definite ideas of human character." We have already touched on Spurzheim's thoughts about portraiture as history, and Akers was prepared to extend this aesthetic from the life masks of the phrenologist to the more enduring effigies of his own profession. Portraiture, by this accounting, need not be regarded inferior in dignity or importance to any other genre.[9] This theme will reappear frequently in the pages that follow, for one consequence of phrenology's influence on the arts was a relaxation of the barriers that separated one category of subject from another. The particular virtue of portraiture was that it testified to its own veracity; any divergence from the unique combination of lines, curves, and planes of an individual's face was bound to reveal inconsistencies. Every form was meaningful, Akers asserted; every feature declared life's triumphs and reversals.[10] Whitman's poetic license granted him the freedom to express the idea succinctly: "Writing and talk do not prove me, I carry the plenum of proof and every thing else in my face."[11]

This plenum of proof often insinuates itself into Victorian portraiture, shoring up fragile surface proprieties with something more substantial. The seated figure of Supreme Court Justice Joseph Story (fig. 5.3), for example, gestures with a decorum appropriate to his station, but deeper implications emerge only after consulting the views of the sculptor, William Story. He writes that his father was unlike most distinguished men, who conceal persistent vices "beneath their towering faculties." The male head, as noted earlier, was usually rendered irregular by the continuous exercise of a few faculties, but in exceptional cases all the mental organs might be fully developed. A life of many triumphs and few reversals had earned Joseph a place among this select company, and the image his son created with chisel and pen reflects this fact. In writing his father's biography, he endowed virtue with a tangibility that readily lent itself to sculptural expression:

> His was not an irregular and precipitous genius, where great defects yawned beside lofty powers, only to lend them greater effect, but a uniform and regular nature, all parts of which were in harmony. It was like some gently sloping mountain, which swells by slow gradations into the upper air;—not like a sheer cliff which startles the imagination to exaggerate its height. His goodness was quite equal to his greatness. He had few defects for friendship to conceal. He was not perfect, for perfection is not allowed to mortal man, but in none did the alloy of humanity ever bear a smaller proportion to the true ore. There was the same harmony of proportion in his mental structure as in his character. His genius was not the result of an exaggeration, or over-development of any par-

FIGURE 5.3. William W. Story, *Joseph Story* (1846, marble, Harvard University, made by order of the corporation)

ticular faculty, or of a preponderance towards one direction, but of completeness of organization and balance of powers. This was in him a singularly exact adjustment of passions and faculties, the motive power of the one being just equal to the distributive power of the other.[12]

This image of the father found its counterpart in the son. Accomplished in poetry, literature, and law, William never feared that diversity would dilute his talent as a sculptor. From phrenology came his lifelong conviction that mental health depended on alternating the exercise of the faculties; excessive reliance on one ultimately undermined the stability of all. The ills afflicting modern society, Story thought, arose from the demands made by specialization. Most of the professional's waking hours were devoted to a single, seemingly meaningless task, so that "a special faculty is trained to the utmost." The man of general culture, the person on whom the continuity and progress of civilization depends, passed unnoticed among the dollar-godded utilitarians. Couching this argument in terms that reflect the anatomical training of a sculptor, Story remarks that the fully developed man, one who has worked every part of his body, will strike a harder blow than the person who has exercised only his arms, and this thought prompts him to "suppose it is the same with the mind as with the body. The fully developed mind will strike the hardest blows."[13] Story's critique of capitalism, then, relies ultimately on phrenology. How like Orson Fowler he sounds in the following: "Drinking runs into mania at last, and money-making is nearly as bad; it becomes a greed that vitiates all one's better tastes, absorbs one's faculties, irritates, excites, and ruins the nerves and becomes a necessity like dram-drinking."[14]

The varied talents of the Renaissance man made him a physiological paradigm that stood in stark contrast to modern degeneracy, and for this reason Raphael figures prominently in Story's poems. In one, a conversation between the young genius and his patron, the Duke of Urbino, enumerates the merits of a life devoted to diverse forms of creativity. The author surely speaks through Raphael in the following lines:

> Life is too short perfection to attain,
> We all are maimed; and do the best we can,
> Each trade deforms us with the overstrain
> Of some too favored faculty or sense,
> O'er-fostered at the others' vast expense.
> Yet why should one Art be the others' bane?
> The perfect artist should be the perfect man.

Further along, the point is emphasized by means of an analogy that was obviously dear to Story:

If I the model of a man should seek,
Where should I find him? Though the blacksmith's arm
Is muscled well, his lower limbs are weak,
His shoulders curved. The student shall I take?
No; he alone will serve who equal strain
Has given each, the body and the brain.

As might be anticipated, the names of Giotto, Da Vinci, Orcagna, and "Angelo" are all invoked as testimony to the benefits of equal strain.[15] These ideas appear not only in Story's poetry; they also inspired much of his sculpture. If *Joseph Story* is a paragon of the virtue of universality, other figures, including *King Saul When the Evil Spirit Was upon Him* (1863, remodeled 1882, Fine Arts Museum of San Francisco) and *Sappho* (1863, Museum of Fine Arts, Boston), are emblematic of the ills that vex modern society. We may judge the faculty responsible for their insanity by adopting a technique employed by phrenologists when circumstances precluded hands-on examination. The behavior or history of an individual suffering from alienation was often sufficiently revelatory of the dysfunctional organ to permit reliable diagnosis. The melancholia of the Jewish king, perhaps the offspring of an overly active *Self-Esteem*, and the unrequited love that has tormented the *Conjugality* of the Greek poet[16] are particular instances of the condition endemic among Story's contemporaries, monomania. When the mind becomes preoccupied with the repetitive cogitations of a single organ, it can no longer sustain the harmony necessary for mental health, or, as Duke Federigo explains:

Besides, the varied tasking of the mind
Not only makes us sane, but keeps us strong.
The noblest faculty when strained too long
Turns to convention,—wearied, seeks to find
In repetition solace and repose.
Tis only the fresh arm that strikes great blows.
Fallow and Change we need, not constant toil,
Not always the same crop on the same soil.[17]

The noblest faculty of Saul and Sappho has been strained too long; they are deranged by persistent, painful memories.

While Story's protagonists are drawn from mankind's earliest annals, they speak eloquently of the malaise prevalent in the nineteenth century. The material abundance of industrial capitalism had cost the soul dearly. No longer free to roam among the faculties as it did during the halcyon days of the Renaissance, it was now shackled by *Acquisitiveness* and a few like organs to a debilitating routine. Such was the folly of self-incarceration, and its consequences could be as detrimental to moderns as the fate that had overwhelmed Story's historical personages. Paradoxically, Joseph Story is more worthy of emulation, more ideal, than the great figures of the distant past. They had permitted a wronged faculty to dictate thought; he had forestalled any potential usurper by fortifying each chamber. Their poses are introspective and withdrawn; his is open and congenial. They warn against single-mindedness; he offers the alternative.

HENRY INMAN

William Story the writer tells much about the imagery and intentions of William Story the sculptor. Our recognition of his father's favorable phrenological organization makes his portrait central to interpreting the artist's career, for subsequent ideal pieces have to be measured by the criteria established in this initial performance. The key Story furnishes, however, is rarely made available by others. We have, for example, little evidence of the deliberations that transpired between Henry Inman and William Wirt (fig. 5.4), but the latter's efforts as a writer and attorney do furnish some clues. The subject sits behind a desk, a position he must have assumed for long hours each day, and while there is nothing particularly novel in this pose, it is not without a touch of incongruity. Despite the fact that Wirt is engaged in writing about his most sensational case, the prosecution of Aaron Burr for treason in 1807,[18] his expression is hardly consonant with the gravity of events that occupy his thoughts. An air of mild amiability lingers over the features, as if the sitter were unmoved by the perils he enumerates. How might we account for this seeming indifference?

Inman imbibed the principles of phrenology with his earliest initiation into the mysteries of the artist's profession. Hence, if Wirt discussed the peculiarities of his own skull, a likely topic given the task at hand, his words would surely have fallen on receptive ears. Several years earlier Wirt had indeed submitted his head to a craniologist. Measurements were recorded, and a drawing was made for the benefit of posterity. At the conclusion the examiner announced that "the organs in front were well developed,—those in the rear comparatively feebly." Like William Rimmer, Wirt was aware "that the intellectual faculties reside in the front of the head, the passions in the back part, but that a full development of the organs of passion [*Amativeness*] is essential to make a bold, daring, strong,

FIGURE 5.4. Henry Inman, *William Wirt* (1832, oil painting, Boston Athenaeum)

enterprising character." While seeking to separate himself from enthusiasts by issuing the standard disclaimer to the effect that he had "no great faith in the science," Wirt goes on to indicate how closely the analysis answered his particular case. He takes no delight in "political wrangling"; he is a man of "peace" and "prudence," preferring, above all, "to paddle my canoe along the smooth surface of a mill-pond."[19] The individual who gazes out from Inman's painting is not the assertive sort usually associated with success in the partisan world of Washington politics. The artist presents his commanding intellect, as proclaimed by the balding brow, while alluding to his deferential nature by the moderation mirrored on his features; in sum, he paints much the same picture as did the phrenologist.

These circumstances remind us that beyond accuracy, phrenology obliged artists also to exercise their interpretative powers in capturing the natural language of the faculties. Not everyone was equal to the challenge. The wooden busts carved by Asa Ames (fig. 5.5), for example, owe whatever animation they possess to the colors that enliven the surface, but this immediacy does not extend to the psychological life. In contrast, the quiet restraint of Wirt's likeness speaks forcefully. The inarticulateness of the former approaches the want of expression present in the phrenological head cut by Ames (fig. 5.6). This object must reflect the artist's enthusiasm for the theory, and it is fair to conclude that the blandness of his portraits is due to an inability to represent values he knew were desirable.[20]

The greater talent of Inman enabled him to redeem even the most inauspicious of faces. One of these was that of Lord Thomas B. Macaulay (fig. 5.7), who, according to Henry T. Tuckerman, was "not a promising subject. His temperament and tone of complexion would prove very ineffective in the hands of an inferior painter. Inman has given so well the noble outline of the head—the swelling curve where phrenologists locate the perceptive organs—and chosen the position so admirably, the eye slightly lifted, that the heavy features have a quiet eloquence which grows upon the spectator."[21] With its slight inclination, the head does indeed give prominence to the faculties just above the eyes, where the perceptive intellect resided. The pose seems calculated to capture the natural language of these organs, which "when active, throw out the chin and lower portions of the face."[22] Tuckerman applauds Inman's ability "to make outlines and tints convey the very personality of a countenance" as an achievement that set him apart from most contemporaries,[23] and a glance back at Ames's work again serves as a reminder that simple adherence to phrenology did not, in itself, guarantee success in this endeavor.

Where theory ends and direct observation takes over in Inman's portraits is an issue that obliges us to confront our assumptions about the

FIGURE 5.5. Asa Ames, *Head of Boy* (1847, painted wood, New York State Historical Association, Cooperstown)

possible impact of phrenology on its followers. If we presume that the doctrine was absorbed during years of study with Jarvis, an ardent advocate of the science, then Inman's works assume a specificity of meaning they would otherwise lack. The two girls who clasp each other in his *Children of Henry Livingston* (fig. 5.8), for example, resemble illustrations of *Adhesiveness* (fig. 5.9), where "two sisters embracing" illustrate its operation.[24] Women responded to this faculty more than men, and what better way to suggest the unfeigned sensibilities of youth than by having the girls assume

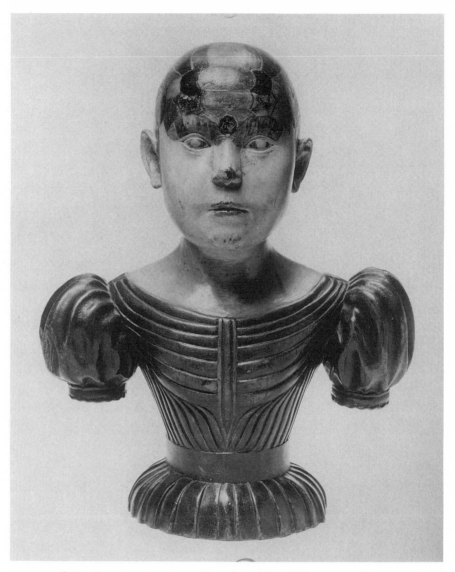

FIGURE 5.6. Attributed to Asa Ames, *Phrenological Head* (1847–50, polychrome pine, collection of the Museum of American Folk Art, New York, N.Y., bequest of Jeanette Virgin)

its natural language? With no documentation to support this proposal, it is made to suggest that a believer in phrenology would regard the range of human emotions as limited to a series of emblematic gestures. Once one begins down this path, however, it is hard to know where to stop. Do the rather nondescript activities of the boys also exemplify the natural language? It may be that Inman, confronted with individuals whose age precluded the sort of exchange he had with Wirt, merely followed his fancy.

FIGURE 5.7. Henry Inman, *Lord Thomas Babington Macaulay* (1844, oil painting, courtesy of the Pennsylvania Academy of the Fine Arts, bequest of Henry C. Carey [Carey Collection])

FIGURE 5.8. Henry Inman, *Children of Henry Livingston* (1827, oil painting, photo courtesy of Richard York Gallery, New York, N.Y.)

FIGURE 5.9.
Adhesiveness, from Mrs. L. N. Fowler,
*Phrenology Designed for the Use of
Schools and Families* (New York:
Fowlers and Wells, 1847), p. 35

REMBRANDT PEALE

We learn more about these considerations from the notes prepared by Rembrandt Peale for a lecture on phrenology delivered at the conclusion of one given by George Combe in 1839. In an account sent years later to *The Crayon*, Peale characterized his own effort as an "ironical lecture against phrenology" but also took the opportunity to reaffirm his belief in the theory, claiming, "Whatever truth there may be in the systems of phrenology, and the minuteness of their claims, it is certain that all artists, especially sculptors, necessarily form conclusions in its favor, without being bound to believe in every tenet. The numerous antique heads of Socrates, himself a sculptor, and those of other great philosophers, are all characterized with craniological accuracy—and nothing is more offensive in the work of a modern tyro in sculpture, than a mal-conformation of skull."[25] In any case the irony mustered on the occasion was mild indeed. It consisted of exhibiting a head copied from Jean Baptiste Greuze (1725–1805) and asking, "What Phrenologist could disturb these luxuriant tresses, to pursue his sober investigations, without being charmed from his purpose by such a soul-beaming countenance! such a holy extacy [*sic*] of expression! the triumph of the Painter's Art."[26] These exclamations would have caused Combe no discomfort, but more to the point are Peale's remarks about his copy of Raphael's *Madonna della Seggiola* (fig. 5.10), a piece he introduced with a dramatic flourish by unveiling it before the audience.

The gesture recalls Charles Willson Peale's famous self-portrait, executed almost two decades earlier, in which he raises a curtain to reveal the natural wonders of his museum. Rembrandt, in contrast, offered a wonder from the hand of man and, unlike the Greuze, now invited scientific appreciation by calling it "a beautiful illustration of Philoprogenitiveness."[27] Since this organ was situated at the back of the brain, where it could not be seen in Raphael's figures, many in the audience may have questioned the basis for this assertion. Peale does not elaborate in his notes, but he was something of an authority on the faculty, having provided Gall with testimony about its development among American Negroes for the latter's examination of his *Love of Offspring*.[28] In the same text Gall praised Raphael for capturing the natural language of the social organs by portraying the Virgin with the posterior region of her head pressed against that of Christ.[29] Returning, then, to Peale's remark on *Philoprogenitiveness*, it may simply refer to the embrace between mother and child frequently found in illustrations of the faculty, or it possibly takes up the more specific evidence supplied by Gall and, by the closeness of the two heads (acknowledging that the point of contact is only approximately that of the faculties concerned), alludes to the magnetism engendered by maternal love. The answer must reside in one of these two alternatives, since it cannot come from scrutinizing the faculty in question.

With these considerations in mind, the viewer of Peale's *Hannah Hansen and daughter, Lydia* (fig. 5.11) gains access to its deeper implications. The image adapts the replica of Raphael, thus evoking "the timeless and sacred quality of the bond between mother and child."[30] From phrenology we learn further that Mary and her modern counterpart Hannah exhibit the natural language of *Philoprogenitiveness*. The artist not only calls attention

FIGURE 5.10. Rembrandt Peale, *Madonna della Seggiola* (after Raphael) (after 1830, oil painting, photo courtesy of Old St. Joseph's National Shrine)

to their mental organization; he also suggests that both are subject to natural laws. Rembrandt's disposition to view even the most sacred subject, the Madonna, in the light of scientific theory was not inconsistent with the Deist predilections of the Peale household. Applied to Hannah and her daughter, this same natural language permitted allusion to faculties that otherwise would not find their way into a painted likeness unless done in profile. The contribution of phrenology ensured that the potential audience for such likenesses extended beyond the immediate circle of

FIGURE 5.11. Rembrandt Peale, *Hannah Hansen and daughter, Lydia* (1831, oil painting, collection of Mr. and Mrs. Nicholas Schaus)

friends and family to engage all who looked to art, even portraiture, for an expression of the universals of human nature.

HIRAM POWERS: THE MALE PORTRAITS

A fortunate circumstance of Hiram Powers's patronage enables us to pursue his devotion to these principles further than with most of his contemporaries. Since his sitters had often returned to the United States to await shipment of their busts or, indeed, never traveled to Italy at all, and consequently sent casts and similar material to the sculptor, both parties were obliged to commit their preferences to writing as part of the process of negotiating a mutually satisfactory outcome. Their letters tell us of directives and decisions that, again, must have been common studio talk but were rarely documented.

The novelty and virtuosity of Powers's busts elevated him to a position of acknowledged preeminence among members of the Florentine artistic community.[31] George Calvert wrote that portraits by other sculptors were "flat and lifeless" by comparison,[32] and Henry Tuckerman thought their unrivaled finish, texture, and "mathematical correctness of detail" filled "the eye and mind with ideas of beauty and meaning."[33] Modern critics have responded with equal fervor but often negatively; one, for example, judges Powers a "banal literalist," an exponent of a "dry naturalism."[34] Whether or not this evaluation is merited, Powers is at least entitled to a fair hearing that takes his own intentions into account.

The rapid material and moral progress of America meant that its citizens more closely approximated the ideal than did those of other nations. During his tour of this country in 1842, Charles Dickens was repeatedly asked whether he "had not been very much impressed by the *heads* of the law-makers at Washington: meaning not their chiefs and leaders, but literally their individual heads, whereon their hair grew, and whereby the phrenological character of each legislator was expressed."[35] It came as no surprise to Powers that the Florentines who gathered around the collection of busts he transported across the Atlantic in 1837 declared that a similar constellation of distinguished heads could not be found in Europe and that Webster's was unequaled in modern times.[36] Part of his success, Powers was forced to admit, stemmed from the fact that he "had such glorious heads to model."[37] The same thought occurred to Henry Tuckerman, who attributed the artist's early prominence to the "rare and emphatic types of American character and physiognomy, such as modern sculptors seldom enjoy."[38]

Recent literature often lists the alterations Powers supposedly imposed on his sitters.[39] Such speculation, however, runs counter to the sculptor's own testimony. Before the bust of Webster (fig. 5.12), an English tourist remarked that "so grand a head had [not] been seen in our day" and asked whether it had been idealized. Powers assured him it had not,[40] and he later explained, in response to criticism of his bronze statue for Boston, that "compasses in a careful hand will not lie, and I measured Mr. Webster's features and thus made myself quite sure of the proportions and they correspond with the general measurements of the cast taken from them after death."[41]

Not content merely with measuring Webster's features, Powers took the

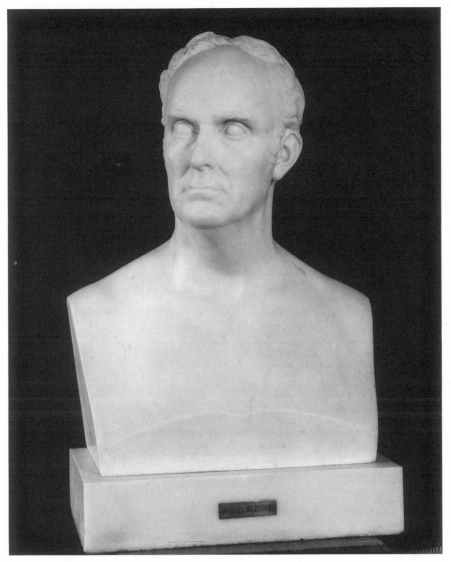

FIGURE 5.12. Hiram Powers, *Daniel Webster* (1836–41, marble, Boston Athenaeum)

same cast to Lorenzo Fowler's London office, where both men marveled at the expansive forehead, a topic we shall return to later, as the phrenologist observed that "language could not be judged very well from the bust[;] still the indications are that the eye must have been prominent and the socket of the eye indicates that the skull was much affected by the brain above in the region of the faculty of language."[42] Obviously the recumbency of the deceased caused the eyes to sink back into their sockets and hence precluded accurate casting, but Fowler was ready to surmise they were of great size. Returning to the marble bust, the alert, large eyes stand out as its most expressive feature, as well they should, for who better embodied the mastery of language than Webster? Hence, claims that Powers deliberately enhanced the undercutting of the eyebrows to enliven the drama of light and shade upon the face should be regarded with caution.[43] To throw the eyes into undue obscurity was to hide the politician's light, his organ of language, under a bushel, and Powers explicitly condemned such modifications in commenting on a bust of Andrew Jackson.[44] From the outset of his career, then, he was committed to accuracy, which, one writer concluded, stemmed from the realization "that the slightest divergence from the particularities of form vitiates the expression."[45] Powers shared with Akers the belief that the portraitist worked for posterity.[46] "Form," he declared, "is the vehicle of spiritual expression. It has meaning" that comes from "all the mental and physical history of the individual."[47]

The merging of formal and spiritual concerns in the above lines raises the issue of Powers's Swedenborgianism. During his Cincinnati years Powers turned to the mystic, and no other feature of his outlook has been so thoroughly examined.[48] One authority contends, "At the same time that Powers's artistic talents developed during the early days of his career, so did his religious awareness unfold. Whenever possible he injected it into his art, and in time of stress and grief, he took refuge in it."[49] Yet no other feature of the artist's philosophy so underscores the need to consider the evolution of Swedenborgian thought in the nineteenth century. Thus the same historian discusses the sculptor's continued allegiance to the mystic "despite occasional flights into the murkier pursuits of phrenology and spiritualism," and while acknowledging that "these deviations were permissible" within the faith, he ignores their implications.[50]

This subject will be considered repeatedly. Initially, Powers's remark about form constituting spiritual expression resembles the integration of phrenology and Swedenborgianism discussed earlier. If his portraits ring true, it is due to the conviction that they reveal more than surface appearances. From this belief arises an intimacy of perception that belies the charges of complacent literalism lodged by modern commentators. The artist shared his ideas with visitors to the studio, discussing the phrenological developments of the busts exhibited there,[51] and one such viewer gives us a striking example of the emotions that the concept of portraiture as history could touch. While gazing at the unprepossessing demeanor of John Slidell (fig. 5.13), diplomat and representative of the Confederacy in France during the Civil War, this observer remarked, "This second, if not first of the exponents of modern ideas of Southernism has a large, square, and originally noble countenance, but it is full of all manner of pride and subtlety. Its wrinkles are spiritual snakes crawling over the whole face from lip to forehead. Its superciliousness is ineffable. The man-stealing, woman-despoiling, child-selling American nobleman appears in every line of his Belial countenance. It is joined to that extreme hauter so characteristic of Southerners of to-day."[52]

The vehemence of this reaction, with its reliance on correspondences to make spiritual snakes of wrinkles, should alert us to the multivalent role of detail in Powers's works. Critics praised his ability to capture "even the most delicate blood-vessels, [and] the finest wrinkles" without sacrificing "the effect of the whole,"[53] and Powers belittled the Italians who emulated his style merely by carving as many wrinkles as possible.[54] By rendering only those details that were consistent with a type, one writer surmised, he achieved a vitality of character that won the approval of the phrenologically inclined.[55]

In carving a bust of Salmon P. Chase, Powers "ventured to subdue the excessive mass of veins on the forehead" not only to comply with the patron's request but also in answer to his own "previous intention."[56] This ability to discriminate between meaningful and extraneous detail confirmed George Calvert's belief that "the faculty for the Ideal is then indispensable to the execution of a good bust."[57] He elaborates elsewhere by asserting that "a man cannot be an artist without imitation; but the faculty of imitation is comparatively superficial, and he who imitates without sympathy learns little, if anything from his model."[58] The gift of sympathy was decisive, for it turned "the other rich faculties into endowments for Art."[59]

Andrew Jackson's wizened visage brought these issues to the fore (fig. 5.14). When Edward Everett suggested that Powers had ignored the example of antique statuary by incising too many lines, Powers retorted that "the wrinkles in Genl. Jackson's face were important to the likeness, I had copied them and should always do so." What if Joseph Nollekens had improved his famous heads of Fox and Pitt? Had straightened a nose or raised a forehead? Would there be any reason for the public to take the trouble to view them? Hardly, and to drive home the point he argued,

The Head of Napoleon by Canova is found to be entirely different from the cast of his real head by Dr. Automarche [*sic*], and but for the latter cast, the Phrenologist would be founding his opinions of Napoleon's character upon false Bumps or premises. What kind of conclusion would the phrenallogist [*sic*] arrive at upon examining the head of Pitt also, had Nollikins [*sic*] been guided by such men as Everett. . . . It is not the artist's opinion of what a great man's face should be that you want. Every man can form that opinion for himself. You wish to see him as he truly is, or was. And I would not walk out of my way to look at a Bust that would please such a man as Mr. Everett.[60]

FIGURE 5.13. Hiram Powers, *John Slidell* (1840, plaster, National Museum of American Art, Smithsonian Institution, museum purchase in memory of Ralph Cross Johnson)

This logic practically eliminates any distinction between aesthetic and phrenological analysis, and years later Powers cited Jackson as confirmation of the coincidence between "crainological signs and the character of those who bear them." His large perceptive organs, indicated by the expanse over the eyebrows, enabled him to sense the public will instinctively. Henry Clay was similarly endowed, but Daniel Webster, who displayed "no marked development of the perceptive faculties," was not. His sympathy

FIGURE 5.14. Hiram Powers, *Andrew Jackson*
(1834, marble, Metropolitan Museum of Art)

for popular sentiment could not counteract the powerful impulse coming from the reasoning faculties located above.[61] Despite a lifelong ambition to occupy the White House, "Black Dan" never realized his goal, while "Old Hickory" served two terms as president. The fate of the nation hung on the brows of its leaders, and these Powers found more intriguing than any fanciful flourishes he might introduce.

The sculptor's treatment of Jackson's mouth particularly disconcerted Everett and a Major Donaldson. Both men thought the abundance of wrinkles, the consequence of dental loss, a feature unworthy of art.[62] Powers disagreed, contending the expression captured the "inflexibility of character," the same "firmness" that had sustained the general through his darkest hours.[63] The Prussian minister Baron Krudener likewise praised the "firmness" that endowed the bust with so much character.[64] This choice of words reflects the infusion of phrenological terminology into everyday vocabulary mentioned in the first chapter. Hence, before a portrait of Jackson one phrenologist exclaimed, "That height above the ear, how unequaled! it is caused by the organ of Firmness."[65] Another, on viewing Powers's bust, noted that the sizable organ of *Firmness* and such companions as *Self-Esteem* had enabled the president to prevail in the rough-and-tumble politics of the day.[66] Here was one of those "grand faces of natural lawyers and judges broad at the back-top" that caught Whitman's eye during his rambles, a face that proved a political asset if we believe Everett's recollection that he was "terrified with the old General's forehead and hair;—not the first man, by the way, who he has frightened."[67]

Powers was likely to respond in a similar fashion. He described an unwelcome customer at the cafe Doney in Florence, for example, as possessing "a strange shaped head—running up high behind and bald[;] he actually harangues the people around him."[68] His own head, he concluded, was "too low for a stump speakers' pedestal."[69] Jackson's prominent *Firmness* would certainly have prompted a search for signs of its influence on the aged hero's features. Illustrations of this faculty in phrenological texts include the same natural language of the mouth, which induced a "perpendicular straightness and stiffness" of the upper lip,[70] and head that ran up high behind, as Powers carved in marble (fig. 5.15). The general's head, then, resolved the doubts many held about democracy, for while large perceptive faculties made him sensitive to the public weal, *Firmness* prevented him from becoming merely an instrument of the mob.

A knowledge of Jackson's character persuaded Powers that it coincided with the visage he beheld, but what was he to do with a stranger? As might be expected, his first priority was accuracy of appearance and proportion. In the case of *Solomon Sturges* (1862, Chicago Historical Society), for example, photographs and measurements were dispatched to Florence. These contradicted Powers's impression, gained during an earlier encounter, that the subject was a tall man with "a large head." He asked that measurements be made again and listed a number of focal points that would ensure precision. These included, among others, the diameter from between the eyebrows to the back of the head, the diameter just above the top of the ears, and the diameter at the orifice of the ears. Much of this was merely intended to attain the desired degree of exactness, but the

FIGURE 5.15.
Firmness, from "Signs of Character,"
*American Phrenological Journal and Life
Illustrated* 42 (1865): 136

repeated reliance on the ear as an anchor recalls the importance of this feature to the phrenologists, while the request that "the convexity of the forehead" be traced on a stiff piece of paper likewise suggests its essential contribution to their analyses.[71]

In preparing to render *Elisha Lichtfield* (1865, Brooklyn Museum), Powers again required measurements and photographs. The latter were to be taken from the front and the sides, but the sculptor was also interested in obtaining a view of the back of the head.[72] Powers complained that Canova's habit of introducing his own features into his portraits had its consequence even for the back of his bust of Napoleon.[73] What is surprising in the case of Lichtfield, however, is that the piece is a relief with the face turned outward, so whatever information Powers acquired from the photograph was never rendered directly. This suggests that the artist was interested in learning about *Amativeness,* that key to male identity. The situation, then, was analogous to Inman's portrait of Wirt; faculties that were not directly visible to the viewer could nevertheless contribute significantly to the natural language.

Other stratagems included requests for measurements taken from the interior rim of a hat and a "paste board trimmed so as to fit the hat."[74] Another correspondent was told that his character had been read from a photograph and handwriting, both being indicative of a bold, straight, "steam engine" type.[75] The hand, like other bodily organs, labored at the behest of the faculties, and their peculiar influence accounted for the singularities of an individual's script.[76] Plaster casts constituted still another important source. Since they had an impersonality akin to photography, one might suppose that their testimony would go unquestioned, but Powers's response to casts taken by Clark Mills indicates that this was not always the case. "You should see his [Mills's] cast from the living face— the upper lids scraped off to open the eyes done apparently with a rusty nail and hastily at that, lumps of dough for the ears—stuck on with the thumb and fingers, so at least they appear and the whole sand papered over! and then the expression! such a stare as they have! They seem petrified in amazement as I really was when I first beheld them—and this is no exaggeration—one of my workmen laughed himself almost into fits at the sight."[77]

The negligence of Mills meant that all hints of the natural language were subsumed in a stupefied expression, while the location of the ear and its orifice would also defy the phrenologist's scrutiny. Such want of precision obviously compromised Powers's ability to characterize his subjects with his customary acumen. Hence the report by Louisa S. McCord that she was dissatisfied with the likeness of her father, Langdon Cheves, as cast by Mills was no doubt read with sympathy. She explained to Powers what he might have anticipated. The image did no credit to her father's "great intellect," his "firmness," and like qualities of mind.[78]

Powers employed the cast in rendering *Langdon Cheves* (1870, Augustine T. Smythe, Charleston, S.C.), but also asked Louisa and her brother to furnish any biographical material they might deem relevant. A verbal account of an individual's moral strengths and weaknesses was often evidence enough for a likeness—so, in any case, claimed the French sculptor and devotee of phrenology, David d'Angers, who stated he could fashion a portrait merely by reading a biography.[79] McCord supplied the sort of information Powers would have thought necessary to rectify Mills's bunglings. We learn that Cheves was "careless in dress, unostentatious in manner, never seeking to be looked at nor even thinking of the effect of his appearances, deficient to a fault in (to speak phrenologically) love of approbation, there was yet about him that calm commanding dignity which the vulgar associate with the idea of royalty, and which the nobler man bows to, even sometimes in spite of himself."[80]

Precisely how these directives found their way into the marble is open to speculation. It is plausible, for example, that Cheves's feeble *Love of Approbation* contributed to the decision to leave the shoulders bare, since this alternative would seem preferable to exhibiting his penchant for being careless in dress. The calm commanding dignity mentioned by Louisa McCord is also there, though few today would likely feel the inclination to bow. The bottom line to this exchange, and the many like it, is that Powers's busts emerged from an accumulation of data that reached the artist in both visual and written form.

Powers, of course, was a man of his age and therefore absorbed its standards governing style and content, but he wished to eschew convention by precipitating the image out of the pool of information he had gathered. Henry Tuckerman praised his busts as "remarkable for their individuality,"[81] and perhaps this insight offers an alternative to the method of analysis usually encountered in modern literature. There we read about the contending influence of classicism and realism, but this discussion generally ignores the artist's stated ambition of making each portrait as singular in form and expression as the prototype.

The dynamic likeness of *Horatio Greenough* (fig. 5.16) has persuaded historians that it inaugurates a "Byronic" phase in Powers's career. From the late 1830s into the 1840s the artist is said to have abandoned the prosaic elements of previous years in favor of a style akin to Romanticism,[82] but one would be hard pressed to discover in this piece a greater quotient of psychological intensity than, for example, the Webster, which was executed in the United States. Nor does the Greenough necessarily stand at the beginning of a series of equally magnetic images that follow.[83] The qualities present in the bust are more convincingly interpreted in light of Powers's perceptions of the peculiarities of Greenough's personality.

Afflicted by insanity throughout his career, Greenough combated its recurrent bouts either by plunging into work or by engaging in his favorite recreation, horseback riding.[84] Both his lucid and benighted selves inhabit the image, although the darker half is rather elusive, appearing in the distant, abstracted gaze and slightly furrowed brow. These features suggest some troubling thought, perhaps a private vision. Powers was present when Greenough succumbed to one such vision. The two men were chatting on the banks of the Arno when Greenough suddenly "started at something apparently before him and exclaimed, 'Did you see that?' 'What?' 'Why that horse.' I saw nothing. 'Is it possible you did not see him?' 'Where?' 'Why just there before us. He rushed across our path and lept into the river!' On this he rubbed his forehead and suddenly became as calm and sensible in his conversation as before."[85] Powers "often heard him [Greenough] make strange remarks," and to ignore such events would betray his belief in portraiture as history. The last part of the incident must have been especially meaningful, for phrenology taught Powers that the hand was often drawn to an agitated faculty. If Greenough rubbed the middle of his brow, he would have massaged *Form*, an organ no doubt overtaxed by his labors as a sculptor and here avenging itself by conjuring up the phantom of his deliverance, horseback riding. This vision, then, derived not from the supernatural world but from the same realm whence came Washington Allston's breakdown and Thomas Cole's dream.

Returning to the bust, the slight furrow between the brows suggests that *Form* is indeed active, while *Ideality* emerges at the angular ridge where the planes of the forehead meet. A love of "intrinsic elegance" rather than mere novelty sprung from this pair;[86] hence Greenough's genius for clas-

sicism. Phrenology did not discourage long-held notions about the precariousness of genius,[87] and behind this Byronic facade lurks the specter of monomania.

The life led by Jared Sparks amidst the groves of academe left him untroubled by the sort of turmoil that beset Greenough. Judging from his portrait (fig. 5.17), Sparks would seem to be endowed with the dispassionate character necessary for the historian. To reach this result Powers had to sift through a variety of images sent to Italy by the family. In doing so he surmised that a bust by Luigi Persico was at odds with the testimony of three daguerreotypes. The former exhibited the prominence of jaw and recession of forehead associated with prognathism. These traits were hardly compatible for someone of Sparks's intellect.[88] Powers noticed further that "in the cast you appear to have the organ of 'self-esteem' large, but the Daguerreotype makes it small."[89] He resolved to rely on the photographs,[90] but the subject's arrival in Florence at the end of 1857 relieved him of the obligation. The resulting marble elicited praise from contemporaries who felt no discomfiture in describing it as an "accurate likeness and a fine specimen of art."[91]

After Sparks's death, his wife, Mary, requested Powers to write down the observations he had shared with her husband (an entreaty that again alerts us to the studio conversations that are now irretrievable). She reminded him that he had perceived a nobility that "surpassed all busts modern or ancient in height or breadth—in intellectual development" and that he had felt obliged to measure constantly in order to make sure he was not exaggerating.[92] In reply Powers assured Mrs. Sparks that he always made careful measurements, commencing with the distances of several parts of the head from the orifice of the ears, where the base of the brain was situated. In other words, he followed the modus operandi of the phrenologists. From these determinations he concluded that the distance to the height of Sparks's forehead equaled Webster's. It may even have surpassed the politician's, but the latter was more fully endowed in the back. Webster was perhaps too sensual and Sparks too deficient in this capacity, but in sum, Powers concluded, "Mr. Sparks' head possessed (phrenologically) all the noble qualities of humanity in the highest degree," while assuring the widow that nothing had been altered for the sake of effect.[93]

A turn around Sparks's bust confirms these assertions. The occiput does

(Opposite)
FIGURE 5.16. Hiram Powers, *Bust of Horatio Greenough* (1854–59 [modeled in 1838], marble, courtesy of Museum of Fine Arts, Boston, bequest of Charlotte Gore Greenough Hervosches du Quilliou)

FIGURE 5.17. Hiram Powers, *Jared Sparks* (1857, marble, Harvard University Portrait Collection, given to Harvard College, 1857, by students under the presidency of Jared Sparks)

indeed fall off precipitously, displaying none of the backward bulge seen in Webster. The sculptor discounted the evidence of the plaster bust that expanded *Self-Esteem*, favoring instead the photographs he received. More important, however, was the deficient sensuality, which translates into a weak *Amativeness*. Lorenzo Fowler's analysis of Webster's death mask confirmed this assessment, for the large organ of *Passionate love* had caught the phrenologist's eye. "Mr. Webster's natural propensities," Powers informed Edward Everett, "leaned strongly to virtue's side. It afforded him greater pleasure to give than to receive and he had not the ready firmness always to resist. Animal propensities like his would have sent to the penitentiary a score of ordinary men."[94] Put more specifically, the senator's powerful intellectual and spiritual faculties restrained "animal propensities" that might otherwise have run amuck. This was an exceptional organization, for as we have seen, *Amativeness* vitalized the entire organic economy, and much of the dynamism in the statue of Webster can be attributed to its workings. By contrast Sparks displays a composure comparable to Inman's portrait of William Wirt, where, also, a feebleness of the "propensities" prevailed. Cloistered in the libraries and lecture halls of Harvard University, Sparks had less need for the abundant energies, or the *Self-Esteem*, that made Webster a force to be reckoned with in the Senate chambers. The former's intellectual prowess was not goaded by a passionate nature into seeking worldly power, and as his bust confirms, he was better suited to the contemplative life.

Although Edward Everett (fig. 5.18) served as both politician and academic, his virtues leaned toward those of Webster, to judge from Powers's forceful representation of him. During his stay in Florence in 1839, Everett seems to have smoothed over any previous misunderstandings he had with Powers, and his conversion to phrenology is suggested by the fact that he escorted George Combe to a school convention during the latter's visit to the United States.[95] Powers undoubtedly noticed the statesman's undistinguished perceptive faculties during their encounters, since the sculptor later singled out this feature as responsible for Everett's inability to sympathize with the common people.[96] His "intellectual head," however, won the admiration of Powers and his associates,[97] but what are we to make of the response of Baroness Myandoff? She did not know Everett, Powers remarked, "but was struck very much with certain peculiarities in your bust, but what she said about it I shall whisper to Mrs. Everett when I get the opportunity."[98] Why this confidentiality unless *Amativeness* was involved? The size of this organ would greatly interest a spouse. This public disclosure of private inclinations led an associate of Combe to opine, "If your science should ever be fully received, I am convinced that wigs or caps would be reckoned quite as much an article of decency as britches."[99]

Once, much to Powers's annoyance, a woman attempted to plant a buss on one of his busts.[100] The crystalline purity of marble could not long endure such displays of affection, but given the evidence, it is easy to understand how such responses might ensue. A comparison of Powers's Everett with Clevenger's (fig. 5.19) makes us realize why the younger artist never quite freed himself of the charge of being unduly swayed by *Imitation*. His Everett is a respectable but rather haggard figure seemingly worn down by life's adversities. Quite a different individual confronts us in the other

FIGURE 5.18. Hiram Powers, *Edward Everett* (1841, marble, National Museum of American Art, Smithsonian Institution, museum purchase in memory of Ralph Cross Johnson)

image; while restrained, he exudes an aura of subdued dynamism. Sensing the potency latent in Powers's busts, Akers claimed that he had mastered the difficulties inherent in representing repose.[101] Clearly, Everett's forehead promises all that the intellect can offer, but pervading the work is something more elemental that endowed it with a magnetism that drew women to its "powerful" manhood.[102]

One authority attributes Powers's success to an ability to engage his subjects in discourse so he might study their fleeting expressions,[103] but this assertion runs up against his confession that he continued to work after Daniel Webster fell asleep.[104] The bust exhibits no evidence of the in-

FIGURE 5.19. Shobal Vail Clevenger, *Edward Everett* (1844, clay or plaster by Clevenger, marble carved by Hiram Powers, Harvard University Portrait Collection, presented to Harvard University as the bequest of Thomas Handasyd Perkins)

convenience, nor does it seem to suffer from the sitter's having to endure repeated applications of the calipers. These facts undermine the image of Powers as a latter-day Gilbert Stuart, regaling his patrons while deftly taking their likenesses. Shoptalk, in any case, was often insufficient to produce the softening of features that occurred when the natural language of the nobler faculties was animated. For this reason Powers advocated viewing the male sitter as a wife does so that one might touch the deeper strains of character and not just the public persona.[105]

Despite the animated expressions often exhibited by Powers's sitters, they gaze into the distance or turn to left or right, rarely taking the viewer into account. This is not a consequence of the omission of the iris; the eyes simply look elsewhere when we stand directly in front of the bust. Stuart, the virtuoso painter and raconteur, gives us the sudden glance or the immanence of speech, as if we had just entered the sitter's domain; each obeys the Lockean imperative and responds to sensory stimuli. Not so with Powers. He prefers rumination; his sitters are motivated by innate faculties and not the presence of others. All the data-gathering discussed above was directed to this end, to coordinating natural language with the idiosyncrasies of organic constitution, or as Edward Everett wrote, "His principle, as practiced by himself, we understand to be to reproduce the man in the best and most accustomed expression of his character. To attain this end, whatever is essentially characteristic in the original, must be preserved, whether it be great or small, feature or wrinkle. The consummate skill of the artist is shown in thus selecting what is thus characteristic, however seemingly inconsiderable, and still more in making these innumerable details work together toward the uniform and appropriate expression and life of the whole." [106] Some measure of Powers's success in this endeavor is provided by the fact that the patrons who were unable to travel to Florence are no less animated than those who did.

Among the plaster heads Powers brought to Italy, that of John Calhoun (fig. 5.20) vied with Webster's for the attention of those who flocked to see the collection. The southerner, however, was endowed with the ample perceptive faculties Powers found wanting in his northern counterpart. These differences appear in a phrenological diagram (fig. 5.21). The profile on the left exhibits a noticeable bulge over the eyes, corresponding to the development of Calhoun, while the next illustrates intellectual faculties of the sort enjoyed by Webster. The talents of Calhoun, Powers thought, had been expended solely in taking the pulse of the South while the legitimate demands of the North went unnoticed.[107] As we have seen, critics were enthralled by the notion that the history of the Confederacy might be read in the mental organization of its heroes; hence Powers was credited by one with disclosing "traits in Calhoun whose existence even his companions had never suspected till they were revealed by the chisel of Powers. In the light that history now throws on that famous bust even the common observer can see the whole Civil War slumbering in that piece of marble." [108] Treachery insinuated itself even into the natural language of such individuals according to Tuckerman, who claimed, "It is a singular coincidence that the bust of the chief envoy of the Southern traitors may also be seen in the studio of Powers; where the true American can compare the shrewd and plausible natural language of these unscru-

FIGURE 5.20. Hiram Powers, *John Caldwell Calhoun* (1836, plaster, National Museum of American Art, Smithsonian Institution, museum purchase in memory of Ralph Cross Johnson)

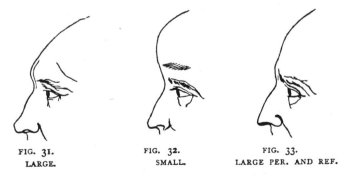

FIGURE 5.21. *Perceptives*, from *Self-Help* (Boston: Cowan, 1874), p. 105

pulous partisans, with the grand, honest, wise physiognomies of the noble fathers and defenders of the Republic."[109]

These issues and those concerning the alterations licensed by phrenology surfaced in 1844 when Powers was commissioned by the legislature of South Carolina to carve a full-length statue of Calhoun. He had modeled the bust years earlier; but since then the senator had allowed his mane to grow, and Powers was no more likely to ignore the implications of such matters than Palmer. Miner Kellogg sent a sketch of Calhoun's current appearance with a note that the politician would defer to the artist's discretion.[110] Powers weighed his alternatives and wrote the following to the committee of overseers:

> You will find that I represent his [Calhoun's] hair shorter than he now wears it. Mr. Kellogg sent me a drawing of his head with long hair, but I did not like it so well; it was shorter when I made his bust; but even then, I thought it too long for the bust. Mr. Calhoun's head is beautifully formed. Nothing could be finer than the outline of it. The concentrated energies of this powerful mind appear to flow and sometimes to flash from his face, where all is angular and masculine — long hair is effeminate and soft. It does not accord with the "cast iron man" — I may add that long hair disturbs the clean and fine outline of his head. It is true that at his fireside and among his friends, Mr. Calhoun's manner is soft and gentle as a child's. His smile is sunshine, and like sunshine it warms while it enlightens all around us. But it is sunshine. It is no ordinary light and heat that is perceived and felt in Mr. Calhoun's relaxed presence. It is the light and heat of melted "cast iron." It may be enjoyed, but it cannot be played with. I have preferred to represent Mr. Calhoun as he is known and understood by the mass of our people, the disinterested and stern statesman of the South. I say nothing of his political views, more than that I believe them to be sincere and honest.[111]

Calhoun's fireside manner, known to his wife and associates, is relinquished here in favor of the stern statesman of the South. While we cannot test these words against the original, it having been destroyed at the end of the Civil War, the surviving bust exhibits a passion that one contemporary described as "demoniac."[112] The angular head described by Powers accords with phrenological teaching about the male skull, and for this reason he took liberties with appearances by shortening the hair, a modification that entailed no alteration of crucial proportions while permitting viewers to see that the head is beautifully formed.

Combined with phrenological tenets is an analysis based on the theology of Swedenborg. Calhoun's presence is like sunshine, warming and

FIGURE 5.22.
Hiram Powers,
Mary Duncan
(front) (1857,
marble, Sargent
House Museum,
Gloucester, Mass.,
photo by the
author)

enlightening all around. The light and heat of the sun correspond to divine wisdom and love, and as such they entered Zeus Franklin's "Phreno-Chart." But note that Powers then employs Calhoun's nickname to take the senator down a peg, placing him in the material realm of cast iron, which when molten sends out light and heat but sears if too closely approached. The leading proponent of slavery is not guided entirely by true spiritual love and wisdom, and Powers's disapproval is apparent in the faint praise he musters, calling Calhoun's views merely sincere and honest (but not good). Before the implications of these ideas can be examined in greater detail, further considerations of gender and portraiture merit review.

THE FEMALE PORTRAITS

The consideration given Calhoun's hair indicates the importance Powers attributed to this feature, and we learn of his deliberations regarding the female coiffure from his correspondence with Mary Duncan (fig. 5.22). The subject, unable to travel to Florence at the time, sent a cast of her head, but Powers found it disconcerting. At some points the size rivaled

Webster's, and this seemed beyond a woman's attainment.[113] Duncan explained that the unusual dimensions were the result of an abundance of hair that she braided around the ears; these tresses, along with the shape of her head and throat, were among her "claims to greatness." Indeed, artists had declared the shape of her head "quite beautiful."[114] But the spread of stories about her Webster-sized cranium was a source of embarrassment, and she urged Powers to refrain from mentioning it "as my acquaintances seem to view it as a capital joke."[115]

Powers answered that he had discussed the cast only to condemn the blunders of the artist who made it, but he also needed more to go on. Could she send photographs with her hair let down and held back in a manner that displayed the ears? He clearly needed this index, but he was willing to go further and assume the duties of her coiffeur, noting, "Although your head may not present such enormous organs of self-esteem, philoprogenitiveness, etc. yet it will lose nothing of its intellectual developments under my hands." Abundant hair, he adds, should be tied behind or otherwise arranged so that it does not enlarge the volume of the head. "Let me see the outline of your entire head," he implores, "and then I shall know what to do."[116]

We can trace Powers's priorities here. The forehead is given due prominence, while the hair conforms to the cranium as it glides past the ear and gathers in a bun over *Philoprogenitiveness* (fig. 5.23). The profile recalls illustrations of those types whose large maternal organ, labeled number three, silently reproached "the unmotherly" (fig. 5.24). There is not that upward inclination in the back characteristic of lawyers and politicians, and thus Powers's conclusion about the negligibility of *Self-Esteem* is confirmed. This faculty was not an attractive feminine attribute, so there was no need for alarm; but the allusion to a small *Philoprogenitiveness* is intriguing. Did Powers know that Mary Duncan's only child had died shortly after birth?[117] Bereft of its natural means of exercise, the organ may have been smaller than thought meet, hence prompting an arrangement designed to gloss over a painful chapter in the sitter's life without actually falsifying it.

Amativeness, the battery that charged all other faculties, was both absolutely and relatively smaller in women than men. It would be unseemly, then, to represent a member of the fair sex overly energized by this organ, and the calm of Mary Duncan is typical in this respect. Women rarely exhibit the magnetism that animates the busts of Webster or Everett. This tendency to individuate male emotions more than female prompted Lorado Taft to praise the "faithful, vivid portraits of men" executed by Powers, while complaining that the women drifted off into a vague ideal.[118] As if in anticipation of this criticism, Powers's friend George Calvert wrote

FIGURE 5.23.
Hiram Powers,
Mary Duncan
(side) (1857,
marble, Sargent
House Museum,
Gloucester, Mass.,
photo by the
author)

VERY LARGE.

DEFICIENT.

No. 143. — THE DEVOTED MOTHER.

No. 144. — THE UNMOTHERLY.

FIGURE 5.24.
*The Devoted Mother
and the Unmotherly*,
from O. S. Fowler,
*The Practical
Phrenologist*
(Boston: O. S.
Fowler, 1869),
p. 74

FIGURE 5.25. Hiram Powers, *Mary Sargent Duncan* (1868, marble, Willard B. Golovin, Germantown, N.Y., photo courtesy of the owner)

"that you cannot say that he does men better than women"; he was equally adept at capturing both "kinds of physiognomies."[119] The emotional current could not be turned up beyond the capacity of the sitter, and the wattage of women was simply lower than men. This belief may have induced Powers to apply leeches behind the ear of his child, Louisa.[120] *Combativeness* and *Destructiveness*, very unfeminine organs, operated in this region, and their energetic assertion in a daughter would have been the source of concern. Phrenologists were prepared for such contingencies and recommended the procedure as the most effective means of quelling renegade faculties.[121]

Drapery was another feature that invited creative adjustment even in the abbreviated format of the bust. The décolletage of the second portrait of Mary Duncan (fig. 5.25) contrasts markedly with the prim elegance of the first. The sitter herself requested the change, expressing the hope that the sculptor would "not neglect the ripple of flesh where the arm joins the bust."[122] She sent Powers a picture of Lord Townley's *Antonia* (36 B.C.– A.D. 36, British Museum), urging him to adopt it as a model, a request that was obviously granted.[123] False modesty was not one of Mary Duncan's vices, but given her familiarity with phrenology,[124] she may have had reasons other than the obvious ones for featuring her physical allure. The Townley piece often appeared in phrenological literature, where, under a variety of titles, it was identified as "representing a perfect female bust" (fig. 5.26). The accompanying text enumerated the virtues of an ample bosom: "Men turn from a flat chest disappointed, as if it lacked something essential. As a face looks badly without a nose, so does the female chest when narrow and flat. Those are poorly ornamented, however rich their toilets, whose breasts are small and flat; while all who have them large, plump, and naturally elevated, are beautiful to behold, though dressed in calico; for bountiful Nature has already ornamented them beyond all

FIGURE 5.26.
Psyche, from O. S. Fowler, *Creative and Sexual Science* (Rochester: New York State Pub. Co., 1870), p. 145

power of art to equal." Ladies so richly endowed might harbor their resources by sound physical management, while the squanderer was advised to "think well and tremble you 'society' mothers before you suppress by artificial means this veritable 'fountain of life' for your darling babe."[125]

In her first incarnation Mary Duncan wears garb reminiscent of the quattrocento; in her second coming she fulfills the promise of physical metaphysics more explicitly by displaying those ornaments that art itself could not equal. Although women were only moderately endowed in *Amativeness*, they enkindled its warmest fires in men, the latter, according to Orson Fowler, being driven by the "male breast-loving instinct"[126] to hurl themselves in lemming-like droves over natural cleavage of the kind displayed by Mary Duncan.

While the similarities between Mary Duncan and the Antonia are readily apparent, the differences also merit attention. The greater expanse of forehead exhibited by the former signals the intellectual development available to modern women. Both are loosely robed, but in keeping with Victorian standards of propriety, Duncan's garment is slightly less revealing. Likewise, the glance avoids the coquettishness of her counterpart; instead, an air of pensiveness lingers over the features. The sunflower petals that encircle Mary Duncan allude to Clytie, the nymph whose infatuation with Apollo caused her to gaze longingly at the sun god as he traversed the heavens. Moved by this devotion, the gods transformed her into a heliotrope or sunflower, and in this metamorphosis she symbolized constancy.[127] Mary Duncan seems to have been affiliated with the Swedenborgian church,[128] and this device may have been intended to allegorize faith. Pagan myth could embody Christian devotion because "the sun of our world derives its heat and light from being perpetually operated upon by the Sun of the eternal world."[129] In several respects, then, the bust of Mary Duncan resembles Powers's Clytie, who wears a tiara of sunflower petals (fig. 5.27); both integrate spiritual content with sensuous form, and the unity of these apparent opposites touches the very core of the sculptor's aesthetic.

POWERS AND SWEDENBORG

One consequence of Powers's belief in physical metaphysics is the difficulty, if not impossibility, of extricating his thoughts about portraiture from those about the ideal. Both modes of expression touched the spirit; Mary Duncan could write Powers about her phrenology and also refer to her head as "my soul's temple."[130] Intimations of the divine appeared in her face as well as that of Clytie; hence much of what follows anticipates the chapter on the ideal.

FIGURE 5.27. Hiram Powers, *Clytie* (1867, plaster, National Museum of American Art, Smithsonian Institution, museum purchase in memory of Ralph Cross Johnson)

Powers's assertion that "the nude statue should be an unveiled soul"[131] has engendered much speculation. One interpretation contends that Powers's imperfect understanding of Swedenborg allowed him to fuse the sensuous earthly body immediately with its spiritual counterpart despite the mystic's insistence that the two were incompatible. The resulting combination of erotic and spiritual, real and ideal, produced "a hieroglyph for the materialized soul and Divine Order," a phrase devised to distinguish this approach from conventional allegorical content, which "unfolds discursively (as in a literary narrative)." In effect, the allure of Powers's figures embodies the soul's beauty directly. Its purity is conveyed by the flawless marble and technical perfection.[132]

If Powers unwittingly indulged in heterodoxy, it went unnoticed by the Swedenborgians. They welcomed him as a distinguished addition to their numbers and noted at his death in 1873 that he had been a practicing member for nearly fifty years.[133] The consequences of this extended discipleship are evident in his writings, and nothing there suggests that his comprehension of the Swede's teachings was clouded. More importantly, the above argument fails to take the doctrine of correspondences into account. According to this theory, "Nature has not the least claim to be a direct revelation of God, any more than the body has to be a direct revelation of the soul." The author of these words, Henry James Sr., goes on to explain that "this visible universe is by no means the true or spiritual creation, but only and at best a lively image or correspondence of it to a sensibly-organized intelligence."[134] The image of the world that presents itself to the eye is not identical to the spiritual realm. Emanations from the latter can only be decoded by the discerning wisdom of the initiate.

One such initiate was Mary Duncan. How else could she understand the deeper implications of the following passage from a letter sent by Powers to explain his decisions about the hair and garment of the first bust, but perhaps even more applicable to the second?

> The serpent who beguiled Eve has never been discharged. He still waits upon her daughters—and through them—operates on men. His invention is exhaustless. We are indebted to him for the waltz and the polka, and the whales in our northern and southern seas will never forgive him for crinoline. For here he has housed at their expense. Under whalebone rafters, he lives secure. He has ample room and his presence is not suspected. Art owes him a grudge however, and it is art which now condemns him. For to make room for himself he has distorted the human form divine—His own form is monstrous, and therefore he cannot appear in the simple garb of nature—but is constantly prompting

the mantua makers of Paris to afford him accommodations and disguises. I hate him as much as I love his victims, and in my attempted likeness of you, my dear lady, I shall leave him out. He shall have nothing to do even in the arrangement of your hair if I can help it and I trust you will perceive how superior simplicity is to all his devices.[135]

The effectiveness of this extravagant imagery depends on the theory of correspondences to transform the body into a microcosm where the cosmic struggle between good and evil unfolds. In order to hide his ugliness, the devil has plundered the oceans of whalebone to furnish the rafters for his abode beneath the accoutrements of fashion. By such devices he distorts the human form divine. Even the hair can be made an accomplice to his machinations, concealing the true mental and spiritual orientation of the phrenological organs. Art, however, can thwart his nefarious designs by exposing the simple garb of nature to all who have eyes to see.

As a sculptor Powers's domain was the human form. Swedenborgianism, filtered through phrenology, transformed that form, whether clothed or nude, into a morality play where fashion contended with nature for dominion over the corporeal realm. Since mankind can know the "creator a posteriori only, i.e. only through an actual experience of the creative presence and power as revealed in the created nature,"[136] the artist who adopted an evident style, who glossed over the particularities of visual experience, sided with the forces of darkness. Only the most natural representation of the body enabled a recognition of the correspondences intended by the divinity. It followed that a palpable rendering of the flesh need not engender immoral thoughts; rather, it was the proper means of discerning the "soul unveiled." This philosophy removed the source of inspiration from the innate ideas of Platonism[137] and located it instead in a rational knowledge of anatomy and physiology. By adopting this stance, Powers could claim the ideal was the real, was nature redeemed by truth and shorn of physical imperfection. "We have deformed her," he declared, "twisted her nose out of joint, crooked her back, warped her legs and carved her feet, and all this by our sensualities."[138]

The consequence of this understanding was to make the entire human form resonant with moral identity, offering the soul unveiled to the eye able to read the code. Many implications follow from this belief. With regard to portraiture it warrants repeating that the most subtle and informative correspondences were registered by the phrenological faculties on the skull. These protuberances were not moral qualities in themselves. *Benevolence* was not an act of benevolence; it merely corresponded to, or gave physical evidence of, the performance of charities. The actual dispo-

FIGURE 5.28. Hiram Powers, *Martha Endicott Peabody Rogers* (1845, Peabody Essex Museum, Salem, Mass.)

sition to do so, however, was an attribute of the soul and thus invisible to mortal eyes. When rendering the ideal nude, Powers could restore the figure warped by fashion to the form intended by the divinity, and as the body was healthy, so was the mind. In modeling a portrait, such as that of Mary Duncan, he could attend to the hair, clothing, and similar features in a manner that would likewise confound the Serpent.

Several other female portraits are also enwreathed, and like Mary Duncan they exhibit a décolletage that accomplished for the body what the coiffure did for the mind. The acanthus leaves that surround Martha Endi-

FIGURE 5.29. Hiram Powers, *Proserpine* (1844 [carved after 1873], marble, National Museum of American Art, Smithsonian Institution, museum purchase in memory of Ralph Cross Johnson)

cott Peabody Rogers (fig. 5.28) symbolize immortality, as they do in his popular ideal bust *Proserpine* (fig. 5.29).[139] The similarity of the two in appearance and content derives from the convergence of portraiture and ideal in Powers's theory. Rogers, however, is more individualized; she is somewhat worn by the burden of years, and mortality is in the details, giving them a tension and sharpness not seen in her mythological counterpart. Although we see through a glass darkly, intimations of the unveiled soul are discernible in both. An admirer of *Proserpine* was so taken by her "mental ability" that a phrenologist was brought in for a consultation.[140] Unfortunately, the results do not survive, but the very fact that someone would even propose the undertaking indicates that Powers composed the features, hair especially, to invite such scrutiny. Apparently his audience also thought the boundary between real and ideal easily traversed. The brow of Rogers offers itself for similar evaluation, and although not quite as regular as that of the goddess, it is elevated.[141]

Perhaps Powers's preferences are most evident in portraits of his relatives, since they were likely to accede to his intentions. In the case of *Anna Barker Gibson Powers* (1862–64, National Museum of American Art, Washington, D.C.), his second daughter, we encounter a woman in her early twenties who exhibits a vertical profile and a serenity that becomes her sex. Her simple garment has a classical aspect without being quite as revealing as that of Mary Duncan. A pendant rests between the breasts and gives this portion of the anatomy due prominence. It is readily apparent that no artificial support is needed here, the mature figure being what the phrenologists liked to call "deep chested." The hair is drawn back from her forehead, and the claim of a child of one patron "that the hair [of the bust] didn't come down so low on the face as mama's"[142] permits us to infer that the sculptor actively intervened in such matters when the habits of the sitter did not meet his standards. Anna's ears remain uncovered, while the hair gathers over the domestic faculties. In rendering his wife, *Elizabeth Powers* (1856–57, National Museum of American Art, Washington, D.C.), Powers played down her physical allure but made the cranium equally accessible to scrutiny. As befitting a matron in the fifth decade of life, her apparel is plain, modest, and seemingly contemporary. Decorum, then, may vary with age and status, but the constant remains the intent to trace the influence of the psyche upon the features.

THE REAL AND THE IDEAL

While each of Powers's sitters retains his or her individuality, each also partakes of larger categories of identity, the most obvious being gender.[143] Men, wrote a contributor to *The Crayon*, were "sublime," with a "rugged brow, full of the severity of thought," while women were "beautiful," exhibiting an "open brow."[144] Much the same dichotomy appears in Powers's oeuvre. His female sitters are individualized but at the same time exhibit that roundness of form and character advocated by John Bell and Erastus Palmer; they are alert, gracious, maternal, and open browed, displaying none of the sharpness that caused another writer for *The Crayon* to complain, "Our women, though smart and intelligent, are too prone to an ill-bred pertness which rather provokes the angularities of the intellect than the more elevated feelings of the heart."[145]

The same angularity of brow in men was, of course, sublime, and no- where was this more true than in the enormous head of Daniel Webster, the contemporary who seemed to embody the greatness of the nation. Here correspondences with the sublimity of the American landscape readily sprung to mind, causing one observer to write,

> Powers studied Webster's face as Church studied Niagara. His vast forehead, his overhanging brows, his massive features, the strong lines about his mouth, were each subjects of long and patient study; and when he had become fully possessed by his great subject he thought as Webster thought, and then the head and features of the grand man simply flowed out through his fingers and took form in marble. This bust by Powers and the *Niagara* by Church, each in its own distinctive sphere, marked an epoch. In looking at one, the beholder hears the awful cataract roar; as he gazes at the other, he sees the great man think. Powers caught Webster in his best mood, when blended thought and feeling threw about him an air of soft refinement.[146]

When Powers traveled to Webster's home in Marshfield, he was awed by a head that struck him as "natural, but one of nature's exaggerations; out of her common way of working, but still her own work."[147] Since the senator was an exaggeration, the artist was all the more bound to tell the truth about it as one of nature's wonders. The steps taken to ensure this end—the use of calipers, casts, and similar devices—have been discussed, but despite these measures, the artist did not escape criticism when his full-length bronze statue of Webster (fig. 5.30) arrived in Boston in 1859. Among certain parties it was bruited about that the mouth was unnatural; the figure, "lank"; the posture, poor; and the trousers, baggy.[148] Actually, the controversy surrounding the Webster had commenced years earlier among those who had seen the piece in Florence, and generally Powers seems to have fared well. In one report we read that

> the action, air, and proportions are all those of the Orator in his finest mood, and in his own proper costume. The colossal man here stands up to the height of his great argument on the Constitution, firmly holding you to the symbol of the Union with one hand, as he reasons from the vital scroll which nerves the other. The identity is complete. No one could hesitate a moment in recognizing it from any point of observation, front or rear. The incomparable bust is an enlarged copy of the

one modeled at Marshfield in Mr. Webster's prime, and is therefore the very presentment of his best condition. In the best judgments here, Art has not bequeathed to us a nobler head.[149]

The details about the modeling offered in this passage suggest that the author discussed the work with Powers. We find the same insistence on the correctness of proportion obtained during the visit to Marshfield that the sculptor was wont to mention. The assertion that identity was as apparent from behind as it was in front alludes to the conclusion drawn by the artist and phrenologists that Webster's "social feelings are all large, Amativeness particularly so—as large as is almost ever found."[150] Stress is also placed on the importance of having rendered the senator during his prime. Powers made the same point, contending that only then was the body sufficiently strong to support completely the labors of the gigantic brain.[151] The orator is seen in his best mood, upholding the Constitution while clasping the symbol of the Union. Again we hear the artist, who at the outset of his labors stated that he intended to depict Webster with his arm partially around the fasces, traditional symbol of unity, defending the union from those who would dissolve it.[152]

The sculpture depicts the orator's finest moment, when during the Webster-Hayne debate he thundered, "Liberty and Union, now and forever, one and inseparable!" Although Powers attributed great importance to the symbolic content of his work, modern commentators have tended to treat it perfunctorily. The fasces, for example, imparted a lesson of great consequence, which is reiterated in the ideal statue *America* (fig. 5.31), where the partially nude figure, intended to personify the greatness of the sculptor's native land, also rests its hand on this emblem of strength through union.[153] In a letter to Nicholas Longworth, Powers made an impassioned defense of this piece against those who had "no great relish for allegorical figures." He pillories General Cass for requiring "every body [to] express his views in direct terms, matter of fact language, and if so, what would he do with the Bible?" The flag, Powers contends, is "emblematical,—figurative—or allegorical," and artists of genius, such as Michael Angelo, Raphael, and Thorwaldsen, among others, all "showed some partiality for 'allegorical figures.'" "Our Savior spoke in figurative language," he adds with a touch of irony, "but we are more enlightened now."[154]

The reason for reviewing this argument at some length is to suggest that Powers was committed to "allegorical sculpture" as opposed to the "hieroglyphic" approach recently attributed to him. Especially relevant is his defense of allegory in Swedenborgian terms. The Swede set out to unriddle Scripture; hence the science of correspondences is premised on the

belief that the Savior spoke in parables, that he clothed spiritual truths in physical images, or allegories. Although ostensibly secular, *America* gestures toward heaven to indicate the providential source of liberty,[155] and there resides another source of Powers's imagery.

Radical uprisings throughout Europe in 1848 stirred the initial impulse to model *America*, or *Liberty*, as the statue was alternately titled, but Powers soon had even more compelling reasons for promoting the virtues of union. Threats of secession by South Carolina in 1849 and dissension over slavery during the subsequent decade took their toll on the sculptor. Initially his wrath was directed at the abolitionists, but the intransigence of the South also aroused his ire. In letter after letter he agonizes over the prospects of a "terrible and bloody civil war,"[156] and he worried as early as 1854 that his statue of *America* would be "out of date unless it goes home soon. She will wander about like a cat in a strange garret and finally hang herself on some tree or more."[157] A few years later the deteriorating situation caused him to fear that "her bundle of sticks may be unloosed and scattered to the four winds of Heaven."[158] Powers's nationalism, the strength of which seems to have grown during his residence in Italy, engendered much of this anxiety; but religious convictions also fanned the fire, and without some cognizance of these, the implications of both the *America* and the *Webster* are likely to be lost.

Like the *America*, the figure of Webster could also engage the sculptor's metaphysical turn of mind. He again invoked the spirit of Swedenborg and the theory of correspondences before his statue, explaining, "There is order and a complete system in creation. God is in the highest, man next, and nature below. The lowest level of the globe is the ocean—and this is a mirror. It reflects upwards and back all that is in man. The lowest level of life is the animal kingdom and it reflects back to man all that is in him. He sees the lion—the tiger, and the ass—images of himself. The fox is a image of man. Van Buren is a fox. The elephant is an [illegible]. . . . Webster was an elephant. Jackson was a lion."[159] While all is not explained, the drift of this remark is clear. Man, the microcosm, finds the imperfect image of himself within the environment. Van Buren, the low man on the totem pole, corresponds to the fox, an unclean animal of the infernal realm in Swedenborg's theology. Webster and Jackson are identified with animals of the spiritual world, and the elephant, which corresponds to "those who are in general knowledge," may also refer to the mental prowess of the senator.[160] Webster, then, stands out not only in the political arena but also in the more rarefied realms of creation.

Swedenborg was on the artist's mind when he commenced a statue of the leading advocate of union at a time when disloyalty seemed to abound.

The mystic's views on patriotism met the sculptor's needs precisely, for consistent with the doctrine of correspondences, he declared, "a society is a composite man. One's own country is the neighbor because the country consists of many societies, and is therefore a still more composite man. And the human race is composed of great societies, each of which is a composite man."[161] He elaborates elsewhere, "Man is born for no other end than that he may perform use to the society in which he is and to the neighbor, while he lives in the world, and in the other life according to the good pleasure of the Lord. The case in this respect is the same as it is in the human body, every part of which must perform some use, even things which in themselves are of no value, such as the many salival fluids, the biles, and other secretions, which must be of service not only to the food, but in separating the excrements and purging the intestines."[162]

Each citizen performs a necessary function in this organic conception of country as composite man. The idea was grafted by subsequent commentators to the perfectionism of the nineteenth century; hence "every well-constructed and well-ordered society is in the human form, and every society which is in the way of improvement and progress tends to this form."[163] As the nation advances, it approaches the celestial ideal where "all constitute one universal man, the strength, health, and happiness of all becomes that of each. Precisely as in the human body, where by the wholesome action of the whole frame, and its universal health, the proper vigor, peace, and comfort of each part are promoted and secured. As these increase and expand in the whole, so they do in all the parts."[164]

The Webster statue, then, provided an opportunity to focus these theological and physiological beliefs. A progressive, harmonious nation corresponds to a healthy human body. The great physical and mental strength of the senator in his prime made him the just embodiment of this concept; he was an elephant, a cerebral Niagara Falls, a man whose gigantic phrenological faculties stunned Europeans and testified to the advanced state of American civilization. Despite all of Powers's grousing about having to clothe the figure in contemporary fashions, he could also claim of the senator and like renowned figures that "for all their physical imperfections their high souls shine out like diamonds as set in lead. We do not see their bodies—and even the coats and breeches fail to kill entirely the inward spirit."[165] Clothing, as a lower form of "body phrenology,"[166] can reveal the unveiled soul to those initiated into the science of correspondences. Physical imperfections are not necessarily removed; rather, one can see through them and recognize the gem set in base metal.

These considerations make apparent the crucial role of the fasces in the Webster statue. If unity is a form of health in which each part functions organically, then disunity is a type of disease that can prove fatal.[167] Webster, the image of health and a champion of union, becomes an allegory of nationhood at the time of its greatest peril.[168]

While observers could claim to find in the clothed figure of *Webster* "a noble exhibition of the high energy which the mind imparts to the muscle,"[169] the flesh of the ideal nude was an even more subtle expression of the mind's intent. *America*'s allegorical attributes include the chains beneath her foot, indicative of the triumph over tyranny; a crown of stars, emblematic of the thirteen original states; and the fasces, suggestive of "union and strength."[170] The last of these virtues were present not only in explicit symbol but also in the physical constitution of the body. Her healthy torso, with breasts "naturally uplifted" and ample hips, exhibits no trace of the feebleness that results from having been a refuge for the devil. Indeed, Powers thought that fashionable ladies would do well to gaze upon his "strong Ideal."[171] This integration of political and corporeal imagery was common among Swedenborgians, and it is easy to imagine *America* illustrating the following lines, written by a prominent theologian to celebrate the triumph of freedom over the tyranny of restrictive clothing:

> Much has been written, and justly, upon tight lacing, as injurious both to the development and stability of the body. But if our ideas be correct, the duty of leaving the chest and the body free, becomes tenfold more imperative than before. If motion be the essence of the life of the organs, and if it extends to the whole frame and to the limbs, then all articles of apparel may fairly be supervised and limited in their pressure, in order to give our persons their lawful liberty. In this case the emancipation of the body itself is a subject of individual and domestic politics of the utmost importance, and the science of every organ should wring a progressive Magna Charta of dress from the kings of fashion.[172]

Following the doctrine of the composite (wo)man, *America* is emblematic of the health of individual citizens and of the state. Powers could also turn this mode of thought around and view his ideal figure as behaving like a mortal. He writes that if the rods of her fasces were scattered, she would be driven to suicide, "her ships will fall to pieces, the stars will fade out upon her head and she will disappear forever upon the face of the earth. America wants a man to take her by the hand just now and lead her out of the [illegible] and there is no man."[173]

When Powers penned these lines in 1854, Webster had been dead for two years, but America was still in need of the guidance his hand could provide. In his sculpted form the orator places his left hand on the symbol of union, as if to complement the same gesture made by *America* with her right. In contrast his Calhoun, the proponent of state sovereignty and regional interests, had as an attribute the palmetto, symbol of the fractious state of South Carolina.[174] *America* with her fasces embodied "Truth, Justice, Union and Freedom," Powers noted, but Calhoun and his palmetto stood solely for the words inscribed on the scroll he held, "Truth, Justice and the Constitution."[175]

What was true at the level of allegory also applied to physical constitution, that is, to the formal configuration of each piece. We have seen that Calhoun's large perceptive faculties, which attuned him to his constituency, were ultimately inferior to the "reasoning faculties" that swelled the upper region of Webster's head, even though the latter's devotion to principle cost him popular sympathy. Webster most closely approximated the composite man because his moral suasion emanated from a sublime forehead that corresponded to all that was good in the new nation. It followed that his advocacy of union would bring the composite man progressively closer to the "celestial man." No female brow could match the senator's in this respect, so Powers turned to personification for his *America*, where beauty, rather than sublimity, conveyed virtually the same message. The bickering of politicians might retard but could never prevent entirely the progress of freedom and improvement throughout the world.[176] And as the contention over slavery worsened, he was elated to hear that Virginia held fast "to the bundle of sticks" and hoped that South Carolina could be induced to do the same. *America*, he thought, might lend its example to the debate, providing in its healthful, "womanly embodiment" a discourse on the superiority of union to the fever of secession that had gripped some quarters of the republic.[177]

Equipped with the precepts of Swedenborg and Spurzheim, Powers was prepared to survey the psychic life of the nation just as Whitman did the pedestrians he encountered on his rambles. Unlike the aristocrat, who might dabble in an occupation, the professional of the Jacksonian era was confirmed in his calling, was assured that what he did to earn money was part of his innate being, by phrenology. Faces disclosed destiny, and since personal and professional choices corresponded to spiritual truths, indeed, comprised the very heaven or hell one was preparing for oneself while still resident in the terrestrial sphere, none of Powers's works, not even the portraits, is entirely devoid of metaphysical content. The confidence that prevails among his sitters need not be viewed as complacency; it wells up from springs that run deeper than self-satisfaction, and from each visage there beams the intimations of a fate that transcends worldly happiness.

With exceptional personages such as Webster and Calhoun, so resonate was the body with the soul's urgent communications that the figure
articulates an ideal of collective identity similar to that found in *America*. 209
Faces
In terms of style, belief in the composite man and the principles of
phrenology permitted an enhanced naturalism to be equated with spiritual expression. While Powers's sitters often exhibit the outward trappings
of antiquity in the form of classical garb, the directives of neoclassicism
do not apply to the head, where scrupulous fidelity to the features contrasts with the modifications introduced by Canova (it should be noted
again that Powers attributed the latter to the artist's egotism). Without
these obvious stylizations, Powers's portraits have drawn the fire of critics
who demand that Art announce its presence with clarion call. The chaste
lines, restrained vitality, and unobtrusive originality of his busts, however,
share a community of interests with other products of Yankee culture
that have been more enthusiastically received. Like Shaker furniture, for
example, his works emerge from that confluence of materialism, pro-
gressivism, and millennialism that constituted an essential component of
antebellum society. Powers's belief that the unique identity of each mortal
was preserved through eternity helped him forge an authentic link between the nuanced treatment of surface and penetration into the depths
of character. The result is one of the major aesthetic accomplishments of
mid-century America. His bust of Everett can stand next to the works of
predecessors such as Stuart or those of successors such as Saint-Gaudens
without suffering from the comparison, but only if we do not insist on
finding qualities that are not there.

The fact that Powers's portraits were intended to prompt questions that
run counter to modern criticism has confounded evaluation. Would this
person make a good politician? A good spouse? A trusted business partner? The answers would seem to be purely conjectural and hence beyond
the pale of visual analysis were it not for the fact that the artist inscribed
them into the formal matrix of his work. He includes a variety of clues
that lead us to the identity of the sitter. The arrangement of the hair, the
shape of the skull, the tenor of expression, and the manner of apparel
all contribute to that effective integration of form and content that is the
foundation of all successful art. The theory that facilitated this integration
was phrenology.

No wonder, then, that the widow of one of Powers's patrons wished
to hang a phrenological reading of her husband next to his marble likeness. Any doubts the visitor might entertain about his or her own analytic
powers could thus be tested against expert testimony.[178] While a recent
textbook claims that looking at nineteenth-century busts "can be one of

FIGURE 5.32. Jeremiah Pearson Hardy, *Catherine Wheeler Hardy and Her Daughter*
(ca. 1842, oil painting, courtesy of Museum of Fine Arts, Boston, gift of Maxim
Karolik for the M. and M. Karolik Collection of American Paintings, 1815–65)

the more numbing experiences in art,"[179] this verdict does not square with
the response of contemporaries to Powers's portraits. According to their
testimony, "Whenever he undertook a new bust he studied his subject till
he became wholly absorbed by it, and could for the time think and feel like
the man himself."[180] George Calvert, whose considerable knowledge of
phrenology made him an especially sensitive interpreter of Powers's work,
wrote that even in the plainest face the sculptor recognized "an inner
lamp of unrevealed beauty, casting up at times into the features gleams
of its light. These translucent moments,—its truest and best states,—the
Artist must seize, in order to effect a full likeness."[181] In weighing these
contending evaluations, some acquiescence to the assumptions intended
to govern our response may tip the scale in Powers's favor.

The sculptor's intent to eschew personal mannerisms recalls Durand's
ambitions, but the analogies with landscape painting do not end here.
Calvert's mention of translucent moments, when the natural language

aligns the inner and outer person, is reminiscent of the response in recent literature to the humble but captivating settings of luminism. We are told that "the light emanating from the core of the [luminist] picture becomes palpable, uniting matter and spirit in the single image."[182] Similarly, the harmony Powers discovers in even the most unprepossessing countenance results from a vision of body and soul joined in an order that will one day reconcile heaven and earth.

This interpretation suggests that the imagery devised during the antebellum years is bound by stronger ties than hitherto surmised. Barbara Novak, for instance, calls attention to the light-filled landscape in a painting by Jeremiah P. Hardy (fig. 5.32) to demonstrate how the values associated with luminism could enter portraiture.[183] On closer examination we notice that the head of Mrs. Hardy projects backward almost to the point of deformity. By turning to *The Devoted Mother and the Unmotherly* (fig. 5.24), which illustrates the bulge of *Parental Love*, we encounter a strikingly similar profile. Little is known about Hardy, an artist who spent most of his career in Maine, but one authority reports that he "rejected the painterly portrait style of his teacher [Samuel F. B.] Morse" in favor of "crisply delineated forms, sharp silhouettes, tight, controlled handling of paint, and a smooth surface."[184] On the strength of the visual evidence, it appears safe to infer that he entertained an interest in the science of Gall and Spurzheim, a consideration that might well have encouraged his abandonment of the inexactitudes associated with the painterly style in favor of a linear manner analogous to that of luminism. Again, we seem to have entered a translucent moment and there witness the divine energy that pervades the environment attain its most comprehensive expression in the verities of the human form.

6

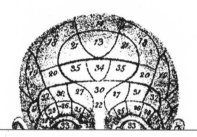

The Index of Natural National Character

America could embrace Daniel Webster because humanity would one day be wedded to the ideal, and the cohabitation seen in Thomas Crawford's pediment for the Senate was the outcome of this conception. There a personification of America rubs shoulders with a revolutionary soldier and a stalwart pioneer (fig. 6.1). The ideal and historical taper into the mundane and modern as the eye travels to the mechanic, the schoolmaster, and the merchant on the left. Such intercourse of noble and mundane types reflects the ongoing decline of social stratification fostered by Jacksonian politics, but the Native Americans on the right are not invited into the community so engendered, for the sculptor has another agenda as well. He wants to shift attention away from conventions of class and direct it toward current perceptions of race and gender. The resulting pyramidal

FIGURE 6.1. Thomas Crawford, *The Progress of Civilization* (1851–63, Senate pediment, U.S. Capitol, Washington, D.C., U.S. Senate Collection)

composition seeks to found national order on scientific theory and natural law rather than on the precarious arrangements fostered by social distinction. It is emblematic of the priorities of racial imagery. Caucasians are central to the endeavor, while other peoples serve as a foil. We better understand the contribution of phrenology to this enterprise if we adopt a like manner of thinking, concentrating first on the center, on the superiority of whites, rather than plunging prematurely into the margins as is so often done in modern histories.

Even so seemingly innocent a piece as *Phrenology at the Fancy Ball* (fig. 6.2) could convey such notions. One partygoer, who has crowned himself with a phrenological bust, examines another dressed in oriental garb. All is evocative of Victorian parlors and a seemingly simpler time, but the group's quaint charm should not blind us to the message it held for contemporaries. Long before John Rogers set hand to clay to recount this yarn, phrenologists had set their hands to his cranium in search of the tales it might tell. Almost four decades earlier he had his head examined after attending a lecture devoted to the topic.[1] The results have not been preserved, but some years later the *American Phrenological Journal* published another analysis that cited a large *Benevolence,* a moderate *Self-Esteem,* and well-developed "artistic and mechanical faculties" as responsible for his success.[2] Rogers probably concurred, for he eyed the heads of associates in like manner, finding, for example, a "wonderful bump of hope" arising from one.[3]

Although *Phrenology at the Fancy Ball* has been called a tongue-in-cheek spoof on the theory,[4] little supports the contention, and the meaning must be sought elsewhere. The reveler on the right has come as Poo Bah from Gilbert and Sullivan's operetta *The Mikado.*[5] Ostensibly, then, he belongs to the "Mongolian" race, but were he actually so, faculties such as *Mirthfulness, Ideality,* and *Causality* would be deficient. Since he is Caucasian, these

FIGURE 6.2. John Rogers, *Phrenology at the Fancy Ball* (ca. 1886, plaster, collection of the New-York Historical Society)

organs can be expected to be reasonably well developed,[6] and "Mr. Phrenology," with his deft digits placed precisely where the testimony is most telling, unmasks the deception. The subject's amusement suggests that the first of these faculties is indeed substantial, and that the examiner has made a "hit."

Rogers's abolitionist inclinations need not have inhibited his belief in the ranking of races. The case of Lydia Maria Child demonstrates how the two commitments might be reconciled. A visit to the American Museum in New York provided this leading abolitionist with the opportunity to scrutinize casts of fifteen Indians. The head of one exhibited remarkable *Destructiveness*, while the facial angle of the rest was inferior. Provided the opportunity to exercise their "moral and intellectual faculties," Child concluded, Indians and Africans would bring their skulls into alignment with those of whites.[7] This is a liberal interpretation of the tenet that all brains, even those belonging to nonwhites, could expand with exercise. While phrenologists would agree, most would assert they expand at different rates and that the gap was ultimately unbridgeable. In either case, Caucasians were the paradigm by which other races were measured, as Rogers's Poo Bah might testify. The consequences of this sort of thinking have only begun to receive the attention they deserve,[8] and as noted above, the most fertile field of inquiry is found in representations of whites. Blacks and Native Americans reside on the outskirts of antebellum art, in caricature or on the margins of genre scenes,[9] where their role is subservient to the priorities set by whites.

POLYGENESIS AND PHRENOLOGY

Those intent on maintaining racial ranking could turn to the Old Testament, where the curse of Ham, whose son was condemned to be "a servant of servants," provided justification for the perpetual enslavement of the dark-skinned.[10] Inquiring spirits, however, were not prone to the pieties of fundamentalism. By subjecting biblical narratives to the harsh light of reason, such individuals hoped to rescue faith from dogma. The preferred stratagem was to question the tenet that held all mankind to be descended from a single, primordial couple. By examining the physical remains (primarily crania) of the ancient inhabitants of the New World and the Near East, supporters of polygenesis, the discipline dedicated to gathering evidence of multiple acts of creation, furnished testimony to the unchanging nature of anatomical organization. If, say, a thousand years passed between the Flood and the construction of the pyramids, then all the differences in mankind would have had to appear in that single period, with none evolving in the succeeding millennia. The mummies and paintings left by the Egyptians evinced a variety of races identical to that seen in the nineteenth century and seemed to discredit those who sought to account for diversity by the effects of climate. Had all sprung from Adam and Eve, as claimed by advocates of monogenesis, and then darkened when they migrated to southern latitudes, why did this not represent an ongoing process, with blacks blanching in the New World and Europeans assuming the features of the Ethiopian as they moved into Africa? And why did skulls from antiquity exhibit the same disparity between the ample Caucasoid and diminished Negroid encountered in the modern world? In other words, partisans of polygenesis cudgeled both religious conservatives and old-fashioned upholders of Enlightenment notions of unity with what they perceived as objective data. They postulated numerous moments of creation in which each race emerged as a distinct and unchanging species arrayed along a chain of being that placed Caucasians on its highest material rung.[11]

The theoretician of this movement was Louis Agassiz, a Swiss-born naturalist who settled in Boston in 1846. Its statistical genius was Dr. Samuel George Morton, whose *Crania Americana* of 1839 and *Crania Aegyptiaca* of 1844 furnished the data on which these arguments rested. By filling the cranial cavity with lead shot which he then emptied into a calibrated beaker, Morton measured the volume of the brain and, after years of collecting and study, claimed to be able to identify race merely on the basis of the size and shape of a skull.[12] Always reticent to draw conclusions, Morton refrained from endorsing forthrightly the plurality of human species, from asserting, for example, that the American Indians, who were the principal subject of *Crania Americana*, were a distinct species and unrelated to Asiatics. Although Morton also equivocated about the claims of phrenology,[13] devotees of the science would have found much in this volume to encourage their efforts.

Evidence of Morton's affiliation with the phrenologists of his native Philadelphia appears repeatedly in his work. In *Crania Americana* he acknowledges, for example, his debt to the writings of Charles Caldwell,[14] to the city's phrenological society, and to George Combe for supplying valuable skulls.[15] Further, insufficient attention has been devoted to Morton's liberal use of the terminology popularized by the doctrine. His references, for instance, to the prominent "faculty of imitation" discovered in the Chinese, the enormous development "in the region of firmness" discernible in Siamese skulls, and the inferior "intellectual faculties" and "imitative faculties" of American Indians attest to a familiarity that undermines his professed reservations.[16] His analysis can glide effortlessly from discussion of cranial shape to matters of racial character, as seen in his assertion, apparently in reference to *Combativeness* or *Destructiveness*, that the mental structure of the aboriginal inhabitants of the New World prevents them from fraternizing with whites.[17] Thus, while hesitating about the particulars, Morton was willing to accept the "fundamental principles" of Gall's system and recognize "a singular harmony between the mental character of the Indian, and his cranial developments as explained by Phrenology."[18]

Lending weight to this endorsement was Morton's invitation to George Combe, who was then in Philadelphia, to append an essay on the phrenological attributes of the crania illustrated in the book. The Scotsman stressed that without phrenology, anthropological analysis was of little value. We have touched on this point before, but its inclusion in this seminal work of scientific racism warrants quotation: "If the size of the brain and the proportions of its different parts be the index of natural national character, the present work, which represents with great fidelity the skulls of the American tribes, will be an authentic record in which the philosopher may read the native aptitudes, dispositions and mental force of these families of mankind. If this doctrine be unfounded, these skulls are mere facts in Natural History, presenting no particular information as to the mental qualities of the people."[19] Identification of the qualitative differences that divided the several families of mankind was phrenology's most substantive contribution to the debate that sundered antebellum society.

Needless to say, Combe confirmed the stereotypes. The Iroquois, for instance, possessed a combination of *Self-Esteem, Firmness, Combativeness, Destructiveness*, and feeble moral organs that prompted them to resist the intrusion of Anglo-Saxons.[20] It is crucial to recognize that such conclusions do not occur in a vacuum; they are accompanied by explicit or tacit comparisons with whites. Hence, a treatise ostensibly devoted to the American Indian actually abounds with inferences about the virtues of Caucasians, and particularly the Germanic branch of the race.[21]

These ideas were picked up by Josiah Clark Nott and George Gliddon, two followers of Morton who did not equivocate in drawing conclusions from his data. The two collaborated on a number of books that represent the most definitive effort to prove polygenesis and establish a hierarchy of races.[22] Their *Indigenous Races of the Earth* repeats Combe's remark included above and reviews various aspects of phrenology,[23] while *Types of Mankind* reports that the Toltec skull is very broad around "the organs of caution, secretiveness, destructiveness," lending much credibility, it is asserted, to the claims of phrenology.[24] Here again, passages devoted to Combe's views indicate the integration of his theories and theirs.[25]

One reason for discussing polygenesis at length is to call attention to phrenology's complicity in its effort to evaluate the relative merits of the several families of mankind. Recent literature devoted to race and the arts in nineteenth-century America ignores this dimension almost entirely. One can leaf through such publications without encountering a single reference to Morton, Nott, Gliddon, Combe, or phrenology.[26] The authors apparently assume we all know what racism implies and that it has remained unchanged over the last century and a half.

While phrenology contributed to polygenesis, the impact of polygenesis on the visual arts is less easily assessed. Morton could state that the average Caucasian skull exceeded the Negroid by seven cubic inches,[27] but the artist would be hard pressed to translate such data meaningfully. On the other hand, phrenology gave these dry statistics a visual dimension; it transformed them into specific shapes and modes of behavior. One other ingredient was needed, however, before this brew would attain its true toxicity.

By 1850 Americans attributed their irresistible sweep across the continent, their Manifest Destiny, more to the superiority of English stock than to the efficacy of democracy.[28] Citing the praise Tacitus lavished on the freedom-loving, warlike German tribes, proponents of Anglo-Saxonism held that these same virtues were a legacy they left to the present inhabitants of England. Phrenology and polygenesis were grafted onto this notion and contributed to the conviction that the stalwart sons and daughters of Albion were destined to bear the torch of civilization to all the benighted races of the planet, displacing those who stood in the way of progress and making lands fruitful that previously had lain fallow for want of ingenuity. Evidence that the skulls of Englishmen and their American descendants were more capacious in the regions occupied by the reasoning and moral faculties came from phrenology, while Morton and his followers affirmed that the species that arose in northern Europe was the most vigorous and intelligent of all mankind. The license for conquest, if one was ever needed, was signed and delivered by the hand of science.

MEN OF GENIUS

In seeking to confirm this interpretation of history, Americans found in Daniel Webster a contemporary who epitomized all that these disciplines held estimable. The present being secured, the past was surveyed for Anglo-Saxon predecessors whose place in the march of progress was uncompromised by monarchical leanings. The obvious candidate was Shakespeare. Rising from humble beginnings, the playwright created an oeuvre that, in William Wetmore Story's words, "holds together all our literature. Our language is embedded in his works; we speak Shakespeare, even when we know it not."[29] England, of course, shared this estimation, and when plans for a proposed national monument were debated there in 1823, one wit opined that craniologists would insist on celebrating the poet's perfect head by constructing a rotunda with a marble skull in the center.[30] Actually, he was not far off the mark.

It was usual to assert that all Shakespeare's faculties were well developed and then add something about his "fineness of texture" and "exquisiteness of temperament."[31] George Calvert put this notion into the larger context discussed above by mentioning that the research of Morton confirmed the racial ranking devised by Johann Friedrich Blumenbach. It is to Gall, Calvert adds, that we owe the understanding of the relationship between the brain's shape and intelligence. One need only compare the humble pate of George III with the magnificent dome atop Shakespeare to confirm the truth of this tenet.[32] The poet emerges from Calvert's essay as a "spiritual earthling," a turn of phrase not unlike Palmer's physical metaphysics, and one characteristic of bardolatry.[33]

By mid-century, then, phrenology was regularly a part of such analysis, as subscribers to *The Crayon* could testify after reading about Mr. Faed's rendering of Shakespeare's "immense forehead."[34] Not everyone, however, was ready to believe that a relatively untutored actor from Stratford-on-Avon was capable of the brilliant displays of erudition that regularly illuminate the plays attributed to him. Was there not some profounder, more subtle mind at work in these pages? Partisans of Francis Bacon found his name encoded in elaborate ciphers within the texts.[35] The matter might be settled, some said, if only the curse inscribed on Shakespeare's tomb, with its imprecations against those who would disturb his mortal remains, could be circumvented. Proponents of exhumation justified their position by claiming it to be "in the interests of science, physical and moral." The attempt to secure an exact likeness of the poet, asserted another, was no "mere relic-mongering" but a project that would greatly benefit posterity.[36] Charles Dickens noted that enthusiasts hoped to display the skull "in the phrenological shop-windows,"[37] and Oliver Wendell Holmes, despite his skepticism, could not suppress the wish that someone would "get round the curse that protects the bones of Shakespeare[.] I should like to see the dome which rounded over his imperial brain. Not that I am what is called a phrenologist, but I am curious as to the physical developments of these fellow-mortals of mine, and a little in want of a sensation."[38]

These issues were bound to arise when artists sought to satisfy the demand for images of the bard, as William Wetmore Story, who modeled a statuette of Shakespeare in the early 1870s (Pierpont Morgan Library), documents. He dismisses the Bacon controversy on the grounds that "the portrait, after all, that forms the frontispiece to the plays does not look like a perfect fool. It is not a bad nor a mean forehead, is it? If the person it represents did not do something remarkable, one cannot help wondering why not, with that great brain and that speaking face."[39] Here, then, was a head equal to that of Justice Story, and a talent that likewise escaped monomania by the exercise of its many large faculties.

Story's mention of a frontispiece to the plays refers to the "Droeshout engraving," an image included in the 1623 folio and thus entitled to serious consideration as the authentic representation of the bard. The claim, however, was challenged by contenders that did not necessarily resemble the print. One was the bust by Gerard Johnson that kept a vigil over the tomb; another, the famed "Chandos" portrait, was a work with a shadowy provenance that entered the National Portrait Gallery in 1856. The discovery of a death mask, rescued in 1849 from a curio shop in Germany, answered the prayers of many who had longed for unequivocal evidence of the dramatist's features.[40] But the testimony of these various likenesses was not easily reconciled.

The steps taken by William Page to devise an image of Shakespeare (fig. 6.3) reveal the lengths to which some might go to ensure accuracy.[41] Any number of Page's acquaintances could have familiarized him with phrenology, while Hiram Powers, who converted him to Swedenborg in 1850, must also have reviewed the deeper ramifications of the science.[42] Significantly, Page's likeness of Shakespeare, even more than the attempts to render Christ, came to represent the culmination of his theories about the potential of portraiture. As his wife wrote in her journal, the bard embodied "an Anglo-Saxon type of beauty which stands up by the Phidian Greek just as bravely as do his plays by Aeschylus."[43] A similar thought had prompted George Combe to study the busts of Shakespeare, Dryden, and Addison, among others, "for the purpose of comparing them with the faculties revealed in their works."[44] The procedure offered another means of penetrating the veil of mystery that shrouded the Elizabethan poet, for as we have seen, literary output corresponded to bodily organization.

This sentiment was echoed in a booklet written by Page to accompany the exhibition of his painting in Chicago. Shakespeare, we learn, represents an English type of manliness; his head was no more Greek than his plays are.[45] Phrenologists would also have applauded Page's contention that portraiture was a branch of history, obliged by its internal logic to tell the truth or be censured before the tribunal of humanity.[46] If this sounds similar to Akers's thoughts on the subject, it may be because that sculptor seemingly adopted many of Page's beliefs.[47] The latter's quest for authenticity sent him to photographs of the mask and then to Darmstadt

FIGURE 6.3. William Page, *Shakespeare Reading* (1873–74, oil painting, National Museum of American Art, Smithsonian Institution/Art Resource, N.Y.)

in 1874 to study the original before preparing a final, life-sized bust of the playwright.[48] Much of the pamphlet is devoted to measurements taken from the cast.[49] This exercise was fundamentally akin to the undertaking of Morton and Combe earlier in the century, but while they sought racial norms, Page endeavored to perpetuate the statistics of racial genius.

Page also consulted the other portraits, valuing the Droeshout and Chandos images over the Stratford bust, whose portly features he believed a consequence of ineptitude.[50] These differences were not inconsequential. Oliver Cromwell's brow needed just a "wedge in the upper loft to expand it to the ideality of Shakespeare's head,"[51] but from this divergence Mars and Apollo went their separate ways. Like Tuckerman, Page saw *Ideality* as a civilizing force; hence the bard's sonnets and plays were "written in his face."[52] A reviewer concurred, stating, "The face and head which Mr. Page had produced from the hints contained in these photographs [of the various portraits and the death-mask] differed so widely from all the other recognized portraits of Shakespeare, and I may add, were in themselves so much more satisfactory to the student of the plays, so much more suggestive of what we might conceive to have been the earthly dwelling-place of the mighty spirit which had created Macbeth, Hamlet, Othello, and Lear."[53] We would do well to remember that a corpulent, Falstaffian Shakespeare based on the Stratford statue entailed a different vision of genius, race, and, ultimately, Manifest Destiny than a lean, pensive, Hamlet type. The latter was decidedly favored and became a model of Anglo-Saxon comeliness.[54] Page sought, according to one reviewer, "to give us a true Shakespeare; to suggest the soul and body of the poet; and this in such fashion that when we look upon the picture we shall say: 'Yes, just such a one he must have been, that highest type of the intellect in man which the modern world has known.'"[55] Consequently, there arose the tendency to measure contemporaries against this prototype. Charles Loring Elliot was frequently subject to the comparison, particularly after a copy of the Chandos portrait circulated in this country,[56] and when Tuckerman wanted to inventory the features that confirmed the creativity of Akers, he wrote that the artist "was small in stature, delicately organized, but, before his invalid days, athletic, agile, and lithe; his head was Shakespearian, in type, the brow being high and broad, and the crown bald; his gray eyes were grave, tender, and magnetic, and his hair silky and sunny, and he wore his beard intact."[57]

The epitome of this refined but athletic organization is found in John Quincy Adams Ward's statue for Central Park (fig. 6.4), a piece commissioned to celebrate, albeit belatedly, the tricentennial of Shakespeare's birth.[58] It was fitting that William Cullen Bryant was invited to deliver an address at the unveiling in May 1872. As a writer, he had been inspired by the bard's example; as a resident of New York, he had been the first to propose that the city set aside a parcel of land for public recreation before the entire island was consumed by development. Phrenology certainly entered his thoughts when he made this proposal, for he feared the "corrupt atmosphere generated in hot and crowded streets" during torrid summer days.[59] Miasmatic airs exhaled from stagnant water had long been viewed as a source of disease, and indeed the land in question possessed this feature. But Bryant focused on the city, describing it in terms comparable to those employed by phrenologists in their critique of the American home. It is overheated and confined, hence replete with noxious human effluvia, which ventilation or, in this case, fresh breezes, could remove. The theme was one to which the poet often returned. When, for example,

FIGURE 6.4.
John Quincy Adams Ward, *William Shakespeare* (1870, bronze, Central Park, New York, N.Y., courtesy of City Parks Foundation)

he was struck by the general good health of the Cuban population despite the warm climate, he attributed it "to the free circulation of air through their apartments. For in Cuba the women, as well as the men, may be said to live in the open air."[60] By prefacing his plea for "beautiful pleasure-grounds" with a discussion of the physiological benefits they would grant, Bryant was adopting a line of argument consistent with George Combe's reasoning.

The words Bryant offered on that spring day summarize the cult of Shakespeare as it had evolved over the preceding half-century. He assured his listeners that the blood coursing through their veins was drawn from the same fount that had nourished the bard and his contemporaries, and that the fabric of their cerebral tissue was woven of the same fibers that formed the warp and woof of English civilization. Turning to the statue, Bryant proposed that

> those who profess to read in the aspect of the individual the qualities of his intellectual and moral character, have always delighted to trace in the face, of which we this day unveil an image to the public gaze, the manifest signs of his greatness. Read what Lavater wrote a hundred years since, and you shall see that he discovers in this noble countenance a promise of all that the critic finds in his writings. Come down to the phrenologists of the present day, and they tell you of the visible indications of his boundless invention, his universal sympathy, his lofty idealism, his wit, his humor, his imagination, and every other faculty that conspired to produce his matchless works.

Bryant was just warming to the subject, for he goes on to compare Shakespeare to Niagara, the first among waterfalls, and while admitting that the playwright was not an American poet, he regards him as the poet of Americans. But even these encomiums did not stanch the flow of adulation. In what may be the most extraordinary application of physical metaphysics, the speaker relied on its premises to envision a phrenological apotheosis, contending, "So it is with those great minds which the Maker of all sometimes sends upon the earth and among mankind, as if to show us of what vast enlargement the faculties of the human intellect are capable, but if rarely in this stage of our being, yet at least in that which follows the present life, when the imperfections and infirmities of the material frame, which is now the dwelling of the spirit, shall neither clog its motions nor keep back its growth. Such a great mind was that of Shakespeare." Shakespeare's vast enlargement of the faculties had always been a source of wonder. Now they served to illustrate the rewards that await humanity in the life to come, and in case any of his auditors missed the point, Bryant repeated it, finding the head a revelation of "the immortal part of man" which shall emerge when "every cause that dims its vision, or weakens its energy, or fetters its activity, or checks its expansion shall be wholly done away, and that subtler essence shall be left to the full and free exercise of the powers with which God endowed it."[61]

Consider the island of Manhattan a microcosm of the nation as a whole in the latter half of the nineteenth century. One portion is heavily populated and the rest sparsely settled. As that population continues to grow and spread, those with a yen for nature's balm and beauty, such as Bryant, see the need to preserve enclaves from the ravages of unthinking development. Particularly telling in this respect is the election of Frederic Church to the park's Board of Commissioners in 1871 to restore its integrity after the depredations inflicted by the corrupt Tweed administration.[62] To continue the proposition, Central Park corresponds to the national park system that was to appear some years later. Within the park the statues created by Ward correspond to the Anglo-Saxon perspective on the New World. Leaving aside the *Seventh Regiment Memorial* of 1869, which was produced to meet pressing needs that grew out of the Civil War, we encounter in *Shakespeare* one whose muscular frame supports the gigantic intellect from which emerged the writings that united kinsmen no matter how widely dispersed over the globe they might be. One such tribe flourished in the hostile clime of Massachusetts; its representative is *The Pilgrim*, executed in 1884 at the behest of the New England Society in the City of New York. As he sets foot on the rocky shore, he brings to the wilderness the culture and art embodied by Shakespeare. His descendants will transform the barren expanses of the continent into a park. But Ward had further thoughts about their potential, ideas that accorded with those expressed by Bryant. "I think nearly every one in America has some idea of the value of art. I believe that our people are naturally more artistic than any other branch of the so-called Anglo-Saxon or North people. They have a native skill and certain other qualities essential to the make-up of either a sculptor or a painter."[63]

No such skill is likely to characterize *The Indian Hunter*, the first figure by Ward to be placed in Central Park. Presented to the city in 1868, it was based on a popular statuette that was modified, enlarged, and cast in 1866.[64] Before modeling the small piece in 1860, Ward traveled to the Dakotas to study the Indians in their native habitat. The resulting sketches were praised as being "amongst the most authentic aboriginal physiogonomical types extant in plastic art,"[65] and in this form, as well as in the finished works, the brow is far less lofty than that exhibited by the bard. A review in *The Crayon*, which Lewis Sharp believes may have inspired

Ward's Indian, is especially revelatory of the assumptions that were later to motivate the Central Park commissions. "Picture the group of Aborigines, who, hiding in the forest, wonderingly watched the landing of the Pilgrims. What attitudes for the sculptor. One of them, perhaps, crawling along on his hands and knees in the snow, holding one hand over his eyes to hide the light, and the other by his side, clutching his bow, peering cautiously through a vista at the approaching strangers. Suppose an Indian hunter in this attitude, crawling along in sight of his prey, beckoning back with his hand behind him his crouching dog, and holding with the other his gun." This is not to suggest that a single program guided Ward's various efforts; rather, there were in circulation during these years certain pervasive beliefs that surface in a variety of literary sources and works of art regardless of the influence, or lack of it, that one had on the other. Hence, the writer of the above description surmises that in the near future "the last red man will have faded for ever from his native land," [66] supplanted, one presumes, by those who trace their lineage back to the likes of Ward's Pilgrim. In one of those exquisite ironies of history, Ward's Dakota Indian was to witness in the early 1880s the construction of the Dakota apartments, so named for their remote locale.

When the National Sculpture Society was incorporated in 1896, it set as one of its objectives the duty of reminding the citizens of New York of their Anglo-Saxon heritage and destiny.[67] By this time the mission was already well under way, and it is important to recognize the place of Shakespeare in this effort. When the park was in its initial stage of development, George Templeton Strong wrote that its outcome depended on "Celts, caravans of dirt carts, derricks, [and] steam engines." [68] Bryant's dedication asked Americans whose "ancestors came from the Old World" to claim Shakespeare as their poet. It goes without saying that this line of reasoning excluded Native Americans entirely—they would eventually vanish from the land—but what of those Irish laborers whose strong backs effected the miraculous transformation of the landscape? Clearly, the cumulative intent of the park's statuary was to encourage them and comparable immigrants to acknowledge the ideology and identity of those who traced their ancestry to the Pilgrims.

In *Highbrow/Lowbrow* Lawrence Levine reminds us that the terms that serve for his title initially were put into circulation by phrenologists. The output of elevated foreheads such as Shakespeare's, he argues, furnished the older, more established portion of the population with a means for guiding the perceptions and aspirations of those new to these shores. His reflections on this development tell us much about the extreme reverence that characterizes Bryant's dedication speech. "Inevitably, in a heterogeneous nation in which the working classes were more and more composed of recent immigrant groups and migrant blacks, the ideology of culture assumed ethnic and racial dimensions."[69]

When Americans turned from the precipitous forehead of Shakespeare to that of Webster, they could take comfort in the notion that, however modest their personal endowments, they at least nestled among the foothills of this mountain range. Yet a rather large gap separated the two peaks, and a third was needed to complete the horizon. Who might serve as a transition between the colonial past, when England put its stamp indelibly on the continent's destiny, and the democratic present, which represented the fulfillment of the freedom-loving inclinations of the Anglo-Saxon race? The answer was readily apparent to anyone who posed the question: George Washington.

Accustomed from birth to comfortable surroundings, Washington was inured to hard work and privation by his stint as a surveyor in the backwoods of Virginia. Sound of body and mind, he was "no eccentric" but an adept in practical matters such as engineering, architecture, farming, soldiering, and statesmanship. The diversity of interests he pursued contributed to the regular growth of all his faculties, which were "large and active." If any area was more conspicuous than the rest, it was the prominence of the perceptive faculties over the reflective, while *Veneration, Firmness, Conscientiousness*, and *Spirituality* endowed the man with the steadfastness necessary to lead his ragtag army to victory.[70] Like Shakespeare and Webster, Washington possessed an auspicious brain that was large and uniformly developed. At most, the organs immediately engaged by his profession were only moderately more developed than the rest.

Washington Irving's popular biography of his namesake provides an example of phrenology's influence on perceptions of the hero. The general's "forehead," we learn, "was of that square mould that accompanies an executive mind, not swelling at the temples, as in the more ideal conformation of poetical men." One could hardly expect the seasoned warrior to be as generously endowed in *Ideality* as Shakespeare. Nor could the former match the latter in *Language*, as the following remark about his eyes confirms: "Not remarkably large as in persons of more fluency, . . . [they] foretold Washington's natural deficiency in language, proclaiming the man of deeds, not words." The years as a surveyor, however, left their trace on his features, for "the distance between the eyes [*Form*] marks a capacity to measure distance and appreciate form and the relation of space." With the sort of flourish common to members of the literary profession, Irving concludes by doubting the capacity of art to capture a soul so profound yet so reticent to reveal its depths.[71]

These words carried sufficient authority with Henry Tuckerman for him to repeat them verbatim near the end of his book on portraits of Washington.[72] The same message, sans doubts, is implanted in the text, with praise going to Washington's perceptive faculties in preference to his "sense of beauty" (*Ideality*). The critic then takes up the general's "sentiment of order" (*Order*) to stress its contribution to his various callings, assuring success of a kind that escaped the unfortunate John Wesley Jarvis.[73] Much that follows in Tuckerman's analysis of specific works depends on his conception of the general's verifiable "mental organization," which, he believes, artists are obliged to respect.

Jean-Antoine Houdon, the French sculptor, enjoyed the decided advantage of having visited Mount Vernon in 1785. Daily observation acquainted him with Washington's features and "his natural language."[74] In this matter Houdon succeeded where the Swedish painter Adolph-Ulrich Wertmuller failed. The latter gave the general an expression of superciliousness or surprise, neither being indicative of his "habitual state of mind."[75] To those who might object that Gilbert Stuart's famed images likewise exhibited a disparity between the configuration of the mouth and "the distinct outline of the frontal region" or "the harmonious dignity of the entire head," a question again of the natural language, Tuckerman responded that this circumstance was a consequence of dental loss and not an oversight on the artist's part.[76] Of further relevance to the themes reviewed in this chapter is the remark that Trumbull managed to portray the "ruddy complexion" that resulted from Washington's repeated exposure to the elements and his "Saxon blood."[77]

But Houdon's piece left much to be desired, for it lacked the "mathematical exactitude" one might expect to find in modern statuary.[78] By this criterion the bust cut by Hiram Powers (fig. 6.5) surpassed its predecessor because "the moulding of the frontal region so significant of extraordinary perceptive organs, would delight a phrenologist; there is an expansive candor in the open look, a sublime dignity in the air, an ingenuous and benign intrepidity in the whole aspect, that corresponds intimately with our exalted impression of Washington's character."[79]

Houdon's *Washington* figured significantly in Powers's calculations, causing him to request a photograph of the statue to "show me the true proportions of Washington."[80] Contemporaries, however, were less struck by the similarities between the two than by their divergence. The Frenchman, one wrote, had thrown the head back in "an arrogant, theatrical way," a fault Powers managed to avoid, thus endowing his piece with a "benevolent expression."[81] This observation draws its substance from tenets associated with natural language. When *Self-Esteem* was active, it did indeed

Figure 6.5. Hiram Powers, *George Washington* (1838–44, marble, Minneapolis Institute of Arts)

cause the head to move upward and backward in obedience to its magnetic pull.[82] The military commander who relinquished the prospect of kingship without qualm would hardly feel the tug of this faculty, though it came to play a crucial role among the populist leaders of a subsequent generation. *Benevolence*, the organ apparently designated by Powers's correspondent, inclined the head forward,[83] and the bust does just that, advancing the profile in front of the shoulders. Such adjustments did not contribute to the physical beauty of the figure, but they did enhance its moral stature and in this sense brought it into closer proximity to the ideal.

Above, Tuckerman emphasizes Washington's perceptive organs; else-

FIGURE 6.6. John Gadsby Chapman, *Portrait of George Washington* (1841, oil painting, collection of the New-York Historical Society)

where he again addresses this theme, appending his thoughts on the importance of physical fitness to the healthy consummation of a promising cerebral organization. The figure that caught the critic's attention was that of the young surveyor in a painting by John Gadsby Chapman (fig. 6.6), but the subject could just as well have been Asher Durand or any American who had found in nature an antidote to the debilitating effects of urban living.

Never had that vocation [of surveyor] greater significance. It drew the young Virginian unconsciously into the best education possible in a

FIGURE 6.7. Rembrandt Peale, *George Washington, Patriae Pater* (ca. 1824, oil painting, U.S. Senate Collection, Washington, D.C.)

new country for a military life. He was thereby practiced in topographical observation; inured to habits of keen local study; made familiar with fatigue, exposure, and expedients, incident to journeys on foot and horseback, through streams and thickets, over mountains, and marshes; taught to accommodate himself to limited fare, strained muscles, and bivouac, the woods, the seasons, self-dependence, and effort. This discipline inevitably trained his perceptive faculties, and made him the accurate judge he subsequently became of the capabilities of land, from its position, limits, and quality, for agricultural and warlike purpose.[84]

Tuckerman sought to emphasize the practical accomplishments of Washington by favoring his perceptive faculties, but the standard line tended to praise the fact that "he had no very shining qualities" while discerning greatness in the balance of all.[85] Rembrandt Peale advanced this thesis in his *George Washington, Patriae Pater* (fig. 6.7).[86] The year was 1823, and Peale, having passed midway through life's journey, determined to devote much of the remainder to this new venture. On examining various portraits of Washington, including those by his father, Stuart, Trumbull, and Houdon, he noticed certain discrepancies that he proposed to reconcile by establishing "the standard National Likeness." The resulting image was followed by many subsequent versions, all intended to prevent the hero's character from fading into oblivion.[87]

Peale's objective was to demonstrate "how far his [Washington's] corporeal features corresponded with his acknowledged mental and moral greatness,"[88] a goal that presumed such correspondences were indeed demonstrable. The date of the project's inauguration merits attention in our efforts to flesh out this rather meager report. It followed shortly after the establishment of a phrenological society in Philadelphia and the delivery of lectures on the topic at the Peale museum by Richard Harlan. These events occurred in 1822, and while Peale must have mulled over the theory earlier, the sudden outburst of enthusiasm among his fellow citizens apparently caused dormant ideas to blossom into a program that would now find a receptive audience. Nor should this accounting ignore the fact that 1822 also witnessed the publication of George Combe's *Essays on Phrenology* in Philadelphia.

This last event is particularly noteworthy because the book contains an introduction by John Bell, and his predilection for drawing on the world of art is again apparent here. He relies on phrenology to justify racial ranking. Why, he asks, did the Egyptians in their sixteen centuries of empire never approach the Greeks "in useful invention or tasteful decoration"? One need only "compare the head of a Copt with a Greek, of an African with an European," or "look at the Sphinx, and the Apollo" to realize that the latter in each instance embodied superior intelligence. There follows a passage that speaks directly to Peale's scheme: "It is a fact, not a little curious, that the ancient artists gave very generally to their gods and heroes, conformation of head corresponding with the present notions of Phrenology: thus Jupiter, the father of gods and men, is represented with an uncommonly lofty forehead: Apollo and Hercules are made to differ from each other, not more in their forms, than in the relative size of their heads and proportional development of these latter." In wording much like Peale's, Bell goes on to stress "this correspondence between cranial feature and affective quality," urging artists to respect the "harmony of proportion in . . . form and feature."[89]

These assertions tell us a great deal about Peale's reasons for including the head of Jupiter above that of Washington. As the former was "the father of gods and men," the latter was the father of his country, and in discussing antique busts of the divinity, phrenologists regularly take up Bell's ideas, stressing the immensity of the Olympian's forehead on the assumption that all faculties were equally developed and hence not in need of particularization. Gall's text, which incorporates Peale's observations on blacks in America, asserts that the ancient sculptors were accustomed to representing the heads of their philosophers, heroes, and gods as larger than those of their athletes or gladiators. This was especially true of Jupiter, and it was no accident that men of genius, such as Franklin, also exhibit a "strongly arched forehead" of remarkable extent.[90] The Jupiter Capitolinus is singled out for its "supreme intelligence"; any comparably endowed forehead would enjoy immunity from the superstitions that bedevil the ordinary mind.[91]

The same thought occurred to Spurzheim, who regarded Jupiter's forehead "more prominent than ever seen in nature,"[92] while Combe describes this feature as "piled up and spread out."[93] As noted in the first chapter, the latter's tour of Peale's studio in early 1839 included an analysis of the equestrian portrait of Washington, and despite the general's wig, the phrenologist remarked that "the anterior lobe of the brain is large in all directions," while concluding that Washington "was one of those rare specimens of humanity in whom nearly all the mental organs are largely developed, and in harmonious proportions."[94] In composing the *Patriae Pater*, then, Peale could expect a portion of its viewers to recognize Jupiter's brow as the epitome of wisdom, and this same audience would find much the same virtue embodied in their first president.

Comparisons between Jupiter and Washington were not uncommon, the most famous being Horatio Greenough's colossal work (fig. 6.8). The sculptor was rare among artists in contesting the claims of phrenology, an attitude seemingly encouraged by his confusion of the theory with polygenesis. Departing from the position of Morton and Agassiz, Greenough wrote that the similarities between the Chinese and North American Indians indicated that they were not distinct species. He simply could not "allow any phrenological observation the authority to shake this belief, for the Anglo Saxon skull has undergone changes on this continent equal to

FIGURE 6.8. Horatio Greenough, *George Washington* (1840, marble, National Museum of American Art, Smithsonian Institution)

the differences between different races."[95] The reasoning here is not entirely lucid but seems to question the tenet held by polygenesists (but not necessarily by phrenologists) that changes in the cranial structure of races occur at a glacial rate, if at all. In any case, this stance contrasts markedly with both Peale's embrace of phrenology and his assertion that the retreating foreheads and thick lips of the Egyptians he happened upon in Marseilles authenticated the types seen in the art of that ancient civilization.[96]

Greenough's image of Washington is essentially unphrenological in its premises. Followers of the theory certainly would have regarded his forcible merging of the two figures as muddled and incongruous in its welding of the mature presidential head to the athleticism of the divinity. Peale's solution, on the other hand, allows the viewer to compare, to recognize differences if any do indeed exist, and ultimately to verify the similarities for oneself. This approach resembles the experience granted the visitor to a phrenological cabinet where a variety of crania awaited judgment. By peremptorily uniting the two identities, Greenough precludes this possibility; authority simply descends from above, and virtue (Washington's or ours) consists in acknowledging the obligation to conform. Peale's more egalitarian spirit invites the audience to weigh the evidence and by such reasoning to participate in the very virtue that accounted for Washington's greatness.

Given the emphasis placed on the universal expansion of Washington's faculties, Peale may be excused if, like Chester Harding, he seems at times to exaggerate the size of the head. His equestrian portrait of 1850 (Dietrich Brothers Americana Corporation) exhibits this tendency, and it is just one of a number of images that testify to his growing preoccupation with the standard National Likeness, a concern that pushed him increasingly into the role of lecturer. While he does not mention phrenology specifically in this context, his criticism does reflect the absorption of its tenets. He takes Robert Edge Pine to task, for example, for making Washington's head too small and narrow. His assertion that the general's profile displayed "unsurpassed benignity" translates Combe's observations on the general's *Benevolence* into layman's terms. Houdon's miscalculations become obvious in this respect when we see how far he causes the chin to protrude, a pose, Peale contends, that makes the forehead appear more retreating than it actually was.[97] Compounding the error was the fact that it also countered the natural language of *Benevolence*, which inclined the upper part of the head forward. We have seen that Powers sought to make adjustments in this matter, and Peale's colossal profile based on the Frenchman's work (1857, Philadelphia Museum of Art) brings the chin into vertical alignment with the brow.

Peale intended to extend the ideas developed in the *Patriae Pater* to a number of paintings of great men. Likenesses of Benjamin Franklin and William Penn were planned, and those of *John Oliver* (1824) and *John Marshall* (1825) were actually executed, the latter with a head of Solon, the lawgiver, in the keystone.[98] In 1832 the portrait of Washington was acquired by Congress and stood in silent judgment over the nation's elected officials. Few could equal the hero's superb organization, as the following response by Horace Mann to Henry Clay's entry into the hall makes clear:

"I have been studying his [Clay's] head—manipulating it with the mind's fingers. It is a head of very small dimensions. Benevolence is large; self-esteem and love of approbation are large."[99] Peale's other images were doubtlessly designed to encourage this method of analysis, and a citizenry so alerted would have more than the promises of politicians to consult when selecting its representatives.

One would suppose that the life mask by Houdon (presently in the Pierpont Morgan Library, New York City)[100] would have settled any possible disagreements about Washington's features, but as Jared Sparks noted in his biography of the general, constant repetition from imperfect casts made it difficult to acquire an accurate likeness. His praise of the plaster bust offered by James DeVille for its fidelity provides another reminder of the service rendered artists by phrenology.[101] In addition to publishing treatises on the science, DeVille ran a large phrenological establishment in London, and like the cast of Coleridge discussed earlier with regard to the Boston Phrenological Society, his wares were intended to set a standard. Washington Irving recommended his copy of Houdon's mask to Emanuel Leutze, and on the author's word the artist acquired a copy. Unfortunately, the source of this account, J. R. Briggs, does not tell us when the encounter took place but does remark that he saw the cast in the artist's possession when the latter was at work in the Capitol, presumably on *Westward the Course of Empire Takes Its Way* in late 1861 or 1862.[102]

The problems associated with rendering American subjects when the artist was separated by the wide Atlantic from the land and its people was a topic of considerable interest to critics of Leutze. Could Dusseldorf offer models equal to the challenge? Not according to a reviewer for *The Crayon*, who complained of Leutze's *Washington Rallying the Troops at Monmouth* (1854, University Art Museum, Berkeley) that "the people are not Americans. There are fine studies of individual heads, but they are strikingly German—as unlike what we should expect a Revolutionary militia to be as could well be."[103] The round head of the Teuton bespoke his ingenuity but also betrayed (for reasons unexplained) a degree of cautiousness[104] that was scarcely consonant with the courage that inspired those who followed Washington. Along this same line is the well-known account given by Worthington Whittredge of his contribution to the famed *Washington Crossing the Delaware* (1850, Bremen Kunsthalle, destroyed 1943). Leutze was seeking American types for the heads and figures and pressed the recently arrived artist into service as the protagonist. The head, however, he painted from Houdon's cast (probably the one mentioned by Briggs),[105] and while that feature is protected from the elements by a hat, the evidence does suggest that Leutze was attentive to claims that the peculiar moral climate of a particular society left its mark on the physical organization of its citizens. The various members of the beleaguered crew whose features are exposed appease the phrenological eye, while *Washington as the Young Surveyor* (exhibited in 1852, Cooper Union, New York) grants a view of the future hero's uncovered brow when the perceptive faculties that were to prove so crucial to his future success were developing.

This tendency to skirt the borders of portraiture, genre, and history is also seen in Thomas Rossiter's series of paintings devoted to the family life of Washington. The artist consulted portraits by Houdon and Stuart and from these concluded that "like the head of Napoleon, Washington's will ever remain a standard from which to compare other men's cranial and facial combinations."[106] Since all the organs were equally enshrined in Washington's noble cranium, his "domestic faculties" deserved acknowledgment along with those that accounted for his military triumphs and statesmanship. The spate of images devoted to life at Mount Vernon evinces the appeal of this idea.

Modern eyes are likely to find these among the least appealing genre (history) paintings of the era. Inserted into a scene redolent of Victorian sentiment, the general, exhibiting the placid demeanor of Houdon's and Stuart's portraits, seems alien to his surroundings. Characteristic of this tendency is William Powell's *General Washington Receiving His Mother's Last Blessings* (fig. 6.9), but our inclination to find such subjects contrived and bathetic may ignore the feature that stirred the greatest admiration among contemporaries. The head that bows in filial devotion is the same that rose so conspicuously above the serried ranks throughout the throes of revolution. Crossing the hearth, the general doffs his tricorn, while the dutiful son can readily be espied by the campfires of those awaiting the morrow's battle; the setting may change, but physical constitution continues to divulge all the dimensions of character. Hence, the pamphlet that accompanied Powell's work alludes to the entire range of the virtues visible in the hero's uncovered brow. Often with genius "certain faculties are abnormally developed; appearing suddenly and in amazing proportions, as mountains are thrown up from the deep by the force of volcanic fires. They remind us of cloudy summits whose bold, irregular outlines and striking features are only softened and rendered comely when 'Distance lends enchantment to the view.'" Washington, however, numbers among the saviors of mankind. "Others may have arrested the world's attention by some abrupt phase of their development; possibly by a reckless success in the business of life; or by some peculiar angularity of mind; but Washington, especially commands our supreme regard on account of the grand equipoise of mental faculties and moral qualities which rendered his character sym-

FIGURE 6.9. William Powell, *General Washington Receiving His Mother's Last Blessings*
(1864, oil painting, New York State Office of Parks, Recreation, and Historic
Preservation, Senate House State Historic Site)

metrical, and his career at once a living illustration of constant action and
undisturbed repose." The author goes on to praise Washington's courage,
firmness, patience, comprehensive judgment, and familial affection. Then,
turning to the matriarch, he asserts that "no woman since the mother of
Christ has left a better claim on the affectionate reverence of mankind."[107]

Readers of this booklet were in effect treated to the phrenological line
on Washington. Even the remark about his mother has the ring of Orson
Fowler's theory of heredity; his observations on this good woman might
stand as a epigram to the picture. "Shall we venerate Washington," he asks,
"and not likewise his parents? Could he have been but for them?" Follow-

FIGURE 6.10. Richard Caton Woodville, *Old '76 and Young '48* (1849, oil painting, Walters Art Gallery, Baltimore, Md.)

ing up on this bit of wisdom he adds, "His mother was one of Nature's noblest women! In other words, she was admirably sexed; and hence her son's genius."[108] Powell testified to her worthiness by giving the superior organization of her son its due.

If the gilded phrases of Bryant's oratory could raise Shakespeare to the promise of bliss in the life to come, Washington bore comparison with the divinity who became a man. Charles Edwards Lester, for example, discerned in Houdon's bust a commingling of benevolence and severity that suggested an affinity with the Savior.[109] But the blessings he bequeathed did not flow equally to all, for the cult of Washington as it evolved in the antebellum years was closely allied with theories about race that were emerging at the same time. What might we hear, for example, if we could eavesdrop on the family gathered in Richard Caton Woodville's *Old '76 and Young '48* (fig. 6.10) and listen to the exchanges between the veteran of the revolution and his grandson, recently returned from the Mexican War? Presiding over the group is a bust of Washington, a progenitor whose like was unknown among the Mexicans. They were, in American eyes, a mongrel race whose intermarriage with the native population diminished their capacity to make productive use of the land, to say nothing of resisting the invaders from the North,[110] and words to this effect must pass among those assembled before us.

The likelihood that matters of race were on Woodville's mind is enhanced by the presence of a group of black servants who enter on the right. Returning for the moment to Crawford's pediment, it is apparent that the Indian (and his Mexican relatives) have now been expelled from the edifice, and in Woodville's painting, only Caucasians occupy the pyramidal grouping in the foreground. To see where the blacks fit in the picture, a glance at *Uncle Tom's Cabin* will convey some notion of attitudes then in circulation even in enlightened circles.

Stowe's novel relies on phrenology regularly to provide the psychological dimensions of the characters. Uncle Tom possesses "an organization in which the morale was strongly predominant, together with a greater breadth and cultivation of mind than obtained among his companions."[111] The particulars of that organization are not detailed, but his penchant for prayer (*Veneration*) and the repeated reference to his "benevolence" (*Benevolence*) fills the most optimistic profile for blacks drawn by phrenology.[112] His counterpart among whites is Augustine St. Clare, a talented, sensitive soul attuned to "the ideal and the aesthetic" and therefore appalled by the brutality associated with slavery. His own plantation is an exception in this respect, but he seems incapable of attending to its efficient management, a consequence, we learn, of his "balance of the faculties."[113] That balance is tipped in favor of *Ideality*, for not only is he responsive to the arts,[114] but his mansion has "been arranged to gratify a picturesque and voluptuous ideality."[115]

In accordance with phrenological teaching, Stowe gives these mental qualities a physical dimension. St. Clare's "blue eyes, golden hair, . . . Greek outline, and fair complexion" contrast markedly with the "black, fiery eyes, coal-black hair, . . . strong, fine Roman profile and rich brown complexion" of his twin brother.[116] These characteristics accord with the standard differentiation between the "Mental" and the "Motive Temperament,"[117] and St. Clare confirms the typology by remarking on his own "abstract ideality" while commending the "pride and courage" of his sibling. When the latter assures him that "the Anglo Saxon is the dominant race of the world," St. Clare worries that slaves whose mixed blood endows them with the "calculating firmness" of their father's race will bridle under servitude and eventually lead those of their mother's race in rebellion against their masters.[118]

One such individual is George Harris, the issue of an interracial liaison who manages to escape to Canada, shooting one of his pursuers in the process. When still in bondage he is "able to repress every disrespectful word; but the flashing eye, the gloomy and troubled brow, were part of a natural language that could not be repressed."[119] Were his masters alert to this natural language, they might have taken measures to prevent flight. He exemplifies Stowe's favoritism toward blacks of mixed ancestry,[120] while his opposite, "Black Sam," who is "three shades blacker than any other son of ebony" on the Shelby plantation,[121] is far more docile, scratching his "woolly pate" to no great end since it contains no "very profound wisdom."[122] One talent, however, is a source of considerable pride; Sam has "a habit o' bobservation" and reminds his companion, Andy, that this "makes all de difference in niggers." So endowed, he is prepared to "see what Missis wanted, though she never let on." Sam is sure that his habit is "what you may call a faculty," explaining, "faculties is different in different peoples, but cultivation of 'em goes a great way."[123] Phrenologists would have agreed, and they were inclined to regard the perceptive faculties of Negroes as among the most developed.[124]

Paradoxically, when Stowe wrote *Uncle Tom's Cabin*, she was not particularly familiar with blacks or the conditions of their existence.[125] Phrenology helped mitigate that want of knowledge by supplying information about mental orientation and its consequences on outward appearances. The importance of the latter for Stowe is suggested by the contention that her "vocation is simply that of a painter, and my object will be to hold up in the most lifelike and graphic manner possible Slavery, its reverses, changes and the negro character, which I have had ample opportunities for studying. There is no arguing with pictures, and everybody is impressed by them, whether they mean to be or not."[126]

Woodville, of course, *did* paint pictures, not under the influence of Stowe, whose novel appeared some years after his image was created, but certainly under the influence of ideas that were also important to her. The combative and aesthetic inclinations of the Anglo-Saxon race are confirmed by the bust of Washington, and we can read many of the same tendencies in the heads that are so prominently featured in the foreground. Again telling is the isolation of youth's profile; it begs commendation of its perpendicularity. Those in the shadows on the right are characterized by the "habit o' bobservation" which "makes all de difference in niggers." Their faculties cause them to watch attentively and respond appropriately, but they are not a part of the procession of history that so animates the conversation of their masters. The peripheral role of blacks in the progress of mankind is suggested by their location on the periphery of the composition, and the same inference can be applied to those whose misfortune it was to test the young warrior's steel.

The blood that united Shakespeare and Washington also flowed through the veins of Daniel Webster. As noted in the preceding chapter, fate had assigned him the task of preserving their legacy by thwarting the designs of secessionists. His command of language rivaled the former's; his statesmanship, the latter's; and when he gazed on the inhabitants of New Mexico in 1848, he judged them "infinitely less elevated in minds and condition than the people of the Sandwich Islands."[127] Manifest Destiny, then, was manifest not only in the seemingly empty lands that invited Anglo-Saxons to transform them into the garden of the world; it was also manifest in the physical organization of the contending parties. About the outcome there could be little doubt; the large-brained descendants of the bard of Stratford-on-Avon and the Cincinnatus of Mount Vernon would sweep aside those whose sole claim to the land rested on their present occupancy of it. Further, phrenology relieved the artist of the necessity of conveying such ideas in scenes of strife and conquest. One had merely to depict the head of one of these paragons to conjure up an entire ideology in the minds of contemporary viewers.

NATIVE AMERICANS

We have encountered Audubon's musings on the similarities between George Combe and Richard Harlan, Tuckerman's remarks on the affinities between Benjamin Paul Akers and Shakespeare, and Lester's thoughts about Washington and Christ. In *Moby-Dick* this method of comparison also serves Ishmael when, on encountering Queequeg, he seeks to learn something about his future shipmate and concludes,

> He looked like a man who had never cringed and never had had a creditor. Whether it was, too, that his head being shaved, his forehead was drawn out in freer and brighter relief, and looked more expansive than it otherwise would, this I will not venture to decide; but certain it was his head was phrenologically an excellent one. It may seem ridiculous, but it reminded me of General Washington's head, as seen in popular busts of him. It had the same long regularly graded retreating slope and above the brows, which were likewise very projecting, like two long promontories thickly wooded on top. Queequeg was George Washington cannibalistically developed.[128]

The last observation suggests that the "savage" was more expansive around the ears, especially in the region of *Destructiveness* and *Alimentiveness*, than his civilized counterpart, but the analysis assures readers that Ishmael's trust in the South Sea Islander is not misplaced.

However worthy his mettle, Queequeg was still the counterfeit of coinage minted with Washington's image, and in such passages Melville addresses an issue then much in circulation. If Caucasians were the gold standard of racial economy, who was silver? Who brass? For Harriet Beecher Stowe, those of mixed parentage represented the next step down, but for the moment let us look at those whose blood was unalloyed. In the visual arts, blacks were rarely cast in the heroic mold; that role was reserved primarily for Indians,[129] whose forceful resistance to incursions into their territories won the grudging admiration of whites.

A number of warriors gained celebrity status in the early years of the republic, and the response of phrenologists to their features did nothing to discourage such adulation. About Black Hawk, the chief for whom a war was named in 1832, one reporter wrote he possessed "a head that would excite the envy of a phrenologist—one of the finest that Heaven ever let fall on the shoulders of an Indian."[130] Perhaps no individual, however, proved more conducive to the alternating currents of admiration and disdain generated by whites than Red Jacket, "the last of the Senecas."[131] The very nature of the epithet attached to his name suggests the ambiguities associated with his reputation, for it evokes the melancholy cultivated by Romantics as they witnessed the demise of ancient tribal ways before the onslaught of civilization.[132] For most, the emphasis was on "last"; as long as the Indians were considered a dying race, the rhetoric of those who decried the adoption of European ways could be tolerated, even savored, as the crepuscular effulgence of a waning people. Red Jacket filled the bill. Famed for his harangues urging the continuance of ancestral customs, he was known as the Demosthenes of the forests.

These circumstances cannot have been far from Robert Weir's thoughts when the elderly Indian entered his studio in New York to pose for a portrait (fig. 6.11). The sitting had been arranged by Dr. John W. Francis, whose efforts on behalf of phrenology were recounted earlier. The figure rendered by Weir offers an imposing presence for one who had long passed his allotted three score and ten. His emblems include a tomahawk, for he shirked not the warpath when occasion demanded, and a large medal personally awarded him by George Washington. Something more striking still, however, caught the doctor's eye, as revealed in a letter to William Dunlap: "His characteristics are preserved by the artist to admiration; and his majestic front exhibits an altitude surpassing every other that I have seen of the human skull. As a specimen for the craniologist,

FIGURE 6.11. Robert Weir, *Portrait of Sa-go-ye-wat-hg, or Red Jacket* (1828, oil painting, collection of the New-York Historical Society)

Red Jacket need not yield his pretensions to those of the most astute philosopher. He affirmed of himself, that he was *born an orator*. He will long
live by the painting of Weir, in the poetry of Halleck, and by the fame of
his own deeds."[133]

Captivated by Weir's image, Fitz-Greene Halleck set pen to paper to see
if he could equal the painter's effort. Gazing on the "thoughtful brow,"
he mused,

> Its brow, half martial and half diplomatic,
> Its eye, upsoaring like an eagle's wings;
> Well might he boast that we, the Democratic,
> Outrival Europe, even in our kings!

The martial half of the brow alludes to *Combativeness* and *Secretiveness*,
visible in the painting thanks to the close-cropped hair, while the diplo-
matic and oratorical skills of the aged Seneca derive from *Language* and
allied faculties. Many of these same virtues, of course, belonged to Washington, but nowhere in the response to Red Jacket is there any mention
of *Benevolence*, that jewel crowning the general's forehead. Halleck dwells
rather on the wrath hidden beneath the outward composure (*Secretiveness*)
and the sorrow stemming from the realization that none will inherit his
name, passion, or throne.[134] Here indeed was a Washington, if not can-
nibalistically developed, then vengefully so. Praise was rarely bestowed
unstintingly on the Indian, and reservations were increasingly prompted
by perceptions based on physical organization.

Francis's evaluation found its way verbatim into William Stone's early
biography of Red Jacket,[135] and so it also appeared in the McKenney-Hall
book of American Indians. This volume adds the observations of a gentleman who encountered the famed chief in 1820 and reported that "his
forehead [was] lofty and capacious."[136] While citing Francis, Tuckerman
extols Red Jacket's "extraordinary cranium" and praises his inborn abilities as an orator.[137] All this had the sanction of Gall, who identified verbal
ability as a particular gift of the American Indian;[138] hence the romance
surrounding Red Jacket was in large part sustained by science.

These motives converged in George Catlin, the chronicler of Native
American culture whose ethnology is not without Rousseauian coloration.
His pilgrimage to portray Red Jacket in 1826 (Gilcrease Institute) takes
on added relevance when seen in light of the commotion stirred by the
latter's lofty forehead. The heroic features of the chief set Catlin thinking
about the need to rescue his people from oblivion.[139] What did that noble
face disclose to arouse such sentiments? Enough is visible beneath the
headdress to satisfy adepts of phrenology as to the orator's talents, but two

years passed before Francis and Weir alerted the world to this fact. Catlin's initial reaction on meeting Red Jacket can best be surmised by reviewing the experiences and training that prepared him for the encounter.

Active in Philadelphia at the outset of the 1820s, Catlin witnessed the halcyon days of phrenology in the city.[140] He befriended Rembrandt Peale as the latter embarked on his standard likeness of Washington,[141] and he was elected to the Pennsylvania Academy in 1824, when John Bell was holding forth on the doctrine's relevance to the arts. Evidence suggesting he absorbed this discourse comes from his account of Pigeon's Egg Head (fig. 6.12), a warrior encountered on his trip to Washington in late 1831. As chance would have it, the two met again after the Indian had relinquished his resplendent native costume, "which was classic and exceedingly beautiful," in favor of a military uniform given him by the president. Bell's admonishments about the detrimental effects of tight, unaesthetic clothing apparently conditioned the artist's reaction to this "full suit of regimentals." "It was broadcloth, of the finest blue, trimmed with lace of gold; on his shoulders were mounted two immense epaulettes: his neck was strangled with a shining black stock, and his feet were pinioned in a pair of water-proof boots, with high heels, which made him 'step like a yoked hog.'" Constricted from head to heel, with waist likewise confined by a thick belt, Pigeon's Egg Head seems blithely unaware of the price he must pay for his foppery. The reader learns that all this finery was soon reduced to tatters as the once-proud warrior took to the bottle and was finally killed as a wizard by tribesmen who thought his tales about the East intolerably tall. Although Catlin never attributes this harsh fate explicitly to habits acquired in civilization, the whisperings of Nemesis are audible throughout his narrative; the initial act of abandoning the healthful customs of his people swept Pigeon's Egg Head down a slope of folly and degradation to an end that somehow seems merited.[142]

The teachings of phrenology on physiology also inform Catlin's short treatise devoted to the subject. Amusingly titled *Shut Your Mouth and Save Your Life*,[143] the book extols the virtues of breathing through the nose. Again the artist condemns the customs of civilized society, specifically the overheating of bedrooms, which causes sleepers, especially infants, to gasp for air through their mouths, thus precluding the purification that occurs in the nasal passage. Much the same message was repeated in the jeremiads on ventilation and excessive heat in American homes delivered by the Fowlers. To this contention Catlin contributed his own observations gathered during his travels. Contrary to received opinion, he notes, infant mortality was actually lower among savages than among the civilized. The

FIGURE 6.12. George Catlin, *Pigeon's Egg Head (The Light) Going to and Returning from Washington* (1837–39, oil painting, National Museum of American Art, Smithsonian Institution, gift of Mrs. Joseph Harrison Jr.)

same might be said of idiocy, lunacy, crooked spine, and like deformities, all because Nature was so woefully ignored by urbanites.[144]

Catlin, like Durand, ventured into the wilds equipped with the precepts of Gall and Spurzheim, justifying his undertaking in terms that reflect this understanding:

The opportunity afforded me by familiarity with so many tribes of human beings in the simplicity of nature, devoid of the deformities of art, of drawing fair conclusions in the interesting sciences of physiognomy and phrenology, of their manners and customs, rites, ceremonies, etc; and the opportunity of examining the geology and mineralogy of this western and yet unexplored country, will enable me occasionally to entertain you with much new and interesting information, which I shall take equal pleasure in communicating by an occasional Letter in my clumsy way.[145]

If Catlin set out to supply physiognomists and phrenologists with useful information, one might assume he would have done so in the case of Red Jacket, but his report offers little that would assist either.[146] The reason for this reticence can be gathered from a letter sent by his sister Eliza to his wife, Clara. "My Baby is now 9 years old," she writes, "a smart lad I can assure you—his big head was a good one as Doct McCall of Utica said when George brought him to our house to lecture upon his Phrenological bumps."[147] The fact that an expert had to be consulted suggests that the artist appreciated the doctrine's utility but did not feel himself to be qualified to conduct examinations. As we have seen, Audubon also suffered such qualms. Both men were prepared to furnish others with relevant data but did not wish to subject their own knowledge of the theory to rigorous criticism. Nevertheless, the science furnishes a most intriguing subtext to Catlin's stated ambitions and is an essential feature in comprehending his perspective on the people he studied.

Catlin occasionally uses phrenological terminology to express notions that verge on the platitudinous. He applauds the prairie nomads for their undeveloped "acquisitiveness,"[148] while the uncultivated condition of the Indian mind, he notes elsewhere, grants the "uninterrupted enjoyment of their simple natural faculties."[149] A report by Major Dougherty is cited, however, to explain that only by schooling designed to inculcate working habits will their "intellectual faculties" be improved to a point where a transition to civilization might become feasible.[150]

The reader who remains cognizant of Catlin's phrenological leanings, however, will also recognize their presence even when the analysis does not delve into the particulars. At times he merely states he has rendered "the shape and character of the head" faithfully,[151] or that it is "fine and intelligent."[152] In the case of the Crow tribe, he is struck by the "semi-lunar" heads, which offer "exceedingly low and retreating forehead[s]"; yet Two Crows, an orator who exhibits this "peculiar" development, conducts his affairs with "extraordinary sagacity."[153] The conviction that Indians who most closely resembled Caucasians were handsomer and smarter than their brethren remained intact despite such experiences. Consequently, "the fine and Roman outline of head" found frequently among the Kioways raises them well above either the Camanchees or Pawnees in his estimation.[154] And when surveying individual members of a tribe, as he did the Wee-Ahs, he notes "intelligent European heads" whenever he encounters them.[155]

In discussing the custom of modifying the shape of an infant's head, Catlin addressed an issue that intrigued and perplexed phrenologists. Were such alterations bound to affect mental acuity, or did the faculties function normally despite their cramped quarters? Gall cautioned midwives against indulging their penchant for fashioning the soft skulls that literally fell into their hands, and he warned of the imbecility that might result. He did not ignore the example set by American Indians but remained by and large inconclusive about the consequences.[156] His examination of the *Instinct of Self-Defense*, however, offered an explanation that satisfied most followers despite the fact that it left the essential question unanswered: "Certain savage races seem to have a confused notion of some advantage in great breadth of this region of the head, and are in the habit of endeavoring, by means of pressure, to increase the breadth of their children's heads between the ears, in the belief that they will thereby become better fitted for war."[157]

Even those unacquainted with phrenology were often able to intuit its principles, and by widening the head around *Combativeness* and *Destructiveness*, a mother could fit out her future warrior with a semblance of ferocity that would later stand him in good stead. This reasoning sufficed for Samuel Morton when he sought to account for the flattened crania of ancient Peruvians he acquired from Titian Ramsay Peale.[158] After conversing with a member of the Cloughewallah tribe whose head had been modified by boards, George Combe surmised that *Destructiveness* and *Secretiveness* were well developed, while *Comparison* and *Causality* were unable to generate ideas of any consequence. The convolutions of the brain, he adds, had been displaced but not destroyed, and the intellectual powers retained "tolerable strength"; nevertheless, the implication that compression did diminish mental acuity remains.[159]

Catlin examines the custom in some detail, explaining that gradual pressure forced the occipital portion of the skull upward and the frontal section downward until the profile at the summit was no more than two inches in breadth. Despite such deformities, and despite personal disapproval, the artist cites witnesses who contended that the individuals so treated were "in no way inferior in intellectual powers to those whose heads are in their natural shape." Further, he is not persuaded that the practice imparts an air of ferocity.[160] Returning to the subject, he stresses the infrequency of the practice, adding that "the mental organs" operate effectively despite the change in form and position.[161] The subject as broached by phrenologists was clearly of concern to Catlin, but their reasoning did not inhibit him from offering his own conclusions.

Phrenology again enters Catlin's narrative when he recounts his experiences among the Mandans, a remote and fabled people inhabiting what is presently the region around Bismark, North Dakota. Enchanted by their ways, the artist remained longer with this tribe than any other, and they came to constitute the core of his romance about the Indian. An epidemic of smallpox in 1838 decimated the population[162] and seemed to destine it for the role of vanishing race, but Catlin's interest had its source elsewhere. Unlike their nomadic neighbors, the Mandans built permanent residences that they protected with fortifications. They were, in Catlin's words, a "civilized race," with light skin and hair of diverse shades. The women exhibited a "most pleasing symmetry and proportion of features; with hazel, with grey, and with blue eyes."[163] Their myths included a Deluge, the appearance and death of a Savior, and the transgressions of a Mother Eve,[164] while their language contained words of foreign origin, resembling Welsh. All evidence pointed to the conclusion that they were an amalgam of a native and a "civilized" race.[165] The clue to the identity of the latter came from the singularities of their tongue. Were they not descendants of Madoc, the Welsh prince who set sail in the early fourteenth century, never to return to his native shore? Could not this party have landed in Florida or at the mouth of the Mississippi, and then married into a local tribe?[166]

Evidence of northward migration came from abandoned towns farther down the Missouri, where Catlin encountered skulls arranged in a circle and left at the mercy of the elements in a manner typical of Mandan memorialization.[167] As he surveyed one such site, Catlin mused, "The great variety of shapes and characters exhibited in these groups of crania render them a very interesting study for the craniologist and phrenologist; but I apprehend that it would be a matter of great difficulty (if not of impossibility) to procure them at this time, for the use and benefit of the scientific world."[168]

Even at a distance Catlin could espy a variety of shapes that bespoke a diversity of character that, according to phrenology, appeared only where social evolution encouraged individuality.[169] Had he the discriminating eye of a trained phrenologist, he might have recognized the squared, broad skulls common among the Welsh and returned with unimpeachable testimony of Madoc's legacy.[170] Behind the glowing descriptions of the Mandans sent east by Catlin lurk assumptions similar to those advanced by Charles Caldwell in a work published some years earlier. Much of Caldwell's text is dedicated to the proposition that men are not all created equal, and that Indians in particular were constitutionally unfit for civilization, a condition mitigated only by intermarriage.[171] Those imposing palisades whose dark silhouettes stood out against the lurid sunsets that stretched across the endless prairie—were they not a dim reflection of the same genius that built the mighty walls of Conway Castle and carved the intricate fretwork of Tintern Abbey?

As a partisan of polygenesis, Catlin could find nothing in the history or "physiological traits" of the Indians to gainsay the theory.[172] If reviewers, then, found the artist's remarks about the Indian excessively sanguine,[173] the perception may have stemmed from recognition of the unacknowledged strains of scientific racism that run through his writings. Quite telling in this respect is Combe's account of a conversation with Catlin in which the latter voiced the same opinions expressed by Caldwell. The Scotsman notes the contradiction between the virtues Catlin ascribed to the natives and the scenes of cruelty and superstition he illustrates, and then continues,

> The pictures, as works of art, are deficient in drawing, perspective, and finish; but they convey a vivid impression of the objects, and impress the mind of the spectator with a conviction of their fidelity to nature which gives them an inexpressible charm. In the portraits, a few of the men are represented with tolerably good intellectual organs, and some of the women with a fair average development of the moral organs. The best, Mr. Catlin suspected to be half-breeds; but the great mass of pure Indians present the deficient anterior lobe, the deficient coronal region, and the predominating base of the brain, by which savages in general are characterized.[174]

Combe did not allow his misgivings about Catlin's abilities to intrude when the latter offered a gift of two skulls from the Blackfoot tribe, and these he donated to Samuel Morton, who found the "phrenological organ of firmness" large in one.[175] The constant pillaging of ancestral burial grounds, Catlin asserts, constituted one of the primary grievances of Indians against whites,[176] yet he was not above spiriting off skulls in the name of science.[177] Hence Morton's reference to this material can be regarded as a consummation of the years of travel in the West. Obviously, monetary considerations were never far from Catlin's thoughts, but he was also serious about furnishing the scientific community with the data it needed to conduct research. His own plans for an ethnological museum included a department devoted to crania so that visitors might trace the connections between physical constitution and mental character in both individuals and races.[178]

During his travels through Europe Catlin readily obliged the phrenologists who were eager to learn more about Native Americans. Shortly after his arrival in London in 1839, his host remarked in anticipation of a meeting with "Professor D, the phrenologist," that "this will be so rich to him—I would not miss him for anything in the world."[179] The subject of this remark was certainly James DeVille, but Catlin left no record of the actual encounter. He is, however, more forthcoming about his meeting in Manchester with Mr. Bally, Spurzheim's erstwhile collaborator and a sculptor in his own right.[180] Catlin describes him as "a gentleman of great eminence and skill in the science of phrenology, . . . who has one of the richest collections of casts from nature in the world."[181] To enhance these treasures, a sitting with the Ojibbeways who had joined Catlin's entourage in 1843 was arranged. The artist volunteered to be the first, "and when his features were covered with a mask of the soft composition, the diversion of the Indians was extravagant. They laughed immoderately, and their jokes were uttered with great fluency; every fresh simile or comment causing another burst of laughter. At length the operation having been performed on the white man, the old chief intimated that he was ready to go through the same process."[182] We are told in this report that the proverbial immobility of the Indian greatly facilitated the process, and Bally was soon able to offer his American guest a set of casts while keeping another for himself. Catlin concludes by hoping that the busts would "continue to be subjects of interest and value."[183]

In Paris Catlin granted an audience to a phrenologist who distributed gifts among the Native Americans and assured them he planned no witchcraft. His findings confirmed the same prominence of *Self-Esteem* that others had previously ascertained.[184] Of especial interest is Catlin's account of the Indians' response, since we are rarely informed on this matter when the sitters are not Caucasians. One member of the party, Jim, decided to turn the tables on the visitor by insisting that he submit to analysis. Finding the skull full of bumps, Jim extracted a great deal of humor at the phrenologist's expense by waving a large knife before his eyes. No doubt there was an element of camaraderie here, but one wonders if the Indian may also have seized the opportunity to dish up some of the same "medicine" that whites had so liberally bestowed on other peoples. In any event, the Frenchman was "delighted to get off without loosing his scalp-lock."[185]

Newspaper reviews suggest that appreciation of the phrenological dimension of Catlin's gallery was not limited solely to adepts of the theory. A critic for the *Philadelphia Herald and Sentinel* thought it an ideal place to "learn what are the dispositions and faculties which belong to the mind and heart of man."[186] The *East India Chronicle* touted the heads as "bold and highly intellectual, and remarkable for their phrenological developments,"[187] a response that reminds us how easily the science could be skewed to the settled opinions of the examiner. While defending Catlin against detractors who claimed he could neither paint nor draw, Charles Baudelaire, himself a dab hand at phrenology,[188] praised the expressions captured by the artist, adding, "the structure of . . . [the] heads is wonderfully well understood,"[189] an observation that goes to the heart of Catlin's enterprise.

THE PHRENOLOGY OF AFRICAN AMERICANS

The paintings by William Sidney Mount have long been praised for their eschewal of the standard caricatures of race so prevalent in his day. Recent analysis, however, stresses the artist's commitment to inequality and surveys the stereotypical behavior enacted by his figures.[190] His images do seem to rehearse the contradictions that arise when a close familiarity with blacks is constrained by a pervasive ideology.[191] Even the noble African American woman who commands the small craft in *Eel Spearing at Setauket* (1845, New York State Historical Association, Cooperstown) is not without ambivalent implications.

The scene is derived from Mount's childhood memories but introduces one significant change. Instead of representing the Negro male, Hector, who actually stood in the skiff's prow, the painter chose to represent a woman. Speculating on the reasons for this adjustment, Albert Boime proposes that a maternal type would have been less "threatening," while the force of Hector's personality, felt before racial attitudes had congealed, remains to impress the figure with its majestic bearing.[192] While this degree of intimacy was missing in Stowe's youth, she and the artist would no doubt have concurred about the mental attributes of the person, male or female, who was so plainly an adept in "the philosophy of a crane," to use Mount's words. One thus endowed would again embody Black Sam's faculty "o' bobservation."

The work of Harriet Beecher Stowe has been discussed in this chapter in order to articulate assumptions about race and phrenology as they influenced the arts. Similar assumptions are evident in Mount's work, but his figures have an experiential dimension rarely apparent in the writer's characterizations. This factor may obscure the racial agenda present in his

FIGURE 6.13. William Sidney Mount, *The Power of Music* (1847, oil painting, Cleveland Museum of Art, Leonard C. Hanna Jr. Fund, 1995)

paintings, yet his conflicted perceptions engender, if anything, a vitality of human presence that finds no precise equivalent in *Uncle Tom's Cabin*. Perhaps consideration of another painting will serve to clarify my meaning.

In *The Power of Music* (fig. 6.13) one of Mount's most dignified blacks leans against a barn door, enthralled by the strains of music wafting from within. It was this circumstance that prompted a critic to remark, "The phrenological hobby of the artist is apparent in the musical bump of the negro, whose organ of tune . . . has been much developed."[193] This judgment may derive as much from the figure's pose as from the critic's actual perception of an expanded faculty, but it has the advantage of coming from someone whose discussion of the hobby, studio, and personal appearance of the painter suggests a certain degree of familiarity with him.[194] The cumulative weight of these disclosures suggests that the reviewer's opinions reflect those of the artist.

Phrenology had long linked the prominence of *Tune* with the African race, and by virtue of this innate talent, blacks were endowed with the ability to listen to and recall music.[195] When Mount's painting was published as a lithograph by the firm of Goupil, Vibert & Co., their flier included comments by a reviewer who "never saw the faculty of listening so exquisitely portrayed as it is here. Every limb, joint, body, bones, hat, boots, and all are intent upon the tune."[196] But is this rapt attention to be condoned? We note to the right that an axe and jug have been set aside, signifying a chore postponed. Phrenologists not only listed the activities associated with the influence of a particular faculty; they also enumerated the "perversions" that might ensue should it become excessively powerful. Among the latter, Orson Fowler identified "excessive fondness for music to the neglect of other things" as a consequence of *Tune*.[197]

The influence of phrenology on Mount and Stowe varied according to the medium of expression favored by each. The latter never entirely disentangles herself from the stereotypes engendered by natural language, and even partisans of *Uncle Tom's Cabin* note its limitations in this respect.[198] In contrast, the artist was obliged by the theory to scrutinize the black face with an intensity that banished all the demeaning conventions then prevalent. Indeed, from this perspective, caricature could falsify character and might even elevate the intellectual capacity of the subject inadvertently. One would be hard pressed, for example, to identify a greater fidelity to the scrupulous reproduction of actual form than the skulls depicted in Morton's *Crania Americana*, yet such accuracy was intended to demonstrate the diminished abilities of the colored races. Since, as we have seen, Mount believed that his precise rendering of cranial structure placed him in the tradition of the old masters, he would have conceived his approach as more profoundly indicative of black inferiority than anything the popular arts could concoct.

In other words, we know how Uncle Tom behaves, but his appearance is largely a construct of the reader's imagination. Mount, however, was encouraged by his medium and the theories he had adopted to render an actual individual. Hence a dichotomy arises between that person's appearance and his behavior; the former is intelligent, reflective, and genial, no doubt the consequence of sympathies that arose as the artist carefully examined the model. That physical presence in the studio inhibited the lapses into conventional thought that were likely to overtake the writer as she sat alone and commenced her task. But the sensitive soul who appears in Mount's work is trapped in his natural language, and in this respect he is as much the victim of innate constitutional dictates as the martyr of *Benevolence* created by Stowe.

Perhaps even more indicative of these contradictions is a series of picturesque figures Mount composed for Goupil, Vibert & Co. to turn into prints. In *The Bone Player* (fig. 6.14), for example, scholars have remarked on the presence of both cliché and dynamic individual likeness in the same painting,[199] and again the resolution is found in the agenda of scientific racism (as opposed to the visceral racism of caricature) he sought to fulfill. That such considerations were indeed on his mind at this time is suggested by a letter in which he mentions another of the series, *Just in Tune* (1849, Museums at Stony Brook), and also thanks his correspondent for sending an autograph of George Combe, adding that it is a token "which I value."[200]

The pose of the bone player conforms to the natural language of *Tune,* which induces an "upward and lateral motion of the head (an indication of the position of the organ)."[201] The slight turn of the forehead does permit the viewer to inspect this faculty, located just above the eyebrow, advantageously. But the virtual identification of African Americans with the organ was not without qualifications. "Our colored population, especially at the South," Orson Fowler explains, "often make hills and dales echo with their peals of song, yet they never learn to sing scientifically, nor from notes, but by means of the instinctive exercise of this faculty."[202] The full potential of *Tune* could only be realized when it was exercised in conjunction with those intellectual faculties that enriched its simple melodies with harmony. Perceiving the narrow foreheads of the Negroes he encountered in America, Spurzheim surmised that, while they might sing better than whites, they would not "go far in music."[203] The rather primitive instrument wielded by the bone player indicates that his performance wants refinement, and while others in the series play banjo and fiddle, they are unaccompanied and without score, giving every indication that they depend on what they pick up by ear. Even the quality of educability, which serves as the theme of *Catching the Tune* (1866, Museums at Stony Brook), where one white whistles while the other follows along on the violin, does not appear to number among the possibilities open to the blacks depicted by Mount. In a letter to the Goupil agent in America, William Schaus, the artist remarked that he would just as soon paint "the characters of some negroes as to paint the characters of some whites," adding, "a Negro is as good as a white man as long as he behaves himself."[204] It is clear, however, that the parameters of behavior were far more restricted for blacks than for whites. The issue had as much to do with innate organization as decorum, and one can imagine that if a string quartet composed of blacks somehow managed to give a Beethoven concert at Stony Brook, the artist and his neighbors would have looked upon the event as a curiosity, if not an impropriety.

FIGURE 6.14. William Sidney Mount, *The Bone Player* (1856, oil painting, courtesy of Museum of Fine Arts, Boston, bequest of Martha C. Karolik for the M. and M. Karolik Collection of American Paintings)

In relating his life's story to William Dunlap, David Claypoole Johnston remarks that a propensity "to indulge in a hearty squall" during infancy was attributed "to an unusual development of the organ of tune." He goes on to question such "phrenological prejudices" and follows with a humorous disquisition on "bumps" that reveals little about his actual orientation toward the theory.[205] It does suggest, however, that he was not averse to using the doctrine as a vehicle of satire, and satire was much his stock-in-trade. Hence he devoted one of his famous *Scraps,* pamphlets that poked fun at the various fashions of the day, to phrenology. Published in Boston late in 1836 and again in early 1837,[206] *Phrenology Exemplified and Illustrated with Upwards of Forty Etchings* appeared when the tide of popularity for the theory was reaching flood proportions in the city.[207] Nothing in the text was designed to discourage the patronage of those caught up in the craze. Its humorous vignettes depict the activities, or natural language, promoted by the faculties, much as George Cruikshank did in a pamphlet on the same topic published a decade earlier.[208] In some instances Johnston's efforts are genuinely funny. *Time* depicts a condemned criminal, his time running out, gazing up at a noose, while the inscription reads, "The natural language of time, says Spurzheim, is turning the eyes upwards." This line is taken almost verbatim from the phrenologist[209] and constitutes just one of many examples that indicate the artist's familiarity with the writings of Gall, Spurzheim, and Combe.

Of particular interest here is the illustration of *Order* (fig. 6.15), with its officer calling a platoon to order. The composition is a variant of one he repeated on several occasions, the best known being the *The Militia Muster* of 1828 (fig. 6.16), which he exhibited in 1829 to some critical acclaim. David Tatham has sketched the background for such scenes in the satires, onstage and elsewhere, of the haphazard training received by civilian reserves during the early years of the republic,[210] but phrenology furnishes another means of entry into the subject.

Somewhere behind Johnston's motley assembly stands Hogarth's famed *The March to Finchley* (1749–50, Thomas Coram Foundation for Children), where, at least in the foreground, efforts at regimentation break down before the temptations offered by the brothel and tavern.[211] In essence the soldiers act upon Lockean motives; their confusion reflects the moral confusion of their environment. No such considerations operate in the images by Johnston. The order of "attention" goes out, and each man complies according to his innate ability to do so. Some succeed, while others scramble about as best they can; the latter, we may suppose, are the least

FIGURE 6.15. David Claypoole Johnston, *Order* (1837, etching, from D. C. Johnston, *Phrenology Exemplified and Illustrated with Upwards of Forty Etchings for the Year 1837* (Boston: D. C. Johnston, 1837)

FIGURE 6.16. David Claypoole Johnston, *The Militia Muster* (1828, watercolor, American Antiquarian Society, Worcester, Mass.)

endowed with *Order.* The interior promptings manifested here make an instructive contrast to earlier notions of the mind as a tabula rasa.

What remains undetermined is the relationship between the watercolor and the print. Was the former, executed almost a decade earlier, also inspired by phrenology? Or was the latter merely an expedient adaptation of a preexisting image? No definitive answer readily offers itself. Charles Caldwell lectured in Boston in 1828 while Johnston resided there, and the artist's letter to Dunlap indicates a familiarity with the discipline before 1834; both facts support but do not establish the first proposal.[212] Whatever the circumstances, the theme lent itself to phrenological interpretation and, at a minimum, furnishes an instance of a composition that acquired such associations as the doctrine's popularity grew. Mount's musicians adhere persistently to a single mode of behavior, fulfilling popular stereotypes as well as scientific prognostications; by contrast, Johnston's would-be soldiers act on a whole spectrum of motives that a weak or strong *Order* might induce. They are more individualized in their mental constitution than blacks and hence behave more diversely while also possessing the potential to learn and improve.

Since Johnston's sunshine patriots wear hats, conclusions about their phrenology come from the natural language they enact. Without the tip supplied by the artist, however, the case for the connection would be weak. In other instances the visual evidence is so compelling and so pertinent to the narrative that inferences hardly require the support of documentary evidence. One such work is Sanford Thayer's *The Connoisseurs* (fig. 6.17), a scene reminiscent of Mount's *The Painter's Triumph* but more given to satire than the latter. The standing figure wearing a fez makes a claim to being a self-portrait, while the rotund form of the prospective client bespeaks a familiarity with creature comforts unknown to the struggling artist. A pretty woman, perhaps a daughter or young wife, urges him to part with some of his lucre in the interest of art. As they discuss the merits of his piece, the artist glances beseechingly toward us, seeking our commiseration. The key to this little drama is found in the patron's head, which finds a close counterpart in the person of "Judas, Jr." (fig. 6.18), who typifies the want of *Benevolence.* Such individuals "care little for the happiness of man or brute, and do still less to promote it; make no disinterested self-sacrifices; are callous to human woe; do few acts of kindness, and those grudgingly, and have unbounded selfishness."[213]

Enough is visible beneath the artist's cap to assure us that he is adequately endowed in *Ideality* and *Sublimity,* and the round head of the woman, made especially apparent by the band she wears, renders her susceptible to the charms of his painting. The skull of the portly visitor,

FIGURE 6.17. Sanford Thayer, *The Connoisseurs* (1845, oil painting, Onondaga Historical Association, Syracuse, N.Y.)

21. BENEVOLENCE.

LARGE.
21

SMALL.

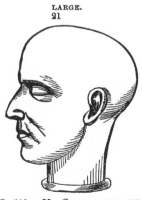

No. 166. — MR. GOSSE — GAVE AWAY
TWO FORTUNES.

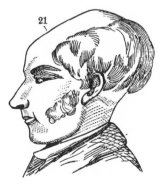

No. 167. — JUDAS, JR.

FIGURE 6.18. *Mr. Gosse and Judas, Jr.,* from O. S. Fowler, *The Practical Phrenologist* (Boston: O. S. Fowler, 1869), p. 122

however, exhibits no such developments, and his response is predictable. "Mr. Thayer," he seems to say, "your picture will add a touch of color to my dining room, but I cannot meet the price. It is simply too dear. Knock off a hundred dollars and throw in that thing hanging on the wall over there and we have a deal."

The operative word among Mount and his friends and patrons was "benevolence." They have the "bump of benevolence" well developed or are compared to Mr. Gosse, that paragon of *Benevolence*. Hence the artist in *The Painter's Triumph* can expect a generous offer to follow the unveiling of his latest creation. Poor Sanford Thayer, however, must sully his aesthetic soul by haggling with a man who is much better equipped than he for the effort. Several factors encourage this analysis. The unobstructed view of the client's profile and its close conformity to phrenological diagrams serve as the initial impetus. These clues reinforce the general tenor of the narrative, which is easily calculated due to the paucity of characters. Their fewness stands in marked contrast to the complexity of Bingham's elections scenes. Block proposed some time ago that the types encountered in these gatherings owed their diversity to the artist's knowledge of phrenology. He wisely refrained from attempting to specify further, for wanting fairly clear indications from the artist himself, the endeavor would soon likely become an exercise in circular reasoning, with the figure's activities providing the phrenological reading, and vice versa.[214]

MARRIAGE AND CHILDREN

In Mount's *The Sportsman's Last Visit* (fig. 6.19), two suitors vie for the favor of a lass who listens demurely to the contender on her right. As the title indicates, there can be little doubt about the outcome. The sportsman, hat on head and gun nearby, is about to depart in the face of the superior claims advanced by his rival. Courtship was then a popular theme on the stage, and this circumstance suggests a source of inspiration;[215] but so does phrenology. Among the institutions it sought to reform, marriage topped the list. They courted disaster who plunged into matrimony without giving thought to their own organic constitution or that of their intended. Where science supplanted caprice, the prospects of wedded bliss rose considerably because no hidden incompatibilities lurked to ensnare the couple after infatuation began to lose its initial luster. Of course, the children also had to be considered. An auspicious mating of harmoniously adapted parents boded well for the republic's future, and the choice Mount's heroine must make is ultimately of greater consequence than that offered the "sovereigns" of Bingham's election series.

The rough-hewn interior with its old-fashioned fireplace was based on

FIGURE 6.19. William Sidney Mount, *The Sportsman's Last Visit* (1835, oil painting, Museums at Stony Brook)

Mount's ancestral home in rural Stony Book, and we may infer that despite her Sunday finery, this woman is no stranger to household chores or the bracing lessons of Nature, an assumption reinforced by the sickle on the back wall. An article saved some years later by Mount alerts us further to the considerations his interest in phrenology would have inspired even at the early date of this painting. There, a "city belle" is described as she prepares to retire for the night by her "simple country" cousin. More ludicrous than lewd is the account of a disrobing that entails the removal of various paddings artfully contrived to conceal malformations of the spine and lower anatomy. "Let me be anything," laments the unfortunate, "anything, rather than the cold, heartless, artificial slave of fashion—anything but a belle."[216] None of that heartlessness mars the unfeigned innocence of Mount's maiden, nor have her days been frittered away before the mirror.

Her suitors are a study in contrast. The bemused sportsman, equipped for the hunt, is no match for his rival, who appears already to have captured his quarry. The latter's intelligent profile, with its thinning hair over a capacious forehead, ample sideburns, high collar, and black suit, resembles images of the Reverend Dr. Tyng (fig. 6.20), an exemplar of the blessings bestowed by lofty moral faculties. Mount did not necessarily intend to specify the identity of his protagonist,[217] but it seems fair to assume that he wished to appropriate much of the cerebral majesty exhibited by Tyng. The minister was commonly contrasted with the likes of Hagarty, a miscreant tutored in his murderous ways by an overweening *Destructiveness*. Mount's sportsman is not so inauspiciously organized, but his attribute, the rifle, and his weakness for the pleasures of the chase are common to emblematic representations of this organ. Further, by facing outward, the disappointed suitor invites assessment of the width of his head. Add the hand that scratches *Destructiveness*, a sure sign of excitement or confusion of the dominant faculty, and a more detailed reading of the narrative

FIGURE 6.20.
Rev. Dr. Tyng and
Hagarty, Murderer,
from O. S. Fowler,
The Practical Phrenologist
(Boston: O. S. Fowler,
1869), p. 110

No. 160. — REV. DR. TYNG.

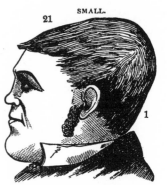

No. 161. — HAGARTY, MURDERER

results than might otherwise be possible.[218] The gentle humor that prevails is intended to impart a lesson the gravity of which differs appreciably from the satirical mode employed, for example, by Francis Edmonds. The comedy of manners enacted in the latter's *The City and the Country Beaux* (ca. 1839, Sterling and Francine Clark Art Institute, Williamstown, Mass.), where the affectation of both suitors is excessive, deprives the maiden of a meaningful choice.

Mount's phrenological hobby, already a matter of notice at this time, enabled him to employ a variety of devices and forms to enrich his narrative. Not everyone, of course, would have picked up on them, but their presence in Harriet Beecher Stowe's *The Minister's Wooing*, first published in 1859, permits us to trace their implications further. Like the scene staged by Mount, the novel addresses issues concerning the importance of complementary temperaments in couples contemplating matrimony. By this means, the phrenologists asserted, the defects of one partner could be compensated by the virtues of the other.

The setting for Stowe's narrative is New England shortly after the revolution, a golden age in the physiological history of the republic because domestic labors had not yet been relegated to Irish servants. The hearths of olden time looked like the one in Mount's painting. They provided far better ventilation than modern iron stoves and were tended by "women whose strong minds and ever-active industry carried on reading and study side by side with household toils."[219] One such person is Katy Stephens, an intensely "matter-of-fact" type who makes "an excellent wife" though one entirely devoid of every "particle of ideality."[220] She marries George Scudder, a man in possession of "a sublime tier of moral faculties" and hence one "of the order of dumb poets." Impractical and thoroughly repelled by the slave trade that proves the most lucrative means of commerce in Newport, George manages to thrive but attains none of the prosperity enjoyed by his less scrupulous neighbors.[221] Despite his unworldliness, or more precisely, because of it, he makes an excellent husband; his talents complement those of Katy, confirming the wisdom of "naturalists" that maintains that "every defect of organization has its compensation, and men of ideal natures find in the favor of women the equivalent for their disabilities among men."[222]

Just as the harmony between Raphael and the Fornarina produced great art, so the "statuesque beauty" of Mary, the daughter of Katy and George, affirms the sanctity of their union. Although adept at household chores, Mary inherits her father's predisposition for deep thought. The "cold New England clime" has honed her "religious faculties" to a sharpness that splits the hairs of Calvinist dogma with a finesse scarcely matched by other parishioners.[223] Her first love is James Marvyn, a youth who cuts an athletic figure and exhibits a "high forehead." He is organized, however, "to do battle with life," and in his "firm and determined mouth" we may recognize a measure of Andrew Jackson's tenacity.[224] Long voyages have endowed him with a knowledge of the world that leads him to regard the sermons of Dr. Hopkins, the local minister, as divorced from reality and consequently unable to meet the emotional needs of his flock.[225]

The disappearance and presumed death of James at sea permits the minister, a man of forty years, to court the affections of Mary. The forehead of Dr. Hopkins, with its "squareness of ideality giving marked effect to its outline," must resemble that of the Reverend Dr. Tyng. But this "ideality had dealt only with the intellectual and invisible"; in other words, the faculty had not been nourished on its intended object. Had the doctor lived in Florence and experienced the exaltation of its great art and architecture, his soul would have been "as rounded and full in its sphere of faculties, as that of Da Vinci or Michel Angelo."[226] Nevertheless, Mary's "veneration" induces her, after many misgivings, to accept Dr. Hopkins's proposal, and she is about to plight her troth when James, quite alive, reappears in town. Recognizing the depth of affection between the two, Dr. Hopkins releases Mary from her vows, thus allowing true love to run its course.

This gesture represents an abandonment of the abstract theology that previously had dominated the doctor's outlook in favor of the balanced philosophy taught by physical metaphysics.[227] It results from the recognition that in this world the spirit cannot be entirely divested of its bodily garb. Both Mary and Dr. Hopkins exhibit a predilection for the contemplative life. She needs someone like James to counterweigh the inclination of her faculties. A similar message runs through Mount's composition. Were the country lass to marry the sportsman, one whose rustic propensities match her own, neither would rise in mental or moral stature. By favoring the refined suitor, one whose organization vies with that of Dr. Hopkins, she effects the commingling of types encouraged by phrenology. Not only will her husband benefit from her innate practicality and good sense, but their children will inherit the strengths of both.

SCHOOL DAYS

Phrenology did not relax its vigilance once a couple was wedded. It also attended to the upbringing of their children, and education, like marriage, was an institution in dire need of reform. What might proponents of the theory think, for example, of Henry Inman's *Dismissal of School on an October Afternoon* (fig. 6.21)? Pervaded by a golden light that enkindles

FIGURE 6.21. Henry Inman, *Dismissal of School on an October Afternoon* (1845, oil painting, courtesy of Museum of Fine Arts, Boston, bequest of Martha C. Karolik for the M. and M. Karolik Collection of American Paintings)

the autumnal foliage, the setting reflects many of the qualities associated with the Hudson River School. To this landscape, however, the artist has introduced a sentimental note, as children dismissed from school gambol about in the great outdoors. Delighted by the evocation of innocence and youth, one reviewer observed, "The subject of the painting is an 'American District Schoolhouse' on the skirt of a wood, with children just released from their tasks, loitering to frolic on the hill-side ere they turn their steps homeward. A blithe and buoyant rout of Youngsters they are, and some of them beautiful withal, as ever set philoprogenitiveness a yearning for the honors of paternity." [228]

These sentences articulate an alternate approach to the criticism previously encountered. Instead of discussing the phrenology of those depicted, the writer focuses on the organization of the observer.[229] The sight of so many youngsters was bound to thrill *Philoprogenitiveness*, or *Parental Love*, as the Fowlers named it. Men were not immune to the promptings of this faculty that, when rendered emblematically, was often represented by a teacher surrounded by adoring students (fig. 6.22). And here the plot thickens. A sign over the schoolhouse door identifies the departing master as Ichabod Crane. On two occasions Irving supplies significant clues about the cranial form of this character. In the first he notes that Crane's "head was small, and flat at top"; in the second he adds that it exhibited only a "scanty strip of forehead."[230] Neither of these observations is complementary, but the mention of flatness suggests that more can be inferred than mere want of acuity. *Benevolence*, a necessary trait for effective pedagogy,[231] would find little room in a skull so shaped. The feebleness of this faculty and that governing the love of children is confirmed by the "sound of the birch" that regularly interrupts the drone of daily recitations. Ichabod was not one to spare the rod,[232] and while Inman's composition might appeal to the *Philoprogenitiveness* of viewers, its protagonist would be unlikely to respond similarly.

At the outset of his career Irving mused that Gall's system proved "your whorson jobbernowl; is your true skull of genius."[233] This statement suggests that the reader might have access to personality traits that remain unperceived by the characters themselves. One such individual is Ichabod Crane, a teacher who has embarked on a profession for which he has no innate affinity. This fact fans the fires of ardor that burn for Katrina Van Tassel, a beauty whose inheritance would free him from the onerous duties of his present occupation were they wed. As things stand, he wields

FIGURE 6.22.
William Howland, *The Good
Schoolmaster Illustrated*
(*Philoprogenitiveness*), from
American Phrenological Journal
17 (1853): 12

the switch with an alacrity that qualifies him for the fraternity of school-masters who appear regularly in paintings of the antebellum era.

The colorful foliage of Inman's scene sets the stage for the events of "a fine autumnal afternoon" recounted by Irving. A Negro servant, perhaps the figure on the left, delivers an invitation to Ichabod Crane to join the Van Tassels in a "quilting frolic." The news transforms the pedagogue's usual lethargy into earnest purposiveness as he hurries through lessons so he can rush home and prepare for the evening's festivities. The nimble err with impunity while the slow are hastened through their recitations by judicious applications of the rod until the moment selected by Inman arrives. "Books were flung aside without being put away on the shelves, ink-stands were overturned, benches thrown down, and the whole school was turned loose an hour before the usual time, bursting forth like a legion of young imps, yelping and racketing about the green, in joy at their early emancipation."[234] Outwardly all seems quite genial, but viewers familiar with the story would know that the events take place in circumstances of neglect prompted by the self-interest of the teacher. This is not a routine dismissal; it has been advanced an hour and is conducted with unseemly haste. Some of the delight reflected in the children's faces no doubt derives from their having escaped the control of a tyrant who rules his tiny kingdom, according to the critic cited above, with a "birchen sceptre."[235] These developments serve to emphasize the fact that the locus of *Philo-progenitiveness* is in the viewer's relationship with the children and not between them and their schoolmaster.

To this point a variety of approaches have been employed to identify the phrenological content residing in works of art. When the artist confesses to the influence, the issue is relatively straightforward. Somewhat more speculative is the evidence of contemporary criticism. If the artist did not announce the connection, at least someone did, and this proves a significant feature in mapping the taste of the time. This mode of interpretation has just been applied to Inman's painting; however, the conclusions in this instance are reinforced by the artist's own interest in the theory. When such data is not available, compelling similarities to the diagrams found in texts, as in the case of Sanford Thayer's work, may sanction the drawing of inferences, and of course these methods are not mutually exclusive.

In selecting Winslow Homer to test another means of probing visual imagery, I want to stress from the outset that he was temperamentally adverse to the wild-eyed utopianism of the antebellum era. His enthusiasms were not worn on the sleeve in the manner of Mount and Powers. But this fact does not preclude the possibility that he documented the impact phrenology had on his environment. In other words, like the

FIGURE 6.23. Winslow Homer, *Snap the Whip* (1872, oil painting, Butler Institute of American Art, Youngstown, Ohio)

Impressionists, he may have recorded recent changes in society and its material circumstances without giving vent to his feelings toward such developments.[236] The detachment cultivated by his French counterparts often introduces an element of ambivalence into their imagery; likewise, Homer's attitude toward his subjects is frequently a matter of conjecture. To be more specific, his taciturnity was legendary, and he rarely furnishes clues about the implications of his scenes. The historian, then, must draw whatever conclusions the evidence warrants. Homer's caricature of his father, for example, suggests a visit to the Fowler museum, but his words tell us nothing about his views on the theory. One suspects he approved its prescription of exercise and fresh air as an antidote to the confinement endured by modern professionals, but even were this not the case, we might still find evidence of phrenology's influence on American life in his paintings.

A comparison of Homer's *Snap the Whip* (fig. 6.23) with Inman's painting of almost thirty years earlier reveals that the world of education had not stood still in the interval. Unlike the children who have been dismissed early to satisfy the whim of Ichabod Crane, Homer's students enjoy recess. They rid their lungs of stale air and invigorate themselves after intervals of sedentary study. We sense here a more nurturing environment and a schedule that is more regulated than the one that prevailed in Sleepy Hollow. What might account for these differences?[237]

During the Jacksonian era it became increasingly apparent that the education system prevalent in America tended to reinforce the disparities of class and thus undermined the pretense of equal opportunity so dear to apologists of the republic. The well-to-do went to private academies, while children of meager means attended public schools, if such were available. The latter offered rudimentary instruction in physical facilities that left much to be desired. Few qualifications were required of the teachers, and one historian cites the example of Ichabod Crane as typical of the benighted and often brutal individuals who entered the profession.[238] The festering of such conditions was perilous to the body politic, and increasingly voices were raised in favor of the "common school." If improved instruction for all were offered in a single institution—hence the appellation "common"—the ills of modern democracy might be remedied. The familiarity between persons of differing social status would diminish class antagonism, while the more demanding curriculum would prepare young minds for the responsibilities of citizenship.[239]

Shortly after Spurzheim arrived in Boston, he set about visiting schools and suggesting measures that would ameliorate conditions. Education, he intoned, should address the physical as well as the moral development of the child, and opportunities for recreation should be a regular part of the schedule. Teachers ought to heed the counsel of *Benevolence* when disciplining students, for coercion was usually ineffective.[240] The Boston Phrenological Society made sure that the wisdom of its mentor would not go unheeded and to that end published reports calling for improved ventilation and playgrounds for the city's schools.[241] The favor shown these ideas became pervasive during Combe's tour of America. In December 1839, for example, he delivered a course on phrenology to fifteen hundred teachers from the Boston area.[242]

Horace Mann, "the father of the American common school," was among the most receptive of those who flocked to hear the phrenologist's words. Shortly before his appointment as secretary of the Massachusetts board of education in 1837, he had been reading Combe's *The Constitution of Man* and reflected that in the next century its author would "be looked back upon as the greatest man of the present."[243] "There will be a new earth, at least, if not a new heaven," Mann wrote Combe, "when your philosophical and moral doctrines prevail."[244] The reports he prepared annually are often interlarded with the phrenological wisdom he hoped would usher in this millennium.

To raise the level of instruction, Mann became an advocate of normal schools, institutions designed to teach the teachers.[245] Women were encouraged to apply because the "domestic faculties" fitted them for the calling, and Mann saw their entry into the schoolroom as a victory of nature over custom. However powerful their "reflective faculties" might be, they were a deformity, he wrote, when not "over-balanced and tempered by womanly affections";[246] hence the opening of new professional opportunities for women was hastened by phrenology.[247]

By introducing physiology into the curriculum of normal schools, graduates could impart its tenets to their young charges.[248] The common schools would then serve as the primary vehicle for spreading information about hygiene to the populace, and Mann extended this principle to his annual reports. There, for example, in words that should, by now, have a familiar ring, he berated the Chinese custom of swathing the foot at birth and the practices followed by the Flathead Indians: "And the victim of Chinese fashion may as well expect to walk or dance with the grace and lightness of a Camilla, or the tribe of Flatheads to attain the intellectual stature of Lord Bacon, or Dr. Franklin, as anyone can expect to enjoy vigor of body, buoyancy of spirits, or energy of intellect, who is doomed by any tyrant whether law or of custom, to interdict the free motion and enlargement of this vital organ, the lungs."[249]

Following Combe's doctrine of ascent from physical to mental concerns, Mann gave physiology priority over all other subjects.[250] Classrooms were to be properly ventilated, for impure air "benumbs and stupefies every faculty,"[251] and ample opportunity was to be afforded for recess.[252] Previously such considerations had gone "almost completely neglected in the schools," and in contemplating "the major role of physical education in our schools and colleges today," one authority notes, "we would do well to remember that it mostly began with phrenology."[253] Even after Mann's resignation in 1848, these issues continued to occupy the board of education. A report published in 1866, for example, commends physical exercise on the grounds that "the mind is invigorated, quickened and strengthened, in a great degree, and the physical nature and moral and intellectual faculties are brought into a healthful and vigorous exercise that they may be educated together and in harmony."[254]

Homer entered the Cambridge school system in 1842, just as the tide of Mann's reform was sweeping Massachusetts.[255] At age six he could hardly comprehend the consequences of the changes going on about him, but their continued influence during the following decades must have had some impact. Whether or not he brought these ideas to *Snap the Whip*, he did bring the eye of the flaneur, albeit one far removed from the usual urban haunts favored by this type. Like his paintings of blacks at this time,[256] Homer's school scenes divulge much about social conditions without indulging in the kind of explicit attitudinizing seen in most genre paintings of the time.

I know of no painting from the antebellum era where children play with the sheer exuberance seen in *Snap the Whip*; even the escapees in Inman's work are restrained by comparison. The same might be said of the youths who appear in images by Bingham, Mount, Edmonds, or Blythe. None exhibits the same vitality and unbridled delight in physical sensations; none enjoys the uninhibited freedom of movement momentarily experienced by those cast off the whip. They whoop and halloo, gallop and tumble, and generally fill their lungs with fresh air as prescribed by reformers. Though not as rambunctious as the boys, the girls with their hoop are also encouraged to join in the activities. All this takes place in a large playground such as Inman's Ichabod Crane did not think to provide his pupils.[257]

The recreation enjoyed by Homer's children should not be seen as antithetical to their book learning, for as Mann stressed, "energy of intellect" depended on the unrestrained exercise of the lungs. Also crucial was the quality of air inhaled in the classroom after recess was over, and again Mann's words and Homer's composition offer intriguing similarities. The reformer recommended that during recess the doors and windows be left opened to ventilate the interior,[258] and the artist complied, leaving the door ajar and the window propped up.

Stepping inside the classroom, we also encounter an environment different from that prevalent in the antebellum era. The men who once dominated have been replaced in Homer's work by women, a development that reflects Mann's understanding of the female brain. In *The Noon Recess* (1873, Warner Collection of Gulf States Paper Corporation, Tuscaloosa, Ala.), one has kept a student inside while the others, seen through the open window, play vigorously in the sunlight. Whatever the misdeed, the boy can thank Mann for having campaigned successfully for the restriction of corporal punishment to a last resort. The threat of birching, which hangs so ominously over Ichabod Crane's tiny fiefdom, has been dispelled.

In the *Blackboard* (fig. 6.24), the curricular innovations advocated by Mann appear. He required candidates at the normal schools to demonstrate a command of the blackboard in order to delineate letters and sentences, to make diagrams that would facilitate the explanation of concepts, and to teach drawing.[259] Education should address all the faculties, and the last of these proposals would benefit *Form* among others.[260] He also thought the endeavor a moderate form of physical exercise capable of consuming some of the excess nervous energy prevalent in children

FIGURE 6.24. Winslow Homer, *Blackboard* (1877, watercolor, National Gallery of Art, Smithsonian Institution, gift [partial and promised] of Jo Ann and Julian Ganz Jr. in honor of the fiftieth anniversary of the National Gallery of Art)

as a consequence of their relatively large proportion of brain to body.[261] Cambridge adopted the measure in 1849, but its consequences for Homer are not known.[262] In any case, he would not have seen the designs on this blackboard during his school days, since they belong to a course of drawing devised in the 1870s by Walter Smith.[263] The painting does testify, however, to the expanding field of knowledge believed necessary for a basic education, a development for which phrenology could take some credit.

Imagine for a moment that you are Horace Mann inspecting some school. You have entered the room depicted by Homer (for the sake of argument, we will ignore the fact that you have been dead for eighteen years): how would you evaluate this teacher? Her placid demeanor is commendable, for transcendental medicine inclines you against an ardent or declamatory presentation. Ladies frequently lack "self-possession," especially when they seek to impress an audience, a misfortune that arises from "having the organ of cautiousness, or love of approbation too much excited, so that they absorb the whole force of the mind, and leave nothing by which the other faculties can be worked."[264] The subject before you is the source of no anxiety in this respect. And the head! How wonderfully it is organized! The reflective faculties are quite adequately developed, but look at the "domestic affections." See how they bulge out behind the ear and overbalance mere intellect! There is but little distance from the ear to *Amativeness*—again, an auspicious sign.[265] Her posture, however, cannot go unnoticed. That slouch is precisely the reason you rebuked Mr. Pierce, the principal of one of the normal schools, for having added an extra hour of study time to the weekly schedule. Did he not know how many "young virgins are sacrificed" in this manner?[266] Your present subject, unfortunately, tends to confirm what Mrs. Stowe wrote about the American woman: "Her arms have no exercise; her chest and lungs, and all the complex system of muscles which are to be perfected by quick and active movement are compressed while she bends over book and slate and drawing-board; while the ever active brain is kept all the while going at the top of its speed."[267]

Homer's precise thoughts while composing this image are unrecoverable, but his aesthetic is comparable to European realism in its desire to record the economic and cultural factors that were transforming society. In Homer's case this ambition caused him to examine the physiological characteristics of different peoples, and if one were writing a book on the topic, it might begin by noting the contrast, then almost a commonplace, between perceptions of the frailty of American women and the buxom health of their English cousins.[268] Did this belief condition his response to the fishmongers of Tynemouth? His early biographer, William Howe Downes, states that Homer found there "young women [who] are not nervous types; they are almost phlegmatic," and these he brought back to the rugged Maine coast where similar environmental conditions as well as racial affinities eased the transition.[269] His later women exhibit a greater robustness than the rather delicate types of the 1870s. What we might consider the adoption of a stereotype, contemporaries would have regarded as a probing of the deeper connections between race, climate, and custom. These factors were of particular consequence for women, since the happiness of future generations was largely the outcome of the nurturing they received in childhood.

CONCLUSION

Ideas of such significance were bound to find their way into the monumental medium of sculpture, and a return to Crawford's pediment for the Senate suggests how they could be integrated into a program intended to project the nation's image of itself on its most hallowed ground. While modeling the Indians, the sculptor ran into the same difficulties encountered by others who attempted this feat while residing abroad. After viewing a set of photographs of the statues in progress sent from Rome, Captain M. C. Meigs, supervisor of the Capitol project, noted the want of authentic types and suggested several publications that might be consulted. Late in 1854 Crawford replied that he was in possession of a cast of "the entire face and head of Osceola the Florida chief," adding that it would secure "in my heads the requisite qualities."[270] Whence came this treasure and what were the qualities it exhibited?

During the Second Seminole War, Osceola earned wide renown for his resistance to the advance of whites into his ancestral lands. He was eventually captured and held in Fort Moultrie, South Carolina, where he died in 1838. The attending physician, Dr. Frederick Weedon, immediately removed and embalmed the chief's head. In justifying the measure the doctor claimed that science was in need of such specimens, contending that even a cabinet containing the skulls of ancient Greeks and Romans would welcome this addition.[271] A cast was made and soon attracted the attention of local phrenologists, one of whom noted that the large development of *Destructiveness* and *Combativeness*, common among Indians, was surprisingly counterbalanced by a prominent *Benevolence. Amativeness* was not remarkable, but both *Philoprogenitiveness* and "Inhibitiveness [*sic*]" were, while the "perpendicular" profile of the forehead was likely to ensure that casts would be "eagerly sought by Artists and men of science."[272]

This prophecy came to pass in the person of Thomas Crawford, and his reasons for valuing the cast can be surmised by comparing the above appraisal with one given of another warrior who fell in the same war that claimed Osceola. The head, we learn, was "one leavened mass of destructiveness, and the basilar region of his brain was so spacious that every other bad quality appertaining thereto found an equal room in it, and merged all difficulties about *Bumps*; while the moral and intellectual organs were supposed too insignificant to merit attention—his forehead, however, though retreating, was strongly marked by the perceptive organs." [273]

The contrast between this more or less typical profile and the noble brow of Osceola explains Crawford's enthusiasm for the latter. It should also blunt some of the modern criticism directed at the finished piece for being too classical in face and form.[274] Phrenology alerted contemporaries to nuances that are less apparent to us, and in Osceola's case the head was comparable to those of the Greeks and Romans.[275] Here, then, was an opponent worthy of "high" art and of the pioneer whose axe fells the forest pedimental. Further, among the requisite qualities the sculptor would have found in the cast were *Philoprogenitiveness* and *Inhabitiveness*, virtues that corresponded well with the proximity of children and the warrior's reluctance to abandon his tribal lands. The dignity of this head enhanced the tragic melancholy of the seated figure, and to eyes attuned to the tenets of phrenology, the natural language associated with this sense of loss would have been less appropriate in one whose features departed significantly from the European mold.

On the far left, opposite the grave that beckons the forest dwellers, is the mechanic. He is followed by a teacher with his student, then by two youths "advancing to devote themselves to the service of their country," then by a merchant, and finally by a soldier of revolutionary vintage. The schoolmaster is reminiscent of illustrations of *Philoprogenitiveness* and of the reforms of Horace Mann. Crawford met Mann in 1843, and what he did not learn from the reformer directly, he would have gleaned from Samuel Gridley Howe, Mann's cohort in the struggle for improved schools and, as mentioned, the artist's brother-in-law.[276] These two men were instrumental in making education relevant to the needs of a progressive democracy, and their thoughts influenced Crawford's when he came to render the subject in marble.

Mann called his reforms "American" to distinguish them from the social stratification prevalent in European educational systems.[277] This characterization accorded perfectly with Crawford's intent to celebrate the "Progress of American Civilization." More specifically, Mann's approach, which addressed both body and mind in seeking to adapt the faculties to their use in this world, was widely promoted as a boon to manufacturers. He advised them that a common school background enhanced the productivity of mechanics and improved the state's economy. To prove his point he collected endorsements from factory operatives in Lowell and elsewhere testifying to the greater efficiency of workers who had received an education, many of whom had ascended from the ranks to assume managerial positions. In gathering this data Mann claimed his purpose was "to show that education has a market value."[278]

Such thoughts inspired the left half of Crawford's pediment, where the classics and "dead" languages that prepared the elite for the church and the bar find no place. Instead, by means of the practical schooling advocated by phrenologists,[279] the mechanic can aspire to become the merchant, as do the two boys who, on leaving school, dedicate themselves to their country. The merchant, in turn, benefits from the labors of the educated mechanic whose goods are competitive around the world, a concept embodied by the globe atop the stack of merchandise. Here productivity and patriotism march hand in hand, declaring the business of America to be business.

Although it would be misleading to insist that every portion of the Senate pediment was carved at the behest of phrenology, one further bit of evidence does suggest its pervasive influence. In reviewing the plaster figures before they were cut into marble, one critic took up a theme so frequently repeated in these pages that it hardly requires commentary: "Prominent among these models is the Genius of America, represented as a female of giant proportions; her dress, not hooped, but loose and flowing; nor is her waist wasp-like, under the assumed compression of a corset! Her breathing apparatus being free from exterior pressure, she exhibits in her countenance no symptoms of pain from obstructed respiration."[280] The "athletic figure of [the] backwoodsman"[281] who stands to her left must have sprung from loins such as these, and Crawford's pediment would almost seem to answer Whitman's manifesto:

> These American states strong and healthy and accomplished shall receive no pleasure from violations of natural models and must not permit them. In paintings or mouldings or carvings in mineral or wood, or in the illustrations of books or newspapers, or in any comic or tragic prints, or in the patterns of woven stuffs or any thing to beautify rooms or furniture or costumes, or to put upon cornices or monuments or on the prows or sterns of ships, or to put anywhere before the human eye indoors or out, that which distorts honest shapes or which creates unearthly beings or places or contingencies is a nuisance and revolt. Of the human form especially it is so great it must never be made ridiculous. Of ornaments to a work nothing outre can be be allowed. . . .

But those ornaments can be allowed that conform to the perfect facts of the open air and that flow out of nature of the work and come irrepressibly from it and are necessary to the completion of the work. Most works are most beautiful without ornament. . . . Exaggerations will be revenged in human physiology. Clean and vigorous children are jetted and conceived only in those communities where the models of natural forms are public every day.[282]

That this subject loomed large in the minds of contemporaries can be surmised from Horace Mann's conviction that "the doctrines of human physiology have come in just in season to save the race from destruction. Had their advent been delayed much longer, it is doubtful whether men would have been able to discover them at all."[283]

Along with pride in the accomplishments of Anglo-Saxons came anxieties that were nearly as pervasive. In 1620, the *American Phrenological Journal* notes, the race numbered but 6 million; now (1860) it had increased tenfold and was fast absorbing or displacing "all the sluggish races or barbarous tribes of men."[284] This is the story of Crawford's pediment, but what was the price for all the mental effort expended on the left? Would the scholar, mechanic, and merchant be able to match the vigor of the woodsman? Only if the proper regimen was followed, one that would yield, in Mann's words, "a race of men and women, loftier in stature, firmer in structure, fairer in form, and better able to perform the duties and bear the burdens of life."[285] Hence the centrality of the personification of America; from one so garbed would come the masses needed for expansion on a global scale.

The Senate pediment, then, provides an apt summation of the themes covered in this chapter. It employs the vanishing aboriginal population as a foil to what was the primary subject of art devoted to racial superiority, the Caucasian race. But where does Topsy fit in this grand scheme? In *Uncle Tom's Cabin* her features likewise serve as a foil to those of Eva in the following passage: "There stood the two children representatives of the two extremes of society. The fair, high-bred child, with her golden head, her deep eyes, her spiritual, noble brow, and prince-like movements; and her black, keen, subtle, cringing, yet acute neighbor. They stood the representatives of their races. The Saxon, born of ages of cultivation, command, education, physical and moral eminence; the Afric, born of ages of oppression, submission, ignorance, toil and vice!"[286] Eva, of course, is doomed to an early grave, and Stowe is careful to delineate the hereditary factors that contribute to her demise. Her spoiled and indolent mother, Marie St. Clare, represents all that is wrong with American womanhood in the author's eyes. Marie's fevered brain constantly contracts the symptoms of one imagined disease after another. This ploy permits her to indulge every whim, running the house slaves ragged while neglecting her own daughter. An overwrought "nervous system" renders her unequal to the slightest adversity, "one snuff of anything disagreeable being, according to her account, quite sufficient to close the scene, and put an end to all her earthly trials at once." [287]

Marie St. Clare is the antithesis of the Scudder women in *The Minister's Wooing*, for she lacks the strength, the "steady nerves, [and] healthy digestion" that were once the birthright of "Yankee women." Idleness causes her misery, but its consequences extend to her child. The "laws of descent" ensure that "the woman who enfeebles her muscular system by sedentary occupation, and over-stimulates her brain and nervous system . . . perpetuates these evils to her offspring. Her children will be born feeble and delicate, incapable of sustaining any severe strain of body or mind." [288] If the Scudders' happiness stems from the diversities of their constitutions, the St. Clares are too alike. Both are "fine-grained, [and] their children . . . too precocious." [289] In summing up his precepts on hereditary descent, a subject that occupied him from the outset of his career, Orson Fowler paid particular attention to "Anglo-Saxon Love-Making Errors." Among these was the fact that "our marriages are far the more unhappy than those of the bulk of mankind." [290] Into such a household comes Eva, and soon she must depart.

Topsy exhibits no such frailty and gives every indication that she will be around long after the narrative concludes. But her future and that of her kind does not find its way into Crawford's pediment. The absence of blacks in this setting confirms their marginal status in the fine arts of the antebellum era. And just as they have no place among the brood of an uncorseted America, so they were ignored by physiological treatises, a fact reflected as well in Stowe's work. We are given ample information about the congenital factors that contribute to little Eva's demise, but Topsy repeatedly claims she "never was born . . . never had no father nor mother." [291] These words epitomize in an oblique manner the convictions held by whites, even those of liberal sympathies, about the generation of black children. Untroubled by tasks that tax the brain and unswayed by fashion, blacks did not deplete the vital resources that assured healthy childbirth. It was, in effect, needless to inquire about parentage, since one was unlikely to discover those quirks and flaws that were integral to the individuality and intellect of Caucasians.

This brings us, finally, to that remarkable last line in the passage from

Whitman included above. Healthy children are jetted and conceived only where the public has daily concourse with images of natural form. In effect this concept places art at the core of human progress. To understand the reasoning behind this notion, we turn in the next chapter to the form that embodied the highest aspirations of nature, the ideal nude.

7

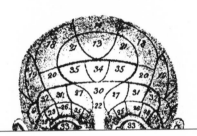

Clear from Our
Very Organization

The warm reception accorded the *Greek Slave* (fig. 7.1) during her nationwide tour in the late 1840s marks a watershed in American culture. Why did this demure nude bask in enthusiastic acclaim when her predecessors had withered before either wintry indifference or blistering criticism?[1] Some change in the social climate induced the public to check its inhibitions at the gallery door and gaze unabashedly upon the disrobed captive. A pamphlet distributed at the exhibition facilitated this response, but this expedient was just part of a larger crusade conducted by the sculptor, Hiram Powers, and the phrenologists to alert Americans to the value of nudity in art. This chapter examines this campaign and its impact on the larger enterprise of creating the ideal figure in the antebellum era.

The pamphlet mentioned above includes an article written

FIGURE 7.1.
Hiram Powers, *Greek Slave* (1846, marble, in the collection of the Corcoran Gallery of Art, gift of William Wilson Corcoran)

by the Reverend Orville Dewey in which the slave is described as "clothed all over with sentiment, sheltered, protected by it from every profane eye."[2] But such eloquence could not dispel the figure's sexual allure,[3] and while the statue met the criteria of ideal art, it also spoke to the more instinctive needs of its beholders. These seemingly antithetical values were reconciled in physical metaphysics, which sanctified the jetting and conceiving of healthy children as the central sacrament of the progressivist's creed; hence the hushed reverence so often described as prevailing among the slave's viewers need not have precluded feelings of a less elevated nature.

Taken captive by the Turks during the recent war of independence, the slave finds herself exposed to the bidder's calculating gaze. A cross by her side bespeaks her moral rectitude, while a locket, presumably containing the image of a lover lost to the ravages of battle, adds a note of pathos. The pose quotes that of the *Venus de' Medici*, an exemplar widely cherished by Victorians, in order to place the figure securely within the realm of Art. These facts are regularly cited in modern histories, where they serve as a prelude to an analysis that usually finds little to redeem the piece. A standard textbook of American art, for example, claims that "without the libretto she remains an ungainly and bloodless manikin."[4]

The repetitiveness of this criticism derives, I believe, from the inordinate weight given Dewey's characterization. All too often historians imagine that the recitation of this mantra grants them the indulgence of taking a few gratuitous whacks at Victorian prudishness, but this approach ignores an abundance of critical discourse that endeavored to establish a meaningful social context for the slave. We have seen that Powers's interest in phrenology dovetailed with his religious beliefs, and on this basis alone the remark about a bloodless manikin seems undeserved. Add to this the further contention that the statue is a "routine adaptation of the *Medici Venus*" and "a triumph of shrewd Yankee merchandising," and the impression is one of an extreme negativity unwarranted by the evidence. Whatever else we may say about the slave, she is the outcome of prolonged meditation on the creator's part, and the depth of these convictions is not sounded by facile commentary.

Phrenology alerted Powers to the frailty of American women, and his reflections on the subject, as we have seen, were motivated by religious and physiological teachings. A passage concerning his statue of Eve bears quoting in this regard because it indicates how the entire body could become an arena where the struggle between good and evil, nature and artifice, unfolds.

Eve might shock the sensibilities of many who found the Slave quite as much as their moral feelings could bear, for Eve is quite "naked," and she does not appear in the least "ashamed." It was very wrong to make her so, but it is now too late to correct an error which Eve herself discovered in season for fig leaves and managed to set all right where all was wrong before. I forgot to do so until too late in the season to get any, and so I had to send her off naked as she came from the chisel of her maker. I trust she will not corrupt the morals of her more perfect and less sinful descendants. She is an old fashioned body, and not near so well formed and attractive in her person as are her granddaughters, at least some of them. She wears her hair in a natural and most primitive manner, drawn back from her temples and hanging loose behind, thus exposing that very ugly feature in woman, the temples. Her waist is quite too large for our modern notions of beauty, and her feet—oh, murder! They are so very broad and large! Did ever a body see such long toes! They have never been wedged in form by the nice and pretty little shoes worn by her lovely descendants—and then how ugly she would appear with clothes on—so ridiculously flat and perpendicular below the waist behind. It would require a cart-load of cotton at least to correct this real formation. But Eve is very stiff and unyielding in her disposition and I am afraid she will refuse to conform to improved ideas of her more refined daughters. In regard to her hair, she prefers convenience to fashion, and she is willing to expose as much of her face as was left destitute of hair by her maker. She will not allow her waist to be reduced by bandaging because she is far more comfortable as she is and besides, she has some regard for her health, which might suffer from such restraint, upon her lungs, heart, liver, etc., etc. She says that in her day women were never seen with such enormous developments in their rear below the waist, and she wonders if it be real or fictitious. In either case, she thinks it decidedly ugly and vulgar, but some allowance ought to be made for these crude notions of hers, founded as they are on the . . . absurdities of primitive days. I could never prevail upon her to wear modern shoes, for she dreads corns, which she says are neither convenient nor ornamental, and as for her nudity, she does not appear to know that she is so, by thus it would appear that she has forgotten the fig leaves.[5]

Much of this derives from phrenology, and although Powers never put his ideas into a single, comprehensive statement, a review of his letters and published remarks reveals a consistent aesthetic deeply indebted to

the theory. In this light, Antonio Canova's *Venus Italica* (fig. 7.2) epitomized the fallacies inherent in traditional aesthetics. Along with the anatomical inaccuracies Powers found in this famed statue, he also criticized the work based on qualitative criteria. The facial angle he judged almost simian, and the distance from the chin to "the organ of self-esteem" was found excessive.[6] A glance at the profile does indeed reveal a posterior region that looms up over the anterior, and the elaborate coiffeur, which Powers disparaged as being "arranged by some French hair-dresser," only compounds the error.

The diagrams published by Erastus Dow Palmer in *The Crayon* some years later were based on much the same premise. While a large *Self-Esteem* and *Firmness* might be commendable in Andrew Jackson, when "prodigious" in a woman (fig. 7.3), she was likely to "be devoted to her own family or particular friends in a way to gratify her personal pride."[7] By contrast, the cranium of the *Greek Slave* displays no such commanding irregularities. Almost circular in profile, it epitomizes feminine virtue, and as in the portraits, the bun is located over the domestic faculties. The close conformity of the hair to the shape of the skull in this and other ideal works caused Lorado Taft to remark that one looked "bald."[8] Adepts of phrenology, of course, would admire the arrangement as conducive to the most comprehensive analysis of the figure.

It was not modern sculpture alone that failed to meet Powers's standards. Like the phrenologists, he took the *Venus de' Medici* to task for its "insipid" expression and insignificant head. "No woman with such a cranium," he declared, "would have sense enough to keep out of a fire."[9] During a stay in Florence, Nathaniel Hawthorne was apprised of the particulars that led the sculptor to this conclusion. A small cranium, yes, but beyond this the forehead was less than mediocre and the ear too low.[10] The latter observation indicates that *Combativeness* and *Destructiveness* were unduly developed for womanly needs and hence inappropriate for ideal art. The author then examined Powers's busts of *Proserpine* and *Psyche* and, after some discussion, acknowledged the greater "beauty, intelligence, feeling, and accuracy" of the modern works.[11]

The Greeks sensed the inner life of the spirit but dimly, Powers told Henry Bellows, and being unaware that the brain was the organ of thought and the seat of the soul, they modeled the head and hair only perfunctorily. It was folly to suppose one could improve on nature, and the real

(Opposite)
FIGURE 7.2. Antonio Canova, *Venus Italica* (1804–14, marble, Palazzo Pitti, Florence, Italy, Alinari/Art Resource, N.Y.)

challenge, as he so often repeated, was to discern her true intentions beneath all the contrivances of fashion. The task was daunting, but science proved a trustworthy guide in avoiding the snares set by convention.[12]

THE BODY OF THEORY

The testimony of contemporaries gives every indication that they were alert to this philosophy when they viewed the *Greek Slave.* They regularly remarked on the differences between it and the famed Venus of antiquity, praising especially the larger head of the former.[13] William J. Clark made much the same point when he sought to distinguish the merits of each, explaining, "It is exceedingly interesting to note that the head is unmistakably American in its type. Consciously or unconsciously Powers refused to go to either ancient or modern Greece for the head of his ideal Greek Slave, but chose a type with which he was more abundantly familiar."[14]

The modernity of the *Greek Slave,* then, resides not merely in the relative contemporaneity of the subject but also in the style. She and the *Eve* were acclaimed by one correspondent for "their assimilation to the spirit of the age."[15] Another wrote of the latter that she was "the Venus de Medici of the new world, if not her eclipse in the Old."[16] To belabor Powers's work for its

SELF-ESTEEM.—THE HAUGHTY LADY.

FIGURE 7.3.
Self-Esteem—The Haughty Lady, from *American Phrenological Journal* 17 (1853): 36

similarity to the Venuses of antiquity, as is often done, is rather like disparaging Manet's *Olympia* for its reliance on Titian's *Venus of Urbino*. In both we are asked not only to recognize the allusion to an older prototype but also how old and new differ. The upshot of this process is a heightened appreciation of the novelty and relevance of the figure. The reaction of viewers to Palmer's *White Captive*, a piece that shares Powers's ambitions, illustrates the response both artists hoped to elicit. "It is original, it is truthful, it is American," wrote one reviewer, "our women may look upon it and say, 'she is one of us,' with more satisfaction than the Greek women could have derived from the Venus de Medici, with its insignificant head and its impossible spine."[17] Likewise, the large head of the slave made her "one of us."

It was not just the head of the *Greek Slave* that rewarded close scrutiny; the body also invited similar examination. Powers, however, was generally satisfied with the physical constitution of the *Venus de' Medici* but was less sanguine about the condition of contemporary women. They were asked to evaluate themselves in light of the example offered by the marble nude, and if their eyes chanced to wander to the apparel draped by the slave's side, another lesson might be imparted. The garment has been identified as the kind worn in Greece at the time,[18] and the smart set could learn much from its lack of hoops, bustle, and whalebone corset. The words of Charles Caldwell are particularly relevant here: "Instances of crooked spine have been fearfully multiplied in fashionable female circles of Europe and America, since the beginning of the present century; while in Greece, Turkey, Persia, Arabia and other parts of Asia, as well as Africa, where no tight forms of dress are thought of, it is almost unknown."[19] Again critics were cognizant of the sculptor's intent, as Henry Tuckerman indicates when he explains that Powers rendered nature as she would present herself "if freed from the conventional blights and boundaries of custom and error."[20] The proximity of dress and healthful body invited inferences about cause and effect.

More was involved, however, than the constraints imposed by fashion, for the anatomy was also subject to emanations transmitted by the brain. To demonstrate this point, Lawrence MacDonald, a Scottish sculptor who befriended George Combe, compared limbs from two ancient statues, one of a virtuous character, the other lascivious, and found that while the first excited moral feelings, the second gave rise to baser sentiments.[21] Such uniformity intrigued the phrenologists, who illustrated, for example, the influence of a "Chuckle Head" on the appendages (fig. 7.4). Powers had this notion in mind when he told Charles Edwards Lester that "the mind forms the features after its own fashioning, and they vary, as a man's character varies."[22] The maxim is crucial to the assessment of his work.

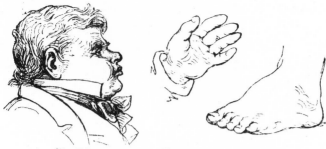

FIGURE 7.4.
A Chuckle Head, etc., from Samuel Wells, *New Physiognomy* (New York: Samuel R. Wells, 1868), p. 742

Fig. 1043.   Fig. 1044.   Fig. 1045.

A chuckle head, a chuckle hand, a chuckle body, and a chuckle foot.

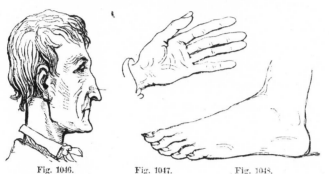

Fig. 1046.   Fig. 1047.   Fig. 1048.

A long head and face, a long hand, a long body, and a long foot.

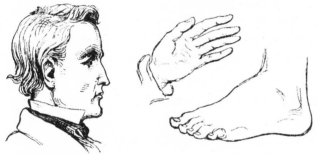

Fig. 1049.   Fig. 1050.   Fig. 1051.

A well-formed or symmetrical head, body, hand, and foot.

The phreno-mesmerists were particularly committed to this doctrine, and none surpassed Joseph Rhodes Buchanan in drawing the connections between mind and body. His science of "Sarcognomy" unriddled the occult language of the entire organic constitution.[23] What resulted was more elaborate than the system devised by Spurzheim and Combe, but in principle the two were not irreconcilable. Buchanan proposed that the moral implications of the bodily frame corresponded with those of the brain. The upper regions in each served the spiritual needs, while the lower attended to the animal functions. Likewise, the anterior mental faculties emanated their positive energy to the front of the torso, while the posterior sentiments prevailed behind.[24]

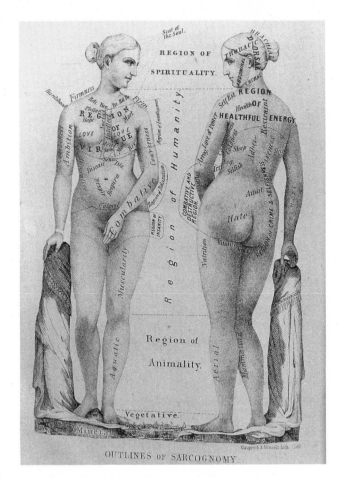

FIGURE 7.5.

Buchanan's System of Anthropology, from Joseph R. Buchanan, *Outlines of Lectures on the Neurological System of Anthropology* (Cincinnati: Buchanan's Journal of Man, 1854)

The diagram devised to illustrate these theories is certainly one of the most startling and revelatory documents about art to come down from the antebellum era (fig. 7.5). Besides illustrating a scale, ascending from mineral to spiritual, of susceptibilities to "nervauric" (mesmeric) influences, the *Greek Slave* maps the entire body in terms of the phrenological faculties. One can only imagine the tact required to locate the corporeal outlet of *Love,* and what could have signaled the location of its opposite, *Hate*? However eccentric it might appear, Buchanan's diagram tells us much about the principles that guided the statue's creation as well as the criteria by which it was judged. No doubt Powers would have disagreed with many of the particulars of the chart, but the underlying concept would have seemed reasonable. Indeed, where else will we find a more graphic demonstration of the unveiled soul? Behind these correspondences stands Swedenborg, for both Buchanan and Powers realized that the Swede's theories offered a standpoint from which phrenology surveyed the spirit's influence on corporeal form.

As noted in the chapter on landscape, transcendental medicine obliged its practitioners to specify what others often presumed was understood. Buchanan's diagram alerts us to the complexities of thought underlying Powers's masterpiece. With it we may begin to wriggle out from under the weight of conventional wisdom and see the statue afresh. Certainly the Reverend Dr. Dewey's words are apposite,[25] but a moratorium on their quotation might inspire scholars to think for themselves and abandon the tiresome condescension toward Victorian theories of sexuality that prevails in discussions of the slave.

It cannot be entirely accidental that the tour of the slave and the publication of Buchanan's illustration coincided with the acquisition and division into territories of vast lands that previously belonged to Mexico. The comparison of Palmer's *White Captive* to the landscapes of Frederic Church, or the head of Webster to Niagara Falls, derived from ideas about the microcosm that might also be applied to the slave as mapped by Buchanan.[26] If the head corresponds to the populous regions of the eastern seaboard, the financial, nervous hub of the union from which flowed the iron rails of commerce, the region of *Virtue*, with its gently swelling landscape, might be said to be the Catskills or the White Mountains of the body, where man resides peacefully in the bosom of nature. Traversing these ranges, we pass through a Cumberland Gap and enter an environment that is less welcoming. Crossing the low lands, the westward pioneer faces the climactic episode of his venture, the challenge of the cordillera of human flesh rising in the *Combative* and *Destructive* region. This is also a region of *Crime* and *Selfishness*, where desperadoes lurk in the shadows, ready to descend on the unsuspecting traveler. Without a reliable guide, he might get lost in the region of *Insanity*, from whose dark declivities many an innocent never returns. Should he survive unscathed, he will have proved his manhood.

The motive for drawing these parallels is less frivolous than may appear on first reading. The one realm Victorians found more mysterious and more awe inspiring than the primeval forests and towering mountains of the West was sexuality. Contrary to the claims of conventional criticism, Powers's statue was *not* not about sexuality;[27] it was a forthright attempt to provide the guidance needed in this unchartered region. Not among his options, however, was the rendering of orgasmic ecstasies of the sort favored by Rococo artists. Roger Cooter's point about phrenology being an effort to inscribe middle-class values into the very structure of the brain can be extended here to include the physiology of sex. This territory could not simply be ignored or denied, nor could it be left untamed; it had to be annexed to the realm of reason. Animal passions could serve positive ends if they were guided by the mind. Sexuality, the Fowlers claimed, was subject to natural laws that were as unrelenting as the law of gravity.[28] This brings us back to the analogy of empire building. To enforce laws, jurisdictions must be drawn as a means of legitimating the authorities tasked with the duty of reining in the promiscuous and unruly frontier elements. The charts designed by Buchanan and other phrenologists were likewise an attempt to mandate the boundaries governing the most volatile personal experiences, to circumscribe physical passion within acceptable parameters. While these attitudes may seem masculine and paternalistic, they actually enjoyed greater currency among women, as we shall see.

The notion that the entire figure was resonant with the same spiritual forces active in the mind helps explain the popularity of sculpture devoted to portions of the anatomy, a phenomenon that has often baffled scholars. Powers executed, for example, several replicas of the slave's right foot, and *Loulie's Hand*, a piece inspired by his infant daughter, sold many copies.[29] One authority characterizes these pieces as the "macabre" outcome of "fetishism"; another, commenting on the marble hand by Powers, sees it as emblematic of "the miracle of birth and childhood."[30] Contemporaries, however, would have discovered levels of meaning unanticipated by these explanations, drawing on phrenology to decode the soul's communications.

This predisposition appears in the letters Miner Kellogg sent while traveling through the Near East. He regularly reports on the natives encountered on his journeys, often to the exclusion of the monuments and picturesque locales he must have seen. In Egypt, he tells Powers, the women are "well formed," wearing loose garments while carrying large jars of water on their heads. Their feet are "well formed with small ankles," and he has yet "to see one having as large ankles as the Venus D' Medici."[31] From Constantinople, the presumed site of the slave's travails, he sent a long disquisition on the virtues of Swedenborg's "transcendental anatomy."[32] So when we learn that George Calvert, an adept in phrenology, possessed a cast of the right big toe of Powers's *Eve*,[33] it is fair to conclude that he felt capable of reconstructing the entire physical and moral constitution of the subject from this small clue.

A search for the larger implications of the *Greek Slave* ultimately leads to the Fowlers because they knew Powers and could have informed him personally about their theories of sexuality.[34] Suggestive in this respect are the frequent references to his work in their texts, but it should be noted that their philosophy of procreation was merely an elaboration of ideas available in the writings of Spurzheim and Combe. The latter's *Con-*

stitution of Man considers the subject at length, and Powers may well have numbered among its readers. For these reasons Combe's book is the best point of departure.

We have seen that Combe considered the principles of hereditary descent as a means of weeding out the physical and moral shortcomings that bedeviled humanity.[35] No doubt he would have approved of the termination of Mary Scudder's betrothal to the elderly pastor in *The Minister's Wooing*, not merely for their contemplative inclinations but also because the disparity in their ages boded ill.[36] While phrenologists adopted the Lamarckian tenet which maintained that acquired qualities of body and mind were transmitted to offspring, they attached a radical interpretation to this belief. For Combe and his followers the endowment of traits need not evolve over prolonged intervals; the process could involve even the most fleeting emotions, including those that might arise during the act of mating.[37] The newborn was greatly influenced by whichever parental faculties were most vigorous at the moment of conception, and for this reason Combe urged the habitual exercise of the moral sentiments so that they might prevail during moments of nuptial bliss.[38]

HEROIC COPULATION

This advice sought to reconcile antithetical attitudes toward sex held by Victorians. On one level sex was seen as animalistic and in need of restraint; on another it was regarded as the gift of God for the purpose of engendering superb children. The gist of the message that reformers such as Combe sought to convey was that sexual intercourse ought to be decidedly vigorous in order to ensure the health and strength of the offspring. Conversely, the act should be approached with the reverence due this most consequential duty and should be performed only infrequently so that the reservoirs of vital fluids would be amply supplied at the requisite moment.[39]

This dictate, with its cautions and conditions, best explains the motives governing the *Greek Slave*. To characterize the statue as embodying beliefs about the "vulnerability" and "passionless" nature of womanhood, as one writer has recently surmised, interprets the scenario with excessive literalism.[40] To be sure, the slave is enchained, but her vibrant strength was intended to rebuke the frailty of contemporary fashionables, who, if they wished, could become as robust and resilient as the nude they were invited to examine. The writer mentioned here apparently assumes that only one attitude toward sexuality prevailed throughout antebellum America, an assumption no more valid then than now.[41] Powers's own words clearly put him in the phrenological camp, and as Martha H. Verbrugge explains, these reformers "supported aspirations for women that stretched, even broke, social custom. They argued that independence and other 'unseemly' qualities were compatible with being female and were essential to being well."[42] Since "being well" is the slave's primary message, she is also an advocate of the independence that comes from nonconformity.

Phrenology granted viewers of the *Greek Slave* the ability to read her virtues not merely as victim or object of erotic fantasy but primarily as a prospective spouse. This potential constitutes her essential identity. She is not "passionless"; on the contrary, her organic constitution makes her an acolyte of what one scholar has called "heroic copulation." Capable of energetic, mutually orgasmic intercourse, she is ideally suited to bring children into the world.[43] We encounter her at one of those intervals of continence requisite for the role, but she served her Greek lover in this capacity, or would have had their relationship been consummated, and, as we shall see, will bestow the same blessing, though perhaps less enthusiastically, on her heathen captors. What distinguishes the sexuality of slave from the ecstasies seen in works such as Auguste Clesinger's *Woman Bitten by a Snake* (1847, Louvre, Paris) is the concept of natural law. Its reasonable principles made the slave a vehicle of progress as that notion was understood by Americans.

Orson Fowler sought to adapt these notions to the American context, and his pronouncements come particularly close to those of Powers. The latter, for example, asserted, "That we are bound to multiply and increase the stock of humanity as a duty is clear from our very organization."[44] The contention that sexuality was an integral part of the identity implanted into mankind by the divinity is implied in this statement. Fowler was more explicit, placing the entire phenomenon under the rubric of "natural law." Sexuality, he noted, permeated every "iota" of the human "constitution," announcing its intent and blessings to all who were not blinded by prudery from recognizing the fact.[45] To validate this assertion he observed that "Michael Angelo, Powers, and every other artist ancient and modern, exemplify this law, that gender ramifies itself upon and throughout every talent, every intellectual manifestation."[46]

We have seen that phrenologists viewed health as crucial to parenting, and the rationale adduced to support this contention is especially pertinent to analysis of the *Greek Slave.* Each member and organ of the body and each faculty of the brain impressed its disposition upon the semen and the egg by means of the "spirituo-sexual magnetism" that circulated not only through the individual bodies of the engendering pair but also between them as the spark that ignited their love.[47] This philosophy alerts us further to the importance of Buchanan's diagram and, even more pertinently, to the labor expended by Powers to ensure the fleshlike qualities of the marble. If every iota of our very organization participates in the formation of the fetus, then none should be glossed over by the conventions of style. It would take, Fowler surmised, only one generation of happy and vigorously consummated marriages to usher in the millennium.[48] The slave was ready to do her part.

In his advocacy of energetic copulation Fowler reasoned, "Power is Nature's first great prerequisite throughout all her functions, into all of which she infuses the utmost vigor possible. Weakness here is her especial abomination, which she punishes with parental and progenal inertia, while sexual power in parents is life, flow, vim, and snap, throughout themselves and their offspring. Every single animal function must be then and there exercised in power, else its inertia would leave it weak in offspring, and this drags all their other functions down to its level."[49] Drawing on resources from all portions of the body, the act of initiating life required "an immense amount of power" to impart a commensurate "momentum" to its issue.[50] Prospective mothers were urged to abandon any passive inclinations and to recognize that their duty consisted in "heartily receiving the life germ."[51]

Beauty itself, Fowler continued, could be explained scientifically, since all that promoted maternal fitness was beautiful to man. A moderate fleshiness, full breasts, and a large pelvis were desirable, while obesity indicated a sluggishness that was inimical to healthful sexuality. The *Greek Slave* (fig. 7.6) epitomized this doctrine, and to it "all ancient and modern attempts bow in acknowledged inferiority." It exhibited the "whole pelvic region large and full, broad from hip to hip, and deep through; besides showing just the kind of breasts, thighs, and limbs here described." Fowler is not asking readers to ignore the figure's nakedness but to scrutinize it closely; nevertheless, he justifies the venture in terms reminiscent of those used by Orville Dewey. "Beauty unadorned," the phrenologist wrote, "is adorned the most."

By placing the *Greek Slave* at the pinnacle of artistic accomplishment, Fowler felt obliged to explain why it surpassed other works, especially the *Venus de' Medici*. The arms of the latter, he notes, obscure more of the torso than in the former, thus diminishing its instructiveness. Her pose, which he describes as a "Grecian bend," also leaves much to be desired. Powers had used the same term, not so much in criticism of the antique statue, but in reference to the unhealthful posture adopted by modern belles who sought to emulate the renowned piece.[52] This coincidence is another similarity that suggests the two men conversed on such topics and testifies to the proximity of their views.[53]

After examining the statue, Fowler confided to readers that "the Greek Slave would choose not a tall, slim, but a thick-set, broad-shouldered man, though perhaps tall, if capacious-chested and prominent-featured."[54] The perfumed effeminacy of the *Apollo Belvedere*, in any case, would not turn her head. Her ardor was much more likely to be aroused by the muscular magnetism of Justice Story.[55] The goal of such analysis was to furnish the nation with perfect individuals; there loomed, however, one ominous development that threatened to bring all Fowler's plans to naught. Declining birth rates among the older stock of Americans meant that those of foreign origin would outnumber the native-born within two generations. If this trend were allowed to continue unabated, he warned, the wheels of progress would come to a halt, and tyranny would rule the land.[56] Fears of this sort nourished the eugenics movement that emerged toward the end of the century, when differentials in the fertility rates of the classes created a siege mentality among its proponents.[57] Prejudices against the Irish, whose numbers surged during the antebellum era, were not discouraged by phrenology's stigmatization of these immigrants as a distinct and inferior race.[58] Powers shared with Fowler the inclination to favor those of English descent; if only the British and Americans could act in tandem, the sculptor mused, "the anglo-saxon race might defie the world in regard to power and lead all the nations in the grand march of Christianity, civilization and science."[59] A generation of women modeled on the example

THE PERFECT FEMALE FORM.

FIGURE 7.6.
Powers's "Greek Slave," from O. S. Fowler, *Creative and Sexual Science* (Rochester: New York State Pub. Co., 1870), p. 152

of the *Greek Slave* would quicken the pace of this march, but there always lurked the possibility of failure, a prospect that prompted Allan Sekula to characterize eugenic ideology as "a utopianism inspired and haunted by a sense of social decline and exhaustion."[60]

Walt Whitman's translation of physiological theory into poetry has served as a leitmotif in this text because it illustrates the similar practices employed by artists of the time. Particularly relevant here is the female persona who appears in the *Leaves of Grass*. She is the Eve to its eugenic Adam, and together they set out to regenerate the continent. Aspiz realized some years ago that her round breasts, broad hips, and serene physical ripeness closely resembled the disposition of Powers's nudes.[61] Whitman must have passed long hours gazing at the *Greek Slave* during the "days and nights" he spent at New York's Crystal Palace, where a version was exhibited in 1853.[62] Such experiences contributed to his description of "a woman's body at auction" in "Children of Adam." Instead of taking the opportunity to condemn slavery, the passage contrasts the "firm-fibred body" of this "teeming mother of mothers" with "the fool that corrupted her own live body" and cannot conceal herself.[63]

How different is this slave from the one who appears in histories of art! Her "perfect body" engenders superb children who are destined to shape the world. She is a "strong and arrogant woman," "well-muscled" and given to "brawny embraces." From the "folds" of her brain come "all the folds of the man's brain."[64] Blessed is she among women as she calls out,

> Come nigh to me limber-hipp'd man,
> Stand at my side till I lean as high as I can upon you,
> Fill me with ablescent honey, bend down to me,
> Rub to me with your chafing beard, rub to my breast and shoulders.[65]

The moment of ecstasy approaches:

> Mad filaments, ungovernable shoots play out of it, the response
>   likewise ungovernable,
> Hair, bosom, hips, bend of legs, negligent falling hands all diffused,
>   mine too diffused,
> Ebb stung by the flow and flow stung by the ebb, love-flesh swelling
>   and deliciously aching,
> Limitless limpid jets of love hot and enormous, quivering jelly of love,
>   white-blow and delirious juice,
> Bridegroom night of love working surely and softly into the prostrate
>   dawn.[66]

The propitious alignment of highly charged genitalia in such arc-lamp-like couplings discharges sparks bright enough to illuminate all creation.

The Galatea most apt to step down from her pedestal and embrace
Whitman's fecundating, bearded Pygmalion would be the *Greek Slave*. From her ample loins emerge "Americanos! conquerors!" with Nordic features and blue eyes that gaze toward a future destined for those of similar appearance.[67] Neither Whitman nor the Fowlers nor Powers, for that matter, seems to have considered any race but their own as endowed with the qualities necessary to establish the millennium.

Whitman's vision of the western forests found in "Song of the Redwood-Tree" resembles Combe's ruminations on nature and fate. The redwoods are emblematic of the race of human giants who will replace them. Each harbors a spermatic treasure; these "deathless germs" obey "occult deep volitions" and promote the universal progress that could only come from the succession of generations that Combe thought the primary benefit of "the institution of death."[68] Both men wrote under the spell of neo-Lamarckian beliefs in a primordial, sexual-evolutionary drive toward perfection operating throughout nature.[69] Both had "learn'd the physiology, phrenology, politics, geography, pride, freedom, [and] friendship of the land."[70] Buchanan's chart, with its delineation of the body as microcosm, comes to mind when Whitman inquires,

> Was somebody asking to see the soul?
> See, your own shape and countenance, persons, substances, beasts,
>   the trees, the running rivers, the rocks and sands.[71]

The poet dedicated himself to producing "poems of my body and of mortality" on the supposition that in doing so he would "then supply myself with poems of my soul and of immortality."[72] The fleshy, unveiled soul created by Powers was similarly motivated, and there is no reason to suppose that he any more than Whitman was confused about the intent.

The life that swarmed upon the earth's surface—indeed, the very planet itself—was created and sustained, according to Orson Fowler, by electricity, "the great motor of the universe" that endlessly spawned matter. Since its positive and negative currents corresponded to the male and female principles, all being was pervaded by sexuality. This agency attained its purest manifestation during intercourse, when the positive male seminal fluid rushed toward the negative female egg; hence the vitality of a child was commensurate with the energy expended in begetting it.[73] When Whitman writes,

On women fit for conception I start bigger and nimbler babes,
(This day I am jetting the stuff of far more arrogant republics.) [74]

we should remember that trajectory of the stuff so jetted was crucial to the happiness of future generations. Ejaculated with the requisite degree of "flow, vim, and snap," [75] it assured the gratitude of posterity, but if feebly propelled, the palsied hand of a wan and haggard progeny would rightfully point an accusatory finger at the forebear whose profligacy had forever precluded entry into those far more arrogant republics. This mode of thinking links the destiny of the body politic directly with the bodies of those who compose it, [76] a doctrine Powers would have also learned from Swedenborgian teachings about the composite man.

THE SLAVE IN AMERICA

While phrenologists sought to identify men whose abundant sexuality suited them for paternity, the brunt of responsibility for ushering in the millennium rested on women destined for motherhood. [77] Shakespeare, Washington, and Webster testified to the reasons for Anglo-Saxon hegemony, but the ideal female nude spoke to the future. Orson Fowler regarded the *Greek Slave* as the epitome of his teaching, and her appearance before large audiences across America was certainly eased by such notions. When reviewers told the public why it should put down hard cash to see the slave, her superior endowments as a harbinger of far more arrogant republics weighed heavily in their reasoning.

The slave was first exhibited in a gallery especially fitted out for her display, with an iron railing, crimson curtains, and a Brussels carpet with a Persian pattern. [78] Skepticism about the venture's prospects abounded at the time of its inauguration in New York in August 1847, but Miner Kellogg, the tour's manager, acceded to the "bump of *pugnacity*" that urged him to persevere. Since no pamphlet had yet been published, he answered questions while operating the rotating pedestal that enabled visitors to appraise the entire body. [79]

In the ensuing months Kellogg remained wedded to the slave, a relationship not lost on visitors who called the statue his "marble wife." [80] However trifling, such comments reveal a disposition to view the figure as a matrimonial prospect. Even the pedestal might serve this end. Such, in any case, was the response of Oliver Wendell Holmes to a similar device employed by Erastus Dow Palmer to display his work. His account of Mrs. Sprowle's party in *Elsie Venner* includes the following: "The dance answers the purpose of the revolving pedestal upon which the 'White Captive' turns, to show us the soft, kneaded marble, which looks as if it had never been hard, in all its manifold aspect of living loveliness."[81] So, he tells his female readers, "you must be weighed in the balance," a thought that may also have inspired "The Greek Slave Waltz" and like tunes that appeared during the years of the slave's celebrity.[82] Despite Powers's advice to Kellogg that he ought to eschew marriage during the tour, since it would add "a male slave to the exhibition,"[83] the latter entertained ideas of wedding "the *first* lady visitor to the slave in this country." She was a Swedenborgian, and the depth of her response to the slave moved its male attendant to conclude, "She was the girl for me."[84]

A troupe of "model artists" began to follow the slave from city to city, portraying her plight in a *tableau vivant* while causing Kellogg to worry about a loss of revenues.[85] This development recalls the oxymoronic character of popular reform discussed by David Reynolds. He describes antebellum society as permeated with contradictions: a democracy weakened by growing class antagonism, a country of vast forests and deteriorating cities, and "a nation of Christians who tolerated the most un-Christian practices."[86] This environment bred "immoral reformers" who thought nothing of lacing their appeals for chastity with salacious tidbits that whetted the very appetites they ostensibly sought to quell.

Powers's own roots sprang from this pungent humus that fertilized much of the art and literature of the antebellum year. The aim of his *Infernal Regions*, a scene of hell enacted by automata, was to illustrate the wages of sin, but the crowds that thronged Dorfeuille's museum in Cincinnati, where it was installed in 1828, thrilled at its spectacle of suffering.[87] The parallels with the gallery devised for the *Greek Slave* are intriguing. Both relied on controlled lighting and moving statuary, though the slave only after the manner of the dervishes. Both employed iron barriers to separate the spectators from the object of their curiosity, but viewers who leaned on the fence before the abyss of Hades were rudely shocked by a jolt of electricity, while prolonged observation of the slave was encouraged by the padding on the horizontal bar. In contrast to its predecessor, the marble nude attained the status of high art, but like the literary figures discussed by Reynolds, including Whitman, Melville, and Edgar Allan Poe, the sculptor's familiarity with the popular traditions of his native land served to enrich his oeuvre.

Whitman campaigned against the "sickly prudishness" that condemned the "model artists,"[88] but a commentator of our own enlightened times characterizes their performances as "pornography [that] reached toward high culture for a veneer of respectability."[89] So much for Victorian squeamishness. In any case, a contemporary newspaper reports the following: "Model artists, or naked women, representing the Greek Slave and other pieces of statuary, are traveling from city to city, and from town to town, exhibiting themselves for money; and strange to say, they drew large audiences even among the ladies!"[90] If such shows were indeed pornographic, and if the feminist theory of the gaze as an instrument of power over the object of its attention applies—indeed, if the *Greek Slave* and, by inference, its impersonators acted as signifiers of the social value of women as commodities exchanged among men[91]—why was she so popular with women?

Quite early in the tour Kellogg noted that two-thirds of the visitors were women.[92] What drew them to a statue that, theoretically, would seem designed to appease the male appetite? Of course it could be argued they had simply internalized the values of the paternalistic society to which they belonged, and this would ring true were the slave regarded merely as a victim. But the weight of contemporary evidence complicates this interpretation considerably. Seen as a paradigm of phrenological teaching, the slave spoke of liberation from the conventions governing sexuality that sought to keep women entirely in the dark on the subject.

The critical dialogue concerning the *Greek Slave* frequently raised issues of race, but we must allow some latitude in such matters because Victorians often associated the concept with nationality. We have already encountered reviewers who stressed her modernity and one who even traced her Yankee descent. Powers's biographer, however, claims that the sculptor's sympathy for the plight of blacks in America made the statue a "widespread antislavery sensation."[93] No documentation is offered in support of this assertion, so one must assume the source is Green's article on the abolitionist reaction to the piece. There it is noted that Powers's stand against slavery came about only after the passage of the Kansas-Nebraska Act of 1854, and the few press notices cited in the text take the statue's exhibition as an opportunity to remind readers of the shame associated with the nation's "peculiar institution" without imputing this motive to the artist.[94] If the work received wide recognition as the symbol of the country's racial wrongs, that fact went unnoticed in New Orleans, where its reception was as enthusiastic as that in Boston.[95]

There was little in the agenda prosecuted by the abolitionists that appealed to Powers, and their zeal made him fear for the Union's survival.[96] Indicative of this mindset is the answer given one visitor to the slave during her tour. When asked why the slave was not black (as good an opening as any abolitionist intent on delivering a harangue might wish), the attendant simply explained that she was Greek, and Greeks were white.[97] Even more telling is Kellogg's letter to Powers recommending the platform of Lewis Cass. The senator from Michigan proposed that the question of slavery be settled by the territories, a stance that caused the abolitionists to bolt from the Democratic Party when he made his bid for the presidency in 1848, and it seems fair to conclude such an exchange would not have taken place between a pair who intended to alert the nation to the evils of the enslavement of blacks.[98]

Even the identity of the *Greek Slave* as Greek turns out to be less clear-cut than might be initially assumed. From the outset her nationality apparently merged in Powers's mind with that of a related ethnic group, the Circassians.[99] Since Kellogg did a painting and a print of a woman belonging to the latter tribe as well, the two men shared ideas on the subject as the slave made her tour of the states.[100] Some indication of the importance of Circassians to the phrenologists was included in the first chapter, but the topic merits further review here. The profile so prominently displayed by the slave was a feature Samuel Morton praised in the Circassians. Its nobility, he states, approached that of the Greeks as well as the beau ideal of classical statuary. They are shepherds, Morton continues in words that again bring Powers's figure to mind, but also fierce warriors who seldom sell their own women to the Turks.[101]

Members of the Edinburgh phrenological society were especially gratified when one of their number donated the skull of a Circassian girl to their collection.[102] The study of Circassian types was made available to a wider audience when James Stewart, "a zealous Phrenologist," engraved William Allan's painting titled *Sale of Circassian Captives in a Turkish Bashaw.* In his first venture into art criticism, George Combe lauded both oil and print for the accuracy of the heads, which, he observed, were "phrenologically correct." The superiority of the Circassians, who are described as "a free people, of the Caucasian race," caught the writer's attention and caused him to contrast their crainia with those of the despot and his entourage. Having access to the collection of the phrenological society, where skulls of both peoples were preserved, doubtlessly encouraged Combe to make this judgment.[103]

These ideas appeared in *The Constitution of Man*, where, after discussing the superiority of "half-breed American Indians" to other members of the tribe, Combe again takes up Persia and Allan's picture. "In that country, it is said that the custom has existed for ages among the nobles, of purchasing beautiful female Circassian captives, and forming alliances with them as wives. It is ascertained that the Circassian form of brain stands comparatively high in the development of the moral and intellectual organs. And it is mentioned by some travelers, that the race of nobles in Persia is the most gifted in natural qualities, bodily and mental, of any class of that people."[104] Here phrenological teaching on the natural laws of heredity conditioned the response to a work of art. By extension the *Greek Slave*, both in her ostensible role and as Circassian, is among those (Turks and Americans) who may also bequeath their children improved prospects by uniting with one of like constitution.

Visitors to their remote realm praised not only the mental attributes of the Circassians but their physical stature and demeanor as well. Perhaps Powers attended the address on the insalubrity of modern life given in 1837 by Samuel Gridley Howe to the Boston Phrenological Society. The lecture was particularly harsh in its condemnation of contemporary mores, calling the milliner and the hairdresser "funguses growing out of a rotten state of society." Then the speaker set his sights on corsets, claiming, "Should a female appear in the streets with her dress arranged so as to show her figure to be in outline like that of Eve, she would be pointed out as a fright." Indeed, he intoned, no greater contrast to our fashionables could be imagined than "the famed beauties of the East." Untouched by the blight of stylish apparel, the bodies of Georgian and Circassian women exhibited a graceful bearing that reproached the artifice prevalent in American society. Ignorance of organic law cast a pall over the nation's future by encouraging the transmission of hereditary infirmities to generations yet unborn.[105] We have encountered these ideas already, but the similarity of Howe's remarks about Eve to the words put in her mouth by Powers, as well as the subsequent reference to Circassians, just as the sculptor followed his statue of the mother of mankind with the slave, is intriguing. Did some acquaintance persuade Powers to attend the discourse, and did these notions come to fruition later when circumstances permitted? We shall never know for sure, but Howe's presentation offers an interesting parallel to the subsequent evolution of the artist's thought.

The contrast Howe established between the fashionably attired American and the natural form of the Circassian was readily available to those who viewed the *Greek Slave*. One had only to glance around the gallery (fig. 7.7) to be reminded of the gap between the clothed and the nude, to see the sad realities of American life and an ideal that might be attained. Powers chose not to transform the spectator into a disembodied eye permitted to witness the gambols of a nymph, the meditations of an Indian maid, or the trials of some biblical heroine, as was usually the case. Instead the viewer is left in a quandary about the reasons for his or her presence at this distressing scene. Even the pleasure derived from examining the exquisite figure is a source of discomfort, for it makes the observer little better than the Turks who presumably jostle at his or her shoulder. In other words, the artist tapped the currents of Calvinism flowing not very deeply beneath the surface of American culture. The statue furnishes a pretext for self-scrutiny, a basic tenet of the old religion, but

FIGURE 7.7.
Robert Thaw,
*Exhibition Room
of the Dusseldorf
Gallery, New York,
1857* (1857,
engraving,
reproduced in the
*Cosmopolitan Art
Journal,* December
1857)

305
*Our Very
Organization*

salvation now comes through physical metaphysics. Not being Moslem, those standing before the captive need only shudder at the customs of heathen nations, but what was the lesson to be learned? Those who came away with a heightened appreciation of their duty as Christians to purify and maintain the living temple of the body were closely attuned to the sculptor's own convictions.

Powers explained his intentions in an interview with Charles Edwards Lester that was published some two years before the slave went on tour. There, in words reminiscent of Howe's, he wished that his countrywomen "could see a Florentine peasant-girl under her broad Tuscan hat, attired in a simple and becoming dress, walking through the streets of New York, by the side of an exquisite of the female gender. It is needless to say, what would be the effect upon the minds of spectators. Her superiority in elegance, and dignity, and true grace (which is always natural), would be so great, no one could fail to perceive it." This image should occasion no levity, nor was it simply a question of taste; bad posture and tight lacing crowded the breast and stomach, causing diseases that annually sent thousands to their graves. Yet, the sculptor continued, before American girls succumbed to "the despotism of fashion," they were better formed and more beautiful than those he had seen elsewhere.[106] We hear echoes of these sentiments in newspaper articles of the day. One reporter remarks that on descending from the gallery, he encountered "two fashionably dressed belles whose tournures were shaking and swinging from side to side as they ascended. 'Twas a sad fall in poetry, from the contemplation of the beauty unadorn'd, we had left above to that *so much* adorn'd we met below."[107] Another reviewer relates that before the statue "a wish unbidden intruded upon our reverie, that all the sex would adopt the same unique fashion."[108]

As noted earlier, the concerns shared by Powers and the phrenologists appear regularly in the popular response to the slave. Historians who have consulted just the pamphlet sold at the exhibition have had limited access to the latter, but the depth of the statue's implications can only be assayed by examining a wider range of sources. One contemporary, for example, evinces a knowledge of the issues discussed above when he opines that "the subject is a female slave, Greek or Circassian, exposed in a state of perfect nudity, for sale."[109] Another records the desire of the citizens of St. Louis "to have a peep at the 'Circassian' before she goes to New Orleans."[110] Some measure of the wide association of the *Greek Slave* with the Circassian race comes as well from the efforts made by several critics to refute it. Were it a female from Georgia or Circassia, one surmised, the form would be "full and swelling, sleepy and indolent," for in those provinces the girls are fatted from youth to enhance their market value to the Turks. Had Powers depicted one such individual, all would have declared his work a failure, but he chose instead a Greek, a race "well-figured" though rarely "full or voluptuous." No unanimity exists, the author concedes, about the attributes that comprise the perfect female figure; in large portions of Asia, for instance, a "superabundance of flesh" is preferred. The slave, however, is not "one of the indolent houris of the East, but a woman full of strong life and health, and with enough apparent strength and muscle to make her capable of an hour's exercise without producing death. He [Powers] has sacrificed part of the voluptuous fullness of the usual, to give us a better picture of the natural and the real."[111]

Some were dissatisfied with the Greek nativity of the slave, even though they might accept its likelihood. Were she Circassian, one reporter reasoned, the complacency of the captive would be understandable, for in that region women were raised in the expectation of their entry into a

Turkish harem. But the features of the slave disclosed her Greek lineage; hence hers was a heritage of antipathy for the Turks and their religion. How, then, could her apparent serenity be explained? For this reviewer at least, the want of emotion was a source of disappointment.[112] Did Palmer intend to forestall such criticism when he depicted the disgust on the face of his *White Captive?* This emotion would preclude any ambivalence about her acquiescence to fate and thus allay the fears of miscegenation harbored by onlookers.

Boyd Reilly, the uncle of Powers's wife, could speak to these questions with authority, having peddled "vapor baths" in Turkey for some years. He asserted that the subject was an actual one, adding, "The present white slaves are generally those who willingly exchange a life of privation, in the huts of their unnatural Circassian and Georgian parents (who sell them like lambs to a butcher) in hope of becoming 'Lights of the Harem,' to some great Pasha, or happily to the Sultan himself."[113] This report helps explain why differences of opinion arose about the ethnicity of the *Greek Slave.* The statue was initially inspired by events surrounding the Greek war of independence; that war having been won, this region no longer provided chattel for the market, but Circassia still did. Associations of slavery with the latter group held sway in the minds of many, while others endeavored to set the drama in a particular moment of recent history and thus preferred the former. Notions of race were fluid, as noted above, and the slave could also be seen as a contemporary American. But whatever the response, underlying attempts to assign an identity was the program of racial improvement advanced by the phrenologists.

Beyond the generalities of race, responses to the *Greek Slave* ranged from concerns about the particulars of the anatomy to questions of the mind's relationship to the body, and again, much of this coincided with the sculptor's professed beliefs. It was Powers, after all, who maintained that an artist's knowledge of the body must be comparable to a physician's, contending that "to represent a leg properly requires almost as much anatomical study and science as to cut off a leg."[114] During the tour, the slave was examined by a committee of physicians who declared the piece "perfect in its anatomical developments."[115] We might at first be inclined to interpret this report as an instance of the aesthetic naivete prevalent among a public still relatively unfamiliar with sculpture, but there may be more going on here than merely a prosaic reckoning of the accuracy of representation. For those involved in transcendental medicine, as Powers was, organic growth was assumed to reach toward a perfection that was never quite attained because of bad habits or want of wisdom in matters of heredity. The above endorsement suggests that, in the eyes of his contemporaries, the sculptor had attained a flawlessness equal to nature itself. This was the realism of a visionary who could recognize and preserve in marble those fragmentary intimations of beauty discernible in humanity as it was presently constituted.

Viewers of the *Greek Slave* sought these clues wherever they might be found. One was relieved to see that the "dainty feet" were unsullied by the "sacrilegious pavement of the slave market" thanks to the garment so rudely torn from the maid's shoulders.[116] Other portions of the anatomy likewise aroused an enthusiasm that verged on religious awe. "One of the hands is alone ample recompense for the nominal price of admission," claims a reviewer, while another calls attention to the right hand as "a perfect *hand*; so of all the limbs, which are wonderfully life-like."[117] Critics were apparently in accord with the physicians mentioned above, for they also praised the features as capable of defying "the nicest scrutiny of the anatomist."[118] Expanding on this response, a writer called attention to the "complete mastery of the anatomy of the human figure" and went on to applaud the "muscular development, erroneously though generally supposed to detract from feminine beauty." The analysis continues along familiar lines, for the author contrasts the "*undulating* grace" of the slave to the "luxuriant development" so often favored by viewers. We hear the physiologist speaking here, telling listeners that the essence of beauty resides in physical fortitude and not mere abundance of flesh, and this insight prompts him to conclude with a "Hurrah then for Republican Art."[119]

In light of Powers's contention that the ideal was merely nature unconstrained and undeformed, passages such as the following take on added meaning: "The anatomy of this figure is astonishingly fine. Every development, even to the slightest, is exquisitely wrought. It is nature itself."[120] Not everyone agreed. There were those who found the anatomy too sharply marked, the consequence, it was supposed, of "a thin and sickly model." This observer adds, "Mr. Powers is not a scientific workman, and therefore cannot produce great ideal works; for in whatever he might attempt there would certainly appear the imperfections of some one or other of the models he employed; the fault of leanness predominates in the Slave."[121] What intrigues here is the author's apparent concurrence with the aesthetic espoused by Powers, maintaining, as he does, that science is the bridge to the ideal, but this does not lead to the same conclusion reached by others. Where they see muscularity and desirable stamina, he discerns only leanness and a want of the abundance they disparaged.

The head and hair were likewise closely scrutinized. Of the latter, one reviewer relates that it "is simply and beautifully bound, according to the classic fashion of her country, leaving the neck uncovered, and the high brow full and distinct." This opinion did not go uncontested; elsewhere it was asserted that the head could not be considered "by any means beautiful; to us it is certainly not pleasing; it is too square; the forehead too prominent for female beauty." [122] Both writers respond to the phrenology of the slave, but the intellect is too assertive for the latter, who perceives an angularity that is more appropriate in the male cranium. Yet another, however, thought Powers's statue more admirable than classical renderings of Venus precisely because the "intellectual and physical beauty [of the slave] are most felicitously blended in its swelling proportions and graceful contours." [123]

Claims for the special merit of the *Greek Slave* rested primarily on the perception that her moral and physical traits were effectively integrated, with each reinforcing the other. Consequently, the notion that the soul might be revealed by the body was no more problematic to critics than to Powers. Hence one contended, "As a work of art, in our esteem it stands higher than any Venus, of any artists, and for this reason, that it seems to be a blending of the spiritual with the sensual in complete harmony. An internal radiance of the soul seems to beam forth and mantle the entire form." [124] This idea was more explicitly stated in the following:

> The bones, slightly apparent in outline at certain points, are clothed by the muscles which are sufficiently developed to give the idea of strength and still not marked by the hard outlines which indicate age or the effects of physical labor: the envelope of fatty tissue appears just thick enough to give plumpness, and a soft fleshlike pulpy appearance to the whole figure. The head might be taken as the beau ideal by the most enthusiastic phrenologist; the features of the face are inexpressibly beautiful, and radiant with the elevated sentiments and conscious dignity of character. [125]

It is often difficult to tell whether this criticism is based solely on the visual testimony of the statue or whether some intelligence of the artist's intentions has guided the account. The following report, for example, relies on physical metaphysics of the kind popular among Swedenborgians, yet the author gives no intimations that he has done anything other than draw inferences from the figure: "He [Powers] believes in nature and in fact, in the yet present Deity, present most in what is most palpable, most actual, most near. His is the healthier kind of genius, whose works are not mere phantoms of a vague idealism, possessing only a subjective validity."

According to this reading, the sculptor sought to represent "a woman of this age, only without the disguises, the fantastic winding-sheets of our conventions which conceal the full divinity of form."[126]

Apprehensions about the winding-sheets of our conventions were not the exclusive preoccupation of Powers and the Fowlers. A number of reviewers point out the potential for the slave to effect much good in this respect. In urging the public to gaze at the statue, one reporter hoped it would be "long and carefully studied by none more than by the fairer sex, upon whom it must have the most salutary effect, by its faultless exhibition of woman's true beauties, and by its tendency to correct many of abuses to which they subject themselves through false notions of dress."[127] Much the same logic appeared in another column: "We recommend our ladies to mark well the waist of this model. They will perceive that it is not at all forced, as they do theirs, by stays and braces of various kinds out of shape. It is proportionally large, as theirs should be, and would be, but for their attempts to improve upon nature."[128]

Some years after the slave's tour, it was reported that A. T. Stewart, the proprietor of a large emporium in New York, concluded after acquiring his version of the *Greek Slave* that "to introduce such an illustrious exemplar of *non*-crinoline and *native* beauty to his customers for emulation" would be detrimental to trade. So the piece was packed off to his mansion, where it was seen "only by the admissible few."[129] Doubtless there were those who considered Stewart's actions socially irresponsible;[130] among them would have been the author of the following passage, which urges every woman to "study its [the slave's] proportions, and compare herself with it, and consider well the contrast, and understand the causes which have made the living, sentient being, and the inanimate marble so essentially to differ. The statue is not merely ideal, as some describe it; it is rather the verisimilitude of that perfection which is now obliterated and lost." Gaze, the article continues, upon "those pledges of maternity, which, in full and fair development, have almost universally disappeared from the living form, [they] stand here a memorial of the grace and beauty and naturalness that have departed." A figure so evidently without "hereditary blemishes" or "defects induced by fashion" represented "one of the most striking appeals ever made to our race, to arrest that progress towards complete physical deformity, the evil effects of which upon health, morals and happiness cannot be overrated."[131]

The range of fears and aspirations expressed above are encompassed in an extraordinary article written for *The Cosmopolitan Art Journal* a decade after the slave made her tour. In reading the following lines it is important to keep in mind that the views expressed would not have been considered mere flights of fantasy or poetic concoctions devised in lieu of serious aesthetic analysis, but an effort to bring to bear advanced theories of physiology and sexuality on a leading work of contemporary art.

> The children of men are conceived in sin, born in iniquity, bred in dis-obedience; and, therefore, the world is peopled with deformities. Let us, for instance, glance at the women of our acquaintance. The majority are ugly; many are good-looking; a few are handsome; and one or two are beautiful. Whose fault is it that all are not? Of themselves and their progenitors. For the sins of our forefathers and foremothers, the living generation are not responsible. No one can help being born ill-shapen and badly constituted; with eyes asquint and nose "out of drawing." But (and this brings me to a practical point) we can make the best of what we are. Health, strength, and beauty, can be cultivated, as well as the faculties of the mind and the heart. The eye can be educated as well as the ear; and the art of beauty may be taught as successfully as the art of music. "How shall it be done?" does some one eagerly inquire? By studying the best models in Nature and Art. Gaze at the living beauty when you can—the perfect statue from the hand of God; and when that happiness is denied, find the truest reflex of it in Art. . . . Power's [*sic*] Greek Slave may improve the symmetry of generations yet unborn. A thing of beauty is not only a joy, but an influence forever.[132]

These words resound from within the temple of beauty, an edifice built by neo-Lamarckians on the ruins of Calvinism. Acolytes need no longer smash idols, rapt admiration now being the preferred mode of worship. Beneath the rotunda stands the *Greek Slave*, a figure whose perfection holds the promise of a physiological millennium where the body, luminous in its health, shall cast out the last shades of sin and corruption.

The influence exercised by the *Greek Slave* was not limited merely to those lucky enough to have seen her during the tour or even to observers of the six life-size marble statues, for smaller replicas, numerous busts, and various marble and plaster renderings of portions of her anatomy, including the feet, hands, and torso, were also in circulation.[133] The list does not end with copies done more or less under the supervision of Powers. Unauthorized versions in the form of Parian ware statuettes, photographs, and even oil paintings supplied by the Fowlers were also produced,[134] to say nothing of the innumerable illustrations that appeared in phrenological manuals and elsewhere. By these means the slave's gentle suasion could be heard in households throughout the land. The extent to which such objects were gazed upon with an eye attuned to their physiological qualities is not readily ascertainable, but some tantalizing evidence relating to the mindset of ordinary viewers survives.

THE LADIES' PHYSIOLOGICAL INSTITUTE

This material comes from the files of the Ladies' Physiological Institute, an organization established in Boston in 1848 to provide the female population with information about the body and its functioning.[135] Attitudes toward health had been evolving rapidly since the 1820s, and unlike their Puritan ancestors, members of the institute did not regard illness as an inevitable part of worldly existence. It was, rather, a sign of the expanding chasm between human affairs and the designs of god.[136] Their outlook is aptly summarized in the following lines:

> The larger meaning of female sickness can be seen in the responsiveness of middle-class Bostonians to antebellum health reform. For many, women's ailments, and sickness in general, demonstrated the precariousness of urban life: the city teemed; children passed way; immigrants proliferated, spread epidemics, and died; women became invalid and infertile. That was physical evidence of deeper problems. Along with others in the urban Northeast, middle-class Bostonians sensed that their world was shifting: familiar routines held true less and less; traditional roles and values were strained; the structure of work, home, and neighborhood began to change. Dis-ease was a social as well as physical condition; the vulnerability of the body mirrored the insecurity of one's private world. Literally and figuratively, middle-class Bostonians came to fear for their lives.[137]

Projected outwardly, such fears were made visible in the club-wielding, heavy-jawed, low-browed, simianized Irish Celts, whose antics wreaked havoc on urban America in the cartoons of Thomas Nast. Like many illustrators of the day, Nast consulted phrenology in devising his stereotypes,[138] and phrenology again came into consideration when Victorians looked inward. During the 1850s the ladies of the physiological institute, for example, purchased a phrenological bust, subscribed to the *American Phrenological Journal,* and acquired the works of Combe.[139] By these means they hoped to gain access to the inner self, finding there a serenity that might stave off the disorders going on in the world beyond the confines of their establishment.[140]

Not content merely with current literature, the institute invited a number of phrenologists, including Orson Fowler, to lecture on diverse topics.[141] In December 1851 he delivered an address on midwifery and re-

FIGURE 7.8. John Absolon, *The United States Section of the Great Exhibition, London, 1851* (1851, lithograph, published in *Recollections of the Great Exhibition*, 1851)

turned on 11 February 1852 to discourse on "Love" or the "Feminine principle." Two weeks later it was proposed that members visit the panorama then showing in Boston of the famed Crystal Palace exhibition taking place in England. This was put to a vote on 3 March, when the date for the outing was set for the twelfth. At the same meeting it was also suggested that Dr. Lydia Folger Fowler, wife of Lorenzo, be requested to give a talk.[142] Was there a thread connecting these activities?

Awaiting the ladies at Amory Hall was the panorama and a narrator who enlivened his account of the scenes "with many gems of wit and humor." "Faithful" renderings of every part of the exposition were included, and since the figures appeared "as large as life," the audience left with "a much more vivid idea of it [the exhibition] than they had ever imagined."[143] One portion featured "The American Division," the very setting where the *Greek Slave* had created a sensation (fig. 7.8). Here was justification enough for the members of the physiological institute to attend en masse. They could now gaze upon the ideal, albeit in a painted reproduction, that had featured so prominently in their meetings, particularly in those attended by the Fowlers.[144] Walt Whitman had "scarcely witnessed a more pleasing sight than the visit of the young ladies belonging to the Brooklyn female seminary to the exhibition of Powers' statue of the Greek Slave, in New York,"[145] and their sisters in Boston would seem to have been equally eager to profit from its teaching.

The annual reports of the institute from the years when the above events occurred stress the importance of study as a means of enhancing personal beauty and grace.[146] This beauty, like that of the slave, was not simply a means of making oneself attractive to men; it also fortified the body, fitting it to endure illness and the perils of childbirth. Beauty was a sure sign of health, and health of strength, but, reformers argued, these virtues were sacrificed when women conformed to the foolish ideals dictated by men and forced their bodies into corsets and their feet into small shoes. These practices made them incapable of challenging male authority.[147] When the physiological institute urged women to abandon "their stupid submission to the requirements of fashion,"[148] it adopted a position consistent with its general emphasis on the need to be fully informed in matters of hygiene, a stance, incidentally, that miffed established male physicians.[149] In other words, it would be simplistic to contend that the *Greek Slave* merely answered the erotic longings of American men; she served several constituencies, and the largest of these was composed of those females who longed to gaze at the figure. By ignoring this factor modern historians have generally failed to recognize the great vitality of the statue; how it addressed the anxieties, some perceived, some real, of its audience; and how it celebrated, as Whitman did, the prospects of democracy. Indeed, any work that both inspired and reflected the values expressed in *Leaves of Grass* cannot be quite as dowdy and routine as has often been maintained.

The assertion that humanity would one day evolve from its present misshapen and diseased state to one of bodily perfection that would usher in the golden age may sound like the prognostications of Whitman or the Fowlers, but in fact it is again drawn from the records of the physiological institute.[150] This organization was not composed of eccentrics or wild-eyed radicals; its members were middle- and upper middle-class women who did not work to earn money.[151] Whether or not these women visited the panorama for the reasons suggested, Parian ware versions of the slave doubtlessly decorated their homes. Phrenology took the expansive ambitions associated with Manifest Destiny and enfolded them within the parlors of Victorian America. There, among the shag carpets and over-stuffed chairs, stood the little nude figure, its example offering a constant reminder to all who entered that they too could become progenitors of far more arrogant republics.

PHYSIOLOGICAL IDEALS

Our previous examination of Erastus Dow Palmer indicates that his philosophy resembled that of Powers, and one is bound to inquire whether other sculptors were similarly motivated. At first glance, Joseph Mozier's *The Wept of Wish-ton-Wish* (fig. 7.9) offers little in common with the *Greek Slave*. Both represent captives, the former having been taken from her familial abode in infancy by Indians, but she is clothed and no longer distressed by her plight. A description of the heroine from James Fenimore Cooper's novel, however, reveals its proximity to Powers's philosophy. There we read the following: "Though the person, from the neck to the knees, was hid by a tightly-fitting vest of calico and the short kirtle named, enough of the shape was visible to betray outlines that had never been injured, either by the mistaken devices of art or by the baneful effects of toil." [152] The injurious devices of art mentioned are the corsets and like fashions that captivity has spared the maid. Phrenology assisted Cooper in his delineation of American society. Aristabalus Bragg, the representative of a class of Yankees whose unreflective "go-a-head-ism" is frequently disparaged in *Home as Found*, is portrayed, for example, as well endowed in "his organ of acquisitiveness." [153] The physical allure described above, which results from moderate exercise and loose garments, likewise serves to criticize American mores, and it must have caught Mozier's attention precisely because it developed a theme already sanctioned by the popularity of Powers' sculpture.

One historian examines Mozier's work in light of the discontent shared by Victorian housewives about their narrowly circumscribed opportunities. Might such women, the scholar asks, find *The Wept of Wish-ton-Wish* a release from their own domestic confinement? She then inquires, "What if the white woman, like Pocahontas, should cross the threshold of the new life willingly? What if her identity proved malleable?" [154] Those who were familiar with the narrative, however, were unlikely to be troubled by the prospect as they gazed on the maiden. Cooper continues the passage quoted above by describing the head of the beautiful captive; her eyes are azure, her hair flaxen, and her "forehead, fuller than that which properly belonged to a girl of the Narragansetts, but regular, delicate, and polished." [155] Notions of malleable identity are perhaps more amenable to our multicultural society than to the one Cooper surveyed. The physical metaphysics of his day made personality and race integral to one's material and moral being and not something put on or cast off like cloth-

FIGURE 7.9. Joseph Mozier, *The Wept of Wish-ton-Wish* (1859, marble, courtesy of Hirschl and Adler Galleries, New York, N.Y.)

ing. Although Cooper's heroine has lived among the Indians most of her life, her full forehead signals the inherited mental prowess of her Caucasian progenitors, while its lack of any irregularities is compatible with her femininity. This identity permeates every fiber of her body and can no more be erased by a change in environment than the blue of her eyes or the wave in her golden hair, both of which are also the result of a fine-textured temperament. Like the Circassians, the Wept of Wish-ton-Wish may serve as an instrument of improvement among her captors, but only at the price of tainting the intellectual reservoirs of her own race, reservoirs amply illustrated in this instance by the close conformity of the hair to the shape of the skull.

The Venus of Joel Hart's *Woman Triumphant* (1865–77, destroyed) [156] has not endured the tribulations faced by the heroines of Powers and Mozier. Yet for all its Rococo ebullience and paganism, the artist declared the subject to be both original and modern.[157] In explaining the many casts of limbs dispersed about his studio, he launched into a refrain we have often heard: "Yes, I am making them all the time. It is very hard to find good models among women, for their forms are usually ruined by the vicious customs of pinching and squeezing, and tightly binding what nature intended to be free." His pursuit of nature, then, entailed an unrelenting effort to discover its vestiges among more than 150 models. Of these the unfettered form of the Italian peasants proved most amenable to his purpose. There was, of course, also the example offered by the statuary of antiquity, but this likewise could not be emulated uncritically, for the sculptor aspired "to represent a woman not only faultless and beautiful in form, but full of mind, of refined intellect, of pure but strong emotions. The Venus de Medici is a voluptuous, sensuous woman—the embodiment of physical beauty that is not illumined and elevated by intelligence." [158] The face that beamed down upon Hart in his infancy would have been more worthy of imitation in this respect, for his mother was described as being "big brained," [159] a trait he no doubt inherited and desired in turn to bestow upon his marble progeny.

Surviving photographs of the statue indicate that the coiffure was similar to that favored by Powers, enabling viewers to judge for themselves just how refined and big brained Hart's Venus really was. But beyond this feature and her obvious shapeliness, the little drama she enacts with Cupid, denying him the promiscuous use of his arrow, is emblematic of phrenological thinking on sexuality. Optimal coitus, it was contended, occurred when *Spirituality*, at the top of the head, held *Amativeness*, at the bottom, in subjugation, permitting the magnetic/spiritual force imparted to the child at this instant to be of the highest possible caliber. Hart's group enacts this tenet allegorically, for Cupid, often the symbol of *Amativeness* in phrenological texts, is held in check by the superior wisdom of a woman whose refined mental attributes distinguish her from the sensuous goddess of mythology.

Critical reaction to Hart's piece acknowledges this distinction; hence it resembles the response elicited by the works of Powers and Palmer. The figure represented, according to one reviewer, a "radical departure from the canons of antiquity" seen in "the Venus of the Capitol or the Venus de Medici." In wording reminiscent of the assurances offered about *The White Captive*, that she was "one of us" (that is, a modern woman), this same writer asserts that Hart had captured "our type of feminine beauty." [160] These claims were likely motivated by the large head that crowns the body, but recent histories have largely ignored this integration of form and content. One account, for instance, characterizes the effort as "confused" because it seeks to express the virtue of chastity by means of pagan ideals of beauty. [161] Members of Hart's generation, however, would have regarded his statue as a more meaningful antithesis to classical form than that achieved by the art of the Middle Ages. As such, it had much to impart to modern viewers.

A LIFETIME OF PHRENOLOGY

The years of Harriet Hosmer's minority coincided with the flourishing of phrenology in America. Born in 1830, she did not encounter the theory as a novel import from Europe; it was simply an integral part of the environment. This circumstance is illustrated by her father's endorsement in 1836 of a petition urging George Combe's appointment to the faculty of the University of Edinburgh. [162] Hiram Hosmer, a physician who practiced in the Boston suburb of Watertown, had every reason to hope that the Scotsman's prescriptions would serve as the proper regimen for his daughter. Having lost a wife and a child to consumption (tuberculosis), he was a subscriber to the belief that such maladies preyed on the weakness of women. As a consequence Harriet was given a horse, a gun, a boat, and permission to rove at will, her father claiming, "There is a lifetime for the cultivation of the mind, but the body develops in a few years, and during that period nothing should be permitted to interfere with its free and healthy growth." [163] The outcome can be judged from the report that "Harriet is a signal instance of what judicious physical training will effect in conquering even hereditary taint of constitution." [164]

Harriet's youth was governed in large measure by perceptions about congenital illness propagated by phrenology. Even her decision to become a sculptor must be viewed in this light, for wielding a heavy mallet provided the sort of exercise someone of her background and disposition required.[165] Her escape from the clutches of fashion was celebrated by Lydia Maria Child, a close friend, in the following manner: "Here was a woman, who, at the very outset of her life, refused to have her feet cramped by the little Chinese shoes, which society places on us all, and then misnames our feeble tottering feminine grace. If she walked forward with vigorous freedom and kept her balance in slippery places, she would do much toward putting those crippling little shoes out of fashion."[166] This inclination was not confined merely to footwear, for she also took to wearing bloomers when the occasion permitted.[167]

In 1847 Hosmer entered Elizabeth Sedgwick's famed academy. Among the inducements behind this move were the fresh mountain air of the Berkshires and the "healthful freedom" afforded by the school.[168] A notion of Sedgwick's philosophy can be garnered from passages of her writings quoted approvingly by Orson Fowler in one of his texts on physiology. Like Spurzheim and Combe, she states that Providence cannot be blamed if "young ladies" decide "to walk in thin shoes and delicate stockings in mid-winter. A healthy, blooming young girl thus dressed in violation of Heaven's laws, pays the penalty—a checked circulation, colds, fever, and death." In words that might have been inspired by Harriet's case, she remarks that "a feeble mother rarely leaves behind her vigorous children." Only avoidance of "indiscreet dressing, tight-lacing, etc." and devotion to "exercise, cleanliness, and pure air" might save such offspring.[169]

These ideas found their way into Harriet's juvenilia. In a mock disquisition on the hen delivered in 1848, for example, she remarks on the fowl's "intellectual *and* illustrative faculties," while mentioning Andrew Combe, George's brother, and the desirability of keeping the "animal propensities" subordinated to those governing the moral sense.[170] Some seven years later she reflected on the benefits of going "to dear Mrs. Sedgwick to study about the 'chain of connection'" of George Combe, an apparent reference to his teachings on man's relation to the environment.[171]

As Hosmer's reputation grew, phrenologists invoked her example as testimony to the truth of their theories. An article in the *Phrenological Journal and Life Illustrated* regularly punctuates statements about her large *Form* and *Constructiveness* with exclamation points, but considerable attention is also devoted to her father's unflagging efforts to ensure she received "good physical training, then and now so much neglected among girls." The reward of his persistence came when his daughter commenced work in the studio he built for her in the backyard, for "the muscular adaptation and strength gained by her vigorous physical exercise greatly contributed to her success in the manipulation of clay."[172] In phrenological circles she became something of an athlete of virtue, a heroine of health, and a living embodiment of Combe's principles. One pamphlet on the perils of tight lacing (which, incidentally, also advertises images of the *Greek Slave* to contrast with a "Deformed Woman," "drawn 'to the Life' from one of our patients") commends her example in these words: "The history of Miss Harriet Hosmer, the eminent sculptress is instructive. Her father, an eminent physician of Watertown, Mass. had lost wife and children of consumption, and fearing a like fate for Harriet, who was now the only survivor, he gave her dog, gun and boat, and insisted on an out-door life as indispensable to health."[173] The author then urges that children be introduced to physiological theory and training as early as possible.

After a residence of three years in Lenox, Harriet returned home at age nineteen, sound of mind and body and determined to pursue a career in art. The reluctance of Boston physicians to instruct a woman in anatomy sent her to St. Louis in 1850 to study with Joseph Nash McDowell at St. Louis Medical College. The fact that McDowell had already taught Powers and Clevenger suggests the kind of training she received, and his devotion to spiritualism must have deepened his relationship with a pupil who also exercised psychic powers.[174] In an interview granted late in life, Hosmer recounted the instruction she found most relevant to her own career: "Dr. McDowell once lectured on the form of a lady who had died from tight lacing. The ribs, instead of diverging diagonally downwards, had been cramped up until they interlaced. This had forced the upper organs up and the lower ones down until death had resulted." This passage is part of a monologue devoted to the advantages of loose clothing, and in it she spoke forthrightly about the goal of her art: "The problem of my life has been, why those who model fashion have made a departure to the opposite extreme of Hellenistic simplicity. Certain it is that those who set fashions for society appreciate Grecian models. The Venus de Medici is as large about the waist as about the chest. But while society leaders will admire that statue, they would weep their eyes away were they compelled to appear in the same unconfining draperies."[175] She concludes with the hope that the wheel of fortune will turn once again in favor of the fashions worn in antiquity.

This statement, with its assertion about the "problem" (direction) of her life, stands as a manifesto uttered in retrospect by the artist. One can imagine her taking such notions with her to Italy in 1852 and discussing them with John Gibson, her mentor in Rome. The English sculptor would have listened sympathetically, for he had served as one of George Combe's hosts during the winter of 1843–44 when the phrenologist traveled south.[176] Another adviser and confidante who had entered Hosmer's circle by 1855 was Anna Jameson, a prolific author and likewise one who shared her thoughts on art with Combe.[177]

These circumstances set the stage for *Zenobia in Chains* (fig. 7.10), a statue of the queen of Palmyra whose heroic defiance of the Roman empire eventually led to her capture in A.D. 273 by Aurelian. The moment selected for depiction was one of those disastrous reversals of fortune that try all the resources of character. Paraded before the Roman populace in a triumphal procession, Zenobia deports herself in a manner befitting her noble rank and station. The attitude of quiet determination in the face of adversity is reminiscent of the *Greek Slave*, and again the viewer must situate him- or herself. Are we to join the gawkers who crowd the city streets, or has the progress of moral culture in the nineteenth century transformed our gaze into one of sympathy?

The fact that *Zenobia* was created by a woman encouraged a personal identification of the artist with her subject that was less available to the male sculptors discussed above.[178] Hosmer researched the history and circumstances surrounding her heroine, and in this endeavor she profited from the assistance of Jameson, who had included a chapter on Zenobia in her book on female sovereigns.[179] Jameson sent a cast from a coin depicting the queen in profile but called attention to the fact that the diadem was "too low on the brow, thus taking from the value and dignity of the face, and that intellectual look which Zenobia had, I suppose as indicative of her talents."[180] Had she said the same to George Combe, the inference would have been as readily understood. Like the phrenologists, Hosmer also opposed those fashions that hid the brow and during a lecture delivered in her later years took the opportunity to bemoan the popularity of "bangs," which, she noted, betrayed "that oval facial contour over which the Greeks raved centuries ago."[181]

The most revealing statement concerning the intent of *Zenobia* comes in a letter Hosmer wrote to her patron Wayman Crow. There she remarks that if he could see in his mind's eye what she gazes on at present, "it would be a huge, magnificent room, not in Mr. Gibson's studio, but close by, with a monstrous lump of clay, which will be, as Combe would have said, 'when her system is sufficiently consolidated,' Zenobia."[182] The importance of this statement has, perhaps, evaded detection due to the offhand manner of its delivery. It encapsulates much of Hosmer's aesthetic while connecting it to the circumstances of her own life.

The mention of Combe and the consolidation of systems is a reference to the embryology discussed earlier in this chapter. As the fetus absorbs the mental and physical traits of its parents, so the clay reflects the mental and physical traits of the sculptor, a process that involves a wide array

FIGURE 7.10. Harriet Hosmer, *Zenobia in Chains* (original 1859, marble, Wadsworth Atheneum, Hartford, Conn., gift of Mrs. Josephine M. J. Dodge [Arthur E.]; this is a reduced version of the original)

of assumptions about these traits and the interrelation of mind and body. In a manner that parallels the criteria of Tuckerman's criticism, Hosmer proposes that the quality of her work reflects the quality of her being, and this resembles in turn the theory of acquired characteristics borrowed from Lamarck by phrenologists. If Harriet's infancy was imperiled by her mother's frailty, she (Harriet) had acquired health by vigorous exercise; now she could impart to her own "child," her *Zenobia*, the ample strength that had made her a model to physiologists. Much has been made of Hosmer as a precursor of the feminist movement in art, but the implications of the above passage as they pertain to the issue remain unexplored.[183] It is in them, however, that we come closest to her own sentiments regarding the relationship between her persona as a woman and that as a sculptor. While colleagues such as Powers often allude to their marble children, none poses the whole act of creation in terms that are so intimately biological and so maternal. One contemporary describes her "watching" a statue's "growth beneath her hand, as a young mother watches, step by step, the progress of her first born; kneading in with the plastic clay all those thousand hopes and fears which, turn by turn, charm and agitate all who aspire."[184] Hosmer's reference to Combe's theories of prenatal growth multiplies the ramifications of this metaphor manyfold while locating her radicalism within the orbit of that practiced by the Ladies' Physiological Institute.

A number of literary sources ancient and modern were available to Hosmer, but the precise passage that inspired the figure is difficult to identify. One might suppose that Jameson's history would have provided the definitive account, but she tells of Zenobia's "delicate form drooping under the weight of her golden fetters." These were so heavy that two slaves were obliged to assist her.[185] The marble Zenobia stands alone and evinces no such fatigue. Although the contribution of William Ware's novel about the queen has been debated, contemporaries made the connection,[186] and the circular distributed at the New York showing in 1864 quoted this source. While Ware mentions the servants and the protagonist's pitiable condition, he also emphasizes her physical stamina, and this can hardly have escaped the artist's notice. "A feebler spirit than Zenobia's," he writes, "and a feebler frame would necessarily have been destroyed" by the ordeal. The passage cited in the leaflet states she was "exposed to the rude gaze of the Roman populace, toiling beneath the rays of a hot sun, and her arms confined with chains of gold." This is an abbreviation of the novel's telling of events, and it pointedly omits the attending slaves who appear at the end of this very sentence.[187] The statue emphasizes Zenobia's solitary plight and the fortitude, both moral and physical, that enabled her to endure it.

The ornateness of Zenobia's drapery has often been viewed as excessive and thus detrimental to plastic values. Indeed, Lorado Taft called the work "a lay figure draped to display an antique garb."[188] While Hosmer did expend considerable labor on the garments,[189] the criticism of this effort overlooks its intent. The thick chains of gold, the abundant jewels, the weighty crown, and the heavy robes are all, paradoxically, counterparts to the nudity of the *Greek Slave*. If the latter exudes resilient health, so do the former, for their burden could only be borne by one who enjoyed great constitutional fortitude. In urging modern women to cast off the shackles of fashion and take up gymnastics, one physiological reformer adopts the philosophy that informed the statue by envisioning Zenobia's

> fine, massive figure [that] is as beautiful in its lines as a Greek statue or one of those early Saxon heroines Beringeria or Brunhilde, whose frame seems as large and strong as the imperious soul it carried. Behind her came thronging the women of the city [Palmyra], each one stalwart and straight under the tremendous burden she carries, and each one evidently as proud of her load as is her noble mistress. Good heavens! if they had worn tight sleeves, and humped shoulders, and eighteen inch corsets, and paniers, and high-heeled, pointed-toe boots, what a romantic interest would have been lost to history forever; for they could no more have shouldered their burdens than you or I could move Bunker Hill Monument.[190]

Years later, in explaining her aesthetic to a Chicago audience, Hosmer encouraged listeners to emulate the "big waists" and "big ankles" of the Venus de Milo and others so abundantly endowed. The reporter recording these remarks goes on to explain the speaker's reasoning in terms that indicate just how closely viewers of the era sought to emulate the marble figures before them. Regarding the desirability of those ample ankles, it was asked, "How can a beautiful statue (that means some of us, of course) be supported on a little pedestal?" It seems that art and the doctrines of physiology were interchangeable in the lessons they could impart, for the writer concludes that "from our training from Miss Hosmer the representative girl of the present period is sure to come from our ranks."[191] A similar thought occurred to Nathaniel Parker Willis when he gazed on *Zenobia* in 1864. American womanhood was evolving toward such ideals, he claimed, for "the sex is undergoing a grand process in the history of this republic."[192]

Hosmer's own "broad forehead and high aims" caught the eye of Elizabeth Barrett Browning when the two first met in Italy.[193] The artist reciprocated by describing Robert Browning as "the ideal we have formed of

FIGURE 7.11. Harriet Hosmer, *The Browning Hands*
(1853–54, bronze, Boston Public Library)

a poet. The broad forehead, the black and slightly waving hair, the keen
and clear eyes, the fresh complexion of faintest olive hue, and very slight,
as yet, the delicate frame."[194] This constellation of features locates the
author in the Nervous or Mental temperament, which phrenologists associated with those who "are very fond of reading and study, of thinking and
reasoning, of books and literary pursuits, of conversation and all kinds of
information."[195] In her delineation Hosmer does not halt with the forehead; she goes on to trace the refined nature throughout the entire body.
Others were prepared to do the same. Samuel Wells characterized Browning's hand as "better adapted to hold the pen than the sword, and may
write with great fervor and brilliancy."[196] These observations can serve to
introduce *The Browning Hands* (fig. 7.11), perhaps the most revered sculpture of its kind from the Victorian era.

Cast in the winter of 1853–54 at Harriet's own bidding, the piece became a prized keepsake and was frequently reproduced.[197] If regarded
merely as a relic of the Browning cult, the cast loses much of the impact it
once delivered. Even the usually sober Nathaniel Hawthorne was moved
to call it a symbol of "the individuality and heroic union of two, high,
poetic lives."[198] Such responses were sanctioned by the belief that every
portion of the anatomy was resonant with character. Deprived of such justification, objects of this ilk tend to wash up on the shores of our time bereft of the life that once animated them. For Hosmer it was as replete with
the identity of two sensitive souls as the other features mentioned above,
and this belief explains her decision not to polish or otherwise finish the
hands when they came from the mold. This resolution was taken "to preserve at the expense of finish all their characteristics of texture."[199] When

we recall that even the surface of the flesh revealed qualities of mind, that the skin of the hardened criminal, for example, was coarser than that of the refined poet, the logic behind Hosmer's decision becomes apparent.

The Browning Hands embodies the virtues of marital fidelity and ideal poetic character. Devotion to the life of the mind is readily visible in the delicacy of the structure and refinement of form. How Robert would have winced had Zenobia clasped him in her firm grip! The influence of the vital spiritual principle can be perceived in the queen's figure as well. Not even her massive garments can conceal the erect posture and sturdy constitution that reprimand a generation whose infatuation with fashion had rendered it oblivious to the distress of the unborn. These same features were especially meaningful to the artist, for they served as a reminder of the benefits she had derived from a lifetime's devotion to the tenets of phrenology. In her old age did she gaze wistfully at the hands cast so many years earlier, finding in their frailty a portent of the relatively brief worldly partnership of two souls now joined in eternity?

WICKED WOMEN

One account of William Wetmore Story's *Venus Anadyomene* (fig. 7.12) claims it was created as a ruse to fool a connoisseur into identifying it as antique, but circumstances suggest that the sculptor had other, more serious intentions in mind when he commenced the piece.[200] In 1859 a statue of Venus posed in the manner of the *Venus de' Medici* was unearthed just outside the walls of Rome. Initially it lacked a head, but this was soon discovered nearby. When the statue was assembled, viewers noted that the head was "not of that disproportionate smallness which strikes the beholder on first contemplating the 'Venus de Medici.'"[201] Story confirmed this judgment, pronouncing the head "larger and in better proportion to the figure than the small, characterless head of her rival."[202] Given his phrenological preferences, the circumstances must have inaugurated a train of thought that sanctioned his only completely nude female.

It has also been proposed that the *Venus Anadyomene* was devised to test a system of proportions Story was then formulating,[203] but no specific evidence linking the sculptor's mystical, arcane theory to the figure has yet been adduced.[204] Elsewhere in his writings, however, pertinent passages do appear. In one of these he bemoans the want of appreciation of sculpture among his contemporaries, explaining that "the public appreciate neither its anatomical accuracy nor its subtle expression of the human form; because the naked figure is so rarely seen, and so unfamiliar, that few are able to say whether it is right or wrong."[205] By contrast, "the Greeks always had the nude before them, and felt no sham mod-

esty in exposing their person." The annual festival of Neptune provided Athenian girls the opportunity to bathe in the sea while all gazed at them without misgiving. On such occasions Phryne, a beauty of great repute, exposed herself to the populace and resembled none more than Aphrodite as she rose from the sea.[206] Depictions of Aphrodite (or Venus) rising from the sea were titled "Venus Anadyomene," and following a prototype established by Apelles, she was shown wringing the water from her hair. Story's reference to this tradition was not merely an instance of learned antiquarianism; the subject was of great relevance to modern civilization, and his lost *Phryne before the Tribunal,* a piece done in 1873, testifies to the ongoing importance of these concerns to the sculptor.[207]

Story goes on to propose that "artists were thus inspired, and all the world educated to a knowledge of the human figure and its nude beauty. When they saw a statue, they could criticise [*sic*] it and feel its beauty or defects." The habit could be cultivated during one's daily routine:

> The Greek dresses, with their long folds and delicate draperies, followed the form and the motions. But how can we in general know whether a statue is right or wrong, who can only judge it by generalities, and lose all the finesse and refinement of the art? In Greece, fashion did not every year rearrange itself, seeking ever the new and the fantastic, as it does with us. There beauty and grace were the ends sought, not mere novelty. For centuries the dresses never changed. They were simple, and modeled on the human figure,—vestes artus exprimentes, —not like ours, grotesque and deforming. The tyranny of scissors had not come. With them, what was beautiful today was beautiful tomorrow, the next month, the next year, the next century. We, on the contrary, worship the Proteus of Fashion. The costume of one season becomes ridiculous in our eyes the next season. We chiffonier everything. We are made of shreds and patches. There is neither dignity nor beauty in our dress, and the outward shows of life are vulgar and ugly.

A series of dichotomies is developed here to emphasize the point. Against the tyranny of scissors Story sets the benign reign of the chisel; the worship of Proteus is opposed to that of the unclad Venus; fashion is contrasted to nature, and the transitory to the eternal. From these a reciprocal relationship between art and nature emerges, each heightening one's sensitivity to the beauties or defects of the other. His avowal of the benefits of public nudity may be merely the daydream of an overdressed age, but in such reflective moments Story, the Brahmin of Boston, sounds very much like the bard of Brooklyn, Walt Whitman.

Most detrimental, in Story's opinion, was the Gallic insistence on "some

hump of deformity on women's dresses: sometimes it is low down, sometimes high up, sometimes behind, sometimes in front, sometimes all
round, but it never is wanting. I suppose no modern dress would be
accepted in Paris without a deformity somewhere."[208] These same sentiments inspired his muse to describe one creature of fashion as

> the thing of laces, and silk,
> And ribbons, and gauzes, and crinoline,
> With her neck and shoulders as white as milk,
> And her doll-like face and conscious mien.
> A lay-figure fashion to fit a dress,
> All stuffed within with straw and bran;
> Is that a woman to love, to caress?
> Is that a creature to charm a man?[209]

The charms of such creatures quickly pale before those of the peas-
ant women,

> All in their festal costumes clad,
> O'er bursting bosoms the busto laced,
> Spanning with scarlet their ample waist.[210]

Excessive mental activity, Story worried, would unfit women for motherhood. "The world now overworks its brain," he warns, "and grows severe
in its wisdom and feeble on its legs, and a morbid irritability of temper
follows as a necessary consequence. When we scorn the body it revenges
itself on the mind; only a healthy, vigorous frame can hold a healthy, vigorous body." American girls, he continues, are thinner and more fibrous
than their English counterparts. The latter exhibit a roundness of muscle
developed during the frequent outings to which they are accustomed.
Their cousins across the Atlantic, however, are "kiln-dried in over heated
rooms," and the solution he proposes is identical to that advanced by
Combe and the Fowlers. The introduction of recreation periods at school
would relieve the bad digestion that results from an overactive brain and a
passive body, and thus quiet the nerves of our irritable national psyche.[211]
Emulation of the *Venus Anadyomene* would also help; free of Parisian fashions, she bathes in the ocean. The benefits of such exercise appear in the
figure, while her head is far more instructive to moderns than the standard set by the *Venus de' Medici.* The small size of Story's piece destined it
for a domestic interior, and there one can imagine it fulfilling a function
analogous to that served by the statuettes of the *Greek Slave.*[212]

The supposed differences between English and American women was a
theme Story returned to repeatedly, each time adjusting the implications

slightly. In one instance he again describes his countrywomen as slighter limbed, fairer, and thinner than the more fully developed British type. He extends this discourse to the hands and feet, where, he contends, the greatest distinctions are found. The American foot is small, thin, high arched, and tendonous in the ankle; the hand exhibits like characteristics. Across the Atlantic, however, hands are plump and ankles full. Those wanting proof need only "take a cast from an American and an English foot, and any one can distinguish them with half an eye. All the attachments, as they are called, are longer and more tendonous in the American than in the English." These observations are then expanded to include their moral implications. The lean Yankee girl, he maintains, is more vivacious and excitable than her English counterpart, whose heavier build accords with the evenness of temper for which the inhabitants of the British Isles are famed.[213]

Without such insights the viewer of Story's "wicked" women is inadequately prepared to appreciate their implications. As his *Venus* illustrates, an erect posture best serves the positive exemplar. We are invited to judge the relative proportions of the head to the body, the fitness of the torso, and so on. A seated or reclining pose obscures much of this and is likewise suggestive of a relaxation of moral rectitude. It can hardly be coincidental that most of Story's protagonists who are so rendered are, from the standpoint of Europeans, dysgenic to some degree. This does not place them beyond the pale of phrenology, but its tenets are more productively engaged in examining the entire organic constitution than in scrutinizing a particular portion of the skull.

Some notion of Story's thinking on this subject comes from his efforts to conjure up the shade of Lady Macbeth. She could not be the tall, dark, imperious figure played by Sarah Siddons but, rather, a woman of medium height and delicate organization, with hair inclining to red and little hands. "Her temperament nervous and sanguine," she is capable of repentance and must act at once on her resolve. The deed done, she breaks down and dies of remorse, a clear indication that her nature "was not wicked in itself" but merely the victim of a sluggish moral sense.[214] We need only open a standard phrenological text to find the same lady in the pages devoted to the Mental or Nervous temperament. Such women exhibit "a high, pale forehead," delicate features, hair that is not "very dark," and soft skin of fine texture. They "lack the rounded outlines, the full bosom, and the expanded pelvis, which betoken the highest degree of adaptation to the distinctive offices of the sex," displaying instead an "emaciation of the muscles" that disposes them to "quickness and intensity of the sensations, the suddenness and fickleness of the determinations, and a morbid impressibility." These words describe not only Lady Macbeth but also much of what we see in Story's *Sappho* and those American girls who might benefit from the example set by the rounder, fuller proportions of English womanhood. Indeed, the phrenologist quoted here chimes in on this point, claiming, "There is at the present day, in this country especially, an excessive and morbid development of this temperament" due to "sedentary habits, lack of bodily exercise," and "a premature or disproportionate development of the brain."[215]

Such fragile types are remote from Story's *Cleopatra* (1858, replica of 1869 in the Metropolitan Museum of Art, New York, N.Y.), a brooding, venomous creature whom Hawthorne described as "voluptuous, passionate, tender, wicked, terrible, and full of poisonous and rapturous enchantment." Ideas about passion and race were also entertained by the artist as he contemplated the piece. Many assumed that, as a member of the Ptolemaic dynasty, Cleopatra was Greek; the artist argued against this, however, citing sources to prove her African descent.[216] His determination on this point derived not merely from a desire for historical accuracy but, perhaps even more profoundly, from convictions about what acts a Greek, as opposed to an Egyptian, Cleopatra was capable of committing. Sappho was his Greek; she was, in his own words, "very tender, very sweet, very sentimental." Jilted once by a lover, her faculties abandon her. Story continues the line just quoted by stating that he went "into Egypt" for *Cleopatra*[217] and in doing so created a more amply endowed figure. The sculptor alludes to her physical attributes in a poem about an artists' model who sits for a painting of Cleopatra:

> With her squared brows, and full Egyptian lips,
> A great gold serpent on her rounded arm.[218]

Like the English girls Story admired, Cleopatra displays a roundness of limb that betokens physical fortitude, though perhaps not the former's high-mindedness.

Cleopatra has survived a series of blows, any one of which would have sundered Sappho. Indeed, even as Cleopatra's empire crumbles and Octavius remains oblivious to her charms, critics could discern a faint smile on her lips, perhaps, they surmised, induced by memories of past lovers or the glory she once knew.[219] Again, phrenology enables us to fathom the mysteries of one so organized. Those belonging to the Vital temperament possess a bust that "is full and rounded" while harboring a penchant for "violent and passionate" behavior. "The whole figure is plump, soft and voluptuous," the writer adds, but unfortunately "this temperament is not so common among American women as could be desired."[220] Certainly

Story's sentiments did not diverge widely from these, and he must have hoped that the brainy women of his native land would become a little more like Cleopatra, while not relinquishing altogether their powers of intellect.[221]

In describing his *Libyan Sibyl* (1861, replica of 1868 in the Smithsonian Institution, Washington, D.C.), Story articulated most fully the qualities of race as they pertained to his work.

> This last winter I finished what I consider my best work—it is so consid-ered by all, I believe—the Libyan Sibyl. I have taken the pure Coptic head and figure, the great massive sphinx-face, full-lipped, long-eyed, low-browed and lowering, and the largely-developed limbs of the Afri-can. . . . The upper part of the figure is nude, and a rich simple mantle clothes her legs. This gave me a grand opportunity for the contrast of the masses of the nude with drapery, and I studied the nude with great care. It is a very massive figure big-shouldered, large-bosomed, with nothing of the Venus in it, but, as far as I could make it, luxuriant and heroic. She is looking out of her black eyes into futurity and sees the terrible fate of her race. This is the theme of the figure—Slavery on the horizon, and I made her head as melancholy and severe as possible, not at all shrinking the real African type. On the contrary, it is thoroughly African—Libyan African of course, not Congo.[222]

In this instance a low brow corresponds with the massiveness of the figure. While it has taken numerous shocks to bring Cleopatra to the brink of suicide, the sibyl can contemplate the enslavement of an entire race and still endure. A contemporary reviewer picked up on these characteristics, noting "the full-bloom proportions of ripe womanhood" that make her the "mother of myriads."[223] Among those myriads will appear Topsy. Like the absent parent of Stowe's little black girl, the *Libyan Sibyl* is hidden in the obscurity of the past, and like the same shadowy being, she has be-queathed all her daughters a physical fortitude and resilience that their masters might envy and emulate.

William Gerdts finds a positive correlation in sculpture between the size of breasts and the progress of the century. The later the date, the larger the bust. This culminates, he adds, in Story's *Salome* (1871, Metropolitan Museum of Art, New York, N.Y.), another of the artist's vengeful protago-nists who unabashedly displays the bountiful attributes of her sex.[224] She is, however, no more generously endowed than her sisters of a decade earlier, and perhaps a more calculated agenda is operative here than mere infatuation with amplitude. Above, I proposed that while Story's women are in some sense dysgenic, their example was not to be eschewed entirely. They do not advocate miscegenation; no right-minded male would contemplate marriage to one of these murderous individuals, whatever their allure. The pleading, rather, is directed to the female audience. Delicately organized Yankee girls might gaze upon these brawny temptresses and learn something about the physical consequences of love. Passion, as we have seen, was essential to the successful outcome of the act of generation, but passion unaccompanied by the endurance necessary to withstand its drain could prove disastrous. One might be less excitable than Sappho and considerably superior to Cleopatra or Salome in matters of morality. Since the latter could be taken for granted, it was the muscular development of Story's wicked women that called for emulation. A little more roundness and fullness of proportion would serve to temper the nervous energy prevalent among the irritable daughters of Puritanism. In essence, this message parallels the one delivered by reformers, for they wanted to disabuse the populace of the illusion that sexual pleasure, passion if you will, was solely the domain of nonwhite females. To enhance the prospects of success, adolescent girls were asked to suspend their brainwork so that they might gather the strength necessary for the impending trials of childbearing.[225]

The most problematic of Story's figures is *Medea* (fig. 7.13), a woman encountered as she contemplates the most unspeakable of crimes, the murder of her children. Clearly there can be no question of eugenics here, but phrenology helps us comprehend her dilemma and perhaps moderates the severity of our condemnation. Useful in this respect is the artist's description of Macbeth's mental state just before he embarks on his fatal course. It "has been too long strained with one thought," Story surmises, "and, as in all men of excitable brain, there comes a moment of reaction."[226] This account relies heavily on the theory of monomania adopted by the sculptor from phrenology, and we may safely assume that Medea is also one "of excitable brain." But what faculty or faculties have been so preoccupied, and what are the consequences?

The Medea of classical legend is a magician and woman capable of great cruelty, visiting her wrath not just on her children but on a number of other persons as well. In Story's poetry Medea's persona is amplified by the variety of emotions that contend with one another as she meditates on the death of her offspring. There we are urged to "see on her dark face and serpent brow, rage, fury, love, despair,"[227] much as we do in the marble figure. Also relevant is the performance of Adelaide Ristori, an Italian actress who, as the lead in Ernest Legouve's *Medea*, had enchanted audiences in Europe and America. Story writes enthusiastically about her performance, and it is difficult to imagine that his sculpture was uninflu-

FIGURE 7.13. William Wetmore Story, *Medea* (ca. 1868–80, marble, courtesy of Museum of Fine Arts, Boston, gift of a friend of the department and the Curator's Fund)

enced by this experience. In the play, Medea is presented as a devoted mother who slays her children only after learning that they are to be removed from her care. The sympathy of this portrayal has led modern critics to stress the commingled elements of compassion and revulsion that are likely to dictate the viewer's response to the statue.[228]

While evoking both these emotions, *Medea* presents the case for the defense. Story, who was a successful lawyer before becoming an artist, labors dutifully on behalf of his client.[229] The phrenologists had investigated infanticide because it seemed so contrary to the "laws of nature." It could be explained, however, as a consequence of feeble *Philoprogenitiveness*, and when this condition prevailed, some mitigation of the punishment was advised.[230] In Story's Medea, on the other hand, the motive apparently derives from an excess of parental affection, from a brain that has been captivated by a single faculty and has now lapsed into insanity.

Those who regarded the mind as a single power made little progress in the treatment of the insane, Spurzheim insisted. Any faculty might induce alienation if, under great tension, it snapped and made demands on mind and body that could not be placated by the powers of reason or volition. Sudden affections of a disagreeable nature were especially perilous in this respect, but if one faculty were deranged, did this preclude the exercise of moral and legal freedom in other areas where the relevant faculties remained unaffected?[231] In probing the organic factors that contributed to insanity and crime (the two were closely linked), phrenology took issue with those who attributed such tendencies to innate depravity and with a penal system that viewed its measures as purely retributive. It was hoped that understanding would make more lenient the exercise of restraint on those whose misdeeds necessitated it.[232]

Also relevant to the *Medea* is Story's account of an Irish immigrant who was brought before the court of his father, Joseph Story, on the charge of infanticide. Alone and desperate on her voyage to America, she could conceive of no greater succor for her babe than to cast it upon the ocean's heaving bosom. The verdict of innocence was predicated on the prisoner's mental derangement at the time of the act, "situated as she was . . . [in] a state very likely to exist in the condition produced by recent delivery, and amid such appalling circumstances. . . . [She] was so near to insanity, that she could not be held legally responsible for what she might have done. It was also shown how directly such entire destitution of all that care, nay of any portion of it, which her recent confinement demanded, went to produce a state of mind which would destroy responsibleness."[233]

Further insight on the subject comes from Oliver Wendell Holmes's *Elsie Venner*, where the heroine, for whom the novel is named, suffers all her life from a congenital proclivity for malevolence brought on by a traumatic encounter between her mother and a rattlesnake. Deep within the womb, the fetus that would become Elsie shared this affliction, and its enduring consequences recall Story's figure: "Here was a magnificent organization, superb in vigorous womanhood, with a beauty such as never comes but after generations of culture; yet through all this rich nature there ran some alien current of influence, sinuous and dark, as when a clouded streak seams the white marble of a perfect statue."[234] Other telling traits include "scowling eyebrows"; a fondness for jewelry, especially a golden torque such as worn by the Gauls; and an inclination to loll about on animal skins. Elsie has, according to the author, much in common with Cleopatra,[235] and while Holmes did not share Story's enthusiasm for phrenology, both men believed that the moral and corporeal person were linked by correspondences.

Suspicion that Elsie has attempted (unsuccessfully) to poison her governess leads to an exchange between the local physician and the town's minister. The latter disparages theories of biological fatalism, which, he believes, tend to loosen the bonds of morality and religion that hold society together. The former responds that, while we must act according to conscience, experience suggests that not all races or individuals are granted the same capabilities for practical freedom of choice.[236] His further reflections on this principle seem to answer the riddle posed by *Medea.*

> The limitations of human responsibility have never been properly studied, unless it be by the phrenologists. You know from my lectures that I consider phrenology, as taught, a pseudo-science, and not a branch of positive knowledge; but for all that, we owe it an immense debt. It has melted the world's conscience in its crucible, and cast it in a new mold with features less like those of Moloch and more like those of humanity. If it has failed to demonstrate its system of special correspondences, it has proved that there are fixed relations between organization and mind and character. It has brought out the great doctrine of moral insanity, which has done more to make men charitable and soften legal and theological barbarism than any one doctrine that I can think of since the message of peace and good-will to men.[237]

The viewer who casts aside the doubts expressed here and adopts its positive assertions will approach the statue with many of the same assumptions that motivated its creator.

Story readily professed his allegiance to phrenology, and its teachings underlie much of his thought. It subjected infanticide to prolonged scrutiny and concluded that it was indeed a form of moral insanity. As the attorney for the defense, the sculptor points to his client and claims she had been abandoned by her husband for another woman. Then, faced with the prospect of having to relinquish her children, the reigning instinct of her existence, *Philoprogenitiveness*, lapsed into a monomania that prompted behavior that was otherwise entirely abhorrent to its nature. This is not a case of congenital deficiency, he tells the jury; on the contrary, because she is so thoroughly a woman, her mind is permeated by the longings engendered by this faculty, and the possibility of losing the object of these yearnings was simply too much to bear. Biology and circumstance exonerate the defendant, just as they did the unfortunate woman acquitted before the court of Judge Story.

Having established his ideal in the *Venus Anadyomene*, Story chose to explore other types. By turning to his wicked women, however, he did not intend to deny their potential to instruct. The smoldering passions of these tigresses might spark kindred emotions in the proper American women who came to see them. There was a time and place for everything, the phrenologists proclaimed, and this included sexual ecstasy when governed by the moral faculties. Viewers were challenged, then, not merely to read the narrative as developed in the secondary details of the statues[238] but to weigh their knowledge of these events against the organic constitution of the protagonist. This involved the integration of iconographic and formal analysis, and Story hoped his contemporaries would familiarize themselves with the particulars of the female anatomy so that they might be equal to the task. Without this physiological dimension to lend meaning to their parts, his actresses tend to be upstaged by their costumes and trappings.

The acts committed by Medea were provoked by *Philoprogenitiveness* rather than *Amativeness*. For this reason, and because she was Greek, she evoked more sympathy than might be granted either Cleopatra or Salome. But in either case, phrenology possessed the virtue of explaining what seemed incomprehensible to many Victorians: the dangerous, vengeful woman. It demonstrated how this apparent violation of feminine character could, in fact, be reconciled with the laws of nature. Indeed, as late as 1927, when Ruth Snyder was tried for murdering her husband in a sensational case described by one historian as being "as subversive to American domesticity as the anarchism of Nicola Sacco and Bartolomeo Vanzetti was to the American political and economic order," a phrenologist was hired by the newspapers to assuage any doubts readers may have entertained about the defendant (who was eventually electrocuted). After examining her photographs, the consultant, Dr. Edgar C. Beall, concluded that she was "a shallow-brained pleasure-seeker, accustomed to unlimited self-indulgence, which at last ends in an orgy of murderous passion and lust."[239] This criminal type bore little resemblance to Medea, but if the spirit of William Story hovered over the proceedings, he must have nodded in assent.

Some three years after these events, while at work on his *Andromeda* (1929–31, Chesterwood), the aged Daniel Chester French granted an interview to a reporter. During their exchange the sculptor voiced opinions that indicate the longevity of the philosophy discussed in this chapter.

> The modern woman . . . has reached a perfection which woman hasn't achieved since the days of Greece. The reason is very simple. She is the first free woman of many centuries. She has intellectual freedom, and she has physical freedom. Her figure has improved marvelously since she got out of stays. In fact, it is almost unbelievable, the difference between the modern woman and woman of my youth. This generation of women which hasn't worn stays is the most nearly perfect that the world has seen in many centuries. Even when she passes her first youth she still has a good figure.[240]

The *Andromeda* could justly claim a lineage that stretched back almost a century previous to her conception, but several developments ensured its rapid demise. While the eugenics crusade had enjoyed two generations of recognition in political and academic circles by 1930,[241] the movement was soon to be discredited entirely by its incorporation into the racial doctrines of the Nazis. Aesthetically, the finely nuanced modeling and realism of the *Andromeda* could not withstand the assaults of modernism, which had long since cast such conventions aside as the vestiges of an earlier, less enlightened age.

Nevertheless, the frank sensuality of French's nude, which makes its predecessors seem positively timid by comparison, can be seen as the consummation of Whitman's vision. Here was the liberated Eve he celebrated in poetry and prose, one who fulfilled as well the prescriptions Orson Fowler had set down for the millennium. But that millennium was not merely physiological; it also entailed transformations in the environment. This goal could be achieved by designing domiciles capable of advancing the physical and mental growth of their inhabitants, and this brings us to the most visible legacy left the American landscape by phrenology, the octagon house.

8

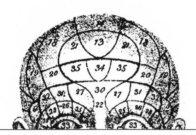

Increase and Multiply

In 1847, as the *Greek Slave* disembarked in New York to begin her tour, Orson Fowler commenced work on his octagonal home, a structure that likewise was meant to offer the citizenry a model.[1] If the slave was to serve by example as the mother of untold millions, then her progeny would require an environment capable of preparing them to assume their place among those destined to quicken the pace of progress. Fowler was not merely building a domicile; he was creating the future. That future materialized near the banks of the Hudson in the town of Fishkill (fig. 8.1) and appeared as well in *A Home for All*, a manual written for those who wished to share the dream.[2] Analysis of Fowler's architectural schemes has relied primarily on this text, but this approach has largely ignored the utopian vision that informed the enterprise. The particulars of the latter he published elsewhere, and only by considering this added dimension do we learn how the octagon house was intended to bring mankind into closer correspondence with the vitalistic principles of nature. A brief venture through this millennial landscape, then, allows us to conclude by surveying the philosophy presented in previous chapters.

Long before Fowler set spade to sod, the urge to do so beckoned from within. He knew that the desire to own a home was innate; its powerful sway originated in *Inhabitiveness* (fig. 8.2).[3] "Every living thing has its HOME," he wrote. The fox has its hole, rats and reptiles burrow in the ground, and even the "very hills make themselves residences." While such projections might seem fatuous, they were a logical consequence of applying the law of correspondences to the subject at hand. Any inclination that arose in the mind had its counterpart throughout nature, but Fowler's primary reason for such recitations was to impress upon his audience the importance of owning a home. If the lowly creatures of the planet managed to provide themselves an abode, how much more incumbent was it upon man to do likewise? No one was exempt from the directive, which weighed particularly heavily on those about to start a family. Everyone, no matter how impecunious, should strive to satisfy *Inhabitiveness*, even if it meant living in a "turf hovel" on a diet of bread and water. Better this than an impaired faculty. Besides, the freedoms guaranteed citizens of the republic ensured that anyone with an ounce of gumption was bound to "rise from poverty to comfort, and then to affluence." Home ownership

FIGURE 8.1. *Residence of O. S. Fowler*, from "Residence of O. S. Fowler," *American Phrenological Journal* 18 (1853): 120

was a crucial ingredient in Fowler's recipe for the renovation of society; hence he regarded it a "sacred injunction."

One faculty alone could not effect the sweeping changes Fowler envisioned, and throughout his writings, as well as those of his colleagues, we encounter maxims that were pertinent to the outcome of his architectural venture. A building loaded down with ornament, with statues and battlements, for example, would engage *Number* excessively, while one that pierced the skies unduly excited *Sublimity* at the expense of the pleasure taken by *Ideality* in beauty.[4] Concord within the domestic circle was largely the responsibility of *Philoprogenitiveness*, and rented rooms rarely afforded the privacy it required to function effectively.[5] As might be expected, *Constructiveness* is frequently discussed, and many attributed the elaborate domiciles built by birds, beavers, and bees to its promptings. But the activities of animals followed in unvarying patterns from one generation to the next, while the mind of man was not bound by such imperious instincts and hence held the promise of improvement.[6]

The offspring of *Constructiveness* reflected the moral tenor of the mind that gave them birth. Fowler observed that "inferior animals, moths, worms, reptiles, etc., make very poor homes." From these lower species the ladder extended upward to mankind, where "the Hottentot, Carib, Malay, Indian, and Caucasian build structures better, and better still corresponding with the order of their mentality." Being the epitome of nature, man could advance beyond his own accomplishments or sink back to a lower level.[7] "The slack, low-minded, and 'shiftless'" man was content to huddle in a hut dug from some river's bank, but for the "spirited, ambi-

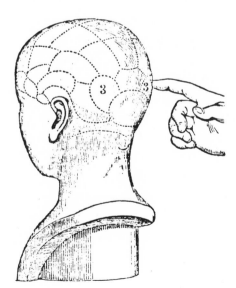

FIGURE 8.2.
Location of Inhabitiveness, from "Inhabitiveness: Its Definition, Location, and Adaptation, Together with the Importance of Having a Home," *American Phrenological Journal and Miscellany* 10 (1848): 55

tious, and enterprising," only a mansion on a splendid eminence would suffice. Indeed, just as the mind impressed its character upon the various bodily members, so "a fancy man will build a fancy cottage; a practical man, a convenient home; a substantial man, a solid edifice; a weak man, an illy-arranged house; an aspiring man, a high house; and a superior man a superb villa." Not only does Fowler extend the chain of being to include architecture; he also proposes that the chain itself could progress with time. Surveying the ruins of Pompeii, he found only two houses above one story. Mankind was then only "little developed,"[8] and their homes were as inferior as the cerebral organization of the Venuses they worshiped in nearby temples. Since progress was a universal law, we might expect that modern buildings would stand to their ancient counterparts as the *Greek Slave* did to the goddesses of paganism; but Fowler found little evidence of a comparable advancement, and he set out to rectify the situation.[9]

There can be little doubt that the frequent references in phrenological literature to the hexagonal cells devised by the *Constructiveness* of bees stood behind Fowler's decision to adopt the octagon as nature's plan for domestic architecture.[10] While claiming this innovation and its combination with the cement wall as his own,[11] he barely acknowledges a long tradition of octagons that extended from colonial times to his own; but he is more forthcoming about his debt to Joseph Goodrich of Milton, Wisconsin, for convincing him of the virtues of gravel.[12] The questions relating to Fowler's originality, or lack of it, have been discussed elsewhere[13] and are of less consequence here than the philosophy that links his architectural ambitions to the physiological considerations delineated in the previous chapter.

While the example of the honeybee may have put Fowler's thoughts in motion, he soon adduced a number of practical and aesthetic reasons for emulating its example. Always a proponent of the practical, he recognized that an octagon required less construction material than a comparable rectangle. The reduced outlay meant that home ownership became an option for a portion of the populace that otherwise would not know the pleasures that attended the exercise of *Inhabitiveness*. Nature also sanctioned his efforts. Her forms were "mostly SPHERICAL"; one need only consider the egg, fruits, tubers, nuts, grains, and similar products of her bounty to realize that their design accomplished much of what the phrenologist proposed to do for architecture. The difficulties involved in raising circular walls, however, caused him to advocate the octagon as a viable alternative. The results, Fowler claimed, were bound to satisfy the eye as well as the wallet, for beauty and utility were inseparable. The truth of this position was confirmed by the almost universal preference for rounded rather than angular shapes; we are told, for instance, that smooth stones are more valued than irregular ones, fleshy persons favored over lean, and apples prized more than chestnut burrs.[14] Whatever the merit of this argument, Fowler's emphasis on utility during an era of ornamental excess has earned him a place in the annals of architecture for anticipating Louis Sullivan's dictum that "form follows function."[15]

Economy and nature, then, sanctioned the octagon as the optimal plan for domestic architecture. Both are invoked, for example, to discourage contemplation of the addition of wings. Not only do such appendages offer scant reward for the expense and effort; they do not answer nature's taste. While wings served the bird admirably, the prospect of a large apple or pear joined on either side by smaller ones was not equally appealing.[16] The implications of this line of reasoning become clearer when Fowler brings the human anatomy into consideration. He argues, for example, against setting the kitchen off from the domicile, calling such outbuildings "wind-riven, out-of-doors, stomach-in-the-foot shanties."[17] The controlling device here is again the theory of correspondences, but this method was especially apt when applied to the skull. Here was a shape that offered a particularly telling analogy to architecture.

This subject appears frequently in the *American Phrenological Journal*, where, for example, one article is devoted entirely to a comparison between the cranium and a castle of many rooms, each occupied by an "appropriate tenant." Inhabitants of the basement are enthralled by "things earthly and material," and because they are given over to "the cultivation of animal feeling," they "do the fighting, the butchering, the cooking, and the rough labor of the entire community." The upper stories are devoted to conserving what society cherishes. Finer distinctions among these dwellers are also made; residents of the anterior apartments of the second story are members of "the historical society, who keep the library, and dispense information." On the third floor reside "philosophical, metaphysical, and analytic characters." One would hardly expect a castle to feature a dome, but there it is, sheltering "the court of justice, of dignity, stability, philanthropy and religion."[18] In other words, the animal, intellectual, and spiritual faculties have taken rooms in the cerebral castle according to their merits. Another article declares "that, while one [man] has a brain but two stories high, and poorly furnished at that, another has one three or even four stories high, well furnished." This distinction is even more pronounced, the author continues, in the case of animals. They are entirely bereft of *Veneration* and hence enjoy "no sense of godliness, nor spiritual insight." He returns again to this analogy in words that also recall Fowler's octagon: "Man has a brain, which, when compared with that of animals, may be likened to a three-story house with a sky-light, while the heads of animals may be compared to a one-story house with a basement and no sky-light."[19]

Fowler generally favored the three-story plan as the house most consistent with his theories, but he was willing to make allowances. Persons of modest means, for instance, might have to settle for a story and a half, but the more affluent should strive for two or three floors if they wished their abode "to appear well proportioned."[20] The cupola or dome advocated by the phrenologist was a complicating factor. On a structure that otherwise rose only two stories, it could be considered the third, fulfilling the function of *Veneration*, particularly when surmounted by a glazed dome. Such was the topping on Fowler's own home,[21] and since a central staircase was located directly beneath, God's good light could filter through the entire structure. Although this was a four-story structure, it did not necessarily violate the brain-building principle, for diagrams of the larger phrenological categories were not limited merely to three major divisions. Refinements were often introduced, and these allowed the reformer some leeway in his plans. Thus, despite the grandeur of his domicile, it was generally in accord with the maxims he set down.

The interior sustained much the same philosophy, although the parallels could be carried only so far. The foundation, Fowler noted, was to a house what the animal and social organs were to the brain,[22] and the functions served by the basement of his home (fig. 8.3) were the least elevated of those the building was intended to serve. There was located the kitchen (K), that "great stomach of the house," while adjoining it were dining (W.D.) and sitting (W.S.) rooms for the servants. Visitors waited in the receiving room (R.R.). There were closets (CL.) and a pantry (P), and coal was kept under the stairs.[23] Other than meeting rather basic, physical needs, it would be difficult to assign each of these chambers a corresponding mental organ, and instead of concentrating on the particulars, it is the larger design that reveals most about the orientation of Fowler's thought. A hall extends through the center, dividing a series of rooms that are more or less symmetrically arranged on either side. This scheme recapitulates the disposition of the faculties, which were likewise evenly distributed in the two lobes of the brain.[24] Just as each faculty was occupied by a specific kind of thought, each room was devoted to a single activity.[25]

Climbing the stairs, we come to "the main pleasure story of the house" (fig. 8.4), where large dining (Di.) and drawing (Dr.) rooms are provided for entertainment on a grand scale. A hundred guests could be seated for dinner, and if more appeared, folding doors between the rooms enabled the host to accommodate the overflow.[26] This feature is reminiscent of

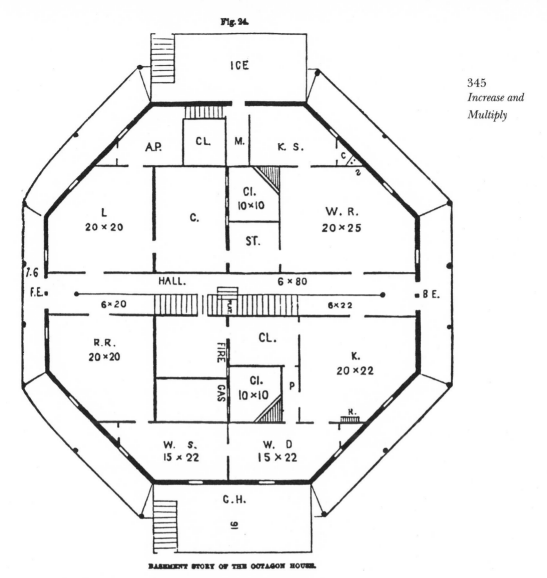

Fig. 24.

BASEMENT STORY OF THE OCTAGON HOUSE.

FIGURE 8.3. *Basement,* from "Description of the Interior of the Residence of
O. S. Fowler," *American Phrenological Journal* 15 (1852): 133

the associations formed among the faculties; they reside adjacent to related functions and cooperate with their neighbors when urged by mutual interest. The dual identity of these rooms, with each governing a single function while reconstituting itself, when obliged, to meet the needs of collective life, resembles both the workings of the brain and the fluid alliances formed among members of Congress.[27] Fowler would not have found this ascent to the macrocosm alien to his way of thinking.

The upper floors (fig. 8.5) are given over primarily to bedrooms and closets, and as suggested earlier, any attempt to draw a precise connection between these functions and the operations of the faculties would be

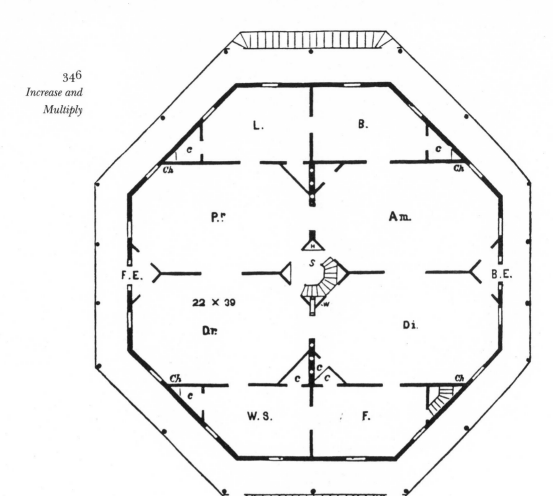

FIGURE 8.4. *Parlor Story,* from "Description of the Interior of the Residence of
O. S. Fowler," *American Phrenological Journal* 16 (1852): 16

forced, although the suggestion that a studio or study might find a place
in this setting accords with the eminence given the intellectual and moral
faculties.[28] The playroom, gymnasium, and dancing room Fowler recom-
mends would presumably also adjoin the sleeping chambers.[29] Whether
or not he actually designated separate rooms for these activities, his advocacy of them as a means of curing the ills that beset "sedentary fashionables and confined operatives" extends the considerations covered by his
architecture to include physiology.

Fowler addressed his text to "practical housekeepers," a term that recalls his own efforts as a practical phrenologist, and it is clear that the
efficiency and comfort he believes essential are not merely ends in themselves. An "unhandy house" was a perpetual irritant to its inhabitants, and

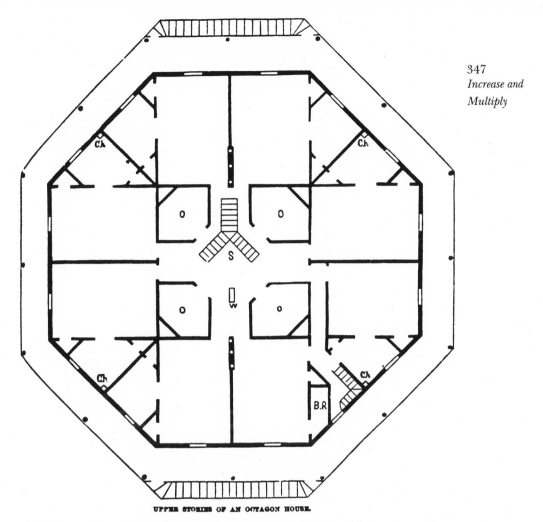

UPPER STORIES OF AN OCTAGON HOUSE.

FIGURE 8.5. *Third and Fourth Stories,* from "Description of the Interior of the Residence of O. S. Fowler," *American Phrenological Journal* 16 (1852): 36

when a wife's temper was soured in this manner, she bestowed a similar disposition on her children, even in their prenatal state.[30] To preclude this possibility, Fowler filled his house with labor-saving devices so that the mother who dwelt within might develop the equanimity requisite for her calling. Maternal steps were reduced, for example, by the inclusion of a speaking tube and a dumbwaiter,[31] but the author was particularly proud of the indoor plumbing he installed. A water closet located beneath the stairs eased nocturnal pilgrimages, while the virtues of fertilizing vegetable gardens and vineyards with excrement are extolled, with physical metaphysics again providing the link between advanced technology and the most primeval, "natural" needs.[32]

Fowler urged the prospective home owner not to stint in acquiring the latest conveniences. By reducing the tedium of household chores, they promoted health and thus represented a far more prudent investment than the thousands of dollars commonly spent on vain ornament.[33] One comfort that also proved an absolute necessity was ventilation. We have already seen how seriously phrenologists viewed this matter, and Fowler heeded the warnings of his predecessors by arranging for the circulation of air throughout the entire structure. The interior bedrooms, for example, expelled their spent air to the central stairway by means of ducts between the floorboards,[34] a solution that enhances the image of the building as an organic entity, inhaling the fresh air of the outdoors and then exhaling the "poisonous carbonic acid gas, generated by the life process." Nor was removal of noxious effluvia the sole reason for ventilation. Overheated rooms and those subject to rapid changes of temperature further imperiled their inhabitants, and he also urged the construction of large chambers to forestall this hazard.[35]

Any examination of Fowler's house would be incomplete without mention of the materials he adopted for the walls. Initially he employed wood, but after examining the gravel walls of Goodrich's hexagonal building in 1850, he began anew. Cement was, he soon realized, "NATURE'S style of architecture." Wood, of course, would also seem to answer this appellation, but Fowler argued that it was expensive and vulnerable to the elements. The stone and lime required for gravel walls were universally available, even in the prairies where trees were scarce, and time only hardened the conglomerate, making it impervious to both weather and vermin. In any case, Nature was no aristocrat; she bestowed her bounty equally on rich and poor, supplying the means for anyone to create an ideal home. Finally, rapid population growth would soon lead to an extensive deforestation that would make wood a scarce commodity.[36]

The implications of this last statement are not drawn in *A Home for All* and must be sought, rather, in a series of articles titled "Progression, a Universal Law," published in the *American Phrenological Journal* of 1852.[37] The gist of these essays involves the assumption that every monad is permeated with the progressive impulse, and as the millennium approaches, the pace of evolution will increase exponentially. This reasoning was hardly Fowler's alone. Many political visionaries of the day shared similar convictions, but the context for his teachings is best sought in those of other phrenologists. Gall addressed the topic when, in reviewing his *Instinct of Generation (Amativeness)*, he contended that "the first and the most universal of all the commands was—Increase and multiply."[38] Fowler took this injunction as confirmation of what had recently been demonstrated by science: that the urge to expand and improve the race was written in the organization of every individual.[39] *Amativeness* operated in each brain, enjoining all to obey this, the earliest biblical commandment.

For his interpretation of progress Fowler relied on *The Constitution of Man.* There Combe proposed that the earth's surface was increasingly capable of supporting organic life, and mankind might ascend to a higher plane as science applied itself to matters of hereditary descent. Fowler's writings demonstrate how much further he was willing to push an idea about which the Scotsman only intimated. Combe implies that humanity may be about to enter a golden age in which a few hours' work every day will suffice to meet its material needs. Moral improvement can be expected to follow, he states, but only if population growth could be restrained.[40] The specter of Thomas Malthus that haunted such warnings, however, did not cloud Fowler's prospects.

Like Combe, Fowler commences his predictions with a glance backward. The gouges in the strata of Mount Holyoke, he remarks, give evidence of the southward advance of glaciers to a latitude they do not presently attain. This suggests that the climate was once colder than at present. Indeed, readers are asked to affirm from personal experience that the world is getting warmer, winters being hardly as severe as those of twenty or forty years ago. Other developments also suggest that the world is accommodating itself to human habitation. Each year the rocky portions of its surface are increasingly made fit for cultivation by the corrosive effects of wind and water. In like manner the mountains are being worn smooth, their substance draining into the valleys to improve the bottomland. Nor are the enriching capabilities of the plant life that covers the continents ever lost; whenever a tree falls, it adds to the sum total of the planet's fertility. The enhanced productivity of the land made possible by this process was requisite for the myriads Fowler envisioned inhabiting the earth.

As noted above, Fowler calculated population growth unconstrained by any Malthusian inhibitions. From a base of 800 million in 1833, the number of humans inhabiting the earth would reach 25.6 billion in 100 years and an astonishing 583.2 billion in 200 years. Such astronomical figures could only be contemplated by assuming that society itself was rapidly improving, a process that would eventually make war and pestilence a dim memory. More importantly, advances in the understanding of physiology would soon spare many from premature death. Parents who had six children, an average according to Fowler, could expect to see all six reach maturity, each in turn having six offspring. Already, he notes, the American continent is being peopled from the Atlantic coast to California, and this trend will continue until "the earth [is] *completely full* of human beings, just as full as can live comfortably."[41]

The reader is bound to ask how hundreds of billions of people could live comfortably when the pressure for scarce resources would seem to make the prospects of eking out even a meager existence rather remote. Fowler answers that such doubts merely reveal the limitations of the inquirer. Resources are unlimited for those who know where to look for them, and returning to the theme mentioned in *A Home for All*, he explains that wood will cease to serve as building material when forested lands are cleared for cultivation. Instead, the bowels of the earth will yield up the "stone, sand, clay, lime, iron, glass &c." needed for tomorrow's houses. Furniture, likewise, will be manufactured from these materials, and coal will supplant wood for heating. Diets will consist of fruit and vegetables, since much more food per unit of land can be secured in this manner than in the grazing of animals. And so it goes; instead of wool, for example, hemp and flax clothing will eliminate the waste of land entailed in pasturing sheep. These measures will enhance the earth's productivity, but they constitute only a fraction of the anticipated changes.

The very presence of vast numbers will, in itself, make the land more fertile. As humans exhale carbonic acid, they nourish the plants that transform such gasses in turn back into oxygen, enriching the atmosphere for animal life. And with so many bodies buried in the earth, it will yield ever more luxuriant harvests. In this context Fowler makes the extraordinary claim that "even now the soil from battlefields is being transported to England in ships, and pays." These words are delivered so matter-of-factly that one is almost inclined to believe them. Whatever the case, they provide the precise physical correspondence to the moral marl that Horace Mann hoped might profit by his contribution.

Whenever human intelligence applies itself, improvement follows. In agriculture the proof of this maxim is apparent in the new hybrid fruits and vegetables that have swelled the bounty of the land. The rate of increase itself can be expected to increase, and if events follow as foreseen, one acre will shelter, clothe, and feed twenty individuals. Every square mile will sustain 12,800, and if we project this figure to the present territory of the United States, we find it supporting some 45 billion citizens, give or take a few hundred million. Those who doubt that northern climes, including Alaska, would prove hospitable to human habitation ignore the fact that the earth is becoming warmer and the mountains are wearing away. On several occasions Fowler celebrates the prospect of a planet "literally all alive with teeming humanity," a world where inconceivable numbers are sustained through infinite ages.[42]

Suppose we were to make the trip from Boston to New York in 1952—

the year when much of what Fowler predicted was supposed to have come to pass—what sights would greet us as we progressed southward? First, we could not expect to travel by horse, since the vast amount of food consumed by this animal made it incompatible with modern civilization. Instead, trains would provide the primary means of transportation, but perhaps we could persuade an obliging citizen to fire up his newfangled steam-carriage and whisk us away. As we rumble over plank roads, the eye feasts on rich gardens and fields sewn with diverse crops. Along either side of the road grow fruit trees, their blossoms perfuming the air while the dense vegetation purifies it. Since the laws of health are universally understood, everyone from merchant and lawyer to factory operative willingly works the soil a few hours a day. Women have abandoned "Frenchified" fashions for the simpler garb that enables them to cultivate their plots, becoming "muscular mothers" in the process. Of course, we can expect numerous "mansions" to fill the landscape, and while this account does not specifically identify these as octagons, the reader had only to turn the journal's pages to encounter excerpts from *A Home for All*.[43]

The image of steam cars rattling over planks as they progress through an environment literally packed with people lends credence to the old adage that nothing ages quite so quickly as the future. But Fowler was merely indulging a penchant that often occupied social thinkers of the day. His vision of a domesticated planet recalls Charles Fourier's plan to cover the entire land surface of the globe with millions of Phalanxes, yet nothing in Fowler's wildest imaginings equals the Frenchman's vision of the seas turning to lemonade as the beasts of the jungle become affectionate, docile creatures.[44] Given the popularity of Fourier in America in the years preceding Fowler's architectural undertaking, it seems likely that the phrenologist sought to match his predecessor in the scale and splendor of his ambitions.[45]

More fundamentally, Swedenborg's ideas on populating the next world were applied by Fowler to this one. Indeed, the mystic's contention that "in the heavens, all perfection increases in proportion to abundance" might be taken as a credo of the phrenological paradise. That abundance derives, according to Swedenborg, from the continuous arrival of souls who, in this manner, bring heaven into closer correspondence with the divine. Unlike earth, however, heaven can never be filled, even though there may be "a million planets in the universe, with a total of 300,000,000 (three hundred million) people on each planet, and two hundred generations within six thousand years." Instead, these spirits perfect the celestial man, filling not only the "individual members, organs, and tissues of the body in general, but in detail and specifically with all the individual component tissues and organs within them, even to individual ducts and fibers."[46]

Since the heavens are conduits for the transmission of divine life, as they grow in perfection, such emissions are more fully received by earth. The New Church theologian who made this assertion concludes that "improvement, eternal progress, is the constant law of the universe."[47] The same thought caused Fowler to exclaim, "O, earth, glorious, God created, God endowed, earth!! The mirror of thy Maker!!! As infinitely perfect as all his combined perfections could render thee! And most perfectly adapted, in every conceivable respect, to become the paradise of man— the heavenly vestibule of entrance upon another state, as infinitely higher than this can possibly become, as this, infinitely adorned by the fostering culture of man is to yonder primeval forests, or miasmatic swamp, full of reptiles and beasts of prey."[48] Utopians often conjured up ideal homes and gardens as the fulfillment of their visions,[49] but Fowler's peculiar integration of metaphysical notions into his system was unique.

The octagon house was a nexus where the infinite potential of the spiritual realm was accommodated to the contingencies of sublunary existence. At a practical level the earth *could* be filled up, and the octagon, by enclosing more space within its walls than the traditional home, made optimal use of the ground it covered in anticipation of a time when the land itself would become the scarcest of resources. The reader of *A Home for All* who remains unaware of Fowler's thoughts about the future may find his comments about buildings that could hold a hundred families inconsistent, for the same text stresses the importance of home ownership. In the case of the larger domiciles, however, he suggests that the buildings could be purchased by associations whose members individually lacked the funds to acquire a private house, or by those tied by the bonds of consanguinity. Although not specified in the text, the proposal apparently anticipates a world where such measures would open more acreage for cultivation.

Another facet of this philosophy emerges in Fowler's proposal that octagons could be attached to one another to form large octagons or decagons.[50] This again entails notions about the microcosm and macrocosm, or as he expressed it, the belief that nature was composed of a series of perfections, each encompassing its predecessor.[51] By projecting this scheme into subsequent centuries, we find that it shapes the entire environment, with one huge octagon composed of smaller octagonal units attached to the next as the population expands. In Swedenborg's heaven the collective form of the diverse societies of angels represents the Divine Man; in Fowler's utopia the individual home reiterates (albeit somewhat imperfectly) the phrenological organization of its inhabitants while joining a chain of like buildings that perpetuate the same structure across the continents.

This glimpse into the future would be incomplete without some account of the spiritual forces driving the evolutionary process. History begins in *Amativeness*. Before the earth could be subdued, it had to be peopled; hence God's first commandment. Other social affections then came into play, including *Philoprogenitiveness, Adhesiveness,* and *Inhabitiveness,* so that the early years of mankind were a time when the lower, posterior region of the brain reigned supreme. The ancients expressed this preoccupation by revering Venus above all other deities and making her statue the object of their most fervent devotion.

The goddess rewarded her worshipers in kind, and with rising populations, the task of subduing could begin. The spirit of history moves forward and now finds itself ensconced in *Combativeness* and *Destructiveness* whence it emboldens humanity to seek conquest and glory. Soon men are consumed by the venture, and the aggressive instincts run roughshod over the social sentiments. But history will not sit idle; it has begun to creep into *Alimentiveness,* with Bacchus being the primary beneficiary. The gluttony and excesses of the later Roman caesars are largely his doing, and given the continued strength of the other animal and domestic propensities, the fall of the empire is seemingly foreordained. The advent of Christianity does not fit very comfortably into this sequence, for it would appear to herald a rather abrupt departure toward *Veneration* and *Benevolence,* but Fowler ignores this inconvenient turn of events and instead identifies the sixteenth century ("about three hundred years ago") as the dawn of a new era dominated by *Acquisitiveness.* With the preeminence of this faculty, pecuniary interests subdue the penchant for violence, the merchant supplants the warrior, and eventually tyranny will be swept aside by the forces of democracy.

Fowler foresees this stage unfolding in the United States, where the forests were already being replaced by "well-cultivated farms" and "thrifty villages." Fate has decreed that "immense treasures of gold" should be discovered in the far West, and this bounty is "destined to pour in for hundreds of years to come, [and] will all be wanted to enable mankind to exchange products, manufactures, &c., back and forth from all parts of the earth." The upshot of these developments is a greater bodily comfort and leisure that, in turn, will facilitate cultivation of the higher faculties as individuals begin to devote increasing portions of their income to charities, the arts, and the like. The octagon, then, can be seen as congruent with the spirit of the age. It gratifies *Acquisitiveness* while serving as the springboard for the next leap in consciousness. We have already encountered the tendency of phrenologists to interpret Manifest Destiny in physiological terms, and Fowler writes that there is no going back; progress must continue ever onward and upward, bringing as yet unexploited regions of the brain under its dominion.[52]

Following the publication of *A Home for All*, a fad for octagon houses took hold in New England, New York, and the Midwest. Madeleine Stern reports that at a least a thousand were built, most by 1857. Individuals attracted by the design need not have consulted Fowler's book, for similar plans soon appeared in carpenter's manuals,[53] and this suggests that not everyone who raised an edifice of this type was necessarily inspired by the ideology it embodied. No doubt affordability was sufficient motivation for some, and of course many devoted phrenologists did not live in octagons. The rest of this chapter will briefly examine the beliefs held by those who did employ this type of architecture as an instrument of reform.

A number of buildings were erected by persons whose association with the Fowlers or the causes they espoused was sufficiently close to permit conjecture about their intentions. Orson, for example, mentions an octagon designed by his engraver William Howland, and it seems likely that the former's millennial enthusiasm rubbed off on his employee.[54] The octagon built in the mid-1860s on Staten Island by William Page doubtlessly reflected his interest in phrenology.[55] Another example "said to have been built by a spiritualist group" in Chautauqua County, New York,[56] would also seem the outcome of numerous connections between the spiritualist and phrenological communities. We saw in an earlier chapter that William Sidney Mount heard Andrew Jackson Davis, the Poughkeepsie clairvoyant, lecture on topics akin to those expounded by Fowler,[57] and both movements entertained like notions about the possibilities of progress. There can be little doubt that Henry S. Clubb was similarly inspired when he organized his Octagon Settlement Company in 1856 at the Fowler headquarters. In the spring of that year the group marched to Kansas under the banner of reform, having declared themselves opposed to slavery and alcohol. When this intrepid band of pioneers arrived in July, it found a plot of some four square miles laid out on an octagonal plan, and they seem also to have contemplated a similar scheme for their homes. But within a year the community dissolved, and with it vanished all hopes of an imminent octagon millennium.[58]

The influence of phrenology on John Humphrey Noyes's utopianism is especially intriguing. Before moving to Oneida in 1848, the group that gathered around Noyes persuaded at least two phrenologists, Orson

Fowler and Nelson Sizer, to lecture on the theory,[59] and the subsequent history of the community suggests that some of the wisdom imparted in these sessions was later put to use by its members. Noyes, for example, came to justify the loosening of marriage vows among his followers on the pretext that the bondage of monogamy was fostered by "amativeness and acquisitiveness."[60] A long-standing affiliation with phrenology also explains why plans to expand Oneida in 1856 included consideration of octagon architecture.[61] But if these utopians sought to embrace Fowler's plans, the admiration was not entirely mutual. He saw no possibility of redemption in free love and reminded readers that there were good phrenological reasons for maintaining the institution of marriage, not the least being the existence of *Conjugality*, which was devised by the divinity to ensure the lifelong bliss of partners rightfully coupled.[62] We come closer to the spirit of Fowler's teachings with the establishment of Modern Times, a town founded on Long Island in 1851 by Josiah Warren and Stephen Pearl Andrews.

Warren first enunciated the principles that were to govern Modern Times, and, paradoxically, these were designed to ensure that there was no governance at all, that the community placed no constraints on the individual. This preoccupation with "Individuality" makes Warren, according to one modern authority, America's first "philosophical anarchist."[63] "Individuality" grew from within, Warren wrote, causing "the practice of mentally discriminating, dividing, separating, disconnecting persons, things, and events, according to their individual peculiarities."[64] A phrenological faculty also bore this name, and Orson Fowler's description of the functions of *Individuality* as "adapted to individual existence, or the thingness of things"[65] confirmed the innate nature of Warren's principle. The contacts between the two men will be reviewed shortly, but in articulating his faith in Individuality, Warren was also attempting to go beyond the reigning *Acquisitiveness* of the age. In moving from this organ to *Individuality* he advanced forward in the head, as required by the exigencies of history, but left to future generations the task of ascending to even more elevated faculties.

To preclude the possibility of exploitation Warren sought to eliminate its source, the dollar. Money represented nothing but itself and hence was subject to changes in value that encouraged speculators to reap profits at the expense of those most vulnerable to such fluctuations. Warren hoped to replace this form of "civilized cannibalism" with a more benign economy based on cost. Cost represented the amount of labor required to produce a commodity. If cost became the medium of exchange instead of value, no one would be able to amass a fortune beyond his or her ability to work. Capitalism would collapse with the introduction of promissory notes based on the premise that one hour's exertion would procure either an hour's labor in return or some item on which an equal amount of effort had been expended. Labor for labor was meant to prevent the vast accumulation of wealth in the hands of a privileged few and replace such inequity with a system that fostered Individuality.[66]

The idea for "labor notes" came from Robert Owen,[67] whose philosophy Warren had ample opportunity to study during his stay at New Harmony in 1825–26. The experiences of these two years convinced Warren that the evils of capitalism could not be extinguished simply by resorting to collective ownership. This alternative merely replaced one form of tyranny with another because it was equally unresponsive to the principle of Individuality.[68] In searching for a third path, he devised two solutions. The first, known as "the time store," was an experimental and preparatory step for the stage that was to follow. Several means of exchange were acceptable at the store where Warren served as proprietor. We need not go into the particulars any further than to indicate that they were devised to deny the middleman the power to inflate prices. This was accomplished by limiting the recompense due the manager to the time spent in concluding a transaction, for which he was reimbursed in kind (hence the name), while the customer also paid cash for the expenses incurred in acquiring and transporting the article. The success of such establishments was intended to convince the community of the viability of Warren's theories and provide recruits for an equity village, whose example, the reformer hoped, would renovate society.[69]

Until 1850 the Midwest had been the primary locus of Warren's activities; there he had set up several stores and two short-lived towns. In this year, however, he found himself in New York City, planning a third community with Stephen Pearl Andrews, a recent convert and an effective proselytizer. Andrews called Warren's doctrine of equitable commerce a "science of society," and to ensure that this system would indeed be viewed as scientific, Andrews relied heavily on phrenology to demonstrate that Individuality was founded on objective criteria. Modern society, he wrote, was constituted in a manner that was positively detrimental to its members. Professional life developed one faculty to the neglect of the rest, and where an organ enjoys extraordinary strength, it deranges the entire system. To prevent the withering of inherent powers, reform movements had to take measures that would bring out the Jack-at-all-trades latent within everyone.[70] By adopting this tack, both Warren and Andrews glided increasingly into the orbit of the phrenologists. Their writings were published and distributed by the firm of Fowlers and Wells, and Samuel Wells endorsed their venture by becoming a charter member of Modern Times, although he later defaulted on the commitment.[71]

Within a few years of its establishment in 1851, Modern Times grew into a pleasant if humble village nestled in the piney woods of Long Island some forty miles east of New York City.[72] The land was infertile and inexpensive, the latter condition being a paramount consideration to an enterprise that intended to house those who previously could not afford their own homes. The proximity of a railroad station meant that prospective recruits might easily satisfy their curiosity—again, an important factor in the founders' minds. The census of 1860 counted a 126 residents occupying a motley array of houses on some 750 acres.[73] No uniform architectural code was enforced, for such measures were antithetical to the spirit of Individuality, but Orson Fowler would have found much to approve as he strolled down the streets. These were lined with cherry and apple trees planted by the residents to enable the wayfarer to partake freely of their bounty.[74] This circumstance alerts us to the fact that the villagers were not quite as bereft of collective will as their declarations might lead the reader to believe. The Fowlers encouraged lining public thoroughfares with fruit trees as a means of alleviating the suffering of the poor. Were this measure widely adopted, it was reasoned, crime would be greatly reduced,[75] and the inhabitants of Modern Times were eager to assist those whose desperate conditions they understood from personal experience.

Although Warren and Andrews eschewed the responsibilities associated with leadership, they nevertheless took steps to ensure that their's would be a Jack-at-all-trades utopia. In order to prevent agriculture on a large scale from dominating the village's economy, residents were permitted to acquire only three acres. Andrews stated that the purpose of this restriction was to create "a town of diversified occupations."[76] Each citizen would own property as Fowler urged and thus satisfy the needs of *Inhabitiveness*, but none could become merely a pawn of a domineering *Acquisitiveness*. Andrews's warnings about mental stability in a society that encouraged the exercise of a single faculty were also answered by this provision. A garden of this size could not occupy all one's waking hours and hence obliged the proprietor to take up several trades, giving faculties that might otherwise have remained dormant a chance to operate. Another benefit that accrued to caring for a small vegetable garden was the opportunity for moderate exercise. The phrenologists were forever hectoring their followers, women especially, on this point, and raising crops instead of slaughtering animals gave positive encouragement to *Benevolence* while holding *Destructiveness* in check.[77] Many of these ideas also appear in *A Home for All*, where both gardening and eating fruit are an integral part of the larger scheme.[78]

Recent advances in the science of physiology encouraged Andrews to inaugurate a science of economics,[79] and from the similarities he concluded that "the Science of Society is to the Community what Physiology is to the Individual."[80] The casual visitor to Modern Times was unlikely to recognize the thread that held the community together, but behind the seemingly haphazard collection of buildings and individuals stood the conviction that economy *was* physiology, that a benign environment was conducive to physical and mental soundness, and vice versa.

There were thirty-three households in Modern Times in 1860,[81] and the surviving evidence suggests that at least some of these followed the maxims set down by Fowler. A number of buildings were made from gravel and concrete, the most prominent being a vocational school called the Mechanical College. In addition to this function, the Jack-at-all-trades structure also served as a print shop, a time store, and Warren's home. It was square, not octagonal, but this plan was preferable, in Fowler's mind, to the traditional rectangle.[82] Warren seems to have approached the project with trepidation, for he worried that the mortar would not have sufficient time to harden between the rains and that the walls would have to be reinforced with wood. Time bore out his apprehensions, for the edifice collapsed in 1870.[83] This sequence of events suggests the following scenario: Fowler, just back from Wisconsin, lectures Warren on the virtues of the gravel wall; the latter wants to introduce advanced techniques into his utopia but is anxious about using a novel material while also attempting to master the complexities of the octagon. The compromise managed, in any event, to shelter him for the duration of his stay in the village.

More soundly built was the residence of William Upham Dame, an octagonal structure that survives to this day.[84] Dame's praise for its "economy of space, no space being lost in acute angles," resembles Fowler's disparagement of the dark corners in rectangular houses.[85] When the residents of Modern Times gathered for a meeting or dancing, they did so on the second floor of Dame's abode, and again these circumstances suggest the practical application of *A Home for All.* Such assemblies surely required a large open area, and Fowler's provision for sliding doors between rooms would have met this need, while the dancing was an activity he promoted as a remedy to the woes besetting sedentary females.

The village school, which opened in 1857, was also octagonal, suggesting again that the villagers hearkened to Fowler's ideas (fig. 8.6), even if they did not adopt them for their own homes.[86] The schoolroom, Orson wrote, was the "corner-stone of our nation's greatness"; hence its shape was no trifling matter. The closer it approached a circle, the better. If the participants in "magnetic and electrical experiments" formed a circle so that their thoughts might harmonize, then how much more important was it for all the pupils in a room to have their attention directed to a single object—the teacher. Thus the young minds of Modern Times were "carried onward and upward illimitably" in just the setting Fowler thought conducive to this end.[87]

Connecting the several buildings that served whatever collective functions were observed by the people of Modern Times was the architectural theory expounded by Orson Fowler. Perhaps the link was fortuitous, but it seems more likely that the intention was to acknowledge the philosophy which united a community that eschewed money and devoted itself to the principles of Individuality: *Acquisitiveness* could only be overcome by those willing to cultivate a wide range of faculties and vocations.[88] A daily reminder of these ideas existed in the person of Dr. Edward Newberry, the resident phrenologist and dentist. Following a pattern often encountered, he was an artist as well, and nineteen heads he rendered in watercolor to illustrate his lectures on phrenology presently grace the town's library. Newberry's perfectionism also included the theory of opposites advanced by the doctrine. Hence he advised the blonde, in choosing

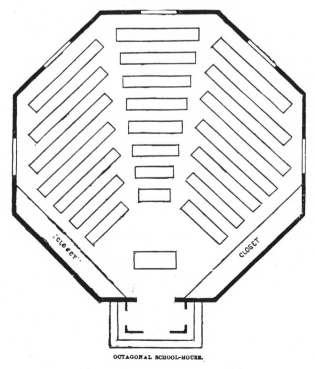

OCTAGONAL SCHOOL-HOUSE.

FIGURE 8.6.
Octagonal School-House, from O. S. Fowler, *A Home for All* (New York: Fowlers and Wells, 1851)

a mate, to seek the brunette; the bilious, the "locomotive"; and so on.[89] One wonders whether the students of the octagon school were jetted and conceived according to the doctor's prescriptions; if so, the cycle would have been complete, with the environment and its inhabitants now attaining the desired integration.

The question was crucial to much of the utopian thinking of the time. The future could not be left to chance; progress rewarded those who followed nature's dictates, and many thought conventional arrangements governing the begetting and rearing of children were calculated to thwart this wisdom. Such sentiments led a number of the town's residents to ignore entirely the bonds of marriage and seek partners among those who seemed most compatible to their needs. The reputation the village acquired of being a hotbed of "free love" so "disgusted the surrounding neighborhood," Warren wrote some years later, "that even the name of the place was something like an emetic."[90] Apparently this opinion came to be shared by a substantial portion of the members of Modern Times, who in 1864 changed the name of their hamlet to Brentwood in an attempt to deflect the invective.[91]

By then Warren had been absent from the community for two years.[92] He never returned but did continue to harbor dreams of a geometrical paradise. His *Practical Application of the Elementary Principles of "True Civilization"* of 1873 includes a design provided by J. Madison Allen for an ideal community based on this approach, albeit hexagonal in this instance. In the *Plan of One Section of a City* (fig. 8.7), a series of private homes, marked *d*, are separated by radiating roads *S*, which also form property boundaries, while a pavilion for public use occupies the central circle. A consideration of the more encompassing *Plan of a Whole City* (fig. 8.8) reveals the logic behind the scheme. Each hexagon is surrounded by six others, the intent being to ensure "that growth will be only a repetition of what has already been done." Anyone with ambitions of vastly expanding his or her tract would likely have them frustrated by this plan, for even if one had the means to acquire more land, the sequence of small, irregularly shaped plots would inhibit the effort. Each family is encouraged to cultivate its own three- to five-acre lot and, beyond that, to mind its own business.[93] No specific indication is given regarding octagon houses, but a design that ordered the environment according to the principles that the bee's *Constructiveness* dictated for the hive would surely have earned Fowler's approval.

When Fowler himself gazed into the future, he saw his own utopian schemes coming to fruition within a hundred years. If, for reasons that will become apparent shortly, I may be permitted to add ten years to his

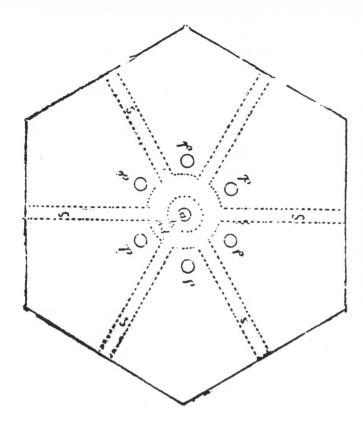

FIGURE 8.7.
J. Madison Allen,
*Plan of One Section
of a City*, from
Josiah Warren,
*Practical Appli-
cation of the
Elementary
Principles of "True
Civilization," to the
Minute Details of
Every Day Life*
(Princeton, Mass.:
Published by the
author, 1873),
p. 46

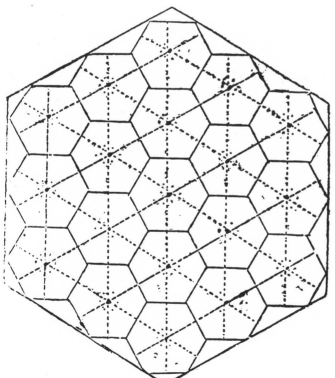

FIGURE 8.8.
J. Madison Allen,
*Plan of a Whole
City*, from Josiah
Warren, *Practical
Application of the
Elementary
Principles of "True
Civilization," to the
Minute Details of
Every Day Life*
(Princeton, Mass.:
Published by the
author, 1873),
p. 47

figure, we might ask what he would have thought of the world in 1962. Where were his far more arrogant republics? Other than the two octagon buildings of Modern Times and the other such edifices that occasionally dot the landscape, the physical environment would hardly have resembled the densely populated garden he envisioned. His notion that planting fruit trees would solve the problem of poverty is just one instance of the many that might be cited where the proposals of antebellum reformers sound quaint and decidedly out of touch with reality. On the other hand, we have seen that the innovations of Horace Mann and others concerned with institutional reform were quite substantial. But beyond these concrete accomplishments it is also possible to identify a less tangible yet enduring legacy of phrenology. This entails what I would consider a healthy inclination to question authority. In this respect the name of Henry Thoreau comes more readily to mind than that of Josiah Warren, but the former's experiment at Walden was relatively brief compared with Modern Times.[94] If phrenology tended to reinforce racial stereotypes, it also mandated George Catlin's ambassadorship on behalf of Native Americans and, in the character of Uncle Tom, helped undermine the foundation of slavery. If it regarded women as the begetters of children, it also managed through organizations such as the Ladies' Physiological Institute to encourage them to take charge of their bodies in ways that offended the staid medical community. Finally, I would like to imagine that Moby-Dick's last furious charge on the *Pequod* was a service rendered by *Firmness* to the cause of animal rights. As suggested at the outset, the contradictions inherent within phrenology made it malleable to the purposes of its interpreters.

It is not overstating the case, however, to suggest that phrenology could persuade persons of goodwill to examine their motives. I hardly wish to imply, for example, that slavery was overthrown at phrenology's behest, but those who adopted its precepts were at least obliged to recognize that blacks were not without virtue. Perhaps we can best judge the legacy it left the twentieth century, evasive though it may be, by briefly examining the career of one individual whose contribution to modern mores was influenced by its example.

To do so, we must return to 1962 and search out Margaret Sanger, famed feminist and pioneer of the birth control movement, while she cradles her great-granddaughter in her arms. As her aged hand glides over the infant's head, she is overcome by the similarity of its phrenological organization to that of her own daughter, a child who had died some forty-seven years earlier. With obvious emotion, she repeats, "Peggy's come back. Peggy's come back."[95] Reincarnation and phrenology converge in this exclamation and remind us that the waning of the nineteenth century, the time of Sanger's youth, witnessed the merging of such doctrines into a larger occult movement.[96] But it must also have had deeply personal meaning for her as well, permitting a tangible contact with a departed daughter while perhaps also reviving one of her most vivid childhood memories.

Sanger has a legitimate place in this narrative because she was an accomplice to her father, Michael Hennessy Higgins, when he committed an act of art. Higgins, a mason whose radicalism and anticlericalism frequently put him at odds with the Catholic hierarchy, decided shortly after the death of his four-year-old son in 1892 to disinter the boy so that he might make a death mask and, by means of its phrenological developments, have a record of the child's soul. Margaret stood guard while her father went about the task in the dead of night. Much of the seeming bizarreness of this incident fades when we recall the frequent connections between phrenology and disinterment in the nineteenth century. Reflecting on the event later in life, Sanger experienced some pangs of remorse and never quite reconciled herself to the lifelessness of the bust,[97] but it may have provided a valuable lesson in physical metaphysics. Although her brother had never been baptized, here was tangible evidence of a soul that possessed, presumably, all the virtues of common humanity despite its failure to comply with strictures of traditional religious teaching. The notion that moral authority comes from within and not from the perfunctory sanction of ceremony would have served Margaret well in her later skirmishes with the Catholic Church.

In any case, Sanger learned about phrenology at an early age from her father.[98] And while increasingly marginalized by the growing professionalization of the medical community in the last decades of the century, the theory answered needs not met by licensed practitioners. The passage of the Comstock Act in 1873, which classified birth control literature as obscene, obliged those enlightened phrenologists who set themselves against conventional morality to operate outside the law.[99] One such individual was Zeus Franklin. Like Orson Fowler, Franklin could, even at this late date, encourage the use of statuary, and particularly the *Greek Slave*, as a means of acquiring physiological knowledge.[100] But he did not share his predecessor's optimism about the prospects of unlimited population growth and ultimately was imprisoned for his advocacy of a woman's right to control her body by preventing conception.[101] Out of this milieu of alternate medicine and mysticism came convictions that fostered Margaret Sanger's beliefs about birth control. As noted above, she never abandoned her faith in spiritualism, and her reference, for example, to the "most wonderful head" of Henry Havelock Ellis[102] suggests a continued interest in the science of Gall and Spurzheim that found its final expression in the examination of her great-granddaughter.

Of course the legacy of phrenology, like that of any mass movement, was a mixed blessing, and it bears asking whether Sanger's occasional flirtations with eugenics did not also trace their roots back to the lessons she learned on her father's knee. Its positive consequences for her, and for American culture in general, can be found in the encouragement it offered the individual to believe in herself. In this respect it pays to look again at the ladies of the physiological institute; they were not radicals, but phrenology helped them articulate their discontents. They willingly braved the disapprobation of established physicians and proceeded to acquire anatomical models and study the *Greek Slave*. How many other women and men, one wonders, were likewise inspired by the marble nude's example to challenge the dictates of conventional wisdom?

The contribution of phrenology to the fine arts was more concrete. Its influence between the third and eighth decades of the nineteenth century was significant among individuals who envisioned mankind's evolution to higher levels. Two developments contributed to the success of this proposition. First, Newton's discoveries placed all phenomena under the domain of rational law; thus disease ran a regular course that could be calculated with the same precision as one measured the effects of gravity. Second, from Protestantism came the belief that the responsibility for health resided in the conscious choices made by individuals; what resulted was a medical pathology that regarded voluntary habits as both the cause and the cure of all maladies.[103] These principles were readily adaptable to aesthetic ends. Thomas Cole, for example, had some notion of them in mind when he declared, "We are still in Eden; the wall that shuts us out of the garden is our own ignorance and folly."[104] This statement echoes Combe's belief that nature had never experienced any cataclysmic disruption of its order. The same laws that prevailed in primeval times are still in effect; it is simply our own moral lassitude that prevents us from enjoying the benefits they promise.

To propose that American art passed through a phrenological stage is not to make inflated claims for the movement's impact. The reader is not being asked to find its influence in every image but, rather, to remain open to the possible meanings it infused in works that strove to articulate the deepest convictions of the age. A decided advantage offered by Gall and Spurzheim's science in this venture is that it was studied enthusiastically by contemporaries. In contrast, a label such as the Hudson River School was a belated invention designed to convey disapprobation;[105] luminism is a relatively recent designation and hence was unknown to the artists it encompasses;[106] neoclassicism is a rather inappropriate term for a sculptural style that aimed to surpass the standards set by antiquity; and Emerson's Transcendentalism gives no evidence of having enjoyed similar popularity. In a culture of correspondences, it bears emphasizing, all natural phenomena exist by virtue of their reference to some feature of the human body, and, as no other doctrine of the day, phrenology offered an itemized inventory of the human anatomy with reference to its physical and spiritual implications.

Perhaps a glance at *Kindred Spirits* (fig. 8.9) can provide some clues on how one might go about identifying the concerns advanced by physical metaphysics. Painted in 1849 by Asher Durand to commemorate the death of Thomas Cole, it can now be seen that these two artists were devotees of phrenology, as was the person for whom the work was destined, William Cullen Bryant. Deep in the forest we encounter Cole as he points out to his companion the beauties of the untrammeled wilderness. Bryant, who was yet to evolve into his bearded self, doffs his hat to exhibit an especially propitious phrenological development. Those who had gazed upon it recognized its contribution to his talent. Edgar Allan Poe remarked on Bryant's "prominent organs of Ideality,"[107] while the *American Phrenological Journal* extolled his *Sublimity* for making him "very fond of contemplating the grand, sublime, extended, eternal, and magnificent, particularly in nature, and in wild and romantic scenery." Certainly the viewer of Durand's image will recognize the poet's powerful intellect, but the journal added that his physical strength made him "less susceptible to diseases, and better able to resist them than most men."[108] This brings us to the crux of the painting, for one of those less resistant men was Thomas Cole.

Cole's sudden death came as a shock to the artistic community, and many lamented the loss in written form or painted image.[109] None of these is more familiar than Bryant's own speech, given to the National Academy in 1848. In delivering a eulogy, the poet could hardly delve into the reasons for the painter's demise other than to note that he had slipped off into "the world of disembodied spirits" with mind undiminished by the disease that had brought his body down.[110] Cole's biographer Louis Legrand Noble explains that Cole contracted an inflammation of the lungs that caused his expiration within a week of the first appearance of the symptoms.[111] But to answer *why* he was stricken, we have to turn to the testimony of E. H. Dixon, who sent his recollections on the matter to the *American Phrenological Journal* some years after the event.

The letter sent by Dixon was written to confirm the truth of phrenology by calling attention to the fact that the resemblance of Frederic Church's talent to Cole's was reflected in the shape of his head. Dixon as-

FIGURE 8.9. Asher B. Durand, *Kindred Spirits* (1849, oil painting, Collection of the New York Public Library, Astor, Lenox, and Tilden Foundations)

serts that he frequently met the elder artist at the house of his brother-in-law, Dr. Ackerley,[112] and then adds that Cole died from pleuro-pneumonia caught during the trips required to return home from his studio. "I cautioned him strongly against walking from his studio," Dixon recalls, "which he kept at a very high temperature, across the brow of a hill to his house." He continues, "He [Cole] used to get absorbed in his great work, and then go a few hundred feet across the hill to reach his house."[113] In other words, the painter of Nature disobeyed one of her fundamental dictates. He allowed himself to become preoccupied with his work while laboring in an overheated, ill-ventilated room and then shocked his lungs by subjecting them to the sharp, fresh atmosphere of the outdoors. This was, so to speak, death by architecture. If Cole was negligent in this respect, he was hardly alone. Even the great Spurzheim, who should have known better, had ruined his health in like manner. According to one biographer, the phrenologist used to exit so precipitously from the warm room where he was lecturing into the cold evening air of the American autumn that he hastened his demise.[114]

Would it be inappropriate for Durand to allude to these circumstances in a painting dedicated to his departed colleague? There are several reasons for thinking not. Combe, whom Durand, Cole, and Bryant all admired, devoted much of his philosophy to the proposition that death be regarded a beneficial institution. As an instrument of progress, its visitation was not simply due to some inscrutable whim of the divinity but operated according to fixed laws. In the case of premature death the deceased bore the brunt of the responsibility. Thomas Cole understood this. Shortly before his death he complained that he had been ailing for want of sufficient exercise.[115] He could also have learned much from the advice he sent Durand: "Your depression is the result of debility, and you require the pure air of heaven. You sit, I know you do, day after day, in a close, airtight room, toiling and stagnating, and breeding dissatisfaction at all you do, when, if you had the untainted breeze to breathe, your body would be invigorated, your spirits buoyant and your pictures would charm even you. This is not all exaggeration, there is much sober truth in it."[116]

The fact that this same passage found its way into Noble's biography of Cole and John Durand's account of his father[117] suggests that its message weighed heavily in the thoughts of both artists and in those of their associates. Turning to *Kindred Spirits*, we notice that the tree in the foreground has broken off at the trunk, and the upper portion now tumbles down a precipice. This is certainly emblematic of the artist's death, but how? I would like to think that there is more involved here than merely the simplistic equation of dead tree to dead man; the circumstances that brought the tree down are also relevant. Unlike its neighbors, this tree has projected itself over the cliff, and the tension on the trunk created by its near-horizontal extension has proved excessive, causing it to snap. Like Cole, it has pushed too far, setting itself against the most universal of laws—gravity—and in such contests the outcome is foreordained. Given Graham's doctrinaire insistence that all premature death was the consequence of some infraction of nature's laws, and given Durand's close association with this reformer and others of like sentiment, the parallel between the tree and Cole would seem to operate at this level as well. Since even such events were part of a benevolent plan set down by the deity, and since death was meaningful not only with regard to the afterlife but also as an instrument of mankind's moral and physical improvement in this sphere, those who reflected on the painting could take comfort in its message while learning from it as well. The golden light that filters through the landscape adds its own amen, confirming the consolation offered by this sermon in physical metaphysics.

If Thomas Cole came to a belated recognition of the seriousness of Dixon's warning, Walt Whitman followed the advice the doctor offered readers of his publications by taking to the open air as a means of resisting infection.[118] This connection serves as one further reminder, if one is needed, of how pervasive phrenology and similar reforms were among creative circles in the antebellum era. It also permits me to conclude by returning to the theme introduced at the outset of this book: we come closer to the vital spirit of the fine arts of that time in the visceral dynamics of Whitman's poetry than in the somewhat cerebral philosophy of Emerson. By refusing to ignore or dismiss the beliefs held by Durand, Cole, and others simply because we do not share them, we discover, paradoxically, that their work speaks more forcefully to us than if we attempt to make it over in our own image.

Notes

INTRODUCTION

1. Much of the following account is from John Davies, *Phrenology: Fad and Science* (New Haven: Yale University Press, 1955), pp. 162–71.

2. G. W. F. Hegel, *The Phenomenology of Mind*, trans. with an introduction and notes by J. B. Baillie. Introduction to the Torchbook Edition by George Lichtheim (1910; New York: Harper and Row, 1967), pp. 338–72.

3. Davies, *Phrenology*, pp. 68–72.

4. Thomas Sewall, *An Examination of Phrenology* (Washington, D.C.: Homans, 1837), pp. 69–72.

5. Herman Melville, *Moby-Dick*, edited with an introduction by Charles Child Walcutt (1851; New York: Bantam, 1986), p. 323.

6. See, for example, Sewall, *Examination of Phrenology*, p. 11.

7. Georges Lanteri-Laura, *Histoire de la phrenologie: L'homme et son cerveau selon F. J. Gall* (Paris: Presses Universitaires de France, 1974), pp. 174–99.

8. Steven Mintz, *Moralists and Modernizers* (Baltimore: Johns Hopkins University Press, 1995), p. xxii.

CHAPTER ONE

1. Quoted in F. O. Matthiessen, *American Renaissance* (1941; London: Oxford University Press, 1968), p. 61.

2. On the fallacies of the physiognomic venture, see E. H. Gombrich, "On Physiognomic Perception," in *Meditations on a Hobby Horse* (London: Phaidon, 1971), pp. 45–55.

3. John Caspar Lavater, *Essays on Physiognomy; Calculated to extend the Knowledge and the Love of Mankind*, 3 vols., trans. C. Moore (London: Symonds, 1797), 1:12.

4. Ibid., 1:9.

5. See John Graham, *Lavater's Essays on Physiognomy: A Study in the History of Ideas* (Berne: Peter Lang, 1979), pp. 45–47.

6. For a brief review of physiognomy before Lavater, see Mary Cowling, *The Artist as Anthropologist* (Cambridge: Cambridge University Press, 1989), pp. 13–17.

7. For writers, see Graeme Tytler, *Physiognomy in the European Novel: Faces and Fortunes* (Princeton: Princeton University Press, 1982); for artists, see Judith Wechsler, *A Human Comedy: Physiognomy and Caricature in Nineteenth-Century Paris* (Chicago: University of Chicago Press, 1982).

8. My narrative of Gall's life and ideas is drawn primarily from Francois Joseph Gall, *On the Origin of the Moral Qualities and Intellectual Faculties of Man*, 6 vols., trans. Winslow Lewis Jr. (Boston: Marsh, Capen and Lyon, 1835); W. Mattieu Williams, *A Vindication of Phrenology* (London: Chatto and Windus, 1894); Charlotte Fowler Wells, *Some Account of the Life and Labors of Dr. Francois Joseph Gall, Founder of Phrenology* (New York: Fowler and Wells, 1897); Bernard Hollander, *In Search of the Soul and the Mechanism of Thought, Emotion, and Conduct*, vol. 1 (New York: Dutton, n.d.); Georges Lanteri-Laura, *Histoire de la phrenologie: L'homme et son cerveau selon F. J. Gall* (Paris: Presses Universitaires de France, 1974); and Anthony Albert Walsh, "Johann Christoph Spurzheim and the Rise and Fall of Scientific Phrenology in Boston, 1832–1842" (Ph.D. dissertation, University of New Hampshire, 1974).

9. For example, see Etienne Jean Georget, *De La Physiologie du System Nerveux, et Specialment du Cerveau*, 2 vols. (Paris: J. B. Bailliere, 1821), 1:133–36.

10. For Gall's views on Lavater, see Gall, *On the Origin of the Moral Qualities,* 5:261–65.

11. Arthur Wrobel, "Phrenology as Political Science," in *Pseudo-Science and Society in Nineteenth-Century America,* ed. Arthur Wrobel (Lexington: University Press of Kentucky, 1987), p. 140.

12. For his criticism of Immanuel Kant, see Gall, *On the Origin of the Moral Qualities,* 5:130.

13. Davies has observed that the aberrations of phrenology were not the consequence of charlatanism but the limitations of nineteenth-century medical science. See John Davies, *Phrenology: Fad and Science* (New Haven: Yale University Press, 1955), p. x.

14. See Roger Cooter, *The Cultural Meaning of Popular Science* (Cambridge: Cambridge University Press, 1984), pp. 24–25.

15. Stephen Jay Gould, *The Mismeasure of Man* (New York: Norton, 1981). See esp. pp. 57–68 for a discussion of the miscalculations involving brain size and intelligence.

16. Cooter, *Popular Science,* pp. 16–17.

17. Ibid., pp. 5, 39–40; see also "Phrenology," *Annals of Phrenology* 2 (1835): 386–87.

18. Gall, *On the Origin of the Moral Qualities,* 5:241–43.

19. This concept parallels the theme developed in M. H. Abrams, *Natural Supernaturalism* (New York: Norton, 1971).

20. Alexis de Tocqueville, *Democracy in America,* 2 vols., the Henry Reeve text as revised by Francis Bowen and corrected and edited with a historical essay, editorial notes, and bibliographies by Phillip Bradley (New York: Vintage, 1962), 2:4.

21. "Introductory Statement," *American Phrenological Journal and Miscellany* 1 (1838): 4. The author goes on to remark that Americans "enquire for facts, in every department of life, with an eagerness which is really a national characteristic."

22. L. Maria Child, *Letters from New York,* 2 vols. (New York: Charles S. Francis, 1843), 1:64.

23. Cooter, *Popular Science,* pp. 70–72.

24. A review of the invention and use of the term "phrenology" can be found in Patricia S. Noel and Eric T. Carlson, "Origins of the Word 'Phrenology,'" *American Journal of Psychiatry* 127 (1970): 694–97.

25. Tytler, *Physiognomy,* p. 34.

26. For the events of Spurzheim's life, and particularly those relating to his trip to America, I have relied on J. G. Spurzheim, *Phrenology, in Connexion with the Study of Physiognomy,* with a biography of the author by Nahum Capen (Boston: Marsh, Capen and Lyon, 1833); Andrew Carmichael, *A Memoir of the Life and Philosophy of Spurzheim* (Boston: Marsh, Capen and Lyon, 1833); Nahum Capen, *Reminiscences of Dr. Spurzheim and George Combe* (New York: Fowler and Wells, 1881); Anthony Albert Walsh, "The American Tour of Dr. Spurzheim," *Journal of the History of Medicine and Allied Sciences* 27 (1972): 187–205; Walsh, "Phrenology and the Boston Medical Community in the 1830s," *Bulletin of the History of Medicine* 50 (1976): 261–73; and Walsh, "Spurzheim."

27. See Cooter, *Popular Science,* pp. 77–78.

28. For a discussion of the differences between Gall and Spurzheim, see J. G. Spurzheim, *Phrenology or the Doctrine of Mental Phenomena,* 2 vols. (Boston: Marsh, Capen and Lyon, 1832), 1:129–30, 196; Davies, *Phrenology,* pp. 8–9; and Walsh, "Spurzheim," pp. 101–7.

29. Gall, *On the Origin of the Moral Qualities,* 1:211.

30. This account derives from "Catalogue, Numerical and Descriptive, of Heads of Men and Animals, which Composed the Collection made by the late Dr. Gall," transcribed by A. A. Royer from a manuscript by Dr. Dauncey, *Phrenological Journal and Miscellany* 7 (1831–32): 30. A more extended narrative is included in "The Phrenological Consultation," *Popular Phrenologist* 7

(1902): 140–42. Here we are informed that the examination took place in 1800 and that up to that time Ceracchi was unaware of the premises of Gall's science. See also Gall, *On the Origin of the Moral Qualities*, 4:170.

31. J. G. Spurzheim, *Mental Phenomena*, 2:138.

32. For Biddle's efforts, see Helen W. Henderson, *The Pennsylvania Academy of the Fine Arts* (Boston: L. C. Page, 1911), p. 11, and Lois Marie Fink and Joshua C. Taylor, *Academy: The Academic Tradition in American Art* (Washington, D.C.: Smithsonian Institution Press, 1975), p. 28.

33. George Combe, *Notes on the United States of North America during a Phrenological Visit in 1838–9–40*, 2 vols. (Philadelphia: Carey and Hart, 1841), 1:188.

34. Ibid., 1:369.

35. For the developments relating to phrenology in Philadelphia, see Walsh, "Spurzheim," pp. 206–15.

36. "History of Phrenology in Philadelphia," *American Phrenological Journal and Miscellany* 2 (1839–40): 477.

37. Bell's election is recorded in the "Minutes of the Meetings of the Board of Directors of the Pennsylvania Academy of Fine Arts," 16 April 1823, Archives of American Art (henceforth AAA), P63/587, Pennsylvania Academy of Fine Arts, Philadelphia. He ceases to appear in the lists of officers of the academy in 1840; see *Exhibition of the Pennsylvania Academy of Fine Arts, 1840* (Philadelphia: T. K. and P. G. Collins, 1840), p. 2.

38. "Notices," *Phrenological Journal and Miscellany* 1 (1823–24): n.p.

39. "Notices," *Phrenological Journal and Miscellany* 2 (1824–25): 649. This quote is included in a letter from John Bell dated 12 August.

40. "Mr. Rolph and the Philadelphia Journal on Phrenology," *Phrenological Journal and Miscellany* 1 (1823–24): 634.

41. A review of this aspect of Biddle's patronage will be found in Nicholas B. Wainwright, "Nicholas Biddle in Portraiture," in *Portrait Painting in America*, ed. Ellen Miles (New York: Main Street/

Universe Books, 1977), pp. 149–56. There we read, for example, that a contemporary, Sidney George Fisher, noted that "his [Biddle's] head and face were stamped with the marks of character and intellect" (p. 149).

42. See J. DeVille, *Manual of Phrenology* (London: J. DeVille, 1835), p. 20. DeVille gathered a collection of crania just to demonstrate this point.

43. Jane Montgomery to Mrs. Biddle, 4 October 1839, quoted in Wainwright, "Biddle," p. 154.

44. Dickson contends that Jarvis must have borrowed the phrenological literature in 1816–17. See Harold E. Dickson, *John Wesley Jarvis, American Painter* (New York: New-York Historical Society, 1949), p. 207.

45. William Dunlap, *A History of the Rise and Progress of the Arts of Design in the United States*, 2 vols., ed. Rita Weiss, introduction by James Thomas Flexner (1834; New York: Dover, 1969), vol. 2, pt. 1, p. 77.

46. Donald R. Thayer, "Early Anatomy Instruction at the National Academy: The Tradition behind It," *American Art Journal* 8 (May 1976): 39.

47. "Notices," *Annals of Phrenology* 2 (1835): 388. The formation of the society is stated to have happened "within the present year," presumably 1834 or 1835. See also "Dr. John W. Francis, Biography and Phrenological Character," *American Phrenological Journal* 27 (1858): 69–70.

48. "Notices," *Phrenological Journal and Miscellany* 1.

49. Both, for example, refer to the "faculty of Imagination" as remaining awake while the others slept. Though this precise term was not used by phrenologists—they would call it "Ideality"—the idea of one faculty remaining awake while others slept was central to Gall's theory, as we have seen. See *Prose Writings of William Cullen Bryant*, 2 vols., ed. Parke Godwin (1884; New York: Russell and Russell, 1964), 1:6, and Samuel F. B. Morse, *Lectures on the Affinity of Painting with the Other Fine Arts*, edited with

an introduction by Nicolai Cikovsky Jr. (Columbia: University of Missouri Press, 1983), p. 53. Also useful is Cikovsky's introduction, pp. 1–38.

50. His tenure, however, was not long; he died in 1829. See Stephen W. Williams, *American Medical Biography* (Greenfield, Mass.: L. Merrian, 1845), pp. 340–41. For more on King and the establishment of the academy, see Thomas S. Cumming, *Historic Annals of the National Academy of Design* (1865; New York: DaCapo, 1963), pp. 25–33, and Eliot Clark, *History of the National Academy of Design, 1825–1953* (New York: Columbia University Press, 1954), p. 25.

51. "Notices," *Phrenological Journal and Miscellany* 2 (1824–25): 650.

52. Samuel F. B. Morse, President of the National Academy of Design, to J. L. Morton, Esq., Secretary of the National Academy of Design, Rome, 2 March 1831, AAA N19/598, New York Public Library, Rare Books and Manuscript Division, Astor, Lenox, and Tilden Foundations. The remarks are contained in a review by Count Hawks le Grice, which Morse includes in his letter.

53. J. Manesia to Asher Durand, 22 August 1832, AAA N19/718.

54. *The Diary of Philip Hone, 1828–1851*, 2 vols., ed. Allan Nevins (New York: Mead, 1927), 1:71.

55. J. G. Spurzheim, "Notes on Scientific Institutions in the United States of America," Boston Medical Library, Francis A. Countway Library of Medicine, Harvard University, Boston, Mass., B MS C22.4.

56. *Diary of Christopher Columbus Baldwin, 1829–35* (Worcester, Mass.: American Antiquarian Society, 1901), p. 199.

57. Robert E. Riegel, "The Introduction of Phrenology to the United States," *American Historical Review* 39, no. 1 (1933): 76. See also Walsh, "Boston Medical Community," pp. 263–65.

58. R. W. Haskins, *History and Progress of Phrenology* (Buffalo: Steele and Peck, 1839), p. 108.

59. Walsh, "Boston Medical Community," pp. 261–73.

60. Walsh, "American Tour," p. 192.

61. John James Audubon, *Delineations of American Scenery and Character*, introduction by Francis Hobart Herrick (New York: Baker, 1926), p. xxxiii.

62. Rembrandt Peale, "Reminiscences," *Crayon* 1 (1855): 370.

63. The funeral ceremonies are recorded in Charles Follen, *Funeral Oration Delivered at the Burial of Gaspar Spurzheim, M.D.* (Boston: Marsh, Capen and Lyon, 1832).

64. "Mount Auburn," *Crayon* 5 (1858): 327.

65. The history of the Boston Phrenological Society is best recorded in Walsh, "Spurzheim," pp. 324–404.

66. Quoted in Jared B. Flagg, *The Life and Letters of Washington Allston* (1892; New York: Benjamin Blom, 1969), p. 106.

67. "Officers of the Boston Phrenological Society for 1835," *Annals of Phrenology* 1 (1834): 399.

68. *Boston Saturday Evening Gazette*, 20 February 1864. This report states that Dr. Mason Warren, the son of John Collins Warren, had invited Rimmer to bring his classes. Certainly the casts assembled by the Boston Phrenological Society would have been of primary interest, since much of the other material in the Warren collection was employed to illustrate the symptoms that accompanied various bodily diseases and was hardly appropriate for artistic purposes. This newspaper article is in the Rimmer scrapbooks, Boston Medical Library, Francis A. Countway Library of Medicine, Harvard University, B MS b44.2.

69. Newspaper clipping, Rimmer scrapbooks.

70. The negative evaluation comes from Alan Burroughs, *Limners and Likenesses* (Cambridge: Harvard University Press, 1936), p. 127. See also Henry T. Tuckerman, *Book of the Artists* (New York: G. P. Putnam and Son, 1867), p. 67, and

William Gerdts, *The Art of Healing* (Birmingham: Birmingham Museum of Art, 1981), p. 40.

71. Walsh, "American Tour," p. 198. The exhibition took place in 1833. Walsh was unable to find any evidence to support the suggestion made by some that Audubon and Rembrandt Peale also executed portraits of Spurzheim.

72. Alvan Fisher to Asher Durand, 14 December[?] 1832, AAA N19/742.

73. "Notices," *Annals of Phrenology* 1 (1834): 528.

74. Frazee carved busts of Nathaniel Bowditch (1833–34), Daniel Webster (1833–34), John Marshall (1834–35), Thomas Handasyd Perkins (1834–35), John Lowell (1834–35), William Prescott (1834–36), and Joseph Story (1834–36). Painted portraits of Marshall and Webster by Chester Harding and of Perkins by Thomas Sully already hung in the Athenaeum. For the particulars of this commission, see Frederick S. Voss, Dennis Montagna, and Jean Henry, *John Frazee, 1790–1852, Sculptor* (Washington, D.C.: Smithsonian Institution Press, 1986), pp. 11–12, 84–102. I wish to express my thanks to Dr. Frederick S. Voss for his suggestion regarding the possible phrenological implications of the Athenaeum patronage.

75. When Dr. John Collins Warren wanted to borrow over a hundred objects from Spurzheim's collection for his lecture at Harvard in 1834, he applied to Ward for permission to use the material. See T. W. Ward to Dr. John C. Warren, 18 April 1834, Files of the Warren Anatomical Museum, Boston Medical Library.

76. J. G. Spurzheim, *Phrenology, in Connexion with the Study of Physiognomy*, pp. 47–48.

77. The phrenologist who made this judgment also remarks that he proceeded with his analysis of Marshall without ever having seen the subject in person, believing that Frazee's bust provided sufficient evidence. See Silas Jones, "Character of Chief Justice Marshall," *American Phrenological Journal and Miscellany* 1 (1838–39): 382–84.

78. Davies, *Phrenology*, pp. 79–105.

79. Horace Mann to George Combe, 25 March 1839, in Mary Mann, *Life of Horace Mann* (1888; Miami: Mnemosyne Publishing, 1969), p. 113.

80. "Lectures of Mr. George Combe in Boston and New York, with a Brief History of Phrenology and Its Present State in the Former Place," *American Phrenological Journal and Miscellany* 1 (1838–39): 121.

81. Walsh, "Spurzheim," p. 404. Loss of the element of novelty and a consequent decline in membership often brought an end to scientific societies. Cooter notes that this fate frequently befell geological societies even though there can be no claim that the discipline was discredited. See Cooter, *Popular Science*, p. 89.

82. Cooter, *Popular Science*, p. 120; see also "Obituary: Death of George Combe," *Providence Daily Journal*, 3 September 1858, and George Combe, *The Constitution of Man Considered in Relation to External Objects*, 5th ed. (Boston: Marsh, Capen and Lyon, 1835).

83. Henry T. Tuckerman, *The Criterion; or the Test of Talk about Familiar Things* (New York: Hurd and Houghton, 1866), p. 116.

84. My account of Combe's life and travels is derived from Combe, *Phrenological Visit*; Charles Gibbon, *The Life of George Combe, Author of "The Constitution of Man,"* 2 vols. (1878; Westmead, Farnborough, Hants, England: Gregg, 1970); and David de Giustino, *Conquest of Mind Phrenology and Victorian Social Thought* (London: Croom Helm, 1975).

85. Some measure of Combe's popularity can be taken from the following statement: "Charles Lyell's audiences rivaled both Combe's and Dickens's" (Taylor Stoehr, "Robert H. Collyer's Technology of the Soul," in Wrobel, *Pseudo-Science and Society*, p. 26).

86. Lillian B. Miller, *In Pursuit of Fame: Rembrandt Peale, 1778–1860*, with an essay

by Carol Eaton Hevner (Washington, D.C.: National Portrait Gallery, 1992), p. 147. Peale states that he met Gall in Paris in 1812. Perhaps this is a slip of the memory; see Peale, "Reminiscences," p. 370. See also Gibbon, *Life of George Combe*, 2:56.

87. Combe, *Phrenological Visit*, 1:208–9.

88. See, for example, Rembrandt Peale, *Portfolio of an Artist* (Philadelphia: Carey and Lea, 1831), p. 177.

89. Peale, "Reminiscences," p. 370.

90. Combe, *Phrenological Visit*, 2:54.

91. The differences between philosophical and itinerant phrenologists are discussed in Davies, *Phrenology*, pp. 30–43.

92. See Donald M. Scott, "Itinerant Lecturers and Lecturing in New England, 1800–1850," in *Itinerancy in New England and New York*, ed. Peter Benes (Boston: Boston University Press, 1986), pp. 67–68, and Carey P. McCord, "Bumps and Dents in the Skull," *Archives of Environmental Health* 19 (1969): 228.

93. Nelson Sizer, *Forty Years in Phrenology: Embracing Recollections of History, Anecdote, and Experience* (New York: Fowler and Wells, 1891), p. 3.

94. As late as 1931 the Psychograph Company of Minneapolis began production of coin-operated machines that provided phrenological readings by means of a helmet placed over the head. See Guenter B. Risse, "Vocational Guidance during the Depression: Phrenology versus Applied Psychology," *Journal of the History of the Behavioral Sciences* 12 (1976): 130–40.

95. Madeleine B. Stern, *Heads and Headlines: The Phrenological Fowlers* (Norman: University of Oklahoma Press, 1971), p. 214. Also cited is Harriet Beecher Stowe's remark to the effect that phrenology was as convenient in treating human nature "as the algebraic signs in numbers" (p. 82).

96. Walt Whitman, *Leaves of Grass*, edited with an introduction by Malcolm

Cowley (1855; New York: Penguin, 1982), p. 18.

97. John Fentress Gardner, *American Heralds of the Spirit* (Hudson, N.Y.: Lindisfarne Press, 1992), p. 17.

98. See Arthur Wrobel, "Walt Whitman and the Fowler Brothers: Phrenology Finds a Bard" (Ph.D. dissertation, University of North Carolina, Chapel Hill, 1968).

99. Thomas Ball, *My Threescore Years and Ten*, edited with an introduction by H. Barbara Weinberg (1892; New York: Garland, 1977), pp. 255, 301–2.

100. Tuckerman, *Book of the Artists*, p. 448.

101. The best history of the Fowler family is in Stern, *Fowlers*.

102. Ibid., pp. 67, 84, 138.

103. Ibid., pp. 49–50.

104. Juliette Tomlinson, *The Paintings and Journal of Joseph Whiting Stock* (Middletown, Conn.: Wesleyan University Press, 1976), pp. 55–57. This material is part of an inventory of his library.

105. Mary Black, "Phrenological Associations," *Clarion* 9 (Fall 1984): 48.

106. Tomlinson, *Joseph Whiting Stock*, p. 26.

107. O. S. Fowler, *Physiology, Animal and Mental* (New York: Fowlers and Wells, 1852), p. 31.

108. Whitman, *Leaves of Grass* (1855), p. 113.

109. Tomlinson, *Joseph Whiting Stock*, p. 58.

110. This possibility has been mentioned by Vlach. See John Michael Vlach, *Plain Painters* (Washington, D.C.: Smithsonian Institution Press, 1988), p. 53.

111. Stern, *Fowlers*, pp. 24–25.

112. Ibid., p. 54. They moved from this location in 1854; as late as 1928 the American Institute of Phrenology was still in operation (ibid., p. 258). The National Academy of Design held its exhibitions at Clinton Hall from 1831 to 1840. See Clark, *National Academy*, p. 32.

113. Philippe Julian, *The Oriental-*

ists, trans. Helga and Dinah Harrison (Oxford: Phaidon, 1977), p. 94.

114. "A Poetical Sketch of Fowler and Wells' Phrenological Museum," *American Phrenological Journal* 32 (1860): 64.

115. My discussion of Mesmer relies on Robert Darnton, *Mesmerism and the End of the Enlightenment in France* (Cambridge: Harvard University Press, 1968).

116. This account of mesmerism in the United States is drawn primarily from Robert Fuller, *Mesmerism and the American Cure of Souls* (Philadelphia: University of Pennsylvania Press, 1982).

117. See, for example, Samuel R. Wells, *New Physiognomy* (New York: Samuel R. Wells, 1868), pp. 54–68.

118. Even the Fowlers identified their practice as "Fowler's practical phrenology."

119. O. S. Fowler, *Fowler's Practical Phrenology* (New York: Fowlers and Wells, 1847), p. 59.

120. A good biography of Buchanan can be found in Hugh M. Ayer, "Joseph Rodes Buchanan and 'The Science of Man,'" *Filson Club History Quarterly* 36 (1962): 32–42.

121. Charles Coleman Sellers, *Mr. Peale's Museum* (New York: Norton, 1980), p. 304.

122. "Letter from Dr. Andrew Boardman, New York, to Mr. George Combe, on Mesmero-Phrenology," *Phrenological Journal and Miscellany* 16 (1843): 163–67. See also *Uncle Sam's Recommendation of Phrenology to His Millions of Friends in the United States* (New York: Harper and Brothers, 1842), pp. 278–79.

123. Henry Inman to J. C. Spencer, 15 June 1842, AAA P22/249, Smithsonian Institution, Washington, D.C.

124. William Gregory, *Animal Magnetism or Mesmerism and Its Phenomena* (1909; New York: Arno Press, 1975), pp. 13–15. Here Gregory cites a nineteenth-century author.

125. Gall discusses this most extensively in Gall, *On the Origin of the Moral Qualities*, vol. 5.

126. Gilbert Stuart Newton, *Portrait of Washington Irving* (1830, oil on canvas, Historic Hudson Valley, Tarrytown, N.Y.). The quote on Irving is from O. S. Fowler, *The Practical Phrenologist* (Boston: O. S. Fowler, 1869), p. 61.

127. Cooter, *Popular Science*, p. 81.

128. For the reflections of Spurzheim on religion and materialism, see J. G. Spurzheim, *Mental Phenomena*, 2:89–115.

129. For biographical material on Swedenborg, I have consulted Benjamin Worcester, *The Life and Mission of Emanuel Swedenborg* (Boston: Little, Brown, 1901); Marguerite Beck Block, *The New Church in the New World*, introduction by Robert H. Kirven (1932; New York: Octagon Books, 1968); and Signe Toksvig, *Emanuel Swedenborg* (New Haven: Yale University Press, 1948).

130. Ernest Benz, "Swedenborg und Lavater: Uber die religiosen Grundlagen der Physiognomik," *Zeitschrift fur Kirchengeschichte* 57 (1938): 165–77; Joan K. Stemmler, "The Physiognomical Portraits of Johann Caspar Lavater," *Art Bulletin* 75 (1993): 153–57.

131. "Character, Organization, and Biography of Emanuel Swedenborg," *American Phrenological Journal and Miscellany* 11 (1849): 114.

132. The doctrine of correspondences is discussed throughout much of Swedenborg's work. Good summaries can be found in Edward Madeley, *The Science of Correspondences Elucidated*, ed. B. F. Barrett (Germantown, Pa.: Swedenborg Publishing Association, 1883), and William L. Worcester, *The Language of Parable* (1892; New York: Swedenborg Press, 1976).

133. The theory of influx is explained in Emanuel Swedenborg, *Angelic Wisdom Concerning Divine Love and Divine Wisdom*, trans. John C. Ager (New York: Swedenborg Foundation, 1982).

134. For the history of Swedenborgianism in America, see Block, *New Church*, and Scott Trego Swank, "The Unfettered Conscience: A Study of Sectari-

anism, Spiritualism, and Social Reform in the New Jerusalem Church, 1840–1870" (Ph.D. dissertation, University of Pennsylvania, 1970).

135. A review of Swedenborg's influence on American artists will be found in Martha Gyllenhaal, Robert W. Gladish, Dean W. Holmes, and Kurt R. Rosenquist, *New Light: Ten Artists Inspired by Emanuel Swedenborg* (Bryn Athyn, Pa.: Glencairn Museum, 1988).

136. Block, *New Church*, pp. 131–32. Both Block and Swank, "Unfettered Conscience," delineate the connections between Swedenborgianism, mesmerism, and spiritualism.

137. Frank Podmer, *Mediums of the Nineteenth Century*, 2 vols. (New Hyde Park, N.Y.: University Books, 1963), 1:15. Published in 1902 as *Modern Spiritualism*.

138. These similarities were noted by Andrew Boardman in George Combe, *Lectures on Phrenology*, with notes, an introductory essay, and a historical sketch by Andrew Boardman (New York: Samuel Colman, 1839), pp. 50–53, and Thomas Sewall, *An Examination of Phrenology* (Washington, D.C.: Homans, 1837), p. 14.

139. On the connections between phrenology and the occult, see Cooter, *Popular Science*, p. 40.

140. James John Garth Wilkinson, *The Human Body and Its Connection with Man* (London: New Church Press, [1851]), p. 25.

141. This occurred in 1855. See Alfred Frankenstein, *William Sidney Mount* (New York: Harry N. Abrams, 1979), p. 296.

142. Andrew Jackson Davis, *The Philosophy of Spiritual Intercourse, Being an Explanation of Modern Mysteries* (New York: Fowlers and Wells, 1855), pp. 17–18.

143. For a discussion of the decline of phrenology within the scientific community, see Lanteri-Laura, *Histoire de la phrenologie*, pp. 175–99. See also Cooter, *Popular Science*, p. 123.

144. Wells, *New Physiognomy*, p. 203.

145. The telegraph metaphor comes from W. F. Evans, *The Mental-Cure, Illustrating the Influence of the Mind on Body Both in Health and Disease and the Psychological Method of Treatment* (Boston: H. H. and T. W. Carteer, 1869), p. 103.

146. For the place of Warren Felt Evans and Swedenborg in the origins of Christian Science, see Gail Thain Parker, *Mind Cure in New England* (Hanover, N.H.: University Press of New England, 1973).

147. Evans, *Mental-Cure*, p. 102.

148. William B. Hayden, *On the Phenomena of Modern Spiritualism* (Boston: Otis Clapp, 1855), pp. 60–63.

149. O. S. Fowler, *Self-Culture and Perfection of Character* (New York: Fowlers and Wells, 1855), pp. 17–18.

150. Frankenstein, *Mount*, p. 296.

151. For Mount's political views, see Joseph B. Hudson Jr., "Banks, Politics, Hard Cider, and Paint: The Political Origins of William Sidney Mount's Cider Making," *Metropolitan Museum Journal* 10 (1975): 108. See also Benjamin Nelson Pfingstag, "Aspects of Form and Time in the Paintings of William Sidney Mount" (Ph.D. dissertation, State University of New York, Binghamton, 1980), pp. 91–92.

152. Entries for March 1854 in the "Spiritualist Diary," in Frankenstein, *Mount*, pp. 288–90.

153. Frankenstein, *Mount*, p. 290.

154. T. S. Mackintosh, *The "Electrical Theory" of the Universe* (Boston: Josiah Mendum, 1846), p. 423. For his library acquisitions, see Donald D. Keyes, "William Sidney Mount Reconsidered," *American Art Review* 4 (August 1977): 128.

155. See O. S. Fowler, *Physiology*, pp. 19–37.

156. G. Spurzheim, *Outline of Phrenology* (Boston: Marsh, Capen and Lyon, 1836), p. iii.

157. William Sidney Mount to James B., April 1857, quoted in Edward Buffet, "William Sidney Mount," *Port Jefferson Times* (1923), AAA SM1/616, Museums at Stony Brook, Stony Brook, New York.

158. For Mount's interest in temper-

ance as part of his larger concern for phrenology, see Pfingstag, "Aspects of Form and Time," pp. 131–40.

159. Andrew Jackson Davis, *The Magic Staff: An Autobiography* (Boston: Colby and Rich, 1857), p. 478.

160. Cooter, *Popular Science*, p. 258.

161. See Allan Sekula, "The Body and the Archive," *October* 39 (Winter 1986): 3–64.

162. Cooter, *Popular Science*, pp. 258–63.

163. Davies, *Phrenology*, 172.

164. Mark Twain, *The Adventures of Huckleberry Finn* (1884; Garden City, N.Y.: Doubleday, n.d.), p. 122.

CHAPTER TWO

1. Nelson Sizer, *Forty Years in Phrenology: Embracing Recollections of History, Anecdote, and Experience* (New York: Fowler and Wells, 1891), pp. 206–7.

2. Stock's inventory reveals that he possessed a "plaster Phrenological head" valued at twelve cents. See Juliette Tomlinson, *The Paintings and Journal of Joseph Whiting Stock* (Middletown, Conn.: Wesleyan University Press, 1976), p. 53.

3. "Columbus, Ill. August 10, 1848— Monday last Mr. J. E. Quidore [*sic*] circulated a prospectus in this place and obtained up to thirty subscribers for the *American Phrenological Journal* as a foundation on which to establish a society" (D. M. Mong, "Phrenology in the West," *American Phrenological Journal and Miscellany* 10 [1848]: 357). The inclusion of the middle initial is somewhat puzzling, since Quidor does not seem to have had a middle name. It seems more probable that this results from some mistake made in the transcription by Mong than that there were two persons with the same relatively rare name in so small a town. Even today the population of Columbus does not exceed five hundred. See David M. Sokol, *John Quidor, Painter of American Legend* (Wichita: Wichita Art Museum, 1973), p. 18. See also Madeleine B. Stern, *Heads and Headlines:*

The Phrenological Fowlers (Norman: University of Oklahoma Press, 1971), p. 68, and, for example, the advertisement in *American Phrenological Journal* 15 (May 1852): 118.

4. Hiram Powers, "On Prejudice," Archives of American Art (henceforth AAA), 1146, Smithsonian Institution, Washington, D.C. (The roll I consulted did not number the individual entries.)

5. In one letter, Powers mentions the arrival in Florence of a Mr. Castle, who had apparently agreed to pick up some pamphlets and then declined to do so, owing, Powers speculates, to the fact that Mr. Castle was a phrenologist himself and may have wished to promulgate his own theories (Hiram Powers to George D. Berney, 20 June 1848, AAA 1133/1243). A second letter to the same correspondent informs him about the bust and indicates that the pamphlets were being circulated (Hiram Powers to George D. Berney, 3 August 1848, AAA 1133/1321).

6. Robert Macnish, *An Introduction to Phrenology* (Glasgow: John Symington, 1837), pp. 229–30.

7. Henry W. Bellows, "Seven Sittings with Powers, the Sculptor," *Appleton's Journal of Literature and Art* 1 (1869): 342.

8. Ibid., p. 343.

9. C. Edwards Lester, *The Artist, the Merchant, and the Statesman of the Age of the Medici and of Our Own Times*, 2 vols. (New York: Paine and Burgess, 1845), 1:144.

10. Bellows, "Powers," p. 343.

11. George Combe, *Phrenology Applied to Painting and Sculpture* (London: Simpkin, Marshall, 1855), pp. 80–81.

12. "The Phrenological Gauge," *Crayon* 3 (1856): 300.

13. Rembrandt Peale, *Notes on Italy* (Philadelphia: Carey and Lea, 1831), p. 253.

14. William Wetmore Story, *Roba di Roma* (London: Chapman and Hall, 1875), p. 182.

15. William Wetmore Story, *Excursions in Art and Letters* (Boston: Houghton Mifflin, 1891), p. 20.

16. William Wetmore Story, *Conversations in a Studio*, 2 vols. (Boston: Houghton Mifflin, 1890), 1:164.

17. Story, *Excursions*, p. 39.

18. Hiram Powers to Captain Grindley, 5 March 1852, AAA 1135/2599.

19. One newspaper report indicates that Powers employed a machine that took several hundred measurements from the head. There is some ambiguity here, since the account does not say whether the head was that of a living sitter or merely a plaster head. In the case of his son and Joe Hart, however, the evidence is less equivocal. See newspaper clipping, R.T., "American Sculptors in Florence," 27 December 1868, AAA 1146.

20. Wayne Craven, *Sculpture in America* (New York: Crowell, 1968), p. 210.

21. Issa Desh Breckinridge and Mary Desh, *A Memorial to Joel T. Hart* (Cincinnati: Robert Clarke, 1885), pp. 20–21.

22. Lester, *The Artist*, 1:76.

23. The first took place in Washington, D.C. See O. S. Fowler and L. N. Fowler, *Phrenology Proved, Illustrated, and Applied* (New York: Fowlers and Wells, 1847), pp. 332–33. A verbatim record of the second examination survives: L. N. Fowler, "Phrenological Description of Hiram Powers," AAA 1146. Both Powers and Lorenzo Fowler were in London for the international exhibition of 1862. See Stern, *Fowlers*, p. 181.

24. Bellows, "Powers," p. 342.

25. Nicholas Longworth to Hiram Powers, 21, 31 August 1836, MSS qP 888 RM, Cincinnati Historical Society, Cincinnati, Ohio, Manuscript Collections (henceforth CHS).

26. Nicholas Longworth to Hiram Powers, 23 September 1838, CHS. This subject was touched on in Craven, *Sculpture in America*, p. 183.

27. Nicholas Longworth to Hiram Powers, 20 March 1839, CHS.

28. Fowler and Fowler, *Phrenology Proved*, pp. 169–70.

29. Mrs. L. N. Fowler, *Phrenology, Designed for the Use of Schools and Families* (New York: Fowlers and Wells, 1847), pp. 126–27.

30. William Dunlap, *A History of the Rise and Progress of the Arts of Design in the United States*, 2 vols., ed. Rita Weiss, introduction by James Thomas Flexner (1834; New York: Dover, 1969), vol. 2, pt. 1, pp. 58–59.

31. George Combe, *A System of Phrenology* (New York: William H. Colyer, 1841), p. 242.

32. Nicholas Longworth to Hiram Powers, 23 September 1838, CHS.

33. Henry T. Tuckerman, *Book of the Artists* (New York: G. P. Putnam and Son, 1867), p. 38.

34. Nicholas Longworth to Hiram Powers, 23 April[?] 1837, CHS.

35. Hiram Powers to Mrs. Powers, 5 April 1837, AAA 1131/685.

36. Hiram Powers to Nicholas Longworth, 5 October 1842, CHS (typed transcript).

37. Hiram Powers to Nicholas Longworth, 18 December 1840, CHS (typed transcript).

38. Hiram Powers to Nicholas Longworth, 5 October 1842, CHS (typed transcript).

39. Nicholas Longworth to Hiram Powers, 23 November 1842, CHS. This quote is included in Craven, *Sculpture in America*, p. 185. Longworth thought, however, that the unfamiliarity of the Italians with Indian subjects might work to Clevenger's advantage.

40. For more on Clevenger's career and his Indian warrior, see Jan Seidler Ramirez, "Shobal Vail Clevenger," in *American Figurative Sculpture in the Museum of Fine Arts, Boston*, introduction by Jonathan L. Fairbanks (Boston: Museum of Fine Arts, 1986), p. 48.

41. Tuckerman, *Book of the Artists*, p. 607.

42. O. S. Fowler, *The Practical Phrenologist* (Boston: O. S. Fowler, 1869), p. 6.

43. He made these remarks to Sophia Peabody, 22 July 1830; see Leah Lipton, *A Truthful Likeness* (Washington, D.C.:

Smithsonian Institution Press, 1985), p. 121.

44. *Diary of Christopher Columbus Baldwin, 1829–35* (Worcester, Mass.: American Antiquarian Society, 1901), p. 97, entry for 12 March 1831. I would like to thank Dr. Frederick Voss for calling my attention to this passage.

45. Lipton, *Likeness*, p. 34.

46. Dunlap, *Rise and Progress of the Arts*, vol. 2, pt. 2, p. 349. William Gerdts has recently affirmed that this took place in 1814, yet as we saw in the first chapter, Jarvis was supposed to have attained his knowledge of phrenology when John Francis returned from Europe in 1816. The disparity remains unexplained. See William Gerdts, *The Art of Henry Inman*, catalog by Carrie Rebora (Washington, D.C.: National Portrait Gallery, 1987), p. 31.

47. F. W. E., "A Phrenological Experience," *American Phrenological Journal* 15 (1852): 52.

48. "Editorial Correspondency," *American Phrenological Journal* 29 (1859): 70.

49. Sizer, *Forty Years*, pp. 215–16.

50. The year was probably 1835, since he became interested in sculpture at that time. See Tuckerman, *Book of the Artists*, 584. Much of this material appears in Charles Colbert, "Clark Mills and the Phrenologist," *Art Bulletin* 70 (1988): 134–37.

51. "Clark Mills and the Equestrian Statue of General Jackson, from the *Southern Patriot*," *American Phrenological Journal* 17 (1853): 77–78. The author says the account was given him by the artist "six or seven years ago."

52. Harold Aspiz, *Walt Whitman and the Body Beautiful* (Urbana: University of Illinois Press, 1980), p. 122.

53. From *Gentleman's Magazine* (1827), quoted in Graeme Tytler, *Physiognomy in the European Novel: Faces and Fortunes* (Princeton: Princeton University Press, 1982), p. 95.

54. Journal entry, 2 November 1826, in *Audubon and His Journals*, 2 vols.,

by Maria R. Audubon, notes by Elliott Coues (1897; Gloucester, Mass.: Peter Smith, 1972), 1:156.

55. Journal entry, 3 November 1826, ibid., 1:157. See also Alice Ford, *John James Audubon* (Norman: University of Oklahoma Press, 1964), p. 192.

56. Journal entry, 28 November 1826, in Maria R. Audubon, *Audubon and His Journals*, 1:166. See also Charles Gibbon, *The Life of George Combe, Author of "The Constitution of Man,"* 2 vols. (1878; Westmead, Farnborough, Hants, England: Gregg, 1970), 1:189. The honor of this designation may have contributed to Audubon's annoyance some years later when a phrenologist stated that the artist had "no coloring." The naturalist declared such pronouncements "quackery"; but this may have been in irritation about a diagnosis that was so contrary to his own understanding, or it may have been merely distrust of an uninformed practitioner. The Fowlers frequently made the same judgment about those they thought unqualified. See entry for 29 September 1842, in *Journal of John James Audubon Made While Obtaining Subscriptions to His "Birds of America," 1840–1843*, ed. Howard Corning (Boston: Club of Odd Volumes, 1929), p. 132.

57. Journal entry, 19 November 1826, in Maria R. Audubon, *Audubon and His Journals*, 1:160.

58. Journal entry, 14 January 1827, ibid., 1:205.

59. "M. Audubon, M. Weiss, Carl. Mar. V. Weber," *Phrenological Journal and Miscellany* 4 (1826–27): 295.

60. Ralph Waldo Emerson, "Fate," in *Selected Prose and Poetry*, edited with an introduction by Reginald L. Cook (New York: Holt, Rinehart and Winston, 1960), p. 258.

61. Dr. Andrew Combe, "On the Influence of Organic Size on Energy of Function, Particularly as Applied to the Organs of the External Senses and Brain," *Phrenological Journal and Miscellany* 4 (1826–27): 178–79.

62. Journal entry, 13 April 1827, in

Maria R. Audubon, *Audubon and His Journals*, 1:231.

63. Macnish, *Phrenology*, p. 125.

64. Journal entries, 11 January, 10 April 1827, in Maria R. Audubon, *Audubon and His Journals*, 1:204, 225.

65. Journal entry, 9 October 1826, ibid., 1:135.

66. John James Audubon, *Ornithological Biography*, 5 vols. (Philadelphia: Carey and Hart, 1832), 2:455.

67. Journal entry, 5 August 1826, in Maria R. Audubon, *Audubon and His Journals*, 1:109–10.

68. See Amy R. W. Meyers, "Observations of an American Woodsman: John James Audubon as Field Naturalist," in *John James Audubon: The Watercolors for "The Birds of America,"* ed. Annette Blaugrund and Theodore E. Stebbins Jr. (New York: Random House, 1993), p. 43.

69. Journal entry, 20 December 1826, in Maria R. Audubon, *Audubon and His Journals*, 1:191. On Audubon and Natty Bumppo, see Annette Blaugrund, "The Artist as Entrepreneur," in *John James Audubon*, p. 31.

70. "Review of *The History and Progress of Phrenology*, by R. W. Haskins," *Eclectic Journal of Medicine* 4 (1840): 310.

71. John James Audubon to Rev. Bachman, 3 March 1837, in *Letters of John James Audubon, 1826–1840*, 2 vols., ed. Howard Corning (1930; New York: Krauss, 1969), 2:151. Audubon does not identify the person to whom he refers.

72. Ford, *Audubon*, p. 298.

73. Journal entry, 20 December 1826, in Maria R. Audubon, *Audubon and His Journals*, 1:191.

74. Meyers, "American Woodsman," p. 44.

75. Theodore E. Stebbins Jr., "Audubon's Drawings of American Birds, 1805–38," in *John James Audubon*, p. 7.

76. Journal entry, 20 February 1827, in Maria R. Audubon, *Audubon and His Journals*, 1:212.

77. Ford, *Audubon*, p. 118.

78. Francois Joseph Gall, *On the Origin of the Moral Qualities and Intellectual Faculties of Man*, 6 vols., trans. Winslow Lewis Jr. (Boston: Marsh, Capen and Lyon, 1835), 3:303. See also "Letter to the Editor on Philoprogenitiveness," *Phrenological Journal and Miscellany* 2 (1824–25): 360–61. This was published shortly before Audubon's appearance before the phrenological society.

79. John James Audubon, *Ornithological Biography*, 1:250.

80. Meyers, "American Woodsman," p. 44.

81. "Animal Phrenology," *American Phrenological Journal* 15 (1852): 32. *Union for Life* was a faculty discovered by the Fowlers; it appears only occasionally on their charts.

82. Michael Harwood, "A Watershed for Ornithology," in *The Bicentennial of John James Audubon*, by Alton A. Lindsey, Michael Harwood, Scott Russell Sanders, Robert Owen Petty, Frank Levering, and Mary Durant (Bloomington: Indiana University Press, 1985), pp. 32–33.

83. Stern, *Fowlers*, p. 82.

84. Tuckerman, *Book of the Artists*, p. 484.

85. Herman Melville, *Moby-Dick*, edited with an introduction by Charles Child Walcutt (1851; New York: Bantam Books, 1986), pp. 321–25.

86. John James Audubon, *Ornithological Biography*, 1:xvi. See also journal entry, 11 January 1827, in Maria R. Audubon, *Audubon and His Journals*, 1:204.

87. John James Audubon to Lucy Audubon, 21 December 1826, in Corning, *Letters*, 1:15.

88. Patricia Hills, *The Painters' America* (New York: Praeger, 1974), p. 12.

89. G. Spurzheim, *Outline of Phrenology* (Boston: Marsh, Capen and Lyon, 1836), n.p. This book was meant to accompany a bust. Mount's copy is inscribed "May 10, 1848" (AAA SM4/857, Museums at Stony Brook, Stony Brook, New York). We do not know precisely when Mount became acquainted with phrenology. It seems likely, however, that he learned of the theory from Inman dur-

ing his brief apprenticeship with this artist in 1827. For the circumstances of Mount's early career, see Alfred Frankenstein, *William Sidney Mount* (New York: Harry N. Abrams, 1979), p. 17.

90. William T. Oedel and Todd S. Gernes, "*The Painter's Triumph*: William Sidney Mount and the Formation of a Middle-Class Art," *Winterthur Portfolio* 23 (Summer/Autumn 1988): 113–19.

91. William Sidney Mount notebooks, 1843–48, AAA SM2/22.

92. Mount notebooks, entry 29, August 1846[?], AAA SM2/136.

93. Ibid.

94. "Rembrandt, to his friend Wm. S. Mount," 25 March 1855, in Frankenstein, *Mount*, p. 294; emphasis added.

95. "Letter from the Spirit of Rembrandt to William Sidney Mount," 29 January 1855, ibid., p. 292.

96. Diary entry, 21 January 1850, ibid., p. 239; emphasis added.

97. On the potential of *Combativeness*, see Fowler and Fowler, *Phrenology Proved*, pp. 75–82. For a previous commentary on this statement by Mount, see Colbert, "Mills," p. 137.

98. William Davis to William Sidney Mount (1866–67), in Frankenstein, *Mount*, p. 421.

99. "Phrenology and Its Foes," *American Phrenological Journal* 31 (1860): 56.

100. William Sidney Mount to Solomon Townsend Nicoll, 8 February 1847, in Frankenstein, *Mount*, p. 150. See also William Sidney Mount to Thomas Addison Richards, 20 October 1848, ibid., p. 233.

101. See Ellwood C. Parry III, "Thomas Cole's Imagination at Work in *The Architect's Dream*," *American Art Journal* 12 (Winter 1980): 55–57; William H. Pierson Jr., *American Buildings and Their Architects* (Garden City, N.Y.: Anchor, 1980), pp. 127–29; and Ellwood C. Parry III, *The Art of Thomas Cole: Ambition and Imagination* (Newark: University of Delaware Press, 1988), pp. 243–48.

102. See Charles Colbert, "Dreaming Up *The Architect's Dream*," *American Art* 6 (Summer 1992): 79–91. Much of what follows is treated in this article.

103. Parry, "Cole's Imagination," p. 42. Cole merely expressed his regrets that his patron failed to appreciate his work, but he offered no justification for the imagery. See Thomas Cole to Ithiel Town, 25 May 1840, AAA ALC 1, box 1, folder 2, New York State Library, Albany, Manuscripts and Special Collections; Howard S. Merritt, "'A Wild Scene': Genesis of a Painting," in *Studies on Thomas Cole, an American Romanticist* (Baltimore: Baltimore Museum of Art, 1967), p. 13; and Tuckerman, *Book of the Artists*, p. 224.

104. Journal entry, 8 August 1835, in *Thomas Cole: The Collected Essays and Prose Sketches*, ed. Marshall B. Tymn (New York: John Colet Press, 1980), p. 134.

105. Thomas Cole, personal notes on chiaroscuro painting, AAA ALC 2, box 4, folder 2. It should be noted, however, that Cole did paint a trompe l'oeil window for his parish church, Saint Luke's, around 1841. Whether this has to do with the fact that his objections were to chiaroscuro painting, as opposed to the window, which employed color, wants further investigation. See Parry, *Art of Thomas Cole*, p. 243.

106. Fowler and Fowler, *Phrenology Proved*, p. 141.

107. Thomas Cole to William A. Adams, 26 February 1840, in *The Life and Works of Thomas Cole*, by Louis Legrand Noble, ed. Elliott S. Vesell (Cambridge: Belknap Press of Harvard University Press, 1964), p. 210. See also Stern, *Fowlers*, p. 82.

108. For Cole's intended treatise, see Noble, *Thomas Cole*, pp. 298–99. His comparison of painting and sculpture is in a letter to John M. Falconer, 29 December 1847, ibid., p. 283; emphasis added.

109. Charles Caldwell, *Elements of Phrenology* (Lexington, Ky.: Meriwether, 1827), pp. 167–68.

110. Journal entry, 30 July 1843, in Tymn, *Thomas Cole*, pp. 174–75. See also Combe, *System of Phrenology*, p. 409.

111. Thomas Cole, journal entry, 29 December 1829, AAA ALC 4, box 6, folder 2.

112. On Tasso, see Combe, *System of Phrenology*, p. 241, and Noble, *Thomas Cole*, p. 251.

113. Noble, *Thomas Cole*, p. 307; emphasis added.

114. "L. N. Fowler's Phrenological Opinion of Mr. Thomas Cole, Phrenological Rooms, 286 Broadway, N. York, 30 May 1837," in Parry, *Art of Thomas Cole*, p. 189. A phrenological analysis of Thomas Cole was published in the *American Phrenological Journal*. This, however, was made from a portrait after the artist's death. There are numerous examinations of artists of this sort that appear in this context; generally, I have not used these unless there is some evidence that they were taken from the living individual. For Cole, see "Thomas Cole, N.A.," *American Phrenological Journal* 13 (1851): 28–30.

115. He concludes that Cole's *Philoprogenitiveness* would restrain the impulse (George Ackerley to Thomas Cole, 10 January 1838, AAA ALC 2, box 4). For Cole's efforts to acquire Combe's works, see George Ackerley to Thomas Cole, 29 August 1834, AAA ALC 2, box 4.

116. L. Niles, *Phrenology, and the Moral Influence of Phrenology* (Philadelphia: Carey, Lea, and Blanchard, 1835), p. 49.

117. Matthew Baigell, *Thomas Cole* (New York: Watson-Guptill, 1981), p. 64. See esp. Parry, *Art of Thomas Cole*, pp. 207–10, 216.

118. O. S. Fowler, *Practical Phrenologist*, pp. 39–40.

119. Robert Macnish, *The Philosophy of Sleep* (Hartford: Silas Andrus and Son, 1847), p. 12. See also J. G. Spurzheim, *Phrenology of the Doctrine of Mental Phenomena*, 2 vols. (Boston: Marsh, Capen and Lyon, 1832), 1:74.

120. Macnish, *Sleep*, pp. 11, 18.

121. William Cullen Bryant, *A Funeral Oration Occasioned by the Death of Thomas Cole, Delivered before the National Academy of Design, New York, May 4, 1848* (New York: Appleton, 1848), p. 27. On Bryant's interest in phrenology, see John Davies, *Phrenology: Fad and Science* (New Haven: Yale University Press, 1955), p. 62.

122. Bryant quoted in John Bigelow, *William Cullen Bryant*, introduction by John Hollander (1890; New York: Chelsea House, 1980), p. 262; emphasis added.

123. Gall, *On the Origin of the Moral Qualities*, 2:321.

124. See Nicholas Powell, *Fuseli: The Nightmare* (New York: Viking, 1973), pp. 37–52.

125. Cole often lamented the restrictions placed on his imagination by popular taste. See, for example, journal entry, 17 July 1841, in Parry, *Art of Thomas Cole*, p. 262.

126. E. Anna Lewis, "Art and Artists of America—Thomas Cole," 340, AAA N650/724.

127. Elihu Vedder, *The Digressions of V.* (Boston: Houghton Mifflin, 1910), p. 8.

128. See, for example, Christian D. Larson, *Brains and How to Get Them* (New York: Crowell, 1913), p. 206.

129. "The Memory of Names Impaired by a Fall on the Forehead," *Phrenological Journal and Miscellany* 5 (1828): 432.

130. J. G. Spurzheim, *Mental Phenomena*, 2:30.

131. Regina Soria, *Elihu Vedder, American Visionary Artist in Rome, 1836–1923* (Rutherford, N.J.: Fairleigh Dickinson University Press, 1970), p. 13.

132. Vedder, *Digressions of V.*, p. 124.

133. Fowler and Fowler, *Phrenology Proved*, p. 361.

134. Vedder, *Digressions of V.*, p. 8.

135. Joshua C. Taylor, "Perceptions and Digressions," in *Perceptions and Evocations: The Art of Elihu Vedder*, by Regina Soria, Joshua Taylor, Jane Dillenberger, and Richard Murray (Washington, D.C.:

Smithsonian Institution Press, 1979),
p. 61.

136. Soria, *Elihu Vedder*, p. 94, and
Russel M. Goldfarb and Clare R. Goldfarb, *Spiritualism and Nineteenth-Century
Letters* (Rutherford, N.J.: Fairleigh
Dickinson University Press, 1978),
p. 110. Soria acknowledges Kate Field's
interest in the occult but does not pursue the matter; see Soria, *Elihu Vedder*,
p. 167. For more on this relationship,
see Taylor, "Digressions," pp. 51–52.
Soria discusses the possibility that Inness
introduced Vedder to the doctrines of
Swedenborg in the summer of 1871. He
seems, however, to have been aware of
the theology earlier; see Soria, *Elihu
Vedder*, p. 94.

137. Soria relates *Memory* to a sketch
done in 1867; see Soria, *Elihu Vedder*,
p. 79.

138. *Planchett's Diary*, ed. Kate Field
(New York: J. S. Redfield, 1868), p. 65.
Field claims only to have edited the communications that came from elsewhere.
When asked about the appearance of
spirits, Field was told, "Whatever our
nature, that is seen in our figure and
face" (ibid., p. 35). For more on the
spiritualist implications of Vedder's
drawing, see Jane Dillenberger, "Between Faith and Doubt: Subjects for
Meditation," in Soria et al., *Perceptions
and Evocations*, p. 115.

139. These events occurred during his
"Cafe Greco days," the three years before
his marriage in 1868. From the tenor of
Vedder's remarks it would seem that his
enthusiasm for Swedenborg, which was
strongest in the years following the Civil
War, waned later in life. See Vedder,
Digressions of V., p. 345.

140. Emanuel Swedenborg, *Heaven and
Hell*, trans. George F. Dole (New York:
Swedenborg Foundation, 1984), p. 463.

141. Trudie Grace, "The Disembodied Head: A Major Theme in European
Art from 1885–1905" (Ph.D. dissertation, City University of New York, 1984),
p. 25. What Grace has to say about the

popularity of such imagery in Europe
holds true also for America; thus she
states, "Thus allusive heads are addi-
tionally significant because they reflect
a major cultural concern: again, man's
non-physical plane—a main facet of
physiognomy, phrenology, spiritism, oc-
cultism, and psychology. Perhaps never
before had so many people in such a
short period become interested in such
a variety of subjects dealing with the
incorporeal dimension" (ibid., p. 243).
Vedder could combine these interests
in his own peculiar manner, as in the
following observation on the popularity
of his illustrations for Omar Khayyam:
"After wondering so much, even at the
risk of having the spirit of Lamb fum-
bling at my bumps, I will say—How
wonderful is the working of the mind"
(Vedder, *Digressions of V.*, p. 231). For
a similar situation in terms of William
Blake's phrenological analysis of his
visionary heads, see Anne K. Mellor,
"Physiognomy, Phrenology, and Blake's
Visionary Heads," in *Blake in His Time*,
ed. Robert N. Essick and Donald Pearce
(Bloomington: Indiana University Press,
1978), pp. 53–74.

142. Theophilus Parsons, *Essays*, 3 vols.
(Boston: T. H. Carter and Son, 1868),
1:64–65. These essays were written over
the preceding two decades.

143. Ibid., 3:199. Another source is
Alfred Lord Tennyson's poem "Break,
Break, Break," which evokes memories
of a departed love as the narrator walks
along the shore. Vedder may have combined these several sources. See Ilene
Susan Fort and Michael Quick, *American Art: A Catalogue of the Los Angeles
County Museum of Art* (Los Angeles: Los
Angeles County Museum of Art, 1991),
p. 151. The painting hardly illustrates
the passage from the poem; rather, it
evokes a similar mood while also employing symbols from other sources that
preoccupied the artist.

144. Soria mentions Vedder's anticipation of Symbolism and Surrealism;

see Soria, *Elihu Vedder*, p. 37. See also Charles C. Eldredge, *American Imagination and Symbolist Painting* (New York: Grey Art Gallery and Study Center, New York University, 1979), p. 57.

145. Soria notes that through his paintings Vedder sublimated the fear, terror, and sorrow he felt as a consequence of the events of his early life; see Soria, *Elihu Vedder*, p. 15. Passages in Vedder's poetry reflect Swedenborgian ideas about memory, hence we read:

> The Mind's a stuff that doth retain
> A form, an impress, or a stain
> That nothing can obliterate:
> A hall-mark on Youth's golden state
>   That must remain.
> [Elihu Vedder, *Doubt and Other Things*
>   (Boston: Four Seas, 1923), p. 26.]

146. Parsons, *Essays*, 3:197.

147. Undated entry in Mount notebooks for 1858–68, AAA SM2/498. Mount's anxieties and interest in phrenology is a major theme in Benjamin Nelson Pfingstag, "Aspects of Form and Time in the Paintings of William Sidney Mount" (Ph.D. dissertation, State University of New York, Binghamton, 1980).

148. Notebook entry, 31 May 1857, in Frankenstein, *Mount*, p. 308.

149. For example, see J. G. Spurzheim, *Mental Phenomena*, 1:13. Mount could have become acquainted with this saying through any number of phrenological publications. An instance among the books in his possession is found inside a volume of poetry called *Flora and Thalia: Gems of Flowers and Poetry*, by "A Lady" (Philadelphia: Carey, Lea, and Blanchard, 1836). Among the advertisements inside is one for a book on phrenology that contains the following quote from Pope: "Man's greatest knowledge is himself to know" (AAA SM4/860).

CHAPTER THREE

1. Meeting of the Stockholders of the Pennsylvania Academy of Fine Arts, 11 February 1835, Archives of American Art, P63/1013, Pennsylvania Academy of Fine Arts, Philadelphia.

2. John Bell, *Health and Beauty* (Philadelphia: Carey and Hart, 1838), pp. 13–15.

3. "On Voluntary Distortion of the Human Figure by Artificial Compression," *Phrenological Journal and Miscellany* 7 (1832): 579.

4. Ibid., p. 583.

5. George Combe, *Notes on the United States of North America during a Phrenological Visit in 1838–9–40*, 2 vols. (Philadelphia: Carey and Hart, 1841), 1:329–30. The was some resistance to Combe's lectures, but generally they were well received; indeed, he was asked to repeat them. Peale adapted Combe's remarks to the needs of the artist by quoting the phrenologist on the selection of models: "The advantage of studying the finest models of the human figure as exhibited in painting and sculpture, is to raise our ideas of the excellence of forms and proportions to which our nature is capable of attaining; for, other conditions being equal, the most perfect forms and proportions are always the best adapted for health and activity. G. Combe" (quoted in Rembrandt Peale, *Portfolio of an Artist* [Philadelphia: Henry Perkins, 1839], p. 163).

6. Bell, *Health*, p. 185.

7. Ibid., pp. 67–71.

8. Ibid., pp. 13–15.

9. Ibid., pp. 226–27.

10. Ibid., pp. 15–19, 214.

11. Ibid., pp. 58–60.

12. Ibid., pp. 94–98.

13. Ibid., pp. 100–105.

14. Bell, in *Essays on Phrenology*, by George Combe, edited with an introduction by John Bell (Philadelphia: Carey and Lea, 1822), p. L, and Francois Joseph Gall, *On the Origin of the Moral Qualities and Intellectual Faculties of Man*, 6 vols., trans. Winslow Lewis Jr. (Boston: Marsh, Capen and Lyon, 1835), 1:49.

15. "Mrs. Thompson's Phrenological Museum, 518 Broadway, Albany,

N.Y.," *American Phrenological Journal* 15 (1852): 48.

16. Thomas W. Olcott, *Address Delivered before the Albany Phrenological Society at Its Meeting in the Female Academy* (Albany: J. Munsell, 1840), p. 3.

17. Henry T. Tuckerman, *Book of the Artists* (New York: G. P. Putnam and Son, 1867), p. 364.

18. John Davies, *Phrenology: Fad and Science* (New Haven: Yale University Press, 1955), p. 93.

19. Amos Dean, *Lectures on Phrenology* (Albany: Oliver Steele and Hofman and White, 1834).

20. E. D. Palmer, "Philosophy of the Ideal," *Crayon* 3 (1856): 19. His wording on physical metaphysics encompasses the "spiritual modification" of the features and seems to apply both to transitory expressions (natural language) and the gradual changes of form that result from prolonged mental development. The diagrams employed to illustrate his meaning engage considerations repeatedly addressed by the phrenologists. There has been some discussion about Palmer's concept of the ideal and his assertion that there are many types of the ideal; see J. Carson Webster, *Erastus D. Palmer* (Newark: University of Delaware Press, 1983), pp. 39–60. Perhaps the best explanation of the sort of philosophy that inspired the artist comes from Harriet Beecher Stowe. She writes, "As to every leaf and every flower there is an ideal to which the growth of the plant is constantly urging, so is there an ideal to every human being,—a perfect form in which it might appear, were every defect removed and every characteristic excellence stimulated to the highest point. Once in an age, God sends to some of us a friend who loves in us not a false imagining, an unreal character, but looking through all the rubbish of our imperfections loves in us the divine ideal of our nature,—loves, not the man that we are, but the angel that we may be" (Stowe, *The Minister's Wooing* [1859; New York: AMS Press, 1967], p. 96). Such notions permitted Palmer to make the traditional concept of the ideal more democratic.

21. Palmer, "Ideal," p. 19; Dean, *Lectures on Phrenology*, p. 53. Palmer seems even more concerned than most phrenologists to deemphasize the upper portion of the occiput with its masculine faculties.

22. Bell, *Health*, p. 238.

23. Mary Roth Walsh, *"Doctors Wanted: No Women Need Apply": Sexual Barriers in the Medical Profession* (New Haven: Yale University Press, 1977), p. 28.

24. "Sketchings," *Crayon* 2 (1855): 24. The newspaper cited is the *Boston Post*, 25 June 1855.

25. See also "High Foreheads, Beauty and Intellect," *American Phrenological Journal* 23 (1856): 61.

26. George Combe, *Phrenology Applied to Painting and Sculpture* (London: Simpkin, Marshall, 1855), pp. 38–39.

27. For more commentary on the large head of the *White Captive*, see *Boston Post*, 14 February 1860. Quoted in Webster, *Palmer*, p. 86; see also p. 184.

28. From the *New York Journal of Commerce*, 12 November 1859. Quoted in Webster, *Palmer*, p. 73.

29. Letter to an unidentified recipient, Florence, Italy, 5 October 1873, published in the *Albany Evening Times*, 24 October 1873. Quoted in Webster, *Palmer*, p. 302.

30. For example, see the reviewer in the *Atlantic Monthly*, January 1860, pp. 108–9. Quoted in Webster, *Palmer*, p. 74.

31. L. J. Bigelow, "Palmer, the American Sculptor," *Continental Monthly* 5 (1864): 258, 260. Quoted in Webster, *Palmer*, p. 74.

32. Wendell L'Amoreux, "Palmer's White Captive: An Art Epistle," *Springfield Republican*, 27 February 1858. Quoted in Webster, *Palmer*, p. 67.

33. For example, in the *New York Commercial Advertiser*, 12 November 1859. Quoted in Webster, *Palmer*, p. 73.

34. Webster, *Palmer*, p. 79.

35. "Palmer's 'White Captive,' " *Atlantic Monthly*, January 1860, p. 109. Much of this is quoted in Webster, *Palmer*, p. 74.

36. This was still a novel concept in the early nineteenth century; see Harvey Green, *Fit for America* (New York: Pantheon, 1986), p. 95.

37. Quoted in Webster, *Palmer*, p. 51.

38. "Palmer's 'White Captive,' " p. 109.

39. Dean, *Lectures on Phrenology*, p. 251.

40. E. B., "American Art," *New York Journal of Commerce*, 26 December 1859. Quoted in Webster, *Palmer*, p. 78.

41. See, for example, David C. Huntington, *The Landscapes of Frederic Edwin Church* (New York: Braziller, 1966), p. 17.

42. Tuckerman, *Book of the Artists*, p. 359.

43. Harriet Beecher Stowe, *Household Papers and Stories* (1864; New York: AMS Press, 1967), p. 330.

44. Margaret Farrand Thorp, *The Literary Sculptors* (Durham: Duke University Press, 1965), p. 145.

45. Webster, *Palmer*, p. 60.

46. For example, see Charles Thomas Walters, "Hiram Powers and William Rimmer: A Study in the Concept of Expression" (Ph.D. dissertation, University of Michigan, 1977), p. 153. Weidman is ambivalent on the matter, stating that Rimmer recognized "the creative aspects of physiognomy and phrenology while rejecting the unscientific tenets of both" (Jeffrey Weidman, "William Rimmer," in *William Rimmer, a Yankee Michelangelo*, by Jeffrey Weidman, Neil Harris, and Philip Cash, foreword by Theodore E. Stebbins Jr. [Hanover, N.H.: University Press of New England, 1985], p. 10).

47. William Rimmer, *Art Anatomy* (Boston: Little, Brown, 1877), pp. 41, 13. The modern edition of this book makes a number of changes in the wording of the original text; hence, it alters "that disgusting protrusion" to "that exaggerated protrusion." Although slight, such transformations do modify the author's intent; the citations here are from the original text. See William Rimmer, *Art Anatomy*, introduction by Robert Hutchinson (New York: Dover, 1962), p. 140.

48. A good review of the state of medicine during Rimmer's life can be found in Philip Cash, "American Medicine in the Time of William Rimmer," in Weidman, Harris, and Cash, *Yankee Michelangelo*, pp. 20–26.

49. J. Cruveilhier, *The Anatomy of the Human Body*, ed. Granville Sharp Pattison (New York: Harper and Brothers, [1844]). A note by Caroline Hunt Rimmer, the artist's daughter, states that "this book was the primary text employed by William Rimmer." The book is presently in Countway Library of the Harvard Medical School, Boston, Mass.

50. Ibid., pp. 751–53.

51. Jeffrey Weidman, "William Rimmer: A Critical Catalogue Raisonne," 7 vols. (Ph.D. dissertation, Indiana University, 1982), 4:1358–59.

52. The source of this information was Daniel Howard; see Truman H. Bartlett, *The Art Life of William Rimmer: Sculptor, Painter, and Physician* (1890; New York: DaCapo, 1970), p. 21.

53. Again, the source is Daniel Howard; ibid., p. 21.

54. For Rimmer's interest in spiritualism, see ibid., pp. 18, 28, and Weidman, "Critical Catalogue," 1:81–82.

55. The report on Rimmer's Swedenborgianism comes from W. J. Linton, a wood engraver in New York, who in 1868 discussed the possibility of collaboration on a book of art anatomy. This fact suggests a considerable degree of familiarity with Rimmer, and the specificity of his remark reminds us that membership in a particular sect was a matter of greater significance in the nineteenth century than it tends to be today. For Linton's statement, see Weidman, "Critical Catalogue," 1:81. Bartlett writes that Rimmer belonged to no church or creed (*Rimmer*, p. 95). This does not invalidate Linton's testimony, for informal associations arose in America that followed

their own interpretation of the mystic's theology. A divisive force within the New Church was spiritualism, and many of the less orthodox believers embraced this creed. It is revealing to compare the range of Rimmer's beliefs with those of Silas Jones, a leader in the New Era movement; besides being a spiritualist and Swedenborgian, he also lectured on phrenology and belonged to a circle of mesmerists. See Scott Trego Swank, "The Unfettered Conscious: A Study of Sectarianism, Spiritualism, and Social Reform in the New Jerusalem Church, 1840–1870" (Ph.D. dissertation, University of Pennsylvania, 1970), pp. 197–204.

56. John Haller, *American Medicine in Transition, 1840–1910* (Urbana: University of Illinois Press, 1980), p. 3.

57. Walt Whitman, "Mediums," in *Leaves of Grass* (New York: Norton, 1965), p. 480.

58. Haller, *American Medicine*, pp. 140–41. Evans was born in 1817, making him one year younger than Rimmer.

59. For information on magnetic cures in the 1840s, see Robert Fuller, "Mesmerism and the Birth of Psychology," in *Pseudo-Science and Society in Nineteenth-Century America*, ed. Arthur Wrobel (Lexington: University Press of Kentucky, 1987), pp. 209–10.

60. William Rimmer, "Stephen and Philip," Rimmer manuscripts and scrapbooks, Boston Medical Library, Francis A. Countway Library of Medicine, Harvard University, Boston, Mass., B MS b44.2, p. 357.

61. For a discussion of this in the context of spiritualism, see W. S. Courtney, "God," *Spiritual Telegraph* 3 (1854): 405.

62. Quoted in Neil Harris, "The Artist as Teacher," in Weidman, Harris, and Cash, *Yankee Michelangelo*, p. 19.

63. Bartlett, *Rimmer*, p. 112.

64. For example, see W. F. Evans, *The Mental-Cure, Illustrating the Influence of the Mind on Body Both in Health and Disease and the Psychological Method of Treatment* (Boston: H. H. and T. W. Carteer, 1869), pp. 39–48.

65. This inscription is at the top of the page in the original edition, suggesting that all the specimens were drawn from this source, while in the modern edition the inscription is placed under the "Skull of California Indian." See Rimmer, *Art Anatomy*, p. 10.

66. Weidman, "William Rimmer," p. 10. Weidman expresses some doubt as to whether "the Museum of Natural History in Boston" is a reference to the Boston Museum, which opened in 1841, or the Warren Museum, also known as the Natural History Museum. But given Rimmer's invitation to the Warren Museum and the kind of collections it contained, the latter seems more likely. See Weidman, "Critical Catalogue," 3:1036.

67. See J. B. S. Jackson, *A Descriptive Catalogue of the Warren Anatomical Museum* (Boston: A. Williams, 1870), p. 699, entries 3157–58. There are many Indian skulls in the collection, and it is difficult to single out the one Rimmer may have consulted; see pp. 702–4.

68. J. W. Jackson, *Ethnology and Phrenology as an Aid to the Historian* (London: Trubner, 1863), pp. 8–9. See also Hugh Honour, *The Image of the Black in Western Art IV: From the American Revolution to World War I*, 2 vols. (Cambridge: Harvard University Press, 1989), 1:160.

69. Combe, *Painting and Sculpture*. It is likely that Rimmer knew this book, and perhaps he attended Combe's lectures during the latter's tour in 1839–40. On this, see Weidman, "Critical Catalogue," 1:130–31. See also "Phrenology in Art," *American Phrenological Journal* 31 (1860): 19–21.

70. The first of these compares Combe's ideas to those of Professor Hart, R.A., who is skeptical about phrenology. See "What Makes an Artist?," *Crayon* 3 (1856): 218–19. This continues in F., "What Makes an Artist?," *Crayon* 3 (1856): 284–85. A more balanced and detailed review is found in "The Phrenological Gauge," *Crayon* 3 (1856): 298–300.

71. Combe, *Painting and Sculpture*, p. 3.

72. "Phrenology in Art," p. 19.

73. See, for example, the remarks in Rimmer, *Art Anatomy*, p. 24.

74. Weidman, "Critical Catalogue," 1:82, 2:478–79.

75. Rimmer, *Art Anatomy*, p. 30.

76. Samuel R. Wells, *New Physiognomy* (New York: Samuel R. Wells, 1868), p. 753.

77. "Phrenology in Art," p. 21. As a Swedenborgian, Rimmer must have thought that Africans held an important place in creation, but this would not have prevented him from adopting paternalistic attitudes toward them. In this respect, and with regard to Rimmer's drawings dedicated to the black regiment from Massachusetts in the Civil War, Honour's observation seems appropriate: "For white abolitionists—whether inspired by a religious ideal of benevolence or a secular notion of justice— were convinced of their own intellectual and moral superiority" (Honour, *Image of the Black*, 1:50; see also p. 74). Indeed, spiritualism and Swedenborgianism were not prepared to relinquish the belief that external form was a reflection of inner, spiritual condition; hence they continued to rely on phrenology and the facial angle to establish the point. See, for example, Hudson Tuttle, *Arcana of Nature; or the History and Laws of Creation* (Boston: Berry, Colby, 1860), pp. 340–51.

78. Wells, *New Physiognomy*, p. 126.

79. Charles Caldwell, *Elements of Phrenology* (Lexington, Ky.: Meriwether, 1827), pp. 269–70.

80. Rimmer, *Art Anatomy*, p. 12.

81. Ibid., p. 16.

82. "Dr. Rimmer's Sixth Lecture," *Providence Daily Journal*, 3 February 1873.

83. *Self-Help* (New York: Cowan, 1874), p. 40.

84. O. S. Fowler, *Creative and Sexual Science* (Rochester: New York State Pub. Co., 1870), p. 991. See also pp. 80–94.

85. Rimmer, *Art Anatomy*, p. 21.

86. Bartlett, *Rimmer*, p. 121.

87. Many of Wells's illustrations were taken from those that had already appeared in the *American Phrenological Journal*, and Rimmer could well have seen them there if he never encountered the book. See also Wells, *New Physiognomy*.

88. For this perspective on women, see O. S. Fowler, *Sexual Science: Including Manhood, Womanhood, and Their Mutual Interrelations; Love, Its Laws, Power, Etc.* (Philadelphia: National Pub. Co., 1870), p. 131.

89. Stowe, *Household Papers*, pp. 321–22.

90. Weidman, "William Rimmer," pp. 70–71, and Weidman, "Critical Catalogue," 2:638. See also Combe, *Painting and Sculpture*, pp. 60–61.

91. William Wetmore Story, *Roba di Roma* (London: Chapman and Hall, 1875), p. 241.

92. O. S. Fowler, *The Practical Phrenologist* (Boston: O. S. Fowler, 1869), p. 67.

93. William Rimmer, XI Lecture of the 2nd series, April 1872, in Bartlett, *Rimmer*, p. 77.

94. Weidman, "Critical Catalogue," 2:637–38.

95. Quoted in Weidman, "William Rimmer," p. 41.

96. On the claims of Thomas Rimmer to the throne of France, see Lincoln Kirstein, *William Rimmer, His Life and Art* (1946–47; New York: Whitney Museum of American Art, 1961), n.p.

97. Combe, *Painting and Sculpture*, pp. 82–83.

98. For a discussion of Thomas Rimmer's last days, see Weidman, "Critical Catalogue," 1:18, and Kirstein, *Rimmer*.

99. Rimmer employed his father's head for the English type in his treatise; see Kirstein, *Rimmer*.

100. Truman H. Bartlett, "Dr. William Rimmer," *American Art Review* (1880): 462.

101. I.B., "Studios in Florence," *Once a Week*, 19 December 1863, p. 721, Rimmer scrapbooks.

102. Gall, *On the Origin of the Moral Qualities*, 5:217-18.

103. Caldwell, *Elements of Phrenology*, p. 114.

104. Charles A. Sarnoff, "The Meaning of William Rimmer's *Flight and Pursuit*," *American Art Journal* 5 (May 1973): 18–19.

105. Marcia Goldberg, "William Rimmer's *Flight and Pursuit*: An Allegory of Assassination," *Art Bulletin* 59 (1976): 234–40; Ellwood C. Parry III, "Looking for a French and Egyptian Connection behind William Rimmer's *Flight and Pursuit*," *American Art Journal* 13 (Summer 1981): 51–60.

106. Weidman, "Critical Catalogue," 2:610; see also Parry, "Egyptian Connection," pp. 52–53.

107. Emanuel Swedenborg, *The Heavenly Arcana* (Boston: Houghton Mifflin, 1907), no. 2832.

108. Ibid., nos. 10208–11.

109. Emanuel Swedenborg, *Heaven and Hell*, trans. George F. Dole (New York: Swedenborg Foundation, 1984), no. 56. It should be noted in this context that Rimmer's words, "Oh, for the horns of the altar," find no exact counterpart in the Bible, where we are told that someone grasped "the horns of the altar." This suggests that the artist did not intend to illustrate a specific passage from the Bible but sought to include all sinners in his meaning, an approach consistent with Swedenborg's analysis of the Bible and the doctrine of correspondences.

110. See Marguerite Beck Block, *The New Church in the New World*, introduction by Robert H. Kirven (1932; New York: Octagon Books, 1968), p. 31.

111. Swedenborg, *Heaven and Hell*, no. 599.

112. Rimmer, "Stephen and Philip," p. 17.

113. Block, *New Church*, pp. 148–49; Frank Podmer, *Mediums of the Nineteenth Century*, 2 vols. (published in 1902 as *Modern Spiritualism*; New Hyde Park, N.Y.: University Books, 1963), 1:15–16;

Henry James Sr., *The Secret of Swedenborg* (Boston: Fields, Osgood, 1869), p. 67.

114. Weidman, "Critical Catalogue," 2:600.

115. Rimmer, *Art Anatomy*, p. 14.

116. In a different context Rimmer takes up the concept of correspondences with regard to the environment. He writes that trees, rocks, mountains, and valleys "are beautiful, only because there is in us a world of beauty to which such things correspond" (Harris, "The Artist as Teacher," p. 19). The fugitive corresponds to his environment, to the malevolence of his pursuer, because he has the world of evil within him. It is possible that the two mysterious shadows on the right of the painting were included to indicate the presence of the two protagonists of "Stephen and Philip." They would then be the narrators who are not actually "in" the scene. This is, admittedly, a matter of speculation; what is needed is a thorough examination and editing of Rimmer's as yet unpublished manuscript.

117. Rimmer, "Stephen and Philip," p. 29.

118. See Jas Wood Davidson, "Swedenborgian Physiognomy," *Phrenological Journal and Life Illustrated* 60 (1875): 218–33; Swedenborg, *Heaven and Hell*, no. 351; and James John Garth Wilkinson, *The Human Body and Its Connection with Man* (London: New Church Press, [1851]), p. 25.

119. Harold Aspiz, *Walt Whitman and the Body Beautiful* (Urbana: University of Illinois Press, 1980), p. 41.

120. James Thomas Flexner, "Tuckerman's *Book of Artists*," *American Art Journal* 1 (Fall 1969): 55.

121. Henry T. Tuckerman, "Allusions to Phrenology, in *The Last Days of Pompeii*," *Annals of Phrenology* 1 (1834): 460–61.

122. Ibid., p. 462.

123. Henry T. Tuckerman, *Artist-Life; or Sketches of American Painters* (New York: Appleton, 1857), pp. 197–98.

124. Henry T. Tuckerman, *The Italian Sketch Book* (New York: J. C. Riker, 1848), pp. 219–27.

125. Tuckerman, *Book of the Artists*, pp. 302, 441.

126. Tuckerman, *Artist-Life*, p. 183.

127. Henry T. Tuckerman, *The Criterion; or the Test of Talk about Familiar Things* (New York: Hurd and Houghton, 1866), p. 68.

128. Tuckerman, *Book of the Artists*, p. 375.

129. Tuckerman, *Artist-Life*, p. 46.

130. Henry T. Tuckerman, *Mental Portraits* (London: Richard Bently, 1853), pp. 333–34.

131. These comments come in a discussion of Audubon and apply generally to Tuckerman's views on the fine arts. See Tuckerman, *Mental Portraits*, p. 336.

132. For a review of this aspect of Whitman's criticism, see Aspiz, *Walt Whitman*, pp. 61, 121–22, 243–45.

133. Henry T. Tuckerman, *Essays, Biographical and Critical; or Studies of Character* (Boston: Phillips, Samson, 1857), pp. 164–80.

134. Tuckerman, *Book of the Artists*, p. 277.

135. Joy S. Kasson, *Marble Queens and Captives* (New Haven: Yale University Press, 1990), p. 8. Kasson compares Tuckerman's criticism to Horatio Alger success stories, but this begs the whole question of artistic organization.

136. Tuckerman, *Criterion*, pp. 69–70.

137. Tuckerman, *Book of the Artists*, pp. 426, 406.

138. Ibid., pp. 104–6; emphasis added.

139. Combe, *Painting and Sculpture*, pp. 26–50.

140. Tuckerman, *Book of the Artists*, pp. 102–4.

141. Ibid., pp. 414–15.

142. Ibid., p. 156.

143. Wells, *New Physiognomy*, p. 106.

144. Tuckerman, *Book of the Artists*, p. 148.

145. L. N. Fowler, "Phrenological Character of Washington Allston," *American Phrenological Journal and Miscellany* 10 (1848): 330.

146. Tuckerman, *Book of the Artists*, p. 152.

147. Ibid., p. 150.

148. Ibid., p. 112.

149. Ibid., pp. 114–16.

150. Ibid., pp. 59–60.

151. Ibid., p. 60.

152. George Combe, *The Constitution of Man Considered in Relation to External Objects*, 5th ed. (Boston: March, Capen and Lyon, 1835), p. 177.

153. Tuckerman, *Book of the Artists*, p. 125.

154. Ibid., p. 406.

155. Ibid., p. 151. For a recent account of these events, see William H. Gerdts, "The Paintings of Washington Allston," in *"A Man of Genius": The Art of Washington Allston, 1779–1843*, by William H. Gerdts and Theodore E. Stebbins Jr. (Boston: Museum of Fine Arts, 1979), p. 80.

156. George Combe, *Moral Philosophy; or, the Duties of Man* (New York: William H. Colyer, 1846), pp. 83–101.

157. Tuckerman, *Book of the Artists*, p. 220.

158. Ibid., p. 137.

159. On Charles Sumner's interest in phrenology, see David Donald, *Charles Sumner and the Coming of the Civil War* (New York: Knopf, 1960), p. 104. I want to thank Lauretta Dimmick for calling my attention to this material.

160. Robert L. Gale, *Thomas Crawford, American Sculptor* (Pittsburgh: University of Pittsburgh Press, 1964), pp. 31–33.

161. [Thomas Crawford], "A Visit to the Relics of Raphael," *Crayon* 2 (1855): 201. Although the essay is unsigned, Dimmick includes it among Crawford's writings; see Lauretta Dimmick, "A Catalogue of the Portrait Busts and Ideal Works of Thomas Crawford (1813?–1857), American Sculptor in Rome" (Ph.D. dissertation, University of Pittsburgh, 1986), pp. 651–52.

162. George Combe, *A System of Phrenology* (New York: William H. Colyer, 1841), p. 175.

163. "Remarks on the Cerebral Development of Raffael D'Urbino, Compared with the Accounts Given of his Character and Genius," *Phrenological Journal and Miscellany* 2 (1824–25): 327–60.

164. "Raphael's Skull," *Phrenological Journal and Miscellany* 8 (1832–34): 476–77.

165. "Skull of Raphael," *Phrenological Journal and Miscellany* 8 (1832–34): 568.

166. Caldwell, *Elements of Phrenology*, p. 164.

167. Combe, *Painting and Sculpture*, pp. 97–114.

168. Tuckerman, *Criterion*, pp. 98–100.

169. Combe, *Painting and Sculpture*, p. 99.

170. Dimmick, "Thomas Crawford," p. 48.

171. "Aesthetics of Dress," *Crayon* 1 (1855): 145.

172. This material on Whitman is from Aspiz, *Walt Whitman*, pp. 122–25.

173. For the comparison of Palmer to Emerson (and Ruskin), see Webster, *Palmer*, pp. 48, 71.

CHAPTER FOUR

1. This philosophy is articulated at length in Archibald Alison, *Essays on the Nature and Principles of Taste*, with corrections and improvements by Abraham Mills (New York: G. & C. & H. Carvill, 1830). Much has been written about Cole's debt to Alison; an insightful review can be found in Earl A. Powell III, "Thomas Cole and the American Landscape Tradition: Associationism," *Arts Magazine* 52 (April 1978): pp. 113–17. See also Ralph N. Miller, "Thomas Cole and Alison's Essays on Taste," *New York History* 37 (July 1956): 281–99. On the declining relevance of Alison among Cole's younger contemporaries, see Howard Merritt, " 'A Wild Scene': Genesis of a Painting," *Baltimore Museum of Art Annual* 2 (1967): 38.

2. Henry T. Tuckerman, "Artists and Authors," *Cosmopolitan Art Journal* 3 (1858–59): 190.

3. Nelson Sizer, *Forty Years in Phrenology: Embracing Recollections of History, Anecdote, and Experience* (New York: Fowler and Wells, 1891), p. 114.

4. J. G. Spurzheim, *Phrenology or the Doctrine of Mental Phenomena*, 2 vols. (Boston: Marsh, Capen and Lyon, 1832), 2:38.

5. Much of the following material comes from Charles Colbert, " 'Razors and Brains': Asher B. Durand and the Paradigm of Nature," *Studies in the American Renaissance* (1992): 261–90. For the interest of French artists in beards, see Etienne-Jean Delecluze, " 'The Beards' of 1800 and 'The Beards' of Today (1835)," in *Nineteenth-Century Theories of Art*, ed. Joshua C. Taylor (Berkeley: University of California Press, 1989), pp. 206–19.

6. Philip Gilbert Hamerton, *Portfolio Papers* (Boston: Roberts Brothers, 1889), pp. 189–90.

7. John Durand, *The Life and Times of A. B. Durand* (1890; New York: DaCapo, 1970), p. 38. The relationship revealed in the letters between the two men was even closer than that implied by John Durand. We find Graham, for example, discussing Durand's work, and art in general, at some length (Sylvester Graham to A. B. Durand, Middlebury, 8 June 1825, Archives of American Art [henceforth AAA], N19/325–27, New York Public Library, Rare Books and Manuscript Division, Astor, Lenox, and Tilden Foundations). See also David B. Lawall, *Asher B. Durand: A Documentary Catalogue of the Narrative and Landscape Paintings* (New York: Garland, 1978), p. xxxvii.

8. Stephen Nissenbaum, *Sex, Diet, and Debility in Jacksonian America* (Westport, Conn.: Greenwood Press, 1980), p. 80.

9. For a good review of Graham's sources and ideas, see ibid.; Sylvester Graham, *A Lecture on Epidemic Diseases, Generally and Particularly the Spasmodic Cholera* (New York: Mahlon Day, 1833), pp. 5–15; and, most exhaustively, Sylvester Graham, *Lectures on the Science of Human Life*, 2 vols. (Boston: Marsh, Capen, Lyon and Webb, 1839).

10. Quoted in Bruce Haley, *The Healthy Body and Victorian Culture* (Cambridge: Harvard University Press, 1978), p. 6.

11. This analysis relies on Charles E. Rosenberg, *The Cholera Years* (Chicago: University of Chicago Press, 1962), pp. 1–98.

12. Graham, *Epidemic Diseases*, pp. 38–41.

13. William Sidney Mount notebooks, 1858–68, n.d. (near 4 March 1867), AAA SM2/0370, Museums at Stony Brook, Stony Brook, N.Y.

14. Nissenbaum, *Sex, Diet, and Debility*, p. 96.

15. John Durand, *Life and Times*, p. 85.

16. Henry T. Tuckerman, *Book of the Artists* (New York: G. P. Putnam and Son, 1867), p. 192.

17. Anon., *A Defense of the Graham System of Living* (New York: Applegate, 1835), p. 29.

18. J. W. Casilear to Asher Durand, New York, 20 August 1832, AAA N19/712.

19. Graham, *Epidemic Diseases*, p. 76.

20. John Durand, *Life and Times*, p. 86. The print was never completed.

21. Sylvester Graham to A. B. Durand, Little Compton, R.I., 23 September 1832, AAA N19/729.

22. Ralph Waldo Emerson, "Nature," in *Selected Prose and Poetry*, edited with an introduction by Reginald L. Cook (New York: Holt, Rinehart and Winston, 1960), p. 40; for Emerson's negative reflections on Graham, see "New England Reformers," pp. 144–45. The contrast developed in this text between Emerson's Transcendentalism and the transcendental medicine of Whitman, Durand, and others parallels the distinctions between the palefaces and redskins discussed in Philip Rahv, "Paleface and Redskin," in *Image and Idea* (Norfolk, Conn.: New Directions, 1949), pp. 1–5.

23. Alvan Fisher to Asher Durand, Boston, 2 April 1834, AAA N19/822. Thus, Fisher writes that his "memory is very tenacious[,] particularly in *acquisitiveness.*"

24. Asher Durand, journal entry for Sunday, 14 June [1840], AAA N20/5.

25. John Dillenberger, *The Visual Arts and Christianity in America* (Chico, Calif.: Scholars Press, 1984), p. 103, and David B. Lawall, *Asher Brown Durand: His Art and Art Theory in Relation to His Times* (New York: Garland, 1977), p. 85.

26. Asher Durand, journal entry for Wednesday, 10 June [1840], AAA N20/3–4.

27. Graham, *Human Life*, 2:602.

28. Asher Durand, journal entry for Monday, 8 June [1840], AAA N20/2–4. Much of this is also included in John Durand, *Life and Times*, pp. 144–45.

29. George Combe, *Notes on the United States of North America during a Phrenological Visit in 1838–9–40*, 2 vols. (Philadelphia: Carey and Hart, 1841), 2:348–49.

30. John Durand, *Life and Times*, p. 146. I have not been able to locate this passage in Durand's journal, but it is difficult to believe that his son merely fabricated the incident. Perhaps it survived in the oral traditions of the family. Yet even if apocryphal, it would still represent an effort by John Durand to link his father with Combe, whom he, John, describes as "the eminent phrenologist and author of *The Constitution of Man*" (John Durand, *Life and Times*, p. 144). The negative evaluation of this encounter comes in Clara Endicott Sears, *Highlights among the Hudson River Artists* (1947; Port Washington, N.Y.: Kennikat, 1968), p. 45. To my knowledge, she is the only one to mention this meeting.

31. Graham, *Human Life*, 1:viii–ix. This similarity obliged Graham to defend himself against charges of plagiarism.

32. Combe, *Phrenological Visit*, 2:297–98.

33. Barbara Gallati, *Asher B. Durand, an Engraver's and Farmer's Art*, introduction by James Thomas Flexner (Trevor Park-on-Hudson, N.Y.: Hudson River Museum, 1983), pp. 50–52.

34. Graham, *Human Life*, 2:135.

35. Daniel Huntington, *Asher B.*

Durand: A Memorial Address (New York: Century, 1887), p. 21.

36. Gallati, Durand, p. 52.

37. Lawall notes that Durand went through a "spiritual crisis" around 1830 as a consequence of his wife's death. We have seen that Graham regarded premature death as the inevitable consequence of disobedience to the laws of nature. Perhaps these circumstances contributed to the decision to execute the Ariadne. From this perspective the print would have served to assuage his grief, and conceivably a lingering guilt, by warning others to avoid the fate that befell his wife. See Lawall, Durand: His Art and Art Theory, p. 103. Durand's response to a woman who was flush with the excitement of a masked ball, that she exhibited "too fair and delicate [a] texture to sustain for the length of years the blighting influence of sensuality and midnight revel," is entirely consistent with Graham's views on the debilitating consequences of modern entertainment (John Durand, Life and Times, p. 154).

38. Huntington, Durand, p. 24.

39. John Bell, Health and Beauty (Philadelphia: Carey and Hart, 1838), pp. 95–96.

40. See J. Gray Sweeney, "The Nude of Landscape Painting," Smithsonian Studies in American Art 3 (Fall 1989): 43–65.

41. Theodore Winthrop, Life in the Open Air (Boston: J. R. Osgood, 1871), p. 71, quoted in Angela Miller, The Empire of the Eye (Ithaca: Cornell University Press, 1993), p. 96.

42. Graham, Human Life, 2:639.

43. John Davies, Phrenology: Fad and Science (New Haven: Yale University Press, 1955), p. 109. It should be noted that Graham collaborated with the phrenologists. Graham demonstrated, for example, that meat eating enhanced the strength of Destructiveness while weakening Benevolence; this and like discoveries gave added weight to arguments favoring vegetarianism. Graham organized his American Vegetarian Society at the Fowlers' New York office. See Graham,

Human Life, 2:325–27, 354–55. See also Madeleine B. Stern, Heads and Headlines: The Phrenological Fowlers (Norman: University of Oklahoma Press, 1971), p. 49.

44. Samuel R. Wells, New Physiognomy (New York: Samuel R. Wells, 1868), p. 281.

45. Ibid., p. 292.

46. As late as 1847, portraits of Durand exhibit him without a beard; see David B. Dearinger, "Asher B. Durand and Henry Kirk Brown: An Artistic Friendship," American Art Journal 20 (Fall 1988): 76–77. Graham's views on beards appeared late in his career, in 1839. Durand must have picked up the idea sometime after this. As this chapter indicates, Durand could have heard this doctrine from a number of sources. The advantage of studying Graham comes from his close association with the artist and his articulation of the tenet within the larger context of vitalism, but, as noted, Durand could just as readily have learned it from others. There is no indication that Durand ever abandoned Graham's theories entirely; indeed, he was quite concerned to learn of Graham's death in 1851. See Asher Durand to "Dear Son" [John Durand], Factory Point, 14 September 1851, AAA N20/662.

47. Graham's remarks on the freedom of primitive peoples resemble Tuckerman's words about Durand's change of career; the reformer states that in such societies there are no artisans confined in narrow apartments, working in constricted positions, with some limbs excessively developed while others remain emaciated from "inactivity." See Graham, Human Life, 1:182.

48. Tuckerman, Book of the Artists, pp. 192–93.

49. Bumble-Bee, "Beard and Costume," Crayon 1 (1855): 412.

50. An informal survey includes, besides Durand, the following (accompanied by the year[s] of the image that exhibits a beard; this does not tell us

precisely when they adopted the custom): Samuel Colman (1860–69), Jasper Cropsey (ca. 1865), Sanford R. Gifford (1868), George Inness (1862), John Kensett (ca. 1864), Jervis McEntee (1870), William Trost Richards (ca. 1904), Aaron Draper Shattuck (1860–69), Jerome Thompson (1852), Worthington Whittredge (1870), and Alexander H. Wyant (1890). See John K. Howat, "A Climate for Landscape Painters," in *American Paradise*, introduction by John K. Howat (New York: Metropolitan Museum of Art, 1987), pp. 49–70. The list is hardly definitive, and the number who grew beards for philosophical reasons is open to question; but it bears keeping in mind that contemporaries attributed the custom to artists.

51. For a review of attitudes toward the latter, see Nicolai Cikovsky Jr., " 'The Ravages of the Axe': The Meaning of the Tree Stump in Nineteenth-Century American Art," *Art Bulletin* 61 (1979): 611–26, and Barbara Novak, *Nature and Culture: American Landscape and Painting, 1825–1875* (New York: Oxford University Press, 1981), pp. 157–65.

52. On the death of Charles Loring Elliott in December 1868, Theodore Tilton wrote "that Elliott's fine face and beard [were] almost the face and beard of Rubens over again." Quoted in Joshua C. Taylor, *William Page, the American Titian* (Chicago: University of Chicago Press, 1957), p. 188.

53. Alfred Frankenstein, *William Sidney Mount* (New York: Harry N. Abrams, 1979), p. 30. For the similarities of Mount's approach to nature and that of Durand, see James Thomas Flexner, *That Wilder Image* (New York: Dover, 1970), pp. 56.

54. Frankenstein, *Mount*, p. 31.

55. Ibid., p. 288.

56. Ibid.

57. Mount notebooks, entry for 26 December 1867, AAA SM2/407–8.

58. S. B. B., "Razors and Brains," *Spiritual Telegraph* 7 (1855): 309–10.

59. Not only did a dozen new urban centers appear in the 1820s, this development was accompanied by the introduction of new entertainments such as the opera and public dance halls. Reformers were quick to point out the danger of breathing "respired air" in such environments. See Harvey Green, *Fit for America* (New York: Pantheon, 1986), p. 78.

60. Harriet Beecher Stowe, *Household Papers and Stories* (1864; New York: AMS Press, 1967), p. 342.

61. Haley, *Healthy Body*, p. 3.

62. A. B. Durand, "Letters on Landscape Painting," *Crayon* 1 (1855): Letter 4, p. 98, and Graham, *Human Life*, 2:267–68.

63. A. B. Durand, Letter 1, p. 2. See also Sylvester Graham, *A Treatise on Bread, and Bread-Making* (Boston: Light and Stearns, 1837), p. 34.

64. A. B. Durand, Letter 6, p. 211.

65. A. B. Durand, Letter 7, pp. 213–14.

66. George Combe, *The Constitution of Man Considered in Relation to External Objects*, 5th ed. (Boston: Marsh, Capen and Lyon, 1835), p. 16.

67. A. B. Durand, Letter 3, p. 66.

68. A. B. Durand, Letter 5, p. 146.

69. A. B. Durand, Letter 8, p. 355.

70. Barbara Dayer Gallati, "*Early Morning at Cold Spring, 1850*," in *American Paradise*, p. 111.

71. Catherine E. Beecher and Harriet Beecher Stowe, *The American Woman's Home*, introduction by Joseph Van Why (Hartford: Stowe-Day Foundation, 1987), p. 49.

72. Mary Mann, *Life of Horace Mann* (1888; Miami: Mnemosyne Publishing, 1969), p. 359, journal entry for February 22, 1852.

73. Beecher and Stowe, *Woman's Home*, pp. 48–49.

74. Reformers noted that in open, sunlit spaces the blood became oxygenated and electrified by deep breathing while the body was vitalized by atmospheric currents; one remarked that this airborne electricity was "an atmo-

spheric emanation from God" (Harold Aspiz, *Walt Whitman and the Body Beautiful* [Urbana: University of Illinois Press, 1980], p. 161).

75. Sylvester Graham, *A Lecture to Young Men* (Providence: Weeden and Cory, 1834), p. 73.

76. Graham, *Human Life*, 1:443.

77. Anon., *Defense of the Graham System*, p. 184.

78. Gallati, "*Early Morning*," p. 111. When the painting was first exhibited in 1850, it was accompanied by a couplet from Bryant's "A Scene on the Banks of the Hudson." For example, see John W. Francis, *Old New York*, with a memoir of the author by Henry T. Tuckerman (New York: W. J. Middleton, 1865), p. 285, and James T. Callow, *Kindred Spirits* (Chapel Hill: University of North Carolina Press, 1967), pp. 68–69. On the similarity of Bryant's style to that of Durand, see Bertha Monica Stearns, "Nineteenth-Century Writers in the World of Art," *Art in America* 40 (Winter 1952): 30–32.

79. William Cullen Bryant, in a letter to an unnamed correspondent in Boston, 27 March 1865, quoted in Charles I. Glicksberg, "William Cullen Bryant and Nineteenth-Century Science," *New England Quarterly* 23 (March 1950): 96.

80. William Cullen Bryant, "Address Delivered at the Opening of the Academy of Design, April 28, 1865," in *Prose Writings of William Cullen Bryant*, 2 vols., ed. Parke Godwin (New York: Appleton, 1884), 2:235.

81. R. Rio-Jelliffe, "'Thanatopsis' and the Development of American Literature," in *William Cullen Bryant and His America*, ed. Stanley Brodwin and Michael D'Innocenzo (New York: AMS Press, 1983), p. 141.

82. In her analysis of landscape painting Barbara Novak asks what the figures in such works are contemplating and "what we assume their contemplation means." She then discusses Emerson's philosophy. I am following a similar methodology but in terms of Durand's familiarity with the tenets of transcen-

dental medicine. See Novak, *Nature and Culture*, p. 196.

83. Combe's reasoning and his reliance on science to support his conclusions is quite distinct from other liberal interpretations of Genesis, for example, that were embodied in the concept of the "fortunate Fall." And while Combe freed humanity from the taint of ancestral sin, he also perceived that death had a place in the fixed structure of the natural laws. Nevertheless he and the phrenologists in general were firmly within the party of "hope" as described in R. W. B. Lewis, *The American Adam* (Chicago: University of Chicago Press, 1966), pp. 55–80.

84. This argument occupies the first twenty pages of his book; the quote will be found in Combe, *Constitution*, p. 14.

85. For a discussion of these ideas in relation to Thomas Cole, see Charles L. Sanford, "The Concept of the Sublime in the Works of Thomas Cole and William Cullen Bryant," *American Literature* 28 (January 1957): 441–46. For a similar review of Durand, see Wayne Craven, "Asher B. Durand's Imaginary Landscapes," *Antiques* 116 (1979): 1124.

86. Combe, *Constitution*, p. 188.

87. Ibid., pp. 169–71, 200–202.

88. Horace Mann to George Combe, 28 February 1842, quoted in Mann, *Horace Mann*, pp. 157–58.

89. For example, see Tuckerman, *Book of the Artists*, p. 193, and Lawall, *Durand: His Art and Art Theory*, pp. 320, 371, 472.

90. See, for example, Novak, *Nature and Culture*, pp. 101–34.

91. Contemporary sources, however, frequently take up this concept, as the following indicates: "To the inhabitants of cities, as nearly all of the subscribers to the Art-Union are, a painted landscape is almost essential to preserve a healthy tone to the spirits" (from *Transactions of the American Art-Union . . . for the Year 1844*, pp. 7–8, quoted in Nancy Rash, *The Painting and Politics of George Caleb Bingham* [New Haven: Yale University Press, 1991], pp. 42–43).

92. Emerson, "Experience," in *Selected Prose and Poetry*, p. 234.

93. Catherine E. Beecher, *Physiology and Calisthenics* (New York: Harper and Brothers, 1856), p. 6.

94. Emerson, "Nature," in *Selected Prose and Poetry*, p. 6.

95. Nissenbaum discusses Emerson's "transparent eyeball" and its divergence from Graham's philosophy; see *Sex, Diet and Debility*, p. 137.

96. Joshua C. Taylor, *America as Art* (New York: Harper and Row, 1976), pp. 111, 116. See also Novak, *Nature and Culture*, pp. 3–17, 265–73. The question of the relationship between Transcendentalism and the painters of the Hudson River School is complex. For related readings, see John I. H. Baur, "American Luminism: A Neglected Aspect of the Realist Movement in Nineteenth-Century American Painting," *Perspectives USA* 9 (1954): 90–98; Barton Levi St. Armand, "Luminism in the Work of Henry David Thoreau: The Dark and the Light," *Canadian Review of American Studies* 11 (1980): 13–30; Gayle L. Smith, "Emerson and the Luminist Painters: A Study of Their Styles," *American Quarterly* 37 (1985): 193-215; Kevin Radaker, " 'A Separate Intention of the Eye': Luminist Eternity in Thoreau's *A Week on the Concord and Merrimack Rivers*," *Canadian Review of American Studies* 18 (1987): 41–60; Kevin Radaker, "Henry Thoreau and Frederic Church: Confronting the Monumental Sublimity of the Maine Wilderness," *Yearbook of Interdisciplinary Studies in the Fine Arts* 1 (1989): 267–83; John Wilmerding, *American Light*, with contributions by Lisa Fellows Andrus, Linda S. Ferber, Albert Gelpi, David C. Huntington, Weston Naef, Barbara Novak, Earl A. Powell, and Theodore E. Stebbins Jr. (Princeton: Princeton University Press, 1989); H. Daniel Peck, *Thoreau's Morning Work* (New Haven: Yale University Press, 1990), pp. 54–60; and Barbara Novak, "Self, Time, and Object in American Art," in *American Icons: Transatlantic Perspectives on Eighteenth-and Nineteenth-Century American Art*, ed. Thomas W. Gaehtgens and Heinz Ickstadt (Santa Monica, Calif.: Getty Center for the History of Art and the Humanities, 1992), pp. 61–91. For less conventional views, see David C. Miller, "The Iconology of Wrecked or Stranded Boats in Mid- to Late Nineteenth-Century American Culture," in *American Iconology*, ed. David C. Miller (New Haven: Yale University Press, 1993), pp. 186–208, and Angela Miller, *Empire of the Eye*.

97. Roger B. Stein, *John Ruskin and Aesthetic Thought in America, 1840–1900* (Cambridge: Harvard University Press, 1967), pp. 117–18.

98. Quoted in Horatio Greenough, *The Travels, Observations, and Experience of a Yankee Stonecutter*, introduction by Nathalia Wright (1852; Gainesville, Fla.: Scholars Facsimiles and Reprints, 1958), pp. 90–91.

99. James John Garth Wilkinson, *The Human Body and Its Connection with Man* (London: New Church Press, [1851]), p. 21.

100. Ralph Waldo Emerson, *Representative Men* (New York: Hurst, n.d.), p. 88.

101. Richard Ruland and Malcolm Bradbury, *From Puritanism to Postmodernism* (New York: Viking, 1991), p. 123.

102. Henry David Thoreau, *Walden, or Life in the Woods*, afterword by Perry Miller (1854; New York: Signet, 1980), p. 73.

103. Ibid., p. 209.

104. The popularity of Combe's lectures with the businessmen of the time is suggested by Julia Ward Howe's discussion of her father's regular attendance of them. See Julia Ward Howe, *Reminiscences, 1819–1899* (Boston: Houghton Mifflin, 1899), p. 22.

105. Kensett, along with Casilear, went to Europe with Durand and thus must also have listened to Combe's discourses. All three artists were engravers who relinquished the burin for the pencil, though Casilear seems not to have grown a beard.

CHAPTER FIVE

1. It was not uncommon at the time for job advertisements to request a phrenological analysis as a requirement for employment. See John Davies, *Phrenology: Fad and Science* (New Haven: Yale University Press, 1955), p. 38.

2. William Cullen Bryant, "The Marriage Blunder," in *Prose Writings of William Cullen Bryant*, 2 vols., ed. Parke Godwin (New York: Appleton, 1884), 1:197.

3. Theodore Bosson to Hiram Powers, 27 February 1835, Archives of American Art (henceforth AAA), 1131/314–15, Smithsonian Institution, Washington, D.C.

4. This account comes from David M. Armstrong, *Day before Yesterday* (New York: C. Scribner's Sons, 1920), pp. 263–65. It is quoted in John H. Dryfhout, *The Work of Augustus Saint-Gaudens* (Hanover, N.H.: University Press of New England, 1982), p. 71.

5. "Portrait Sculpture," *Crayon* 2 (1855): 166. Greenough received the commission for the statue of Franklin in 1853. It was placed in front of the Boston State House.

6. Hiram Powers to Sidney Brooks, 28 February 1868, AAA 1143/1408.

7. Benjamin Paul Akers, "The Danae," *Crayon* 2 (1855): 65.

8. Benjamin Paul Akers, "Letter, Florence, June 10," *Crayon* 1 (1855): 102.

9. Benjamin Paul Akers, "Our Artists in Italy," *Atlantic Monthly*, January 1860, pp. 5–6.

10. Ibid., February 1861, p. 133.

11. Walt Whitman, "Song of Myself," in *Leaves of Grass* (New York: Norton 1965), p. 55.

12. William Wetmore Story, *Life and Letters of Joseph Story*, 2 vols. (Boston: Little, Brown, 1851), 2:557.

13. William Wetmore Story, *Conversations in a Studio*, 2 vols. (Boston: Houghton Mifflin, 1890), 1:140–43.

14. Ibid., 1:138.

15. William Wetmore Story, "A Contemporary Criticism in which Federigo di Montafeltro, Duke of Urbino, Gives His Views to Raffaele," in *Graffiti d'Italia* (New York: Charles Scribner, 1868), pp. 135–37.

16. See I Samuel 18:8–10, and William Wetmore Story, "Sappho," in *Poems* (Boston: Little, Brown, 1856), p. 286. For more on Story's *Saul*, see Jan M. Seidler, "A Critical Reappraisal of the Career of William Wetmore Story (1819–1895), American Sculptor and Man of Letters" (Ph.D. dissertation, Boston University, 1985), pp. 372–74.

17. Story, *Graffiti*, p. 137.

18. William H. Gerdts, *The Art of Henry Inman*, catalog by Carrie Rebora (Washington, D.C.: National Portrait Gallery, 1987), p. 92.

19. William Wirt to William Pope, Washington, 23 March 1828, quoted in John Pendleton Kennedy, *Memoirs of the Life of William Wirt*, 2 vols. (Philadelphia: Lea and Blanchard, 1849), 2:243. I would like to thank Dr. Frederick Voss for alerting me to this passage. Some indication that Wirt's allegiance to phrenology was greater than professed in this letter comes from the announcement that he was among the founders of the phrenological society in Washington. See "Notices," *Phrenological Journal and Miscellany* 3 (1825–26): 325.

20. For Ames and his interest in phrenology, see Mary Black, "Phrenological Associations," *Clarion* 9 (Fall 1984): 51–52, and Sharon C. Hollander, "Asa Ames and the Art of Phrenology," *Clarion* 14 (Summer 1989): 28–35.

21. Henry T. Tuckerman, *Artist-Life; or Sketches of American Painters* (New York: Appleton, 1857), p. 108.

22. O. S. Fowler, *The Practical Phrenologist* (Boston: O. S. Fowler, 1869), p. 60.

23. Tuckerman, *Artist-Life*, p. 109.

24. Samuel R. Wells, *New Physiognomy* (New York: Samuel R. Wells, 1868), p. 132.

25. Rembrandt Peale, "Reminiscences," *Crayon* 1 (1855): 370–71.

26. Rembrandt Peale, "Ironic" Lecture on Phrenology, p. 3. I would like to thank the Heritage Collectors' Society of Hatfield, Pennsylvania, for making this material available.

27. Ibid., p. 1.

28. Francois Joseph Gall, *On the Origin of the Moral Qualities and Intellectual Faculties of Man*, 6 vols., trans. Winslow Lewis Jr. (Boston: Marsh, Capen and Lyon, 1835), 3:284.

29. Ibid., 5:272. Gall mentions Raphael's *Madonna of the Rabbit*.

30. Lillian B. Miller, *In Pursuit of Fame: Rembrandt Peale, 1778–1860*, with an essay by Carol Eaton Hevner (Washington, D.C.: National Portrait Gallery, 1992), p. 74.

31. Sylvia E. Crane, *White Silence* (Coral Gables, Fla.: University of Miami Press, 1972), p. 197.

32. George H. Calvert, *Scenes and Thoughts in Europe* (New York: Wiley and Putnam, 1846), p. 88.

33. Henry T. Tuckerman, *The Criterion; or the Test of Talk about Familiar Things* (New York: Hurd and Houghton, 1866), p. 342.

34. Crane, *White Silence*, p. 269.

35. Charles Dickens, *American Notes: A Journey* (1842; New York: Fromm, 1985), p. 118.

36. Hiram Powers to William C. Preston, 25 March 1839, AAA 1146. Much of what follows appears in Charles Colbert, " 'Each Little Hillock Hath a Tongue': Phrenology and the Art of Hiram Powers," *Art Bulletin* 68 (1986): 281–300.

37. Hiram Powers to "Uncle" Boyd (Reilly), n.d., AAA 1146.

38. Henry T. Tuckerman, *Book of the Artists* (New York: G. P. Putnam and Son, 1867), p. 278.

39. Charles Thomas Walters, "Hiram Powers and William Rimmer: A Study in the Concept of Expression" (Ph.D. dissertation, University of Michigan, 1977), pp. 40–41, 52.

40. Hiram Powers to Edward Everett, 12 October 1858, AAA 1139/1156.

41. Hiram Powers to Edward Everett, 14 March 1859, AAA 1139/1489.

42. L. N. Fowler, "Phrenological description of the character of Daniel Webster from a cast of his head taken after death in possession of Hiram Powers," n.d., AAA 1146.

43. John S. Crawford, "Physiognomy in Classical and American Portrait Busts," *American Art Journal* 9 (May 1977): 58.

44. C. Edwards Lester, *The Artist, the Merchant, and the Statesman of the Age of the Medici and of Our Own Times*, 2 vols. (New York: Paine and Burgess, 1845), 1:55–56.

45. Calvert, *Scenes and Thoughts*, p. 88.

46. Hiram Powers to Mrs. Austin, 1 January 1850, AAA 1134/0748.

47. Hiram Powers, unpublished essay, AAA 1146.

48. Most particularly in Donald Martin Reynolds, *Hiram Powers and His Ideal Sculpture* (New York: Garland, 1977), and Donald Martin Reynolds, "The 'Unveiled Soul': Hiram Powers's Embodiment of the Ideal," *Art Bulletin* 59 (1977): 394–414.

49. Richard P. Wunder, *Hiram Powers, Vermont Sculptor, 1805–1873*, 2 vols. (Newark: University of Delaware Press, 1991), 1:47.

50. Ibid.

51. "Mr. Hiram Powers' Studio Florence," 26 June 1865, manuscript, AAA 1146.

52. Gilbert Haven, "Powers and His Marbles," *Independent*, [1863], box 6, MSS qP 888 RM, Cincinnati Historical Society, Cincinnati, Ohio, Manuscript Collections (henceforth CHS).

53. Calvert, *Scenes and Thoughts*, p. 88.

54. Edward Everett, "Powers, the Sculptor," *Littell's Living Age* 15 (1847): 99.

55. Ibid., pp. 98–99.

56. Hiram Powers to Salmon P. Chase, 20 April 1868, box 1, CHS. See also Wunder, *Hiram Powers*, 2:224.

57. Calvert, *Scenes and Thoughts*, pp. 91–92.

58. George H. Calvert, *The Life of Rubens* (Boston: Lee and Shepherd, 1878), p. 40.

59. Calvert, *Scenes and Thoughts*, p. 89.

60. Hiram Powers to Nicholas Longworth, 19 February 1835, Washington, Powers Letters to Longworth, CHS.

61. Henry W. Bellows, "Seven Sittings with Powers, the Sculptor," *Appleton's Journal of Literature and Art* 1 (1869): 471.

62. Lester, *The Artist*, 1:65.

63. Ibid.

64. Bellows, "Powers," p. 360.

65. *Uncle Sam's Recommendation of Phrenology to His Millions of Friends in the United States* (New York: Harper and Brothers, 1842), pp. 121–22.

66. "Phrenological and Physiological Organization and Character of Andrew Jackson," *American Phrenological Journal* 7 (1845): 248–52.

67. Edward Everett to Hiram Powers, 12 June 1844, AAA 1132/611.

68. Hiram Powers to Miner Kellogg, 27 February 1848, box 2, CHS.

69. Hiram Powers to "Dear Cousin," 23 July 1853, AAA 1136/804.

70. "Our New Dictionary of Phrenology and Physiognomy," *American Phrenological Journal and Life Illustrated* 42 (1865): 136.

71. Hiram Powers to R. Sturges, 12 October 1862, AAA 1141/1178–81. See also Wunder, *Hiram Powers*, 2:95–96.

72. Hiram Powers to Elisha Lichtfield, 9 June 1865, AAA 1142/1242.

73. Bellows, "Powers," p. 471.

74. Hiram Powers to Julius Converse, 10 February 1873, AAA 1145/471. For the phrenological thought on this subject, see "Heads and Hats," *American Phrenological Journal* 31 (February 1860): 26.

75. Hiram Powers to Edmund J. Nieman, 6 November 1861, AAA 1141/607.

76. "Autographs as Types of Character," *Crayon* 3 (1856): 124.

77. Hiram Powers to Samson Powers, 1854, AAA 1136/1174.

78. Louisa S. McCord to Hiram Powers, 13 January 1860, AAA 1140/519.

79. Graeme Tytler, *Physiognomy in the European Novel: Faces and Fortunes* (Princeton: Princeton University Press, 1982), p. 106.

80. Louisa S. McCord to Hiram Powers, 9 February 1860, AAA 1140/565.

81. Tuckerman, *Book of the Artists*, p. 289.

82. Wayne Craven, *Sculpture in America* (New York: Crowell, 1968), pp. 114–15. See also Matthew Baigell, *A Concise History of American Painting and Sculpture* (New York: Harper and Row, 1984), p. 115.

83. Hence a second current in the analysis of Powers's portraits discovers all the qualities of his mature style in the work done at the outset of his career. This evaluation seems more accurate. See Jan Seidler Ramirez, "Hiram Powers," in *American Figurative Sculpture in the Museum of Fine Arts, Boston*, introduction by Jonathan L. Fairbanks (Boston: Museum of Fine Arts, 1986), p. 35.

84. Nathalia Wright, *Horatio Greenough, the First American Sculptor* (Philadelphia: University of Pennsylvania Press, 1963), pp. 108–9.

85. Powers does not indicate when this took place. See Hiram Powers to Edward Everett, 12 January 1853, AAA 1136/432. Greenough's bouts of insanity began as early as 1827.

86. George Combe, *A System of Phrenology* (New York: William H. Colyer, 1841), p. 233. The features mentioned are best seen in front of the original bust.

87. J. G. Spurzheim, *Observations on the Deranged Manifestations of the Mind, or Insanity* (London: Baldwin, Cradock, and Joy, 1817), pp. 107–8.

88. Hiram Powers to Jared Sparks, 15 August 1857, AAA 1139/274.

89. Hiram Powers to Jared Sparks, 11 September 1856, AAA 1138/698.

90. Hiram Powers to Jared Sparks, 29 January 1857, AAA 1138/1012.

91. Jared Sparks to Hiram Powers, 18 May 1858, AAA 1139/808.

92. Mary Sparks to Hiram Powers, 26 January 1867, AAA 1143/771.

93. Hiram Powers to Mrs. Sparks, 20 May 1867, AAA 1143/929.

94. Hiram Powers to Edward Everett, 30 October 1858, AAA 1139/1220.

95. Charles Gibbon, *The Life of George Combe, Author of "The Constitution of Man,"* 2 vols. (1878; Westmead, Farnborough, Hants, England: Gregg, 1970), 2:30.

96. Bellows, "Powers," p. 471.

97. Sidney Brooks to Hiram Powers, 23 February 1865, AAA 1142/842.

98. Hiram Powers to Edward Everett, 30 April 1849, AAA 1134/286.

99. Gibbon, *Life of George Combe*, 1:264.

100. Clara Louise Dentler, "White Marble: The Life and Letters of Hiram Powers, Sculptor," p. 151, AAA 1102/1555, National Museum of American Art, Smithsonian Institution, Washington, D.C.

101. Akers, "Our Artists in Italy," p. 6.

102. O. S. Fowler, *Creative and Sexual Science* (Rochester: New York State Pub. Co., 1870), p. 116.

103. Wunder, *Hiram Powers*, 1:67.

104. Lester, *The Artist*, 1:67–68.

105. Hiram Powers to Rev. Samuel G. Olmstead, 13 January 1857, AAA 1138/979. See also Hiram Powers, "Perception of Likeness," *Crayon* 1 (1855): 229–30.

106. Everett, "Powers, the Sculptor," p. 99.

107. Bellows, "Powers," p. 471.

108. Henry Boynton, "Hiram Powers," *New England Magazine* 20 (1899): 530.

109. Tuckerman, *Book of the Artists*, p. 289.

110. Miner Kellogg to Hiram Powers, 16 March 1848, box 2, CHS.

111. Hiram Powers to H. Gourdin, Esq., 7 April 1850, AAA 1134/1006.

112. William Ware, *Sketches of European Capitals* (Boston: Phillips, Sampson, 1851), p. 130.

113. Hiram Powers to C. F. Hampton, 12 March 1856, AAA 1138/274.

114. Mary Duncan to Hiram Powers, 8 May 1856, AAA 1138/470–71.

115. Mary Duncan to Hiram Powers, 9 August 1856, AAA 1138/624.

116. Hiram Powers to Mrs. Duncan, 20 August 1856, AAA 1138/661.

117. Wunder, *Hiram Powers*, 2:34.

118. Lorado Taft, *The History of American Sculpture* (1903; New York: Macmillan, 1924), p. 68.

119. Calvert, *Scenes and Thoughts*, p. 93.

120. Hiram Powers, journal entry, 29 March 1842, AAA 1146.

121. W. Mattieu Williams, *A Vindication of Phrenology* (London: Chatto and Windus, 1894), p. 121.

122. Mary Duncan to Hiram Powers, 19 July 1867, AAA 1143/1040.

123. Wunder, *Hiram Powers*, 2:35.

124. For example, see Mary Duncan to Hiram Powers, 15 April 1857, AAA 1138/1185.

125. O. S. Fowler, *Creative and Sexual Science*, pp. 146–47.

126. Ibid., p. 146.

127. Wunder, *Hiram Powers*, 2:35, 129.

128. There is mention of her making a conversion to the faith. The faith is not identified, but why mention this to Powers? Why not identify the religion, unless it was Swedenborgianism? The evidence is admittedly vague. See Mrs. Austin to Hiram Powers, 12 October 1856, AAA 1138/788.

129. Edward Madeley, *The Science of Correspondences Elucidated*, ed. B. F. Barett (Germantown, Pa.: Swedenborg Publishing Association, 1883), p. 313.

130. Mary Duncan to Hiram Powers, 8 June 1856, AAA 1138/530.

131. Hiram Powers to Elizabeth Barrett Browning, 7 August 1853, quoted in Reynolds, "'Unveiled Soul,'" p. 394.

132. Reynolds, "'Unveiled Soul,'" pp. 393–414; Reynolds, *Hiram Powers*, esp. pp. 212–37; H. W. Janson, *Nineteenth-Century Sculpture* (New York: Harry N. Abrams, 1985), p. 82; Martha Gyllenhaal, Robert W. Gladish, Dean W. Holmes, and Kurt R. Rosenquist, *New Light: Ten Artists Inspired by Emanuel*

Swedenborg (Bryn Athyn, Pa.: Glencairn Museum, 1988), pp. 10–12.

133. "New Church Worthies," *New Church Messenger*, 18 February 1885, newspaper clipping, box 6, CHS.

134. Henry James Sr., *The Secret of Swedenborg* (Boston: Fields, Osgood, 1869), pp. 122, 115.

135. Hiram Powers to Mrs. Duncan, 7 September 1857, AAA 1139/366.

136. James, *Secret of Swedenborg*, p. 66.

137. For Swedenborg's disagreement with the notion of innate ideas, see Emanuel Swedenborg, *The Economy of the Animal Kingdom* (New York: New Church Press, 1955), 2:272, #292.

138. Hiram Powers to York Atlee, 1 June 1855, AAA 1137/1014.

139. Wunder, *Hiram Powers*, 2:189.

140. Dentler, "Powers," p. 149.

141. In the case of Anstiss Derby Rogers Wetmore (1848, New York, Dr. William H. Gerdts) Powers not only carved acanthus leaves; he also uncovered the breasts. To defend herself against charges of immodesty, the sitter insisted that this rather daring step was taken at the sculptor's suggestion, so that she could display "ideal form and finish" (Wunder, *Hiram Powers*, 2:106). Unfortunately, Powers's thoughts on this intriguing piece are not preserved. Judging from the marble, Wetmore was no raving beauty; her cranium is regular in form, however, and perhaps this was the source of his remarks on the ideal, if he did indeed utter them.

142. George W. Hughes to Hiram Powers, 20 November 1844, AAA 1132/822.

143. While stressing this individuality, George Calvert offers some observations that sound very much like those stated by Palmer: "Each face is, so to speak, an offshoot from a type; each is a particular incarnation of an ideal" (Calvert, *Scenes and Thoughts*, p. 90).

144. "The Nature and Use of Beauty," *Crayon* 3 (1856): 161–62.

145. "A Glimpse into Home Matters," *Crayon* 7 (1860): 86.

146. Boynton, "Hiram Powers," pp. 529–30.

147. Lester, *The Artist*, 1:67.

148. Edward Everett to Hiram Powers, 15 February 1859, AAA 1139/1425.

149. "From Italy—Statue of Mr. Webster," *Boston Daily Advertiser*, 5 August 1856.

150. Madeleine B. Stern, *A Phrenological Dictionary of Nineteenth-Century Americans* (Westport, Conn.: Greenwood Press, 1982), p. 398.

151. Hiram Powers to Edward Everett, 11 April 1854, AAA 1137/145.

152. Hiram Powers to Edward Everett, 23 July 1853, AAA 1136/810.

153. For the symbolism of "America," see Wunder, *Hiram Powers*, 2:118; see also Vivien Green Fryd, "Hiram Powers's America: 'Triumphant as Liberty and in Unity,'" *American Art Journal* 18, no. 2 (1986): 55–75. Powers also wanted his "George Washington as a Master Mason" to have a fasces, but this proposal was rejected by the patrons. See Wunder, *Hiram Powers*, 2:206–7.

154. Hiram Powers to Nicholas Longworth, 24 June 1857, quoted in "Letters of Hiram Powers to Nicholas Longworth, Esq., 1856–1858," *Quarterly Publication of the Historical and Philosophical Society of Ohio* 1 (April/June 1906): 47–48.

155. Fryd, "Hiram Powers's America," p. 66.

156. Hiram Powers to Edward Everett, 22 June 1854, AAA 1137/314.

157. Hiram Powers to York Atlee, 3 September 1854, AAA 1137/464–65.

158. Hiram Powers to Edward Everett, 7 January 1857, AAA 1138/962.

159. Hiram Powers to Edward Everett, March 1854, AAA 1139/1475.

160. Emanuel Swedenborg, *The Apocalypse Explained* (New York: Swedenborg Foundation, 1972), 6:307, #1200, and Emanuel Swedenborg, *The Spiritual Diary of Emanuel Swedenborg*, trans. George Bush (New York: Swedenborg Foundation, 1971), 4:160, #4705.

161. Quoted in *The Essential Swedenborg*, ed. Sig Synnestvedt (New York:

Swedenborg Foundation, 1984), pp. 59–60.

162. Ibid., p. 48.

163. Theophilus Parsons, *Essays*, 3 vols. (Boston: T. H. Carter and Son, 1868), 1:107. A note inside dates this work to 1856.

164. Ibid., 1:113.

165. Hiram Powers to York Atlee, 1 June 1855, AAA 1137/1014.

166. From the *Quarterly Review* of 1847, quoted in Helene E. Roberts, "The Exquisite Slave: The Role of Clothes in the Victorian Woman," *Signs* 12 (1977): 554.

167. Parsons, *Essays*, 1:113.

168. Powers asserted that it would take wise men to heal the maladies of disunion at this time. See Hiram Powers to George Calvert, 22 June 1851, AAA 1135/2070.

169. "The Webster Statue," *Boston Evening Transcript*, 4 August 1856.

170. Wunder, *Hiram Powers*, 2:118.

171. Hiram Powers to Edward Everett, 14 May 1851, AAA 1135/1954–55.

172. James John Garth Wilkinson, *The Human Body and Its Connection with Man* (London: New Church Press, [1851]), pp. 96–97. The original dedication dates from 1851.

173. Hiram Powers to York Atlee, 3 September 1854, AAA 1137/465.

174. Wunder, *Hiram Powers*, 1:196.

175. Hiram Powers to Rev. Philip Slaughter, 11 April 1852, AAA 1135/2708–9.

176. Hiram Powers to Edward Everett, 23 May 1850, AAA 1134/1170.

177. Hiram Powers to Philip Slaughter, 29 May 1851, AAA 1135/1987–88.

178. Dentler, "Powers," p. 148. No mention is made of the persons involved. For the thoughts of phrenologists on this, see O. S. Fowler, *Hereditary Descent: Its Laws and Facts* (New York: O. S. and L. N. Fowler, 1843), pp. 181–82.

179. Milton W. Brown, Sam Hunter, John Jacobus, Naomi Rosenblum, and David M. Sokol, *American Art* (New York: Harry N. Abrams, 1979), p. 245.

180. Boynton, "Hiram Powers," p. 529.

181. Calvert, *Scenes and Thoughts*, pp. 90–91.

182. Barbara Novak, *American Painting of the Nineteenth Century* (New York: Harper and Row, 1979), p. 106.

183. Ibid., p. 95.

184. Matthew Baigell, *Dictionary of American Art* (New York: Harper and Row, 1979), p. 152.

CHAPTER SIX

1. The lecture was given in Cochituate, Massachusetts, in March 1848. See David Wallace, *John Rogers, the People's Sculptor* (Middletown, Conn.: Wesleyan University Press, 1967), p. 25.

2. "John Rogers, the Sculptor," *American Phrenological Journal and Life Illustrated* 49 (1869): 229–30. See also William H. Gerdts, *The Art of Healing* (Birmingham: Birmingham Museum of Art, 1981), p. 42.

3. The remark was made in August 1853 about Mr. Amory. See Wallace, *John Rogers*, p. 38.

4. Ibid., p. 253.

5. Ibid.

6. Samuel R. Wells, *New Physiognomy* (New York: Samuel R. Wells, 1868), pp. 381–85.

7. L. Maria Child, *Letters from New York*, 2 vols. (New York: Charles S. Francis, 1843), 1:247–51.

8. See Hugh Honour, *The Image of the Black in Western Art IV: From the American Revolution to World War I*, 2 vols. (Cambridge: Harvard University Press, 1989), 1:22.

9. Ibid., 2:26.

10. Genesis 10:18–27. For more on this, see Stephen Jay Gould, *The Mismeasure of Man* (New York: Norton, 1981), pp. 70–72.

11. For a review of these concepts, see William Stanton, *The Leopard's Spots* (Chicago: University of Chicago Press, 1969). This is the source of much that follows.

12. Ibid., pp. 28–29.

13. Ibid., pp. 37–41.

14. Samuel George Morton, *Crania Americana: or, A Comparative View of the Skulls of Various Aboriginal Nations of North and South America* (Philadelphia: Dobson, 1839), pp. iv, 83.

15. Ibid., pp. 201, 239, 247.

16. Ibid., pp. 45, 49, 81.

17. Ibid., pp. 24, 82.

18. Ibid., p. i.

19. George Combe, "Phrenological Remarks on the Relation between the Natural Talents and Dispositions of Nations, and the Developments of their Brains," in Morton, *Crania Americana*, pp. 274–75.

20. Ibid., p. 282.

21. Ibid., pp. 271–73.

22. See Stanton, *Leopard's Spots*, pp. 45–182. See also "The Phrenology of Nations," *American Phrenological Journal* 27 (1858): 51–53.

23. J. C. Nott and George R. Gliddon, *Indigenous Races of the Earth* (Philadelphia: Lippincott, 1857), pp. 239–41.

24. J. C. Nott and George R. Gliddon, *Types of Mankind* (Philadelphia: Lippincott, Grambo, 1854), p. 291.

25. For example, see ibid., pp. 463–65.

26. For example, see Albert Boime, *The Art of Exclusion* (Washington, D.C.: Smithsonian Institution Press, 1990). Mention of phrenology, characterizing its conclusions as "extravagant," is made in Guy C. McElroy, Henry Louis Gates Jr., Janet Levine, Francis Martin Jr., and Claudia Vess, *Facing History*, ed. Christopher French (San Francisco: Belford Arts, 1990), p. 35.

27. Stanton, *Leopard's Spots*, p. 40.

28. Reginald Horsman, *Race and Manifest Destiny* (Cambridge: Harvard University Press, 1981), p. 1. Much of what follows is taken from this text.

29. William Wetmore Story, *Conversations in a Studio*, 2 vols. (Boston: Houghton Mifflin, 1890), 1:91.

30. The remark came in a pamphlet titled "The First Sitting of the Committee on the Proposed Monument to Shakespeare," written by "Zachary Craft" (Charles Kelsall) and published in 1823. Quoted in Louis Marder, *His Exits and His Entrances: The Story of Shakespeare's Reputation* (Philadelphia: Lippincott, 1963), p. 35.

31. Charles Caldwell, *Elements of Phrenology* (Lexington, Ky.: Meriwether, 1827), p. 167. Also see Wells, *New Physiognomy*, p. 527. Wells, however, supposes Shakespeare wanting in "Christian spirituality."

32. George Calvert, *Brief Essays* (Boston: Lee and Shepard, 1874), pp. 78–87.

33. Ibid., pp. 144–47.

34. "Faed's Milton and Shakespeare," *Crayon* 2 (1855): 375.

35. Marder, *His Exits and His Entrances*, pp. 170–72.

36. Ibid., pp. 190–91.

37. Letter of 13 June 1842, quoted in Gary Taylor, *Reinventing Shakespeare* (New York: Weidenfeld and Nicholson, 1989), p. 194.

38. Hjalmar O. Lokensgard, "Oliver Wendell Holmes's 'Phrenological Character,'" *New England Quarterly* 13 (1940): 714.

39. Story, *Conversations*, 1:173.

40. Marder, *His Exits and His Entrances*, pp. 187–207.

41. For a discussion of Page's several images of Shakespeare, see Joshua C. Taylor, *William Page, the American Titian* (Chicago: University of Chicago Press, 1957), pp. 257–58, 280.

42. Ibid., pp. 110–13. Taylor's discussion of Page's interest in Swedenborg is exemplary, but he does not consider the place of phrenology in this context.

43. Ibid., pp. 195–96.

44. Charles Gibbon, *The Life of George Combe, Author of "The Constitution of Man,"* 2 vols. (1878; Westmead, Farnborough, Hants, England: Gregg, 1970), 1:171. This took place in 1824.

45. William Page, *A Study of Shakespeare's Portraits* (London: Chiswick Press, 1876), p. 69.

46. Ibid., p. 75.

47. Taylor, *William Page*, pp. 185–87.

48. Ibid., p. 200.

49. Page, *Shakespeare's Portraits*, pp. 53–55.

50. Ibid., p. 72. See also Taylor, *William Page*, pp. 197–98.

51. Page, *Shakespeare's Portraits*, p. 62.

52. Taylor, *William Page*, p. 201, and Page, *Shakespeare's Portraits*, p. 75.

53. John S. Hart, "The Shakespeare Death-Mask," *Scribner's Monthly* 7 (1874): 309.

54. Taylor finds this "strange" and attributes it to a belief among contemporaries that there radiated from the poet an aura of moral perfection that caused them to vaunt him above all as a model for the race. See Taylor, *William Page*, p. 196.

55. D. O. C. Townley, "Living American Artists," *Scribner's Monthly* 3 (1872): 604. Tuckerman notes that others followed the procedure adopted by Page. Richard Greenough consulted several portraits, particularly the Chandos version, in creating his bust of the bard. Tuckerman describes this as being "an ideal head of intense beauty and truth" (Henry T. Tuckerman, *Book of the Artists* [New York: G. P. Putnam and Son, 1867], p. 593).

56. Col. T. B. Thorpe, *Reminiscences of Charles L. Elliott, Artist* (n.p., n.d.), p. 8.

57. Tuckerman, *Book of the Artists*, p. 618. The beard was associated with Caucasian superiority; see William C. Rogers, "The Natural History of Man," *American Phrenological Journal* 18 (1853): 7.

58. Lewis I. Sharp, *John Quincy Adams Ward, Dean of American Sculpture* (Newark: University of Delaware Press, 1985), pp. 177–81.

59. Bryant letter of 1845, quoted in Henry Hope Reed and Sophia Duckworth, *Central Park: A History and a Guide* (1926; New York: Clarkson N. Potter, 1967), p. 3.

60. *Prose Writing of William Cullen Bryant*, 2 vols., ed. Parke Godwin (New York: Appleton, 1884), 2:121.

61. Ibid., 2:300–309.

62. Frederick Law Olmstead Sr., *Forty Years of Landscape Architecture: Central Park*, ed. Frederick Law Olmstead Jr. and Theodora Kimball (1928; Cambridge: MIT Press, 1973), p. 92.

63. Remark made in 1899, quoted in Sharp, *John Quincy Adams Ward*, p. 19.

64. Ibid., pp. 147, 165.

65. Tuckerman, *Book of the Artists*, p. 582.

66. "The Indian in American Art," *Crayon* 3 (1856): 28, quoted with accompanying opinions in Sharp, *John Quincy Adams Ward*, p. 146.

67. Michele H. Borgart, "The Importance of Believing in Purity," *Archives of American Art Journal* 24 (Winter 1984): 6.

68. Remark made in 1858, quoted in Reed and Duckworth, *Central Park*, p. 33.

69. Lawrence W. Levine, *Highbrow/ Lowbrow* (Cambridge: Harvard University Press, 1988), pp. 219–22.

70. Wells, *New Physiognomy*, p. 714.

71. Washington Irving, *The Life of George Washington*, 4 vols. (New York: Crowell, n.d.), 4:333.

72. Henry T. Tuckerman, *The Character and Portraits of Washington* (New York: Crowell, n.d.), p. 92.

73. Ibid., p. 23.

74. Ibid., p. 46.

75. Ibid., p. 67.

76. Ibid., p. 60.

77. Ibid., p. 51.

78. Ibid., p. 46.

79. Ibid., p. 76.

80. Hiram Powers to Sidney Brooks, 30 January 1850, Archives of American Art (henceforth AAA), 1134/847, Smithsonian Institution, Washington, D.C.

81. George P. Marsh to Hiram Powers, 15 February 1864, AAA 1142/344.

82. Nelson Sizer, *Forty Years in Phrenology: Embracing Recollections of History, Anecdote, and Experience* (New York: Fowler and Wells, 1891), p. 115.

83. O. S. Fowler, *The Practical Phrenologist* (Boston: O. S. Fowler, 1869), p. 60.

84. Henry T. Tuckerman, *Essays, Biographical and Critical; or Studies of Character*

(Boston: Phillips, Samson, 1857), pp. 5–6.

85. Robert Macnish, *An Introduction to Phrenology* (Glasgow: John Symington, 1837), p. 191.

86. Lillian Miller explains that "prevailing theories concerning physiognomy and phrenology help explain why he [Rembrandt Peale] believed a 'standard likeness' was so important" (Lillian B. Miller, *In Pursuit of Fame: Rembrandt Peale, 1778–1860*, with an essay by Carol Eaton Hevner [Washington, D.C.: National Portrait Gallery, 1992], pp. 146–48).

87. See Carol Eaton Hevner, *Rembrandt Peale, 1778–1860: A Life in the Arts*, with a biographical essay by Lillian B. Miller (Philadelphia: Historical Society of Pennsylvania, 1985), p. 66.

88. Rembrandt Peale, "Washington and His Portraits" (1858), AAA 88/186, Smithsonian Institution, Washington, D.C.

89. George Combe, *Essays on Phrenology*, edited with an introduction by John Bell (Philadelphia: Carey and Lea, 1822), pp. xlviii–lii.

90. Francois Joseph Gall, *On the Origin of the Moral Qualities and Intellectual Faculties of Man*, 6 vols., trans. Winslow Lewis Jr. (Boston: Marsh, Capen and Lyon, 1835), 2:220–24.

91. Ibid., 5:131–37.

92. J. G. Spurzheim, *Phrenology or the Doctrine of Mental Phenomena*, 2 vols. (Boston: Marsh, Capen and Lyon, 1832), 1:356.

93. George Combe, *Lectures on Phrenology*, with notes, an introductory essay, and a historical sketch by Andrew Boardman (New York: Samuel Colman, 1839), p. 50.

94. George Combe, *Notes on the United States of North America during a Phrenological Visit in 1838–9–40*, 2 vols. (Philadelphia: Carey and Hart, 1841), 1:208–9.

95. Horatio Greenough, *The Travels, Observations, and Experience of a Yankee Stonecutter*, introduction by Nathalia Wright (1852; Gainesville, Fla.: Scholars' Facsimiles and Reprints, 1958), p. 85; for Greenough's hostility to phrenology, see his letter to John Collins Warren, 1 March 1839, in *Letters of Horatio Greenough, American Sculptor*, ed. Nathalia Wright (Madison: University of Wisconsin Press, 1972), p. 245.

96. Rembrandt Peale, *Notes on Italy* (Philadelphia: Carey and Lea, 1831), pp. 39–40.

97. Rembrandt Peale, "Washington and His Portraits," *American Magazine of History* 20 (December 1888): 16–17 (lecture read on 16 June 1857).

98. Hevner, *Rembrandt Peale*, p. 66.

99. Journal entry, 11 December 1849, in Mary Mann, *Life of Horace Mann* (1888; Miami: Mnemosyne Publishing, 1969), p. 282.

100. For information on this piece, see John S. Hallam, "Houdon's *Washington* in Richmond: Some New Observations," *American Art Journal* 10 (November 1978): 73.

101. Jared Sparks, *The Life of Washington* (Boston: Ferdinand Andrews, 1839), p. 391.

102. J. R. Briggs, "General Washington's Head: Was It Large or Was It Small?," *American Phrenological Journal and Life Illustrated* 49 (1869): 407.

103. "Leutze's Washington at the Battle of Monmouth," *Crayon* 1 (1855): 22.

104. "Blackwood and Phrenology: Was Napoleon's Head Small?," *American Phrenological Journal* 27 (1858): 54.

105. *The Autobiography of Worthington Whittredge*, ed. John I. H. Baur (1942; New York: Arno Press, 1969), p. 22.

106. Among the scenes were *Washington Reading to his Family under the Trees at Mount Vernon* (1859); *Palmy Days of Mount Vernon* (exhibited at Yale University, 1867); *The Library at Mount Vernon* (exhibited at Yale University, 1867); and *Washington and Family in the Summer House at Mount Vernon* and *Washington and Lafayette at Mount Vernon* (Metropolitan Museum of Art, 1859). The quote comes from T. P. Rossiter, *A Description of the Picture of the Home of Washington after the War*.

Painted by T. P. Rossiter and L. R. Mignot with Historical Sketches of the Personages Introduced (New York: n.p., 1859), p. 4. Cited in Mark Edward Thistlethwaite, *The Image of George Washington* (New York: Garland, 1979), p. 142. Thistlethwaite discusses this quote in relation to the contemporary interest in phrenology.

107. *Washington Receiving His Mother's Last Blessing: Painted by William H. Powell, Engraved by Henry Cousins* (New York: W. Shaus, 1864), pp. 1–6.

108. O. S. Fowler, *Sexual Science: Including Manhood, Womanhood, and Their Mutual Interrelations; Love, Its Laws, Power, Etc.* (Philadelphia: National Pub. Co., 1870), p. 58.

109. C. Edwards Lester, *The Artist, the Merchant, and the Statesman of the Age of the Medici and of Our Own Times*, 2 vols. (New York: Paine and Burgess, 1845), 1:93.

110. See Horsman, *Manifest Destiny*, pp. 210–13.

111. Harriet Beecher Stowe, *Uncle Tom's Cabin*, edited and introduced by Ann Douglas (1852; New York: Penguin, 1985), p. 79.

112. For examples of references to Tom's benevolence, see ibid., pp. 68, 79, 272. Phrenologists praised the *Benevolence* of African Americans and often thought our "peculiar institution" detrimental to the faculty in both blacks and whites. See Stanton, *Leopard's Spots*, p. 36, and Combe, *Phrenological Visit*, 1:260. It is possible the individual frequently selected as the embodiment of *Benevolence*, Eustache, a slave who assisted in the rescue of four hundred whites during the slave revolt on the island of San Domingo, was to some extent behind the creation of Uncle Tom. Suggestive in this respect is Stowe's repeated references to the uprising in the novel. Of course other, more immediate individuals also contributed to the creation of Tom; one was Josiah Hanson, but several models may have come together in the fictional character. For Eustache, see "Our New Dictionary of Phrenology and Physiognomy," *American Phrenological Journal and*

Life Illustrated 41 (1865): 109. This material is drawn from publications of an earlier date; see also Honour, *Image of the Black*, 1:115–16. On the San Domingo uprising, see Stowe, *Uncle Tom's Cabin*, pp. 391–92; for Hanson, see Harriet Beecher Stowe, *A Key to Uncle Tom's Cabin* (1853; Port Washington, N.Y.: Kennikat, 1968), p. 26.

113. Stowe, *Uncle Tom's Cabin*, pp. 239–40.

114. Ibid., p. 337.

115. Ibid., pp. 252–53.

116. Ibid., p. 334.

117. Fowler, *Practical Phrenologist*, pp. 34–41.

118. Stowe, *Uncle Tom's Cabin*, p. 392.

119. Ibid., p. 56.

120. Thomas F. Gossett, *Uncle Tom's Cabin and American Culture* (Dallas: Southern Methodist University Press, 1985), pp. 66, 74.

121. Stowe, *Uncle Tom's Cabin*, p. 95.

122. Ibid., p. 97.

123. Ibid., p. 103.

124. William C. Rogers, "The Natural History of Man," *American Phrenological Journal* 18 (1853): 5.

125. Richard Ruland and Malcolm Bradbury, *From Puritanism to Postmodernism* (New York: Viking, 1991), p. 183.

126. Letter from Harriet Beecher Stowe to Gamaliel Bailey, March 1851, cited in *New Essays on Uncle Tom's Cabin*, edited and introduced by Eric J. Sundquist (London: Cambridge University Press, 1986), p. 9.

127. Quoted in Horsman, *Manifest Destiny*, p. 276.

128. Herman Melville, *Moby-Dick*, edited with an introduction by Charles Child Walcutt (1851; New York: Bantam Books, 1986), p. 55.

129. Ellwood Parry, *The Image of the Indian and the Black Man in American Art, 1590–1900* (New York: Braziller, 1974), pp. xiii, 36.

130. Quoted in Cyrenus Cole, *I Am a Man, the Indian Black Hawk* (Iowa City: State Historical Society of Iowa, 1938),

p. 26. The source is not listed. For a more detailed analysis of Black Hawk, one that found his *Combativeness* and *Destructiveness* very large, see "Phrenological Developments and Character of the Celebrated Indian Chief and Warrior, Black Hawk," *American Phrenological Journal and Miscellany* 1 (1838): 54.

131. Much of the account that follows comes from Jadviga da Costa Nunes, "Red Jacket: The Man and His Portraits," *American Art Journal* 12 (Summer 1980): 5–20.

132. Most famous in this respect is Cooper's *The Last of the Mohicans*, where, incidentally, we read of Uncas, the next-to-the-last-of-the-Mohicans, that he possessed a "dignified elevation of his receding forehead." See James Fenimore Cooper, *The Last of the Mohicans*, introduction by Richard Slotkin (1826; New York: Penguin, 1986), p. 53. For a discussion of Romantic attitudes toward Indians, see Robert F. Berkhofer Jr., *The White Man's Indian* (New York: Vintage, 1979), pp. 71–111.

133. William Dunlap, *A History of the Rise and Progress of the Arts of Design in the United States*, 2 vols., ed. Rita Weiss, introduction by James Thomas Flexner (1834; New York: Dover, 1969), vol. 2, no. 2, pp. 395–96.

134. Fitz-Greene Halleck, "Red Jacket, a Chief of the Indian Tribe, the Tuscaroras, on Looking at His Portrait by Weir," in *The Poetical Writings of Fitz-Greene Halleck*, ed. James Grant Wilson (New York: Appleton, 1869), p. 46. For Halleck's association with John Francis, see James Grant Wilson, *The Life and Letters of Fitz-Green Halleck* (New York: Appleton, 1869), p. 262.

135. William L. Stone, *The Life and Times of Red Jacket* (New York: Wiley and Putnam, 1841), p. 376.

136. Thomas L. McKenney and James Hall, *The Indian Tribes of North America*, 3 vols., ed. Frederick Webb Hodge and David I. Bushnel Jr. (1934; St. Clair Shores, Mich.: Scholarly Press, 1970), 1:15, 26.

137. Tuckerman, *Book of the Artists*, p. 142.

138. Gall, *On the Origin of the Moral Qualities*, 5:145.

139. Marjorie Catlin Roehm, *The Letters of George Catlin and His Family* (Berkeley: University of California Press, 1966), p. xvi.

140. For Catlin's background, see William H. Truettner, *The Natural Man Observed: A Study of Catlin's Indian Gallery* (Washington, D.C.: Smithsonian Institution Press, 1979), pp. 62–93. Truettner rightly stresses Catlin's links with the scientific community of Philadelphia but does not include the phrenological society in his review.

141. Harold McCracken, *George Catlin and the Old Frontier* (New York: Dial, 1959), p. 23.

142. George Catlin, *North American Indians*, 2 vols. (Edinburgh: John Grant, 1926), 2:222–27.

143. George Catlin, *Shut Your Mouth and Save Your Life* (London: Trubner, 1873).

144. Ibid., pp. 5–12.

145. Catlin, *North American Indians*, 1:17–18.

146. Ibid., 2:119–21.

147. Eliza (Catlin) Dart to "Sister Clara," Green Lake, Feby 23, 1845, in Roehm, *Letters of George Catlin*, p. 303.

148. Catlin, *North Americans Indians*, 1:133.

149. Ibid., 1:96.

150. Ibid., 2:29–30.

151. Ibid., 2:49.

152. Ibid., 2:133.

153. Ibid., 1:57–58.

154. Ibid., 2:84.

155. Ibid., 2:114.

156. Gall, *On the Origin of the Moral Qualities*, 3:11–17.

157. Ibid., 4:27.

158. Morton, *Crania Americana*, pp. 107–16.

159. Combe, *Phrenological Visit*, 2:48–50.

160. Catlin, *North American Indians*, 2:125–27, 47.

161. George Catlin, *Rambles among the Indians* (London: Gall and Inflis, [187-? (in pencil)]), pp. 144–48.

162. Catlin, *North American Indians*, 2:293.

163. Ibid., 1:105–7.

164. Ibid., 1:200–206.

165. Ibid., 2:295–97.

166. Ibid.

167. Ibid., 2:11–12.

168. Ibid., 1:103.

169. W. Byrd Powell, "Remarks on Watchfulness," *American Phrenological Journal and Miscellany* 1 (1839): 474.

170. Wells, *New Physiognomy*, p. 405.

171. Caldwell, *Elements of Phrenology*, p. 240.

172. Catlin, *Rambles among the Indians*, pp. 298–312. See also Brian W. Dippie, *Catlin and His Contemporaries: The Politics of Patronage* (Lincoln: University of Nebraska Press, 1990), p. 235.

173. Horsman, *Manifest Destiny*, p. 146.

174. Combe, *Phrenological Visit*, 1:70. A few days later Combe went to see Chantry's *George Washington* in Boston and remarked on the "moral and intellectual greatness" of the figure (1:74).

175. Morton, *Crania Americana*, pp. 201–2.

176. George Catlin, *Catlin's Notes of Eight Years' Travels and Residence in Europe*, 2 vols. (New York: Burgess, Stringer, 1848), 2:93.

177. Catlin, *North American Indians*, 2:6–7.

178. Dippie, *Catlin and His Contemporaries*, pp. 140–41.

179. Catlin, *Travels and Residence in Europe*, 1:41.

180. See William Bally, *Sixty Phrenological Specimens Approved and Described by the Late Dr. Spurzheim* (Nottingham: Alfred Barber, 1833).

181. Catlin, *Travels and Residence in Europe*, 1:120–21.

182. From the *Manchester Guardian*, 22 November 1843, quoted in "Intelligence," *Phrenological Journal and Miscellany* 17 (1844): 110.

183. Catlin, *Travels and Residence in Europe*, 1:120–21.

184. See, for example, Combe, *Lectures on Phrenology*, p. 178.

185. Catlin, *Travels and Residence in Europe*, 2:247–49.

186. Ibid., 1:233; no author or date is given.

187. Ibid., 1:216–17; no author or date is given.

188. David de Giustino, *Conquest of Mind Phrenology and Victorian Social Thought* (London: Croom Helm, 1975), p. 33.

189. Charles Baudelaire, "The Salon of 1846," in *Art in Paris, 1845–1862*, ed. and trans. Jonathan Mayne (London: Phaidon, 1970), p. 71.

190. For an example of the first attitude, see Bartlett Cowdrey and Herman Warner Williams Jr., *William Sidney Mount* (New York: Columbia University Press, 1944), p. 6. For the latter, see McElroy et al., *Facing History*, pp. xiii–xvi.

191. In 1864, for example, he wrote, "When a republican calls you a Copperhead in a fair argument, then as a compliment, call him a nigger head" (Alfred Frankenstein, *William Sidney Mount* [New York: Harry N. Abrams, 1979], p. 382).

192. Boime, *Art of Exclusion*, p. 97.

193. W. Alfred Jones, "A Sketch of the Life and Character of William S. Mount," *American Whig Review* 14 (1851): 125. There is some ambiguity in the author's statement. He mentions both *The Power of Music* and *Music is Contagious* (also known as the *Dance of the Haymakers* [1845, Museums at Stony Brook]) and then states, "They represent the love of music at different periods of life. The phrenological hobby of the artist is apparent in the musical bump of the negro, whose organ of tune in the second picture has been much developed." This would seem to imply that the "organ of tune" is developed in both, but more so in the latter. The quote testifies to the assumption among contemporaries that the faculty was large among blacks, a

conclusion reinforced by the activities of both figures. Similar reasoning is employed in David Carew Huntington, *Art and the Excited Spirit* (Ann Arbor: University of Michigan Museum of Art, 1972), p. 7.

194. Jones, "Mount," pp. 126–27.

195. Gall, *On the Origin of the Moral Qualities*, 5:73; see also O. S. Fowler and L. N. Fowler, *Phrenology Proved, Illustrated, and Applied* (New York: Fowlers and Wells, 1847), p. 31.

196. From the *Literary World*, 5 June 1847, quoted in "Subscription leaflet by Messrs Goupil, Vibert and Co., 'The Power of Music,'" (n.p., n.d.), AAA SM1/666, Museums at Stony Brook, Stony Brook, New York.

197. O. S. Fowler and L. N. Fowler, *The Illustrated Self-Instructor in Phrenology and Physiology* (New York: Fowlers and Wells, 1853), p. 118. Whether this applies as well to the whites in the barn is another question. In this respect, the pitchfork leaning against the wall is suggestive.

198. See, for example, Jane Tompkins, *Sensational Designs* (New York: Oxford University Press, 1985), p. 135.

199. See Frankenstein, *Mount*, p. 407.

200. W. S. Mount to George Hart, Stony Brook, 2 December 1849, quoted in ibid., p. 236.

201. Mrs. L. Miles, *Phrenology, and the Moral Influence of Phrenology* (Philadelphia: Carey, Lea, and Blanchard, 1835), pp. 134–35.

202. O. S. Fowler, *Phrenology and Physiology Applied to the Cultivation of Memory* (New York: n.p., 1844), pp. 70–71.

203. J. G. Spurzheim, "Notes Concerning Scientific Institutions and Arts," Boston Medical Library, Francis A. Countway Library of Medicine, Harvard University, Boston, Mass., B MS b44.2, fd. 3. See also Gall, *On the Origin of the Moral Qualities*, 5:225.

204. W. S. Mount to William Schaus, Stony Brook, 9 September 1852, in Frankenstein, *Mount*, p. 164.

205. Dunlap, *Rise and Progress of the Arts*, vol. 2, pt. 2, p. 328.

206. For the dates of publication, see Malcolm Johnson, *David Claypoole Johnston* (Boston: An exhibition held by the American Antiquarian Society, Boston College, the Boston Public Library, and the Worcester Art Museum, 1970), p. 8.

207. D. C. Johnston, *Phrenology Exemplified and Illustrated with Upwards of Forty Etchings for the Year 1837* (Boston: D. C. Johnston, 1837).

208. George Cruikshank, *Phrenological Illustrations: An Artist's View of the Craniological System of Doctors Gall and Spurzheim* (London: George Cruikshank, 1826).

209. Spurzheim, *Mental Phenomena*, 1:341.

210. David Tatham, "David Claypoole Johnston's *Militia Muster*," *American Art Journal* 19, no. 2 (1987): 7–13.

211. For an account of this subject, see Ronald Paulson, *Hogarth: His Life, Art, and Times*, abridged by Anne Wilde (New Haven: Yale University Press, 1974), pp. 262–65. The disciplined ranks in the background do not deny the following interpretation. They as well conform to an external motive, military regimentation. Neither foreground nor background rehearses the scenario employed by Johnston.

212. As early as 1819 Johnston did a military caricature; no information has been offered regarding its relationship to later works. See Johnson, *Johnston*, p. 6.

213. Fowler, *Practical Phrenologist*, p. 123.

214. There is evidence that Bingham was interested in phrenology. For example, in discussing his engraver, John Sartain, and the progress he was making on *The Country Election* in 1854, Bingham writes, "His *hope* is so large, that he promises more than he can perform" (George Caleb Bingham to Major J. S. Rollins, 1 February 1854, in "Letters of George Caleb Bingham to James S. Rollins," ed. C. B. Rollins, *Missouri Historical Review* 32 [January 1938]: 176; emphasis added). Some informative work has been done on Bingham and phrenology; see Henry Adams, "A New Interpretation

of Bingham's *Fur Traders Descending the Missouri,*" *Art Bulletin* 65 (1983): 676–77, and Elizabeth Johns, "The 'Missouri Artist' as Artist," in *George Caleb Bingham,* by Michael Edward Schapiro, Barbara Groseclose, Elizabeth Johns, Paul C. Nagel, and John Wilmerding (New York: Harry N. Abrams, 1990), p. 129. The latter discusses the phrenological organization of the players in *The Checkers Players* (1850, Detroit Institute of Arts). For Bloch's remarks, see E. Maurice Bloch, *George Caleb Bingham: The Evolution of an Artist* (Berkeley: University of California Press, 1967), p. 133.

215. See Sarah Burns, "*Yankee Romance*: The Comic Courtship Scene in Nineteenth-Century American Art," *American Art Journal* 18 (Winter 1986): 53–75. She does not claim, however, that Mount's scene illustrates a particular play, only that it derives from the artist's familiarity with the theater (p. 64).

216. Betsy Green, "The City Belle by a Simple Country Lass," *The Rover* 3 (1844): 8, AAA SM4/903.

217. There are, however, indications that Tyng was a person of some interest to Mount. Included in his notes is a newspaper clipping concerning an address delivered by Tyng to a temperance association of policemen. See newspaper clipping, "Temperance Meeting of Policemen," n.d., AAA SM1/666.

218. Burns, for example, states that Mount does not indicate who is the better man; this may be true, but he is concerned with those attributes that signal the better husband for the woman in the scene. See Burns, "Comic Courtship," p. 67. For scratching behind the ear as a sign of loss of courage, see Gall, *On the Origin of the Moral Qualities,* 5:276.

219. Harriet Beecher Stowe, *Household Papers and Stories* (1864; New York: AMS Press, 1967), pp. 264–66.

220. Harriet Beecher Stowe, *The Minister's Wooing* (1859; New York: AMS Press, 1967), pp. 10–11.

221. Ibid., pp. 5–6.

222. Ibid., p. 10.

223. Ibid., p. 21.

224. Ibid., p. 32.

225. Ibid., p. 72.

226. Ibid., p. 92. As with Tuckerman, *Ideality* was for Stowe a principal means of connecting the material and spiritual worlds. When religion neglects the former (and when it neglects the fine arts), it is reduced to arid speculation.

227. When the doctor releases Mary from her obligations to him, James remarks, "Sir, this tells on my heart more than any sermon you ever preached" (ibid., p. 556). Incidentally, the enigma of Aaron Burr, who appears in the novel as a seducer despite his strong moral faculties (p. 271), would have been resolved in the minds of contemporary readers familiar with phrenological literature because there he stood as the embodiment of *Amativeness*; see Fowler, *Practical Phrenologist,* p. 67.

228. William P. Jones, *New York Evening Gazette,* 24 November 1845, quoted in *Catalogue of Works of the Late Henry Inman, with a Biographical Sketch* (New York: Van Norden and King, 1846), p. 14.

229. For this mode of criticism, see George Combe, *Phrenology Applied to Painting and Sculpture* (London: Simpkin, Marshall, 1855), pp. 3–4.

230. Washington Irving, *The Sketch-Book* (N.p.: Spencer Press, 1936), pp. 368, 384.

231. "The Good Schoolmaster," *American Phrenological Journal* 17 (1853): 12.

232. Irving, *Sketch-Book,* p. 369.

233. Washington Irving, *A History of New York* (New York: Library of America, [1809 ed.]), p. 549. I would like to thank Dr. Michael Black of Baruch College for alerting me to this reference.

234. Irving, *Sketch-Book,* p. 383.

235. Jones, quoted in *Henry Inman,* p. 15.

236. This approach was suggested by Robert L. Herbert, *Impressionism: Art, Leisure, and Parisian Society* (New Haven: Yale University Press, 1991).

237. This analysis parallels that taken by Nicolai Cikovsky in his review of

the school theme. But whereas Cikovsky seeks the source of this imagery in relatively distant sources, such as the writings of Jean-Jacques Rousseau and Heinrich Pestalozzi, I look at the immediate American setting of Homer's own childhood and particularly at the changes inaugurated by Horace Mann. See Nicolai Cikovsky, "Winslow Homer's School Time 'A Picture Thoroughly National,'" in *Essays in Honor of Paul Mellon*, ed. John Wilmerding (Washington, D.C.: National Gallery of Art, 1986), pp. 47–69.

238. E. I. F. Williams, *Horace Mann, Educational Statesman* (New York: Macmillan, 1937), p. 190.

239. Much of this account comes from Lawrence A. Cremin, *The American Common School* (New York: Teachers College, Columbia University, 1951).

240. Charles Follen, *Funeral Oration Delivered at the Burial of Gaspar Spurzheim, M.D.* (Boston: Marsh, Capen and Lyon, 1832), pp. 19, 24.

241. "Review of *Remarks on the Influence of Mental Cultivation and Mental Excitement upon Health*, by Aramiah Brigham," *Annals of Phrenology* 2 (1835): 499–500.

242. John Davies, *Phrenology: Fad and Science* (New Haven: Yale University Press, 1955), p. 84.

243. Mary Mann, *Horace Mann*, pp. 71–72, 132.

244. Horace Mann to George Combe, 11 February 1839, in ibid., p. 111.

245. William Jolly, *Education: Its Principles and Practices as Developed by George Combe* (London: Macmillan, 1879), pp. lxiii, lxxiii. This discusses the influence of Combe on normal schools.

246. Horace Mann, *Sixth Annual Report Covering 1842* (1843; Washington, D.C.: Horace Mann Fund, 1949), p. 24.

247. Horace Mann, *Fourth Annual Report Covering 1840* (1841; Washington, D.C.: Horace Mann Fund, 1949), p. 45.

248. See Robert B. Downs, *Horace Mann, Champion of Public Schools* (New York: Twayne, 1974), pp. 71–72. It is noted here that the textbook employed

was written by Andrew Combe, George's brother.

249. Horace Mann, *Sixth Report*, p. 141.

250. Ibid., p. 100.

251. Horace Mann, *Fourth Report*, p. 94.

252. Ibid., p. 106. This advice comes in a letter sent by Samuel G. Howe, 9 December 1840.

253. Robert Clifton Whittemore, in *Makers of the American Mind*, quoted in Downs, *Mann*, p. 69.

254. "Abstract of School Committees' Reports," in *Twenty-Ninth Annual Report of the Board of Education* (Boston: Wright and Potter, 1866), p. 61.

255. For a discussion of Homer's schooling, see Gordon Hendricks, *The Life and Works of Winslow Homer* (New York: Harry N. Abrams, 1979), pp. 18–19.

256. Richard J. Powell, "Introduction: Winslow Homer, Afro-Americans, and the 'New Order of Things,'" in *Winslow Homer's Images of Blacks*, by Peter H. Wood and Karen C. Dalton (Austin: University of Texas Press, 1988), p. 9. There we read that Homer did not have much to say about his "darkey pictures," but Powell goes on to indicate that they document the circumstances faced by blacks in the 1870s.

257. Hendricks identifies the site of Homer's scene as in New York. See Hendricks, *Homer*, p. 80. A literalist might contend that this disassociates the setting from Mann's reforms, which took place in Massachusetts. The actual locale is not particularly relevant to this argument; certainly Homer meant his appeal to be universal. Even at a literal level of interpretation, it might be noted that Mann's reforms were quickly picked up in New York; see Downs, *Mann*, p. 117.

258. Horace Mann, *Fourth Report*, p. 106.

259. Horace Mann, *Fifth Annual Report Covering 1841* (1842; Washington, D.C.: Horace Mann Fund, 1949), pp. 44–46.

260. Mary Mann, *Horace Mann*, p. 556.

261. See Diana Korzenik, *Drawn to Art*

(Hanover, N.H.: University Press of New England, 1985), p. 46.

262. Hendricks, *Homer*, pp. 18–19.

263. Cikovsky, "Homer's School Time," pp. 57–59.

264. Horace Mann to Misses R. and E. Pennell, Boston, 1841 (no day given), in Mary Mann, *Horace Mann*, p. 152.

265. Years later Homer read George du Maurier's novel *Trilby*, and while the evidence of this book does not bear directly on the creation of the *Blackboard*, it does tell us about the code of physical appearances Homer knew late in life and would likely have known at the time he painted this image. When Trilby, a famed artists' model, decides to give up her shady occupation and reform herself, we learn that "she let her hair grow, and made of it a small knot at the back of her head, and showed her little flat ears which were charming, and just in the right place, very far back and rather high." This passage comes in a book where phrenological concepts appear with some regularity. The aspiring artist, Billee, for example, in a monologue with his pet dog, Tray, asks about "your bump of—wherever you keep your fondness [*Amativeness*]." See George du Maurier, *Trilby* (New York: Harper and Brothers, 1894), pp. 131, 171. Regarding the books owned by Homer, see David Tatham, "Winslow Homer's Library," *American Art Journal* 9 (May 1977): 94.

266. Horace Mann to C. Pierce, Boston, 7 May 1846, in Mary Mann, *Horace Mann*, p. 250.

267. Stowe, *Household Papers*, pp. 309–10.

268. Indeed, Homer explained that he sought out the fisherwomen of Cullercoats because "there are none like them in my country in dress, feature, or form." In attempting to expand on this comment, Franklin Kelly turns to a popular novel, Charles Reade's *Christie Johnstone* (published in a number of editions between 1855 and 1878), which deals with the allure of such women as viewed by contemporary culture. Primary among

their attractions was the fact that "they had never known a corset!" Kelly goes on to speculate whether Homer may have read this book, but even if not, such ideas were in circulation. See Franklin Kelly, "A Process of Change," in *Winslow Homer*, by Nicolai Cikovsky Jr. and Franklin Kelly, with contributions by Judith Walsh and Charles Brock (Washington, D.C.: National Gallery of Art, 1995), p. 177.

269. See William Howe Downes, *The Life and Work of Winslow Homer* (Boston: Houghton Mifflin, 1911), pp. 229–30. For others who fled the ethnic mix of New York City to join the Anglo-Saxon fishing communities of Maine in the late nineteenth century, see Gail Thain Parker, *Mind Cure in New England* (Hanover, N.H.: University Press of New England, 1973), p. 93. For related ideas, see Saul E. Zalesch, "Against the Current: Anti-Modern Images in the Work of Winslow Homer," *American Art Review* 5 (Fall 1993): 120–25.

270. Thomas Crawford to M. C. Meigs, 3 December 1854, quoted in Robert L. Gale, *Thomas Crawford, American Sculptor* (Pittsburgh: University of Pittsburgh Press, 1964), p. 135.

271. Dr. Frederick Weeden to Dr. Valentine Mott, St. Augustine, Florida, 2 October 1843, quoted in Mary McNeer Ward, "The Disappearance of the Head of Osceola," *Florida Historical Quarterly* 33 (January–April 1955): 200.

272. From the *Charleston Mercury*, 21 March 1838, quoted in John M. Goggin, "Osceola: Portraits, Features, and Dress," *Florida Historical Quarterly* 33 (January–April 1955): 175.

273. "A Lieutenant of the Left Wing," *Sketch of the Seminole War, and Sketches during a Campaign* (Charleston: 1836), republished in *The Indian and the White Man*, edited with an introduction by Wilcomb E. Washburn (Garden City, N.Y.: Anchor, 1964), p. 280.

274. See, for example, Sylvia E. Crane, *White Silence* (Coral Gables, Fla.: University of Miami Press, 1972), pp. 362–63.

275. Another contemporary remarks on the Grecian nose and "intellectual mold" of the forehead; see M. M. Cohen in 1836, quoted in Goggin, "Osceola," p. 177. It undoubtedly helped perceptions of Osceola's mental organization that his father was English. See James D. Horan, *The McKenney-Hall Portrait Gallery of American Indians* (New York: Bramhall House, 1972), p. 244.

276. Crane, *White Silence*, pp. 316–17, and Downs, *Mann*, p. 138.

277. Mary Mann, *Horace Mann*, p. 92.

278. Journal entry for 14 September 1841, quoted in ibid., p. 151. See also Downs, *Mann*, pp. 111–14.

279. De Giustino, *Conquest of Mind*, pp. 169–72.

280. "Statuary for the Capitol Extension," *Boston Daily Advertiser*, 1 October 1856.

281. This characterization of the woodsman is from Crawford's programme; see Crane, *White Silence*, p. 360.

282. Walt Whitman, *Leaves of Grass*, edited with an introduction by Malcolm Cowley (1855; New York: Penguin, 1982), pp. 17–18.

283. Horace Mann to Dr. Jarvis, Washington, 14 April 1852, quoted in Mary Mann, *Horace Mann*, p. 362.

284. "The Anglo-Saxon Race," *American Phrenological Journal* 31 (1860): n.p.

285. Quoted in Downs, *Mann*, p. 75.

286. Stowe, *Uncle Tom's Cabin*, pp. 361–62.

287. Ibid., p. 274.

288. Stowe, *Household Papers*, p. 321.

289. O. S. Fowler, *Creative and Sexual Science* (Rochester: New York State Pub. Co., 1870), p. 433.

290. Ibid., p. 477.

291. Stowe, *Uncle Tom's Cabin*, p. 355.

CHAPTER SEVEN

1. The history of the nude in the early Republic will be found in E. McSherry Fowble, "Without a Blush: The Movement toward Acceptance of the Nude as an Art Form in America," *Winterthur Portfolio* 9 (1974): 103–21; see also William H. Gerdts, *The Great American Nude* (New York: Praeger, 1974).

2. Orville Dewey, "From the *Union Magazine*, October 1847," in *Powers' Statue of the Greek Slave* (New Orleans: Norman's Print, 1849), p. 14.

3. A discussion of the sexual appeal of the slave is included in Linda Hyman, "*The Greek Slave* by Hiram Powers: High Art as Popular Culture," *Art Journal* 35 (Spring 1976): 216–23.

4. Milton W. Brown, Sam Hunter, John Jacobus, Naomi Rosenblum, and David M. Sokol, *American Art* (New York: Harry N. Abrams, 1979), p. 232.

5. Hiram Powers to Sidney Brooks, 4 December 1849, Archives of American Art (henceforth AAA), 1134/657–58, Smithsonian Institution, Washington, D.C. This is included in a letter about sending the *Eve* to America. Much of this is published in Richard P. Wunder, *Hiram Powers, Vermont Sculptor, 1805–1873*, 2 vols. (Newark: University of Delaware Press, 1991), 1:187. No commentary is provided.

6. C. Edwards Lester, *The Artist, the Merchant, and the Statesman of the Age of the Medici and of Our Own Times*, 2 vols. (New York: Paine and Burgess, 1845), 2:201.

7. "Self-Esteem," *American Phrenological Journal* 17 (1853): 36.

8. Lorado Taft, *The History of American Sculpture* (1903; New York: Macmillan, 1924), p. 66. This is in reference to the *California*.

9. Newspaper clipping, n.d., Louisville, Kentucky, AAA 1146.

10. Nathaniel Hawthorne, *Passages from the French and Italian Note-Books* (Boston: Houghton Mifflin, 1884), p. 305.

11. Ibid., pp. 305–6.

12. Henry W. Bellows, "Seven Sittings with Powers, the Sculptor," *Appleton's Journal of Literature and Art* 1 (1869): 359–60. See also Hiram Powers to Captain Grindley, 5 March 1852, AAA 1135/2599.

13. For example, see Andrew McFarland, *The Escape* (Boston: B. B. Mussey,

1851), p. 177. Much the same was said about his *Eve*; see Sylvia E. Crane, *White Silence* (Coral Gables, Fla.: University of Miami Press, 1972), p. 197.

14. William J. Clark Jr., *Great American Sculptors* (Philadelphia: Gebbie and Barrie, 1878), pp. 49–50. Powers had his own ideas about the American head; it was, he maintained, less wide than the English and exhibited less distance between the brows and eyes. See "National Types of Beauty," *American Phrenological Journal and Life Illustrated* 48 (1868): 21.

15. A. G. Hoyt to Hiram Powers, 30 September 1844, AAA 1132/759.

16. George Harris to Hiram Powers, 21 January 1844, AAA 1132/405.

17. This appeared in the January 1860 issue of the *Atlantic Monthly*, pp. 108–9. Quoted in J. Carson Webster, *Erastus D. Palmer* (Newark: University of Delaware Press, 1983), p. 74.

18. Samuel A. Roberson and William H. Gerdts, "The Greek Slave," *Museum* 17 (Winter, Spring 1965): 5.

19. Charles Caldwell, *Thoughts on Physical Education* (Boston: Marsh, Capen and Lyon, 1834), p. 121.

20. Henry T. Tuckerman, *Book of the Artists* (New York: G. P. Putnam and Son, 1867), p. 294.

21. G. C., "Notice of Laurence Macdonald," *Phrenological Journal and Miscellany* 7 (1832): 159.

22. Lester, *The Artist*, 1:65.

23. Joseph R. Buchanan, *Outlines of Lectures on the Neurological System of Anthropology* (Cincinnati: Buchanan's Journal of Man, 1854), pp. 359–60.

24. Ibid., p. 360.

25. It should be noted that Dewey's analysis goes on to discuss the intellectual beauty of the slave's face; see Dewey, *Powers' Statue*, p. 15.

26. Buchanan discusses his theory and its relation of man to the material world as "medical geology" (Buchanan, *Anthropology*, p. 88). For a discussion of (wo)man as the microcosm, see pp. 372–75.

27. Some discussion of the sexual ambiguities surrounding the *Greek Slave* can be found in Joy S. Kasson, *Marble Queens and Captives* (New Haven: Yale University Press, 1990), pp. 46–72.

28. O. S. Fowler, *Sexual Science: Including Manhood, Womanhood, and Their Mutual Interrelations; Love, Its Laws, Power, Etc.* (Philadelphia: National Pub. Co., 1870), p. 26.

29. Wunder, *Hiram Powers*, 1:170–71.

30. William H. Gerdts, *American Neo-Classic Sculpture: The Marble Resurrection* (New York: Viking, 1973), p. 140, and H. W. Janson, "Pars Pro Toto: Hands and Feet as Sculptural Subjects before Rodin," in *The Shape of the Past: Studies in Honor of Franklin D. Murphy*, ed. Giorgio Buccellati and Charles Speroni (Los Angeles: University of California Press, 1981), p. 300.

31. Miner Kellogg to Hiram Powers (Memphis[?]), Upper Egypt, 23 January 1844, box 2, MSS qP 888 RM, Cincinnati Historical Society, Cincinnati, Ohio, Manuscript Collections (henceforth CHS).

32. Miner Kellogg to Hiram Powers, Constantinople, 21 June 1845, box 2, CHS.

33. Wunder, *Hiram Powers*, 1:171.

34. Again, for the contacts between Powers and the Fowlers in Washington, see O. S. Fowler and L. N. Fowler, *Phrenology Proved, Illustrated, and Applied* (New York: Fowlers and Wells, 1847), pp. 332–33. By this time the Fowlers had developed their sexual theories; see Harold Aspiz, "Sexuality and the Pseudo-Sciences," in *Pseudo-Science and Society in Nineteenth-Century America*, ed. Arthur Wrobel (Lexington: University Press of Kentucky, 1987), p. 149.

35. George Combe, *The Constitution of Man Considered in Relation to External Objects*, 5th ed. (Boston: Marsh, Capen and Lyon, 1835), pp. 161–64.

36. George Combe, *Moral Philosophy; or, the Duties of Man* (New York: William H. Colyer, 1846), p. 104. Stowe acknowledges this when she has the black servant react to Mary's release by

Dr. Hopkins from her vows by claiming, "Dar's a good deal more reason in two young, handsome folks comin' togeder dan dar is in _____" (Harriet Beecher Stowe, *The Minister's Wooing* [1859; New York: AMS Press, 1967], p. 544).

37. See Harold Aspiz, *Walt Whitman and the Body Beautiful* (Urbana: University of Illinois Press, 1980), pp. 193–202, and Aspiz, "Sexuality and the Pseudo-Sciences," pp. 150–51.

38. Combe, *Constitution*, pp. 159–63.

39. Aspiz, "Sexuality and the Pseudo-Sciences," pp. 147–48.

40. Kasson, *Marble Queens*, p. 63.

41. Kasson, in *Marble Queens*, considers a series of ideal works without reference to the reforming intentions present in them. For a review of the alternate, re-form approaches to sexuality, see Aspiz, *Walt Whitman*.

42. Martha H. Verbrugge, *Able-Bodied Womanhood* (New York: Oxford University Press, 1988), p. 47.

43. Aspiz, "Sexuality and the Pseudo-Sciences," p. 152.

44. Hiram Powers to Charles Eaton, 1 January 1855, AAA 1137/618.

45. Fowler, *Sexual Science*, p. 105.

46. Ibid., p. 98.

47. Ibid., pp. 181–82, 701.

48. Ibid., p. 232.

49. Ibid., p. 679.

50. Ibid., p. 126.

51. Ibid., p. 681.

52. Lester, *The Artist*, 2:193.

53. Fowler's views will be found in Fowler, *Sexual Science*, pp. 168–71.

54. Ibid., p. 486.

55. Ibid., p. 166.

56. Ibid., p. 275.

57. G. R. Searle, "Eugenics and Class," in *Biology, Medicine, and Society, 1840–1940*, ed. Charles Webster (Cambridge: Cambridge University Press, 1981), p. 217.

58. Dale T. Knobel, *Paddy and the Republic* (Middletown, Conn.: Wesleyan University Press, 1986), pp. 122–27.

59. Hiram Powers to Collie [Collin?], 8 June 1865, AAA 1142/1229.

60. Allan Sekula, "The Body and the Archive," *October* 39 (Winter 1986): 54.

61. Aspiz, *Walt Whitman*, p. 218.

62. Justin Kaplan, *Walt Whitman: A Life* (New York: Bantam, 1982), pp. 180–81.

63. Walt Whitman, "Children of Adam," in *Leaves of Grass* (New York: Norton, 1965), p. 99. Vance remarks on the similarity of these lines to Palmer's *White Captive*; see William L. Vance, *America's Rome*, 2 vols. (New Haven: Yale University Press, 1989), 1:241.

64. Whitman, "Unfolded out of the Folds," in *Leaves of Grass*, p. 391.

65. Whitman, "Faces," ibid., pp. 466–67.

66. Whitman, "Children of Adam," p. 96.

67. Whitman, "Starting from Paumanok," in *Leaves of Grass*, pp. 16–17. On Whitman's racial views, see Aspiz, *Walt Whitman*, pp. 139, 190–92.

68. Whitman, "Song of the Redwood Tree," in *Leaves of Grass*, p. 208, and Aspiz, *Walt Whitman*, p. 199.

69. Aspiz, *Walt Whitman*, p. 206.

70. Whitman, "By Blue Ontario's Shore," in *Leaves of Grass*, p. 349.

71. Whitman, "Starting from Paumanok," p. 23.

72. Ibid., p. 18.

73. Fowler, *Sexual Science*, pp. 705–24.

74. Whitman, "Song of Myself," in *Leaves of Grass*, p. 74.

75. Fowler, *Sexual Science*, p. 679.

76. Aspiz, "Sexuality and the Pseudo-Sciences," p. 145.

77. Fowler, *Sexual Science*, p. 800. Combe stressed the mother's role; see Combe, *Moral Philosophy*, p. 121.

78. Wunder, *Hiram Powers*, 1:219–20.

79. Miner Kellogg to Hiram Powers, 20 August 1847, box 2, CHS.

80. Miner Kellogg to Hiram Powers, 26 January 1848, box 2, CHS. In reporting this, Kellogg adds with mild amusement that Powers need not worry that she is in danger, since he (Kellogg) drinks neither wine nor spirits. The phrenologists would have approved of his behavior as a "husband."

81. Oliver Wendell Holmes, *Elsie Venner: A Romance of Destiny* (Boston: Houghton Mifflin, 1895), p. 94.

82. "The Greek Slave Waltz," by Jullien, sheet music issued at the time of the Great Exhibition of 1851; see Wunder, *Hiram Powers*, 1:248, 272.

83. Hiram Powers to Miner Kellogg, 2 December 1848, box 2, CHS.

84. Miner Kellogg to Hiram Powers, 12 July 1850, box 3, CHS.

85. Miner Kellogg to Hiram Powers, 26 February, 14 April 1848, box 2, CHS. Passing reference is made to these events in Wunder, *Hiram Powers*, 1:227, 229.

86. David S. Reynolds, *Beneath the American Renaissance* (Cambridge: Harvard University Press, 1988), p. 86.

87. Wunder, *Hiram Powers*, 1:50–53, and Crane, *White Silence*, p. 177.

88. David S. Reynolds, *Walt Whitman's America* (New York: Knopf, 1995), p. 211.

89. Kasson, *Marble Queens*, p. 60.

90. *Daily Commercial*, 2 November 1848 (from the *Western Christian Advocate*, "Powers' Greek Slave"), box 6, CHS.

91. Kasson, *Marble Queens*, pp. 66–68. The theory of the male gaze has recently been questioned in Frederick Turner, *The Culture of Hope* (New York: Free Press, 1995), p. 141, and Wendy Lesser, *His Other Half* (Cambridge: Harvard University Press, 1991), esp. pp. 53–80. It would be interesting to know more about the man who, under the spell of a mesmerist, imitated the slave. See Wunder, *Hiram Powers*, 1:235.

92. Miner Kellogg to Hiram Powers, 14 December 1847, box 2, CHS.

93. Wunder, *Hiram Powers*, 1:208.

94. Vivien M. Green, "Hiram Powers's *Greek Slave*: Emblem of Freedom," *American Art Journal* 14 (Autumn 1982): 31–39.

95. Kasson, *Marble Queens*, p. 66. It is interesting to contemplate in this context the *tableau vivant* presented during the Civil War by an organization of southern women for the benefit of Confederate soldiers. Its title was *A Turkish Slave Market*. Certainly this cannot

have been intended to call attention to the wrongs of slavery in the South, and Powers's statue of the slave seems likewise to have been viewed in terms of a similar disassociation. See Drew Gilpin Faust, *Mothers of Invention* (Chapel Hill: University of North Carolina Press, 1996), p. 26.

96. Hiram Powers to George Calvert, 22 June 1851, AAA 1135/2070.

97. Miner Kellogg to Hiram Powers, 14 April 1848, box 2, CHS. Wunder prints this letter without comment; see Wunder, *Hiram Powers*, 1:228.

98. Miner Kellogg to Hiram Powers, 6 November 1848, box 2, CHS.

99. Wunder, *Hiram Powers*, 1:207–8.

100. On Kellogg's work on this subject, see Tuckerman, *Book of the Artists*, p. 423. Also see Miner Kellogg to Hiram Powers, 31 December 1847 and 19 April 1849, box 2, CHS.

101. Samuel George Morton, *Crania Americana: or, A Comparative View of the Skulls of Various Aboriginal Nations of North and South America* (Philadelphia: Dobson, 1839), p. 8.

102. "Proceedings of the Phrenological Society, 1824, Feb. 19—Notice of John Thurtell," *Phrenological Journal and Miscellany* 1 (1824): 487.

103. George Combe, "Phrenology Applied to Criticism in the Arts," *Phrenological Journal and Miscellany* 2 (1824–25): 204–5.

104. Combe, *Constitution*, pp. 162–63.

105. "Extracts from a Discourse on the Social Relations of Man Delivered before the Boston Phrenological Society, by S. G. Howe, 1837," in *Reminiscences of Dr. Spurzheim and George Combe: A Review of the Science of Phrenology, for the Period of Its Discovery by Dr. Gall to the Time of the Visit of George Combe to the United States*, by Nahum Capen (New York: Fowler and Wells, 1881), pp. 187–97.

106. Lester, *The Artist*, 2:194–96.

107. Newspaper clipping, "Power's [*sic*] Statue of 'The Greek Slave,'" box 6, CHS.

108. Newspaper clipping, "Powers's Statue of the Greek Slave," box 6, CHS.

109. *Evening Mirror,* New York, 5 November 1847, box 6, CHS.

110. Newspaper clipping, "The Greek Slave," box 6, CHS.

111. H.M., "The Fine Arts," *Literary World,* 24 December 1847, box 5, CHS.

112. Newspaper clipping, "The Greek Slave," box 5, CHS.

113. "The Greek Slave Again," *Daily Commercial,* Cincinnati, 19 December [?], box 5, CHS. Also see Boyd Reilly, "For the *Cincinnati Commercial* 'Powers' Greek Slave,' " n.d., box 5, CHS.

114. Hiram Powers to Theodore Dehon, 25 December 1859, AAA 1140/480.

115. Newspaper clipping, box 6, CHS.

116. "The Fine Arts," *Literary World,* box 6, CHS.

117. "Power's [*sic*] Last Effort" and "The Greek Slave," *Atlas,* Cincinnati, 26 October [?], box 6, CHS.

118. "Powers Greek Slave," box 6, CHS.

119. "Correspondence of the *Cincinnati Gazette,* Powers and his Statue of the Greek Slave" [probably Judge Burnet (in pencil)], box 6, CHS.

120. ["Noah's Sunday Times" (in pencil)], box 6, CHS.

121. "The Greek Slave Again," *Literary World,* [15 January 1848 (in pencil)], box 6, CHS.

122. "The Greek Slave," *American,* Baltimore, 20 April 1848, box 6, CHS, and *Illustrated London News,* 23 August 1851, pp. 241–42; quoted in Wunder, *Hiram Powers,* 1:264.

123. *Boston Daily Times and Bay State Democrat,* 22 June 1848, box 6, CHS.

124. "The New Era of Industry," Boston, 6 July 1848, box 6, CHS.

125. "Art Review for *The American,* Powers's Greek Slave," box 6, CHS.

126. Newspaper clipping, "The Greek Slave in Boston," [8 July 1848 (in pencil)], box 6, CHS.

127. Newspaper clipping, "The Greek Slave," box 6, CHS.

128. Newspaper clipping, "The Fine Arts," box 6, CHS.

129. "Greek Slave purchased by A. T. Stewart," *Cosmopolitan Art Journal* 3 (1858–59): 139.

130. For more on Stewart's patronage, see Kasson, *Marble Queens,* pp. 25–29.

131. *Olive Branch* (Rev. Thomas F. Norris, editor, publisher, and proprietor), 5 August 1848, box 5, CHS.

132. Belle Brittan, "Belle Brittan on Beauty," *Cosmopolitan Art Journal* 3 (1858–59): 35.

133. For a listing of these, see Wunder, *Hiram Powers,* 2:157–77.

134. For the Fowlers' involvement, see John Davies, *Phrenology: Fad and Science* (New Haven: Yale University Press, 1955), p. 84.

135. Much of the following comes from Verbrugge, *Able-Bodied Womanhood.*

136. Ibid., p. 55.

137. Ibid., p. 21.

138. For an account of this tendency, see L. Perry Curtis Jr., *Apes and Angels: The Irishman in Victorian Caricature* (Washington, D.C.: Smithsonian Institution Press, 1971), esp. pp. 11–12.

139. Records of the Meetings of the Ladies' Physiological Institute of Boston and Vicinity, from 1 January 1851 to May 1854, p. 90, MC 236, Schlesinger Library, Radcliffe College, Cambridge, Mass. See also Verbrugge, *Able-Bodied Womanhood,* p. 52.

140. For more on this, see Verbrugge, *Able-Bodied Womanhood,* p. 26.

141. Ibid., p. 57.

142. Records of the Meetings, pp. 89, 99, 101, 102.

143. "The Crystal Palace," *Boston Daily Advertiser,* 20 January 1852.

144. It would be interesting to know if the ladies of the institute visited the slave during her trip to Boston in 1848 and 1849, but the records of activities from this time are incomplete. A second tour of New England by the slave took place in the fall of 1851; Wunder does not mention Boston as a destination. See Wunder, *Hiram Powers,* 1:252.

145. This was written for the *Eagle* in 1846[?]. Quoted in Reynolds, *Walt Whitman's America*, p. 211.

146. Records of the Meetings (1851), p. 34.

147. Verbrugge, *Able-Bodied Womanhood*, p. 46.

148. Records of the Meetings (1851), p. 41.

149. The idea that women might study an anatomical model to comprehend their own bodies was, for example, one source of distress. See Verbrugge, *Able-Bodied Womanhood*, p. 61.

150. Records of the Meetings (1852), p. 132.

151. Verbrugge, *Able-Bodied Womanhood*, p. 63.

152. James Fenimore Cooper, *The Wept of Wish-Ton-Wish* (New York: W. A. Townsend, 1859), p. 369.

153. James Fenimore Cooper, *Home as Found* (New York: W. A. Townsend, 1860), p. 28.

154. Kasson, *Marble Queens*, p. 97.

155. Cooper, *Wept of Wish-Ton-Wish*, p. 369.

156. Reproduced in Vance, *America's Rome*, 1:244.

157. Wayne Craven, *Sculpture in America* (New York: Crowell, 1968), p. 199.

158. Issa Desh Breckinridge and Mary Desh, *A Memorial to Joel T. Hart* (Cincinnati: Robert Clarke, 1885), pp. 19–20.

159. Ibid., p. 39.

160. Ethelbert Dudley Warfield, "The Place in Art of 'Woman Triumphant,'" in Breckinridge and Desh, *Joel T. Hart*, pp. 33–35.

161. Vance, *America's Rome*, 1:245.

162. *Testimonials on Behalf of George Combe as a Candidate for the Chair of Logic in the University of Edinburgh* (Edinburgh: John Anderson, 1836), p. 138.

163. Cornelia Carr, *Harriet Hosmer: Letters and Memories* (New York: Moffat, Yard, 1912), p. 1.

164. "Harriet Hosmer," *Cosmopolitan Art Journal* 3 (1858–59): 214.

165. L. Maria Child, "Harriet Hosmer, a Biographical Sketch," *Ladies Repository* 21 (January 1861): 4, in Harriet Hosmer papers, M 60, Schlesinger Library, Radcliffe College, Cambridge, Mass.

166. L. Maria Child, "Miss Harriet Hosmer," *Boston Daily Advertiser*, 19 October 1857.

167. Dolly Sherwood, *Harriet Hosmer, American Sculptor, 1830–1908* (Columbia: University of Missouri Press, 1991), p. 4.

168. Carr, *Harriet Hosmer*, p. 2.

169. Quoted in O. S. Fowler, *Physiology, Animal and Mental* (New York: Fowlers and Wells, 1852), pp. 45–46.

170. Harriet Hosmer, "Lecture 1st on the Hen," ca. 1848, Hosmer papers, M 60, box 2.

171. Harriet Hosmer to Harriet Hosmer Carr, March 1855, quoted in Carr, *Harriet Hosmer*, p. 55. A footnote here makes the connection with Combe.

172. "Harriet Hosmer, the Woman Eminent in Sculpture," *Phrenological Journal and Life Illustrated* 54 (1872): 169–71. Stern indicates that it was Nelson Sizer who examined Hosmer. See Madeleine B. Stern, *Heads and Headlines: The Phrenological Fowlers* (Norman: University of Oklahoma Press, 1971), p. 225.

173. R. T. Trall, *The Health and Diseases of Women* (New York: R. T. Trall, 1862), p. 15.

174. Robert J. Terry, "Recalling a Famous Pupil of McDowell's Medical College, Harriet Goodhue Hosmer, Sculptor," *Medical Alumni Quarterly* [Washington University, St. Louis, Mo., 1943? (in pencil)], Hosmer papers, M 60. For Mcdowell's experiments in the occult, see Emma Hardinge (Britten), *Modern American Spiritualism* (New York: Published by the author, 1870), p. 354.

175. "Harriet Hosmer" [St. Louis Daily Globe and Democrat 12, 13, 1888 (in pencil)], Hosmer papers, M 60, box 3.

176. Charles Gibbon, *The Life of George Combe, Author of "The Constitution of Man,"* 2 vols. (1878; Westmead, Farnborough, Hants, England: Gregg, 1970), 2:170.

177. Fiona Pearson, "Phrenology and Sculpture, 1820–1855," *Leeds Arts Calender* 88 (1981): 20. On Combe's discussions with Jameson, see Gibbon, *Life of George Combe*, 2:212.

178. Susan Waller, "The Artist, the Writer, and the Queen: Hosmer, Jameson, and Zenobia," *Woman's Art Journal* 4 (Spring/Summer 1983): 21–29. Much of what follows is taken from this text.

179. Mrs. Jameson, *Memoirs of Celebrated Female Sovereigns* (New York: Harper and Brothers, 1836), pp. 57–65.

180. Anna Jameson to Harriet Hosmer, 10 October [?], Hosmer papers, M 60, box 1. See also Carr, *Harriet Hosmer*, p. 150.

181. Newspaper clipping, Hosmer papers, M 60, box 3.

182. Harriet Hosmer to Wayman Crow, December 1858, quoted in Carr, *Harriet Hosmer*, p. 140.

183. See Sherwood, *Harriet Hosmer*, p. 177.

184. "Harriet Hosmer," *Cosmopolitan Art Journal* 3 (1858–59): 216.

185. Jameson, *Memoirs*, p. 64.

186. Sherwood, *Harriet Hosmer*, pp. 231–32.

187. William Ware, *Zenobia: or, The Fall of Palmyra* (New York: C. S. Francis, 1854), pp. 274–78, and " 'Zenobia by Harriet Hosmer' Now on Exhibition at the Fine Arts Institute Derby Gallery, No 825 Broadway, New York," [1864? (in pencil)], Hosmer papers, M 60, box 1.

188. Taft, *American Sculpture*, p. 208.

189. For example, she consulted an eighth-century mosaic of the Virgin for the garments; see Waller, "The Artist," p. 23.

190. Andrew Jackson Davis, *Beyond the Valley: A Sequel to "The Magic Staff"* (Boston: Colby and Rich, 1885), pp. 194–95. This quote is from an unnamed female advocate of physiological training.

191. Newspaper clipping, Hosmer papers, M 60, box 3.

192. Nathaniel Parker Willis, *New York Evening Express*, 17 November 1864, quoted in Joseph Leach, "Harriet Hosmer: Feminist in Bronze and Marble," *Feminist Art Journal* 5 (Summer 1976): 13.

193. Quoted in Carr, *Harriet Hosmer*, p. 34. Hosmer's spiritualist abilities were also a feature Elizabeth Browning appreciated; see Russel M. Goldfarb and Clare R. Goldfarb, *Spiritualism and Nineteenth-Century Letters* (Rutherford, N.J.: Fairleigh Dickinson University Press, 1978), p. 114.

194. Quoted in Carr, *Harriet Hosmer*, p. 49.

195. O. S. Fowler, *The Practical Phrenologist* (Boston: O. S. Fowler, 1869), p. 40.

196. Samuel R. Wells, *New Physiognomy* (New York: Samuel R. Wells, 1868), p. 304.

197. Jan Seidler Ramirez, in *American Figurative Sculpture in the Museum of Fine Arts, Boston*, introduction by Jonathan L. Fairbanks (Boston: Museum of Fine Arts, 1986), p. 161.

198. From *The Marble Faun*, quoted in Sherwood, *Harriet Hosmer*, p. 92.

199. Quote from Harriet Hosmer, no source given, ibid., p. 92.

200. For a review of this work, see Ramirez, *Sculpture*, pp. 119–22.

201. "Foreign Art Gossip," *Cosmopolitan Art Journal* 3 (1858–59): 130.

202. William Wetmore Story, *Roba di Roma* (London: Chapman and Hall, 1875), p. 338.

203. Ramirez, *Sculpture*, p. 121.

204. We do find this useful bit of information: "The head of the Venus de' Medici is, however, notoriously too small for the body" (William W. Story, *The Proportions of the Human Figure* [London: Chapman and Hall, 1866], p. 27).

205. William Wetmore Story, *Conversations in a Studio*, 2 vols. (Boston: Houghton Mifflin, 1890), 2:323.

206. Ibid., 1:22.

207. Jan M. Seidler, "A Critical Reappraisal of the Career of William Wetmore Story (1819–1895), American Sculptor and Man of Letters" (Ph.D. dissertation, Boston University, 1985), p. 620.

208. Story, *Conversations*, 1:25.

209. William Wetmore Story, *Graffiti d'Italia* (New York: Charles Scribner, 1868), p. 408.

210. William Wetmore Story, "Castle Palo," in *Poems* (Boston: Little, Brown, 1856), p. 24.

211. Story, *Roba*, pp. 532–33.

212. Story's *Bacchus* of 1863 was designed as a companion piece to the *Venus*. See Ramirez, *Sculpture*, p. 110. Whether it also had a physiological tale to tell we do not know; if so, it would be a rare case of the male nude serving this purpose.

213. Story, *Conversations*, 2:325.

214. William Wetmore Story, *Excursions in Art and Letters* (Boston: Houghton Mifflin, 1891), pp. 259–64.

215. Wells, *New Physiognomy*, pp. 106–8.

216. Seidler, "William Wetmore Story," p. 483.

217. William Wetmore Story to Charles Eliot Norton, 3 May 1862, quoted in Henry James Jr., *William Wetmore Story and His Friends*, 2 vols. (New York: Grove Press, [1903]), 2:72.

218. Story, "The Confessional," in *Poems*, p. 74.

219. Seidler, "William Wetmore Story," pp. 468–69.

220. Wells, *New Physiognomy*, pp. 105–6.

221. Thoreau expressed much the same idea that runs through Story's work when he stated, "So, we are told, the New Hollander goes naked with impunity, while the European shivers in his clothes. Is it impossible to combine the hardiness of these savages with the intellectualness of the civilized man?" (Henry David Thoreau, *Walden, or Life in the Woods*, afterword by Perry Miller [New York: Signet, 1960], p. 13).

222. William Wetmore Story to Charles Eliot Norton, 15 August 1861, quoted in James, *William Wetmore Story*, 2:70–71.

223. Notice from the *London Athenaeum*, quoted in Mary E. Phillips, *Reminiscences of William Wetmore Story* (New York: Rand, McNally, 1897), pp. 132–33.

224. William H. Gerdts, *The Great American Nude* (New York: Praeger, 1974), pp. 89–91.

225. Cynthia Eagle Russett, *Sexual Science* (Cambridge: Harvard University Press, 1989), pp. 117–18. For a discussion of this concept in Victorian literature, see Athena Vrettos, *Somatic Fictions* (Stanford: Stanford University Press, 1995), p. 53.

226. Story, *Excursions*, p. 272.

227. Story, *Graffiti*, p. 158.

228. Ramirez, *Sculpture*, pp. 122–25, and Kasson, *Marble Queens*, pp. 223–34.

229. On Story's tendency to think like a lawyer, see Alert TenEyck Gardner, *Yankee Stonecutters* (1945; Freeport, N.Y.: Books for Libraries, 1968), p. 35.

230. J. G. Spurzheim, *Phrenology or the Doctrine of Mental Phenomena*, 2 vols. (Boston: Marsh, Capen and Lyon, 1832), 1:157.

231. J. G. Spurzheim, *Observations on the Deranged Manifestations of the Mind, or Insanity* (London: Baldwin, Cradock, and Joy, 1817), p. 99. This is the argument of much of the book.

232. Hewett C. Watson, *Statistics of Phrenology: Being a Sketch of the Progress and Present State of That Science in the British Islands* (London: Longman, Rees, Orme, Brown, Green, and Longman, 1836), p. 66.

233. William Wetmore Story, *Life and Letters of Joseph Story*, 2 vols. (Boston: Little, Brown, 1851), 2:598.

234. Holmes, *Elsie Venner*, p. 397.

235. Ibid., p. 99.

236. Ibid., p. 317.

237. Ibid., pp. 226–27.

238. For the critical reaction to Story's use of detail, see Seidler, "William Wetmore Story," pp. 474–79.

239. Ann Jones, "She Had to Die!," *American Heritage* 31 (October/November 1980): 20–24.

240. "At 80 Starts His Masterpiece,"

New York Sun, 21 April 1930, quoted in Michael Richman, *Daniel Chester French, an American Sculptor* (New York: Metropolitan Museum of Art, 1976), p. 197.

241. Allan Chase, *The Legacy of Malthus* (New York: Knopf, 1977), p. 21.

CHAPTER EIGHT

1. Walter Creese, "Fowler and the Domestic Octagon," *Art Bulletin* 28 (1946): 100. This article remains the primary scholarly discussion of Fowler's architectural endeavors.

2. O. S. Fowler, *The Octagon House: A Home for All*, introduction by Madeleine B. Stern (1853; New York: Dover, 1973). I have also consulted O. S. Fowler, *A Home for All* (New York: Fowlers and Wells, 1851).

3. What follows is from "Inhabitiveness: Its Definition, Location, and Adaptation, Together with the Importance of Having a Home," *American Phrenological Journal and Miscellany* 10 (1848): 55–59. This text is similar to that in O. S. Fowler, *Octagon House*, pp. 9–12.

4. M. B. Sampson, "On the Primary Function of the Organ of Ideality," *American Phrenological Journal and Miscellany* 1 (1839): 300–302.

5. "The Analysis and Grouping of the Social Faculties," *American Phrenological Journal and Miscellany* 12 (1850): 109.

6. George Combe, *Lectures on Phrenology*, with notes, an introductory essay, and a historical sketch by Andrew Boardman (New York: Samuel Colman, 1839), pp. 342–43.

7. O. S. Fowler, *Octagon House*, p. 9.

8. Ibid., pp. 9–12.

9. Ibid., p. 4.

10. Fowler specifically discusses the hexagonal cells of bees, ibid., p. 7.

11. Ibid., pp. 3–4.

12. Ibid., p. 19.

13. See Creese, "Domestic Octagon," pp. 89–102. Also see John Davies, *Phrenology: Fad and Science* (New Haven: Yale University Press, 1955), pp. 114–17, and

Madeleine B. Stern, *Heads and Headlines: The Phrenological Fowlers* (Norman: University of Oklahoma Press, 1971), pp. 86–98.

14. For the above argument, see O. S. Fowler, *Octagon House*, pp. 82–88.

15. Creese, "Domestic Octagon," p. 99.

16. O. S. Fowler, *Octagon House*, p. 73.

17. Ibid., p. 100.

18. "Perfection of Character," *American Phrenological Journal* 23 (1856): 106–7.

19. "Instinct and Reason," *American Phrenological Journal and Life Illustrated* 40 (1864): 12–13.

20. O. S. Fowler, *Home for All*, p. 58.

21. O. S. Fowler, *Octagon House*, p. 126.

22. O. S. Fowler, *The Practical Phrenologist* (Boston: O. S. Fowler, 1869), p. 63.

23. O. S. Fowler, *Octagon House*, pp. 116–23.

24. David Handlin notes the resemblance to phrenological charts but does not follow up on the implications in terms of Fowler's larger philosophy. See David P. Handlin, *The American Home: Architecture and Society, 1815–1915* (Boston: Little, Brown, 1979), p. 336.

25. O. S. Fowler, *Octagon House*, p. 65.

26. Ibid., pp. 123–29.

27. For example, see "Debate of the Faculties," *American Phrenological Journal* 13 (1851): 49–50.

28. O. S. Fowler, *Octagon House*, p. 130.

29. Ibid., p. 65.

30. Ibid., p. 14.

31. Ibid., p. 122.

32. Ibid., p. 137.

33. Ibid., pp. 128–29.

34. Ibid., p. 130.

35. Ibid., pp. 61–62.

36. For Fowler on gravel walls, see ibid., pp. 16–55.

37. There can be no doubt that the articles are by Fowler despite the fact that they are unsigned. For similar passages elsewhere in his writing, see, for example, O. S. Fowler, *Sexual Science: Including Manhood, Womanhood, and Their*

Mutual Interrelations: Love Its Laws, Power, Etc. (Philadelphia: National Pub. Co., 1870), pp. 34, 417.

38. Francois Joseph Gall, *On the Origin of the Moral Qualities and Intellectual Faculties of Man*, 6 vols., trans. Winslow Lewis Jr. (Boston: Marsh, Capen and Lyon, 1835), 3:141.

39. [Orson Fowler], "Progression, a Universal Law: Its Application to the Individual, the Race, and the Universe, Including the Ultimate Destiny of Each," *American Phrenological Journal* 16 (1852): 38.

40. George Combe, *The Constitution of Man Considered in Relation to External Objects*, 5th ed. (Boston: Marsh, Capen and Lyon, 1835), p. 222.

41. [Orson Fowler], "Progression, a Universal Law: Its Application to the Individual, the Race, and the Universe, Including the Ultimate Destiny of Each," *American Phrenological Journal* 15 (1852): 81–82. The repeated emphasis on six children as the optimal number may have contributed to Whitman's claim, when answering those who thought him a homosexual, that he had fathered six illegitimate children. See Harold Aspiz, *Walt Whitman and the Body Beautiful* (Urbana: University of Illinois Press, 1980), p. 217.

42. [Orson Fowler], "Progression," 15:105–7.

43. Ibid., 15:125–27.

44. Mark Holloway, *Heavens on Earth* (1951; New York: Dover, 1966), p. 138.

45. See Creese, "Domestic Octagon," p. 101.

46. Emanuel Swedenborg, *Heaven and Hell*, trans. George F. Dole (New York: Swedenborg Foundation, 1984), no. 415–20.

47. Theophilus Parsons, *Essays*, 3 vols. (Boston: T. H. Carter and Son, 1868), 1:113.

48. [Orson Fowler], "Progression," 15:127.

49. Dolores Hayden, *Seven American Utopias: The Architecture of Communitarian Socialism* (Cambridge: MIT Press, 1976), pp. 9–28.

50. O. S. Fowler, *Home for All*, pp. 86–88.

51. [Orson Fowler], "Progression," 15:125.

52. Ibid., 16:38–40.

53. Stern, *Fowlers*, pp. 95–96.

54. O. S. Fowler, *Octagon House*, pp. 108–15.

55. Joshua C. Taylor, *William Page, the American Titian* (Chicago: University of Chicago Press, 1957), p. 184.

56. Ruby M. Rounds and Stephen P. Leonard Sr., *Octagon Buildings in New York State*, foreword by Carl Carmer (Cooperstown: New York State Historical Association, 1954), p. 5, #12.

57. Andrew Jackson Davis had a vision of Orson Fowler as an architect on 16 January 1847; see Stern, *Fowlers*, p. 87.

58. Creese, "Domestic Octagon," p. 102. For more on this community, see "The Octagon Style of Settlement," *American Phrenological Journal* 22 (1855): 17.

59. Fowler says that he lectured to Noyes before the formation of the Oneida community; see O. S. Fowler, *Sexual Science*, p. 316. Sizer states that he lectured to the group while they were still in Putney, Vermont; see Nelson Sizer, *Forty Years in Phrenology: Embracing Recollections of History, Anecdote, and Experience* (New York: Fowler and Wells, 1891), pp. 206–9.

60. John Humphrey Noyes, *History of American Socialism* (1870; New York: Hillary House, 1961), p. 626.

61. Hayden, *Seven American Utopias*, pp. 207, 223. These schemes apparently never went beyond the planning stage. An octagon *was* built at Hopedale; see p. 335.

62. O. S. Fowler, *Sexual Science*, pp. 257, 263. See also "Free Love Reviewed," *American Phrenological Journal* 29 (1859): 49–50.

63. Madeleine B. Stern, *The Pantarch: A*

Biography of Stephen Pearl Andrews (Austin: University of Texas Press, 1968), p. 73.

64. Josiah Warren, *Equitable Commerce* (Utopia, Ohio: Amos E. Senter, 1849), p. 2.

65. O. S. Fowler, *Practical Phrenologist*, p. 137.

66. Warren, *Equitable Commerce*, pp. 7–29.

67. Josiah Warren, *Practical Details in Equitable Commerce*, 2 vols., preface by Stephen Pearl Andrews (New York: Fowlers and Wells, 1852), 1:15.

68. Warren, *Practical Details*, 1:71; see also Josiah Warren, *Practical Application of the Elementary Principles of "True Civilization," to the Minute Detail of Every Day Life* (Princeton, Mass.: Published by the author, 1873), p. 30.

69. See Warren, *Equitable Commerce*, and Josiah Warren, *True Civilization an Immediate Necessity and the Last Ground of Hope for Mankind* (Boston: J. Warren, 1863).

70. Stephen Pearl Andrews, *The Science of Society, No 2: Cost, the Limit of Price. A Scientific Measure of Honesty in Trade, as One of the Fundamental Principles in the Solution of the Social Problem* (New York: Fowlers and Wells, 1852), pp. 151–52.

71. Roger Wunderlich, *Low Living and High Thinking at Modern Times, New York* (New York: Syracuse University Press, 1992), p. 29. For more on Modern Times, see also Charles Colbert, *"Fair Exchange No Robbery*: William Sidney Mount's Commentary on 'Modern Times,'" *American Art* 8 (Summer/Fall 1994): 29–41.

72. See Warren, *Practical Application*, and Wunderlich, *Low Living and High Thinking*.

73. Wunderlich, *Low Living and High Thinking*, p. 114.

74. Ibid., p. 45.

75. "Benevolence: Its Definition, Location, Function, Adaptation, and Cultivation," *American Phrenological Journal and Miscellany* 10 (1848): 181.

76. Warren, *Practical Details*, p. vi.

Eventually many went on to add extra land, usually just a fourth acre; see Wunderlich, *Low Living and High Thinking*, p. 119.

77. See "Women, and the Kitchen Garden," *American Phrenological Journal* 13 (1851): 133–34; O. S. Fowler, *Education and Self Improvement, founded on Physiology and Phrenology* (New York: O. S. and L. N. Fowler, 1844), p. 244; "Fruit as an Article of Diet—Its Propagation," *American Phrenological Journal and Miscellany* 10 (1848): 96–97.

78. See, for example, O. S. Fowler, *Octagon House*, pp. 139–46.

79. Andrews, *Science of Society*, p. viii.

80. Ibid., p. 22.

81. Wunderlich, *Low Living and High Thinking*, pp. 114–15.

82. See O. S. Fowler, *Octagon House*, pp. 68–69.

83. Wunderlich, *Low Living and High Thinking*, pp. 32–33.

84. Ibid., pp. 37–38, 89.

85. O. S. Fowler, *Home for All*, p. 33.

86. For the circumstances regarding the school at Modern Times, see Wunderlich, *Low Living and High Thinking*, pp. 50–51.

87. O. S. Fowler, *Octagon House*, pp. 151–52.

88. The census of 1860 lists a variety of occupations, including a harness maker, a carpenter, a shoemaker, and a painter, but, presumably, these people would also have tended their gardens, which were the mainstay of the economy. See Wunderlich, *Low Living and High Thinking*, pp. 39–40.

89. Ibid., pp. 41–42.

90. Warren, *Practical Application*, p. 20.

91. Wunderlich, *Low Living and High Thinking*, p. 183.

92. Ibid., p. 182.

93. Warren, *Practical Application*, p. 45.

94. There is no evidence in Thoreau's writing that he was aware of Modern Times; see Wunderlich, *Low Living and High Thinking*, pp. 151–56.

95. Ellen Chesler, *Woman of Valor:*

Margaret Sanger and the Birth Control Movement in America (New York: Simon and Schuster, 1992), pp. 462–63.

96. For Sanger's ties to spiritualism and Theosophy, see ibid., p. 172.

97. Ibid., pp. 27–28.

98. Ibid., p. 33.

99. Ibid., p. 37.

100. Prof. Zeus Franklin, *Private Marriage Guide* (Boston: Mutual Benefit Co., n.d., [ca. 1883]), p. 22.

101. Prof. Zeus Franklin, Elizur Wright, and Alfred E. Giles, *Prosecution and Persecution of Dr. Zeus Franklin* (New York: Mutual Benefit Co., 1883), pp. 229–30.

102. Sanger, in reference to meeting Havelock Ellis in 1914, quoted in Chesler, *Woman of Valor*, p. 111.

103. For Fowler on physiological laws acting like that of gravity, see O. S. Fowler, *Sexual Science*, p. 26. See also Harvey Green, *Fit for America* (New York: Pantheon, 1986), pp. 63–64.

104. Thomas Cole, "Essay on American Scenery, 1835," in *American Art, 1700–1960*, ed. John W. McCoubrey (Englewood Cliffs, N.J.: Prentice-Hall, 1965), p. 109. Cole is referring here to the despoiling of the American wilderness, but like Durand's reliance on Graham, his mode of reasoning parallels that of Combe.

105. See Kevin J. Avery, "A Historiography of the Hudson River School," in *American Paradise: The World of the Hudson River School*, introduction by John K. Howat (New York: Metropolitan Museum of Art, 1987), pp. 3–20.

106. For the use of the word "luminism," see John Wilmerding, introduction to *American Light* (Princeton: Princeton University Press, 1989), pp. 7–19.

107. Davies, *Phrenology*, p. 121.

108. L. N. Fowler, "Phrenological Character of William Cullen Bryant," *American Phrenological Journal and Miscellany* 11 (1849), 14–20, republished in Madeleine B. Stern, *A Phrenological Dictionary of Nineteenth-Century Americans* (Westport, Conn.: Greenwood Press, 1982), pp. 7–9.

109. On the reaction to Cole's death, see J. Gray Sweeney, "The Advantages of Genius and Virtue," in *Thomas Cole: Landscape into History* (Washington, D.C.: National Museum of American Art, 1994), pp. 113–35.

110. William Cullen Bryant, *A Funeral Oration Occasioned by the Death of Thomas Cole, Delivered before the National Academy of Design, New York, May 4, 1848* (New York: Appleton, 1848), pp. 41–42.

111. Louis Legrand Noble, *The Life and Works of Thomas Cole*, ed. Elliot S. Vesell (Cambridge: Belknap Press of Harvard University Press, 1964), p. 306. Noble, an Episcopalian minister and Cole's spiritual adviser, demonstrates how persons of this religious persuasion could be sympathetic to phrenology.

112. Cole's own letters confirm this acquaintance. See, for example, Maria Cole to Thomas Cole, 12 April 1842, Archives of American Art, ALC 2, box 4, New York State Library, Albany, Manuscripts and Special Collections.

113. E. H. Dixon, "Cole and Church: A Remarkable Resemblance," *American Phrenological Journal and Life Illustrated* 39 (1864): 53.

114. Andrew Carmichael, *A Memoir of the Life and Philosophy of Spurzheim* (Boston: Marsh, Capen and Lyon, 1833), p. 48.

115. Written 1 February 1848; see Noble, *Thomas Cole*, p. 285.

116. Thomas Cole to Asher Durand, 11 September 1836, in Noble, *Thomas Cole*, p. 164.

117. John Durand, *The Life and Times of A. B. Durand* (1890; New York: DaCapo, 1970), p. 141.

118. See Aspiz, *Walt Whitman*, pp. 60–67.

Bibliography

ARCHIVAL MATERIAL

Archives of American Art (AAA)
Smithsonian Institution, Washington,
D.C.
AAA 1102 (Clara Louise Dentler,
"White Marble: The Life and
Letters of Hiram Powers,
Sculptor")
AAA P22 (Henry Inman papers)
AAA 88 (Rembrandt Peale papers)
AAA D10 (Rubens Peale papers)
AAA 1131–46 (Hiram Powers
papers)
New York State Library, Albany, Manu-
scripts and Special Collections
AAA ALC 1–4 (Thomas Cole
papers)
New York Public Library, Rare Books
and Manuscript Division, Astor,
Lenox, and Tilden Foundations
AAA N19–N20 (Asher B. Durand
papers)
Pennsylvania Academy of Fine Arts,
Philadelphia
AAA P63 (Minutes of the Board of
Directors and Stockholders)
Museums at Stony Brook, Stony
Brook, New York
AAA SM1–SM4 (William Sidney
Mount papers)
Boston Medical Library, Francis A.
Countway Library of Medicine, Har-
vard University, Boston, Massachu-
setts
B MS b44.2 (Manuscripts and Scrap-
books of William Rimmer)
B MS C22.4 (J. G. Spurzheim, "Notes
on Scientific Institutions in the
United States of America")
Files of the Warren Anatomical
Museum
Cincinnati Historical Society, Cincinnati,
Ohio, Manuscript Collections (CHS)
MS qP 888 RM, boxes 1–6 (Hiram
Powers letters)

Heritage Collector's Society, Hatfield,
Pennsylvania
Rembrandt Peale, "Ironic" Lecture on
Phrenology
Schlesinger Library, Radcliffe College,
Cambridge, Massachusetts
M-60, Harriet Hosmer papers
MC-236 (Records of the Ladies'
Physiological Institute of Boston
and Vicinity)

BOOKS, ARTICLES,
AND DISSERTATIONS

Andrews, Stephen Pearl. *The Science of
Society, No 2: Cost, the Limit of Price. A
Scientific Measure of Honesty in Trade, as
One of the Fundamental Principles in the
Solution of the Social Problem.* New York:
Fowlers and Wells, 1852.
Aspiz, Harold. "Sexuality and the
Pseudo-Sciences." In *Pseudo-Science and
Society in Nineteenth-Century America,*
edited by Arthur Wrobel, pp. 144–
65. Lexington: University Press of
Kentucky, 1987.
———. *Walt Whitman and the Body Beauti-
ful.* Urbana: University of Illinois Press,
1980.
Audubon, John James. *Delineations of
American Scenery and Character.* Intro-
duction by Francis Hobart Herrick.
New York: Baker, 1926.
———. *Ornithological Biography.* 5 vols.
Philadelphia: Carey and Hart, 1832.
Audubon, Maria R. *Audubon and His Jour-
nals.* 2 vols. Notes by Elliott Coues.
1897. Gloucester, Mass.: Peter Smith,
1972.
Bartlett, Tuman H. *The Art Life of William
Rimmer: Sculptor, Painter, and Physician.*
1890. New York: DaCapo, 1970.
———. "Dr. William Rimmer." *American
Art Review* (1880): 461–68, 509–14.
Beecher, Catherine E. *Physiology and*

Calisthenics. New York: Harper and Brothers, 1856.

Beecher, Catherine E., and Harriet Beecher Stowe. *The American Woman's Home.* Introduction by Joseph Van Why. 1869. Hartford: Stowe-Day Foundation, 1987.

Bell, John. *Health and Beauty.* Philadelphia: Carey and Hart, 1838.

Bellows, Henry W. "Seven Sittings with Powers, the Sculptor." *Appleton's Journal of Literature and Art* 1 (1869): 342–43, 359–61, 402–4, 470–71, 595–97; 2 (1869): 54–55, 106–8.

Benz, Ernst. "Swedenborg und Lavater: Uber die religiosen Grundlagen der Physiognomik." *Zeitschrift fur Kirchengeschichte* 57 (1938): 165–85.

Black, Mary. "Phrenological Associations." *Clarion* 9 (Fall 1984): 45–52.

Block, Marguerite Beck. *The New Church in the New World.* Introduction by Robert H. Kirven. 1932. New York: Octagon Books, 1968.

Boynton, Henry. "Hiram Powers." *New England Magazine* 20 (1899): 519–33.

Breckinridge, Issa Desh, and Mary Desh. *A Memorial to Joel T. Hart.* Cincinnati: Robert Clarke, 1885.

Buchanan, Joseph R. *Outlines of Lectures on the Neurological System of Anthropology.* Cincinnati: Buchanan's Journal of Man, 1854.

Caldwell, Charles. *Elements of Phrenology.* Lexington, Ky.: Meriwether, 1827.

Calvert, George H. *The Life of Rubens.* Boston: Lee and Shepherd, 1878.

———. *Scenes and Thoughts in Europe.* New York: Wiley and Putnam, 1846.

Capen, Nahum. *Reminiscences of Dr. Spurzheim and George Combe: A Review of the Science of Phrenology, for the Period of Its Discovery by Dr. Gall to the Time of the Visit of George Combe to the United States.* New York: Fowler and Wells, 1881.

Carmichael, Andrew. *A Memoir of the Life and Philosophy of Spurzheim.* Boston: Marsh, Capen and Lyon, 1833.

Carr, Cornelia. *Harriet Hosmer: Letters and Memories.* New York: Moffat, Yard, 1912.

Cash, Philip. "American Medicine in the Time of William Rimmer." In *William Rimmer, a Yankee Michelangelo,* by Jeffrey Weidman, Neil Harris, and Philip Cash, pp. 20–25. Foreword by Theodore E. Stebbins Jr. Hanover, N.H.: University Press of New England, 1985.

Catlin, George. *Catlin's Notes of Eight Years' Travels and Residence in Europe.* 2 vols. New York: Burgess, Stringer, 1848.

———. *North American Indians.* 2 vols. Edinburgh: John Grant, 1926.

———. *Rambles among the Indians.* London: Gall and Inglis, [187?].

———. *Shut Your Mouth and Save Your Life.* London: Trubner, 1873.

Chesler, Ellen. *Woman of Valor: Margaret Sanger and the Birth Control Movement in America.* New York: Simon and Schuster, 1992.

Child, L. Maria. *Letters from New York.* 2 vols. New York: Charles S. Francis, 1843.

Colbert, Charles. "Clark Mills and the Phrenologist." *Art Bulletin* 70 (1988): 134–37.

———. "Dreaming Up *The Architect's Dream.*" *American Art* 6 (Summer 1992): 79–91.

———. " 'Each Little Hillock Hath a Tongue': Phrenology and the Art of Hiram Powers." *Art Bulletin* 68 (1986): 281–300.

———. "*Fair Exchange No Robbery*: William Sidney Mount's Commentary on 'Modern Times.' " *American Art* 8 (Summer/Fall 1994): 29–41.

———. " 'Razors and Brains': Asher B. Durand and the Paradigm of Nature." *Studies in the American Renaissance* (1992): 261–90.

Combe, George. *The Constitution of Man Considered in Relation to External Objects.* 5th ed. Boston: Marsh, Capen and Lyon, 1835.

———. *Essays on Phrenology.* Edited with an introduction by John Bell. Philadelphia: Carey and Lea, 1822.

———. *Lectures on Phrenology.* With notes,

an introductory essay, and a historical sketch by Andrew Boardman. New York: Samuel Colman, 1839.

———. *Moral Philosophy; or, the Duties of Man.* New York: William H. Colyer, 1846.

———. *Notes on the United States of North America during a Phrenological Visit in 1838–9–40.* 2 vols. Philadelphia: Carey and Hart, 1841.

———. "Phrenological Remarks on the Relation between the Natural Talents and Dispositions of Nations, and the Developments of their Brains." In *Crania Americana; or, A Comparative View of the Skulls of Various Aboriginal Nations of North and South America,* by Samuel George Morton, pp. 269–91. Philadelphia: Dobson, 1839.

———. *Phrenology Applied to Painting and Sculpture.* London: Simpkin, Marshall, 1855.

———. *A System of Phrenology.* New York: William H. Colyer, 1841.

Cooter, Roger. *The Cultural Meaning of Popular Science.* Cambridge: Cambridge University Press, 1984.

Cowling, Mary. *The Artist as Anthropologist.* Cambridge: Cambridge University Press, 1989.

Crane, Sylvia E. *White Silence.* Coral Gables, Fla.: University of Miami Press, 1972.

Craven, Wayne. *Sculpture in America.* New York: Crowell, 1968.

Creese, Walter. "Fowler and the Domestic Octagon." *Art Bulletin* 28 (1946): 89–102.

Cruikshank, George. *Phrenological Illustrations: An Artist's View of the Craniological System of Doctors Gall and Spurzheim.* London: George Cruikshank, 1826.

Cruveilhier, J. *The Anatomy of the Human Body.* Edited by Granville Sharp Pattison. New York: Harper and Brothers, [1844].

Darnton, Robert. *Mesmerism and the End of the Enlightenment in France.* Cambridge: Harvard University Press, 1968.

Davies, John. *Phrenology: Fad and Science.* New Haven: Yale University Press, 1955.

Davis, Andrew Jackson. *The Philosophy of Spiritual Intercourse, Being an Explanation of Modern Mysteries.* New York: Fowlers and Wells, 1855.

Dean, Amos. *Lectures on Phrenology.* Albany: Oliver Steele and Hofman and White, 1834.

De Giustino, David. *Conquest of Mind Phrenology and Victorian Social Thought.* London: Croom Helm, 1975.

DeVille, J. *Manual of Phrenology.* London: J. DeVille, 1835.

Diary of Christopher Columbus Baldwin, 1829–35. Worcester, Mass.: American Antiquarian Society, 1901.

Dimmick, Lauretta. "A Catalogue of the Portrait Busts and Ideal Works of Thomas Crawford (1813?–1857), American Sculptor in Rome." Ph.D. dissertation, University of Pittsburgh, 1986.

Dunlap, William. *A History of the Rise and Progress of the Arts of Design in the United States.* 2 vols. Edited by Rita Weiss. Introduction by James Thomas Flexner. 1834. New York: Dover, 1969.

Durand, A. B. "Letters on Landscape Painting." *Crayon* 1 (1855): Letter 1, 1–2; Letter 2, 34–35; Letter 3, 66–67; Letter 4, 97–98; Letter 5, 145–46; Letter 6, 209–11; Letter 7, 273–75; Letter 8, 354–55; 2 (1855): Letter 9, 16–17.

Durand, John. *The Life and Times of A. B. Durand.* 1890. New York: DaCapo, 1970.

Evans, W. F. *The Mental-Cure, Illustrating the Influence of the Mind on Body Both in Health and Disease and the Psychological Method of Treatment.* Boston: H. H. and T. W. Carteer, 1869.

Everett, Edward. "Powers, the Sculptor." *Littell's Living Age* 15 (1847): 97–100.

Follen, Charles. *Funeral Oration Delivered at the Burial of Gaspar Spurzheim, M.D.* Boston: Marsh, Capen and Lyon, 1832.

Ford, Alice. *John James Audubon.* Norman: University of Oklahoma Press, 1964.

Fowler, Mrs. L. N. *Phrenology, Designed for*

the Use of Schools and Families. New York: Fowlers and Wells, 1847.

Fowler, O. S. Creative and Sexual Science. Rochester: New York State Pub. Co., 1870.

———. Education and Self Improvement, founded on Physiology and Phrenology. O. S. and L. N. Fowler, 1844.

———. Fowler's Practical Phrenology. New York: Fowlers and Wells, 1847.

———. Hereditary Descent: Its Laws and Facts. New York: O. S. and L. N. Fowler, 1843.

———. A Home for All. New York: Fowlers and Wells, 1851.

———. The Octagon House: A Home for All. Introduction by Madeleine B. Stern. 1853. New York: Dover, 1973.

———. Phrenology and Physiology Applied to the Cultivation of Memory. New York: n.p., 1844.

———. Physiology, Animal and Mental. New York: Fowlers and Wells, 1852.

———. The Practical Phrenologist. Boston: O. S. Fowler, 1869.

———. Self-Culture and Perfection of Character. New York: Fowlers and Wells, 1855.

———. Sexual Science: Including Manhood, Womanhood, and Their Mutual Interrelations; Love, Its Laws, Power, Etc. Philadelphia: National Pub. Co., 1870.

[Fowler, Orson]. "Progression, a Universal Law: Its Application to the Individual, the Race, and the Universe, Including the Ultimate Destiny of Each." American Phrenological Journal 15 (1852): 81–82, 105–7, 125–27; 16 (1852): 2–3, 38–40.

Fowler, O. S., and L. N. Fowler. The Illustrated Self-Instructor in Phrenology and Physiology. New York: Fowlers and Wells, 1853.

———. Phrenology Proved, Illustrated, and Applied. New York: Fowlers and Wells, 1847.

Frankenstein, Alfred. William Sidney Mount. New York: Harry N. Abrams, 1979.

Fuller, Robert. Mesmerism and the Ameri-can Cure of Souls. Philadelphia: University of Pennsylvania Press, 1982.

———. "Mesmerism and the Birth of Psychology." In Pseudo-Science and Society in Nineteenth-Century America, edited by Arthur Wrobel, pp. 205–22. Lexington: University Press of Kentucky, 1987.

Gall, Francois Joseph. On the Origin of the Moral Qualities and Intellectual Faculties of Man. 6 vols. Vol. 1, The Connection of their Manifestation. Vol. 2, The Plurality of the Cerebral Organs. Vol. 3, Discovering the Seat of their Organs. Vol. 4, Organology. Vol. 5, Organology. Vol. 6, Critical Review of Some Anatomico-Physiological Works, with an Explanation of a New Philosophy of the Moral Qualities and Intellectual Faculties. Translated by Winslow Lewis Jr. Boston: Marsh, Capen and Lyon, 1835.

Gerdts, William H. The Art of Healing. Birmingham, Ala.: Birmingham Museum of Art, 1981.

———. The Art of Henry Inman. Catalog by Carrie Rebora. Washington, D.C.: National Portrait Gallery, 1987.

———. The Great American Nude. New York: Praeger, 1974.

Gibbon, Charles. The Life of George Combe, Author of "The Constitution of Man." 2 vols. 1878. Westmead, Farnborough, Hants, England: Gregg, 1970.

Gould, Stephen Jay. The Mismeasure of Man. New York: Norton, 1981.

Graham, John. Lavater's Essays on Physiognomy: A Study in the History of Ideas. Berne: Peter Lang, 1979.

Graham, Sylvester. A Lecture on Epidemic Diseases, Generally and Particularly the Spasmodic Cholera. New York: Mahlon Day, 1833.

———. Lectures on the Science of Human Life. 2 vols. Boston: Marsh, Capen, Lyon and Webb, 1839.

Green, Harvey. Fit for America. New York: Pantheon, 1986.

Gregory, William. Animal Magnetism or Mesmerism and Its Phenomena. 1909. New York: Arno Press, 1975.

Gyllenhaal, Martha, Robert W. Gladish, Dean W. Holmes, and Kurt R. Rosenquist. *New Light: Ten Artists Inspired by Emanuel Swedenborg.* Bryn Athyn, Pa.: Glencairn Museum, 1988.

Haller, John. *American Medicine in Transition, 1840–1910.* Urbana: University of Illinois Press, 1980.

Harris, Neil. "The Artist as Teacher." In *William Rimmer, a Yankee Michelangelo,* by Jeffrey Weidman, Neil Harris, and Philip Cash, pp. 14–19. Foreword by Theodore E. Stebbins Jr. Hanover, N.H.: University Press of New England, 1985.

Haskins, R. W. *History and Progress of Phrenology.* Buffalo: Steele and Peck, 1839.

Hayden, William B. *On the Phenomena of Modern Spiritualism.* Boston: Otis Clapp, 1855.

Hevner, Carol Eaton. *Rembrandt Peale, 1778–1860: A Life in the Arts.* With a biographical essay by Lillian B. Miller. Philadelphia: Historical Society of Pennsylvania, 1985.

"History of Phrenology in Philadelphia." *American Phrenological Journal and Miscellany* 2 (1839–40): 476–77.

Hollander, Sharon C. "Asa Ames and the Art of Phrenology." *Clarion* 14 (Summer 1989): 28–35.

Holmes, Oliver Wendell. *Elsie Venner: A Romance of Destiny.* Boston: Houghton Mifflin, 1895.

Honour, Hugh. *The Image of the Black in Western Art IV: From the American Revolution to World War I.* 2 vols. Vol. 1, *Slaves and Liberators.* Vol. 2, *Black Models and White Myths.* Cambridge: Harvard University Press, 1989.

Horsman, Reginald. *Race and Manifest Destiny.* Cambridge: Harvard University Press, 1981.

James, Henry, Jr. *William Wetmore Story and His Friends.* 2 vols. New York: Grove Press, [1903].

James, Henry, Sr. *The Secret of Swedenborg.* Boston: Fields, Osgood, 1869.

Johnston, D. C. *Phrenology Exemplified and Illustrated with Upwards of Forty Etchings for the Year 1837.* Boston: D. C. Johnston, 1837.

Kasson, Joy S. *Marble Queens and Captives.* New Haven: Yale University Press, 1990.

Kirstein, Lincoln. *William Rimmer, His Life and Art.* 1946–47. New York: Whitney Museum of American Art, 1961.

Lanteri-Laura, Georges. *Histoire de la phrenologie: L'homme et son cerveau selon F. J. Gall.* Paris: Presses Universitaires de France, 1974.

Lawall, David B. *Asher B. Durand: A Documentary Catalogue of the Narrative and Landscape Paintings.* New York: Garland, 1978.

———. *Asher Brown Durand: His Art and Art Theory in Relation to His Times.* New York: Garland, 1977.

Lester, C. Edwards. *The Artist, the Merchant, and the Statesman of the Age of the Medici and of Our Own Times.* 2 vols. New York: Paine and Burgess, 1845.

Lipton, Leah. *A Truthful Likeness.* Washington, D.C.: Smithsonian Institution Press, 1985.

Lokensgard, Hjalmar O. "Oliver Wendell Holmes's 'Phrenological Character.'" *New England Quarterly* 13 (1940): 711–18.

McCord, Carey P. "Bumps and Dents in the Skull." *Archives of Environmental Health* 19 (1969): 221–29.

Macnish, Robert. *An Introduction to Phrenology.* Glasgow: John Symington, 1837.

Madeley, Edward. *The Science of Correspondences Elucidated.* Edited by B. F. Barrett. Germantown, Pa.: Swedenborg Publishing Association, 1883.

Mann, Horace. *Annual School Reports.* Washington, D.C.: Horace Mann Fund, 1949.

Mann, Mary. *Life of Horace Mann.* 1888. Miami: Mnemosyne Publishing, 1969.

Marder, Louis. *His Exits and His Entrances: The Story of Shakespeare's Reputation.* Philadelphia: Lippincott, 1963.

Martin, James J. *Men against the State.* Foreword by Harry Elmer Barnes. New York: Libertarian Book Club, 1957.

Melville, Herman. *Moby-Dick.* Edited

with an introduction by Charles Child Walcutt. 1851. New York: Bantam, 1986.

Miles, Mrs. L. *Phrenology, and the Moral Influence of Phrenology.* Philadelphia: Carey, Lea, and Blanchard, 1835.

Miller, Lillian B. *In Pursuit of Fame: Rembrandt Peale, 1778–1860.* With an essay by Carol Eaton Hevner. Washington, D.C.: National Portrait Gallery, 1992.

Morton, Samuel George. *Crania Americana; or, A Comparative View of the Skulls of Various Aboriginal Nations of North and South America.* Philadelphia: Dobson, 1839.

Nissenbaum, Stephen. *Sex, Diet, and Debility in Jacksonian America.* Westport, Conn.: Greenwood Press, 1980.

Noble, Louis Legrand. *The Life and Works of Thomas Cole.* Edited by Elliot S. Vesell. Cambridge: Belknap Press of Harvard University Press, 1964.

Novak, Barbara. *American Painting of the Nineteenth Century.* New York: Harper and Row, 1979.

———. *Nature and Culture: American Landscape and Painting, 1825–1875.* New York: Oxford University Press, 1981.

Oedel, William T., and Todd S. Gernes. "*The Painter's Triumph*: William Sidney Mount and the Formation of a Middle-Class Art." *Winterthur Portfolio* 23 (Summer/Autumn 1988): 111–27.

Page, William. *A Study of Shakespeare's Portraits.* London: Chiswick Press, 1876.

Palmer, E. D. "Philosophy of the Ideal." *Crayon* 3 (January 1856): 18–20.

Parry, Ellwood C., III. *The Art of Thomas Cole: Ambition and Imagination.* Newark: University of Delaware Press, 1988.

———. "Thomas Cole's Imagination at Work in *The Architect's Dream*." *American Art Journal* 12 (Winter 1980): 41–59.

Parsons, Theophilus. *Essays.* 3 vols. Boston: T. H. Carter and Son, 1868.

Peale, Rembrandt. *Notes on Italy.* Philadelphia: Carey and Lea, 1831.

———. *Portfolio of an Artist.* Philadelphia: Henry Perkins, 1839.

———. "Reminiscences." *Crayon* 1 (1855): 369–71.

Pfingstag, Benjamin Nelson. "Aspects of Form and Time in the Paintings of William Sidney Mount." Ph.D. dissertation, State University of New York, Binghamton, 1980.

Phillips, Mary E. *Reminiscences of William Wetmore Story.* New York: Rand, McNally, 1897.

Podmer, Frank. *Mediums of the Nineteenth Century.* 2 vols. Published in 1902 as *Modern Spiritualism.* New Hyde Park, N.Y.: University Books, 1963.

Prose Writing of William Cullen Bryant. Edited by Parke Godwin. 2 vols. Vol. 1, *Essays, Tales, and Orations.* Vol. 2, *Travels, Addresses, and Comments.* New York: Appleton, 1884.

Reynolds, David S. *Beneath the American Renaissance.* Cambridge: Harvard University Press, 1988.

Reynolds, Donald Martin. *Hiram Powers and His Ideal Sculpture.* New York: Garland, 1977.

———. "The 'Unveiled Soul': Hiram Powers's Embodiment of the Ideal." *Art Bulletin* 59 (1977): 394–414.

Riegel, Robert E. "The Introduction of Phrenology to the United States." *American Historical Review* 39, no. 1 (1933): 73–78.

Rimmer, William. *Art Anatomy.* Boston: Little, Brown, 1877.

Seidler, Jan M. "A Critical Reappraisal of the Career of William Wetmore Story (1819–1895), American Sculptor and Man of Letters." Ph.D. dissertation, Boston University, 1985.

Sharp, Lewis I. *John Quincy Adams Ward, Dean of American Sculpture.* Newark: University of Delaware Press, 1985.

Sherwood, Dolly. *Harriet Hosmer, American Sculptor, 1830–1908.* Columbia: University of Missouri Press, 1991.

Sizer, Nelson. *Forty Years in Phrenology: Embracing Recollections of History, Anecdote, and Experience.* New York: Fowler and Wells, 1891.

Soria, Regina. *Elihu Vedder, American Visionary Artist in Rome, 1836–1923.*

Rutherford, N.J.: Fairleigh Dickinson University Press, 1970.

Spurzheim, J. G. *Observations on the Deranged Manifestations of the Mind, or Insanity*. London: Baldwin, Cradock, and Joy, 1817.

———. *Phrenology, in Connexion with the Study of Physiognomy*. With a biography of the author by Nahum Capen. Boston: Marsh, Capen and Lyon, 1833.

———. *Phrenology or the Doctrine of Mental Phenomena*. 2 vols. Boston: Marsh, Capen and Lyon, 1832.

Stanton, William. *The Leopard's Spots*. Chicago: University of Chicago Press, 1969.

Stemmler, Joan K. "The Physiognomical Portraits of Johann Caspar Lavater." *Art Bulletin* 75 (1993): 151–68.

Stern, Madeleine B. *Heads and Headlines: The Phrenological Fowlers*. Norman: University of Oklahoma Press, 1971.

———. *The Pantarch: A Biography of Stephen Pearl Andrews*. Austin: University of Texas Press, 1968.

———. *A Phrenological Dictionary of Nineteenth-Century Americans*. Westport, Conn.: Greenwood Press, 1982.

Stoehr, Taylor. "Robert H. Collyer's Technology of the Soul." In *Pseudo-Science and Society in Nineteenth-Century America*, edited by Arthur Wrobel, pp. 21–45. Lexington: University Press of Kentucky, 1987.

Story, William Wetmore. *Conversations in a Studio*. 2 vols. Boston: Houghton Mifflin, 1890.

———. *Excursions in Art and Letters*. Boston: Houghton Mifflin, 1891.

———. *Graffiti d'Italia*. New York: Charles Scribner, 1868.

———. *Life and Letters of Joseph Story*. 2 vols. Boston: Little, Brown, 1851.

———. *Poems*. Boston: Little, Brown, 1856.

———. *Roba di Roma*. London: Chapman and Hall, 1875.

Stowe, Harriet Beecher. *Household Papers and Stories*. 1864. New York: AMS Press, 1967.

———. *The Minister's Wooing*. 1859. New York: AMS Press, 1967.

———. *Uncle Tom's Cabin*. Edited and introduced by Ann Douglas. 1852. New York: Penguin, 1985.

Swank, Scott Trego. "The Unfettered Conscience: A Study of Sectarianism, Spiritualism, and Social Reform in the New Jerusalem Church, 1840–1870." Ph.D. dissertation, University of Pennsylvania, 1970.

Swedenborg, Emanuel. *Angelic Wisdom Concerning Divine Love and Divine Wisdom*. Translated by John C. Ager. New York: Swedenborg Foundation, 1982.

———. *Heaven and Hell*. Translated by George F. Dole. New York: Swedenborg Foundation, 1984.

Taylor, Joshua C. *William Page, the American Titian*. Chicago: University of Chicago Press, 1957.

Thorp, Margaret Farrand. *The Literary Sculptors*. Durham: Duke University Press, 1965.

Tomlinson, Juliette. *The Paintings and Journal of Joseph Whiting Stock*. Middletown, Conn.: Wesleyan University Press, 1976.

Tuckerman, Henry T. "Allusions to Phrenology in *The Last Days of Pompeii*." *Annals of Phrenology* 1 (1834): 459–64.

———. *Artist-Life; or Sketches of American Painters*. New York: Appleton, 1857.

———. *Book of the Artists*. New York: G. P. Putnam and Son, 1867.

———. *The Criterion; or the Test of Talk about Familiar Things*. New York: Hurd and Houghton, 1866.

———. *Essays, Biographical and Critical; or Studies of Character*. Boston: Philips, Samson, 1857.

———. *The Italian Sketch Book*. New York: J. C. Riker, 1848.

———. *Mental Portraits*. London: Richard Bently, 1853.

Tytler, Graeme. *Physiognomy in the European Novel: Faces and Fortunes*. Princeton: Princeton University Press, 1982.

Vedder, Elihu. *The Digressions of V.* Boston: Houghton Mifflin, 1910.

Verbrugge, Martha H. *Able-Bodied Womanhood.* New York: Oxford University Press, 1988.

Vlach, John Michael. *Plain Painters.* Washington, D.C.: Smithsonian Institution Press, 1988.

Wallace, David H. *John Rogers, the People's Sculptor.* Middletown, Conn.: Wesleyan University Press, 1967.

Walsh, Anthony Albert. "The American Tour of Dr. Spurzheim." *Journal of the History of Medicine and Allied Sciences* 27 (1972): 187–205.

———. "Johann Christoph Spurzheim and the Rise and Fall of Scientific Phrenology in Boston, 1832–1842." Ph.D. dissertation, University of New Hampshire, 1974.

———. "Phrenology and the Boston Medical Community in the 1830s." *Bulletin of the History of Medicine* 50 (1976): 261–73.

Walters, Charles Thomas. "Hiram Powers and William Rimmer: A Study in the Concept of Expression." Ph.D. dissertation, University of Michigan, 1977.

———. "Sculpture and the Expressive Mechanism." In *Pseudo-Science and Society in Nineteenth-Century America,* edited by Arthur Wrobel, pp. 180–204. Lexington: University Press of Kentucky, 1987.

Warren, Josiah. *Equitable Commerce.* Utopia, Ohio: Amos E. Senter, 1849.

———. *Practical Application of the Elementary Principles of "True Civilization," to the Minute Details of Every Day Life.* Princeton, Mass.: Published by the author, 1873.

———. *Practical Details in Equitable Commerce.* 2 vols. Preface by Stephen Pearl Andrews. New York: Fowlers and Wells, 1852.

———. *True Civilization an Immediate Necessity and the Last Ground of Hope for Mankind.* Boston: J. Warren, 1863.

Watson, Hewett C. *Statistics of Phrenology: Being a Sketch of the Progress and Present State of That Science in the British Islands.* London: Longman, Rees, Orme, Brown, Green, and Longman, 1836.

Webster, J. Carson. *Erastus D. Palmer.* Newark: University of Delaware Press, 1983.

Weidman, Jeffrey. "William Rimmer." In *William Rimmer, a Yankee Michelangelo,* by Jeffrey Weidman, Neil Harris, and Philip Cash, pp. 3–13. Foreword by Theodore E. Stebbins Jr. Hanover, N.H.: University Press of New England, 1985.

———. "William Rimmer: Critical Catalogue Raisonne." 7 vols. Ph.D. dissertation, Indiana University, 1982.

Wells, Samuel R. *New Physiognomy.* New York: Samuel R. Wells, 1868.

Whitman, Walt. *Leaves of Grass.* Edited with an introduction by Malcolm Cowley. 1855. New York: Penguin, 1982.

———. *Leaves of Grass.* New York: Norton, 1965.

Wilkinson, James John Garth. *The Human Body and Its Connection with Man.* London: New Church Press, [1851].

Wrobel, Arthur. "Phrenology as Political Science." In *Pseudo-Science and Society in Nineteenth-Century America,* edited by Arthur Wrobel, pp. 122–43. Lexington: University Press of Kentucky, 1987.

———. "Walt Whitman and the Fowler Brothers: Phrenology Finds a Bard." Ph.D. dissertation, University of North Carolina, Chapel Hill, 1968.

Wunder, Richard P. *Hiram Powers, Vermont Sculptor, 1805–1873.* 2 vols. Newark: University of Delaware Press, 1991.

Index